Opera in Context

Opera in Context

Essays on Historical Staging
from the Late Renaissance
to the Time of Puccini

Edited by Mark A. Radice

AMADEUS PRESS
Reinhard G. Pauly, General Editor
Portland, Oregon

ISBN 1-57467-032-8

Printed in Hong Kong

AMADEUS PRESS
The Haseltine building
133 S.W. Second Avenue, Suite 450
Portland, Oregon 97204 U.S.A.

Library of Congress Cataloging-in-Publication Data

Opera in context : essays on historical staging from the late
  Renaissance to the time of Puccini / edited by Mark A. Radice.
        p.   cm.
    Includes bibliographical references (p.   ) and index.
    Contents: Dalle macchine— la maraviglia : Bernardo Buontalenti's
Il rapimento di Cefalo at the Medici Theater in 1600 / by Massimo
Ossi — Opera and ballet in seventeenth-century French theaters :
case studies of the Salle des machines and the Palais royal theater
/ by Barbara Coeyman — Theater architecture at the time of Henry
Purcell and its influence on his "dramatick operas" / by Mark A.
Radice — Handel's Haymarket Theatre / by Mark Stahura — Mozart
and two theaters in Josephinian Vienna / by Malcolm S. Cole — The
Neues Schauspielhaus in Berlin and the premiere of Carl Maria von Weber's
Der Freischütz / by E. Douglas Bomberger — Paradise found : the
Salle Le Peletier and French grand opera / by Karin Pendle and
Stephen Wilkins — Verdi's operas and Giuseppe Bertoja's designs at
the Gran teatro La Fenice, Venice ; Richard Wagner and his search
for the ideal theatrical space / by Evan Baker — Realism on the
opera stage : Belasco, Puccini, and the California sunset / by Helen
M. Greenwald.
    ISBN   1-57467-032-8
    1. Opera—Production and direction.   I. Radice, Mark A.
MT955.054   1998
792.5'023 — dc21   97-2712
                                                                CIP
                                                                MN

Contents

List of Figures

Illustrations are from the authors' collections unless otherwise indicated.

Acknowledgments

To thank each and every person who contributed to the present volume would require another volume of equal size. I would, however, express my particular gratitude to each of the contributing scholars. Their knowledge, experience, patience, and help have had an impact not only on the pages that follow but also upon my own scholarship. To Reinhard G. Pauly, whose kind invitation to compile a book-length study on the historic staging of opera motivated this collection of essays, I am grateful. To Karen Kirtley, editorial director of Amadeus Press at the time, I extend thanks for her excellent advice, patience, good sense, and flexibility. Frederick T. Estabrook, the manager of Ithaca College's Graphic Design Services, was an invaluable aid in sorting through the problems resulting from the extensive iconography employed in these essays. Margaret D. Ericson (Tufts University), Betty Birdsey (Ithaca College), and the interlibrary loan staff of Ithaca College helped to procure essential bibliographic resources. Mary I. Arlin, Graham Stewart, and David Weil provided much assistance in dealing with computer hard- and software. Oxford University Press and the editors of *The Musical Quarterly* graciously granted permission to reproduce my Purcell essay, which first appeared in volume 74 (1990) of that journal. Lanny Collins assisted greatly with numerous editorial details, and Eve Goodman effected a last round of miraculous transformations by the most subtle modifications. To her and all the staff at Amadeus Press, I am deeply grateful.

Introduction

For most of the history of the genre that we call "opera," composers have worked with specific circumstances in mind. The musicians, dancers, and theaters involved in the premiere productions of most operas would have been known to the composer at the time that work on the score was in progress. In many cases, political events, national holidays, or festivities of one sort or another would also have played a significant role in determining the subject matter, the production schedule, and other details of the projected theater event.

Some operatic scores depend upon the environment from which they sprang, so that even relatively slight modifications to any component of the theater piece result in diminution—if not utter destruction—of the creators' intentions. In countries that had a limited number of opera houses, or even a single one, we often find that the operas composed for performance in a particular house were carefully tailored to take the best advantage of its physical properties. Orchestral seating patterns, audience capacities, acoustical properties, stage dimensions, lighting facilities, the nature of the scenery, costuming, and the countless other ingredients each contributed something unique to the production as a totality.

The surviving details of particular opera houses and productions are, obviously, variable. We are fortunate to possess some rather specific information relating to the Dorset Garden Theatre, the building where Henry Purcell's "dramatick operas" were produced. His scores are best understood in the context of that theater; otherwise, the admixture of spoken drama, song, instrumental music, and spectacle may seem like a bewildering hodgepodge. Any opera enthusiast knows, too, that Wagner was sufficiently concerned with achieving optimal integration of all elements to have concluded that nothing short of a theater designed to meet his exact requirements would suffice. The Bayreuth Festspielhaus has become legendary, and even now, more than 100 years since the first performance of the complete *Ring* cycle in the theater in 1876, ticket-seeking opera lovers may apply for many consecutive years in vain for an opportunity to hear Wagner's music in his own theater. In cases like these two, our examination of any score or libretto must be in relationship to specific staging conventions. Nuances of stage action may find parallels or counterparts in the instrumental accompaniment, in the lighting, or in one or another of the simultaneous theatrical events.

A somewhat different historical situation has prevailed in Italy since the seventeenth century. That country was blessed with many important operatic centers, often with more than one opera house. Theater architecture thus achieved a certain degree of uniformity that enabled lyric theater pieces to be transplanted with relative ease from one opera house to another. In dealing with Italian opera, therefore, it is helpful to have some understanding of general practices as well as of the specifics of particular houses.

Examining the original context of a work clarifies the rhymes and reasons of actions and operatic reactions. Adjustments—let us hope judicious ones—can be made with full understanding of their consequences. These adjustments, many of them owing to the physical differences in our present-day opera houses, may facilitate effective productions of repertoire that has gone by the wayside for want of a congenial theatrical environment rather than because of any intrinsic musical or dramatic weaknesses. Other adjustments, possible because technology enables us to do more than any seventeenth-century producer or set designer could have managed, may revitalize some element of the opera to which our hard-to-impress, twentieth-century eyes have become blind.

The purpose of these essays is to inspire and inform anyone interested in operatic repertoire, including opera enthusiasts, scholars, and especially singers, producers, directors, set designers, and conductors, with cogent descriptions of particular theaters' physical properties and of the theatrical traditions in which the master composers originally worked. Each essay in the collection explores the relationship between a specific opera or type of opera and the performance space, stage design, and staging techniques that gave birth to it. For the purpose of this book, "staging" will not include "acting," except peripherally.

With the single exception of my study of Purcell's operas for the Dorset Garden Theatre, each essay in this volume has been written specifically for this book. In recruiting scholars to write these articles, I have turned to specialists whose research backgrounds qualify them to speak with authority on their topics. I have also attempted to include representative operatic productions from each historical epoch treated and from diverse national schools of opera. Though the works of Gluck, Jommelli, Traetta, and other masters have not been

covered in these pages, we hope, nevertheless, that these case studies will provide a starting point for all who are interested in learning about historic staging
techniques.

Read from cover to cover, these essays offer a comprehensive history of
staging techniques that have been used for opera production over the centuries.
Yet to ensure that the essays may also be read individually, we have kept the use
of technical terms—both musical and theatrical—to a minimum and have normally included precise explanations within the body of the text. Notes gathered
at the back of the volume provide more detailed information; for example,
explanations of antique units of measurement and primary sources for translated
excerpts. Unless otherwise indicated, translations are by the author of the essay
in which they appear. For the reader's convenience, measurements have been
given according to both American usage and the metric system.

The methods of inquiry and the bibliographical resources employed by
the various contributors to this volume will doubtless prove useful to others
wishing to pursue further research in historic staging. Consequently, the
bibliography is divided into two categories: (1) general studies of theaters,
theater architecture, staging, costume design, lighting, and musical theater and
(2) specific studies that relate most particularly to the topics covered within the
individual chapters.

While it may not be possible—or even desirable—to duplicate a given
opera's original performance context, we hope that the information and the
insights contained in this collection of essays will, at least, enable twentieth-
century opera practitioners to devise suitable contexts for lyric theater pieces—
contexts that will demonstrate an awareness of the myriad ways in which
sights, sounds, and stories were integrated; contexts that will reveal why the
lyric theater, from antiquity to the present day, has provided a forum for the
expression of the most profound human emotions.

Mark A. Radice
Ithaca College
February 1997

CHAPTER ONE

Dalle macchine . . . la maraviglia: Bernardo Buontalenti's Il rapimento di Cefalo at the Medici Theater in 1600

Massimo Ossi

The "Theatrical Game" and the Flexible Theater of the Renaissance

From the machines, therefore, comes *maraviglia*, which is the principal means of understanding, . . . from the noble and graceful tale comes the moral, and those human and divine customs which, through the expression of proper decorum, purge the minds of the spectators, leading them toward justice and even true love. These last also result from the excellence of the words themselves, which are the images of thoughts, and from the exquisite and varied music, which is perfectly adapted to the characters and to the concepts.[1]

Among the components of dramatic entertainments—machines, story, music, and poetry—Michelangelo Buonarroti, chronicler of the Florentine wedding festivities for Maria de' Medici and Henry IV of France in 1600, attributed to machines an essential role in the success of the entire production. Without the *maraviglia* engendered by the wonders of stagecraft, the spectators' minds could not become receptive to the persuasive powers of the other arts. Buonarroti was by no means alone in emphasizing stage effects: the anonymous author of *Il corago,* a manuscript treatise on the role of the theatrical director (*corago*) written sometime during the late 1620s, considered them integral to the invention of the plot, recommending that in writing the libretto the poet should take care to choose a subject that allowed the creation of stage machines suitable to both the occasion and the means of the patron.[2] In focusing the production around spectacular effects and in insisting that the libretto be written in conjunction with the visual structure of the entertainment, *Il corago* codified what Bernardo Buontalenti and the poets who collaborated with him, chiefly Giovanni Bardi and Gabriello Chiabrera, had conceived and put into practice from at least as early as the mid 1580s.[3]

Central to the aesthetics of early opera was a kind of competition between the audience and the architect in which the former tried to figure out the means by which the stage effects were carried out, while the latter endeavored to hide them.[4] It is clear from accounts of early seventeenth-century operas that the audience expected to be beaten at what Nino Pirrotta has called the "theatrical game," and that much of the enjoyment inherent in the genre derived from this fact. The virtuosity involved in transforming an ordinary room into a theater appropriate for a particular production was part of the game.[5] As the author of *Il corago* boasted, almost any space could be adapted to house an operatic production:

> It has happened that in the same room in which a prince was received with public ceremony, including religious observances during the morning, within the space of four hours, while the prince lunched elsewhere, a stage with its scenery could be made to appear so that the play could be given to the admiration of the visiting prince and of all who attended.[6]

The ease with which stages could be built allowed for the flexible use of rooms, making it possible for even the lesser nobility to mount productions that, "while not lacking in costly splendor, must have been relatively miniature."[7]

Florence is a good case in point: approximately 145 theatrical events that took place between 1590 and 1656 are documented in Robert and Norma Weaver's *Chronology of Music in the Florentine Theater, 1590–1750;* the locations of three-fifths of them (eighty-seven) are known.[8] Thirty-eight of those took place on occasional stages in private residences. These were of several types: the smaller Medici palaces, such as Poggio Imperiale, where Francesca Caccini's *La liberazione di Ruggiero* was produced out-of-doors in 1625, with Giulio Parigi's last stage designs; or private residences in and around Florence, such as the Palazzo Corsi, where Jacopo Peri's setting of Rinuccini's *La Dafne* was given in 1600 before it was staged at Palazzo Pitti, or the Ninfeo, near Fiesole, otherwise known as the Camerata. This was the meeting place of Giovanni Bardi's circle, where Vincenzo Panciatichi's *tragicommedia, L'amicizia costante,* was performed with its *intermedii* in 1600. In addition to these peripheral (or off-court) productions, twenty-eight others took place in the Palazzo Pitti, where the most commonly used space was the Sala delle commedie, also known as the Salone di Don Antonio, a smaller multi-purpose room with a raised platform at one end, in which stage machinery could be set up as needed and where in 1600 *L'Euridice* was first performed for a very restricted audience.[9] A similar arrangement could also be found in the cavernous Salone del Cinquecento in the Palazzo Vecchio, where Emilio de' Cavalieri's setting of Battista Guarini's "Dialogo di Giunone e Minerva" was performed during a banquet in celebration of Maria de' Medici's wedding in 1600.[10] The flexibility with which private rooms were treated extended to sacred settings as well: in 1619 and 1620, in the private chapel of the archduchess, the architect Giulio Parigi staged sacred productions that included a sky which opened to reveal a vanishing perspective of heaven, a spring that fed into the sea, cloud machines, and flying angels.[11]

The Permanent Theater in the Salone grande at the Uffizi in Florence

Because of their size and proportions, certain rooms, such as the Sala delle commedie in the Palazzo Pitti, were used for theatrical productions more often than others. Among these, the Salone grande in the Uffizi in Florence was in continuous use for theatrical productions for at least half a century, beginning in 1586 when Duke Francesco specifically requested that the room be used to stage Giovanni Bardi's *L'amico fido* and the architect Bernardo Buontalenti outfitted it as a theater.[12] The last performance documented in the *Chronology of Music in the Florentine Theater* as having taken place there, Andrea Salvatori's *La flora* set to music by Marco da Gagliano, dates from 1628, although the room may have remained in use after that.[13]

Joseph Furttenbach, who was in Florence sometime after 1610, left a description of the Uffizi theater and of the kinds of productions that were mounted in it:

> From windows there, one can see into the *Theatro* where princely plays are presented in lovely well-contrived scenes appropriate to the action. With great dexterity the whole scene may be changed. Such varied spectacles as these have never been equaled in our times. I present here in plate 14 such a scene, a street open to a great distance, shown by means of perspective art. Here the actors present their play. At the end of the act the whole scene changes into a pleasure garden, a sea, a wood, or some other place, with such dexterity that those who are watching can not see the change and think that they have lost their senses. . . . Such changes of scene often are made six or seven times in the same play. How the clouds appear to the accompaniment of lovely music, and the *Dii* [*sic*] (gods) are let down to earth in the many forms traditional to poetry, would take too long to tell.[14]

In addition to Furttenbach, two other witnesses, Bastiano de' Rossi and Michelangelo Buonarroti, have left descriptions of the Medici theater. De' Rossi published two accounts of its layout, first in 1586 in conjunction with the celebrations for Virginia de' Medici's wedding to Cesare d'Este, and again in 1589 when Girolamo Bargagli's play *La pellegrina* was performed with its famous *intermedii* on the occasion of the marriage of Grand Duke Ferdinando I and Christine of Lorraine.[15] Buonarroti was the official chronicler for the festivities of 1600 when the centerpiece, Ottavio Rinuccini's *Il rapimento di Cefalo* fully set to music by Giulio Caccini, eclipsed all other events, including the now more famous *Euridice* by Jacopo Peri with insertions by Caccini.[16] A later source, an engraving by Jacques Callot, shows a stage design by Giulio Parigi, Buontalenti's successor, for the first *intermedio* of *La liberazione di Tirreno e d'Arnia,* performed in 1616 in conjunction with the wedding of Caterina de' Medici and Ferdinando Gonzaga, Duke of Mantua (figure 1.1).[17]

The *salone* (figure 1.2) was rectangular, 180.7 feet (55 meters) long, 66.6 feet (20.3 meters) wide, and 45.7 feet (13.9 meters) high.[18] It was quite a large hall: by comparison the theater at Sabbioneta near Mantua, built in 1588 by the architect Vincenzo Scamozzi, was an intimate room, about 107 feet (32.6 meters) long and 44.2 feet (13.5 meters) wide, with only 62 feet (18.9 meters) between the back wall and the foot of the stage (figure 1.3).[19] According to de' Rossi the floor sloped, like that at Sabbioneta, toward the stage from a height at the far end of about 4 feet 4 inches (1.3 meters). The slope was intended to give the spectators at the back of the hall a clear view of the scene in spite of the great length of the room (about 142 feet [43.3 meters] from the far wall to the foot of the stage in 1586, 132.5 [40.4 meters] when the stage was moved forward by some 10 feet in 1589).[20] De' Rossi does not tell us whether the slope was integral to the design of the room before 1586, or if Buontalenti added it over an existing, level floor when he converted it in 1586.[21] The latter solution seems more likely, allowing the greatest flexibility in the use of the theater: for example, a wooden, overlaid floor could have been easily modified when the new stage was installed in 1589.[22]

In 1600 the main entrance was in the middle of the back wall under the platform for the court, at floor level as at Sabbioneta. Presumably this was its original location, since in 1589 the space above it was occupied by a gallery for off-stage musicians.[23] Callot's illustration, however, suggests that by 1616 the door was no longer at floor level but had been moved to the top of the seats— one figure is seen descending the bleachers, which appear to slope rather steeply away from the entrance, and others sit below the doorway, which is in the foreground. This perhaps was the level of the ducal balcony at the time of *Il rapimento di Cefalo,* with the actual structure projecting out into the hall from the opening that forms Callot's foreground.

The stage, located at the end opposite the main door, was as wide as the hall, and, according to de' Rossi, it was about 38 feet deep (11.6 meters) and 9.5 feet (2.9 meters) high at the proscenium end in 1586; in 1589 its depth was increased to 47.5 feet (14.5 meters). Buonarroti does not comment on the size of the stage in 1600, but the scale and the number of machines that required operation from below and behind it for *Il rapimento di Cefalo* suggest that it was

PRIMO INTERMEDIO DELLA VEGLIA DELLA LIBERATIONE DI TIRRENO FATTA NELLA SALA DELLE COM
DIE DEL SER.™° GRAN DVCA DI TOSCANA IL CARNOVALE DEL 1616. DOVE SI RAP.™ IL MONTE D'ISCHIA CON IL GIGANTE
TIFEO SOTTO.

Figure 1.1. Jacques Callot, "Primo intermedio della veglia della liberatione di Tirreno."

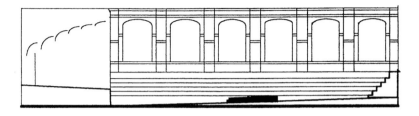

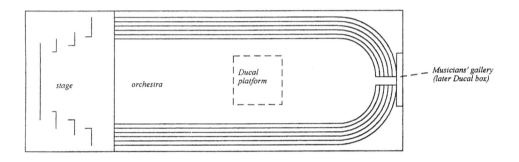

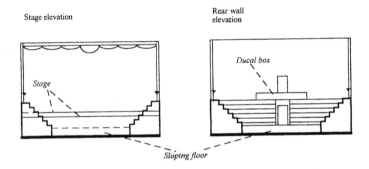

Figure 1.2. Plan and elevations, based on Buonarroti's description and Callot's engraving, of the Teatro Mediceo in the Uffizi. Placement of the ducal box in 1589 and 1600.

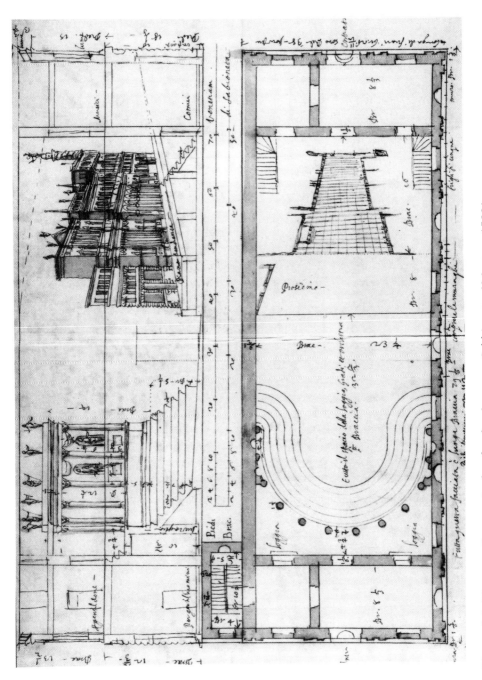

Figure 1.3. Vincenzo Scamozzi, plan for the theater at Sabbioneta (Mantua, 1588).

at least as large as that needed in 1589. The relationship between the seats and the stage in Callot's engraving suggests that in 1616 the stage was still about 9 feet (2.7 meters) high.[24] From the very beginning, the theatrical setup in the *salone* was ambitious: the stage in 1586 was about twice as high as was recommended by both the anonymous author of *Il corago* and the architect Nicola Sabbatini, according to whom the stage should reach no higher than the middle of an average man's chest, or about 4.5 feet (1.4 meters).[25] By way of comparison, the stage at Sabbioneta was placed at chest height.[26] None of the descriptions mentions whether the stage itself sloped; it seems likely that it did, both because of its height and because all instructions for stage construction assume this to be standard.[27] The end facing the audience was enclosed by a partition on which in 1586 were painted *trompe l'oeil* stairs and three fountains.[28] By 1616 these were replaced with real stairs and two ramps, allowing the dancers to move between the orchestra and the stage.

Sabbatini cautions that the stage should be set up so as to have plenty of room on both sides, as well as above, under, and behind, to allow for the working of the machines, some of which required considerable space. For example, a machine capable of delivering a cloud toward the front of the stage would have needed as much as 20 feet (6 meters) behind the stage for the lever and counterweights necessary to its operation.[29] The space above the stage was delimited by the vault of the sky, which could be either a single piece or divided into sections. The former solution blocked off the upper space, whereas the latter allowed access to the rafters for running machines and for altering the appearance of the sky, either by slipping new panels with different cloud patterns over the original ones or by rolling painted cylinders that created the effect of clouds moving. More importantly, the open rafters made it possible to operate machines there as needed; depending on the requirements, several men may have had to climb up among the rafters and move about.[30] In spite of its technological sophistication, the Uffizi theater had no wing space other than what was behind the flats, and the depth of the stage would have allowed little room for the operation of cumbersome machines behind it.

Just as the Uffizi theater had relatively little wing space, it had no designated space for musicians. Unlike other rooms in which musicians were placed either in boxes along the side walls or in front of the stage, all available space in the Medici theater was either taken up by the seats or left open for the audience or for the performers.[31] Descriptions are conspicuously silent on the placement of instruments in the *salone,* even when *sinfonie* are mentioned, and Callot's engraving shows no musicians, although the scene depicts a *ballo.*[32] The only exception was de' Rossi's mention in 1589 of the off-stage chorus, which sang from a balcony above the main entrance at the back of the hall. Accompaniment for the singers, then, must have come from behind the scenes. This was a common enough arrangement, but it must have severely limited the resources available for such productions as *Il rapimento di Cefalo,* and indeed it was judged inadequate because the music was simply too weak to fill the room.[33] Conventional wisdom, expressed in such contemporary documents as the prefaces to Emilio de' Cavalieri's *Rappresentazione di anima et di corpo* and Marco da Gagliano's *Dafne,* warned that the number of instruments be determined by the proportions of the hall and stage.[34] Furthermore, the large audience would have had a considerable sound-dampening effect. Finally, Buontalenti's sets appear to have made it difficult to establish visual and perhaps even aural contact between singers and instrumentalists, compounding the problems posed by the subtleties of the new recitative style.[35]

Before a performance, the spectators' view of the stage was blocked by an elaborate and richly decorated curtain.[36] It parted in the middle and the two halves moved into recesses on either side of the hall; this was unusual at a time when typically the curtain either fell to the foot of the stage—sometimes with disconcerting results—or, less commonly, was raised.[37] The speed with which the curtain disappeared was invariably the cause of admiring remarks—it was essential that it should disclose the scene suddenly, causing the greatest surprise possible. For the remainder of the work the curtain remained open, so that all scene changes took place in full view of the audience. Buontalenti exploited the mechanics of set transformations and incorporated them into his arsenal of spectacular effects.

The placement of the seats in these ephemeral theaters was also under the direct control of the *corago* and reflected the social structure of the court. Along the sides and back wall of the Uffizi theater were wooden bleachers for the audience; in 1600, according to Buonarroti, the seats at the end opposite the stage were curved in a half-oval, in a plan that was perhaps not unlike that of the theater at Sabbioneta and of the later Teatro Farnese (1628) in Parma.[38] Buonarroti also indicates that these seats were reserved for the ladies. The orchestra served two main purposes, both illustrated in Callot's engraving: first, it accommodated a considerable number of spectators either standing or seated on temporary benches (primarily men, although Callot shows both men and women), and second, it served as a dance floor whenever the stage action involved a *ballo,* when the dancing tended to migrate from the stage to the orchestra.[39]

The court sat in a reserved area, probably a temporary structure that could be rebuilt to suit the needs of the various entertainments being staged in the room. As Barnard Hewitt has noted, the focus on a single patron around whom the entire event was choreographed was the one feature of court entertainments that most distinguished them from those produced in the public theaters of the later seventeenth century.[40] According to Sabbatini,

> persons of culture and taste should be seated on the floor of the hall, as near the middle [where the royal seat was located] as possible in the second or third rows. They will have the greatest pleasure there, since

in such a position all the parts of the scenery and the machines are displayed in their perfection, and they will not be able to see the defects which are sometimes discerned by those on the steps or at the sides.[41]

For the 1586 production, the duke and his retinue sat on a square platform 23 feet (7 meters) on each side and 22 inches (55.9 cm) high, set up in the middle of the orchestra 57 feet (17.4 meters) from the stage. Elegant chairs (*ricche, e splendidissime sedie*) were placed on it for the royal patrons, and the stand was covered with red and gold velvet and oriental carpets. The placement of the seats for the court was almost certainly a function of the set design, since the duke's seat was typically located so that his eye would be level with the vanishing point of the set's perspective. In 1586 Bardi's *L'amico fido* opened with a large-scale panoramic view of Florence that depended for its effect on an accurate perception of perspective depth.[42] For Bargagli's *La pellegrina* in 1589, which also used a panoramic set, this time with a view of Pisa, the royal box was moved farther back, but remained on the floor of the hall.[43] *Il rapimento di Cefalo,* by contrast, consisted entirely of scenes in which the overall effect and the movement of machines took prominence over the perspective scenery, which consisted of broad landscape views without buildings, and the court sat on a balcony high in the middle of the back wall, where in 1589 there had been a gallery for a group of off-stage singers. This new location presumably showed Buontalenti's designs and machinery to their greatest advantage. No special area for the court appears in Callot's print, where a *ballo* is shown taking place on the floor of the theater.

The number of spectators such a hall could accommodate remains open to speculation. According to Buonarroti the audience for the performance of *Il rapimento di Cefalo* in 1600 numbered 3,000 gentlemen and 800 ladies of the court. The stands could indeed accommodate about 800 spectators on six tiers, even allowing space for the door and for the ducal balcony.[44] This corroborates Buonarroti's estimate of the number of ladies in attendance; how 3,000 gentlemen could have been made to fit into the orchestra is less clear. Assuming that the proportions in the theater at Sabbioneta, which had five tiers of seats each one *braccio* (1.9 feet [58.4 cm]) deep, were representative, the six-tiered stands in the Uffizi would jut out 13 feet (4 meters) on either side, leaving about 40 feet (12.2 meters) free in the middle and 120 feet (36.6 meters) from the stage to the seats along the far wall, for a total area of 4,620 square feet (429.6 square meters).[45] If the audience were seated on benches, the maximum capacity of the orchestra was about 1,100−1,200 people, assuming that each bench took up 2 feet (61 cm) of space and that the entire floor was used. This, however, was impossible, given that the set for the Prologue of *Il rapimento di Cefalo* extended beyond the front of the stage. The only other possibility, supported by Callot's print, is that those in the orchestra stood. This solution might have allowed 3,000 people to crowd onto the floor, and Buonarroti does report that the audience suffered from overcrowding.[46]

In 1586 the walls of the *salone* were decorated with plant motifs, giving the room the appearance of a "delightful garden"; the windows were covered with panels depicting images derived from classical antiquity.[47] According to de' Rossi's descriptions, the room was repainted in 1589 with a new design based on large, arched sections that framed *faux* metal statues standing against painted views of the sky. This décor seems to have remained the pattern for the ensuing quarter-century or so. Buonarroti's account mentions that the main pictorial feature of the *salone* was a series of *logge* "with vast blue skies that seem all air," which presumably filled the arched sections; above the seats, probably on the same parapet of false marble that de' Rossi had described in 1586, were statues "representing all types of poetry and other figures."[48] Buonarroti did not dwell on the paintings and the statues that ringed the hall because they were *stabili ornamenti* (permanent decorations) presumably well known to his readers.[49] Callot's illustration, although it does not reproduce the mural decorations, shows the same basic design that had been first described by de' Rossi in 1589, an alternation of columns and arched sections above the balustrade on which the statues were placed.[50]

After the stage machinery, lighting was the next most notable feature of Buontalenti's theater. The sets for *L'amico fido* were characterized by unusually realistic lighting, and Buontalenti was credited with discovering a method for achieving it: "our architect was the first to find a way of lighting [the stage]."[51] The hall lights were equally impressive: according to Buonarroti, they numbered "more than one thousand" (*più di migliaja*). Even allowing for hyperbolic propaganda from the court chroniclers, it is clear that the theater was brilliantly lit.[52] Twenty-four lamps hung from the room's ceiling; a series of lamps, spaced about every 15 feet (4.6 meters), projected from the walls above the seats; and lamps hung in front of the stage opening. In 1586 twenty-four floor lamps lined the orchestra, marking the steps that gave access to the seats. To compensate for the sloping floor and to keep the lights level with the seats, which did not follow the slope of the floor, the floor lamps ranged in size from 5.5 feet (1.7 meters) high at the far end to about 10 feet (3 meters) at the end closest to the stage. Their number was reduced to eighteen in 1588, and by 1600 they seem to have been removed: Buonarroti makes no mention of them, and they do not appear in Callot's print. In addition, the stage itself had lights in the ceiling, behind the flats, and in the proscenium arch. In 1589 footlights were added behind the balustrade that enclosed the front of the stage.

With so many lights, heat and smoke—not to mention the danger of fire, Sabbatini's most dreaded contingency—were a constant problem; consequently the room was provided with openings in the ceiling, in the stage, and in the walls (its windows, although hidden, could be opened), through which the fumes could be vented.[53] Even so, Buonarroti notes that by the fourth act of *Il rapimento di Cefalo*, the spectators were suffering from overcrowding and were relieved when the theater was filled with the great scented winds that accompanied the underground setting.[54]

Spectacular though the room may have been, it was the stage machinery, as Furttenbach's description makes clear, that made the reputation of the Uffizi theater and of its architect. Buonarroti gave a general impression of the effects that were possible and of the complexity of the trap room required to make them work:

> No movement of machines was missing, whether across the stage, or circular, or rising, or descending, or even moving forward, or [opening and] closing in various ways, for huge weights held them aloft. . . . A visitor to the hidden places where [the machines] were placed and were run . . . would have seen each trap and mechanism, whether small or large, made of metal or wood, beautifully executed and functioning with unimagined ease, in spite of the large number of men required to operate all of them in time to such musical cues as specific passages or the ends of numbers.[55]

Perhaps the most spectacular production mounted in the Uffizi theater was Chiabrera's *Il rapimento di Cefalo,* praised in the official French account of the wedding as having "filled the ears of all and the eyes of the spectators with such admiration that they were astounded."[56] It consisted of a Prologue and five acts, and, according to Buonarroti's official description, required eight scene changes (see table 1.1) and a prodigious number of machines—so many of them working at once that the chronicler at one point refers to the action on the stage as "that chaos of machines" (*quel caos di macchine*).[57]

Buonarroti's glowing official account of Buontalenti's technical wizardry fails to mention, for obvious reasons, that the entertainment did not go off entirely smoothly in spite of its ambitious program. It was marred by technical and artistic problems, prompting reports that "the movement of machines was not always felicitous," and that the new style of recitative singing, both in *Euridice* and in *Cefalo,* was rather boring.[58] Buonarroti himself, during the preparations for the wedding festivities for Cosimo de' Medici and Maria Magdalena of Austria in 1608, for which he had written the play *Il giudizio di Paride* and two *intermedii,* made veiled references to examples of shoddy execution in earlier years, and Giovanni de' Bardi, who was also involved in the 1608 production, explicitly referred to the entertainments of 1600 as examples of what could happen without adequate rehearsal.[59] Their reports are corroborated by Emilio de' Cavalieri's recollections, which suggest that Buontalenti's designs were not realized adequately, and that Caccini's music was inadequate to the theater.[60] That things did not always go smoothly, and that pitfalls lurked in all machines can easily be gathered from Sabbatini's reminders, liberally sprinkled throughout his *Pratica di fabbricar scene,* to attend to all details and to put the most trustworthy workers in charge of the machines with moving parts, as well as from similar cautionary comments in *Il corago.*[61] Problems with malfunctioning

Table 1.1. Scenes in Chiabrera's *Il rapimento di Cefalo*

Act/scene	Setting	Action
Prologue	Mount Helicon	Muses. Scene change: mountain "deflates."
I	Woodland 1	Dawn. Cefalo and his party. Divided cloud machine.
II	Woodland 1	Titone (changing cloud).
	Seascape	Sea monsters, cloud chase, celestial choir (amorini). Sunset.
III/i	Woodland 2	Cefalo and Aurora.
III/ii	Woodland 3	Lights off on stage and in the theater. Night's chariot, celestial bodies, Zodiac.
IV/i	Woodland 4	Daylight. Scene unfolds: gradual opening of caves; underground treasures.
IV/ii	Woodland 4	Cloud chase: "contest between machines"— Apollo and Cupid. Celestial choir ("100" on stage).
V/i	Woodland 4	Clouds moving, hunters' chorus.
V/ii		
(Postlude)	Theater	Pyramid of Fame and the Tuscan cities.

machines were sure to find their way into ambassadorial dispatches and official correspondence, and in light of the competitive atmosphere that surrounded the artistic productions at state functions, as well as of their ambitious technical requirements, it is surprising that relatively few reports of gaffes (or worse) have made their way into the annals of early opera.[62] The mixed artistic success of the operatic experiments in 1600 seems to have been responsible at least in part for the conservative direction of subsequent Medici entertainments, which returned to the earlier format of the play with *intermedii*.[63]

Bernardo Buontalenti's *Il rapimento di Cefalo*

The opening of the curtain in *Cefalo* revealed Mount Helicon, covered in vegetation and 38 feet high (11.4 meters). Indeed, it was so large that it occupied the entire area of the stage and spilled over its edge, taking up a significant portion of the theater floor with massive boulders.[64] Set upon a stage 9 feet high (2.7 meters), a 38-foot (11.6-meter) mountain would have reached into the theater's rafters. The actual construction must have been somewhat smaller, however, because there had to be room at the top for a mechanical Pegasus, which during the opera struck the ground and started the flow of the Muses' sacred spring.[65] How the curtain hid the boulders that took up part of the orchestra is not clear, and Buonarroti is silent on this point. The rest of the scene consisted of sky and clouds; the front slopes of the mountain formed three paths leading up its sides. Water from the fountain fell into a large bowl decorated with golden masks, and from there it flowed, with many smaller jets, into brooks and other fountains on the mountainside.[66] The air vents—especially those built into the stage—could also be used to generate breezes for scenic effects, and according to Buonarroti the sprays of the various fountains on Mount Helicon were gently blown about by them. The mountain was fully practicable. The Muses and Apollo appeared among the luxuriant vegetation below the top; Calliope sat by the fountain, under its spray, and then descended along a curving path to the foot of the mountain. From there she delivered the Prologue, and then returned to her seat by the spring.

The first act opened in a woodland setting, showing a broad perspective of plains, tall woods, mountain peaks, and deep caves. The change of scene itself was clearly calculated to astound the audience:

> All of a sudden the great mountain caved inwards, and in a sense it almost deflated, as if it had been a very light thing; and yet it had sustained great weight. The Muses, still making music, were hidden in it, and were not seen again; the clouds that had been behind it rose quickly up to the sky. Thus the stage floor and the first perspective came into view, with wide plains, high and shady woods, and open and deep caves.[67]

The lights were doused to represent very early morning just before dawn; in this setting, resting on rocks, were Cefalo and his hunting party. The first act required a relatively simple setup: the woods and caves were probably painted on flats;[68] Aurora descended on a cloud machine "with varied, slow, and sweet motion, turning and revolving" (*travolgendosi*) from an opening in the heavens accompanied by increased stage lighting that represented the rising sun. Buonarroti relates that as her cloud descended, it divided itself into "several lesser clouds which seemed to be playfully born from it" (*altre nugolette, che da quella parevan nascere sorgenti e scherzanti*). After delivering Aurora, "it closed inward upon itself, calmly rising to the heavens, and it could be seen rotating upon itself with elegant artifice, and becoming smaller as it went." (*Tutta in sè rientrava chiudendosi, tranquillamente al cielo tornandosi, si vedeva per grazioso artificio in sè medesima sè travolgendo, sempre più andar menomando.*) This scenic display probably took place in the manner described by Sabbatini.[69] What must have really surprised the audience, however, was that Aurora's entrance was accompanied by sprays of scented mist that rained not only upon the stage but throughout the theater as well.

The set remained unchanged for the second act, which began with the appearance of Titone seated on another cloud, from which he delivered his lament on Aurora's infidelity, "Chi mi conforta ahimè! chi più consolami?" His cloud was quite large, and it changed shape and size several times while crossing the width of the entire stage, resembling "now a porpoise, now a horse, now a woods, a mountain, or perhaps other unknown shapes." Its motion was not in a straight line but along a wavy path "as happens naturally" (*come adiviene naturalmente*), suggesting that perhaps rather than being mounted on a hinged beam or a slide, as were Sabbatini's various cloud mechanisms that permitted only linear motion, Titone's was suspended from the ceiling with cables, such as those shown in designs for the Teatro Farnese in Parma.[70] Observers were filled with "greatest marvel" (*grandissima maraviglia*) at the sight of the "ethereal machine" (*piumosa machina*), which perhaps distracted them from Titone's recitation of his marital woes.

As the cloud was about to slip out of sight, the scene changed to a seascape with islands and mountains on the horizon. The waves, which occupied the main part of the stage, were seen foaming and colliding with each other while making loud, gurgling noises. On one side of the stage, a whale 26.5 feet (8 meters) long arose from the depths carrying the figure of Oceanus, while on the opposite side there appeared the chariot of the sun, equally large as the whale, and drawn by four horses. Both machines came up through trapdoors, the whale "shaking itself and straining to swim upwards," and the horses, "raising at first only their heads . . . later, beating the water quickly with their feet, they appeared to gain the surface by degrees. They were gasping and frothing, shaking their heads, their manes flying, and could not be stopped."[71]

The whale had silver scales and a moveable tail with which it slapped the sea sending spray in all directions. Its belly filled with water and made the sea around it bulge; when it dipped its head beneath the waves, it drank water that was then ejected into the air. Its head shook, its mouth opened and closed, water streamed from its teeth along with brilliantly colored fish writhing about. Its eyes turned, it retracted and moved its spines, and it flapped its fins—which Buonarroti calls "ears . . . attached to its large jaws" (*orecchie . . . alle larghe ganasce appiccate*) and which were shaped like a bat's wings. The outward appearance of the whale was typical of such creatures: engravings of a whale with sea gods in the Pitti Palace in 1579 and in the Arno in 1608 depict animals that fit Buonarroti's description almost exactly.[72] A later design for a sea monster for the Teatro Farnese in Parma (1628) shows a spring coil that was to give mobility to the tail, a hinged mouth, and, for the body, a barrel in which a man could sit to operate its various moving parts. Sabbatini describes a method for making a fish spout water by blowing large quantities of shredded silver or pulverized talc through a funnel.[73] Around the whale swam Tritons, blowing into shells from which water streamed and slapping the waves with their tails. Buonarroti mentions, without describing them, other marvels that made up this *caos di macchine,* and his imprecision frustrates us with a tantalizing glimpse of what Buontalenti could do when he pulled out all the stops: "In the sky above and in the air, clouds could be seen, and all around, changing scenes, and below, a large flooded space cut through by other behemoths that writhed."[74]

After a brief exchange between Apollo and Oceanus, the focus of the scene shifted from the sea to the sky where Cupid had appeared and landed on a large cloud after first flying about the vast space above the scene. Cupid's wide ranging movements, like those of Titone's cloud earlier, were probably made possible by suspending him from cables rather than by using a fixed seat mounted on a beam. Flanking Cupid were a number of *amorini,* at first divided into two choirs and subsequently arranged into a circle ringing Cupid's cloud for the chorus that concluded the act.[75] After the disappearance of both the whale and Apollo's chariot, the sea, which was probably made of cloth,[76] became transparent with the sunset's afterglow, "as it would have done had it been [made of] transparent glass" (*sì come trasparente vetro avria fatto*); the stage lights, however, seem to have remained undimmed until the arrival of Night.

The third act returned to the sylvan setting of the first, but with different scenery, as Buonarroti is careful to point out. This was the setting for a brief dialogue between Cefalo and Aurora, and immediately following their exit, the scene changed again in preparation for Night's entrance. A new set of flats, representing dark woods, ruins, wild crags and "horrid, frightening" caves was put in place, and the lights were dimmed. Night appeared on a chariot drawn by two owls; its four wheels consisted only of spokes that ended with stars, and as it rose it completely darkened the sky and the rest of the stage. Most astonishingly, however, it was at this point that the whole of the theater also went dark and remained so for the duration of Night's scene.[77] Just enough light was left on the stage to make out its scenery, as if by dim moonlight. The sky was punctuated with stars, which could be seen between the clouds, and a silver moon traversed its vault, occasionally disappearing between the clouds. Shooting stars were represented by "vapors" that fell quickly here and there. Once Night had reached her station high in the sky, the circle of the Zodiac appeared and, turning, stopped above her, showing only those constellations visible during the spring. Each of its signs moved independently from the others, and above each stood a singer in angel costume. At the end of the exchanges between Night and each of its signs, the Zodiac continued its motion through the sky. Night disappeared behind a cloud, and the stage and theater were lit once again.

A new woodland set was needed for the fourth act, and as soon as it was in place, the earth began to tremble, vapors arose from it, and rocks fell away to reveal a large cave, which penetrated so deep below the stage that the spectators, "seeing so much space under the stage, could not understand where the other machines that had come up and moved about it could have been housed and how they could have been made to move."[78]

In the opening could be seen mines with their ores, gems, and rocks of various colors, twisted roots hanging among the stones, and seeds, some of which were shown actually growing, while waters and sulfurous springs flowed and bubbled in great quantity. Cool, scented winds blew throughout the theater, bringing relief to the spectators. A mound of earth emerged from the split hillside, and its surface moved "as a mole disturbs the earth"; it cracked and opened, and from it came forth Berecintia to lament the disappearance of the sun. Cupid arrived on a cloud to comfort her and remained on stage after her exit. Buonarroti is not entirely clear on the setting at this point, but his indication "the scene having returned to its mark" (*la scena tornata a segno*) suggests that the great cave may have closed, leaving the spectators free to turn their attention to the sky, which had opened revealing Mercury in all his splendor. A "beautiful contest between machines" ensued in which Mercury on his cloud chased Cupid all over the sky. In the end, Cupid gave up and joined Mercury on his cloud. As they had in previous acts, the clouds changed shape; when Cupid boarded Mercury's, he sat on the end of it, and the cloud "in order to hold him better, grew in size at the end where he was, so that he ended up in the middle." As it ascended bearing the two gods, other clouds appeared, including one so "splendid and enormous" that it could barely be held aloft. Once it reached the middle of the stage, it opened, exposing its resplendent interior where twenty-five musicians were hidden. Together with those held by other cloud machines, these brought the total number of musicians on stage to about 100 for the closing chorus of the fourth act. In the make-believe world of the *intermedii,* however, many of the figures that appeared in the distance were not real: puppets and cut-outs were used to solve the problems of space, weight, and scale in cloud machines and broad perspectives, such as the panoramic views of Florence and Pisa, where figures were seen moving in the distance.[79]

The scene remained unchanged for Act V, in which most of the action involved cloud machines, including one that emerged from below the stage, rose quickly upwards, changed shape to something resembling "a vase without a pedestal" to reveal fully its occupants, Cupid and Aurora, and continued its ascent at a gentler pace. With Aurora's return to the heavens, and the hunters' chorus that followed, the story came to an end. Not so the entertainment, however; Buontalenti had one more spectacular effect in reserve. The setting changed to a "magnificent and great half-oval theater," with Doric columns, and niches for golden statues, and cornices—a mirror image of the Uffizi theater itself. From various entrances, famous historical figures came in to take their seats in the stands, awaiting the arrival of Fame's chariot. Unexpectedly, she emerged from the stage floor standing on a globe representing the world, and her platform continued to grow into a pyramid, larger and larger until it reached the sky. On its tiers stood sixteen young women representing the cities under the grand duke's rule. Buonarroti estimated its height at an impossible 47.5 feet (14.5 meters)—nearly 10 feet (3 meters) higher than Mount Helicon in the Prologue and 1.5 feet (45.7 cm) higher than the theater as de' Rossi had described it. Nevertheless it seems certain that it reached the rafters (leaving room for Fame on her globe at the top). Its effect astounded the spectators, both because it was the largest of all machines in a production that had already pushed stagecraft to its limits and because none could understand where its bulk could possibly have been hidden. Fame sang in praise of Grand Duke Ferdinand, then disappeared among the clouds; the pyramid began to subside into the stage floor. As it descended, it exposed by degrees a Florentine lily, red with golden accents and as high as the pyramid itself had been. After Fame's disappearance a chorus, sung by the cities of the Grand Duchy, closed the production.[80]

Buontalenti deployed his arsenal of technical resources according to a plan consisting of three overlapping cycles: the first regulated the succession of the different scene types; the second, the tempo of the stage action; and the third, the alternation of light and darkness. In the first cycle, spectacular effects (such as the bulk and trappings of Mount Helicon, the seascape, and the caves) alternated with relatively predictable set designs that might almost be considered "background scenes"—the woodland settings (*scene satiriche*) that return throughout, although always in a different form. As table 1.1 shows, the two types of scene alternate in an almost regular progression. After the spectacular setting of the Prologue, Cefalo is seen in the woods with his huntsmen; the seascape and ensuing cloud chase, with their emphasis on mechanical sea monsters and flying machines, take up the whole of Act II, followed in the first scene of Act III by a return to the *scena satirica*. For the second scene of the third act, the set shifts to yet another forest (now with an appropriately unsettling character) that functions as background for the nocturnal effects that accompany Night's appearance. With the return of daylight, another woodland setting frames the underground treasures revealed in the first scene of Act IV. This same setting provides a neutral backdrop for the cloud chase in the second scene and for the continuation of cloud activity in the first scene of Act V. The imposing allegory of Tuscan cities, nominally part of the fifth act but in reality an epilogue outside the story, balances the Prologue in size, character, and type of setting. Buontalenti's (and Chiabrera's) strategy—the use of an element of fixed character against which spectacular scene changes are given relief—was characteristic of the play with *intermedii,* in which the set for the play (such as the condensed panoramic views of Florence and Pisa in, respectively, *L'amico fido* and *La pellegrina* in 1586 and 1589) remained constant and the *intermedii* provided an ever-changing succession of extravagant effects between acts.

Under Buontalenti's direction, the scene changes themselves acquired an unprecedented dramatic presence.[81] Because the curtain remained open throughout the production, the scenery changes had to be carried out in full view of the audience, and they contributed to the sense of *maraviglia* that Buonarroti considered essential. Seeing Mount Helicon "deflate" itself left the audience wondering how it could have supported its "great weight" in the first place; the sudden dousing of the house lights, achieved without visible mechanism for doing so, added to the mystery of the Night scene; and the rise of the pyramid of Tuscan towns was astonishing because it continued to grow until it reached a size unimagined by the audience. That one could see the transformation and yet not divine its workings was integral to the success of the "theatrical game."

Scene changes also paced the spectacle. The collapse of Mount Helicon, the opening of underground vistas, and the emergence of the pyramid all unfolded gradually, creating suspenseful, miniature subplots that took center stage and directed the attention of the audience away from the actors and singers, and toward the workings of the architect's theater.[82]

Acting, in Buontalenti's productions, was directly linked to the movement of the machines and to the effects that they could create. As Cesare Molinari has shown in his analyses of the *intermedii* of 1586 and 1589, Buontalenti's conception of the theater was primarily a mechanical one and derived from a long tradition of animated scenes dating back to antiquity and encompassing such mechanized spectacles as *crèche* scenes.[83] Stage action in the *intermedii* and in *Cefalo* resulted, in large measure, from machines carrying actors, or sometimes even puppets, from place to place.[84] Acting was relegated to a secondary function, both in the earlier *intermedii* and in *Il rapimento di Cefalo*. Character interaction was carefully circumscribed and took place primarily in the forest landscapes where Aurora and Cefalo had their meetings.

The second cycle, which controlled the tempo of onstage activity, was closely allied with the deployment of the machines. After a relatively static Prologue, which depended on the setting for its effect, the pace picked up with the introduction in the first act of predictable devices (cloud machines) and the establishment of the plot. After the measured pace of this beginning, the increasingly frenzied and less predictable activity of the seascape and cloud chase of the second act brought the action to its first climax. The woodland scene at the beginning of the third act provided a lull after the preceding chaos, and the various machines of Night in the second scene (her chariot, the celestial bodies, and the Zodiac), reinforced by the fantastic effects of the darkened theater, intensified the pace once again. The return to the *scena satirica* provided a break and a transition to the next spectacular high point, the opening of the great caves. Here, for a significant period, the focus shifted entirely to mechanical developments, which unfolded with a measured tempo that heightened the *maraviglia* of the effects being revealed. The brilliance of the subterranean landscape was then juxtaposed, as suddenly as logistics permitted, with another high-spirited sky chase in the second half of the fourth act, the intensity of which gradually wound down into the fifth. The rising of the final pyramid balanced, in reverse, the surprising collapse of Mount Helicon, and, as in the Prologue, the overall scene formed a static tableau.

Light, the third component of the plan for *Il rapimento di Cefalo*, was key to Buontalenti's design—perhaps not surprisingly in a work whose central character is Aurora (Dawn).[85] Molinari has analyzed the cycle of light and darkness in *Il rapimento,* showing that not only does the alternation of the two play a structural role in the production, but that an acute sensitivity to the quality of light in its various shadings, from dawn to near-darkness and from the harsh brilliance of the final scene to the sunlit air of the seascape, was also an important theme in this and other productions by Buontalenti.[86] His treatment of light reached well beyond the confines of the stage itself. For the night scene in the third act of *Il rapimento di Cefalo,* all the main lights, both on stage and in the theater, had to be dimmed and at the end restored as quickly "as lightning." The accomplishment of this amazed the audience both because of the large number of lamps involved and because the effect was achieved without the spectators' being aware of how it was done. A similar effect had marked the opening of *La pellegrina* in 1589, and de' Rossi had remarked on it: "With remarkable uniformity, the lights that ringed the hall lit up all at once, without anyone's discerning the fires' being kindled or any other tricks, and the wonderful play began immediately."[87] Light was also a means of mediating between audience and stage: for the night scene, the audience did not merely see a representation of Night—they were plunged into her realm.[88]

The blurring of the distinction between stage and spectators, already evident to a small extent in the 1589 *intermedii,* was an important component of *Il rapimento* and was carried out on several fronts.[89] The sets for the Prologue spilled out onto the orchestra so that: (1) when Calliope sang she did so not from the remove of the elevated stage but from the level of the audience itself; (2) the breezes of the Prologue and the underground scene originated within the stage and blew throughout the theater; and (3) the dews accompanying Aurora's entrance rained on the spectators as well as on the stage. By reaching beyond the confines of the stage and bringing the audience into physical contact with the transformations of the scene, and thus with the story itself, Buontalenti heightened the illusion of reality and "naturalness" of his machines.

With its lavish staging, *Il rapimento di Cefalo* eclipsed its more modest competition *L'Euridice,* which took place in the smaller Salone di Don Antonio in the Palazzo Pitti and required only two scene changes, from woodland to underworld and back.[90] Advance billing for *Cefalo* was much the same as that for other early operas. Its novelty rested on the fact that it was sung throughout: as the Venetian ambassador Nicolò da Molin reported, it was to be "one of the most inventive plays ever produced, all in music and with wonderful *intermedii.*"[91] Molinari makes the point that Molin's confusion regarding the nature of the entertainment in question (a play with *intermedii*) is indicative of the new conception of the *intermedii* as a dramatic unit that blurred the distinction between plays and between-acts *tableaux.*[92] Indeed *Il rapimento di Cefalo* was closer to the *intermedii* that Buontalenti had perfected than to *L'Euridice. Cefalo*'s structure, consisting of linked but self-contained episodes, was not far removed from that of the earlier *intermedii,* and its repertoire of scenes drew on an established stock of spectacular situations. The 1589 *intermedii* had already included a representation of Mount Helicon, complete with Pegasus on top (second *intermedio*) and a seascape with Tritons and other sea creatures (fifth *intermedio*). The representations by Giulio Parigi for Buonarroti's *Il giudizio di Paride* included two large architectural settings comparable to the theater and pyramid of *Il rapimento di Cefalo,* Fame's palace (in the first *intermedio;* like the pyramid, it was massive and could be made to disappear, probably into a trap) and the temple of Peace (the last, in which Peace emerged, seated on her throne, from a trap); a seascape with exotic monsters (the fourth); and natural settings (the second and third).[93] *Cefalo* lacked a representation of hell, which had been common to the 1586 and 1589 *intermedii;* the fifth *intermedio* for *Il giudizio di Paride,* Vulcan's furnace, offered a variation on this theme. From a technical point of view, however, the splitting of the earth for the great underground cave in the fourth act recalls the opening of the chasms of hell in the second *intermedio* for *L'amico fido* and in the fourth for *La pellegrina.*[94] Finally, the pacing of the action and of the scene changes, together with the fundamentally mechanical conception of the scenography, followed schemes established in the *intermedii* of 1586 and 1589.[95]

In the end, as Tim Carter has argued, *Il rapimento di Cefalo* was a dead-end of sorts: for both political and artistic reasons, the Florentines, under the direction of Giulio Parigi, returned to the format of the play with *intermedii* for all their subsequent spectacular entertainments, while *L'Euridice,* which followed in the tradition of the sung pastorale, became the model for other early operas, most notably Monteverdi's *L'Orfeo.* Nevertheless, *Cefalo,* Buontalenti's last production for the Medici court, was a kind of *summa* of his achievements as a designer, an encyclopedic and brilliant catalog of the scenographic possibilities available to generations of *coraghi* well into the seventeenth century.[96]

CHAPTER TWO

Opera and Ballet in Seventeenth-Century French Theaters: Case Studies of the Salle des Machines and the Palais Royal Theater

Barbara Coeyman

A Comprehensive Approach to French Baroque Opera

Many historical and performance practice issues of French Baroque opera and ballet can be illustrated by examining two important and very different theaters, the Salle des Machines in the Tuileries Palace and the theater in the Palais Royal.[1] A greater understanding of these performance sites facilitates scholarly research of the repertoire and modern productions in historical style. The seventeenth-century reception of the repertoire certainly occurred on several levels, and any given production had multiple meanings. Modern interpretations of extra-musical meanings—sociological, cultural, and political undercurrents, for example—may often be clarified through information about the *look* and setting of the production.[2]

Productions in France during the Baroque period, perhaps more so than those in other countries, resulted from the combination of various artistic media, of which visual and kinesthetic elements—dance, costumes, mechanical effects, and scenery—were in many cases perhaps even more prominent than the music. An examination of the physical settings for productions can inform us of these many arts. Theaters also provide excellent venues in which to imagine the human participants—audiences and performers alike—at past performances and to clarify factors such as the placement of performers on stage, the acoustics in the hall, and the capacities of the stage and audience areas, information not included in the primary sources of music and text alone. Finally, a comprehensive approach to repertoire initiated through theater research also helps dispel misconceptions developed through past scholarship that focused largely on the music in the French Baroque repertoire.

In this essay I explore some of the structural features of French theaters; explain how these structures served performances; place the meanings of these settings in a social and political context; and consider the struggle between French and Italian features in the French theaters of the seventeenth century. An overview of seventeenth-century Parisian theaters and a discussion of general characteristics of French theaters precedes our principal discussion of the Salle des Machines and the theater in the Palais Royal.

Early Baroque Lyric Theater in France:
The Quest for a National Style

Seventeenth-century French musical theater can be understood as an art form in search of codification from the viewpoint of its artistic contents as well as of its physical settings of repertoire.[3] In this case study of two very different theaters, we explore some facets of this search, hoping through an exploration of both the wide range of possible meanings for the repertoire and the theater usage to suggest what it was like to have experienced the original productions.

The theater in the Palais Royal was the most important and busiest hall in Paris during the seventeenth and early eighteenth centuries. In contrast, the occasional use of the Salle des Machines can be explained through very different social, political, architectural, and musical issues. The Palais Royal, first a court and then a public site, was always too small, even after remodelings. The Salle des Machines, always a court setting, was too big. Ironically, the former enjoyed nearly uninterrupted use for 125 years, supporting innumerable performances, whereas the latter was used for only three musical-theater productions during a period of sixty years. The intimacy of the Palais Royal probably was much better for sound, whereas the spaciousness of the Salle des Machines likely provided better spectacles and audience comforts. The Palais Royal was relatively flexible in its ability to accommodate the increasing professionalism that became apparent in ballet and in opera during the course of the century, but the Salle des Machines hearkened back to expansive halls which were intended primarily to support court ballets within the context of large social celebrations.[4]

Promoted by Cardinal Richelieu in the 1630s, the opening of the Palais Royal hall in 1641 represented an important new direction in French musical theater. Twenty years later, the Salle des Machines had the potential of taking over as Paris's principal theater because it offered solutions to the problems of size and lack of facilities that plagued the smaller Palais Royal. However, the death of Cardinal Mazarin in 1661—just as the Salle des Machines was being completed—doomed the theater's chances for success, as many old ways of royal life gave way to Louis XIV's new agendas. The young monarch refocused Paris's musical-theatrical life toward the Palais Royal, which, in 1674, became the home of the French national opera for the next ninety years.[5]

The coincident events and individuals associated with these two theaters suggest a relatively small artistic and social circle in Paris's theatrical life.[6] The designer Carlo Vigarani worked on both theaters, and the audiences in both were probably, to some extent, the same individuals, attending the theater not only to see, but also to be seen. Neither theater survives today, but we can reconstruct each setting in our minds' eyes by perusing some of the vast documentation that has been left behind by artists and observers from the seventeenth century. Our re-creation process is supported by the descriptions of productions at these theaters. Since most of this repertoire has not been discussed in detail to date and modern performances are rare, our exploration of these theaters also expands our understanding of this repertoire.[7]

The Nature of Seventeenth-Century French Lyric Theater Productions

The theaters in both the Tuileries and the Palais Royal typify the architectural, the artistic, and the social aspects of theatrical life in France in the seventeenth century. These halls illustrate what Lawrenson describes as a search for self-identity in theaters during a century of transition from the heavily attended yet private, social court entertainments of the late Renaissance, to the professional, public productions of the eighteenth century. The changing milieu of French theater resulted in a corresponding architectural instability: most seventeenth-century French auditoriums for opera had no particular style, and the Salle des Machines, the most distinctive hall from this epoch, embodied a type of architecture that apparently did not work. This unsettled quality of French theater design contrasts with the more nearly uniform design of most Italian structures of the same period.

This situation is filled with irony: the powerful, centralized Bourbon government, for whom spending apparently knew no limits, stood in contrast to the many smaller, separate Italian cities that supported opera with at least as much enthusiasm as the French government. In some ways the French theater practice remained more unstable than the Italian owing to the much stronger influence of court theater and to the influence of court patronage in France. The emergence of French theatrical identity was helped along by the professionalization of opera during the final quarter of the century, at which point the theater in the Palais Royal provided a commodious, if not ideal, setting for the new French repertoire.[8]

The French search for focus in theater construction and in repertoire during the seventeenth century is explainable by the varied conditions of performance.

The fundamentally ad hoc approach to musical-theatrical performance, at least until the time of Lully's takeover of Perrin and Cambert's patent, meant that many performing conditions were far from ideal and would have been inconsistent from site to site. Many productions, for court and public, appeared in temporary structures of varied sorts. Some theaters were erected on twenty-four hours' notice and were torn down just as quickly. Others were used for only a few years.

This relaxed approach to physical settings was reinforced by the installation of many theaters, temporary or permanent, within preexisting chambers that imposed limitations on theater designers and prevented them from tailoring a site to a particular genre or style. In contrast, most Italian theaters by this time were conceived of and built as integral units intended specifically for opera. One ramification of the French way, even for the longer-standing structures such as the Salle des Machines and the Palais Royal, was that they were continually subjected to whimsical changes made to accommodate the repertoire at hand, but renovations were seldom carried out within the context of a long-term strategic plan. This casual attitude toward theaters in France had another consequence: many buildings, including the Salle des Machines and the Palais Royal, fell into disrepair because of disuse. Alternating periods of use and dormancy often depended upon nothing more than whims of royal patrons. On the other hand, some theaters served double duty as ballrooms and meeting halls.[9]

This makeshift approach to productions was usually more apparent in court theaters than in public halls. The court's frequent travels to royal *châteaux* around Paris meant that productions might occur with little lead time, under a wide range of conditions. It is probably no exaggeration to say that any room in a French royal palace was a potential setting for musical theater during the seventeenth century, the often informal settings of court chambers, in particular, reaffirming the thin line between theater and real life, and between observer and performer. The favor of powerful individuals also accounts for some of the casual, fluid approach to physical facilities: the preferences of persons such as Louis XIV or Mazarin could make or break artistic ventures overnight, both at court and in public theaters.[10]

Many historic studies of French musical theater of the Baroque have suggested that productions were always large, spectacular, and well-planned; and that they were presented before huge audiences. My view of the variability and fluidity in sites suggests quite the opposite. Some French Baroque repertoire was intimate, organized quickly or even spontaneously, and often presented in small, sometimes downright cramped, ill-equipped settings. Regardless of the scope and quality, nearly all Baroque theaters were much smaller than the modern halls in which Baroque repertoire is performed today. An awareness of conditions in the original theaters can inform the modern performer's approach to presenting music, dance, stage sets, and other elements of these entertainments, and can help to identify those aspects of original productions that can remain and those which are best modified to meet the different conditions of today's settings.

Some features of both the Salle des Machines and the Palais Royal reveal specifically French conventions; other aspects of these two theaters appear throughout Europe during the Baroque. Most theaters of the period were rectangular, but the proportions between length and width in the majority of French sites are distinctive. Some French theaters approach a length twice their width. Many of these long, narrow rooms had functioned well as great halls, but when remodeled into theaters, they presented many obstacles to productions. For example, their long-and-narrow proportions virtually required one-point-perspective scenery in order to provide a reasonably coherent view of the stage to a respectable number of spectators. One-point perspective also enhanced the sense of depth in scenery, especially important on the smaller stages. A theater based on one-point perspective also complemented the strict social hierarchy in the French culture of the day: views of the stage were more nearly complete from seats in proximity to the king and royal family, who were seated in the ideal, center seats, usually in the first balcony.[11] In several French theaters, upper stages helped extend sight lines and provided a scenery and performance area separate from the main stage. Long, narrow theaters also resulted in a large proportion of the seats' being placed close to the side walls: visibility of the stage from these sides was inherently problematic, even with one-point-perspective scenery, but was improved by rounding out the back corners of the auditorium into a horseshoe shape, as found in both theaters examined in this essay.[12]

The shapes and sizes of the preexisting spaces in which many French theaters were installed, along with single-point-perspective scenery, influenced the visibility of the stage and, in turn, the seating capacities of theaters.[13] Overall it appears that French theaters had lower audience capacities than most Italian Baroque theaters. On the other hand, seating estimates for most French settings vary tremendously in part because many seats were on seat banks.[14] Generally the percentage of total seats in boxes was lower in French theaters than in Italian halls: the narrower the theater, the greater the likelihood that walls of boxes lined up along the sides of the room would impede the visibility of the stage. Such obstruction of sight lines could be minimized by lattice work partitions in boxes, and higher balconies often contained seatbanks or bench seating rather than boxes in order to eliminate dividers between boxes. Also, as Riccoboni pointed out, whereas many Italian theaters contained four or five levels of boxes, the smaller, French settings typically had no more than three levels, in part due to the height of rooms in which theaters were installed, and also because the visibility of the stage, especially in single-point perspective, decreases as one moves to higher boxes. Furthermore, contemporary dress certainly must have influenced seating capacity, but Riccoboni's report that hooped skirts took up so much room that a woman often needed an entire box to herself may be extreme. Riccoboni also observed that in many French theaters there could be either standing or seating in both the pit and the amphitheater. There could also be standing or seating in both the pit and the orchestra.[15] In some theaters there was also audience seating on stage, although Riccoboni suggests that spectators sitting on stage during an opera would get in the way of the machinery.[16]

In most French theaters built before 1800, relatively little floor space was devoted to anything other than the stage or the audience seating area. There was surprisingly limited room in which to circulate, mingle, and socialize, activities which contemporary reports suggest were integral to the theater experience during the *ancien régime*.[17] While separate areas for social interaction were not so crucial in court theaters (because adjoining palace rooms could be used for promenading), even the public theater in the Palais Royal included very little circulating and congregating area. Designers seemed compelled to devote as much of their limited space as possible to stage and seating rather than to circulation, and, even at that, the Palais Royal public theater was too small.[18] Additionally, as both architectural plans and written commentaries suggest, most French theaters apparently provided relatively meager backstage facilities such as changing rooms for performers, de Pure's description of the Salle des Machines excepted.[19] On the whole, however, questions such as how casts were accommodated when not on stage and what audiences did when not watching or listening to the performance require much more scholarly investigation.

In the first half of the seventeenth century, machinery in France was based on Italian practice. In fact, before Jean Bérain's appointment to the Paris opera in 1680, most stage designers were Italian. Even though the French continued spectacular opera production longer into the eighteenth century than the Italians did, the French machinery was never as good as the Italian, even in the more permanent French settings.[20] Many commentators note, however, that what the French lacked in stage settings they made up for in dancing.

One wonders how elaborate some settings were: visual documents of productions, some drawn or engraved before and others after the fact, cannot always be taken for absolute truth, since many artists endorsed by the monarch were encouraged to make their renderings look as good as possible in order to impress readers, some of whom may not have attended the performances. In many court settings, scenic effects must have been minimal, especially in some of the smaller and less well-equipped rooms where tiny stages were installed on short notice. Furthermore, in Parisian theaters, machinery was often not intended for a particular production or, in some cases, even for a particular site. The recycling of scenery, costumes, and machines was especially common during the vogue for machine plays in the 1640s and 1650s.[21]

Court and Public Theaters in Seventeenth-Century France

An overview of sites used for musical theater in Paris in the seventeenth century establishes a context for our case studies and also illustrates the connections among various theaters and artists in the city. Additionally, theatrical life in France, more so than in Italy, illustrates fundamental differences between court and public theaters and productions. Up to 1674, our story is marked by diversity and even downright instability, since musical-theater productions were located in a wide range of physical settings within the various royal *châteaux*. After 1674, there is more focus, as attention shifted to the public theater in the Palais Royal, while productions at court diminished in scope and frequency during the second half of Louis's life.[22]

Court performances could appear in virtually any room of a royal *château*. Most palaces around Paris occupied by the court on a regular basis—especially the Louvre, Fontainebleau, Chambord, Marly, and Saint Germain-en-Laye—contained several apartments or chambers that regularly accommodated performance. Several of these buildings also had auditoriums intended to function as theaters.[23] Royal palaces also hosted outdoor performances from time to time.

One of the oldest court theaters, built in 1548 in the Hôtel de Bourgogne in Paris, served a range of theatrical functions: this hall was used by touring theatrical companies by the mid sixteenth century; Catherine de' Medici brought Italian actors there frequently; farces were presented in the hall in 1607.[24] Bapst suggests that the Hôtel de Bourgogne was disagreeable for spectators since it was built in the shape of a half bowl. It was smaller than the theater in the Petit Bourbon, although better decorated. In 1610 only two or three different sets of scenery were used for all shows. By 1631 the royal comedians remodeled the decrepit hall in Italian style, and in 1634 new decorations were made. The theater was remodeled again in 1647.[25]

The great hall in the Hôtel du Petit Bourbon was built in 1574 and opened as a performance site in 1576. Located across the street from the Louvre, the hall was used for relatively large court musical and theatrical gatherings that could not be accommodated in the smaller chambers in the Louvre. In 1581 the hall was the site of the first court ballet, the important *Ballet comique de la reyne* by Baltasar de Beaujoyeulx. The well-known view of a meeting of the Estates General in 1614 suggests the immense capacity of the hall.[26]

The room was converted to a theater sometime around 1614, with the addition of seating on the floor of the amphitheater as well as in three rows of balconies. Curiously, only a few works are known to have played there in the years following these renovations: the *Ballet de Renaud* in 1619 and the *Ballet de la reyne representant* [*sic*] *le soleil* in 1621. However, after remodeling by Giacomo Torelli, the theater was used frequently during the 1640s and 1650s. Important productions there were the opera *La finta pazza* in 1645 and the machine play *Andromède* in 1650.[27] The hall served Molière's company from 1658 until October 1660, when the entire palace was torn down to make room for the eastward expansion of the Louvre.

As a consequence of his own personal interest in drama, Richelieu legitimized French theater as a cultural institution by establishing the Académie Française in 1635.[28] To promote theater performances, Richelieu also established additional performing sites for the French companies. He saw to the building of several theaters, such as the Théâtre du Marais (1634), home of Corneille's troupe, in a disused tennis court.[29] In 1637 he called for the building of two theaters in his palace, the so-called Palais Cardinal. (After Richelieu's death in 1642, it became known as the Palais Royal.) The smaller of these theaters was to hold 600, the larger 3,000 spectators.[30] Only one of these halls was realized, the theater that we examine in this essay, in conditions much less grand than were Richelieu's visions. The machine play *Mirame* inaugurated the Palais Royal hall in 1641, and later that year, the *Ballet de prosperité des armes* played there.[31]

Following Richelieu's lead, his successor, Cardinal Mazarin, lent equal support to theater. Motivated as much by his own political ambition as by France's artistic needs, Mazarin assisted in both the development and the professionalization of French musical theater, albeit on his own Italian model. Mazarin had learned the importance of fine quality theater from the strong Italian tradition he had experienced in Rome, particularly in the theater in the Barberini Palace, built in 1632.[32] He also anticipated—wrongly, it turned out—that promotion of Italian theater would in turn help win popularity for his Italian methods of running France's government. Most important for the future of French theater, he recognized how sorely Paris lacked adequate performing spaces for theater and music.

To help remedy this situation, Mazarin imported many Italian artists to Paris: for example, in the early 1640s, the Italian Comedians played in Paris; and in 1644 Mazarin requested that the duke of Parma send Torelli to Paris to build adequate performance venues for the Italian performers.[33] Mazarin's importation of Italian opera in the 1640s directly influenced his decision to remodel the Palais Royal—what I describe below in this essay as phase two of the theater's history.

Torelli's improved hall opened in 1646 with Cavalli's *Egisto*. In 1647 Luigi Rossi's opera *Orphée* appeared, the same story which had run as a successful machine play in 1642. To Mazarin's chagrin, the opera was derided for being too Italian and too costly. Consequently, most of his Italian musicians were forced to leave Paris the summer after the production and were also libeled in print in verses called *Mazarinades* published during the course of the Fronde, the French civil war of the late 1640s and early 1650s.

Throughout the 1650s, the court also used various chambers in the Louvre, primarily for two reasons: as a conscious move to combat the public outcry over the high cost of *Orphée,* and also to relocate some productions away from Mazarin's palace into Louis XIV's territory. Many court ballets appeared in the Louvre. Also, the Petit Bourbon theater accommodated a number of productions that were too large for either the Louvre or the Palais Royal: the opera *La finta pazza* played there in December 1645. In 1653 Lully's first big success, the *Ballet des proverbes,* appeared in the larger hall; and in 1654 Carlo Caproli's Italian opera *Le nozze di Peleo e di Theti* [*sic*] was moved from the Palais Royal to the Petit Bourbon to accommodate the anticipated large crowds.[34]

At the end of the 1650s, several events influenced theater development in Paris for the remainder of the century. In 1659—on the heels of relative internal stability after the Fronde, the signing of the Peace of the Pyrenees, and the engagement of Louis XIV to the Spanish Princess Marie Thérèse—Mazarin commissioned the writing of a new Italian opera, *Hercule amoureux* (*Ercole amante*) by the composer Francesco Cavalli and the librettist Francesco Buti for the king's wedding, planned for 9 June 1660.[35]

Cavalli, summoned from Venice in August 1659 and having arrived in Paris in July 1660, was able to employ some of the gifted Italian singers, such as Anna Bergerotti, Giuseppe Melone, Giovanni Francesco Tagliavacca, and Atto Melani, already in Paris. Initially Mazarin promoted the Palais Royal as the location for this production. However, realizing that this room and all other existing theaters in the city were inadequate to hold such a splendid festival, and knowing that Molière's company would soon move there owing to the impending demolition of the Petit Bourbon, Mazarin took advantage of the circumstances and promoted a new, grander theater.

This new hall—which would be named the Salle des Machines—was marked by controversy from its inception. Probably at the urging of Francesco Buti and his niece, the duchess of Mantua, Mazarin turned his back on Torelli, who to that date had not built an entire theater, only having remodeled existing interiors, and the cardinal looked to Italy for another designer. From Modena Mazarin recruited the Vigarani family: Gaspare and his sons Carlo and Ludovico. They may have been chosen because of their reputation not only as stage designers, but also as builders of complete buildings, and as planners of grand, outdoor tournaments. Their greatest achievement as theater builders to that point, the Ducal Theater in Modena, was already well known in France by the time of Mazarin's invitation. This theater, built in 1654, was constructed on a grand scale and could hold 3,000 spectators.[36]

Arriving in Paris at the beginning of July 1659, the Vigaranis were reluctant to follow Mazarin's suggestion that they erect a large wooden theater at the Palais Royal. Instead, they persuaded the cardinal to relocate the theater site to the expanding Tuileries Palace, west of the Palais Royal beyond the Louvre.

At the beginning of August, they submitted plans to the king, and building started on 19 September 1659. Apparently there were numerous differences of opinion between the French and Italian builders. Supporting the idea of a complex theater as envisioned by Mazarin and based on their success with the theater at Modena, the Vigaranis opted for the more durable stone materials being used at that time in construction work in other sections of the Tuileries Palace.[37] They placed the stage of the new theater in an existing pavilion built during Catherine de' Medici's rule, whereas the auditorium was installed within the current construction led by Le Vau.[38] Some of their letters suggest that they had already started building stage machinery as early as the final months of 1659, simultaneous with the construction of the theater.

While the Vigaranis' decision to move the theater to the Tuileries was a sound one, it delayed Mazarin's anticipated completion date of November 1660, when Louis was to return to Paris with the queen. While initially the work seemed on schedule—in July the completion was forecast for August, and the *Gazette de France* reported that the king had inspected and approved the construction site in September—not even the outside walls were finished until October.[39] Apparently the Vigaranis were caught off guard by the scope of the job and also by the French climate.[40] Further, since the walls of the building in progress were already standing, Vigarani had no control over the external dimensions of the theater; he could only control internal structures such as the size of the stage. These unexpected conditions astronomically increased the cost of the project to 120,000 *livres.* The theater was nowhere near completion by November. Consequently, the premiere of Cavalli's new opera, which he apparently composed during his first twelve months in Paris, was also delayed. Instead, another work by Cavalli, the Italian comedy *Xerxes* (text by Buti), played four times in the Haute Gallerie of the Louvre. *Xerxes* appeared in a temporary theater constructed in one month by Carlo Vigarani using tapestries rather than painted sets.[41]

The Salle des Machines opened in February 1662 with Cavalli's new opera, *Hercule amoureux.*[42] Ironically, this production went on without Mazarin, who died in March 1661. In spite of opposition to Italian opera, it was imperative that the production of *Hercule* go ahead as planned, if only because of the immense financial investment at that point.[43] Reviews of the opera's eight performances ranged from very supportive to highly critical.[44] Overall, however, the naysayers prevailed, probably in part because of the absence of Italian opera's principal supporter, Mazarin. Colbert found the expenses for *Hercule* exorbitant.

By this time Louis XIV understood well the usefulness of the performing arts in supporting his autocratic control of France. Lully was not far behind in staking his own claim for power through French art and music, discrediting yet further Mazarin's opera. The court's means of disassociating from Italian theater traditions included moving productions not only away from the Salle des Machines but by totally removing them from Paris. During the 1660s, settings in the palaces at Saint-Germain-en-Laye, Fontainebleau, Chambord, Compiegne, and Versailles witnessed court ballets, new genres such as Molière's *comédie-ballets,* and new operas by Lully.[45]

With Italian opera grossly discredited, Cavalli, the Vigaranis, and the Italian singers beat a hasty retreat from France, arriving back in Italy in May 1662 after *Hercule* closed.[46] However, Carlo Vigarani returned to Paris in August 1662 and became chief organizer of the king's *fêtes*. In August 1672 Carlo signed a contract as Lully's chief machinist and partner in the Académie de Musique, a collaboration which lasted until 1680.[47] Torelli did not leave France immediately, suffering a yet more ignoble conclusion to his tenure in Paris. After being supplanted from the circle of royal artists by the Vigaranis, Torelli sought new sponsorship by designing sets for the production of *Les fâcheux* presented in July 1661 by France's finance minister Nicolas Fouquet at Vaux-le-Vicomte. Two months later, Fouquet was arrested and Torelli departed Paris for good.[48] While his French productions may not have gained as much recognition as his work in Italy, by the end of his fifteen years in Paris, Torelli had done more than any other designer to advance French stage production techniques.

Understandably, tensions between Torelli and the Vigaranis were strong: Torelli probably authored the libelous *Riflessione sopra la fabbrica del nuovo teatro* against the Vigaranis; and the Vigaranis were probably responsible for the destruction of some of Torelli's stage machinery taken from the Petit Bourbon theater.[49]

The Salle des Machines was not used for another production until 1671 when the *tragédie-comédie* and accompanying ballet *Psiché* by Molière, Corneille, Lully, and Carlo Vigarani appeared.[50] Whether any changes were made to the hall following the performances of *Hercule* is unclear, as are the reasons for returning to this site for the 1671 production. In spite of the even greater expense for *Psiché*—130,000 *livres*—the production played there only twice, after which the hall was closed to musical theater for the remainder of Louis XIV's reign.[51] It was not used again until 1720, during the Regency of Louis XV, as the site for *Les folies de Cardenio,* a court ballet that included the first and last appearance of the young king in a dancing role.

The return to the hall made political sense as an affirmation of the Regency's reestablishment in Paris—away from the Versailles of Louis XIV. For the production of *Cardenio,* the theater was remodeled. The cost of the ballet and remodeling was nearly 150,000 *livres.*[52] However, the ballet marked several finales: the demise of court ballet in France; the end of strongly propagandistic musical theater; and the close of the Salle des Machines as a site for musical theater.[53] After *Cardenio* there were no more ballets in the hall, and only marionette theater during the 1730s. In 1763 Jacques Soufflot and Anges Jacques Gabriel remodeled the Salle des Machines as the temporary home of the Paris Opera after a fire destroyed the Palais Royal theater: once again the lives of the two theaters intersected.

It is ironic that the Salle des Machines, built to celebrate the wedding of France's greatest monarch, was used only three times in fifty-nine years; in contrast, the Palais Royal theater—in many ways less accommodating for the court or the public—regularly supported productions for over a century. Molière's move to the Palais Royal in 1660 brought a third round of remodeling to the theater, which was used jointly by his company, an Italian troupe, and court productions during the remainder of that decade.

The Palais Royal thus became the home of the Paris Opera in 1673. Pierre Perrin's 1669 patent, establishing the first Académie d'Opéra, had failed, and by March 1672 Lully had replaced him as the new director of the Opera. Molière's sudden death after the fourth performance of *Le malade imaginaire* in January 1673, coupled with Louis's retirement from dancing in 1671, signaled a new direction for French musical theater. Lully's acquisition of the Palais Royal theater seemed a foregone conclusion. His remodeling of the opera house brought about both its fourth and final stage of reorganization and some level of closure in the French search for theatrical identity, as Parisians acquired a site reasonably on par with Italian theaters. Lully's new opera house opened on 19 January 1674 with a production of his second opera, *Alceste*.[54]

The Salle des Machines

Let us now examine specific theaters: (1) the Salle des Machines in the Tuileries from 1659 to 1721; and (2) the theater in the Palais Royal in its four stages of development—as it appeared when it opened in 1641, as it was remodeled in 1645 by Torelli, during the years from 1660 to 1674 when Molière was in control of the theater, and from 1674 until the end of Lully's career.

Examining these halls can clarify many of our ideas about the history of French theaters and also illustrate the French-Italian dialogue in Paris in the seventeenth century. Clearly the range of topics that can be addressed by examining opera in context is broad: my present descriptions are directed primarily at understanding how architectural aspects of the theaters accommodated the human beings using the theaters. Our considerations must minimally include stages, auditoriums, audience seating, and circulation spaces.

While used far less frequently, the Salle des Machines can be reconstructed in much greater detail than can the Palais Royal. That sources for the Salle des Machines are so numerous is curious since the hall was so little used. At the same time, documentation pertaining to the Palais Royal is sparse, even though it was used more frequently. These two case studies illustrate that the frequency of use of a hall should not be equated with its historical importance or with its efficacy as a theater.

In this essay, the descriptions of repertoire performed in each hall augment the remarks about the perception of these theaters by composers, performers, and audiences alike.[55] Because neither the theaters nor the repertoire discussed here have received much critical attention to date by music or theater historians, this essay significantly expands our understanding of both the productions and the theaters.[56]

This description of the Salle des Machines is based primarily on two sets of images: (1) Blondel's engraved view of the auditorium (drawn possibly as early as 1710) and (2) a drawing of the entire Tuileries Palace (made sometime around 1700 and currently located in the National Archives in Paris). These are complemented by a variety of written descriptions.[57] The latter is chronologically closer to the productions of 1662 and 1671 that we discuss, and it offers a view of both the auditorium and the stage. Blondel's engravings are much more detailed but include only the auditorium. Blondel's view also provides little information about the theater's relation to the palace itself, and he does not describe access points, hallways, and other details. The Archives' drawing depicts the three levels of the theater: here we reproduce only the level of the main stage and auditorium, shown in figure 2.3 below.[58]

The Layout of the Salle des Machines

Bounded by gardens on the west, by a courtyard on the east, and by the wings of the Tuileries Palace on both ends, the Salle des Machines occupied a huge space roughly 260 feet by 58 feet (79.2 meters by 17.7 meters).[59] This space was divided unequally, the stage and backstage occupying about 146 feet (44.5 meters), the auditorium spanning the remaining 114 feet (34.7 meters; see figure 2.1). Hallways between the palace's exterior walls and the theater walls along its two sides and back were relatively narrow, measuring approximately 6.5 feet (2 meters) wide. On the first floor, entry to the building from the outside apparently was through a set of doors on the garden (west) side of the building, but this access led only into the hallway on that same side, not into any space that could be called a lobby.[60] From that hallway one could straight-away enter the auditorium near the orchestra at stage right, or turn right, up a flight of steps to the first balcony of seats. From the mezzanine level in between the first and second balconies, internal exits from the rear of the auditorium led to the chapel on the courtyard side and to a gallery on the garden side.

According to de Pure, the height of the stage was about 24 feet (7.3 meters) and the area above the stage within the mansard roof for flying machines and for other machinery was about 37 feet (11.3 meters). The area below the stage for traps and machinery measured about 15 feet (4.6 meters). The auditorium was about 57 feet (17.4 meters) high and accommodated three balconies.[61] De Pure also described secret stairs and galleries for the king, who, as both actor and spectator, could walk directly from the stage to his private box after dancing. De Pure also indicated private rooms (adjacent the stage) for the king, noble-men, and ladies of the court. There were also backstage rooms for craftsmen.[62]

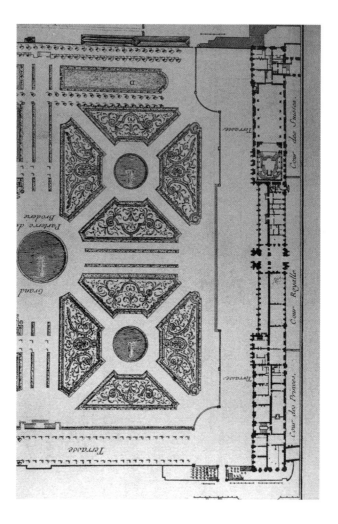

Figure 2.1. Plan of the Tuileries Palace and adjacent gardens c. 1660 from Blondel, *L'architecture française,* vol. 4 (1756), book 6, illus. 1, plate 23. The figure has been inverted in order to position the plan with east to the left.

The raked stage inclined a bit in excess of 40 inches (1 meter) from front to back.[63]

Blondel described the theater décor as breathtaking.[64] Two pairs of Corinthian columns with beautiful bases and capitals, one set back from the other, established the front of the one-point-perspective scenery in front of the proscenium arch (see figure 2.2). Magnificent columns, carved *putti,* and *fleurs de lis* lined the side and back walls of the theater. Décor was supervised by Charles Errard, one of the favorite royal artists at the time of the building of the Salle des Machines. He also

Figure 2.2. Elevation of the Salle des Machines from Blondel, *L'architecture française,* vol. 4 (1756), book 6, illus. 1, plate 30.

painted some of the interiors of the Palais Royal in the 1645 remodeling under Torelli. The ceiling was beautifully decorated, and, according to several reports, the décor was constantly changing.[65] De Pure said the ceiling was built very solidly, and Albert Babeau, author of one of the best historical studies of the hall to date, cites a report from 1757 stating that the ceiling decoration, designed by Le Brun and painted by Noel Coypel, measured 12 feet by 15 feet (3.7 meters by 4.6 meters) and contained fourteen round panels.[66] At one point the ceiling panels depicted Louis as Jupiter restraining Mars so that Love could triumph.[67]

Curiously, much of the surviving information about the Salle des Machines —especially Blondel's text and drawings—focuses on the auditorium rather than on the stage, even though the stage was apparently the more innovative portion of Vigarani's work, the site of the machinery which gave the room its name.[68] My description of the auditorium is based primarily on Blondel's plan and description, augmented by information drawn from the Archives' drawing of 1700. Blondel's engraving of the auditorium does not differ substantially from the 1700 drawing. His detailed descriptions of the auditorium and his plans and elevations of the room provide one of the most precise explanations of auditorium usage in Baroque theaters. In figure 2.3, the letters appearing on Blondel's plan in elaborate script are original; those in the bold, sans-serif type have been added for clarity.

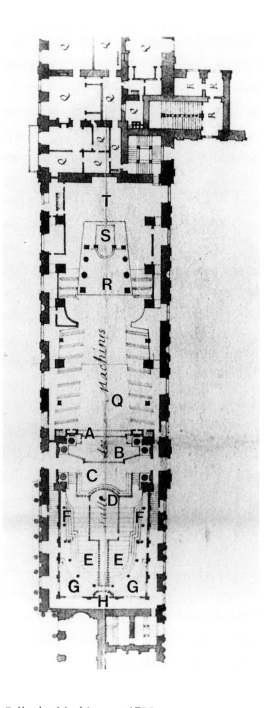

Figure 2.3. The Salle des Machines, c. 1700.

The court's strict social hierarchy is reflected in the arrangement of the auditorium. A row of candles [A] delineated the stage from the auditorium—fantasy from reality—and also provided light for the area Blondel calls "the place in the orchestra for the music" (*le lieu de l'orquestre pour la musique*) [B]. The orchestra, measuring approximately 16 feet by 45 feet (4.9 meters by 13.7 meters) at its greatest width and depth, was the largest in any historic French theater investigated to date.[69] Next to the orchestra was the parterre [C] for the king's guards, reached from either side hallway by ascending three steps. Above these side doorways on both sides were prominently placed boxes, surrounded by four columns, *putti,* and *fleurs de lis* (see figure 2.2).[70] Higher than the parterre by three seat banks was the loge of the king [D]. Behind the king on fifteen low risers and on three rows of seat banks lining the sides and rear [E] was seating for the court, with a center aisle leading to stairs at the rear descending to the ground floor. From these seat banks, doors on each side led to the hallways. Between the two pairs of side doorways were three elevated boxes [F] for the officers of the *maison du roi.* Six rows of seat banks at the rear of the room (not labeled on Blondel's plan; my [G]) were for the public. Above the doorway at the rear was the theater's largest box, for the monarch (my [H]).[71] Blondel included illustrations of both upper balconies, but did not describe them in his text. The first balcony was reached from the outer hallway through two doors above the rear side doors on the amphitheater level, and consisted of twelve boxes each roughly 6 feet by 10 feet (1.8 meters by 3 meters) connected to one another.[72] From the six boxes at right angles to the stage, the view of scenery must have been limited to the depth of only a few flats. Behind the six other boxes at the rear, the balcony also contained three rows of seat banks. Blondel does not specify the height of balconies, but his rear elevation suggests that there was ample room in these boxes. The second balcony ran continuously around the perimeter of the amphitheater without the delineation of boxes as on the first balcony. The second balcony contained two seat banks at the rear. The *livret* of *Psiché* indicated that thirty chandeliers lighted the auditorium.[73]

Reports of audience capacity in the theater vary greatly. Blondel suggests 6,000, but some others pushed the figure as high as 8,000.[74] One wonders what percentage of seats, even at 6,000, was occupied at a single performance. Many diaries and other personal accounts suggest that some spectators attended multiple performances of the same opera or ballet, so it is theoretically possible that the hall was filled to capacity for each performance. What were Vigarani's motivations, or Mazarin's, for that matter, in designing such a large hall, which acts more as a great common space for the people of Paris, as Vigarani said, than as a setting for intimate court gatherings?[75] Perhaps the immensity of the theater was an even greater deterrent to its regular use than were the acoustics: the hall may simply have been too hard to fill.

Our information about machinery and scenic effects comes largely from the
Archives' drawing (figure 2.3). The first floor drawing indicates that the main
part of the stage [Q], from the candles to the edge of the upper stage [R],
measured over 90 feet (27.4 meters)—approximately eighty percent of the
length of the auditorium—and 58.5 feet (17.8 meters) wide.[76] The width of the
opening between flats at the front of the stage was about 33 feet (10 meters).
Eight pairs of flats lined the stage in one-point perspective and provided entry
points to the stage for the performers. Behind this main stage was the upper
stage, which was about half the depth of the main stage, or approximately
45 feet (13.7 meters). The height of this upper stage above the main stage is
impossible to determine from the Archives' plan: our only source of information about heights in the theater, de Pure, said nothing about the upper stage.[77]
In the Archives' drawing, three pairs of flats line the upper stage, and five pairs
of columns support the structure. The ground floor drawing of the stage also
indicates supports for machinery at the front center on the main stage, and the
four main supports of the upper stage carry through to the ground floor as well.
All flats also appear in this lower level, and all structural supports also continue
beneath the stage. Further, the Archives' drawing suggests that the center rear
of the trapezoidal portion [S] of the upper stage was raised. Presumably the area
next to and behind [T] accommodated people, costumes, props, and perhaps
some of the dressing rooms mentioned by de Pure. From this backstage, there
were also several exits to other parts of the palace. How and where performers
entered this upper stage is unclear.

Comments about productions from eyewitnesses suggest the scope of visual
effects possible with this machinery. Menestrier reported that the machines were
quite magnificent, enabling gods and goddesses to make fantastic ascents and
descents.[78] The first act of *Hercule amoureux* attracted the attention of de Pure,
who cited one machine measuring 45 feet by 60 feet (13.7 meters by 18.3 meters)
that held the entire royal family—thirty dancers as the fifteen imperial families
of France—plus sixty unspecified performers. De Pure also notes the folly of
this maneuver, should the machine have malfunctioned. The largest clouds
reportedly could hold 300 performers at once.

In view of this elaborate system of machinery, it is instructive to reevaluate
some of the accepted explanations for the theater's disuse. The conventional
interpretation, in modern histories, for why the hall did *not* work for opera and
ballet is that acoustics were poor. It seems difficult to accept the notion that a
stage designer of Vigarani's caliber could have built a theater that was as
deplorable as some reports suggest.[79] It seems clear that Vigarani intended that
visual components be central to productions in this Salle des *Machines.* Therefore, even if acoustics were weak, could sound alone generate the negative
impression which has been left about the theater in our historical records?

Some contemporary critics were supportive of the theater: the *Gazette de
France* of February 1662, in its report on *Hercule,* praised both sight and sound

in the theater; Germain Brice's *Description de la ville de Paris,* as early as 1684 and as late as the 1757 edition, reported that the hall was among the most magnificent structures in Europe, a room in which everyone could see and hear well.[80] Some of the negative opinions were generated by critics years after the fact, perhaps through hearsay. For example, Blondel, who apparently never witnessed a performance in the hall, reported poor acoustics.[81]

Apparently some of the negative reports emanated as much from social and political controversies as from artistic conditions.[82] The building was caught in that French identity crisis, in the transition from communal, court-based standards of production in the first half of the seventeenth century, to the more theatrical, professional orientation at the end of the century.[83] During the height of the French vogue for stage machinery, it seems that Vigarani and Cavalli gave the audiences of Paris what they thought they wanted in a theater and in theater production, combining many artistic ideals under one roof. Unfortunately the designer, the composer, the hall, and the repertoire all received poor public acclaim, perhaps because all were too Italian. Critics after the fact imparted more importance to sound than either Vigarani or Cavalli apparently ever intended for the theater.[84]

Three Productions at the Salle des Machines:
Hercule amoureux, *Psiché*, and *Cardenio*

Examining the look of productions explains much about how a theater accommodated performers and impressed spectators.[85] *Hercule amoureux* played in the hall eight times in 1662: 7, 14, and 18 February; 18, 22, 25, and 29 April; and 6 May.[86] No iconographic documentation of the production survives: while several different versions of the *livrets* were published, none contains images of the performance. Including construction costs, the production was the court's most expensive musical-theatrical undertaking to that date.

Menestrier viewed *Hercule amoureux* as a paradigm for musical-theater pieces and suggested that its general features be emulated in other ballets. For him there were three principal pleasures in this work: spectacle, in the scenery of the mountains, sea, and sky; singing, in concerts by characters such as La Lune and La Fleuve; and dance, by the fifteen royal families of France. The libretto of *Hercule* clearly indicates the centrality of spectacle for the production. Although the opera was apparently sung totally in Italian, French influence is evident throughout the score, particularly in Cavalli's significant use of chorus, in his inclusion of dances composed by Lully, and in the implementation of the conventional French five-act structure.

Based on the story of Hercules (i.e., Louis) in love, the ballet's Prologue and five acts include a total of eighteen *entrées*—most at the end of acts—which function as supports for the dramatic action and not merely as *entr'acte* spectacle. Some of the negative reports about acoustics may have been prompted by the amount of solo singing in Italian. Perhaps the real problem, though, was with the style of the repertoire rather than with the sound *per se*.[87]

From information in *Hercule*'s published *livret*, we can gain some impression of how the stage in the Salle des Machines accommodated stage settings. Unfortunately, while *livrets* can offer reasonably complete descriptions about settings on the opera stage, they usually provide no information about the time frame in which such sets appeared: how much time any given mechanical action lasted or how long it took to change flats, for example. The reported six-hour performance time for *Hercule* could be explained, in part, by the time needed in setting up the elaborate scenic effects or by time-consuming changes of sets.[88] A greater understanding of the relative amounts of time taken for visual versus aural components of the production might inform our interpretation of comments by members of the audiences about the opera and the theater.[89]

Hercule contained seven different stage settings.[90] Dancing appeared in eighteen *entrées*, eleven of these after Act V of the opera, somewhat like a grand finale in the court ballet tradition. Additionally, thirteen different mechanical effects appeared during the production, some of these providing a way for performers to enter onto or to exit from the stage area, others helping to delineate scene changes.

According to the printed *livret*, personnel in *Hercule* was considerable.[91] Roles in the production consisted of 185 dancing parts and twenty-eight parts for solo singers; the size of the orchestra is unspecified, but the King's Twenty-Four Violins could have been accommodated easily in the theater's orchestra pit, and the chorus could have been the sixty extras on the machine de Pure described.[92] Of the dancers, forty-one were nobles (eighteen men and twenty-three women, from some of the best French families) and at least sixty were professionals. Solo singers numbered twelve (four men, eight women, mostly Italians).[93] Curiously—unlike some other productions at court, including ballets of the 1650s and *Psiché* in 1671—*Hercule* apparently contained no scene in which all the nearly 200 performers appeared together. The largest *entrée* of dance in *Hercule* presented only twenty-two of the dancers, a relatively meager number for such a grand stage.[94]

The scenic course of the opera may be summarized as follows: The Prologue must have been one of the focal points of the ballet, possibly the scene to which de Pure alludes.[95] The sixteen dancers in the Prologue included the king and the new queen representing the house of Austria in one of her few dancing roles ever at court. Other noble dancers represented the imperial families of France. The setting for the Prologue is the rocky terrain of the mountains, through which flow fourteen rivers under the domination of France. In the distance—perhaps the upper stage—is the sea, over which the Moon descends in a machine representing the sky. As the Moon sings of the glory of the houses of France, another machine carrying the fifteen imperial families descends. The sea retreats and opens up the stage for two *entrées* of dance, after which the dancers return to the sky.

In Act I, presumably with the same scenery as the Prologue, Venus and a chorus of graces descend from heaven on a machine. On their return, Junon appears in the clouds on a peacock, and on her return, eight dancers representing storms and thunder emerge from the clouds. Act II begins in the grand palace of Eocalie, and in scene vi changes to a grotto of sleep, where solo singers and a chorus accompany Junon's descent and twelve dancers representing dreams appear. Act III is set in a flower garden. Venus descends on a cloud that immediately disappears. With her magic wand, she causes herbs and flowers to spring up out of the earth. In scene v, Junon and Sommeil ascend into the air and then come down to pick up Hercule, while Mercure flies in to wake him. The exit of the magic chair opens up the sixteen statues in the garden to reveal the demons they have been harboring, and the dance of the demons closes the act. The setting for Act IV is the sea, beside which is the tower where Illus is imprisoned. A Page arrives on a small bark to talk to Illus, who, in a fit of depression, throws himself into the sea. Junon returns to the sky on a throne surrounded by clouds. Neptune, in a grand shell drawn by seahorses, saves Illus to the accompaniment of a celebratory chorus. Finally Illus descends to the stage in a machine of Junon, who returns to the sky. Six zephyrs then dance. In scene vi, the setting changes to a cypress garden full of magnificent sepulchers. Yole visits her father Eutyre's tomb, which immediately falls into ruin and from which the spirit of Eutyre disappears. Twelve women of Yole's court and phantoms from the tombs dance the act's closing *entrée*. Act V takes place in Hell. Pluton (played by Louis), Proserpine, and twelve furies dance. Scene ii changes to the temple of Hymen. Jupiter ascends to the sky, then Junon descends. A chorus of stars and planets offers the final music that occurs at Hercule's wedding, which is then celebrated in eight ballet *entrées,* presumably with the same stage setting as that of the last act of the opera. Apparently this finale was another focal point of the production, with spectacle generated by dancing, costumes, and many instruments, rather than by scenery changes.[96] These concluding *entrées* resemble a French court ballet: in fact, audiences may have preferred this part of the production over Cavalli's Italian opera.

The production of *Psiché* at the Salle des Machines was an important juncture in the history of that theater. While acoustics may not have been as bad as some critics reported, the absence of other repertoire in the hall until January 1671 nevertheless suggests some problem (whether architectural, acoustical, political, or social) in using the theater—especially in light of the great financial investment it represented. The return to the theater for the January 1671 performances of *Psiché* can be interpreted in various ways. In part, the revival of the Salle des Machines can be viewed as the court's attempt at giving the structure new life, perhaps even at justifying its existence at a time when other sections of the Tuilieres Palace were being actively used.[97] Additionally, on the heels of the grand Versailles *fêtes* of 1664 and 1668, the return to the Salle des Machines may reflect an attempt at relocating grand spectacles to Paris, as suggested in reports about *Psiché,* just at the time when Louis was deciding to move his court permanently to Versailles. The festival-like scope of the production of *Psiché* may have been influenced by these outdoor events at Versailles. Some observers even suggested that Louis XIV called for *Psiché* because he wanted to see the machinery representing Hell again. The production cost of *Psiché*— 130,000 *livres*—nearly doubled the price of *Hercule.* After 1671 the hall lay dormant for the remainder of Louis's reign.[98] In March 1671, Molière's company replayed *Psiché,* this time in the Palais Royal, newly renovated especially for the spectacle.

The *livret* for *Psiché* includes a two-page description of the hall.[99] Paralleling other sources already cited, this description focuses on the auditorium—specifying its dimensions—the location of the royal family, the decorations, and other details while virtually excluding commentary about the stage. The *Gazette* cited the scenery in *Psiché* as evidence that no other court in Europe could provide such magnificent décor.

Consisting of a Prologue and five acts, *Psiché* resembles *Xerxes* and *Hercule,* but differs being in French. Mechanical effects and *divertissements* of music and dance appear within each of the five acts, and four *entrées* of dancing follow the final act. However, the production was more French in style than *Hercule* in that it also included *entrées* of dance between each act and far more elaborate scenic and mechanical effects. Unlike *Hercule, Psiché* was not associated with any particular court celebration. (The *Gazette* reports that the only special audience members were a papal nuncio and some ambassadors.) *Psiché* played in the Salle des Machines only twice, on 17 and 24 January.[100] The length of time for the production is not indicated in any descriptions or reports.[101]

The *livret* indicates that *Psiché* included at least nine settings of scenery, eleven uses of machinery, and nine *entrées* of dance. As is typical, the Prologue and the Finale are the most spectacular sections. In the Prologue, the stage represents a seaport with fields at the front, a harbor with several towers, a few vessels in the port, and a village in the distance. Three machines descend, enveloped in clouds, and then open to span the width of the stage. Two graces emerge from the two smaller machines. From the largest machine come Venus, her son, and six young *amours,* accompanied by thirty-four singers and twenty-six dancers. Amour circles in the air several times before getting lost in the clouds.

Scenery for Act I is a grand cypress alley lined with tombs of the kings descended from Psiché's family and covered by a triumphal arch. The third scene of the act includes an Italian concert by ten flutes, three singers, and twelve dancers. No mechanical effects are described for the first act, but for the first *intermede,* the scene changes to a desert with horrible rocks, where only a "lugubrious" concert by three singers ensues. In the final scene of Act II, Psiché is elevated into the clouds by a whirlwind. The setting remains unchanged. The *intermede* after the act shows the grand vestibule of a palace, eight cyclopes and eight fairies dance. The highlight of Act III is a zephyr who flies around the entire stage. Three singers and sixteen dancers as zephyrs and *amours* follow. The setting of Act IV changes to a garden with a variety of fruit trees and rare flowers. In an alcove appear several vaults decorated with shellfish, fountains, and statues. At the end of the scenery is a magnificent palace. In scene i of this act, Psiché's two sisters are carried away on a cloud as wide as the entire stage, and in scene iii, Psiché, lamenting love's resistance, stands in a garden that is then transformed into a field with a broad river. The *intermede* to this act is set in Hell. Boats bob agitatedly on a sea of flames. The infernal palace of Pluto, surrounded by fire, appears in the midst of the boats. Twelve furies and four goblins fight together in dance but are quelled by Psiché's arrival in Hell. The setting for Act V continues in Hell, into which Amour descends, followed by Venus in a chariot. The act closes with Jupiter's arrival by machine and his order that Psiché return to heaven.

The ballet's finale, which includes four *entrées* of dance, singing, and mechanical effects, shows the full potential of the stage the way no other performance did. The setting changes to the sky, in which the grand palace of Jupiter appears. In three successive perspectives, one sees palaces of other gods. Two clouds emerge carrying Amour and Psiché. Cupids followed on five additional machines. Simultaneously, Jupiter and Venus fly through the air near Amour and Psiché. The action culminates in a stage that is full of clouds holding 300 gods, who sing, dance, and play instrumental music to celebrate the wedding of Amour. Several pieces of *récitatif* lead to a chorus accompanied by trumpets and drums; then follow four *entrées* of dancers with musicians. Each *entrée* is led by a mythological figure that would have been well known to French audiences of the time: Apollon, Bachus, Mome, and Mars.

The number of singers and dancers in these four *entrées* was huge, giving the production the semblance of a grand court ballet. The fact that most of the performers appeared in only one *entrée* suggests that the personnel for court productions was virtually unlimited. Such numbers probably could not have been accommodated in smaller halls.

In Apollon's *entrée,* nine dancing muses are accompanied by nineteen instruments, apparently on stage. They are followed by ten dancing shepherds while various songs are sung. The retinue of Bachus is accompanied by an instrumental ensemble of thirty (presumably on stage), and includes solos and ensembles with such figures as Bachus, Silene, and satyrs. The entourage of Mome is accompanied by twenty-nine different instruments accompanying six dancing *polichinelles* and six *matassins.* After their entertainment, Mome sings. The followers of Mars are accompanied by an orchestra of forty-six(!) players. The instrumental ensemble accompanies a solo song and twelve dancers. A grand finale reunites all 239 singers, dancers, and instrumentalists on stage—probably one of the largest ensembles ever convened on the stage of the Salle des Machines. These 239 performers played a total of 660 roles in the entire ballet. How such numbers may have been coordinated without the benefit of modern technology is one of the many questions about theater production in the Baroque that awaits research.

Why did *Psiché* play only twice in the Salle des Machines? Perhaps two performances were enough to accommodate all who wanted (or were expected?) to attend, or perhaps the room really was too large to support the solo singing of opera. Perhaps productions were just easier in the Palais Royal. Could the theater have reminded audiences negatively of the bygone era of Italian opera? If the production of *Psiché* could not win over French audiences and producers to this hall, what could?

Detailed analysis of the third and final ballet given in the Salle des Machines, *Cardenio,* will probably clarify little more about the room. Of much smaller scope than the previous two works, there really was no physical need to use the theater for this ballet. The ballet required far fewer performers, and most were children. The *intermedes* in which they danced were short compared to those of the earlier ballets, nor were mechanical gimmicks or elaborate changes of scenery required.

The court's return to the Salle des Machines after fifty years of productions elsewhere can be interpreted politically more easily than artistically: it gave the young King, Louis XV, an opportunity to appear on the same stage where Louis XIV had starred as a young dancer. For the 1720 ballet, the hall had to be renovated yet again in what seems like a fruitless waste of money, since after *Cardenio* there were no more ballets in the room, and only marionette theater during the 1730s.[102]

The Historical Significance of the Palais Royal

As France's first public opera house, the Palais Royal theater stands as the embodiment of significant aesthetic, social, political, and personal developments in Paris's artistic life in the seventeenth century. The opening of the theater in 1674 as the home for public opera signaled both a reorientation of musical theater and a new focus in theater architecture. Noble amateurs were increasingly replaced on stage by professional performers; performers and audiences grew distinct; and productions moved first from makeshift locations to temporary theaters, and then from temporary structures to what were essentially "permanent" theaters. The Italian style, which had plagued the Salle des Machines, gave way to a new French manner, as Lully moved from court servant to public entrepreneur. A comprehensive history of the Palais Royal theater and its repertoire is waiting to be written: this overview offers a beginning to that history.[103]

The Palais Royal theater presents very different issues from the Salle des Machines, and so complements the overview of French theatrical practice and the French search for theater identity described earlier. The Palais Royal was in almost continuous use from 1638 to 1763—a longevity that stands in contrast to the history of the Salle des Machines. Furthermore, the Palais Royal's varied service, first to the court and then to the public, provides a setting with which a wide range of contextual issues is associated. Its long roster of repertoire includes nearly every opera or ballet of the French Baroque. While not nearly as grand as the Salle des Machines—and probably less accommodating to performers and to audiences alike—the Palais Royal more accurately reflects French Baroque principles of theater design prior to 1800. Though it was a strikingly different theater from the Salle des Machines, the Palais Royal theater nevertheless had some features in common with the Salle des Machines: both theaters were installed in a preexisting site and were, therefore, subject to conditions and limitations that each site imposed; and both were remodeled by the Vigaranis, Carlo bearing particular responsibility for the Palais Royal.

In relation to other theaters in Paris, the Palais Royal also reflects many of the social and political influences at work in Parisian artistic practice during the *ancien régime*. It seems that musical theater kept coming back to the Palais Royal: even the fire of 1763 did not prevent a return to the site, albeit in a newly built hall. As Sauval wrote, the theater remained "the most royal" (*le plus royal*).[104]

Studying the Palais Royal also complements our examination of the Salle des Machines because the two theaters provide source materials almost inversely proportional to their use. Overall, individual sources document the functioning of the Salle des Machines much more precisely than those relating to the Palais Royal. On the other hand, owing to the duration and consistency of its use, the number of surviving sources that deal with the Palais Royal is much greater. The first three phases of the history of the theater in the Palais Royal remain scantily documented, especially through plans and drawings. On the other hand, the hall's fourth and longest phase, as the Paris Opera, is much more carefully recorded. In this essay I focus on the theater during the seventeenth century and summarize its four stages of development. Again, I briefly include some repertoire to suggest the hall's facilities during this century in which French theater was searching for definition.[105]

The Original State of Le Mercier's Theater in the Palais Royal

Built by Le Mercier starting in 1637, the first theater in the Palais Royal (then called the Palais Cardinal; see note 103) was completed in 1641.[106] Sauval's description, though published eighty years later, remains the most extensive written record of the original room. Two important pieces of iconography suggest what the room looked like in its pristine state: Stefano della Bella's view of the setting of *Mirame,* the play that opened the theater, reveals single-point-perspective scenery, a proscenium arch, and six steps up to stage level. The frequently reproduced view of *Le soir* dating from about 1641 represents the same proscenium arch and stage, as well as the hall's communal setting around the perimeter with the royalty on the main floor in the center.[107] Two balconies each holding a single row of seated spectators flank the sides of the stage. Spectators apparently do not have a very good view of the stage since they sit at right angles to it. A third balcony appears to encompass the entire perimeter of the room, but contains no spectators. *Le soir* also seems to indicate an ensemble of instrumentalists in the second balcony closest to the stage, a common feature in French theaters before areas specifically built for the orchestra were placed next to the stage.[108] In *Le soir* the royal family is shown in the center of the floor, perhaps having the best view of the stage, even though they are below it by the space of the six steps. The seated royalty, not the stage, seem to be the focal point of the room—particularly for the spectators in the side galleries.

Sauval's description, somewhat incompatible with information in *Le soir,* is of a theater oriented toward a stage at one end.[109] Sauval says the room was about 115 feet (35 meters) long.[110] The room had a small elevated stage at one end, with an amphitheater occupying about 65 to 70 feet (19.8 to 21.3 meters), which left a depth of approximately 45 to 50 feet (13.7 to 15.2 meters) for the stage. Bjurström points out that this stage was about as deep as that in the Petit Bourbon, and, at 65 feet (19.8 meters), actually a bit wider.[111] The smaller auditorium in the Palais Royal accounts for why the Petit Bourbon was often the preferred site. Sauval also reported twenty-seven rows of stone steps running parallel to the back wall (i.e., not in horseshoe shape). Those steps must have provided cramped seating, since they measured only 5.5 inches (14 cm) high and 22.6 inches (58 cm) from front to back, but their small size meant that the hall accommodated three times as many spectators as the Greek and Roman theaters on which it was modeled. From its earliest form through all phases of remodeling, seating for the audience remained confined. Although Sauval does not mention balconies, there would have been ample height for those as depicted in *Le soir,* since twenty-seven stone steps would reach a height of only 12.5 feet (3.8 meters), and, in any case, would not interfere with the balconies on the side.

Apparent discrepancies in the information provided by *Le soir* and Sauval may help support Lawrenson's thesis regarding the search for identity in French seventeenth-century theaters. This single hall may have been intended both as a communal room with a focus from side balconies toward the center of the floor, and also as a space with a proper elevated stage at one end—for what Lawrenson identifies as "unpolarized" versus "staged" events.[112] Even after three more phases of remodeling, in some ways this tension built into the room never went away.

There is very little surviving information about productions in this first phase of the theater's history, but scholars suspect that stage settings were minimal. Bjurström reports that *Mirame* played with a single set, but did use a curtain and several mechanical effects.[113] Research to date indicates that at least three court ballets—the *Ballet de la prosperité des armes de France* of 1641, *Le libraire du Pont-Neuf ou les romans* of 1643 or 1644, and the *Ballet de l'oracle de la sibile de Pansoust* of 1645—also played in the hall during this first phase.[114] Surviving *livrets* are the principal sources of information about these works, but the *livrets* offer minimal information about stage settings and mechanical effects. None seems to have required any more than generic scenery since these ballets consisted primarily of successive *entrées* of dancing by courtiers for other courtiers. One important question that remains unanswered is whether dancing in these examples of the *ballet à entrées* could have occurred both on stage, in the new theatrical way, and in the center of the floor, as in court ballets known to that time.

The Theater in the Palais Royal as Modified by Torelli

The start of our second phase of building on the Palais Royal theater is marked by the arrival in Paris during June 1645 of Giacomo Torelli. Torelli's influence changed forever the look of French theater: his building and remodeling transformed French performance sites from all-purpose halls to well-equipped theaters, and his stage settings provided visual effects previously unknown to French audiences.

Torelli's first remodeling in Paris was a transformation of the theater in the Petit Bourbon. His first production, *La finta pazza,* played in that hall in December of 1645, and it is believed that *Egisto* also had sets by Torelli.[115] Torelli then turned to the Palais Royal, which he remodeled sometime between his arrival and March 1647, according to similar standards as in the Petit Bourbon: he rebuilt the stage to handle more complicated mechanical effects, opened up side walls of the stage, and probably changed the perspective through new flats.[116] Whether it was Torelli in this second phase or Molière in the third phase who gave the orchestra its own place in front of the stage is unclear. Additionally, there is uncertainty as to when the twenty-seven rows of stone steps were removed: they are uncharacteristic of Italian theater style, but they may have remained until Molière's installation of boxes.

The new production of the Italian opera *Orphée* (with music by Rossi, a libretto by Buti, and choreography by Balbi) appeared five times between March and May 1647 to inaugurate Torelli's hall.[117] Prunières reports that the day after the second performance of the opera, Torelli installed an extra floor over the auditorium for a ball, placing the twenty-four instrumentalists in a machine floating above the dance floor.[118] Many of the sets for *Orphée* were used again for the machine play *Andromède* in 1650, which was to have appeared in the Palais Royal but was moved to the Petit Bourbon. Torelli also may have assisted with several court ballets performed in the Palais Royal: in 1648 the

Ballet du dérèglement des passions played there for one performance, in 1651 the *Ballet de Cassandre* appeared there for four or five performances, and *Les fêtes de Bacchus* ran five times.[119]

While interest in the theater may have been rejuvenated in 1651 after the worst of the Fronde's political unrest had ended, this flourish was temporary, not unlike vacillations in the use of the Salle des Machines ten years later. Perhaps owing to associations with Mazarin and to memories of the high costs of productions he sponsored, the Palais Royal theater was not used again by the court throughout the remainder of the 1650s. Instead, court productions appeared in the Petit Bourbon, in the Louvre, and at Fontainebleau. By the time of Molière's move to the Palais Royal in 1660, the hall was in disrepair. This circumstance undoubtedly contributed to Mazarin's resolve to present the king's wedding celebration in a totally new setting.[120]

According to Bjurström, Mazarin's opponents found *Orphée* boring, and they criticized its expense. The favorable response of the public, however, suggests satisfaction with the new look in French stage design.[121] Because Mazarin's enemies took every opportunity to use the theater against him, estimates for the costs of the remodeling and for the productions therein vary tremendously: for *Orphée,* reports range from 90,000 to 400,000 *livres.*[122] The *Gazette* reported the production through headlines advertising "wonderful variety of scenery, machines, and other novelties, previously unknown in France" (*merveilleux changemens de théâtre, des machines, et autres inventions jusqu'à present inconnues à la France*). France had traditionally been short on scenic effects, wrote the *Gazette,* so these new ornaments were thought to be quite admirable. For the performance on 29 April before the Danish ambassadors, new machines that made the production even more remarkable were added. For the final performance on 8 May, marvelous decorations are again noted.[123]

Scenic and mechanical effects in *Orphée* seem on par with those reported in *Hercule* and include ten different settings of scenery probably designed by French artists and six different spectacles using machinery probably built by Torelli.[124] The Prologue is set in a city, with battles on land and sea in progress. French troops destroy an enemy wall, whereupon Victory descends from the heavens on cloud machines. Act I is in a grove, which, according to the *Gazette,* appears to be one hundred times deeper than the stage actually is.[125] Two turtle doves on the backs of vultures fly in. In the fourth scene, Venus, cupids, three graces, and many *amours* descend on a cloud. To accommodate the wedding feast in scene vii, the back of the set opens to reveal a sumptuous table.[126] A ballet danced by Hymenees and a chorus closes the act. Act II is the richest, with the setting changing in an instant in scene iii to a beautiful palace with marvelous architecture. The scene is ornamented by dancing. Scene iv changes to avenues set in perspective. After Apollo and Amour fly off the stage, the setting changes in scene viii to a temple in the background. In scene x, nymphs holding castanets dance, and in scene xii, Apollon descends and returns to the heavens. Act III appears on deserted land full of rocks and caverns. The ground shakes when Euridice's ghost meets Aristée. The scene changes to Pluton's underworld as Orphée begins his descent to retrieve Euridice, and a great dance by demons, animals, monsters, owls, turtles, and snails ensues. As Euridice returns to Hades, the set changes instantaneously to the Elysian fields. The following settings then appear in quick succession: in a landscape with rocks, trees, panthers, and other beasts gathered around, Orphée sings his plight. Following, in a landscape by the sea, Venus arrives in a shell. The sea appears at the rear as the finale uses the entire cloud machinery for the final appearance of Jupiter and other gods.

The Theater in the Palais Royal under the Management of Molière

The third phase of the Palais Royal's remodeling began in 1660 with the demolition of the Petit Bourbon. Molière's company moved into the Palais Royal in 1660, more or less necessitating the court's construction of the Salle des Machines. Under the direction of the *surintendant* of buildings, Antoine de Ratabon, Molière instigated two phases of remodeling: the first, in 1660, was apparently intended to make the hall quickly usable after its decade of dormancy; in 1670 more long-term repairs were implemented.[127] The nature of these remodelings is known primarily through written accounts: it appears that no plans survive.

The records of Molière's company suggest the decrepit state into which the room had fallen in the nine years that it was closed during the 1650s. By 1660, for example, three beams were decayed, and half of the room was in ruin.[128] The greatest addition in Molière's renovation was his installation of loges, retrieved from the Petit Bourbon, in the galleries on the first two levels of the Palais Royal. In 1671, at a cost of 2,000 *livres,* additional machinery was added for Molière's *comédie-ballets;* a third ring of loges was installed; the hall was repainted; and the ceiling was redecorated.[129] Additionally, as Barbara Mittman has pointed out, benches for spectators were placed on the stage, a common practice in French theaters at the time.[130]

Other important modifications were made to the structure; however, we are not certain about the precise time these changes were made. Some may have occurred during Molière's tenure. The most significant alterations included raising and expanding the stage by knocking out the stone steps leading to it, remodeling the parterre and two rings of boxes, and building or enlarging the orchestra area to accommodate Molière's twelve instrumentalists. Additionally, Jean Gourret suggests that it was Molière who added the public exit into the small dead-end alley running next to the palace, the *cul-de-sac de l'opéra* (see figure 2.4).[131]

During the 1660s the hall was shared between Molière's company and the Italian comedians. The court occasionally presented a production there—for example, the *Ballet des arts* in 1663 and *Les amours desguisés* in 1664—but it also

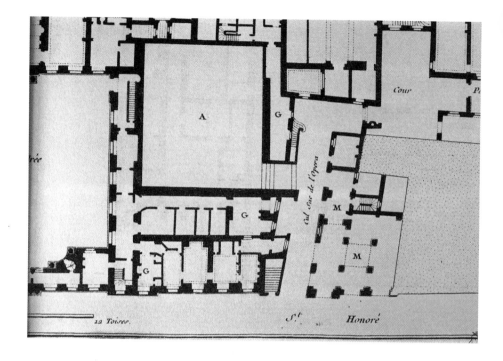

Figure 2.4. Plan of the first floor of the Palais Royal from Blondel, *L'architecture française,* vol. 3 (1754), book 5, illus. 9, plate 2.

relied on other sites, including private apartments in the Palais Royal, in the Louvre, and at Fontainebleau, as well as outdoor settings built specifically for the *Fêtes de Versailles.* Even though Lully and Molière initiated their professional partnership at the Palais Royal in 1664 with the *comédie-ballet* entitled *Le mariage forcé,* most of their productions were mounted elsewhere: *Le sicilien* appeared at Saint-Germain-en-Laye, and *La princesse d'Elide* played at both Saint Germain-en-Laye and Versailles—suggesting that Lully may not have wanted to operate in Molière's territory.

Settings for the *Ballet des arts* are indicative of the greater theatrical orientation of court ballets of the 1660s, perhaps inspired by the new equipment in the theater. In the course of this ballet's seven *entrées,* décor includes a grove; the sea, onto which Junon descends on a machine; a gallery; a forest; a porcelain room; and finally a machine delivering gods from the heavens.

The Theater in the Palais Royal as a Public Opera House

Here we can provide only a small part of the story of the Palais Royal during its ninety years as Paris's public opera house. The principal architectural sources that inform this part of our discussion are three: a set of six drawings from around the year 1700 depicting various plans and elevations of the theater; a sketch dating from about 1752 for a proposed expansion; and Blondel's plan of the theater of 1752 (figures 2.4 and 2.5).[132] A watercolor painted by Saint-Aubin in 1747 depicts Lully's *Armide*. This is one of the few images in which the theater is being used for opera.[133] These and other iconographic and written sources provide more information relating to the Palais Royal in its fourth phase than we have from any other period of the theater's history.

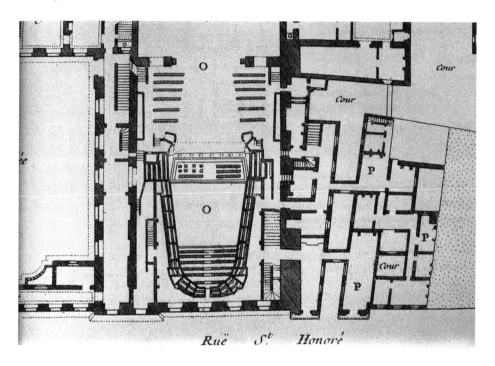

Figure 2.5. Plan of the ground floor of the Palais Royal showing details of the theater's interior from Blondel, *L'architecture française*, vol. 3 (1754), book 5, illus. 9, plate 3.

Henri LaGrave's thesis that public theaters present very different questions and issues from court theaters is borne out by the story of the Palais Royal. Even though the inauguration of the hall in 1674 as the new home of the Paris Opera marked a turning point for the theater, tensions between this new public orientation and its original private communal spirit remained for the entire life of the theater. The remodeling under Lully was pervasive and sought to transform the theater into a respectable home for the Académie Royale de Musique: a legitimized physical structure helped establish the viability of the new artistic institution as well as the new genre of opera that it sustained. Paris's musical-theater setting had come full circle: forty years after Richelieu's vision for legitimized theater, the country finally found a home for its national opera. With the opening of a public hall, court productions diminished in complexity and frequency. Spectacular effects were left for the opera, while the court during the final forty years of Louis's reign turned increasingly to private chamber performances.

Carlo Vigarani reappeared on the theatrical scene, this time as the principal designer of this new French-style setting, and as the partner of Lully. Their partnership ended in 1680, but Vigarani continued to work in Paris. Jean Bérain took over as the principal designer and machinist, and he remained in that post until his death in 1711.

Relative to late seventeenth-century French standards, the improvements that had been made to the Palais Royal gave Paris a viable theater the likes of which it had not yet known. Moreover, it was larger than most theaters for court.[134] However, as La Grave suggests, by the eighteenth century, the theater in the Palais Royal fared poorly when contrasted with theaters in other parts of Europe—particularly those in Italy and in other French cities such as Bordeaux and Lyon. It did not take long for the Palais Royal to revert to its status of inferiority as other halls advanced in their potential for supporting the most progressive ideals of French opera.[135] La Grave proposes that the unsatisfactory conditions of the Palais Royal prevented its entry into writings about theater architecture of the mid eighteenth century, a time when analyses of other theaters abounded. At that point, the theater was well known for its difficult entrance, cramped seating, limited circulation, and questionable mechanical facilities.[136]

Presumably most of Vigarani's remodeling of the 1670s remained until the fire in 1763. Blondel's plan (see figure 2.5), for example, probably the most studied view of the theater, surely depicts Vigarani's theater.[137] Profiting from what Cordey interprets as poor judgment in the building of the Salle des Machines, Vigarani strove for the best in visibility and in acoustics. The most important features of his design included rounding out the loges on all three levels at the rear of the auditorium, as in the Salle des Machines, to increase views of the stage and to improve acoustics; and enlarging the area for the musicians of Lully's orchestra, which, at approximately forty members, was three times the size of Molière's ensemble.[138] On stage, the space above the theater was completed, and weak beams were repaired to accommodate machinery. Two pillars on stage that interfered with the movement of scenery were removed, and additional seats for the audience were placed on the stage. Lully also ordered the complete repainting of the room in order to enhance its appearance as well as to eliminate memories of Molière.[139] This remodeling seems to have been completed by 14 November 1673, and the hall opened on 18 January 1674 with the production of *Alceste*.[140] Half of Lully's expenses of 3,000 *livres* was for décor alone.

The room was divided nearly in half for stage and auditorium. Estimates of the capacity and conditions vary immensely. La Grave's figure of 1,300 spectators is credible, although conditions could have varied considerably during the many decades in which the hall was used. La Grave estimated that there were 600 standing places and 700 seats. While his calculations may be conservative — some observers said as many as 4,000 (!) could be accommodated in the room — even 1,300 meant amazingly cramped quarters.[141] Standing room in the raked parterre, occupied exclusively by men in St. Aubin's drawing, measured only 24.5 by 42.5 feet (7.5 meters by 13 meters). Most seating was on backless benches, even in the theater's boxes.[142] Rows of benches filled the amphitheater. The two rows of loges contained fifteen boxes apiece, and each box held two or three benches. Additionally, there were boxes over the stage. These boxes are clearly depicted in St. Aubin's watercolor. The ceilings over the boxes were low, but the use of lattice-work rather than solid partitions at once improved the view of the stage and, at the same time, gave a feeling of spaciousness to the occupants of the boxes. Sight-lines from many boxes remained partial: even the horseshoe shape of the auditorium was not enough to moderate proportions between the stage and the auditorium to an acceptable level.

The stage measured 56 feet (17 meters) deep and 30 feet (9 meters) wide at the proscenium, about half the workable area of the stage in the Salle des Machines. The number of flats varies in different plans, but several images show six rows before the back partition wall, and, in the 1752 expansion drawing, four more flats behind the wall. The side elevation shown in the Archives' drawings indicates an area below the stage approximately as deep as the height of the proscenium above the stage. The space between the top of the auditorium and the external roof line is about the same distance as the height of the auditorium, but the amount of this height that could have held machinery is not indicated on plans.[143] Beijer argues that because of this relatively small stage, scenery required a greater sense of illusion to achieve an appearance of depth comparable to that in the Salle des Machines; this illusion was accomplished by placing flats closer and closer together as one approached the rear of the stage. Beijer evaluates this stage as incredibly small in relation to audience capacity — a very small space, indeed, and with limited equipment given the fantastic apparitions that it was supposed to sustain.

The nature of the specific scenery and machines that Vigarani installed is unknown. In any case, his machinery apparently served the first years of opera in the theater well enough to ensure the survival of the genre in France.

One of the greatest criticisms of the theater, especially as a public building, was its small entrance from the outside (see figure 2.4), reminiscent of the entry into the Salle des Machines. The problem was unavoidable, though, as no amount of ingenuity on Vigarani's part could have readjusted the relationship between the theater and the public streets. No entry was possible through the front wall along rue St. Honoré, since seating inside was pushed as far as possible toward this wall. The only external access to the auditorium was next to the orchestra pit, as in the Salle des Machines. This side access had been adequate for the hall as a court theater, since royalty could also enter the theater directly from the palace (i.e., stage right). However, as a public theater, audiences had to negotiate the infamous *cul-de-sac de l'opéra,* the dead-end alley running nearly parallel on the east (i.e., stage left) side of the hall. This passageway measured only 10.75 feet (3.3 meters) wide: it is difficult to imagine carriages getting very close to the entry. The problem was exacerbated by the position of the theater's ticket window along this side.[144]

Inside the building, conditions were not much better. There was no grand foyer, only six steps leading directly into the auditorium at parterre level or a quick left turn up stairs leading to the first loges.[145]

Literally hundreds of operas by most of the important French composers of the *ancien régime* appeared in this theater during its roughly ninety-year lifetime as the Paris Opera.[146] Scenic effects can be generalized from descriptions in *livrets,* but most of these do not include names of performers, so personnel on the public stage are much more difficult to clarify than were those at court. There are few reports about acoustics, but I suspect that the room served French opera at least as well as the Salle des Machines and probably better. Its close quarters may have been just right for seventeenth- and eighteenth-century French music.

Trends, Consequences, and Unanswered Questions

Clarifying the architectural structures of these two important theaters in Paris helps us to understand more about the nature of the musical-theatrical repertoire performed therein. We have viewed the seventeenth century as a period of transition in French theatrical life, as a time of searching for definition in both repertoire and in the nature of a theater as a physical structure. In Paris, perhaps more than in other European cities of this period, theater architecture and repertoire were strongly influenced by social and political factors. This search for definition was driven most by a quest for a national style in French musical theater, in a country whose arts were supported by French monarchs but where, ironically, theater in its many dimensions was led by Italian artists and by their artistic styles for most of the century. French national opera did not become a reality until well after the earliest Italian productions, and, oddly enough, the distinctively "French" manifestation of the genre was the creation of a native Italian, Jean Baptiste Lully.

Over the course of the seventeenth century, many transformations thus took place: a growing distinction between court and public performances, with the finances and the physical resources for productions increasingly restricted as opera became a paying matter; the establishment of permanent rather than temporary theaters; a movement from productions intended to provide opportunities for social interaction to performances in which the piece being presented was the essential matter; and, correspondingly, the replacement of the courtier on stage by the professional performer. Finally, the root of French national opera, the ballet, was subsumed into Lully's operatic manner as an integral element.

By the beginning of the eighteenth century, it appeared that Parisian theaters had come of age and had settled in with the best of those in Italian cities and even elsewhere in France. During the course of the eighteenth century, however, a game of catch-up once again began. Perhaps not until the Garnier opera house of the 1860s, or maybe even the Bastille Opera of the 1990s, have Paris's opera theaters found an identity—or have they?

Much more research remains to be done before modern scholars, performers, and observers can gain a comprehensive understanding of the physical settings for French Baroque musical theater. Among such work let us hope for further analysis of the use or disuse of the Salle des Machines; a comprehensive, critical history of the Paris Opera in the Palais Royal, as an artistic institution and as a structure at the center of Paris's cultural life for over a century; a first-ever critical study of the life and works of the Vigarani family, as generators of both Italian and French theatrical standards; and a clearer picture of just who went to the opera, and so received the musical, dramatic, social, and political messages that were delivered by opera in context.

CHAPTER THREE

Theater Architecture at the Time of Henry Purcell and Its Influence on His "Dramatick Operas"

Mark A. Radice

The Nature of English Opera

Late seventeenth-century English opera is generally regarded with skepticism by present-day audiences. These operas—or semi-operas as they are somewhat disparagingly called—do not conform to our contemporary aesthetic, which requires a text that is continuous in its development of a coherent plot. The spoken dialogue of the play often bears only the most casual relationship with the musical entertainments (called *masques*) that were inserted at the ends of acts. Moreover, digressions were commonly introduced into the story line in order to create opportunities for spectacular stage effects. These features are generally regarded as flaws in the typical semi-opera, or dramatick opera, as they are more appropriately called. This term, with its distinctive spelling, was the designation used during the seventeenth century to indicate entertainments of this sort. I shall retain that term here.

Of the composers who made significant contributions to this genre, Henry Purcell must be reckoned as the supreme master. Nevertheless, Purcell's only work that has remained a staple in the operatic repertoire, *Dido and Æneas,* is atypical among Purcell's extended theater pieces because of its very limited orchestral resources and its consistent use of *stile recitativo* for the delivery of the narrative texts. The fact that this opera was composed for Josiah Priest's school for young gentlewomen in Chelsea rather than for the public theater in London also sets it apart from Purcell's other extended dramatic compositions, all of which were composed after *Dido and Æneas.*

That Purcell's dramatick operas were greatly admired by the theater goers of his time can easily be documented. What is more difficult to explain is why these theatrical masterpieces were successful during the seventeenth century whereas, in our day, productions of the dramatick operas are usually partial ones presented by a college opera workshop or *collegium musicum*.

Doubtless this lack of appreciation results from a performance style incompatible with Purcell's actual intentions. Though great headway has been made in recent years in restoring the ornamentation and authentic instrumentation of Purcell's day, music scholars have paid virtually no attention to what is perhaps the single most important element that motivated these theatrical extravaganzas: the theater itself.

The intricacies of Restoration theaters must be studied in order to understand Purcell's typical stage works. Fortunately, during Purcell's career as a composer for the stage, London had but a single theater that might be considered an opera house: the Dorset Garden Theatre. Contrary to the theatrical practices described in the first two chapters of this book, England's nobility were cautious not to give the general public the impression that their attendance at theatrical entertainments was a burden to the state. King Charles II patronized public theaters in order to spare the national treasury the production costs of lavish entertainments at the court. In the years immediately following the Restoration, rather few court masques were given, and consequently, the Dorset Garden Theatre assumed a certain importance as a cultural institution. Though this essay is not primarily concerned with the impact of politics on Restoration theater, one consequence of paramount importance in this particular relationship is the fact that London's opera house was in no way a temporary or makeshift structure. Rather, it possessed certain architectural features and distinctive facilities to which I now turn our attention.

The Dorset Garden Theatre

It was for the Dorset Garden Theatre that Purcell produced his great dramatick operas of the early 1690s.[1] The architectural make-up of this theater has been discussed by only a few theater historians, and their findings have not had any significant impact on the musical community. An examination of the stage, scenery, and musical facilities in this theater sheds light on Purcell's scores and shows that the seventeenth-century dramatick opera followed conventions that were every bit as stylized as the better-understood conventions of Italian Baroque *opera seria*. The knowledge of these conventions also reveals that what might appear at first as a confused jumble of music, scenery, and drama—the very antithesis of the *Gesamtkunstwerk*—is indeed a coordinated theatrical event that has just as much potential to amuse, entertain, and delight today as in Purcell's time.

Any reconstruction of the Dorset Garden Theatre must ultimately rest upon three fundamental pieces of evidence: (1) the Morgan and Ogilby maps of London; (2) a series of engravings by Dolle for the playbook of *The Empress of Morocco* showing the façade of the theater and the interior view of the stage in five other representations (see figures 3.1 to 3.5); and (3) a casual description of the interior written by the French tourist François Brunet. The reliability of these sources is often suspect. Dolle's engravings were made to conform to *quarto* pages, and so scale, as it appears in these engravings, may be distorted. Doubts regarding the accuracy of Dolle's representations have been raised by Diana De Marly's research into the identity of the architect for the Dorset Garden Theatre. After noting a number of architectural peculiarities in Dolle's rendering of the façade, the author concludes: "The final result shown in the

Figures 3.1 to 3.5. Dolle engravings showing the interior of the Dorset Garden Theatre. Courtesy of the Houghton Library, Harvard University.

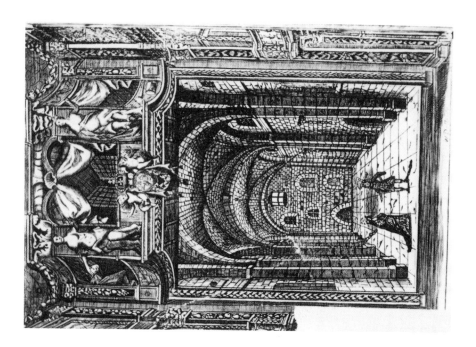

Figure 3.3.

Figure 3.2.

Figure 3.5.

Figure 3.4.

engraving . . . is clearly not the work of an architect. Alternatively, the engraving may be the work of an incompetent artist."[2] Similarly, Brunet's observations on the theater's design, though often quite specific, were intended primarily for his personal use, in the manner of a diary account. They can in no way be applied to a reconstruction of the Dorset Garden Theatre with the authority of an architectural blueprint revealing precise dimensions for the components of this Restoration theater. Despite the evident inadequacy of these sources, they may yet provide us with certain general conventions relating to the Dorset Garden Theatre's design. These conventions can be helpful in constructing a mental image of the building if they are applied in a manner that is not dogmatic.

Beyond these three pieces of evidence, insight into the theater's design can sometimes be gathered from stage directions included in productions that were mounted at the Dorset Garden. Caution is again necessary, though, for as one critic has pointed out, "the stage directions in . . . play[s], no less than the illustrations of *The Empress of Morocco,* are essentially advertising. Let us beware . . . of exaggeration and calculated misinformation."[3]

In this study I have used information relating specifically to the Dorset Garden Theatre whenever possible. In some cases, I have had to look to other documents which, although they do not relate to the Dorset Garden Theatre or its facilities, nevertheless represent an authentic conception of English theatrical practices in Purcell's time.

The old Theatre Royal and the Dorset Garden Theatre date from approximately the same time: the former opened in the year 1663, the latter in 1671. Apparently "the Theatre [Royal] was 112 feet [34.1 meters] in length from east to west, and 59 feet [17.9 meters] in breadth from north to south."[4] On Thursday, 25 January 1672, the Theatre Royal was destroyed by fire. Christopher Wren, who probably designed the Dorset Garden Theatre not long before, was entrusted with the task of developing plans for a new Theatre Royal.

The dimensions of the first Theatre Royal on this site were used as a starting point for the new theater.

> With the addition of the scene-room on the rear, the width of the new theatre was the same, but the length was increased to 140 feet [42.7 meters]. The size of the scene-room is therefore seen to be 58 feet by 28 feet [17.7 meters by 8.5 meters]. . . . the scene room was provided with a cellar—perhaps for the storing of "machines."[5]

Wren's plans for the Theatre Royal at Drury Lane have been preserved among his papers now in possession of the Codrington Library of All Souls College, Oxford (see figure 3.6).[6]

Figure 3.6. Christopher Wren drawing showing the cross-section of a theater. Courtesy of the Warden and Fellows of All Souls College, Oxford.

To formulate a picture of the exterior of an English Baroque theater, we should also consider two other theaters, the Salisbury Court Theatre, which was built in 1660, and Lisle's Tennis Court Theatre. The former was situated on a plot measuring 42 feet by 140 feet (12.8 meters by 42.7 meters).[7] These dimensions would suggest a structure approximately the same length as the Theatre Royal, but somewhat narrower. The lower limit of exterior dimensions can be seen in the latter theater, which was constructed on what Colley Cibber (1671–1757) referred to as "a Tennis *Quaree* Court, which is of the lesser sort."[8] Since the length of a standard *quaree* court was 100 feet (30.5 meters), the exterior of Lisle's Theatre must have measured approximately 75 feet (22.9 meters) in length and 30 feet (9.1 meters) in width.[9]

It is unfortunate that Wren's plans for the Dorset Garden Theatre have not survived. Dolle's engravings showing both the exterior and the interior of the building were made for an edition of Elkanah Settle's play *The Empress of Morocco*, which had its premiere performance at the Dorset Garden Theatre in 1673. From the exterior drawing of the Dorset Garden Theatre and on the basis of the Morgan and Ogilby map that was drawn to scale in the year 1677, it may be suggested that the building was 140 feet (42.7 meters), or perhaps slightly more, in length, and between 50 and 60 feet (15.2 to 18.3 meters) wide.[10]

The exterior view shown in the above-mentioned engraving from Settle's play is also important because from it we can get an idea of the traffic patterns within the building. To the left and right of the central door, a U-shaped corridor led around the ground level and opened into the seating area at a pair of doors, one on either side, located in line with the first row of seats, immediately in front of the stage. From the central door of the façade, a windowed staircase led up to the second and third levels of the house. These upper stories contained public seating and private apartments. From 1671 until 1694 or 1695, one of these apartments was inhabited by Thomas Betterton, the manager of the Duke's Company, with whom Purcell collaborated on his first large-scale dramatick opera, *The Prophetess, or, The History of Dioclesian*, Z. 627.

A rather detailed account of the interior of the house was given by the French traveler François Brunet in his memoirs entitled *Voyage d'Angleterre* [unpublished] in 1676.[11] Brunet states that the benches for the audience were arranged as in an amphitheater and that the house contained three galleries, the first two of which were divided into seven private boxes holding twenty people apiece.[12] Brunet makes no mention of doors leading into the theater; presumably there were no central doors at the extreme rear.[13] It will be seen that each tier of boxes could accommodate 140 persons. The highest gallery was not divided into boxes; as a result, more people could be seated on this level than on either of the two lower galleries. Taken collectively, the galleries could accommodate at least 420 persons quite comfortably. Using Wren's design for Drury Lane once again as our guide, it would seem that the floor seating had room for about twice as many people as one of the galleries. A full house would therefore be an audience of approximately 700 or 800 persons.[14] The typical English Restoration theater was significantly smaller than contemporaneous Continental theaters. These smaller theaters meant, of course, that a relatively small ensemble could fill the house with sound. Similarly, the demands placed upon the vocalists were greatly reduced. It is for this reason that the countertenor voice was far more useful to the English composer than to his Continental colleagues.

Another feature of the Restoration playhouse that distinguished it from Continental theaters of the day was the presence of a large forestage (i.e., the stage area in front of the proscenium arch) which protruded twenty feet or so. This thrust stage was clearly a continuation of theatrical traditions established during the Elizabethan era.[15] Colley Cibber, one of the most articulate voices to speak about the theatrical traditions of the English Baroque, explains why this additional stage area was so useful and laments its loss, an event that took place during the course of his career.

> The usual station of the actors, in almost every scene, was advanc'd at least ten foot nearer to the audience than they now can be; because, not

only from the stages being shorten'd in front, but likewise from the additional interposition of those stage-boxes, the actors (in respect to the spectators that fill them) are kept so much more backward from the main audience than they us'd to be. But when the actors were in possession of that forwarder space to advance upon, the voice was then more in the centre of the house, so that the most distant ear had scarce the least doubt or difficulty in hearing what fell from the weakest utterance. All objects were thus drawn nearer to the sense; every painted scene was stronger; every grand scene and dance more extended; every rich or fine-coloured habit had a more lively lustre. Nor was the minutest motion of a feature (properly changing with the passion or humor it suited) ever lost, as they frequently must be in the obscurity of too great a distance. And how valuable an advantage the facility of hearing distinctly is to every well-acted scene, every common spectator is a judge. A voice scarce raised above the tone of a whisper, either in tenderness, resignation, innocent distress, or jealousy suppress'd, often have as much concern with the heart as the most clamorous passions; and when on any of these occasions such affecting speeches are plainly heard, or lost, how wide is the difference from the great or little satisfaction received from them! To all this a master of a company may say, I now receive ten pounds more than could have been taken formerly in every full house. Not unlikely. But might not this house be oftener full if the auditors were oftener pleas'd?[16]

The disappearance of the thrust stage from English theaters marked the end of an era. Interestingly enough, the dramatick opera as a genre disappeared at approximately the same time. Sir John Vanbrugh (1664–1726), whose style of architecture derived from the manners of Wren and Hawksmoor, designed the Haymarket Theatre (1704), which served as the principal London opera house in the early eighteenth century. In this house, which will be examined in chapter four, Vanbrugh imitated the Continental design, reducing the thrust stage to a more modest apron stage and placing a seating area for the orchestra in front of the apron.

During Purcell's time, the lighting for the thrust stage included a series of footlights which were constructed in a wonderfully ingenious way. A trough of iron or tin was placed at the front of the stage. This trough was filled with oil; in it were placed circular pieces of cork through which holes had been punched. A metal or glass collar was anchored in each hole, and a wick was run through it. This system of footlights (called floats) had advantages over candles. There was no necessity for a stage hand to be bothered with replacing the candles as they melted down. So long as the trough was kept filled with oil, the footlights could burn indefinitely.[17]

The forestage, on which the great majority of the dramatic action took place, was flanked on both sides by a series of doors and balconies through which the various characters entered upon or left from the stage.[18] These doors and balconies could also form an integral part of the set; one of these balconies might have been used for the balcony scene in Shakespeare's *Romeo and Juliet*. From stage directions given in contemporary plays, we can see that these balconies could also serve the musicians. In Dryden's *The Kind Keeper, or, Mr. Limberham,* which was performed at the Dorset Garden Theatre in March of 1678, we find the stage direction "Musick at the Balcony overhead." One of the characters then exclaims, "Hark! there's Musick above!"

As Wren's plan for Drury Lane shows, the forestage and the stage area behind the proscenium were constructed on a gently sloping angle. This angle aided the scene painters in creating the perspective scenes which were placed behind the proscenium arch. This entire stage, both before and behind the proscenium arch, was cut up with trapdoors. A typical Restoration production involved

> an elaborate and intricate system of trapdoors some of which must have been of very considerable size; and such indeed actually did cut up the stage of Dorset Garden. . . . In the Restoration theatre very great use was made of the traps, and a point that must be most carefully borne in mind is that the large traps through which set pieces of scenery of some size, often with characters grouped upon them, rose or sank, were on the further side of the proscenium, that is to say within the curtain line; whilst the apron stage had smaller traps through which one character, or perhaps two characters together, might sink or appear from below. Restoration tragedy is very lavish in its employment of the supernatural, and it would, I think, hardly be any exaggeration to say that unless there be some specific stage direction to the contrary, all apparitions, all ghosts and demons, one might almost say all supernatural visitants, rose on to the stage through a trap-door.[19]

Purcell and his librettists put these trapdoors to good use—and often. They could easily be utilized in staging Act II of *King Arthur,* where the stage direction indicates that "*Oswald employs a magician (Osmond) and his attendant sprites to harass the Britons and lead them astray into bogs and pitfalls.*" A sprite, Phillidel, sings the lines "If you step no danger thinking, / Down you fall, a furlong sinking." Here we might imagine a flurry of stage activity, as dancers suddenly drop out of sight to reemerge at some other place in the magical landscape. Staging the famous "Frost Scene" (which takes place in the next act) without these trapdoors would be unthinkable. The text sung by the figure of the Cold Genius clearly alludes to the traps with the lines that run "What Power art thou, who from below / Hast made me rise, unwillingly and slow / From beds of everlasting snow?" Moreover, the instrumental prelude that Purcell wrote to accompany the ascent of the character of the Cold Genius from the substage area is among the most remarkable pieces of descriptive music ever written; its strange harmonic motion would be utterly meaningless without the corresponding spectacle that is the prelude's *raison d'être.* The traps are also employed in *The Fairy Queen,* most notably in Act V where we find the stage direction, "*Six Pedestals of China-work rise from under the Stage; they support six large Vases of Porcelain, in which six China-Orange-Trees.*"

In his "Conjectural Reconstruction of the Dorset Garden Theatre," Edward A. Langhans points out that Dorset Garden had more elaborate and extensive trapdoor machinery than any other Restoration theater.

> One can safely guess that there was at least one small trap (about 3′ by 6′ minimum [.9 by 1.8 meters]) on the forestage, two medium traps (about 4′ by 8′ minimum [1.2 by 2.4 meters]) upstage of the curtain line but downstage of the first set of shutters, and two small traps (3′ by 6′ [.9 by 1.8 meters]) and one large (about 5′ by 10′ minimum [1.5 by 3 meters]) trap upstage of the shutters, probably between the first and second set of shutters. For many appearances through traps, ladders in the substage would have sufficed, but some of the traps, especially the large ones, must have been equipped with some kind of elevator mechanism. A fairly spacious area under the stage would obviously have been necessary.[20]

The uses to which this substage area might have been put are not clear. In the above-mentioned study, Langhans (p. 86) suggests that the very minimum height of the substage—that would be the area closest to the first row of audience seats—was 5 feet 6 inches (1.7 meters); the extreme rear of the substage area reached a maximum height of 8 feet 9 inches (2.7 meters). Some of this space would presumably have been occupied by stage machinery used in operating the traps. Langhans (p. 78) indicates that the remaining area may have served for storage. What is clear is that the substage area was more than ample and could easily have accommodated a musical ensemble. Documentation of the use of the substage area by musicians may be found in the writings of the indefatigable diarist Samuel Pepys, who observed such an experiment. When Killigrew built his Theatre Royal, which was in use from 1663 to 1672, he imitated the theaters on the Continent by placing the orchestra before the stage in what would become its present-day location. This transformation probably involved removing the front of the substage and placing the orchestra, for the most part, in the substage area; apparently some musicians overflowed onto the floor of the theater. Pepys comments upon the newly opened facility in his entry for 8 May 1663.

To the Theatre Royall, being the second day of its being opened. The house is made with extraordinary good contrivance; and yet hath some faults, as the narrowness of the passages in and out of the pit, and the distance from the stage to the boxes, which I am confident cannot hear. But for all other things it is well. Only, above all, the Musique being below, and most of it sounding under the very stage, there is no hearing of the basses at all, nor very well of the trebles, which surely must be mended.[21]

Pepys's criticisms make clear the fact that theatrical traditions died hard. The location of the main orchestra on the floor in an area approximating a pit must be regarded as anomalous throughout the seventeenth century in England; music sounding from the substage area would have been reserved exclusively for special effects—we might even say "sound effects."

About 20 feet (6 meters) upstage was the proscenium arch. This arch separated the forestage, where the drama proper took place, from the portion of the stage behind the proscenium, which was reserved primarily for the musical portions, special effects such as grand entries, and scenic displays. The depth of the scenic stage at the Dorset Garden Theatre was apparently far greater than in most late seventeenth-century English theaters. In his study "The Dorset Garden Theatre: A Review of Facts and Problems," Robert D. Hume calls our attention to a stage direction in *The World in a Moon* that specifies that the depth of the stage was 50 feet (15.2 meters) to the back wall. Hume contends that this depth was calculated from the curtain line, not the front of the forestage (p. 11).[22] As we shall see, there are good reasons for concluding that the scenic stage area was indeed thus generously proportioned.

If we examine the engravings from *The Empress of Morocco,* which represent the interior of the Dorset Garden Theatre, we see that figure 3.5 shows the drawn curtain at the left and right of the proscenium. Typically, the curtain in a Restoration theater was a looped curtain that divided at the middle. The use of the curtain, however, differed greatly from its present-day function. Normally, the curtain was divided at the beginning of the play and remained open to the end. If a tableau scene showing the *dramatis personæ* momentarily frozen were presented—as is the case with the scene from *The Empress of Morocco* in figure 3.5—the curtain was lowered slightly to emphasize this. It should be stressed that the curtain was not closed during the scene changes; these metamorphoses were considered an important part of the spectacle and were accomplished in public view.

The Restoration theater incorporated many traditions established in the first half of the seventeenth century. Scenery, in particular, relied very heavily upon the innovations made by Inigo Jones in the staging of court masques between 1605 and 1613. Jones had studied in Italy, and it was he who first made extensive use of Italian scenic devices in England.

He [Jones] had established what was to remain for centuries the stock type of scenic decoration. . . . he prepared a series of flat side wings running on grooves and also a set of back "shutters" which could be moved along with the side wings in order to reveal a change of scene. With these side wings and back shutters we are on the threshold of the modern theatre; indeed, the methods employed by Jones are precisely those which may still be seen employed by a number of provincial touring companies.[23]

Jones was also responsible for the introduction of the proscenium arch to England.

The Hall Theatre was smaller than Dorset Garden, but the plans for this theater nevertheless suggest the general layout of scenes.

Behind the proscenium are four pairs of wings, arranged in triangular formation, backed by a pair of shutters. This completes an ordinary set for an indoor or street scene. When greater depth is wanted for a vista or "prospect," the shutters can be withdrawn to reveal one or more relieves . . . placed between them and a back-cloth which marks the full depth of the stage. Corresponding to each section of wings and shutters are upper portions for clouds. The wings are set at intervals of 3 or 3½ feet [.9 to 1 meter], the shutters 17 feet [5.2 meters] from the front of the stage; the first relieve is 2 feet 7½ inches [.8 meter] behind the shutters, and the other relieves and back-cloth follow at equal space of 1 foot 8 inches [.5 meter]. The dimensions of the wings, commencing with the pair nearest the frontispiece, are given as 3 feet 5 inches by 21 feet 6 inches [1 meter by 6.6 meters], 5 feet 3 inches by 18 feet 6 inches [1.6 meters by 5.6 meters], 6 feet 8 inches by 15 feet 6 inches [2 meters by 4.7 meters], and 6 feet 6 inches by 13 feet [1.9 meters by 4 meters]; of the shutters as 15 feet by 12 feet 2 inches [4.6 meters by 3.7 meters].[24]

These "wings" and "shutters" were simply flat wooden frames with canvas stretched over them. The tops of these flats were attached to an upper guide, and the bottoms rested in grooves in the stage floor itself. A mixture of oil and soap was applied to these grooves in order to keep the flats moving smoothly.

Rather early on in the Restoration, shutters provided in addition to the back-shutter were placed at wing positions so that the stage area behind the proscenium arch could be divided into a series of inner stages.

The position of the back shutters was extended beyond their old central position, for there are indications that they could be closed at other positions farther down-stage—there was possible provision made

for them behind every pair of wings—thus permitting shallow Front
Scenes as well as the deeper scene. Behind such front scenes it was possible to set furniture, or groups of players, for discovery at the opening
of the flats. In some masques the shutters were further divided
horizontally into two storeys. The Upper Back Shutters might then
open independently to show a view beyond into heaven . . . while the
Lower Back Shutters parted to disclose a distant landscape beneath. . . .
This system may have persisted well into the next century, for in 1736
Fielding has an interesting allusion to an imaginary scene-painter
named Mynheer Van Bottom-Flat.[25]

In the specific case of the Dorset Garden Theatre, we lack any concrete
evidence verifying the use of a dispersed shutter system. Some scholars argue
that "there were shutters at the first wing position at Dorset Garden."[26] Others
contend that there was no shutter immediately behind the proscenium arch.
Langhans supposes that there were two shutters, the first of which was approximately 15 feet (4.6 meters) beyond the proscenium arch, and the second,
approximately 20 feet (6 meters) beyond.[27] Such an arrangement would create
three distinct areas behind the curtain line: the scenic area, the inner stage, and
the deep inner stage.[28] In the last analysis, no definitive number of shutters in
the Dorset Garden can be determined; nonetheless, details of Purcell's scores
indicate that Langhans is correct in supposing that there were three areas behind
the proscenium arch. Such an arrangement would work splendidly in Act II of
The Fairy Queen where the text reads "May the God of Wit inspire, / The Sacred
Nine to bear a part; / And the Blessed Heavenly Quire / Shew the utmost of
their Art. / While Eccho shall in sounds remote, / Repeat each Note, / Each
Note, each Note." The text in question is scored for three solo voices: alto,
tenor, and bass. The score at this point contains the dynamic indications *loud,
soft,* and *softer.* Though this passage is usually performed only by three soloists
observing the dynamics to suggest an echo, a more effective way of rendering it
(and one that would indeed be "witty") would be to take the hint of the text
and increase the number of soloists to nine, placing three in the scenic area,
three in the inner stage, and three in the deep inner stage.

Shutters dividing the area behind the proscenium arch would also be useful
for rendering the countless stage directions requiring "the sound of distant
trumpets"; hardly any battle scene in the Restoration theater repertoire is complete without this sound effect. Clearly the shutters and flats provided additional
possibilities for locating musicians out of view of the audience.

Flat scenes were a mainstay in Baroque theater. In addition to the simple flat
scene, there was also the cut flat, in which a portion of the flat was cut away to
reveal a smaller scene behind. Most frequently, the cut flat involved a window
or a door.

The reference to "provincial touring companies" cited previously may
suggest that these Restoration scenes were simple and inexpensive, but paintings

for theaters often reached a very high level of refinement. In his entry for 1 February 1669, Samuel Pepys gives the following account:

> I went to a Committee of Tanger, but it did not meet; and so I meeting Mr. Povy, he and I away to Dancres to speak something touching the picture I am getting him to make for me. And thence he carried me to Mr. Streeters the famous history-painter over the way, whom I have often heard of but never seen him before; and there I found him and Dr. Wren and several virtuosos looking upon the paintings which he is making for the new Theatre at Oxford; and endeed, they look as they would be very fine, and the rest thinks better than those of Rubens in the Banqueting-house at White-hall, but I do not so fully think so— but they will certainly be very noble, and I am mightily pleased to have the fortune to see this man and his work, which is very famous—and he a very civil little man and lame, but lives very hansomely.[29]

If we may judge from the fee that was awarded to the scene-painter Isaac Fuller in a dispute with Thomas Killigrew in 1669, it is no wonder that Streeter lived "hansomely." Killigrew, the manager of the King's men at Drury Lane, commissioned Fuller to paint the "Scheane of an Elizyum" for a production of John Dryden's *Tyrannic Love, or, the Royal Martyr.* According to Killigrew, the scene—probably placed on a back shutter—was

> painted very meanly & inconsiderably & not at all answerable to what became such a play or to the curiosity wherewith the said Isaack ffuller agreed to paint the same by reason whereof the said play when it was acted was disparaged & lost its reputacon & not halfe the company resorted to see the acting thereof which wold have come in case the said Scaene had been painted according to the said Agreemt.

When Fuller protested, Robert Streeter was called in as a consultant; according to his judgment, the work was of good quality. The case eventually went to court, and the jury found for Fuller and valued the work, which had been painted over a period of six weeks, at 335 pounds 10 shillings—a substantial sum by Restoration standards.[30]

The Restoration theater had not only flat scenes but also set scenes. These were scenes in which three-dimensional objects were set up in advance behind a pair of shutters. When the shutters were drawn apart, the set scene was revealed. The other possibility for a set scene involved a transformation of the stage by the use of the traps.

A third type of scene, which seems to have appeared at precisely the time Purcell began working at the Dorset Garden Theatre, was the drop scene. Indeed, these scenes were unique to the opera stage. Montague Summers gives the following information:

There occur in Betterton's elaborate opera, *The Prophetess; or The History of Dioclesian,* Dorset Garden, April–May, 1690, a number of extremely significant and interesting stage directions. . . . At the commencement of Act III, 2, we find: *A Curtain falls representing the entrance into the inner parts of a Magnificent Pallace. A noble Arch; behind it two Embroider'd Curtains, part of the first ty'd up on either side, the farther Curtain hanging down. Figures of Diana on each side of the Arch standing on large Pedestalls.* Act IV, scene i, is "Scene *the Great Curtain.*" At the end of the scene Drusilla *waves her Wand thrice. Soft Musick is heard. Then the Curtain rises, and shews a stately Tomb.* . . . The conclusion that these curtains, first seen on the London stage in 1690, were "drops" is unavoidable. "Drops" were used in the French theatre at least as early as 1664, and probably rather before that date. But it must be emphasized that "drops" were never employed by Inigo Jones in the Caroline Masques, nor throughout the whole reign of Charles II, and to talk of "drops" before 1690 is wholly erroneous. When these "drops" known as "curtains" were first introduced they were only utilized as something quite extraordinary, a device wholly belonging to opera rather than to the regular stage.[31]

Some special scenic effects used particular sorts of lighting. One type of scene that is encountered with regularity in the stage works of this period is the so-called glory. Quite simply, this was a wooden frame covered with taffeta (i.e., a shiny silk fabric—it is frequently used nowadays as the lining of bill-folds) behind which lights were placed.[32] This device created an aura around the personage represented in front of the glory. The same basic mechanism could also be used to represent the sun, moon, or other celestial bodies. In Purcell's *The Fairy Queen,* a glory could have been used for the sunrise that takes place at the opening of Act IV, as well as for the appearance of Juno at the opening of Act V. The text of the Chinese Man's song clearly alludes to this effect.

> Thus the gloomy world
> At first began to shine,
> And from the power divine
> A glory round it hurled,
> Which made it bright
> And gave it birth in light.

Stage lighting included lanterns and candles in addition to the footlighting system described above. The lanterns were composed of sheets of mica (referred to in contemporary accounts as "Muscovy glass") on three sides with reflecting plates at the rear as well as on the top and bottom. These lanterns were arranged on wires over pulleys behind the proscenium and the various scenes.[33] Sconces of tin with candlesticks were also employed. These were attached to the backs of the flats in great number.[34] One stage hand, called a snuffer, was responsible for keeping all the candles lit.

General house lighting was supplied by chandeliers. In the old Drury Lane Theatre, there were also windows as well as a glazed cupola over the audience seating area. I doubt, however, that Wren would have included a cupola in the design of the Dorset Garden Theatre owing to the fact that the one in Drury Lane leaked during heavy rains.[35]

The Musick Room

At this point we come to what is, from the standpoint of the musician, the crucial factor in Restoration theater architecture: the placement of the main orchestra. In this matter too, the English playhouse relied upon traditions established in the period of Johnson and Shakespeare. In the Elizabethan theater, the main stage protruded into the audience seating area so that it was surrounded by the audience on three sides. In the theaters built during the Restoration, the first row of audience seating was immediately in front of the forestage; as a result, there was no possibility of having the orchestra in a pit as we do today. Instead, a special "musick room" was used. Placement of this musick room varied somewhat from one theater to another.

In the Globe and Fortune theaters, "the orchestra had habitually performed in the 'music-room,' evidentially one section of the gallery which extended over the back wall of the stage."[36] This practice—or something quite like it—can be seen in later seventeenth-century theaters.

> Court practice cannot be taken to prove anything for the public stage, but it is some help to know what was done at Whitehall. Webb's plans for the remodelling of the Cockpit show a music-room above the central arch of the Palladian facade.
>
> In the Hall Theatre there was a bewildering variety of music-seats. One of the *Mustapha* plans shows tiers of seats above the relieves, and these I believe remained in use until the theatre was destroyed, for repairs in November, 1693, included "mending the boards above the Scenes and the floore where the Musick playes." These seats could be concealed by "oval shutters," presumably representing clouds, for they are sometimes called "ye Musick seate in ye Clowds."[37]

Dance halls—or masking halls as they were called during the seventeenth century—also positioned the orchestra in this way. An engraving in Beaumont and Fletcher's *Wit at Severall Weapons* depicts a masking hall and, at the extreme rear above, the musick room (see figure 3.7).[38] Four musicians are pictured within this room, which, as the engraving shows, had windowed shutters that

Figure 3.7. Frontispiece from Beaumont and Fletcher's *Wit at Severall Weapons* showing the "musick room." Courtesy of the Harry Ransom Humanities Research Center, The University of Texas at Austin

could be closed when the musick room was not in use. Sir William D'Avenant's mansion was equipped with such a masking hall. It was in this hall that his *First Day's Entertainment at Rutland House* was given.[39]

We learn the placement of the musicians for this event from a contemporary account that states that "the Musick was aboue in a loouer hole railed about and couered w*th* Sarcenetts to conceale them."[40] Another work of D'Avenant's, *The Cruelty of the Spaniards in Peru*, contains a stage direction that clearly shows the location of the musicians: "The Priest waves his Verge, and his Attendant, with extraordinary Activity, performs the *Somerset:* and afterwards, waving his Verge toward the Room where the Musick are plac'd behind the Curtain, this Song is sung."

These examples, to which numerous others could be added, bear out an important fact: the main body of musicians in seventeenth-century English theaters was located either in seats above the scenes or in a musick room above the proscenium arch. When the musick room was placed above the proscenium arch, as in the Dorset Garden Theatre, it was part of the theater's permanent structure; however, the seats above the scenes were constructed in a simple manner and may even have been portable. They consisted of several tiers arranged in the manner of bleachers. These seats were hidden by the "clouds" that were included as part of the scenery. Such placement of the musicians was a purely English phenomenon that resulted from the equally peculiar English thrust stage.

The negative sentiments expressed by Pepys (cited above as one reaction to Killigrew's removal of the band from the musick room) must have represented the general public's reaction at the time. We know that a substantial remodeling of the Theatre Royal occurred in early 1666.[41] One of the changes made at this time must have been the addition of a musick room, for when this theater was destroyed by fire in January 1672, the following ballad was written about the incident:

> But on a sudden a *Fierce Fire* 'gan rage,
> In several scenes, and overspread the stage.
> The *Horrors* waiting on the dismal sight
> Soon taught *th' players to th' life to act a Fright*
> The *Boxes* where *splendours* us'd to surprise
> From constellations of *bright ladies'* eyes,
> A different blazing lustre now is found
> And the music-room with whistle flames doth sound.
> Then catching hold o' th' roof it does display
> Consuming fiery trophies every way.[42]

Seventeenth-century documents confirm the use of permanent musick rooms in other English theaters as well. The Duke's men, managed by William D'Avenant, worked at the Lincoln's Inn Fields Theatre. This building was opened in 1661 and remained in use until 1671, when the company moved into a new theater. Pepys's diary entry of 7 November 1667 specifically mentions the musick room of the Duke's Theatre at Lincoln's Inn Fields.

> Up, and at the office hard all the morning; and at noon resolve with Sir W. Penn to go see *The Tempest,* an old play of Shakespeares, acted here the first day. Sir W. Penn and I afterward by ourselves, and forced

to sit in the side Balcone over against the Musique-room at the Dukes' House, close by my Lady Dorsett and a great many great ones: the house mighty full, the King and Court there, and the most innocent play that ever I saw, and a curious piece of Musique in an Echo of half-sentences, the Echo repeating the former half while the man goes on to the latter, which is mighty pretty.[43]

The new Duke's house of 1671, which is the theater pictured in the engravings from *The Empress of Morocco,* was located in Dorset Garden. (During the years when Purcell was active at this theater, it was known as the Queen's Theatre rather than the Duke's Theatre.)[44] The engravings of the theater's interior all show the musick room directly above the proscenium arch. There can be no doubt that this room housed the musicians, since musical instruments are pictured to the left (a viol with its bow) and to the right (a trumpet and a drum) beneath the windows. Musical numbers such as the Act IV duet and symphony for the entry of Phoebus in *The Fairy Queen* rely for their effect upon the use of this musick room. The text of the duet alludes to the placement of the instruments: "Let the fifes and the clarions, and shrill trumpets sound, / And the Arch of high Heav'n the Clangor resound."

Similarly, one wonders whether the musick room might have been used for vocal portions such as the trio and chorus "We brethren of air" in Act II of *King Arthur.* This would accord well with Dryden's division of characters—specifically mentioned in his prefatory remarks—into "airy" spirits and "earthy" spirits. Such a positioning of the voices would also correspond with one of Dryden's basic aesthetic premises, earlier elaborated in his preface to the 1685 publication of *Albion and Albanius,* that even supernatural characters must behave in a consistent fashion. "What was attributed by the Heathens to one Power," he wrote, "ought not to be performed by the other. . . . To conclude, they [i.e., supernatural characters] must all act according to their distinct and peculiar characters."

In 1928, when he wrote his well-known study *The Foundations of English Opera,* Edward J. Dent quoted the first stage direction in Shadwell's *The Tempest* (1674?), which specifies that "The Front of the Stage is open'd, and the Band of 24 Violins, with the Harpsichals and Theorbo's which accompany the Voices, are plac'd between the Pit and the Stage." Dent argued that this positioning of the orchestra indicated that

the presence of a band of instrumentalists was accepted as a recognized convention: that instead of the musicians being either invisible agents . . . or visible actors taking part in the play . . ., the music which they made was to all present as normal a constituent of the mental atmosphere as the oxygen which entered the lungs of audience and actors alike.[45]

Dent's supposition that the orchestra was customarily positioned on the floor in the general public's view at the Dorset Garden from about 1674 onward was prompted primarily by considerations of space. There can be no doubt that such an orchestra as the one described by Shadwell would not have fitted into the space of a typical Restoration musick room in a home or theater, whether private or public. Nevertheless, the musick room of the Dorset Garden Theatre was probably considerably larger than most. Dolle's engravings of the interior of the theater consistently show the musick room spanning the entire width of the proscenium arch—roughly 25 to 30 feet (7.6 to 9.1 meters).[46] As indicated earlier, the depth of the scenic stage area at the Dorset Garden was specified by Elkanah Settle as 50 feet (15.2 meters) in his play of 1697, *The World in the Moon*. This would have been an unusually deep scenic stage in any English theater of the period, and I suspect that one of the reasons for this depth was that the first 8 to 10 feet (2.4 to 3 meters) of the scenic stage could not be used for the much-loved flying machines owing to the presence above the proscenium arch of the musick room. If we assume a depth of 8 feet (2.4 meters) and a width of 25 feet (7.6 meters), the area of the musick room was 200 square feet (18.6 square meters). A closer look at the Dolle engravings of the interior will show that a portion of the musick room also projected forward from the proscenium arch. We have no specific dimensions for this area that protruded, but in all likelihood, it would have permitted sufficient space for several players. Clearly, a musick room of these dimensions would have offered ample passage space as well as seating area for a band of two dozen players and the *continuo* group.

The Virtue of Extravagance

The arguments and evidence here presented lead to the conclusion that the Dorset Garden Theatre was a theatrical amusement park. It could accommodate grand spectacles for the delight of the eye. The house also exhibited a "bewildering variety of music-seats" such as Boswell observed in connection with the Hall Theatre. Because of the thrust stage, the relationship between the performers and the audience was intimate. A wide variety of stage machinery was available not only for the entire length and width of the stage but also above and below it.

The librettos of Purcell's dramatick operas make frequent references to special staging effects as well as to the diverse physical locations of the performers and musicians. The Restoration dramatists who created these stage works were themselves stage players in most cases—indeed, they really *had* to be since firsthand experience of the finer points of the theater's properties was essential.

The dramatick opera as a genre demonstrates a remarkable interdependence of text, music, and the theater *per se*. Certain types of scenes—for instance, those using trapdoors, flying machines, or echo effects—were vital elements in seventeenth-century English operas in much the same way that rage arias were vital to eighteenth-century *opera seria* and *preghiera* scenes to the operas of the nineteenth century. Indeed, the "problem of English opera" was not a "problem" at all: it was an essential diversity that made such extravaganzas appealing.

The Dorset Garden Theatre had the most extravagant facilities in London at the time, and Purcell's music is wonderfully coordinated with the theatrical properties of that building. Perhaps nothing short of a Purcell Festspielhaus would suffice for performing a dramatick opera in an authentic seventeenth-century style; nevertheless, our examination of Purcell's playhouse shows that there was an inherent unity in this genre. The unity was not to be found in logically developed story lines that present-day audiences normally expect; the unity stemmed instead from the intoxicating array of sensory stimulants—constantly changing—that filled the mind alternately with marvel, fancy, and awe. Within the context of the Dorset Garden Theatre, extravagance became a virtue.

CHAPTER FOUR

Handel's Haymarket Theater

Mark W. Stahura

George Frideric Handel spent nearly his entire opera career in one theater, the Haymarket opera house in London. Called the Queen's Theatre under Queen Anne, and the King's Theatre under George I (after 1714), the Haymarket Theatre was built in 1705 by John Vanbrugh for Thomas Betterton's company of actors.[1] By the time Handel arrived in England in 1710, Queen Anne had granted the Haymarket management a monopoly on opera in England. The Haymarket remained Handel's operatic home from 1710 to 1739, with only a single, involuntary break from 1734 to 1737 (when another opera company performed at the Haymarket and Handel conducted operas at Covent Garden). Thirty of Handel's forty-four operas were written for the Haymarket Theatre.

The Haymarket Theatre as a Structure

The opera house of eighteenth-century London was significantly smaller than contemporaneous opera houses of continental Europe. Figure 4.1 shows a scale section and plan of the Haymarket Theatre, drawn by C. P. M. Dumont in 1764.[2] The interior, including the performing space, stage, and audience seating area, was approximately 108 feet (32.9 meters) long by 53 feet (16.2 meters) wide.[3] The theater was divided almost exactly in half by the proscenium arch.

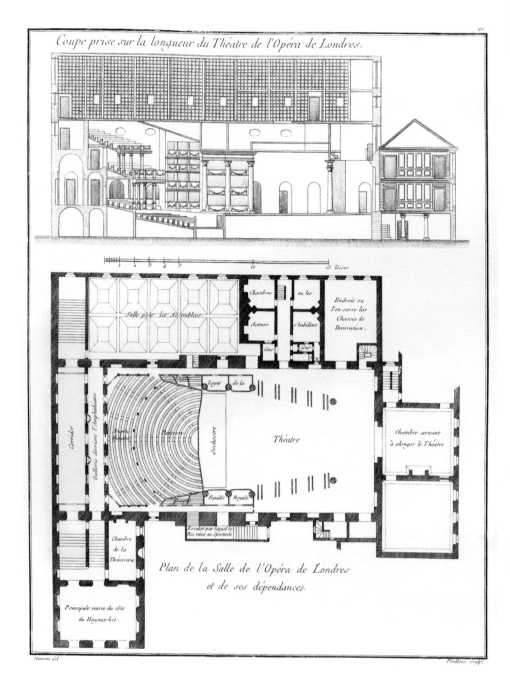

Figure 4.1. Elevation and floor plan of the Haymarket Theatre by C. P. M. Dumont, 1764. Courtesy of the British Library.

By comparison, Hamburg's Opernhaus am Gänsemarkt, where Handel worked for three years, was 160 feet long and 66 feet wide (48.8 meters by 20.1 meters), with an 80-foot (24.4-meter) stage depth.[4]

The Haymarket's stage extended 13 feet (4 meters) in front of the proscenium arch and narrowed to 40 feet (12.2 meters) wide owing to the stage boxes. It was on this forestage that the principal actors did most of their performing. The rear seats on the auditorium's main floor were only 48 feet (14.6 meters) from the front of the stage, and the back row of the second gallery, some 27 feet (8.2 meters) above the auditorium floor, was barely 16 feet (4.9 meters) farther away. The ceiling, 25 feet (7.6 meters) above the stage in front of the proscenium arch, rose to 34 feet (10.4 meters) above the pit.[5] Thus the space for the principal performance area (the forestage) plus the audience was only 53 feet (16.2 meters) wide, 61 feet (18.6 meters) deep, and 34 feet (10.4 meters) high.[6] Handel's theater was an intimate space.

The Haymarket Theatre was well suited to opera for several reasons. Reports indicate that the acoustics of the Haymarket space were very sympathetic to opera. In his memoirs, Colley Cibber notes that while speech was garbled by the liveliness of the acoustics, "the Swell of an Eunoch's holding note, 'tis true, might be sweeten'd by it."[7] This advantage was unaffected by major renovations in 1707–8, which were designed to add seating and mitigate the reverberation in the hall.[8] The orchestra pit also encouraged opera performance, being the largest in a London theater at the time: it spanned the full width of the forestage (40 feet [12.2 meters]) and was 12 feet (3.7 meters) deep, with the instrumentalists seated on the same level as the front row of the audience. Although new theaters were built throughout the eighteenth century, none supplanted the Haymarket Theatre as the English home to Italian opera: the building remained opera's primary locale in England until its destruction by fire in 1789.[9]

Main-floor seating for the audience was on semicircular benches.[10] There were no aisles *per se,* even on the edges of the auditorium. Instead, breaks in the fabric seat-covering of the benches allowed spectators a step, enabling them to get from row to row.[11] The only potentially bad seats on the main floor were in the "front boxes" (at the rear of the main floor), where small supporting pillars for the upper galleries might interfere with sight lines. The front boxes, however, afforded a better view of the full stage, since they were raised slightly in comparison to the pit. The two galleries had equally good sight lines (the first gallery, like the front boxes, having some supporting pillars with which to contend).

Of course, the twelve stage boxes (on the sides of the forestage) were the best seats in the house. The lowest stage boxes were the royal boxes, given a separate entrance. These boxes were also the only places in the hall without bench seating. Presumably free-standing chairs were used. Although the won-

ders of the perspective scenery were denied these patrons, close contact with
the performers and possible views of the machinery in action more than compensated for this deficiency. The worst seats in the house, in terms of sight lines
to the stage, were the side boxes. These twenty-four small boxes hugged the side
walls of the house to such an extent that their occupants would have seen little
beyond the proscenium arch. Patrons in the side boxes were afforded two
advantages, however: (1) they were removed from the hoi polloi among the
audience on the main floor, and (2) they had the best view of the other opera
patrons. These boxes were likely used by those more interested in the social
attractions of opera than in the musical ones. (Since, however, singing was
restricted to the forestage, side-box patrons would have had a perfectly good
view of the performance, if not the scenery.) Prices for opera tickets early in
Handel's London career reflect the desirability of these various seats: 10s. 6d. for
stage boxes, 8s. for front or side boxes, 5s. for the pit, 2s. 6d. for the first gallery,
and 1s. 6d. for the second gallery.[12]

The variability of seating capacity with bench seating has generated a wide
range of capacity estimates by modern scholars.[13] The most reliable figures are
Judith Milhous's estimates that use box office receipts and financial records to
document actual attendance rather than speculative seating potential. She
extrapolates the normal capacity of the hall at 670–940 people.[14] Handel's
opera performances rarely sold out and were usually less than half full.[15]

Little is known about the auditorium lighting in the Haymarket Theatre.
If Graham Barlow's hypothesis about the Thornhill design for the original
Haymarket ceiling (before the 1707–8 renovations) is correct, only two chandeliers hung from the ceiling.[16] Even with substantial chandeliers, the audience
area would not have been well lighted—especially the boxes and farther reaches
of the galleries. Dumont's section and plan of the theater does not show any
lighting apparatus, but this is certainly because chandeliers would obstruct the
view of architectural details. Significantly, however, Dumont's section view
shows no indication of wall sconces in the auditorium. The omission is a
striking one since the indication of sconce locations would not have obscured
any decorative detail.

Dumont's plan was evidently incomplete in regard to the lighting of the
theater. Jean Jacques Fougeroux, who attended three Handel operas in 1728,
reports that

> The sides of the auditorium are decorated with columns, along which
> are reflectors with arms and many candles, just like the columns that
> support the gallery at the rear of the hall. Instead of chandeliers there
> are some ugly wooden hanging candleholders, suspended by rope such
> as one sees at rope dancing. Nothing could be more ugly, [but] there
> are, however, candles everywhere.[17]

Yet even this light may not have provided all the illumination for the audience: in Henry Fielding's *Amelia* (1751), the heroine sits in the first row of the first gallery at a Handel oratorio performance. There she meets an amiable gentleman, who procures and holds a candle to facilitate her reading of the libretto (book 4, chapter 9). Thus, portable illumination was also possible. Fielding's phrasing—"He procured her a book [libretto] and wax-candle"—implies that candles, like librettos, were offered for purchase at the theater. Since dimming the house lights was not possible with the Haymarket's candle illumination, the audience members could read their purchased librettos (which included both Italian and English texts) throughout the performance.[18]

Stage Facilities

Before we consider the stage capabilities of the Haymarket Theatre, a brief overview of Handel's operas will prove useful. The operas Handel composed for the Haymarket Theatre do not all call for extensive and elaborate staging. Four of Handel's earliest operas composed for London—*Rinaldo* (1711), *Teseo* (1713), *Silla* (1713), and *Amadigi* (1715)—and two later ones—*Orlando* (1733) and *Alcina* (1735)—however, call for a multitude of special stage effects. The characters in these works include sorcerers, magicians, and deities, who are capable of supernatural feats (flying, disappearing, creating, or destroying on command). These works clearly call for the full physical resources of the theater: traps, flies, machines, and special effects of all sorts.

In the great majority of Handel's operas, few special effects are required, although an occasional vision or earthly beast may appear. Many of these works, in fact, use only straightforward and often interchangeable sets, such as a royal chamber, a courtyard, or a garden. This contrast with the earlier, effects-heavy operas may have been the consequence of budgetary constraints: after the founding of the Royal Academy in 1720, with its newly recruited, expensive, Continental singers, the norm switched from complex to more simple productions. Perhaps it was decided that the company's money should be spent on the salaries of the vocalists rather than on elaborate machinery and effects. Although the sets for these works were rich in detail and changes of lighting were not uncommon, very little sub- and super-stage machinery was required.

While the more visually complex of Handel's operas require technical effects of all kinds, little is known about the working mechanisms of the stage.[19] (Extant plans of the theater, including Dumont's, do not provide any detail about the traps, flies, or other mechanical apparatus called for in Handel's operas.) One would certainly expect the theater to have had the usual complement of traps for its time, including a midstage grave trap (so-called owing to its use in the graveyard scene in Shakespeare's *Hamlet*) and several single, or corner traps. Single traps could be adjacent and used together to form a larger unit. The exact number, placement, and disposition of the traps at the Haymarket Theatre are not known. Based on playbooks of the Betterton company and the design of the Hampton Court Theatre (a contemporary theater of a similar size), Graham Barlow has proposed four corner traps, three adjacent, single traps downstage center, and a grave trap upstage center.[20]

The librettos of Handel's operas call for traps, primarily of the corner or single-trap variety. There are no open grave scenes, and few effects require larger traps. For example, in *Rinaldo* (1711), Handel's first London opera and one of the most lavish, two furies disappear downward in Act I, mermaids submerge in Act II, and the mountainside battle scene in Act III includes many appearances and disappearances from the ground.[21] Interestingly, throughout Handel's operas almost no principal players are required to appear or disappear through traps—perhaps the subterranean conditions were not suitable to the health, costuming, or egos of the singing stars.

It was entirely suitable, however, for a star to enter on a flying chariot or cloud. This happens in most of the operas with deities or magicians. In *Teseo* (1713), no traps are required, but Medea, Theseus, and Minerva invariably enter upon or exit from the stage via the flies.[22] In *Silla* (1713), only inanimate objects are moved on the traps; all human performers remain above ground.[23] These examples show that the theater must have had a well developed fly system.[24]

Scenery normally consisted only of flats and drops. The Haymarket Theatre had five pairs of grooves for wing flats on each side of the stage, parallel to the front of the stage. The space between the stage-right and stage-left grooves gradually narrowed toward the back, helping to provide the illusion of depth. These grooves (seen on Dumont's plan as dark lines) could have been either stage-mounted slats for sliding flats back and forth or slots cut into the stage floor. This latter would have been part of a newly developed scenery-moving system in which flats and shutters were mounted on wooden poles connected through the floor to under-stage carriages (also called chariots). The underground system was employed at another London theater Handel used for opera, John Rich's Covent Garden Theatre, built in 1732. A Covent Garden inventory of 1744 indicates that the theater had stage-mounted slats for the shutters (the last set of wing flats upstage) and under-stage carriages for the other sets of wing flats.[25] The carriage system had two distinct advantages: first, through ropes and pulleys, it allowed the automated simultaneous changing of wing flats; and second, flats could be built and run on the carriages at angles or perpendicular to the slot, creating actual side walls to the scene.[26] Whether the Haymarket Theatre had either this system or simply onstage slats is unknown. The high expectations for scenery in Italian opera argue strongly for the carriage system.

Scene changes were effected by switching sets of flats, shutters, and drops.

If only onstage grooves were present, this was accomplished either by introducing new flats or drops in front of those previously seen, or by removing a front set of flats or drops to reveal the new set behind. These changes happened in full view of the audience, and were signalled backstage by a bell so that they could happen all at once.[27] Drops and shutters could use cutouts (such as archways) to allow further drops or the vista stage beyond to be seen. Transparencies and projections, used for subtle (and changeable) color effects, were available in English theater, but their use specifically in Handel's operas is not demonstrable.

Above the wing flats and shutters, borders were hung to mask the fly space. These could continue the motif of the scenery depicted on the wing flats (providing, for instance, foliage for trees, or a pediment for a series of columns), or they could contain some less specific image (such as a simple sky border that might be used for any outdoor scene). Drops could be lowered from any wing or shutter position, allowing other scenes or machines to be brought in behind. Thus the depth of the scenes could be varied, reserving the full depth of the stage for maximum effect.

The prime effect sought by scene designers of the day was a sense of distance and of size.[28] Following the example of Italian opera companies and using Italian designers for their productions, English companies likewise strove to dazzle their audiences with scenic effects, most notably effects using perspective.[29] The narrowing of the stage area between the flat grooves was but one factor. Tapering was carried out vertically in the wing flats as well, providing another reason for acting to be confined largely to the forestage: full-size humans toward the rear of the scene would expose the tricks of perspective in the diminishing rear wing flats and drops. The importance of the illusion of distance and volume on stage is demonstrated by the fact that by 1719 Vanbrugh purchased the adjoining house for use as a vista stage, adding 29 feet (8.8 meters) to the scenic depth.

Machinery on the stage (as opposed to that used for flying) would have to be brought on from the rear of the stage. There was essentially no wing space except that between the most upstage set of grooves. The space that existed outside the grooves was undoubtedly taken up with the assortment of flats needed for the evening's production. Even beyond the back grooves, there was slightly over 15 feet (4.6 meters) of wing space on each side for hiding a bridge over a river (*Radamisto*), a mountain (*Rinaldo,* and *Giulio Cesare*), or a fiery porch (*Amadigi*). Larger pieces, such as the mountain or porch (both of which split apart during a scene) may have been brought on in pieces from both wings and connected on stage. This assembly operation, carried out behind a drop, would have allowed the complete machine to be revealed when the drop was raised. There was a 25-foot (7.6-meter) span between the back grooves through which to wheel larger machinery forward.

A special piece of scenic equipment built into the Haymarket Theatre was a system using real water on stage. Handel's operas are full of fountains—certainly actual water—and rivers, which may have been partly real and partly scenic. Both *Radamisto* and *Muzio Scevola* call for lead characters to dive into a river, which may have consisted of an open trap with a slide; a separate splash of water would provide the visual effect.[30] This system was a true drawing card. It apparently had a kind of cooling effect that was most welcome during heat waves: an advertisement on 16 May 1711 for the opera *Clotilda* finishes with the observation, "and by reason of the Hot Weather, the Waterfall will play the best part of the Opera." An ad for Handel's *Rinaldo* later in the month concludes, "The Water Scene as 16 May."[31] The fountains are often called upon in Handel's librettos to rise from the ground, providing confirmation that any piping used was both flexible and situated beneath the stage.

Stage lighting in the Haymarket Theatre used a combination of candles and oil lamps. The forestage—again, where most of the performing took place—was lighted by footlights and chandeliers. The footlights were almost certainly oil lamps, mounted on a recessible tray (for dimming the forestage lighting).[32] The number, size, and intensity of these footlights are unknown. Theaters of the day traditionally had chandeliers over the forestage, and the Thornhill ceiling design postulated by Barlow to be the original Haymarket ceiling indeed has two chandelier openings located just under 10 feet (3 meters) in front of the proscenium arch—near the front of the forestage.[33]

Behind the proscenium arch—in the scene, as opposed to the stage in front of the arch—were certainly also chandeliers, but the number and size of these are not known. Since these were adjustable in height (required for candle trimming and replacement), raising the chandeliers into the flies would partially darken the stage. Each wing flat was illuminated by candles mounted on the back of the next wing downstage. The 1744 inventory at Covent Garden, for instance, lists eight candleholders for each wing. This wing lighting could be varied more than lighting anywhere else in the theater. Darkening the stage could be accomplished by putting shields or blinds over the wing candles—tricky to do all at once for a scene change. Another system for varying the light was to mount the candleholders on a turnable post, so that the candles could be turned away from the stage when darkness was needed.[34] Colored screens and glasses could also be used on these lights, although these techniques were not widely used until later in the century.

Special lighting and sound effects were used in Handel's operas as well. In Act I of *Amadigi,* the stage directions read: "The Scene grows Light on a sudden." Sudden illumination could be effected by quickly adjusting the normal lighting (raising the footlights, turning the wing candles, and lowering the stage chandeliers). A dash of sulphur judiciously thrown on an open flame would have provided a flash to cover the adjustments. This last trick may also have been used for lightning effects. Lightning and thunder are required in *Rinaldo, Teseo, Silla* and *Amadigi*. Thunder was accomplished by rolling balls or a stone on a wooden floor or down a wooden ramp—a "thunder run."[35]

Rinaldo: A Case Study

As an example of the full resources of the Haymarket stage put to use, I will conclude with a commentary on the stage directions for Handel's first London opera, *Rinaldo,* one of his most scenically elaborate scores.[36] These stage directions will allow us to explore the application of the devices and techniques that we have discussed within the context of a specific Handel opera. Passages from the original libretto describe the scenes and effects. Commentary after these passages will focus on the possible method(s) used to accomplish what is described. Handel's original, Italian names for the principal characters are used here even though the libretto's scene descriptions substituted English spellings.

> Act I. scene i. *The City of Jerusalem besieg'd, A Prospect of the Walls, and a Gate on the plainest side of the Town. Part of the Christian Camp on the right side of the Stage.*

This was likely a shallow scene, since many supernumeraries and a chariot-drawn hero will issue from the gate in the succeeding scenes.[37] The city walls were either a pair of shutters or a drop. (A working gate in a set of angled wing flats representing the walls—if a system of under-stage carriages were present—would be quite difficult.) The Christian camp could have been either wing flats, or, less likely, actual tents. Sky borders would mask the fly space.

> Scene ii. *A Trumpet sounds, and the City Gate being thrown open, discovers a Herald, attended by two Guards, who advances toward Godfrey, &c.*

There is no music for this trumpet call in Handel's score; it was likely a standard trumpet fanfare by one or more of the four trumpets indicated in other parts of the score.

> Scene iii. *Argantes from the City, drawn through the Gate in a Triumphal Charriot, the Horses white and led in by arm'd Blackmoors. He comes forward attended by a great Number of Horse and Foot Guards, and descending from his Chariot addresses himself to Godfrey.*

A working chariot is called for, but Sir Richard Steele reported in *The Spectator* of 16 March 1711 that Argante actually entered on foot. The number of supers attending a leading character often reflected the rank of that character:

the extant "prompt copy" of *Radamisto*, for example, implies a total of at least twenty-six supernumeraries for that production. A "great number" of supers is mentioned here, in line with Argante's position as king of Jerusalem.

> Scene v. *Armida in the Air, in a Chariot drawn by two huge Dragons, out of whose Mouths issue Fire and Smoke.* [Later in scene:] *The Chariot being descended, The Dragons rush forward, and draw her toward Argantes, who advances to meet her.*

The fire and smoke from the dragons' mouths were produced by a boy hidden inside the machine, who (according to Steele) did not completely keep himself or his candle hidden. This effect requires that the walls of Jerusalem be at least one set of wings behind the proscenium to allow room for this flying entrance. Armida sings an aria from the sky, implying a certain stability in the machinery. This is also a rare, unarguable instance of singing behind the proscenium arch. The chariot must roll once landed, requiring a bit more sophisticated chariot than one with painted wheels.

> Scene vi. *A delightful Grove in which the Birds are heard to sing, and seen flying up and down among the Trees.*

Flats and shutters are changed. If a drop had been used for the city walls in the previous set, much of this scene could have been in place behind the drop. A border of tree foliage may have been used along the top instead of a sky border. Real sparrows and chaffinches were used in the premiere production, eliciting the comment from Steele that they "either get into the Galleries or put out the Candles." Joseph Addison, in *The Spectator*, No. 5, complained that this effect was an unfortunate mixture of realism with illusion. Handel composed a long and colorful opening *ritornello* (approximately two minutes long) to the aria that begins this scene in order to allow the audience to enjoy the spectacle.

> [Middle of scene vii] [Rinaldo and Armida] *have drawn their Swords, and are making at each other; when a black Cloud descends, all fill'd with dreadful Monsters spitting Fire and Smoke on every side. The Cloud covers Almirena and Armida, and carries 'em up swiftly into the Air, leaving in their Place, two fright-ful Furies, who having grinn'd at, and mock'd Rinaldo, sink down, and disappear.*

The specification of two furies remaining after the two leads leave in the cloud may indicate the approximate size of this machine. The other monsters in the cloud could have been painted, allowing fire and smoke to issue from their mouths more easily than from humans. The fire and smoke were likely produced by the same boy (or boys) who served in the dragons earlier. One larger or two smaller traps are needed to end the effect. Handel composed a quick-tempo

"Prelude" (approximately thirty seconds long) to accompany this series of effects.

> Act II. scene i. *A Prospect of a Calm and Sunshiny Sea, with a Boat at Anchor close upon the Shore; at the Helm of the Boat sits a Spirit, in the Shape of a lovely Woman. Two Mermaids are seen Dancing up and down in the Water.*

The grove scenery is replaced by sky and ocean views. Sea effects were common in plays as well as in opera: the ocean was a set of rotating battens set just above the floor, covered with irregular cloth padding.[38] Both the woman and the mermaids sing later on, so these are not cutouts or mannequins. Since in this scene Rinaldo is invited, and finally agrees, to board the ship, this piece of scenery must have been both large enough to accommodate him, and, at least partly, real (as opposed to flats).

> [Middle of scene iii.] [Rinaldo] *breaks violently from* [Goffredo and Eustazio's] *Hold, and enters the Boat; which immediately steers out into the open Sea, and Sails out of Sight; Then the Mermaids leave Singing and disappear. Godfrey and Eustatio, seem confounded at the Accident.*

The ship has to move through the "ocean," meaning that it was a cart that could be moved by hidden personnel. With the wave battens in place, a cart could not sail upstage or downstage, but simply off into the wings. The mermaids "disappear" in the English translation given above, but in the Italian libretto (on the facing page in the original libretto), *si sommergono nel Mare* (they submerge themselves in the sea). The Italian implies the use of traps for their exit, though they could also have ducked out of sight behind the wave battens.

> Scene iv. *A Delightful Garden in the Enchanted Palace of Armida.*

New wing flats, borders, and shutters would appear.

> Scene vii. *Armida changes herself into the Likeness of Almirena, and follows Rinaldo, weeping.*

During this and the next two scenes, Armida changes back and forth from herself to Almirena several times, requiring rapid metamorphoses. It is unlikely that these transformations were accomplished by means of a trap or drop. Rather, the illusion was either simply acted or suggested by minimal costume changes (Almirena's hat or sash, etc.) or a mask. (She sings both recitatives and arias while in the form of Almirena, so any mask used could not have covered her mouth.)

Act III. scene i. *A dreadful Prospect of a Mountain, horridly steep, and rising from the Front of the Stage, to the utmost Height of the most backward Part of the Theatre; Rocks, and Caves, and Waterfalls, are seen upon the Ascent, and on the Top appear the blazing Battlements of the Enchanted Palace, Guarded by a great Number of Spirits, of various Forms and Aspects; In the midst of the Wall is seen a Gate, with several Arches supported by Pillars of Chrystal, Azure, Emeralds, and all sorts of precious Stones. At the Foot of the Mountain is discover'd the Magicians Cave.*

[Later in the scene] *Godfrey and Eustatio, with drawn Swords, and follow'd by their Soldiers, ascend the Mountain, regardless of the Magician who calls after them.*

[Still later] *Godfrey, Eustatio and the Soldiers, having climb'd half way up the Mountain, are stopp'd by a Row of ugly Spirits, who start up before 'em; The Soldiers, frighted, endeavour to run back, but are cut off in their Way by another Troop, who start up below 'em. In the midst of the Confusion, the Mountain opens and swallows 'em up, with Thunder, Lightning, and amazing Noises. Godfrey, Eustatio, and the Soldiers who escape, return in great Confusion to the Magician's Cave.*

[Still later] *they reascend the Mountain, while the Magician stands at his Cave Door, and sings, to encourage 'em. The Spirits, as before, present themselves in opposition, but upon the Touch of the* [magic] *Wands, vanish upward and downward, with terrible Noises and Confusion. They gain the Summit of the Hill and entering the Enchanted Arches, strike the Gate with their Wands; when immediately the Palace, the Spirits, and the whole Mountain vanish away, and Godfrey and Eustatio are discover'd hanging on the sides of a vast Rock in the middle of the Sea; with much Difficulty they reach the Top, and descend on the other Side.*

. . . As soon as the Magician sees the Enchantment ended, he goes into his Cave.

This scene, which could be set during the break between acts, explicitly requires the full depth of the stage (the vista stage was probably not available in 1711; see p. 101 above). The mountain could not have been a simple ground-cloth on the raked stage, as this would have made "climbing" impossible. It was certainly a huge machine.[39] The fact that Goffredo and Eustazio actually climb the mountain and reach its summit requires that exaggerated perspective from front to back be avoided. The Magician's cave was probably not an integral part of the mountain machine, since it remains after the mountain disappears. It may have been a flat on a downstage side, with a cutout for the entrance. The blazing battlements, the arches, and the gate of the enchanted palace could have been either part of the machine or a painted backdrop (this gate does not have to open, only to disappear when struck—perhaps using a new drop; furthermore, the description of the arches seems more to stimulate the imagination than to describe physical details). Alternately, since the men are said to enter the arches (presumably under the blazing battlements), these features could have been on a set of shutters with cutouts for the arches, with a painted wall and gate on a drop behind. The waterfalls, on the other hand, were almost certainly real.

The spirits appear from within the mountain: traps or hiding places must have been built into the machine. The opening of the mountain could have been simply a separation of the pieces of the machine that made up the scenery (rolled apart, then together again). The indication that the spirits vanish upward and downward when touched by the magic wands implies the use of the flies as well as traps in the machine. Then too, "upward" may allow the spirits to disappear over the summit of the mountain, on foot.

The mountain set had to be built to vanish quickly, however. The "vast Rock" that is revealed could have been a set-within-a-set, with the front of the mountain machine breaking away to reveal the rear portion alone. The challenge lies in hiding these downstage portions of the mountain—they had to be small enough to fit between and outside of the wing grooves. This change had to be coordinated with the reintroduction of the wave battens to represent the sea. The mountain machine might have been built to straddle them.

The larger bits of action in this sequence are covered by music in Handel's score. During the first ascent, the audience would have heard a *sinfonia* in two contrasting sections (slow/fast; approximately five and a half minutes in length). The second ascent, as described in the stage directions, is accompanied by an aria sung by the Magician. It is significant that no singing is required of characters while they are on the mountain: singing was generally confined to the area in front of the proscenium. An additional *ritornello* accompanies the change to the next scene.

> Scene iii. *The Enchanted Garden, Armida, Rinaldo, Almirena.* [Later in scene] *Armida lifts her Arm to Stab Almirena, and Rinaldo draws his Sword and is striking at her, when two Spirits rise to her assistance, and seize upon him.*

This scene probably did not use the full depth of the stage as space had necessarily to be reserved for the following one. Traps—possibly two of them—are required. Steele reports, for either this particular scene change or that in Act II scene iv, that some of the wing flats or shutters missed their cue: "we were presented with a Prospect of the Ocean in the midst of a delightful Grove."[40]

> Scene iv. *Godfrey and Eustatio enter the Garden. . . . A dreadful Host of Spirits rise and fill the Stage, but Godfrey and Eustatio putting out their Wands, the whole Prospect of the Garden vanishes in a moment; leaving in its Place the View of a wild and open Country, with the City of Jerusalem on the side which is built upon Rocks. A Highway is discover'd from the City Gate, which leads in several Turns and Windings down the Mountains.*

More traps are indicated. The vanishing of the garden, with the description of "open Country," suggests a greater depth to this revealed scene—perhaps the raising of a drop along with the changing of the side wings. The description places the city "upon Rocks," and subsequent directions call for groups to march down a "Mountain" or "Hill." These indications imply a ramp or set of steps down from the gate in the wall of the city. The gate is subsequently used for a military procession, so it must have been a working gate.

[Later in the scene] *Rinaldo draws his Sword to wound Armida, who vanishes under the Stroke.*

This description does not indicate how Armida vanishes. Clever staging could have placed her near a wing for a fast exit—perhaps with a flash of light (sulfur) to distract the attention of the audience. It is unlikely (remembering the observation made earlier that lead characters remain above ground) that a trap was used.

Scene v. *Argantes at the Hills Foot, follow'd by three Generals.*

This stage direction does not explicitly say that Argantes comes through the gate mentioned in the succeeding description, but such an entry would make sense given the stage apparatus at hand.

[Later in the scene] *the Pagan Trumpets sound a March, and the Army is seen to pass the Gate, and in military Order descend the Mountain, at whose Foot they pay the usual Compliments of War, as they pass by, to Argantes and Armida.*

Again, the gate must be a working one for this action (or, like Argante's chariot at the beginning of the opera, be a disappointment to the audience). Handel wrote a twenty-two-measure march (about one and a quarter minutes in length) using four trumpets and tympani to accompany this pageantry.

Scene ix. *The Christian Trumpets sound, and the Army in Military Pomp and Order, marches over the Stage, saluting their General as they pass.*

Another *Marcia* (thirty-two measures long, lasting a bit over thirty seconds) accompanies this parade.

Scene x. *Argantes marching his Troops, and ranging them in Order of Battel [sic].*

Supernumeraries sufficient for two groups of soldiers are required.

Scene xi. *The Armies attack each other and form a regular Battle, which hangs in the Balance, til Rinaldo having Storm'd the City, descends the Mountain with his Squadron, and assaults the Pagans in the Rear, who immediately fly, and are pursued by Rinaldo.*

Handel wrote a *Battaglia* movement (forty-seven measures long and lasting about two minutes) depicting this scene.

Most of the scene changes in the opera have no musical accompaniment, occurring between arias and recitatives; furthermore, the machinery may have been quite noisy. Magical transformations are given no music at all, perhaps reflecting a desire to focus attention on the visual spectacle. The thunder and lightning in the third act are the only sound and lighting effects indicated. In fact, Steele criticized these, reporting only "a very short Allowance of Thunder and Lightning."

Handel's operas and the extant data concerning his primary theater combine to sketch practical guidelines for producing his operas. The singing was confined almost entirely to the forestage. Combined with the small size of the auditorium, this provided an intimacy of performance virtually unknown today. The *dramatis personæ* of the opera were supplemented with hosts of supernumeraries whose numbers helped remind the socially alert audience of the relative rank of the various characters on stage. Lead singers not only kept to the front of the stage but also avoided the substage area, a part of the theater apparently suitable only for laborers and supers. The absence of music to accompany many of the visual effects and scene changes points to a deliberate separation of musical and visual events, allowing only one element to command attention at any given time. The balance of these components, kept in line by Handel and his production team through many financial and artistic changes, brought the late eighteenth-century English art of operatic stagecraft to its zenith.

CHAPTER FIVE

Mozart and Two Theaters in Josephinian Vienna

Malcolm S. Cole

The Houses and the Repertoire

Of Mozart's seven operatic masterpieces, four opened in Viennese theaters between 16 July 1782 and 30 September 1791. For this chapter, I have chosen to focus on three of these products of genius:

1. *Die Entführung aus dem Serail.* Premiered 16 July 1782 at the court-operated Royal and Imperial Burgtheater (for production details, please see table 5.1).
2. *Le nozze di Figaro.* Premiered 1 May 1786, also at the Burgtheater; a second production took place on 29 August 1789 (see table 5.2).
3. *Die Zauberflöte.* Premiered 30 September 1791 at Emanuel Schikaneder's privately operated suburban theater in the princely Starhemberg Freihaus on the Wieden (see table 5.5).

Some references will be made to Mozart's *Don Giovanni,* which reached the Burgtheater on 7 May 1788, roughly six months after its Prague premiere, and to *Così fan tutte,* produced at the Burgtheater on 26 January 1790 (tables 5.3 and 5.4 respectively). Additional Da Ponte and Schikaneder collaborations with other composers invite passing attention, as does another Viennese house connected with Mozart's work: the Kärntnertor Theater.

A practical, knowledgeable theater man, Mozart composed his operas with specific conditions in view. Far from dreaming fantasies unrealizable with earthly forces, he knew his emperor, his librettists, the current operatic genres, the singers, the theaters, and the famous (or infamous) Viennese taste. In Andrew Steptoe's words, "Mozart's universality was paradoxically linked to an especial concern with the minutiae of production."[1]

A consideration of Mozart's operas in their theatrical context can yield plentiful information about a fascinating time and place, the Viennese houses in which Mozart principally worked, and the several traditions and conditions that shaped his mature efforts. Concentrating, then, on the two theaters and three works—*Entführung, Figaro,* and *Zauberflöte*—I offer a survey of Mozart's operatic landscape with frequent pauses to examine representative issues in the late eighteenth-century Viennese equation of drama, spectacle, and music. In this manner, we can begin to understand some of the ways in which Mozart integrated stories, sights, and sounds in response to his theatrical environment, and in the process gain insights useful to today's singers, producers, directors, set designers, and conductors.

The Context

Mozart's Viennese decade falls within that period of European history known as the Enlightenment, a hailing of reason, tolerance, and progress.[2] In Austria, more specifically, Mozart's residency coincides almost exactly with the reign of Joseph II (1741–90; co-regent, 1765–80; emperor, 1780–90), who fostered comparable ideals, to include fraternity, forgiveness, and freedom from superstition. In a memoir of 1765, this remarkable ruler articulated a cardinal working principle: "Great things have to be accomplished at one stroke."[3] True to his word, he instituted sweeping reforms in many areas, including theater.[4]

Whether court-operated or privately owned, Viennese theater experienced a golden age. "The theatre [the Burgtheater] . . . was crowded with a blaze of beauty and fashion," Michael Kelly enthused in 1783.[5] "Our National Theatre . . . is always well attended," the ever-watchful Johann Pezzl concurred in 1786; "the members of high society are present in their finery."[6] Likewise, the suburban theaters proved irresistible. " 'Is the playbill for the Kasperl there yet?' asks the government worker as he enters his office. 'We'll see you over there, today they're performing *Cosa Rara.*' "[7]

Joseph viewed theater as both entertainment and an arm of policy. Spoken drama, he reasoned, could provide a cornerstone in the development of a new German culture based on the German language. He was right! "It was in the field of drama that the new [Austrian] culture asserted itself most speedily and most successfully."[8] The better to accomplish his aims, Joseph reorganized the court theater operation. In 1776, at a stroke, he created the German National Theater in the Burgtheater, making it the permanent home of German drama.[9] In 1778 he instituted the German National Singspiel. With Mozart's *Entführung* (1782), a direct result of the emperor's policy, the enterprise achieved its greatest triumph, at the very moment it was foundering. So, in 1783, again at a stroke, the disappointed Joseph established an Italian *opera buffa* troupe in the Burgtheater. As Pezzl put it in retrospect, "in 1783 the Emperor . . . restored to them [his subjects] an Italian opera company, which is still the leading entertainment."[10] Mozart, then, returns to *opera buffa* because of the emperor, his policies, and his tastes.

Da Ponte and Mozart knew and respected this emperor who participated so actively in his theater operation, maintained such cordial relations with his principals, and favored comic opera so strongly. Da Ponte, his heart "aleap with a thousand enthralling sentiments of joy, reverence[, and] admiration," testifies ecstatically that the fact he pleased Joseph upon their first meeting was "the soul of my inspiration, the guide of my pen, in most of the dramas composed by me for his theatre."[11] In recent years, writers have stressed Mozart's career-long attachment to the emperor.[12] Similarly, they have advanced a picture of a politically aware Mozart, a man of bold vision.[13] Considering the Act I finale of *Don Giovanni,* Clemens Höslinger theorizes that the seemingly insignificant textual phrase *Viva la libertà* becomes magnified musically and dramatically to represent "Da Ponte's and Mozart's scarcely veiled personal tribute to Joseph II, to his ideas of liberty (freedom) and enlightenment."[14]

Meanwhile, for a broader audience, a venerable tradition of improvised, often irreverent comedy perpetuated Baroque theater in Vienna. Three great players ensured this tradition's survival in the eighteenth century: Joseph Anton Stranitzky (1676–1726), the Viennese "Hanswurst";[15] Gottfried Prehauser (1699–1769); and Joseph Felix von Kurz (1717–84), the Viennese "Bernardon." Once again, Joseph enters the picture. In 1776, at a stroke, he instituted *Schauspielfreiheit* (*Spektakelfreiheit*): the relaxing of licensing laws that allowed privately run theaters to operate in the suburbs. Here, the theater historian Franz Hadamowsky asserts, is "the hour of birth of the Viennese private theater" (*die Geburtsstunde der Wiener Privattheater*).[16] After its failure at the Burgtheater, "German opera re-emerged in the suburban theatres in the new form of a revived and reformed Viennese popular comedy."[17]

As a result of *Schauspielfreiheit,* three suburban theaters of lasting importance arose, two of concern here: Karl Marinelli's Theater in der Leopoldstadt (1781) and Christian Rossbach's Freihaus Theater auf der Wieden (1787).[18] In the ensuing competition between the houses, Marinelli at first held a tremendous advantage because he employed Johann La Roche (1745–1806), the Viennese "Kasperl." "Coarse, clumsy, grimacing, graphic and obscene," La Roche thrilled the crowds and even the emperor.[19] Then in 1789, a worthy rival assumed direction of the Freihaus Theater; as a writer, Emanuel Schikaneder catered to Viennese public taste.[20] As a comic actor, he triumphed as Anton, the stupid gardener, and eventually as Papageno.

With Da Ponte banished by 1791, "Mozart turned to a new literary collaborator, a new theater, and a new genre."[21] Here, in Schikaneder's arena, he found that "Viennese taste" against which his father had railed in 1768, long before this particular building existed. Leopold Mozart had deplored the Viennese love of "foolish stuff, dances, devils, ghosts, magic, clowns, Lipperl, Bernardon, witches and apparitions."[22] Twenty-three years later, all these elements plus modish "oriental" exoticism are the very ingredients incorporated in *Zauberflöte,* his artistic declaration of independence from the court theater.[23] Mozart, the supreme alchemist, has turned the base elements, scornfully dismissed by his father, into gold.

The Drama

Before its spectacle can dazzle the eye, before its music can enchant the ear, an opera requires a libretto. In Vienna, Mozart collaborated with (Johann) Gottlieb Stephanie the Younger (1741–1800), Lorenzo Da Ponte (1749–1838), and Emanuel Schikaneder (1751–1812). How we evaluate these poets as dramatists will naturally color our perception of their credibility. If we judge one or more of them to be hacks, the temptation arises to tamper with their products because we believe that we know better.

Fascinating characters all, these were capable, experienced, professional theater people. "One of the most successful and popular playwrights of his time" (*Einer der erfolgreichsten und beliebtesten Bühnenschriftsteller seiner Zeit*)[24] and from 1779 the director of the National Singspiel, the Austrian dramatist and actor Stephanie wrote or adapted nearly twenty librettos, for Umlauf, Dittersdorf, and others. Of their working relationship, Mozart reported, "However badly he may treat other people, . . . he is an excellent friend to me."[25]

In response to Joseph's question, how many plays (libretti) had he written, Da Ponte "responded frankly: 'None, Sire.' 'Fine! Fine!' he rejoined smiling. 'We shall have a virgin Muse!'"[26] Truly a beginner, operatically speaking, when appointed court poet and librettist to the newly founded Italian theater, Da Ponte quickly learned his craft through trial and error.[27] He proved particularly skilled in adapting work by other writers and in suiting a libretto for the intended composer, be he Salieri, Martín y Soler, or Mozart.

Of the trio of librettists, Schikaneder is arguably the most interesting because even his contemporaries disagreed about his true stature. In 1792 he published several of his dramas, an ill-considered decision in that he wrote not for readers but for the stage. Divorced from the scenic effects and character portrayals he envisioned, his verse invited merciless lambasting. His own candid statement further tarnished his image: "I write to amuse the public and do not wish to appear learned. I am an actor—a director—and work for the box office." (*Ich schreibe fürs Vergnügen des Publikums, gebe mich für keinen Gelehrten aus. Ich bin Schauspieler—bin Direkteur—und arbeite für meine Kasse.*)[28] One contemporary critic labeled him "an utterly miserable dramatic scribbler" (*vollkommen elender dramatischer Sudler*).[29] Christian August Vulpius, the Weimar court theater poet and Goethe protégé, offered "improved" versions of Schikaneder's librettos, including *Zauberflöte*. Goethe himself, on the other hand, freely conceded that Schikaneder "understood to a high degree the art of making effective use of contrasts and of producing grand theatrical effects" (*in hohem Grade die Kunst verstanden habe, durch Kontraste zu wirken und grosse theatralische Effekte herbeizuführen*).[30] Developing shortly after Mozart's death, a Schikaneder legend was subsequently endorsed by the full weight of Otto Jahn's magisterial authority. Unlettered, dissolute, nearly bankrupt, so the story goes, Schikaneder begged his Masonic lodge brother Mozart to set a libretto, the opera to be performed in the "confined premises" (*engen Local*) of his theater—"little better than a wooden shack" (*nicht viel besser als eine Holzbude*).[31]

The Viennese music historian Egon von Komorzynski toiled half a century to bring "light into the jungle of legends."[32] Although tending at times to gild the lily, he unearthed the materials needed for an objective yet sympathetic appraisal of Schikaneder's achievement. Schikaneder, warts and all, emerged as one of the outstanding theater figures of his period.[33] Acknowledging his accomplishments, one can only hope that today's director will resist the dual temptations of trivializing Schikaneder's work and, worse yet, tampering with it.[34]

A compelling reason for preserving the original order of events in Mozart's operas, even if another ordering might suggest itself,[35] is the composer's active participation in the process of constructing the libretto. A theater devotee— "My sole entertainment is the theatre"[36]—he actually puttered with libretto writing, notably *Die Liebesprobe,* a three-act *Lustspiel* in the style of the Viennese popular comedy.[37] A tantalizing fragment, with its Herr von Dumkopf, Kasperl, Wurstl, and the witch Slinzkicotinzki, it reveals Mozart's concern for stage directions, sound effects, and pratfalls. Mozart's correspondence confirms his involvement in *Idomeneo* and *Entführung*. Given the significantly higher quality of librettos produced by Da Ponte and Schikaneder for Mozart than for other composers with whom they collaborated (like Salieri, Martín y Soler, or Winter), a reasonable surmise is that he helped them too. And yet, neither man incontestably acknowledged such assistance. Linking the subject matter with Joseph's abolition of monasticism, Da Ponte claimed *L'arbore di Diana* as "the best of all the operas I ever composed, both as regards the conception and as regards the verse: it was voluptuous without overstepping into the lascivious; and it interested, as a hundred repetitions of it testify, from beginning to end."[38] For public consumption, Schikaneder rhapsodized that *Zauberflöte* was "an opera which I thought through diligently with the late Mozart" (*eine Oper, die ich mit dem seligen Mozart fleissig durchdachte*).[39] In private conversation, Ignaz Franz Castelli reported, Schikaneder groused that the opera would have been an even bigger success "if Mozart had not spoiled so much of it for me."[40] In any event, ten years before *Zauberflöte*, Mozart confided to his father: "The best thing of all is when a good composer, who understands the stage and is talented enough to make sound suggestions, meets an able poet, that true phoenix."[41] For Mozart, Schikaneder proved to be that phoenix.

Whatever their idiosyncrasies, Stephanie, Da Ponte, and Schikaneder plied their craft honorably. Study of their finished librettos is vital because the portrayal of character begins there with texts that the poets, in consultation with Mozart, calculated to fit a particular operatic genre, each with its own conventions. Before examining these genres, we turn our attention to some general issues of text and translation.

A production team must consult texts that are as complete and accurate as scholarship can render them, including the recitatives for the Italian operas, the dialogue for the German operas, and the full stage directions for both. For such investigation, the *Neue Mozart Ausgabe* provides the foundation.[42] In conjunction with it, other sources may prove useful as well. For example, recommending Kurt Pahlen's edition of the Stephanie / Bretzner libretto of *Entführung,* Thomas Bauman calls attention to the revised version of the poetic texts that arose in north and central Germany, "emendations of some sixty-four lines of [Stephanie's] text, without disturbing a note of Mozart's music."[43] Considering the Act I finale of *Don Giovanni,* Julian Rushton writes, "The Prague libretto of 1787 contains a number of stage-directions which are not normally all reproduced, but which alone make perfect sense of the dance-scene and its sequel."[44] Similarly, a comparison of the *Zauberflöte* text actually set by Mozart with a readily available facsimile of the 1791 libretto printed by Ignaz Alberti demonstrates the additions, deletions, and alterations of various kinds, such as the presence in Alberti's publication of only two stanzas, not three, for "Der Vogelfänger bin ich ja," Schikaneder's magnificent gift to himself![45]

The librettos of Mozart's operas illustrate three different operatic genres: *Singspiel* for the Viennese court (*Entführung*), *opera buffa* (*Figaro*), and Viennese popular theater (*Zauberflöte*). Further enriching these basic genres are additional traditions, notably *opera seria* and *opéra comique.* Concerning *Entführung* Mozart wrote, "I know this nation—and I have reason to think that my opera will be a success."[46] For their venture, Stephanie and Mozart adapted Christoph Friedrich Bretzner's (1748–1807) *Belmont und Constanze, oder Die Entführung aus dem Serail,* which appeared in print in 1781. Set in Turkey, the libretto perpetuates the European vogue for "oriental" subjects, a vogue fueled by eyewitness accounts and by eastern literature itself.[47] Because of its newness, *Singspiel* for the Viennese court lacked the traditional models of *opera buffa* and popular Baroque theater. Retaining the simple plot of the original, the collaborators adjusted the story. Apparently, Stephanie did exactly what Mozart asked, achieving in the process a compromise between the typically North German "comedy with ariettas" and the paradigm for libretto construction that Stephanie developed for German opera and eventually published in 1792.[48] The alliance between spoken and musical traditions caused Mozart great unease.[49] Still, the transformation of Bretzner's original to a pattern in the Italian manner successfully fulfilled aims both practical and dramatic. Practically, it aided the opera's chances for success in Vienna. No less a partisan than Tobias Philipp Freiherr von Gebler (1726–1786) reported that music for the new stage would have to be "of the sort that we are used to here by Piccinni, Anfossi, Paisiello, and to an extent Grétry."[50] Dramatically, it allowed the addition of many new numbers, both solo and ensemble, thus increasing Mozart's opportunities for musical characterization and for the depiction of relationships and confrontations between the strongly etched personalities.[51]

Opera buffa—Schubart's "beautiful monster" (schöne Ungeheuer)—was a thoroughly conventional genre, having standard plot devices, stock characters and vocal types, and particular kinds of musical numbers.[52] Its characters tend to fall into three broad groups: buffo (comic), indebted to the commedia dell'arte (Bartolo); serious, drawn from the upper middle class and the aristocracy and emphasizing traditions of opera seria (the Countess); and mixed, characters introduced to unify a plot and link the serious and comic characters (Elvira).[53]

While the serious undeniably has its place, "the chief thing must be the comic element"—Mozart stresses—"for I know the taste of the Viennese."[54] In selecting La folle journée, ou Le mariage de Figaro by Pierre Augustin Caron de Beaumarchais (1732–1799), Da Ponte and Mozart chose dangerously but well. Da Ponte added buffo detail, muted overt political content, and concentrated the action.[55] Well aware of his task, he commented:

> I was writing an opera, and not a comedy [that is, a spoken play]. I had to omit many scenes and to cut others quite considerably. I have omitted or cut anything that might offend good taste or public decency at a performance over which the Sovereign Majesty might preside.[56]

Worried nonetheless about the opera's length, Da Ponte begs the audience's indulgence, explaining the collaborator's desire "to offer as it were a new kind of spectacle to a public of so refined a taste and such just understanding."[57] How new was Figaro? The aria remains "the normative dramatic structure," with texts for Francesco Benucci, the primo buffo, that require special attention.[58] New, certainly, was the increased number of ensembles and the expansion of the ensemble finales. From a study of Viennese librettos, John Platoff has discovered that most scenes consist of an active part written in dialogue and a concluding reactive portion cast as a tutti.[59] Thus, the finale unfolds as a succession of "cycles" of action and expression, cycles that an informed director can reinforce visually. Da Ponte has memorably described these madly dashing, act-ending complexes: "Everybody sings; and every form of singing must be available—the adagio, the allegro, the andante, the intimate, the harmonious and then—noise, noise, noise; for the finale almost always closes in an uproar."[60]

The suburban theaters catered to the general public's ongoing infatuation with Baroque comedy.[61] Among their attractions was German opera with its indebtedness to the tradition of the Viennese popular theater and its hallowed low-comedy figures, its scenic transformations, and its delight in magic and the other paraphernalia enumerated by Leopold Mozart in 1768. Combining elements from two realms—the lighter *Volkskomik* fare and a weightier stock projecting the splendor and pomp of Baroque opera and embracing the fairy tale—Schikaneder developed a "Magic Flute" formula: a generally lofty, serious opera that included comic episodes, magic and machines, exotic setting, Enlightenment ideals of clemency, tolerance, and liberty, and a basic theme of trial and purification.[62] With its exotic setting and its trial by fire and water for the hero, *Der Stein der Weisen, oder Die Zauberinsel* (The philosopher's stone, or the magic island, 1790; music by Schack and Gerl) established the tone. This recipe is, of course, realized most magnificently in *Zauberflöte* itself, that "happy blend of fantasy, mysteriousness, high drama and cheerful comedy."[63] A host of literary influences has long been recognized; additional candidates continue to be proposed, for example, Chrétien de Troye's Arthurian romance, *Yvain, ou Le chevalier au Lion*.[64] To this multiplicity of influence, Mozart responded with a dazzling variety of musical types and a range of structural designs unmatched in his other mature operas.[65]

From three categories of written source-material—the literary antecedents, the libretto, and, on occasion, Mozart's correspondence—a production team can proceed beyond the character conventions of a genre and discover the singular personalities created for Mozart's musical attention. Three sketches serve to illustrate this process.

In an "oriental" setting like that of *Entführung*, the librettist was free to portray extremes of benevolence (Bassa Selim) and cruelty (Osmin). On two occasions, Mozart refers to Osmin in the correspondence, once branding him "a rude churl and a sworn foe to all strangers," and later in praising Stephanie's poetry as "perfectly in keeping with the character of stupid, surly, malicious Osmin."[66] In the libretto, one sees Osmin both through others' eyes and as he projects himself. Among the choicer epithets directed at him are: "churlish old boor!" (Belmonte); "damned watchdog," "old grouch" (Pedrillo); "old bully," "bellows of a face," "old dodderer," and "stupid old idiot" (Blonde). Evident from his own lines are his hearing handicap, suspicion, bluster, spite, sadistic streak, revenge fantasies, violent temper, intolerance of strangers, gullibility, and helpless infatuation.[67] Mozart expanded Osmin's role expressly for the celebrated Johann Ignaz Ludwig Fischer (1745–1825) both because he had an "excellent bass voice" and because he had the "whole Viennese public on his side."[68] For Fischer, Mozart created "O wie will ich triumphieren," a gloating revenge fantasy in which Fischer's beautiful deep notes "glow."

For the *femme de charge* Marcellina (Marceline) in *Figaro*, the correspondence provides no assistance, but Beaumarchais's preface to *La folle journée* does:

"a spirited woman who was born rather mettlesome, but whose faults and experience have reformed her character" (*Marceline est une femme d'esprit, née un peu vive, mais dont les fautes et l'expérience ont réformé le caractère*).[69] A difficult individual who seeks to cause trouble—"always bitter and provocative" (*Toujours amère et provocante*), Bartolo grumbles after her first lines in the play—she begins as a *buffa* type in the opera, a laughing stock who is humiliated in the trade of insults with Susanna (No. 5, "Via, resti servita"). "A spiteful tongue"—Susanna remarks—"decrepit old witch," "old frump," "putting on high and mighty airs because you've read a couple of books." Yet, upon discovering that Figaro is her long-lost son, Marcellina undergoes a remarkable transformation. She remains a comic figure, but Beaumarchais and "to an even greater degree Da Ponte, make her a lovable one."[70] To render this transformation convincing to an audience, Marcellina's Act IV aria, "Il capro e la capretta," must be preserved, even though commentators such as Julian Rushton, citing the opera's length and the placement of the aria, argue that "major statements by minor characters are out of place when everything is tending to a conclusion."[71] Including Basilio's "In quegli anni" (also customarily cut), Allanbrook rightly observes, "The arias . . . form an important preface to Figaro's angry soliloquy. . . . Viewed in this light both arias—Marcelina's especially—are crucial to the theme of feminine friendship which is the matter at the opera's heart."[72]

The one character in these three operas whose name remains (possibly) in some doubt is Monostatos—or, as Hans-Josef Irmen contends—Manostatos, a Moor residing in yet another exotic locale, Egypt.[73] His literary ancestry can be traced generally to several sources and specifically to Torgut, the "very hideous black slave" (*sehr hässlicher schwarzer Sclave*) who appears in Christoph Martin Wieland's "Adis und Dahy," from *Dschinnistan*.[74] Although he figures in only 109 of the story's 1,110 lines, his repulsive, sharply etched portrait furnishes a model for Monostatos, complete with the traits of "lust, crudeness, mendacity, and tattling" (*Lüsternheit, Roheit, Verlogenheit und Angeberei*).[75] Like Monostatos, he holds a high opinion of himself, especially of his ability to charm ladies and add them to his list. He too is punished instead of rewarded for doing his duty.[76] Based on a theme by Joseph Myslivecek and conceived for the actor Johann Joseph Nouseul, Monostatos's sole aria, "Alles fühlt der Liebe Freuden" (No. 13), masterfully illustrates the *alla Turca* style so popular in Vienna.[77]

From the earliest planning stages, all three genres raise a formidable production issue for modern companies: the achievement of an acceptable balance between the diverse individuals and the myriad incidents of intrigue and plot, on the one hand, and, on the other, the communication of an overarching dramatic theme or themes. Few would disagree that Mozart's recurring calls for clemency, forgiveness, liberty, and tolerance project Enlightenment thought on stage. While the advocacy of more specific meaning in the individual operas is not a central concern of this chapter, a few examples will serve to illustrate the point I wish to make. *Entführung* projects themes of love and society, Brigid Brophy claims.[78] *Figaro* has recently drawn dramatically contrasting responses from three scholars. For Giorgio Pestelli, "[Mozart] disposed once and for all of Arcadia and the dull remnants of pastoral life. . . . *Le nozze di Figaro* immersed itself . . . in the swift, bustling rhythm of city life."[79] For Wye Allanbrook, Arcady is central. As a radiant romantic comedy, with the two women's friendship at its heart, "[*Figaro*] in fact turns out to be a special vision of the refuge offered by the pastoral world to true lovers."[80] For Volkmar Braunbehrens, "*Figaro* served as a signal, a convenient form of propaganda that furthered the goals of Josephine policy."[81] As for *Zauberflöte,* whether choosing to establish a serious Masonic tone or create a lighter, fairy-tale atmosphere, as Constanze Mozart herself advocated, the director can generate a compelling dramatic thrust by viewing the opera as a quest for wisdom guided by friendship and supported by love.[82]

The isolation of a major idea or ideas may indeed inspire the present-day director to forge a powerful unity from seemingly disparate elements. Laudable as such efforts are, one must not overlook an important principle of dramatic organization recognized in Mozart's time and common to all operatic genres then cultivated. In Steptoe's concise formulation, it is:

> The orientation of acting around a series of 'points' in each work: celebrated passages, individual lines, or even single words would elicit a massive response. They became the pivots of an interpretation, . . . a series of dramas of the moment.[83]

Deploring the dramatic limitations of most Italian singers and referring to the ensemble finales of *Figaro,* Adolf Knigge noted:

> What is more, the finest strokes must needs appear in the finales, where it is impossible for every singer to sing so distinctly and also to act so well, that many a *pointe* is not lost; and that is certainly a pity in the case of a piece written with such wit.[84]

The librettist and the composer carefully calculated these points on which an opera's success depended. As his/her point approached, the actor / singer would move to the front of the stage, the better to be seen and heard.[85] The audience, however inattentive it may have appeared, was primed for them. Thus, today's production people incur a responsibility to be equally aware of them, highlighting them with adequate preparation, appropriate motion, and effective lighting, so that many a *pointe* is clearly and forcefully projected.

The Casts

In the sphere of opera, four components invite attention: the casts, the theaters, the productions, and the audiences. Mute on the page, no matter how vividly drawn, an opera's characters must be brought to life by singers and actors, with support from additional theater personnel backstage and in the pit, all directing their efforts toward pleasing an audience.

In Vienna, Mozart wrote for three troupes: the German company, in the Burgtheater from 1778; the Italian company, which replaced the German in 1783; and Emanuel Schikaneder's company, resident in the Freihaus Theater from 1789. The casts of the original productions of Mozart's most important Viennese operas are listed in tables 5.1 through 5.5. Whatever the conduct of its members offstage, each company functioned as a well-organized, disciplined team with individual responsibilities clearly spelled out as in Da Ponte's "Rules Most Necessary to the Theater Direction" (*Ordine necessarissimo in una direzione teatrale*) or in Schikaneder's set of "Instructions and Rules" (*Vorschriften und Gesetze*).[86] Observers extol the effectiveness of these troupes. "It can boast of no great beauty," John Owen reported of the Freihaus Theater in 1792.[87] "Its principal excellence arises from the musicians and singers, who support the whimsical performances here exhibited."

Table 5.1. *Die Entführung aus dem Serail,* K. 384. Johann Gottlieb Stephanie der Jüngere (after C. F. Bretzner); prem. 16 July 1782 at the court-operated Burgtheater, cond. by Mozart.

Singspiel in three acts, set on the Pasha's country estate in Turkey

Constanze	Caterina Cavalieri[a]	sop.
Blonde	Therese Teyber	sop.
Belmonte	Johann Valentin Adamberger[b]	ten.
Pedrillo	Johann Ernst Dauer	ten.
Bassa Selim	Dominik Jautz	speaking
Osmin	Johann Ignaz Ludwig Fischer	bass

[a] Mozart authorities are divided in their spelling of her name as "Catarina" or "Caterina."

[b] In older lists, one sometimes reads Valentin Joseph Adamberger. Today, authorities such as Robert Marshall, *Mozart Speaks,* and H. C. Robbins Landon, ed., *The Mozart Compendium,* specify Johann Valentin.

Table 5.2. *Le nozze di Figaro,* K. 492. Lorenzo Da Ponte (after Beaumarchais); prem. 1 May 1786, Burgtheater, cond. by Mozart; a second production, 29 August 1789.[a]

Opera buffa in four acts, set on the count's estate at Aquasfrescas outside Seville

Figaro	Francesco Benucci	barit.
Susanna	Nancy Storace	sop.
Marcellina	Maria Mandini	sop.
Cherubino	Dorotea Sardi-Bussani	sop.
Count Almaviva	Stefano Mandini	barit.
Countess Almaviva	Luisa Laschi-Mombelli	sop.
Dr. Bartolo	Francesco Bussani	bass
Antonio	Francesco Bussani	bass
Don Basilio	Michael Kelly	ten.
Don Curzio	Michael Kelly	ten.
Barbarina	Anna Gottlieb	sop.

[a] Most notable among the several changes made for the Vienna revival are the *Rondò,* K. 577, and the Aria K. 579 for the new Susanna, Adriana Ferrarese del Bene, née Gabrielli.

Table 5.3. *Il dissoluto punito, ossia Il Don Giovanni,* K. 527. Lorenzo Da Ponte (after several sources); prem. 29 October 1787, Prague National Theater; first Vienna performance, 7 May 1788, Burgtheater, cond. by Mozart.[a]

Dramma giocoso (*opera buffa* in Mozart's thematic catalog) in two acts, set in seventeenth-century Seville

Don Giovanni	Francesco Albertarelli	barit.
Commendatore	Francesco Bussani	bass
Donna Anna	Aloisa Lange	sop.
Don Ottavio	Francesco Morella	ten.
Donna Elvira	Catarina Cavalieri	sop.
Leporello	Francesco Benucci	bass
Masetto	Francesco Bussani	bass
Zerlina	Luisa Laschi-Mombelli	sop.

[a] Mozart substituted "Dalla sua pace," K. 540a, for Ottavio's original "Il mio tesoro." He added "In quali eccessi / Mi tradì," K. 540c, for Elvira and the duet "Restati qua / Per queste tue manine," K. 540b, for Zerlina and Leporello. In addition to various adjustments and additions to the Act II recitatives and the end of Leporello's aria, "Ah pieta," the Epilogue was omitted.

Table 5.4. *Così fan tutte, ossia La scuola degli amanti,* K. 588. Lorenzo Da Ponte (no known source); prem. 26 January 1790, Burgtheater, cond. by Mozart.

Opera buffa in two acts, set in eighteenth-century Naples

Ferrando	Vincenzo Calvesi	ten.
Guglielmo	Francesco Benucci	barit.
Don Alfonso	Francesco Bussani	barit.
Fiordiligi	Adriana Ferrarese del Bene	sop.
Dorabella	Louise Villeneuve	sop.
Despina	Dorotea Sardi-Bussani	sop.

Table 5.5. *Die Zauberflöte,* K. 620. Emanuel Schikaneder; prem. 30 September 1791 at Schikaneder's privately operated Freihaus Theater auf der Wieden, cond. by Mozart.

Grosse Oper in two acts, set in ancient Egypt. Stage scenery by Joseph Gayl and Herr Nesslthaler[a]

Tamino	Benedikt Schack	ten.
Papageno	Emanuel Schikaneder	barit.
Queen of Night	Josepha Weber-Hofer	sop.
Pamina	Anna Gottlieb	sop.
Sarastro	Franz Xaver Gerl	bass
Three Ladies	Fräul. Klöpfer, Hofmann,	
	Elisabeth Weinhold-Schack	sops.
Three Boys	Nanette Schikaneder,	
	Matthias Tuscher,	
	Master Handlgruber	
Speaker	Herr Winter	
Three Priests	Urban Schikaneder	speaking
	Johann Michael Kistler	ten.
	Christ. Hieronymous Moll	bass
Monostatos[b]	Johann Joseph Nouseul	ten.
Papagena	Barbara Reisinger-Gerl	sop.
Three Slaves	K. L. Giesecke,	
	Wilhelm Frasel,	
	Herr Starke	
Two Men in Armor	Johann Michael Kistler	ten.
	C. H. Moll	bass

[a] One occasionally will see "Resslthaler" as in Rudolph Angermüller, *Mozart's Operas,* p. 229.

[b] For Hans-Josef Irmen's fascinating theory, see note 73. Should the Moor's name properly be "Manostatos"?

A striking feature of the companies, generally speaking, is the youth of several of their members. At the premiere of *Figaro,* for example, Gottlieb (Barbarina) was twelve, Storace (Susanna) twenty, Laschi-Mombelli (the Countess) about the same age—she was born around 1766—and the double-cast Michael Kelly (Basilio, Don Curzio) twenty-four.[88] The male stars were older, Mandini (the Count) about thirty-six and Benucci (Figaro) a relatively venerable forty-one. Young but well-trained voices amply filled the modestly proportioned Viennese theaters of the time.[89] Because roles were allocated on a hierarchical basis, the status of the vocalist mattered more than his / her voice type.[90] Therefore, the *prima donna* would automatically appropriate for herself the major female part. That Nancy Storace, the *prima buffa,* played Susanna confirms the primacy of that role. The youthful coloratura Luisa Laschi-Mombelli played the Countess. The implication for modern performance is clear: since both women are young, today's interpreters should resist any temptation to sing the Countess's arias too slowly, in a manner reminiscent of an older, more mature lady like the Marschallin in *Der Rosenkavalier.*[91]

As for the individual singers, on whom the opera's success chiefly depended, Mozart's oft-cited tailoring simile remains apt: "I like an aria to fit a singer as perfectly as a well-made suit of clothes."[92] Simply put, he catered to strength; he concealed weaknesses. Mozart, the emperor, and others attest that each company had principals who could really sing: Adamberger, Cavalieri, and Fischer of the German company; Benucci, Mandini, and Storace of the Italian company; Hofer and Schack of the Freihaus Theater troupe.[93] Of *Figaro,* Michael Kelly reported, "It was allowed that never was opera stronger cast."[94] In another place, he calls Mandini and Benucci "the two best comic singers in Europe," an assessment seconded by Pezzl, who considered them "the most accomplished buffo actors one can see."[95]

Eyewitnesses, including Mozart, cite pros and cons suggesting that dramatically credible interpretation mattered more than sheer beauty of tone and perfection of technique (although they too were much appreciated). Johann Valentin Adamberger (1743–1804) possessed a voice that "would have had none too great a compass, yet 'its congenial expression, its feeling, and its soul' were praised" (*keinen allzu grossen Umfang gehabt hätte, man lobte jedoch 'den sympathischen Ausdruck, das Gefühl und die Seele derselben'*).[96] Concerning the "flexible throat" of Caterina Cavalieri (1760–1801), Gebler remarked in 1780–81 that she had "a strong and pleasant voice, in both the high and the low notes, a combination which one seldom encounters, [she] sings equally well the most difficult passages" (*eine starke und angenehme Stimme, mit tiefen und hohen Tönen, die man selten beysammen antrift, singt ebenfalls die schwehrsten Passagen*).[97]

For both her singing and her physical appearance, Nancy Storace (1765–1817) drew both effusive praise and some unkind criticism. She had "a pretty, voluptuous figure, beautiful neck, and [was as] good as a Bohemian girl," Count Carl Zinzendorf noted on one occasion, while remarking on another that she sang like an angel.[98] Admitting that she sang very well, Pezzl offered this contrary view of her appearance: "her figure was not advantageous: a thick little head, without any feminine charm, with the exception of a pair of large and nearly expressionless eyes."[99] In Burney's judgment, the voice of this "lively and intelligent actress" had "a certain crack and roughness" and "a deficiency of natural sweetness."[100] Lord Mount Edgecumbe believed that "in her own particular line . . . she was unrivalled, being an excellent actress, as well as a masterly singer."[101] Whatever her perceived shortcomings, through intelligence, wit, and charm she moved audiences with her comic portrayals, as Franz Kazinczy enthused: "Storace, the beautiful singer, enchanted eye, ear, and soul." (*Storace, die schöne Sängerin, bezauberte Auge, Ohr und Seele.*)[102]

A particular favorite of the emperor and the Viennese public, Francesco Benucci (1745–1824) was the greatest *buffo* bass of his generation, "the strength that emboldened Mozart to conceive of writing an opera on the scandalous Figaro play."[103] Worth more than two Storace's, in the emperor's opinion, "probably he was the finest artist for whom Mozart wrote, and as a *buffo* outshone his contemporaries as singer and actor."[104] In an illuminating study, John Platoff has analyzed the Viennese repertoire created for Benucci, especially those expansive *buffo* pieces which afforded "a talented singer and actor an extended opportunity for comic expression."[105] "Aprite un po' quegli occhi," Figaro's "outburst of jealous rage in Act IV of *Le nozze di Figaro,* exemplifies with particular clarity the two-part structure of the buffa aria, with the opening stanzas . . . setting the scene for a subsequent outburst of comic energy."[106]

Composer, flutist, and singer, Benedikt Schack (1758–1826) impressed Leopold Mozart: "He sings excellently, has a beautiful voice, easy and flexible throat, and beautiful method. . . . This man sings really very beautifully."[107] Even the great actor Friedrich Ludwig Schröder, who committed to print some candid remarks about members of the Freihaus-Theater troupe, found Schack "a good tenor, but with Austrian accent and suburban declamation" (*ein braver Tenorist, aber mit Österreichischer Mundart und Vorstadtsdeclamation*).[108]

All these singers had received Italian training, the elements of which are available to present-day vocalists in treatises ranging from Pier Francesco Tosi (1723) to Manuel Garcia (1847), and including Johann Adam Hiller's *Anweisung zum musikalisch-zierlichen Gesange* (1780), now available in Suzanne Beicken's translation.[109] For the aspiring singer, Hiller prescribed proper training (a three-year program at least), purity of intonation, evenness through the registers, *portamento* (connection of tones "without a gap or break [and] no unpleasant slur or pull through smaller intervals" [p. 34]), and a clear pronunciation of syllables and words: "well spoken is half sung" (*Gut gesprochen, ist halb gesungen*).[110] Although a sustained examination of performance practice lies outside the scope of this chapter, the serious interpreter of Mozart's operas must utilize the uniquely twentieth-century knowledge explosion in this subject area. Drawing upon materials like the contemporary reports sampled above, the treatises, and the methods, scholars and performers continue to examine the parameters of pitch, rhythm and tempo, phrasing and articulation, ornamentation and improvisation, and *continuo* realization.[111] With increasing frequency, their results are manifest in sound recordings using period instruments.[112]

The Theaters

What of the vanished buildings in which these masterworks premiered? Soon after 1800, the Freihaus Theater had disappeared, replaced by a housing tract;[113] demolition of the Burgtheater followed in 1889. In their heyday, neither venue functioned exclusively as an opera house. Both were versatile spaces that accommodated spoken theater, ballet, and academies as well. From preserved evidence—documentary, anecdotal, and iconographic—and from studies of other contemporary theaters, notably the still operative Drottningholm Court Theater, much useful information emerges.[114]

In the 1780s, the Burgtheater's exterior would have appeared to Mozart as it does in the nineteenth-century photograph reproduced as figure 5.1. Its three high bay windows and the ornamental balcony were but a façade enlivening the

Figure 5.1. Burgtheater, St. Michael's Square, nineteenth-century photograph of the backstage wall and façade.

back wall of the stage.[115] Depending upon the source consulted, the building was somewhere between 125 to 144 feet (38.1 to 44 meters) long, 33.5 to 49 feet (10.2 to 14.9 meters) wide, and 39.5 to 46 feet (12 to 14 meters) high. That scholars working from the same drawings derive strikingly different dimensions is hardly surprising, although scarcely noted in print. Numerous obstacles hinder the determination of precise figures. To begin with, the drawings themselves have not always been rendered to exact scale. Then comes the conversion process, with concomitant rounding off: from old Austrian units of measurement such as the *Klafter* or *Schuh* to meters, from meters to feet and inches. Finally, writers sometimes fail to specify exactly what it is that they are reporting. For example, to which drawings are they referring? Is the auditorium width being calculated from side wall to side wall, or perhaps from loge front to loge front? Offered in table 5.6 below are the measurements proposed in several representative studies.

Under the supervision of the court architect Franz Anton Hillebrandt, the oft-renovated structure's interior underwent a facelift completed in mid April 1779.[116] This was the house as Mozart found it. A contemporary visitor's report ushers us inside: "Here I must also mention the Burgtheater, which doesn't look like anything from the outside, but on the inside is decorated almost too elegantly and with almost too much gilt—and is not large enough for Vienna."[117] A color scheme of white and gold prevailed, with red carpet in the boxes and red seat cushions. With a capacity of approximately 1,350, this prototypal "box, pit, and gallery" arrangement was somewhere around 74 feet (22.6 meters) long.[118] Spectators sat (or stood) in the front (*noble*) parterre, the second parterre, and the four tiers surrounding the auditorium pictured in figures 5.2 through 5.4.

Helpful though they are, iconographic materials and architectural measurements ultimately cannot capture the feel of the space, its cramped quarters, its narrow stone staircases (an hour was required for emptying a full house), its smells, its temperature, and its ever-present danger of fire.[119] Nonetheless, theater historians and musicologists express a virtually unanimous conclusion: although an "architectural mishap" in some respects, the house's dimensions, relatively low ceiling, seating arrangement, and wood paneling combined to create a clear, bright acoustic conducive to hearing "the words and the highly articulated musical detail of rapidly sung passages. . . . The best way to achieve this [acoustic clarity] is for the audience to be seated as close as possible to the stage."[120] Mozart certainly concurred: "You have no idea how charming the music sounds when you hear it from a box close to the orchestra—it sounds much better than from the gallery."[121]

The clarity of sound was further enhanced by the large amounts of sound-absorptive material provided when an audience in full costume crowded into boxes around the wall and on the parterre, all in a

Table 5.6. Burgtheater Dimensions

Writer	Total length feet (meters)	Auditorium length	Auditorium width	Height	Stage length	Stage width	Proscenium
Angermüller	144 (44)	62 (18.9)	49 (14.9)	39.5 (12)	41.5 (12.6) +26 (7.9)	56 (17.1)	—
Baker		62 (18.9)	33.5 (10.2)	40 (12.2)	41.5 (12.6) +31 (9.5)	56 (17.1)	27.5 (8.4)
Heartz	125 (38.1)	—	49 (14.9)	46 (14)	—	—	—
Hennings		79 (24.1)	34 (10.4)	39.5 (12)	—	—	—
Michtner		—	—	—	49 (14.9) +26 (7.9)	—	30+ (9.2)
Morrow	125 (38.1)	74 (22.6)	39 (11.9)a 49 (14.9)	—	49 (14.9)	—	—
Schindler		—	35 (10.7)	40 (12.2)	—	—	27.5 (8.4)
Singer		72 (21.9)	44 (13.4)	39.5 (12)	—	—	—

a See figure 5.2 below for the 1779 floor plan offered as plate 5 in Morrow, *Concert Life in Haydn's Vienna*, p. 74. Morrow also shows Burgtheater dimensions derived from a 1778 floor plan (p. 75). She cites an interior width of approximately 49 feet and a "wall to wall" distance of approximately 39 feet. Another table of comparative dimensions of five Viennese theaters (p. 90) indicates only a house width of 49 feet.

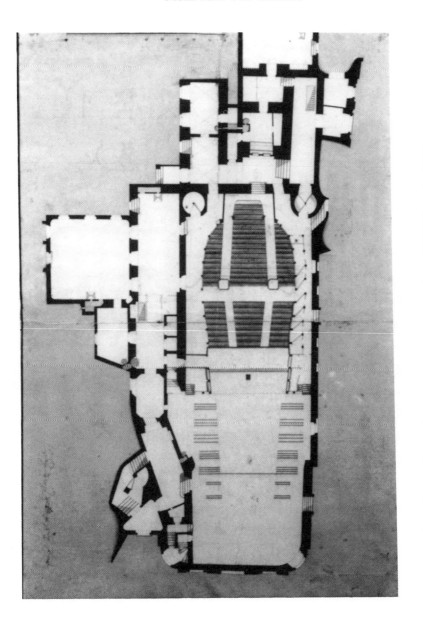

Figure 5.2. Burgtheater floor plan, parterre, drawing by Joseph Hillebrandt, 1779.

Figure 5.3. Burgtheater auditorium, cross-section, drawing by Joseph Hillebrandt, around 1778.

Figure 5.4. Burgtheater interior, around 1820, anonymous colored engraving.

comparatively small space. There was consequently little danger of excessive reverberation to obscure musical detail and speech intelligibility.[122]

Focusing upon spoken drama, Herta Singer has calculated a reverberation time of 1 to 1.3 seconds depending upon audience size.[123] In concise summaries, both Singer and Michtner emphasize the abundant use of wood that yielded a bright acoustic.[124] Fred Hennings warmly echoes the prevailing sentiment of all who study this place: "this most intimate and pleasant of all public auditoriums" (*diesem intimsten und gemütlichsten aller öffentlichen Audienzsäle*) ideally matched the style of Mozart's operas.[125]

Destroyed by fire on 3 November 1761, the Kärntnertor Theater was quickly rebuilt, to a plan of the court architect Nikolaus Franz Leonhard Pacassi.[126] It reopened 9 July 1763. An imposing front invited patrons into a room that the indefatigable music traveler Dr. Charles Burney found "lofty. . . . The height makes it seem short, yet, at the first glance, it is very striking."[127] Once again, scholars disagree about the house's exact dimensions. The auditorium stretched somewhere between 60.5 feet (18.4 meters) to 69 feet (21 meters) deep by 31 feet 3 inches (9.5 meters) wide, measuring from the fronts of the side boxes. Like the Burgtheater, the Kärntnertor Theater auditorium's first floor consisted of a parterre divided into two sections and an orchestra "pit" of 6.5 feet (2 meters) that separated the parterre from the stage area. Unlike its counterpart, the Kärntnertor Theater had five tiers surrounding the parterre. Characteristically, these tiers included boxes and gallery space (each writer advances a slightly different total of boxes). With a capacity of approximately 1,000, then, the Kärntnertor Theater was shorter, narrower, and, to judge from Burney, higher than the Burgtheater. Beginning in the 1770s with Burney and Müller, visitors and authorities alike praised the Kärntnertor Theater for its splendid scenes and decorations. From proscenium to back wall, the stage length was approximately 39.5 feet (12 meters), its width 65.5 feet (20 meters) wall to wall, and its proscenium opening 42.5 feet (13 meters) wide by 36 feet (11 meters) high. Five wings were set in perspective, while the stage allegedly included thirteen traps.

Like its proprietor, the Freihaus Theater took an unwarranted pummeling from Jahn.[128] Far from being a "miserable shack," "little better than a barn," it was in fact a substantial structure of brick and stone, with a tile roof and an interior of wood paneling. The floor plan is shown in figure 5.5. Apparently unknown to Jahn and even to Rommel, an inventory compiled in connection with a legal action of 1794 provides abundant information about the building and its appointments.[129] Its interior disposition was as follows:

The stage
the proscenium
the *parterre noble* consisting of
    18 benches with backs [covered with] red fabric
    5 benches without backs [covered with] red fabric
    1 wooden partition with fabric between parterre and *parterre noble*
    1 of the same in the orchestra
        [that is, between *parterre noble* and orchestra]
In the parterre
    28 upholstered benches without backs
    4 unupholstered benches without backs
In the *noble* gallery
    8 benches with backs upholstered with red fabric
In the second gallery
    12 upholstered benches on the sides
    5 long [upholstered] benches in the middle
        In addition 20 boxes
    Right 6 small
       3 large
    Left 10 small
       1 large[130]

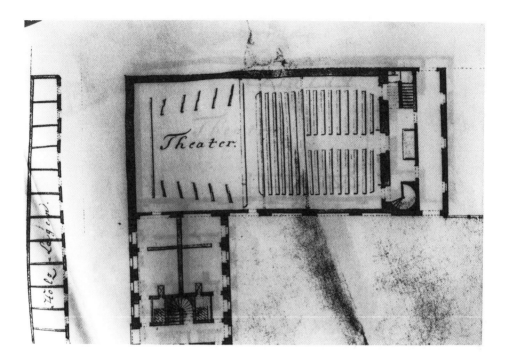

Figure 5.5. Freihaus Theater floor plan, drawing by Andreas Zach, 1789.

Designed by the *Landschaftsbaumeister* [district architect] Andreas Zach, the house was somewhere between 98 to 125 feet (30 to 38.1 meters) long by 49 to 56 feet (14.9 to 17.1 meters) wide, with a capacity of about 1,000 spectators. (Additional information about the dimensions of the Freihaus Theater is included in table 5.7.) In 1853 Ignaz Franz Castelli recalled this long, rectangular building, with its two parterres and two galleries: "The auditorium was painted quite simply and on the stage to either side of the proscenium stood two life-size figures, a knight with a dagger and a lady with a mask."[131] While it too must have been favorable acoustically, given its size, design, and manner of construction, I know of no study comparable to Herta Singer's for the Burgtheater. Even with the addition of a third gallery in 1794, the auditorium—approximately 44 to 47 feet (13.4 to 14.3 meters) long—could not be expanded sufficiently to match Schikaneder's ambition. So, armed with a privilege granted by Joseph II in 1786, he abandoned this house, which had served so honorably, and erected his temple to German art, the Theater an der Wien (1801).

Burgtheater and Freihaus Theater alike were illuminated by candlelight during performances. Chandeliers hung over the auditorium and stage. Providing further light were wax candles and oil lamps mounted in the foot-

Table 5.7. Freihaus Theater Dimensions

Writer	Total length feet (meters)	Auditorium length	Auditorium width	Height	Stage length	Stage width	Proscenium
Angermüller	98 (30)	—	49 (14.9)	—	39.5 (12)	33 (10.1)	29.5 (9) x 13 (4)[a]
Baker	125 (38.1)	47 (14.3)	56 (17.1)	—	43.5 (13.3)	56 (17.1)	31 (9.4)
Deutsch	98 (30)	—	49 (14.9)	—	39.5 (12)	—	—[b]

[a] Angermüller, *Mozart's Operas*, p. 226. Cited this way in the original German edition as well, surely the figure "4" is an error.
[b] Deutsch's figures are accepted by Honolka, Komorzynski, Morrow, and Spiesberger. Morrow further indicates an auditorium length of 44 feet (13.4 meters).

lights (along the edge of the stage) and on the sides of the wing wagons.[132] As is so often the case, eyewitness accounts are contradictory. In 1781 Georg Friedrich Brandes found the Burgtheater house lighting superior to that of the Comédie-Française, while twelve years later Johann Friedel complained, "The loges are small, poorly decorated, and illuminated still worse."[133]

The facilities of both theaters allowed elaborate productions. The Burgtheater stage was approximately 41.5 to 49 feet (12.6 to 14.9 meters) deep, with a width of perhaps 56 feet (17.1 meters) wall to wall and a proscenium opening of 27.5 to 30 feet (8.4 to 9.2 meters), width and height. Included were seven banks of wings set in perspective and at least seven sets of traps. Rendered for a different purpose, an engraving by Johann Ernst Mansfeld, included here as figure 5.6, appears in Joseph Richter's satirical *Bildergalerie weltlicher Misbräuche* (1785). It shows "the prompter's box and the sparsely decorated flats to the side of the Viennese stage that first welcomed Figaro."[134] Another view of the auditorium can be seen in figure 5.7. Slightly over eight feet (2.5 meters) deep, the orchestra "pit" could hold up to forty musicians seated in parallel rows facing a common desk. Recently recovered account books reveal that during the 1782/83 season (*Entführung*), thirty-five musicians were on the Burgtheater payroll. For the 1786/87 season (*Figaro*), the number is thirty-four.[135] According to the Dresden Plan, woodwinds on one side of the pit faced strings on the other. In the Turin Plan, winds and strings were distributed across the pit.[136] Were Viennese listeners simply unaccustomed to Mozart's orchestral richness, or did a balance problem exist between pit and stage? The emperor expressed this caveat to Carl Ditters von Dittersdorf: "He [Mozart] has only one fault in his pieces for the stage, and his singers have very often complained of it—he deafens them with his full accompaniment."[137]

"The Burgtheater was among the best technically equipped theaters in Mozart's time."[138] Surely, its capabilities would have matched Sweden's Drottningholm Court Theater with its "unusually well-stocked box of conjuror's tricks, whose contents are made of nothing but the simplest materials: pinewood and linen."[139] Among the devices and the machinery necessary to operate them, Mozart could have counted on a curtain, backcloths, flats and flat machinery, ceilings, traps, cloud machine, wave machine, wind machine, thunder box, and lighting effects. Particularly astonishing were the alternations between shallow and deep sets, as in *Don Giovanni*.[140] "A shallow scene can be successively deepened to reveal at last an infinite perspective onto a sky or distant horizon."[141]

The Freihaus Theater's orchestra pit was just under seven feet (2.1 meters) deep, with room for up to forty musicians, like the Burgtheater. Its stage was 39.5 to 43.5 feet (12 to 13.3 meters) deep and 33 to 56 feet (10 to 17.1 meters) wide, with a proscenium of approximately 31 feet (9.4 meters). Also equipped with traps, the stage accommodated five or six sets of wings on chariots in the stage floor with three sets of wing wagons for each wing, set in perspective.

Figure 5.6. Joseph Richter, *Bildergalerie weltlicher Misbräuche* (auditorium in the Burgtheater), engraving by Johann Ernst Mansfeld, 1785.

Reproduced in figure 5.8 is the only known view of this stage, Ignaz Albrecht's copperplate engraving of a scene from Schikaneder's *Der Stein der Weisen*. Of its production capabilities, an anonymous writer reported, "The interior of the house is well fitted out, the machines on stage well placed so that large-scale transformation scenes can be carried out."[142] With the turn of a handle, Schikaneder could indeed execute the wondrous *Verwandlungen* (transformations), that is, scene changes, which were a staple of Viennese machine comedy. *Zauberflöte* demanded thirteen transformations, to include the machinery for flying drops and persons—the three spirits and their flying machine, a theatrical

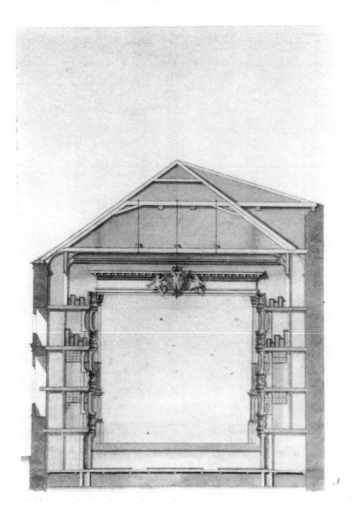

Figure 5.7. Burgtheater proscenium, drawing by Joseph Hillebrandt, around 1778.

response to the rage for balloon ascents.[143] *Babylons Pyramiden* (Babylon's pyramids), the height of Schikaneder's extravagance, demanded twenty-one.

While frustratingly vague written remarks survive in abundance, with the one possible exception to be discussed below, no known iconographic material documents the sets or costumes created for the Viennese runs of the three productions addressed in this chapter.[144] Because of its significance for the German National Singspiel, Ignaz Umlauf's *Die Bergknappen* (1778) was illustrated by Carl Schütz. Its scenery, designed by Alessio Cantini, "signals the wish for scenic reform. The area has its—narrow—boundaries; it portrays the site of the action realistically throughout."[145] Generic sets were the norm for standard fare, with

Figure 5.8. Freihaus Theater interior, engraving by Ignaz Albrecht, 1791.

new wings, borders, and drops made when necessary. For something special like *Figaro*, lavish illustrations of sets and costumes accompanied the first edition of Beaumarchais's play.[146] Though these illustrations were contemporaneous, the place is Paris, not Vienna. Closer to Vienna, Medardus Thoenert's famous engraving of Luigi Bassi as Don Giovanni presumably portrays a set from Domenico Guardasoni's original Prague production.[147] For more exotic fare, iconographic materials must be used with extreme caution. For example, H. C. Robbins Landon has convincingly dissociated from any connection with Esterháza that famous gouache long thought to depict a performance of Haydn's *L'incontro improvviso*, an appealing model for *Entführung*.[148] If Landon's speculation is correct and the painting does "represent one of the 'Turkish' operas by Gluck given at Vienna, such as *Le cadi dupé* (1761) or *Le rencontre imprévue* (1764)," the place is right but the date some twenty years too early.[149]

All three operas arose during a period of costume reform that sprang up in response to a desire, largely French and Italian at first, for dress reasonably appropriate to the time, customs, and circumstances of a given drama. According to Michtner, "In Vienna it was Noverre who pointed to the individual expressive power of genuine period costumes, just as F. L. Schröder, in 1781, included stage clothing as a primary means of expression in an individual and realistic play."[150] Beaumarchais devoted a section of his *Figaro* preface to characters and costuming. Marcellina's clothing, for example, "is that of the Spanish duennas, of a modest color, a black bonnet on her head."[151] As with sets, the costuming for "oriental" opera is more speculative. For instance, I have been unable to connect with Vienna in any way the wonderful illustrations of Constanze, Belmonte, and Selim reproduced in *Heritage of Music,* volume I.[152] Not to be overlooked for *Zauberflöte* is iconography portraying fanciful costumes from the early to mid 1790s, for example: the feathered Papageno figure, with cage, who poses in the Alberti libretto; the Friedrich John engraving of Act I, scene xvii, which depicts the Prague production of 1792; the *Kalenderkupfer* of 1793 which represents, presumably, the Hamburg production of 1793; the S. Richter engravings of costume designs from Leipzig, 1793; and the Franz Wolff engraving of a Papageno costume from Mannheim, 1794.[153]

With iconographic materials in such short supply, the librettists' stage directions furnish an invaluable guide to production. Stephanie's, on the whole, are simple and functional, as in Act III of *Entführung: "Square in front of the Pasha Selim's palace. On the right, the palace; opposite, Osmin's dwelling; in the background the sea. It is midnight. Belmonte, Pedrillo."*[154] Da Ponte's directions confirm the shift from the Baroque court spectacle once so admired in Vienna to the close-ups of individuals and their interactions in *opera buffa.* See, for example, the final direction of *Figaro,* Act I, scene vi: *"The Count goes to hide behind the chair: Susanna interposes herself between the Page and him. The Count pushes her gently aside. As she moves, the Page passes in front of the chair and curls up inside it: Susanna covers him with her dress."*[155]

Often more poetic than his poetry *per se,* Schikaneder's directions invite close study. Projecting an at-times cinematic fantasy, they communicate a vision of his heritage. As Otto Rommel reminds us, Baroque theater is representational.[156] For Schikaneder, theater scenes are the natural means of expression. Through them a legendary view of life takes shape in a naive, childlike way. What might Schikaneder have known of an exotic place like ancient Egypt? Historical authenticity was not yet an issue, Siegfried Morenz contends; the earliest history of *Zauberflöte* scenery reveals a Baroque, generally "legendary-oriental" (*märchenhaft-orientalisch*) approach, like Wieland's fairy tales.[157]

Recently, combining stage directions with a careful reading of the iconographic record, the theater historian Evan Baker has made a welcome effort to translate production generalizations into specific staging techniques.[158] He selects three of the six Peter and Joseph Schaffer engravings published between January and July 1795 in the *Allgemeines Europäisches Journal:*[159] Papageno presenting his catch of birds, the grand entrance of Sarastro at the end of Act I, and the trials in Act II. Whether or not these engravings depict the original Freihaus Theater production, they clearly represent an early staging.[160] Schikaneder's direction for Act II, scene xxviii, reads:

> *The scene changes to two great mountains. In one is a waterfall in which one hears rustling and splashing; the other spews fire. Each mountain has a fence with openings through which one can see the fire and water. Where there is fire, the horizon must be bright red; black fog lies where there is water. The side flats are rocks. Each scene completed by an iron gate. Tamino is lightly clothed and without sandals. Two men in black armor lead Tamino in. On their helmets is a flame. They read to him the transparent script which is inscribed on a pyramid. This pyramid is in the middle, right at the top, near the fence.*[161]

In Baker's hypothetical reconstruction, several flats (recycled from the beginning of the opera) depicting rocky landscapes are mounted in the first and third wings. An additional set of painted flats with the "iron gates" is mounted in the second wings. The fence was probably a self-standing unit. A drop depicting the "transparent script" on the pyramid is hung upstage of the waterfall and the mountain of fire. Baker continues:

> The waterfall was in two parts: the upper part was a painted flat mounted on a chariot, and the lower part was probably devised after an old theater trick of a moving device manually operated by a stagehand. The mountain of fire was more than likely a painted flat with transparent red cloth hung over an opening. The cloth was alternately gently and roughly shaken by another stagehand to create the rippling effect of fire; the illumination from the candlelights behind the red cloth conjured the color of fire.[162]

In determining how far forward in the years following Mozart's death one might profitably press in the search for other potential production models, we must heed Morenz's caution:

> The next generation [that is, post-1791], . . . culminating in K[arl] Fr[iedrich] Schinkel (1815) [*sic;* should read: 1816], is concerned with historical accuracy in the sense of strict classicism. . . . Because this is so, it appears unproductive for the producers of *Zauberflöte* themselves to seek precise models from antiquity for the scenery.[163]

Listed in table 5.8 are representative productions from 1792 to 1818.[164] In these landmark ventures, however, the findings of archaeology and the restless tide of Romanticism already occasioned settings very different from Schikaneder's Baroque, *märchenhaft-orientalisch* conception.

Table 5.8. Selected Productions of *Zauberflöte,* 1792–1818

City	Theater	Director	
Prague	Nostitz Theater	1792	Mihule's Company
Munich	Salvatortheater	1793	Giuseppe Quaglio
Hamburg	Deutsches Theater	1793	Fried. Lud. Schröder
Leipzig	Städtisches Theater	1793	Carl Benjamin Schwarz
Weimar	Ducal Court Theater	1794	Goethe; adaptation by C. A. Vulpius; Georg Melchior Kraus, director of scenic workshop
Mannheim	A. W. Iffland's National Theater	1794	Trinkle (prompter) noted staging details in his ledger[a]
Vienna	Freihaus Theater	1798	Schikaneder, a new production with 12 magnificent sets by Vincenzo Sacchetti
Vienna	Kärntnertor Theater	1801	Lorenzo Sacchetti
Berlin	Royal National Theater	1816	Karl Friedrich Schinkel
Weimar	Ducal Court Theater	1817	Goethe; Friedrich Christian Beuther
Munich	Hof- und Ntnl. Theater	1818	Simon Quaglio
Vienna	Kärntnertor Theater	1818	Antonio de Pian

[a] Reproductions of Trinkle's jottings appear, for example, in Angermüller, *Mozart's Operas,* p. 229, and in *New Grove Dictionary of Opera,* vol. 3, p. 1118.

The Theater Goer

As Morrow has said, "Viennese society offered a myriad of diversions and entertainments, among which the theater ranked first and foremost."[165] Inseparable from the spectacle displayed in the theater is the object of a company's efforts, the audience it sought to attract. Audiences of the time included a broad cross-section of Viennese society. Through surviving records such as subscription rosters and lists of complimentary tickets, a vivid picture of the

Burgtheater's audience emerges.[166] Aristocrats, artists, intellectuals, and military officers mingled in the *parterre noble*. Anyone who could afford a ticket crowded into the second parterre. The high nobility monopolized the loge levels, members of the middle class, critics, and connoisseurs filled the third floor, while a rowdier element frequented the upper gallery. To the suburban theaters, Verena Keil-Budischowsky observes, "went not only the bourgeoisie of that place but also the aristocracy and even the imperial court took pleasure in the rather coarse jokes of the Kasperliades and Zauberposses."[167]

Confronting Mozart were matters of professional intrigue and audience etiquette that, mercifully, no longer bedevil today's director. That cabals threatened either to torpedo or at least to compromise *Entführung* and *Figaro*, accounts by Mozart himself, his father, Michael Kelly (who implicates three members of the Italian company), and the anonymous reviewer of the *Wiener Realzeitung* attest.[168] The reviewer singles out those "obstreperous louts in the uppermost storey [who] exerted their hired lungs with all their might to deafen singers and audience alike with their *St!* and *Pst!*"[169]

Under even the most favorable conditions, audiences behaved differently then. Omitted in Emily Anderson's translation, the continuation of Leopold Mozart's letter of 30 January–3 February 1768 is revealing:

> A gentleman, even a nobleman with decorations, will clap his hands and laugh so much over some ribald or naive joke of Hanswurst as to get short of breath; during the most serious scenes, however, . . . he will prattle so loudly to his lady that other honest people in the audience cannot understand a word.[170]

The Mansfeld engraving, mentioned earlier in connection with the facilities of the Burgtheater, supplies a delightful iconographic reinforcement of Richter's satire. For example, "A cavalier with fixed telescope looks at the beautiful priestess so that he loses not a word of her moral philosophy."[171] We see also some young ladies chatting—they have sufficient moral philosophy!—and a farmer, who must ask why the audience is laughing. As an audience member, Mozart himself could misbehave: "I talked a lot; but that quite contrary to my usual custom I chattered so much may have been due to... Well, never mind!"[172]

Mozart aimed to please the audience as a whole: "short, lively and written to please the Viennese," he characterized the first Janissary chorus from *Entführung*.[173] He even catered to specific segments of it, for example, by including his Turkish tattoo *per i signori viennesi*. Further, he shares with his father his thinking about the concluding trio of Act I: "It must go very quickly—and wind up with a great deal of noise, which is always appropriate at the end of an act. The more noise the better."[174] Although an audience could powerfully focus its attention upon those carefully prepared "points" in an opera, it too could generate a great deal of noise during a performance. Conversation was the least offender. In 1775 a law was passed according to which "'not only repeated whistling, but also stamping with feet, stamping and beating with walking sticks on the floor, benches and partitions of all places' [sic] was punishable by imprisonment."[175] To signal its enthusiasm and acceptance, on the other hand, an audience demanded encores, a practice undoubtedly gratifying to the composer but ruinous to dramatic flow and so time-consuming that in 1786 the emperor decreed through Count Franz Xaver Wolf Rosenberg-Orsini that only solo numbers were to be encored.[176] Mozart recognized and appreciated a deeper tribute to his art. Having informed Constanze that the usual numbers and also the trio of the boys had been encored during that evening's performance of *Zauberflöte,* he adds: "But what always gives me most pleasure is the *silent approval!*"[177]

The Music

"In the opera the chief thing is the music," Mozart wrote on one occasion; on another, he declared more expansively, "In an opera the poetry must be altogether the obedient daughter of the music; . . . there [in Italian comic opera] the music reigns supreme and when one listens to it all else is forgotten."[178] Whether stated simply or poetically, then, the verdict is identical: as undeniably important as drama and spectacle are, for Mozart music was the crucial component of the operatic equation. While the sustained investigation of performance practice issues and the technical analysis of Mozart's music are not objectives of this volume, a production team must be aware of certain musical conventions operative during Mozart's time if it is to coordinate the drama, staging, and singing most effectively.

Mozart's ability to convey drama through music remains unsurpassed. In the small, he excelled in vocal and orchestral tone painting, responding sensitively both to general mood and to specific textual nuances as he reported about "O wie ängstlich, o wie feurig," Belmonte's poignant aria in *Entführung.*[179]

In the large, as Leonard Ratner and Wye J. Allanbrook have established, Mozart relied upon a vocabulary of characteristic, essentially rhythmic gestures or rhetorical topics—subjects for musical discourse—to set his characters in motion on the stage.[180] Accompanying Allanbrook's impressively drawn metrical spectrum is a corresponding affective spectrum and a class or social hierarchy.[181] For example, Figaro's dancing school, "Se vuol ballare," is an aria in two sections designed by Mozart to display Figaro's intelligence, wit, and boldness of imagination.[182] Recognizing that the sections are a minuet followed by a contredanse and knowing that this sequence was common in middle-class dance halls, the director will be better equipped to devise appropriate gestures for the aria, making it clear that Figaro has transported his victim from the salon "onto his own turf."[183]

The shape of an opera is of particular interest to me. "Mozart," John Eliot Gardiner observes, "was clearly prepared to be a ruthless editor of his own creations when it came to matters of dramatic pacing and verisimilitude."[184] Others, I believe, are well advised to preserve Mozart's order of events intact. In connection with the drama component, I have touched on the issues of unauthorized cuts and on the rearrangement of Mozart's sequence of events. Another issue is even thornier today because the composer is no longer here to adjust a score for the resources at hand. In catering to the members of a particular company, Mozart himself sometimes altered his original music-dramatic conception. Therefore, his substitute numbers and his additional numbers require the serious consideration of today's directors and performers. A decision to preserve the original components, to substitute for them, or to mix them affects the shape and tone of the opera in question.

Of the seven available *Figaro* alternatives recognized by Alan Tyson, the two most arresting are the substitute arias Mozart composed for the 1789 revival, with a new Susanna, Adriana Ferrarese Gabrieli del Bene.[185] "Un moto di gioia," K. 579, replaced, "Venite, inginocchiatevi" (No. 12), while a lengthy coloratura *rondò*, "Al desio di chi t'adora," K. 577 (complete with autograph cadenza), replaced "Deh, vieni, non tardar" (No. 27), the "garden" aria. In a balanced modern view, Tyson writes: "New numbers for a new singer in an opera's revival, however effective purely as vocal pieces, may seem a little inappropriate to the stage character as we have hitherto viewed him or her."[186] As always, Mozart built to suit. Ferrarese was more of a coloratura than Storace. Besides, as Daniel Heartz has commented, she could not act: "The dressing-up song had to be replaced. She just couldn't do all that action at the same time as singing, and so she got this little waltz song which stands completely outside the action."[187] In choosing between the first pair of arias—No. 12 and K. 579—in fairness, one cannot simply dismiss the 1789 composition as an obvious musical and dramatic disfigurement, "a grotesque sacrifice to the flexible throat of Da Ponte's ghastly mistress."[188] Rather, one must decide whether or not a different text and musical characterization are desirable. Mozart himself equivocated: "The little aria, which I composed for Madame Ferraresi, ought, I think, to be a success, provided she is able to sing it in an artless manner, which, however, I very much doubt. She herself liked it very much."[189] As for the other pair, by inserting the two-tempo *Rondò*, K. 577, the kind of vehicle a *seria* star of the 1780s and 1790s would have expected, a director shifts "the center of dramatic and musical interest away from the Countess and toward Susanna."[190]

Unlike *Figaro, Don Giovanni* exists in two authentic versions, one each for Prague and Vienna.[191] Today, "what is normally done is [the one for] Prague with Nos. 10a and 21b slotted in defiance of authenticity and sense."[192] Still open is the intriguing question of how to conclude this opera, with the Epilogue or without it? Here, the production decision profoundly affects the tone of the entire opera. Julian Rushton, pointing out that the Epilogue is missing from the 1788 Viennese libretto, raises the possibility that the common nineteenth-century practice of omitting this *scena ultima* may have Mozart's authority. In 1788, Mozart and Da Ponte tried various ways of ending the opera: "There is no way of knowing which the authors finally preferred."[193]

In sum, a wealth of information awaits the potential participants in productions of Mozart's Viennese operas. Throughout this resplendent decade (1782–1791), the composer collaborated with three capable librettists, each working within a specific theatrical tradition, one relatively new, the others already established. Mozart's hand altered all three irrevocably. Even when taking conventional character types as their point of departure, the poets developed remarkably individual personalities for realization in sound by Mozart's magical music. The professionals who sang this music were artists whose voices Mozart knew intimately and to whose requirements he adapted, even to the point of composing new arias and ensembles or revising extant ones. The results appeared in theaters equipped for mounting productions designed to attract audiences eager for spectacle. Because of its dimensions, structure, and acoustical properties, the Burgtheater, with its auditorium as centerpiece, was the ideal space for Mozart opera.[194] So too was the Freihaus Theater, the building of brick, stone, tile, and wood paneling.

Anyone contemplating the production of a Mozart opera today might profitably visualize Josephinian Vienna. Imagine mingling with the expectant public crowded into the Freihaus Theater on those historic fall evenings of 1791, ready to share the excitement generated by a new popular comedy carefully calculated for the Viennese taste. Imagine the delight of hearing an experienced ensemble of singers and players render Mozart's music in bright, lively tempos, calling to life a host of fascinating characters.[195] Cognizant of Schikaneder's genius for effect, imagine the eager anticipation of scenic transformations miraculously achieved through Baroque stagecraft. The most spectacular he saves till last: "One hears the loudest chords; thunder, lightning, storm. Immediately, the entire stage becomes a sun."[196] In Schikaneder's well-equipped theater, this transformation (*Verwandlung*) would have been breathtaking. Rather than render a lifeless recreation based on the Schaffer engravings, for example, modern directors and performers must seek to recapture the vibrant eighteenth-century spirit that bubbles beneath the surface. Then, audiences of today, like their counterparts two centuries ago, can fully register what Mozart called their "*silent approval!*" of, in Wagnermann's words, this "culmination of the Austrian achievement in the age of Enlightenment."[197]

CHAPTER SIX

The Neues Schauspielhaus in Berlin and the Premiere of Carl Maria von Weber's *Der Freischütz*

E. Douglas Bomberger

Seldom in the history of music have auspicious occasions coincided with the production of significant compositions. More typical are the memorable occasions marred by undistinguished music or the inauspicious premieres of what are later recognized to be great works. A rare exception to this rule was the premiere of Carl Maria von Weber's *Der Freischütz* on 18 June 1821, the first opera produced in Berlin's Neues Schauspielhaus, designed by the distinguished architect Karl Friedrich Schinkel (1781–1841). The work changed the course of German Romantic opera and became the most-performed composition in the history of the Berlin Opera. The building introduced significant innovations in theater construction and became a cornerstone of theatrical life in Berlin for over a century. The simultaneous inauguration of the two was more than coincidence, though. An examination of both works shows that their unique strengths were complementary and that each contributed to the initial success of the other.

The Genesis of the Opera and the Theater

Both the opera and the theater had their origins in the year 1817. As Friedrich Wilhelm Jähns points out in his thematic index, *Der Freischütz* had the longest gestation period of any of Weber's operas—not because of a lack of inspiration but because of a variety of hindrances, foremost among which were his responsibilities at the court in Dresden.[1] The idea for the opera had been in Weber's mind since at least 1810 when he had asked his friend Alexander von

Dusch to prepare a libretto from the *Freischütz* legend as told in the *Gespensterbuch* (vol. 1) of Johann August Apel and Friedrich Laun, published in Leipzig earlier that year.[2] The plan did not come to fruition, however, until Weber enlisted the services of the Dresden poet Friedrich Kind (1768–1843), who completed the libretto within ten days in 1817.[3] Weber's diary entries show that the composition of the opera was divided into four segments: July–August 1817, April 1818, September–December 1819 (with one day in March also devoted to *Der Freischütz*), and February to May 1820.[4] On 12 August 1819, Weber wrote to Count Carl von Brühl (1772–1837), *Intendant* of the Berlin Opera, that he hoped to produce the opera that winter,[5] but Brühl delayed the premiere until 1821 in order to use it to showcase the Neues Schauspielhaus. This theater also had its origins in 1817 owing to the fact that the previous building, the Nationaltheater, burned to the ground in that year.

The Nationaltheater, located in the Gendarmenmarkt in central Berlin, had been built in 1800 by Karl Gotthard Langhans (1732–1808), who was also architect of the Brandenburg Gate. The theater was quite large, with room for approximately 2,000. The proscenium opening was 41.5 feet (12.6 meters) wide and 34 feet (10.4 meters) high, and the depth of the stage was 85 feet (25.9 meters).[6] From the beginning, certain problems with the theater became evident. Because of the size and oblong shape of the auditorium, the acoustics were poor, making it difficult to hear the actors onstage. The exterior of the building was also less than attractive visually, as shown in figure 6.1, earning it the nickname of *Koffer* (trunk).[7] Schinkel proposed an extensive renovation in 1813 that would have altered the interior and would have attempted to solve the acoustical problems.[8] The plans were not immediately implemented, though, and on 29 July 1817 the theater was destroyed by fire.[9]

The burning of the Schauspielhaus was fortuitous because it afforded Schinkel the opportunity to design an entirely new building. The architect had for several years considered the problems of Baroque theater construction and had sought solutions to what he considered the two most important: poor acoustics and poor sight lines. Schinkel's ideas for reform in theater construction were highly original, and although not fully implemented until after his death, they had a significant impact on the reshaping of interior space in the nineteenth century.

Karl Friedrich Schinkel and Theater Reform

Schinkel's early ideas on theater reform may be found in a variety of documents: a letter to the general director of Berlin's royal theaters, August Wilhelm Iffland (1759–1814); two drafts of a lost memorandum; two detailed drawings of a proposed renovation of the Schauspielhaus; and two rough sketches that were not prepared for publication.[10] These items were apparently produced

Figure 6.1. Nationaltheater, built by Karl Gotthard Langhans, 1800/01, destroyed by fire, 29 July 1817. Courtesy of the Märkisches Museum, Berlin, Abteilung Berliner Theater-, Literatur- und Musikgeschichte.

before the burning of the Schauspielhaus.[11] As a group, they present a thorough picture of Schinkel's ideas, which were remarkably forward-looking for the time.

The focal point of Schinkel's reform was the role of the proscenium. It was his goal to turn this traditional barrier between actors and audience into a connecting link that would make the theater an organic whole. The traditional boxes in the proscenium wall above the stage were to be replaced with a row of Corinthian columns, thus improving both acoustical projection and visual unity. The added depth of the proscenium area would thereby create a new zone on the stage that would serve three functions: as a connecting link between stage and auditorium, as a visual and acoustic focal point, and as a performance area with a different significance from the rest of the stage.[12] This new proscenium area has obvious advantages but has one serious drawback—the removal of the proscenium boxes. As Marvin Carlson notes in his study of the semiotics of theater architecture:

The custom of seating certain privileged spectators on the stage seems to have begun in the early seventeenth century. No seating in the theatre provided a less satisfactory view of a perspective setting, or of the actors, who tended to work essentially in a downstage line near the footlights, but the occupants of this space shared with the actors the regards of the rest of the audience and indeed even of the inhabitant of the royal box.[13]

In Berlin, one of the proscenium boxes was a royal box, allowing the king to choose between his box in the center of the first balcony or the box on the stage.

Along with this radical change in the proscenium area, Schinkel proposed eliminating the wing-and-fly scenery so crucial to Baroque theaters. In calling for this change, he was echoing Goethe, E. T. A. Hoffmann, and others who believed this sort of perspective scenery was flawed because it was only effective when viewed from one point in the theater.[14] Schinkel advocated a wider, shallower stage with painted backdrops to suggest the scenes. He argued that this arrangement would simplify productions and save money, since there would be less scenery to paint, less machinery to maintain, and fewer stagehands needed to operate the machinery. The scenery would also not be as bulky, allowing more scenes to be available for performances at any given time. Additionally, Schinkel's backdrop scenes would open up the wings to give a larger stage area and more room for entrances and exits.[15]

Schinkel also proposed two significant changes in theatrical lighting, one on stage and one in the auditorium, both of which are now standard practice. The first was the introduction of lighting from above rather than from below. Clearly this modification presented problems in the days before electric lighting because of both the difficulty of accessing the lamps and the potential fire hazards. Schinkel defended this proposal on aesthetic grounds, though, with the sensible argument that "light falling from above will be much more natural than light rising from below."[16] The second innovation was the lowering of the auditorium lighting during performances in order to focus attention on the stage.

Evident in the drawings is a raked auditorium floor, creating an amphitheatrical setting. Schinkel was impressed by the model of the Greek theater and also by the proposals of his friend, the architect Friedrich Gilly (1772–1800).[17] Following Gilly's lead, Schinkel experimented with a semicircular arrangement of the auditorium; however, the limitations of the previously existing structure precluded a semicircular renovation of the Schauspielhaus. Both amphitheatrical seating and a semicircular auditorium provide optimal sight lines. The drawback is again a social rather than an artistic one—audience members cannot see each other as readily as in a horseshoe-shaped theater. We will see that Schinkel was able to include a semicircular auditorium in the Neues Schauspielhaus but did not use amphitheatrical seating. The combination of these two features of auditorium construction would not become reality until the construction of the Festspielhaus in Bayreuth.

A final proposed change had major significance for operatic productions:

> The lowering of the orchestra about two feet [.6 meter] deeper is of the greatest advantage for the impact of the music. The individual instruments are blended together better through the enclosed space in which they find themselves, and [they] come out as a full harmony. . . . This is especially important in that the voices, which are now often completely covered by the overpowering of the closer orchestra, will dominate the scene more. Also, the musicians who work before the stage will not be so obtrusive, but will form a very advantageous dividing area between audience and stage.[18]

This passage predates the building of the Bayreuth Festspielhaus by over half a century. By lowering the floor of the orchestra pit only two feet, Schinkel would not achieve the degree of blending found in Bayreuth, but it is evident that he recognized the acoustical advantages to be gained from such an arrangement.

Taken together, these ideas represent a radical rethinking of theater construction for the early nineteenth century. Many of Schinkel's ideas were incorporated into the Festspielhaus in Bayreuth, but others would not be fully realized until the twentieth century. In assessing Schinkel's importance to the history of staging, Klaus Wever credits him with a direct influence on all the major trends of the nineteenth century and an indirect influence on many of those of the twentieth century.[19]

Theory Transformed to Reality: The Construction of the Neues Schauspielhaus

With these proposals on record, Schinkel was an obvious choice to design the Neues Schauspielhaus. Indeed, Brühl proposed Schinkel as architect in a report to the king dated two days after the fire.[20] Schinkel responded with a memorandum to Brühl on 15 January 1818 outlining his ideas and requirements.[21] On 2 April the king commissioned Schinkel to draw plans for the proposed theater, and on 30 April Brühl and Schinkel were entrusted with the project. In the summer, Schinkel presented the king with drawings and a detailed description of the building. The cornerstone was laid on 4 August, and the theater was finished two-and-a-half years later.[22]

Despite the apparently enthusiastic support of Brühl, Schinkel's idealistic plans for theater reform were dealt a serious blow by this man whose position as *Intendant* of Berlin's royal theaters gave him equally strong ideas on what was necessary for the new theater.[23] Brühl describes the early stages of their planning in a letter:

> It had long been my wish to be involved in negotiations with our excellent Schinkel, because I consider him without exaggeration to be one of Germany's most brilliant and gifted architects. At first he did not seem inclined to it, for the same reason that all negotiations with architects are difficult—namely, *his ideas on theater and the stage, on drama, poetry, and dance were so different from what was and is* that I could never hope to come to an understanding with him. Several months passed, and he did not seem to want to get to work, because he was likewise afraid of all obstacles and did not believe he could get through. About two months ago he nevertheless fulfilled my wish and request. He sketched a theater design based on what I had explained to him in writing about the *necessary convenience of theater services* and on what the laws of *architectural beauty* demand![24]

Added to Brühl's intractability was the king's command to keep the cost as low as possible. In his memorandum to the king, Schinkel stressed the economy of his design with several points. Although the previous building had been burned completely, he was able to salvage a significant amount of building material. He used the same foundations and the old walls, except for the section directly around the stage, which was not strong enough to bear the extra weight. He also proposed reusing the six portals from the entrance (although without mentioning that they would need to be grooved and fitted with Ionic capitals). An additional saving was gained by the fact that only the central section of the building, that housing the theater itself, would be of the height necessary for a theater. The two side wings, one of which housed a concert hall and the other dressing rooms, rehearsal rooms, and scene shops, would be much lower, thus reducing the cost.[25] The exterior view of the completed building, shown in figure 6.2, illustrates this difference in height among the three sections.

The Neues Schauspielhaus clearly represented a compromise for Schinkel. In meeting the king's demands for economy and Brühl's demands regarding the interior arrangement of the theater, he was required to sacrifice many of the reform ideas noted above. The resulting theater, though, combined both beauty and practicality while retaining some of Schinkel's ideas.

Perhaps the most brilliant idea Schinkel had in building the new structure was to rotate the axis of the theater 90 degrees. Figure 6.3 shows the floor plan of the Langhans Nationaltheater, while figures 6.4 and 6.5 show floor plans for the ground and auditorium levels of Schinkel's Neues Schauspielhaus. The rotation alleviated the extreme oblong shape of the old building and produced

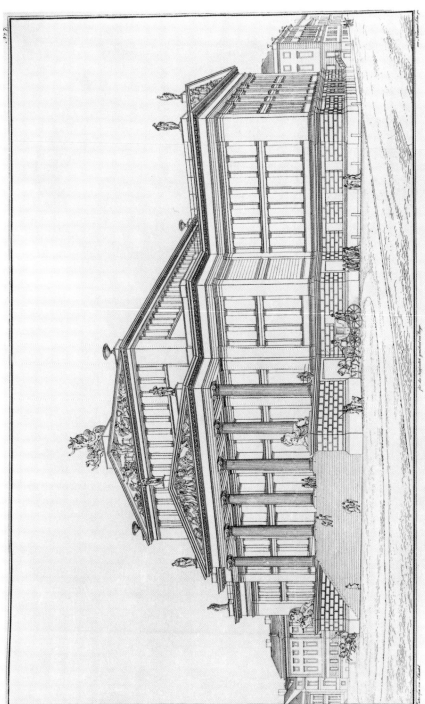

PERSPECTIVISCHE ANSICHT DES NEUEN SCHAUSPIELHAUSES ZU BERLIN.

Figure 6.2. Perspective view of the exterior of the Neues Schauspielhaus, built by Karl Friedrich Schinkel, 1818–21. Courtesy of the Märkisches Museum, Berlin, Abteilung Berliner Theater-, Literatur-, und Musikgeschichte.

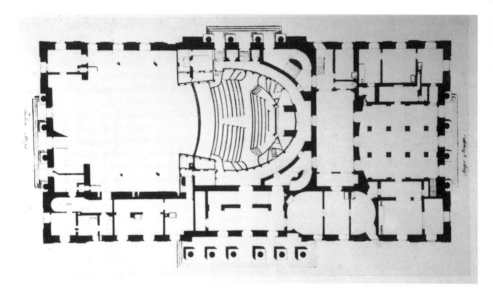

Figure 6.3. Floor plan of the Langhans Nationaltheater.

a shape that was much closer to Schinkel's earlier proposals. Although he was not allowed to eliminate the wing-scenery, the stage was not nearly so deep, meaning that it was dominated more by the painted backdrop. Figure 6.6 shows the stage as it was decorated for the dedication ceremony on 26 May 1821. The backdrop was a painting of the theater with the two churches that flank it in the Gendarmenmarkt. Ironically, this setting approximates what the stage might have looked like had Schinkel's ideas about the proscenium been followed. Although the king was not willing to give up the traditional proscenium boxes (shown on both walls above the orchestra pit), Schinkel used a row of columns in the wings to illustrate what the proscenium would have looked like had they followed his 1813 proposal for remodeling the old theater.

As seen in Schinkel's ideas above, he considered the proscenium pivotal in the construction of a theater. In this case there were special conditions to be met. The Neues Schauspielhaus was to be reserved for plays and small-scale operas, while the Königliches Opernhaus on Unter den Linden would continue to be used for all large operas and ballets. The king therefore requested a proscenium opening of 36 feet (11 meters), and in Schinkel's words:

> This predetermined dimension now dictated all other measurements, creating additional difficulties. To be sure, there were advantages of a theater this size, but as far as the box office was concerned, it was a disadvantage. With a stage so small, the audience size had to be limited for every seated spectator to be able to enjoy the performance fully. In

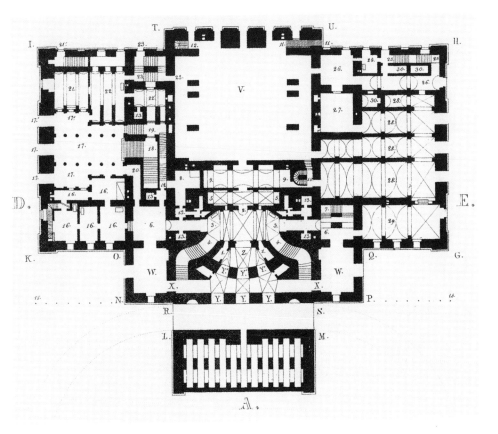

Figure 6.4. Floor plan of the Neues Schauspielhaus, built on the same foundations as the Langhans Nationaltheater. A: ground level. Courtesy of the Märkisches Museum, Berlin, Abteilung Berliner Theater-, Literatur-, und Musikgeschichte.

such cases one cannot extend the auditorium to the back, for the best boxes—those opposite the stage—would thus be too far removed and the spectator would miss the words and would not be able to enjoy the acting, unless he had an opera glass. Deep side boxes in such a long auditorium would not be practical either, because only a small part of the stage can be seen from them and even then only with continuous turning of one's head toward the stage, which is highly uncomfortable and tiring. The more the form approaches a semicircle, the better it is for hearing and seeing, as proven by the ancient theaters. Thus, the form of the half circle was proposed. From almost all boxes the spectator looks directly onto the stage. The boxes had to be shallower on the sides than in the center, so that one could see well from all seats in a

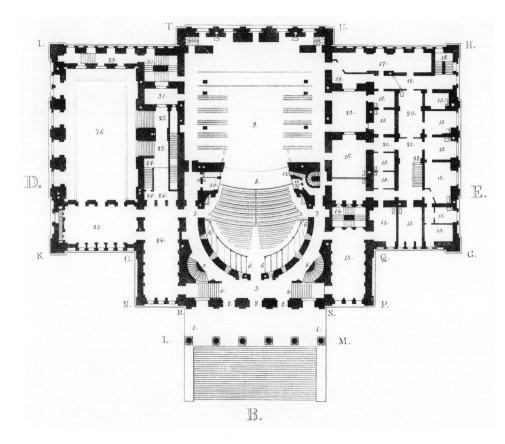

Figure 6.5. Floor plan of the Neues Schauspielhaus built on the same foundations as the Langhans Nationaltheater. B: stage / auditorium level. Courtesy of
the Märkisches Museum, Berlin, Abteilung Berliner Theater-, Literatur-, und
Musikgeschichte.

box. In regard to the unobstructed view of the stage, the goal is completely achieved by this means; however, because of the limited size of
the room due to the semicircle and the above-noted small proscenium
opening, the desired number of spectators could not be accommodated.
In order not to give up the other advantages of this form, there was no
other means of gaining seats than to place so-called balconies in front
of the boxes and a bit lower. These balconies certainly accommodate a
great number of spectators in very pleasant seats. However, it cannot be
denied that the boxes have lost, due to this revision, insofar as they have
receded more to the back. The spectators sitting in the boxes are now
less visible by the audience than before. Also, the people sitting in
the boxes see less of the other spectators so that, at least as far as the

Figure 6.6. Interior view of the Neues Schauspielhaus, showing the stage decoration for the dedication ceremony on 26 May 1821. Courtesy of the Märkisches Museum, Berlin, Abteilung Berliner Theater-, Literatur-, und Musikgeschichte.

entertainment during the intermission is concerned, the boxes are less valuable. However, for some people these recessed boxes might be quite valuable since they can enjoy the theater completely in private. Nevertheless a majority of people go to the theater for reasons of vanity and out of the desire for distraction, so at first there were frequent objections to these more hidden boxes. But in time another side emerged, and it is exactly the most hidden box seats that have become the most popular.[26]

The auditorium of the Neues Schauspielhaus (shown in figure 6.7) had distinctive characteristics that could be advantages or disadvantages, depending on the type of work presented. First, unlike in the typical horseshoe-shaped theaters of the day, all seats had good sight lines. As Schinkel wrote in his initial proposal to the king, "The auditorium is arranged so that the boxes have almost all the theater directly before them, and the worst seat can survey all the front portion of the stage and more than half of the background."[27] Second, the relatively shallow stage in conjunction with the shallow boxes and the semi-circular shape of the auditorium meant that all seats were unusually close to the stage. Schinkel pointed out that the distance from the royal box to the grand drape was 60 feet (18.3 meters) in the Nationaltheater and only 50 feet (15.2 meters) in the Neues Schauspielhaus. Third, along with proximity to the stage came improved acoustics. For theater goers accustomed to the poor acoustics of the old Nationaltheater and the cavernous space of the Königliches Opernhaus, the acoustical presence of the voices and instruments must have been a revelation. Finally, the theater would have seemed more intimate for at least three reasons. The stage of the Neues Schauspielhaus was 1,300 square feet (120.9 square meters) smaller than its predecessor, bringing the actors much closer to the audience.[28] Also, the new theater had fewer than 1,000 seats and could accommodate only about 1,200 including standing room, as opposed to the 2,000 that could fit into the old theater. Most important, of the seats in the Neues Schauspielhaus, only about a third were in boxes, as opposed to nearly three-fourths in the opera house.[29] Carlson notes that from the earliest days of public opera houses, boxes were associated with the aristocracy, and later, with opera houses in general, which were more exclusive than playhouses. He observes that

> the removing of the partitions and the converting of this upper area into a gallery in the French or English style were invariable signs that the theatre was seeking a more democratic audience, perhaps even that it was considering giving up the performance of opera altogether.[30]

Figure 6.7. Auditorium of the Neues Schauspielhaus, Berlin, as viewed from the stage. Courtesy of the Märkisches Museum, Berlin, Abteilung Berliner Theater–, Literatur–, und Musikgeschichte.

The new theater, then, was ripe for a work that was intimate rather than majestic, that would appeal to the common people rather than to the nobility, and that had the sort of crisp dialogue that could benefit from the superb acoustics of the Neues Schauspielhaus. That work, which Brühl had the foresight to schedule as the first opera in the new theater, was *Der Freischütz*.

A New Opera Suited to a New Theater: *Der Freischütz*

Weber had been working intermittently on the opera since 1817 with the expectation of producing it in Berlin. He had been negotiating with Brühl on specific dates since early in the compositional process, but the premiere was delayed repeatedly. Already in July 1820, Weber had received the first half of the fee of 80 Friedrichs d'or, but on 9 November 1820, he wrote to Brühl, "I look forward with impatience to your gracious reply, highly born sir; may it bring me the assurance that the poor freeshooter might finally be able to step freely into the world." When this letter did not produce the intended result, he wrote on 25 December that he had contracted with the *Intendant* at Braunschweig to produce it there.[31] Kind was requesting permission to publish the libretto in an upcoming collection of his works, which also increased the urgency.[32] Under this pressure, Brühl was finally able to arrange for the premiere of *Der Freischütz* as the first opera given in the Neues Schauspielhaus.

The reason for Brühl's foot-dragging was not a lack of enthusiasm for Weber's work—in fact the opposite was true—but was rather his relationship with the new music director at Berlin, Gasparo Spontini (1774–1851). As early as 1815, Brühl had opposed the hiring of Spontini in favor of a German music director, preferably Weber. The king ignored his advice and in August 1819 hired Spontini without consulting his *Intendant*. When the Italian composer arrived in Berlin in May 1820, he immediately came into conflict with Brühl over a variety of issues. Because of this, the latter informed Weber that *Der Freischütz* could not be presented until after Spontini had introduced his opera *Olympia*, a work that would require three months' rehearsal.[33] Before either had been performed, then, these two operas were figuratively, if not literally, set in opposition.

Spontini had introduced his monumental opera *Olimpie* at the Paris Opera on 22 December 1819. It had not been as successful as some of his earlier works, in large part because of the tragic ending of Act III. For the Berlin premiere, he commissioned E. T. A. Hoffmann to prepare a German translation with a completely reworked third act. Spontini composed new music for this act, and it was this version that was presented to the Berlin public on 14 May 1821 at the Königliches Opernhaus. The rehearsal period was exceptionally long, and the cost of the production was exorbitant, but the lavish spectacle suited the taste of the king perfectly. The public, though, was of a different opinion, as noted by Weber, already in Berlin for rehearsals of *Der Freischütz*, in letters to Kind of 27 May and 31 May:

> The performance of Olympia is the most *sumptuous* that one can imagine. It cost over 20,000 talers.[34] Spontini was called out after the first performance and showered with wreaths. The second performance was snubbed *quite coldly*.[35] . . . What your friends say about Olympia is completely true. The most indicative is what Zelter said about it, ["]When I come out of the opera, the fire alarm is a melodious pleasure and relief.["][36]

Despite his feelings about the work and despite the adversarial position in which he was cast, Weber was publicly supportive of Spontini's opera. According to his diary, he attended six performances of *Olympia* in the month following its premiere, including two in the week prior to the premiere of *Der Freischütz*. (Coincidentally, his lodgings at 34 Behrenstraße were precisely equidistant from the front entrances of the Königliches Opernhaus and the Neues Schauspielhaus.)

The Production of *Der Freischütz*: Rehearsals

When Weber, his wife, and their favorite dog arrived in Berlin on 4 May 1821, he still did not know the exact date of his work's premiere.[37] The first rehearsal took place on 9 May, but was not followed by another for nearly two weeks because of rehearsals and performances of *Olympia*. The composer had previously estimated that the opera could be mounted with only two to three weeks of uninterrupted rehearsals;[38] however, circumstances in Berlin stretched out the rehearsal period to twice that. It is possible to recreate the exact distribution of rehearsal time from Weber's diary entries:

9 May	10:00 A.M. first rehearsal of *Freischütz*.
21 May	9:00 A.M. went through the choruses with Eunike.
	11:00 A.M. to 1:30 P.M. rehearsal.
22 May	10:00 A.M. rehearsal.
23 May	10:00 A.M. rehearsal, then conference until 3:00 P.M.
24 May	10:00 A.M. rehearsal with the four principals.
25 May	11:00 A.M. four principals with chorus, previously with chorus alone.
26 May	10:00 A.M. rehearsal with four principals and chorus.
29 May	10:00 A.M. *Freischütz* orchestra rehearsal.
30 May	10:00 A.M. orchestra rehearsal.

2 June	10:00 A.M. principals, chorus and reading rehearsal.
8 June	10:00 A.M. principals with chorus.
9 June	5:30 P.M. to 11:00 P.M. rehearsal in the theater.
12 June	10:00 A.M. to 2:00 P.M. dress rehearsal of *Freischütz*, without first horn and Hildebrand [*sic*], then conference until 3:30 P.M.—another postponement of the opera!!!
14 June	8:00 A.M. rehearsal of the Wolf's Glen, then dress rehearsal from 10:00 A.M. to 2:00 P.M.
17 June	8:30 A.M. to 12:30 P.M. dress rehearsal.

Weber had only fourteen rehearsals with the actors, a stark contrast to the lavish preparations for *Olympia*.[39] *Der Freischütz*, though, was a completely different kind of opera. With its simple, folk-like melodies, spoken dialogue, and small cast, the rehearsal requirements were not nearly so great. In addition, Weber had an unusual cast that drew from the strengths of the royal opera company and the royal theater troupe.

The Cast

The four principal characters were played by some of the opera company's best singers. Caroline Seidler (1790–1872), in the role of Agathe, was one of the most popular singers in the royal opera company. According to Carl Ledebur:

She possessed a pure, clear and extremely pleasing voice of two full octaves and great facility; her outward appearance was very attractive, and if her acting was not suited to large dramatic performances, it was nevertheless superb in lively, graceful roles.[40]

The other female role, Ännchen, was played by a veteran of the Berlin stage, Johanna Eunike (c. 1798–1856). She came from a theatrical family and had played soubrette roles with great success since her early teens. Her light voice and youthful demeanor made her a particular favorite with the Berlin public. The part of Ännchen was originally very small, but Brühl convinced Weber and Kind to add another scene for Eunike. The result, "Einst träumte meiner sel'gen Base," was completed in late May, after Weber had a chance to learn the strengths of Eunike's voice.

Heinrich Stümer (1789–1857), well known for his performance of the Evangelist's part in Mendelssohn's 1829 revival of the St. Matthew Passion, created the role of Max, performing it ninety-six times before his retirement in 1831.[41]

Heinrich Blume (1788–1856) performed the role of Caspar in the premiere and in 111 subsequent performances.[42] He was equally popular in operatic and theatrical roles, and was one of Berlin's hardest-working performers. After listing his roles Ledebur adds,

> This list of his roles shows that there were only a few operas given in which he did not participate. These almost superhuman efforts, since he also played in very many plays, etc., were unable either to exhaust his physical strength or to prevent him from participating in most concerts for charity with the greatest willingness.[43]

The rest of the cast was a mix of actors and singers: August Wiedemann (Kilian), Hillebrand (Samiel), Lebrecht Gottlieb Rebenstein (Ottokar), and Carl Wauer (Cuno). Friedrich Beschort was originally scheduled to stage the opera and play the role of Ottokar, but he was replaced by Rebenstein for the premiere. His *Regiebuch,* with stage directions and diagrams for the placement of furniture, is preserved in the archives of the Berlin Staatsoper, albeit in badly mutilated form because of years of alterations in the course of hundreds of performances.

As noted above, this experienced cast needed only fourteen rehearsals to mount *Der Freischütz,* but the various scheduling conflicts stretched the time from first rehearsal to final dress to over five weeks. The last two rehearsals were the result of yet another postponement. Originally scheduled for 14 June, the opera's premiere was rescheduled for 18 June because of the king's command for two additional performances of *Olympia* on 13 and 15 June.[44]

Opening Night

Word of the new opera had begun to leak out, and by opening night, excitement was at a fever pitch. Weber's son Max reported in his biography that there were crowds at every entrance four hours before the doors were opened, and that the police were needed to prevent injuries in the rush. The audience, in contrast to that which had been at the opening of *Olympia,* consisted mostly of students, artists, and middle-class citizens, with very few uniformed officers.[45] The court did not attend the opening-night performance.[46] The premiere was an unqualified success, and Weber's diary entry for that evening shows his relief and happiness:

> In the evening, as the first opera in the Neues Schauspielhaus, Der Freischütz opened to the most unbelievable enthusiasm. Overture and Volkslied repeated on demand. In all, fourteen of seventeen musical numbers noisily applauded. All went splendidly, and [the performers] sang with all their hearts. I was called out and took Mme. Seidler and Mlle. Eunicke [*sic*] with me since I could not get hold of the others. Poems and wreaths flew. Glory to God alone.[47]

Special Effects

Throughout the rehearsal process, the main point of concern for Weber seems to have been the pivotal Wolf's Glen scene. On 27 May, the day after the dedication ceremony for the Neues Schauspielhaus, he reported in a letter to Kind:

> Now, according to his majesty's express command, only old things may be given until my opera can be staged. This will hardly happen before 8–10 June, since the Wolf's Glen scene requires far too much Spanish machinery. By the way, machine master and decorator Gropius's[48] ideas and plans for it are all marvelous and imaginative, and it will no doubt be unrivaled in its presentation.[49]

Four days later he reported further, "On the musical side, *Der Freischütz* is going admirably; everyone is working with love and enthusiasm. The set and machine work, though, is holding us up frightfully."[50]

The Wolf's Glen scene was indeed complex in its premiere, utilizing the most advanced special effects available in 1821. The scenery, intended to reflect the wildness of nature, is shown in figure 6.8. The problems of staging the scene were not finally solved until the rehearsal devoted to the Wolf's Glen scene on 14 June. Weber was so pleased with the final result that he wrote an extensive description of the effects for the Dresden director Hellwig in preparation for the premiere in that city. His description holds many useful insights for those who produce the opera today:

> *Act II Finale.* Only one of the two thunderstorms can be used, since the whole theater is built so that the moon itself has little more room in the background.
> *The skull* is hidden.
> *The wooden owl* sits still and moves its head and wings. The eyes [are] transparent.
> Samiel appeared in Berlin *in a rock.* Kaspar makes his circle somewhat to the side, in order to keep the largest portion of the stage free for the apparitions. On the wings is a boulder painted on muslin [scrim]. Behind this is a device that can light it rapidly from behind. As long as it is *dark,* Samiel remains invisible behind it, but when it is lighted, the muslin (or coarse brown gauze) is transparent. Here Samiel was attired in a long scarlet mantel as well as a transparent red skull, with his hat on top, to reveal him in this moment in all his horror as the Prince of Hell.
> *The skull with the hunting knife* vanishes through a trapdoor, and up through the same door comes the small hearth with gleaming coals, etc.

Albert Frisch, Berlin W

Decoration Nr. 5. **Wolfschlucht**, gemalt von Gropius.

Figure 6.8. Stage decoration for the Wolf's Glen scene of *Der Freischütz*, designed by Carl Wilhelm Gropius. Courtesy of the Deutsche Staatsoper, Berlin.

Brushwood is not put on the fire, since it makes too much odor. On the other side lies some Bengali fire powder or something else that burns green, which Kaspar now and then throws on the coals unobserved by the audience.

The crag on which Max appears was completely downstage because of the singing, but mounted very high. In order not to cover the scenery it had the following form:

and Max climbed down behind.

The apparitions of the mother and Agathe played by children were also in the rocks in the background, likewise behind scrims, and only appeared with the lighting of lamps mounted beside them, visible and invisible as needed.

Since the skipping of the forest birds can easily be laughable, they were followed by snakes and toads moving on the floor and bats whizzing by on wires.

The boar can be half hidden. It runs in a channel behind *Kaspar* over the stage. It does not need to have moving parts, since it goes over so fast that no one will notice.

The *fiery wheels* are light wheels of ribbon on a frame which run in a channel above the stage:

To these wheels, which naturally turn on an axle, small rockets are attached. As soon as these are ignited the wheels spin rapidly by themselves.

The wild hunt consists of figures of hunters, dogs, deer as skeletons or with twisted necks, etc. painted on linen, white and gray, and then cut out and pasted on muslin and pulled in long strips and trains under the flies over the stage. Since one does not see the muslin, all figures float free in the air.

At the end all rain, crash, and thunder machines must be set in motion. The *will-o'-the-wisps,* little sponges soaked in alcohol, and the flames out of the earth must be numerous. In the rear wings they dropped out real fir trees that crashed and crackled.

Samiel stands behind the dried-up tree and holds his arm behind its branch in such a way that Max is already grasping him when the tree vanishes.[51]

This production used an array of special effects that are unfamiliar to modern theater goers. These effects fall into two general categories: the flames of various colors and intensities and the machines for creating special sounds.

The various flaming concoctions are of particular interest and were available in almost unlimited variety. Düringer and Barthels's *Theater-Lexicon* of 1841 describes the mixing of these substances and their theatrical uses in considerable detail, providing recipes for *bengalisches* (Bengali), *blaues* (blue), *gelbes* (yellow), *griechisches* (Greek), *grünes* (green), *rothes* (red), and *weisses Feuer* (white fire), which was also known as *Indianisches Feuer* (Indian fire).[52] The principal ingredients of these recipes are saltpeter, sulfur, resin, and pitch in various proportions, with the color provided by arsenic, sulfuric acid, and other agents. The *Lexicon* gives five different methods of creating green fire, although the one recommended for theatrical use is a mixture of 130 parts *salpetersaurer Baryt* (barium nitrate), thirty-two parts *Schwefel* (sulfur), and fifty parts *Chlorkalischwefel* (probably a mixture of potassium chlorate and sulfur). Bengali fire, said to have been discovered by the British in the East Indies and refined for use in the theater, consisted of twenty-four parts saltpeter, seven parts flowers of sulfur, and two parts red arsenic. The fumes from Bengali fire are so noxious that the editors add this warning, which also attests to the growing fame of Weber's opera by 1841:

> Should such fire be required in the course of a performance (in which it usually takes place at the end of an act), as for instance in *Der Freischütz*, all the backstage windows, especially the upper ones, must immediately be opened at intermission so that the fumes will dissipate quickly, since as noted, they already cause the actors or singers enough difficulties at the moment of use.[53]

Weber's description of the Wolf's Glen scene mentions three separate sound effects. The *Donnermaschine* (thunder machine) normally consisted of a large drum set in a metal frame, which was struck with a double-headed mallet. (The method for recreating thunder varied greatly in different theaters, though. A sheet of iron or copper could be shaken thus imitating the rolling of thunder, but this method was only effective for small rooms. A *Donnerwagen* [thunder wagon] consisted of a wheeled rectangular wooden box that was filled with stones and was drawn back and forth over an uneven portion of the stage. A fourth means of recreating thunder consisted of using paper that was stretched over a wooden frame, dampened, and then struck with the hands as it was being dried over a coal fire. This was by far the most complicated, but it yielded the widest variation in tone quality through the use of frames of different sizes and through different rates of drying.)[54]

The *Einschlagemaschine* (crash machine) created a sound similar to that of the *Donnermaschine,* but through two different methods. The first consisted of alternating boards and sheets of iron tied at each end on two ropes to create a series of parallel pieces about half an ell (22.5 inches or 57.2 cm) apart resembling a rope ladder, which was then mounted on a pulley in the ceiling. The entire contraption was dropped on a hollow wooden floor to create a crash whose length depended on the number of pairs of boards and sheets of iron in the stack. The other method consisted of dropping stones or nuts through a channel in the floor onto a large drum of sheet metal with a leather drumhead.[55]

The *Regenmaschine* (rain machine) was mounted above the stage and could be operated from stage level by pulling a cord. It normally consisted of a wooden drum containing dried peas and was covered with a sieve of parchment or wire. When this drum was set in motion, it created the sound of rain. A similar effect could be achieved by simply shaking a wire sieve containing a few dried peas.[56]

The Wolf's Glen Scene: Lessons from the Premiere

Weber's attention to the Wolf's Glen scene in rehearsals and in his letter to his director in Dresden suggests that the staging of this scene is the central problem in any production of Der Freischütz. The success or failure of this one scene determines the believability of what is in itself an incredible story. This scene epitomizes the goal of leading the audience to the suspension of disbelief. While modern directors may not wish to duplicate the special effects used in the premiere, certain principles must be retained in order to create an effective Wolf's Glen scene.

First, Weber recognized that there were many things in this scene that could appear ridiculous, were it lacking a careful balance between fantasy and reality. It seems to have been the goal of the directors to create an atmosphere that was serious enough to inspire fear and belief in the audience but not so serious as to seem absurd. Finding this balance is crucial to planning the scene, and most accounts indicate it was effective in the Berlin performances.

Second, the element of surprise is essential to an effective staging of this scene. While the use of scrims is familiar to theater goers today, it was apparently new to Weber's audience, to judge from the detailed descriptions he gave to Hellwig. The startling appearances of Samiel and the apparitions, combined with the barrage of flying creatures, kept the audience in Berlin at a peak of anticipation. The principle that made this scene effective in 1821 is the same principle that makes the latest science-fiction movie effective today—the viewer is constantly surprised by dazzling special effects.

Finally, the original staging of this scene also had the potential of arousing real fear in the audience. Devil worship alone was certainly enough to make most viewers uncomfortable, but the special effects also had an element of danger. The liberal use of flames, smoke, and rockets could not help but remind the audience of the fate of the Nationaltheater four years previously, and the choking fumes from the exotic chemical compounds surely added to the sense of fear. Although Schinkel's precautions against fire in the new building were well known,[57] the sight of open flames and the smell of smoke must have contributed to the sense of awe—and consequently belief—inspired by this scene.

The subsequent history of Der Freischütz is one of unqualified success. The work immediately caught the imagination of the public and was performed throughout Germany.[58] On the occasion of the fiftieth Berlin performance of the opera on 28 December 1822, Brühl sent Weber a collection of pictures of costumes from the opera and an honorarium of 100 talern.[59] Weber returned the honorarium with the cynical comment:

> This case, so unusual in the annals of theater, has also merited a special distinction, especially since rumor has it that these fifty full houses have brought the box office proceeds of 30,000 talern.[60] From this the composer was allocated a gift of 100 talern.[61]

The opera continued to be successful after Weber's death, and by 1928, the year of the 185th anniversary of the Berlin opera, it was the most-performed work in the history of the company.[62] The opera has never been as successful on stages outside of the German-speaking countries, but nonetheless its music is beloved throughout the world. As Zelter wrote to Goethe, "The music is meeting with great success and is in fact so good that the public does not find the clouds of charcoal and powder smoke intolerable."[63]

There is no question that the music is appealing enough to stand on its own merits, but it is also clear that the opera's early success as a stage work was helped by the unique features of the Neues Schauspielhaus. Because of the excellent acoustics, the dialogue was much more effective in the new theater than it would have been in the opera house or in the previous theater. The clarity of sound served to underscore the strengths of a cast consisting in part of singing actors. The machinery above the stage and the fire safety precautions allowed special effects that would have been difficult if not impossible in the previous theater. The new arrangement of fewer boxes and more areas of gallery seating also underscored this work as opera for the ordinary person. It served to attract the sort of audience who appreciated a work in the vernacular with a rustic, folk atmosphere. Finally, the smaller stage, shallower auditorium, and lowered orchestra pit brought actors and audience closer together, a feature that is crucial in this most intimate of operas. It might be argued that the larger the theater, the less likely the spectators are to be drawn into believing what is essentially an unbelievable story. A careful consideration of the circumstances surrounding the first production of *Der Freischütz* may therefore be the most important preparation for anyone involved in a production of this deceptively simple work.

CHAPTER SEVEN

Paradise Found:
The Salle le Peletier
and French Grand Opera

Karin Pendle and Stephen Wilkins

On 29 February 1828, audiences at the Salle le Peletier—Paris's Opéra—
witnessed the dawn of a new era. *La muette de Portici*, with libretto by Eugène
Scribe, score by Daniel-François-Esprit Auber, and sets by Pierre-Luc-Charles
Ciceri, marked not only the beginning of the development known as French
grand opera but also the rebirth of a house that, less than a decade earlier,
seemed to be dying. Now it appeared restored to life, rejuvenated by an infusion
of the Romantic spirit in the form of dramatic and scenic elements developed
on the boulevard stages in conjunction with the presentation of melodramas and
spectacles d'optique. Historical plots, local color, a dramaturgy based on the
concept of the musico-visual tableau, modern dancing styles, masses of people
on stage, and scenic wonders hardly attempted before at the Opéra—all were
components of a work which can only be described as a blockbuster. Though its
score lacked the grandeur that would characterize later grand operas by Rossini
or Meyerbeer, *La muette de Portici* marked the beginning of a new synthesis
of theatrical arts which was to become the basis of Europe's most influential
nineteenth-century operatic genre.

No type of theater suffers more from the tendency to approach such works
simply as a combination of literary drama and music than does French grand
opera. For grand opera depended for its very life upon being realized on the
stage—not just any stage, but that of the Salle le Peletier, which uniquely
possessed the resources to reveal the scores of Auber, Meyerbeer, or Halévy as
total works of art. When Giacomo Meyerbeer posed the question, "Where but
at Paris can one find such immense resources put at the disposal of an artist who
wishes to compose truly dramatic music?"[1] he was taking for granted that such

171

music could only be created in collaboration with librettist, designer, machinist, choreographer, and *metteur en scène*. Though French grand opera could well be thought of as a joining of equals among the arts, it would not be inappropriate to consider the visual side of the production as the glue that held the other elements in place.

Before discussing specific works and ways in which their productions relied on the facilities available at the Opéra, we shall consider some elements of dramatic theory that help explain why the particular spectacles of French grand opera were so effective and so well received. Michael Walter has pointed out the relevance of Victor Hugo's concept of *couleur du temps* to a consideration of the formative influences on Meyerbeer's *Les Huguenots*.[2] Since many of the ideas expressed in Hugo's *Preface to Cromwell,* which discusses this concept, were already part of Parisian stage practice in the boulevard theaters and *spectacles d'optique*, this 1827 document represents not so much a prescription for the future of the Romantic stage as an articulation of ideas that were making their way from the popular spectacles to the subsidized stages. Hugo advocated what dramatists like Pixérécourt had been attempting for some time, though without the refinement that came to characterize productions of Romantic dramas or grand operas. Regarding a drama's setting as an important part of its message, Hugo wrote: "exact locality is one of the first elements of reality. . . . The place where the catastrophe takes place becomes a terrible and inseparable witness to it . . . [a] sort of mute character."[3]

He is, of course, speaking not of "reality according to nature" but rather of "reality according to art."[4] Such a reality ought not to be grafted onto a generic plot, as Hugo believed to be the case with much that passed for *couleur locale*. Instead, the work ought to be "radically impregnated" with a *couleur du temps,* a more all-encompassing sort of local color "at the very heart of the work, from which it spreads outward, of itself, naturally, equally, . . . into all the corners of the drama, like the sap which rises from the roots to the last leaf of the tree." *Couleur du temps* "ought to be somehow in the air, in such a way that is perceived at once when one enters, and when one leaves, one changes century and atmosphere."[5] To evoke this *couleur du temps,* the creator should choose "not that which is beautiful, but that which is *characteristic.*"

Whether Hugo's ideas directly affected the designers, librettists, or composers who wrote for the Opéra is unimportant; these ideas were current, and Hugo was merely their codifier. Throughout grand opera's most innovative period—from 1828 to the early 1840s—its creators made consistent efforts to reproduce the actual historical atmosphere in which events took place. Though at times this atmosphere was essentially new-created, at other times exact models of historical buildings appeared on the stage—the cloister in *Robert le diable,* for example, or the country chateau in *Les Huguenots'* second act. This attitude toward stage design was intended to result not in spectacle for its own sake, then, but spectacle as an important component of the expressive power of the work.

In conjunction with the general principle of a scenic *couleur du temps,* Eugène Scribe created librettos which were not only dramaturgically smooth and musically viable, but scenically oriented as well. He modeled the frame- work of these librettos on his own technique of the well-made play, on which he mounted not just opera's customary recitatives and musical numbers but larger units, tableaux, in the manner of boulevard *mélodrames* and *spectacles d'optique.*[6] These tableaux could be described as mimed stage pictures, intended to make the action visually clear at the same time that they provided the basis for the broad musical forms that underscored this movement. In cultivating these large musico-dramatic units, Scribe changed the structural emphasis in French opera from dialogue and declamation to a succession of stage pictures reflecting the desired *couleur du temps.* Dramatic purposes were furthered not only by stage action *per se,* but also by a succession of tableaux that contrasted, often very strongly, with one another.

Indeed, contrast is an essential ingredient of grand opera, according to Louis Véron, director of the Opéra from 1831 to 1835. In his evaluation of Scribe's contributions to the creation of the genre, he states:

> For a long time people have thought that nothing was easier to write than an opera libretto—a great literary error. An opera in five acts can live only with a very dramatic action, putting into play the grand passions of the human heart and powerful historical interests. This dramatic action, moreover, ought to be intelligible to the eyes, like the action of a ballet. The choruses must play an impassioned role and be, so to speak, one of the interesting characters of the piece. Each act ought to offer contrasts in sets, in costumes, and especially in skillfully prepared situations. . . . *La Muette de Portici, Robert le Diable, Gustave III, La Juive, Les Huguenots, Le Prophète* by M. Scribe offer that fertility of ideas, those grand dramatic situations, and fulfill all conditions for variety in staging required of the poetics of an opera in five acts.[7]

Clearly, Véron believed that the manner in which the drama was laid out had a great deal to do with the type of music and *mise en scène* that came to charac- terize grand opera.

Scribe's refinement of these dramaturgical devices coincided with the advent, toward the end of the 1820s, of new subject matter in French opera. Romanticism had everywhere opened people's eyes to the existence of histori- cal and supernatural worlds beyond their own. These themes entered French opera decisively with *La muette de Portici* and brought with them an insistence on historical and geographical accuracy in sets and costumes and on the archi- tectural grandeur suggested by distant places and eras—Hugo's *couleur du temps.*

Though we can never know every detail of an opera's original *mise en scène,* numerous sources exist that provide a foundation upon which valid production decisions can be made. The Bibliothèque de l'Opéra is the repository of numerous sketches and *maquettes* of costumes and settings from the nineteenth century,[8] many of them corresponding to images in engravings that appeared in such popular journals as *L'illustration*.[9] Also available in Parisian archives are inventories of set pieces for certain operas,[10] records of production expenses, and printed librettos and scores containing handwritten annotations on how certain scenes were staged. Contemporary reviews provide valuable descriptions of the staging. More valuable still are the scenic librettos which began to appear in 1828 and which contain such information as *plantation* diagrams (the arrangement of set pieces on the stage), directions for stage movement, and descriptions of sets and costumes.[11] The approximately 140 *livrets de mise en scène* published by Louis Palianti between 1830 and 1870 deal with grand operas and *opéras comiques* from the period and can be supplemented by the numerous manuscript production books that have been preserved.[12]

Setting the Scene

> This spectacle now unites, with the enchanting effect of the sets, the astonishing art of the machinist, the luxury and authenticity of the costumes, all the pomp of the performance and the foremost talents in song and dance. Without equal in Europe, the Opéra is for this very reason a national spectacle, and one ought not to be astonished at the interest the government shows in it. It is the temple that the Muses, that enchantment have erected. Everything must contribute to this magical whole which pleases, captivates, and carries one's senses away.[13]

Thus did Alexis Donnet describe the new "temporary" opera house designed by François Debret (1770–1850) and erected on the grounds of the Hôtel de Choiseul on Paris's Rue le Peletier in 1821. The need for the new house had arisen the preceding year, when the Duke of Berry was assassinated at the former theater, the Salle Montansier, on the Rue Richelieu. As the duke had received the last rites of the church in the anteroom of the old hall, it was deemed improper to continue to use the building for secular purposes. Searching the city for a suitable plot of land for a new opera house, the government hit upon the gardens of the Hôtel de Choiseul, as it already owned the property and hence need not go to great expense for a theater that would be used, it thought, only until a permanent house could be designed and erected.[14] To economize even further, Debret was ordered to use as much of the interior of the old house as he could salvage. The columns, the fronts of the loges, the cornices, the cupola, and much of the stage machinery were carefully transferred to the Salle le Peletier, making the new interior "almost the exact reproduction of the old one."[15] There were modifications, of course, for Debret had made his interior more nearly circular and had enlarged the height and depth of the stage while at the same time keeping its proportions essentially the same as before. This too was an economy measure, making possible the reuse of set pieces from the Salle Montansier to remount works from the old repertoire.[16]

The Salle le Peletier opened on 16 August 1821 with two old standbys: Catel's *Les Bayadères* of 1810 and Gardel and Steibelt's one-act ballet, *Le retour de Zéphire*. While one might expect to find a festive new work opening the new house, the directors reasoned that the audience would be so taken up with the hall itself that they would pay little attention to a new piece anyway—hence the tried and true.[17] Indeed, the hall was thoroughly scrutinized. Though many found its exterior ugly and to some degree even laughable,[18] most were well satisfied with the elegant, acoustically excellent interior, the well-equipped stage, and the expanded corridors and foyers.

> At the Opéra, everything is grandiose. The hall is the most beautiful that I have ever seen; it forms a vast circle of which a quarter is occupied by the proscenium stage. Twice, the long line of the loges is interrupted by double columns between which small loges are located. The rich gilding, the beautiful paintings on the ceiling and on the walls, [and] the brilliant lighting complete the most dignified impression. On the chandelier there are seventy gas jets and on the eight [light fixtures] attached to the columns, seventy-two.[19]

The new structure measured 257 feet (78.3 meters) in length by 102 feet (31.1 meters) in width, with a façade measuring 180 feet (54.9 meters) across. The façade, 64 feet (19.5 meters) high, followed the Palladian model of columns, porticoes, and arcades. The initial vestibule, a one-story arcade, led to a two-story arrangement of glassed-in porticoes crowned by a series of statues of eight of the nine Classical Muses, each 6.5 feet (2 meters) in height (figure 7.1, far left). Universally condemned on aesthetic grounds was the functional awning on the lower level, needed to protect arriving and departing patrons from rain or snow. The mansion that was already on the property was turned into administrative offices, dressing rooms, and rehearsal rooms (figure 7.1, far right).

The essentially circular auditorium was 70 feet (21.3 meters) in diameter from the forward edge of the stage apron to the back of the first tier of loges. Whereas the seating capacity in the Salle Montansier had been approximately 1,300,[20] the Salle le Peletier ranged, through periodic renovations, from 1,400[21] to as many as 1,950 seats.[22] The height from the lowest portion of the parterre to the top of the cupola was 63 feet (19.2 meters). The cupola rested on the eight interior columns transferred from the Salle Montansier. The loges were

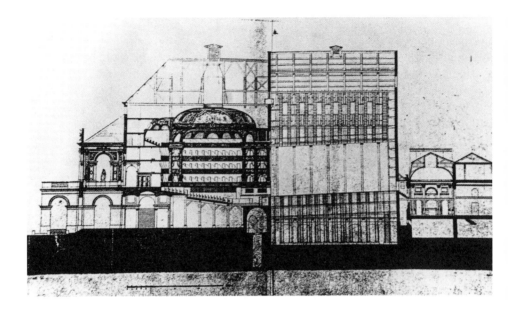

Figure 7.1. Engraving of a cross-section of the Salle le Peletier, from Donnet, *Architectonographie des théâtres de Paris.*

variously decorated with bas-reliefs in gold and white and canopied tapestries in gold and blue. The ground floor of comfortably spaced, bench-type seats was steeply raked, falling to the orchestra area.

The orchestra was placed on the main floor immediately in front of the stage apron.[23] The conductor stood chest high to and facing the stage next to the prompter's box, turning his face to the orchestra only for selected numbers such as the overtures or the ballets.[24] There were about eighty orchestra members in the employ of the Opéra throughout the 1830s and 1840s.[25] The magnificent proscenium arch separated the auditorium from the stage, with a stone wall surrounding the curtained arch. Since fire was the eternal predator of theaters, the stone wall supported two reservoirs of water, and a fire curtain was maintained. Four pumps could also draw from a large cistern just beneath the floor area occupied by the orchestra.

The arrangement of multilevel loges dictated the great size of the proscenium arch, 45 feet (13.7 meters) high by 41 feet (12.5 meters) wide. This proscenium opening could be adjusted by means of flexible arrangements of painted drops and borders suspended from the flies and brought in from the wings. A permanent house curtain, which was seldom lowered between scenes or even acts, was painted by Ciceri and depicted Lully receiving the *privilège* from Louis XIV. Early in the operation of the theater, however, there were also special movable curtains painted to reflect the subject of the opera.[26] The curtains opened, at last, to reveal grand opera's crown jewel—the magical stage itself.

Imagine viewing the playing area of the stage from above (figure 7.2). The stage of the Salle le Peletier was divided into twelve *plans,* each approximately 6 to 8 feet (1.8 to 2.4 meters) deep.[27] The elliptical apron, running across the full width of the proscenium, measured 9 feet (2.7 meters) from the front to the back at its deepest point. The stage floor was raked at a rate of 2 inches (5.1 cm) for every 4 feet (1.2 meters) of depth. The apron and stage together

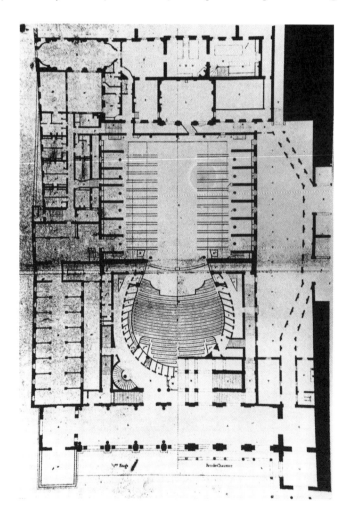

Figure 7.2. Engraving of the interior floor plan of the Salle le Peletier, from Donnet, *Architectonographie des théâtres de Paris.*

created an impressive playing area, 98 feet (29.9 meters) deep. The stage width, including the wings, was approximately 100 feet (30.5 meters) but the actual playing width would most often be about half that, due to the use of flats brought in from the wings.[28]

Each *plan* of the stage included a series of parallel sections that could be variously opened and closed. A *grande rue*—a series of large trapdoors running the width of the stage, from wing to wing—could be opened from below, by means of levers, to any width as needed (see figure 7.6 below). Single doors were 4 feet (1.2 meters) deep and 3 feet (.9 meter) wide. *Costières*—grooves in the stage floor about 1.5 inches (3.8 cm) wide—also ran the width of the stage. They were used for the movement of flats from the wings onto the stage. They were usually left open, though they could be closed manually with wooden slats, especially for the ballet. In addition, *trappillons* (also referred to as *petites rues*)—hinge-covered openings about 1 foot (.3 meters) deep, again running the full width of the stage—were the means by which flats stored in the substage area could pass up through the floor to the stage (figure 7.3).

Each *plan* was separated from the next by an immobile section of flooring. The most-used sections of the stage (the third through eighth *plans*) featured one *grande rue*, two *trappillons*, and three *costières* each, while the less-used areas (first, second, and ninth through twelfth *plans*) contained a *grande rue*, one *trappillon*, and two *costières* (see figure 7.4). One begins to appreciate the complex possibilities for settings with, theoretically, forty-eight sets of flats moving onto the stage by means of *trappillons* or *costières*.

The multilevel, scaffold-like structures above and below the stage conformed to the stage floor's *plan* arrangement (see figure 7.1, right half of theater). The *dessous* (substage) comprised three levels totaling more than thirty feet (9.1 meters) in vertical depth, each level raked at the same degree as the stage itself. The heavy, hand-operated machines for raising and lowering set pieces and people were located on the lower two levels (figure 7.3, bottom tier), while the traps of the *grande rue* and the *chariots* (wheeled frameworks which passed through the *costières* and supported the flats; figure 7.5) were operated from the highest level of the substage. These various substage levels were visible to each other through open scaffolding, and coordinating cues were whistled to the workmen during set changes.

The *cintre* or flies rose 102 feet (31.1 meters) above the stage and comprised four scaffold-like levels and additional storage areas (figure 7.1, upper right half of the theater). The curtains (including the fire curtain), power drums, pulleys, counterweight mechanisms, canvas drops, webs of rigging, open cylinders containing gas jets with reflective metal above the flames to illuminate the stage below—all of these occupied the brave stagehands who carried out their duties from the flies, watched for fires, and occasionally fell from the precarious framework.

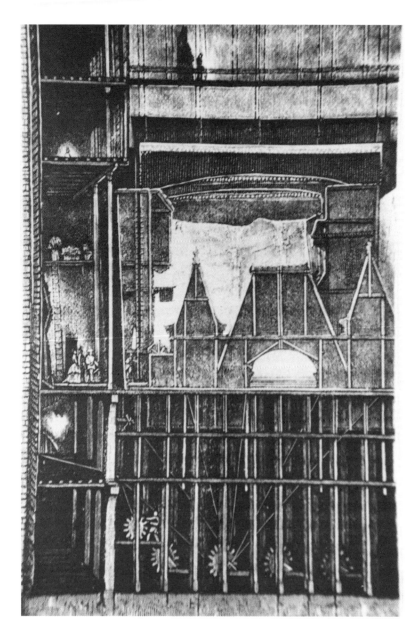

Figure 7.3. Cross-section of the stage at the Opéra, showing the substage area and the back of a *ferme* being raised to stage level by means of gears and pulleys on the lowest level of the *dessous*, from Moynet, *L'envers du théâtre*.

Figure 7.4. A section of the eighth and ninth *plans*.

Germain Bapst points out that all designs for the Opéra had to conform to the distribution of the twelve *plans*.[29] Working through the creation of an imaginary set, one moves from upstage to downstage. The most distant device from the audience, be it on the sixth, ninth, twelfth, or other *plan,* was likely to be the painted canvas backdrop or, in some cases, a curved, panorama-like structure such as that used in Act V of *La Juive.* These painted cloths were more than superficial, functional images. They respected all the rules of perspective and reflected a growing refinement in the use of chiaroscuro techniques to add depth and texture through implied light and shadow. This backdrop could be preceded at a distance of one or more *plans* by some relatively tall painted flats or *fermes* (more substantial and heavier than simple flats) brought in from the wings or up from the *dessous* (figures 7.3 and 7.5). From the same sources, additional *fermes*, slightly lower and one or more *plans* farther downstage, could represent shorter ranks of scenery. Theoretically, all twelve *plans* could be utilized in this way. In addition, the basically parallel alignment of set pieces could be broken by flats that could swivel on pivots or were provided with hinged wings. The true artistry and talent of the designers is evident when one realizes that each scenic layer had to make coherent sense as part of the whole—perspective, integration into the over-all design, coordination of chiaroscuro effects—not only from the rear center of the auditorium but from a nearly 270-degree semi-circle of amphitheater viewers.

Designers also introduced innovative *practicables* (structures) on which the performers could move to various heights above the stage. Such *practicables*

Figure 7.5. Backstage at the Opéra, showing a large *ferme* with stationary wing supported by two *mâts* (long vertical bars) on *chariots* (wheeled mechanisms below the stage), from Pougin, *Dictionnaire historique et pittoresque du théâtre.*

ranged from the magnificent staircase in Act II of *Les Huguenots* and the steps of Munster Cathedral in *Le prophète* (see below, figure 7.13) to interior galleries, rocks, and other natural formations. Then came the smaller additions of furniture, curtains, carts, and finally the costumed soloists, chorus members, and even animals.

The maturity of grand opera was not immediate, however. It developed through an adolescence of imagination and means. When the Salle le Peletier opened its doors, it was company policy to reuse, inasmuch as was possible, the sets and costumes created for works already in the repertoire in the service of the new. When Ciceri became the Opéra's *peintre en chef* in 1816—a position he held until 1848—he had two functions: "to furnish the 'watercolor sketch and the *plantation* of all set designs for all new works' and to restore the painted cloths from earlier productions."[30] Indeed, since so many works in the Opéra's repertoire at that time called for a kind of generic "classical" setting, there was no reason why the drops and set pieces from one work, suitably restored, could not be used for another work. The situation was self-perpetuating: not only was there no reason to try something new, there was every economic reason for maintaining the status quo.

Nevertheless, over time, innovations did occur, many of them at the hands of the increasingly restless Ciceri. Among the more far-reaching changes, the spectacular (and spectacularly expensive) production of Isouard's *Aladin, ou La lampe merveilleuse* (1822) introduced gas lighting onto the Opéra's stage. By 1833 all stage lighting was done by gas. Brighter, more variable, and more easily controlled than oil lamps, gaslights encouraged technicians and designers at the Opéra to attempt more striking effects, often taking their cues from ideas first presented at Daguerre's diorama or at the boulevard theaters.[31] "By means of gas," wrote Deshayes approvingly, "one can obtain a truly magical gradation of light, and one is not obliged to resort to shocking unrealities when the action demands that one pass from day to night."[32] Better lighting also brought the softening of the extreme gestures and facial expressions that had been a part of the acting style in use when oil lamps made such exaggerations necessary. In addition, costumes could make use of fabrics and colors that were not effective on stage under the old lighting conditions.[33] Moreover, the new methods of lighting seconded French grand opera's requirements in the area of stage composition. Now that the center stage could be lit as effectively as the forestage, the entire playing area could be used for the movement of characters, crowds, or scenery, exactly the sort of movement required in grand opera.

During its first half-decade, however, the Salle le Peletier saw no innovations in *mise en scène* that could equal, much less surpass, those of the boulevard theaters. These theaters—the Gaîté, the Ambigu-Comique, and the Porte-Saint-Martin—had been working since Revolutionary days to create new scenic marvels, new interactions between theatrical media, and new approaches to stage movement.[34] Erupting volcanoes had appeared on these stages over a decade before *La muette de Portici*'s Vesuvius. The same is true of historical and local color, freedom in *plantation,* the use of free-standing set pieces (*fermes* and *practicables*), and changes in stage composition. Though the Opéra could not have been unaware of developments on the boulevard stages, it proved extremely slow to adopt any of their innovations. This inaction was the legacy of Napoleon's policies toward theaters, under which those houses having official approval to exist were stereotyped, producing only the types of works for which they had been established. The Opéra's reluctance to trespass on the boulevard theaters' grounds thus deprived the company of the very transfusion that would have brought it back to life in the early 1820s.

Beginning in 1825, an amazing concurrence of developments in the Parisian theatrical world led to the renewal of the Opéra, its repertoire, and its production values. In that year, Baron Isidore Taylor took over as director of the Comédie-Française. Taylor, an experienced man of the theater, introduced historical accuracy to the *mise en scène* of even Classically oriented dramas and began to cultivate the Romantic playwrights. By 1830 he had staged Alexandre Dumas's *Henri III et sa cour,* Alfred de Vigny's *Le more de Venise,* and Hugo's *Hernani* in full-blooded productions that Meyerbeer and Scribe might envy. With Baron Taylor at its helm, the Comédie-Française demonstrated how a theater of the first rank could absorb influences from the secondary theaters to its great advantage.

An event of great importance for the musical revitalization of the Opéra occurred in 1826: Rossini began to write for the company. Not only were his *Siège de Corinthe* (1826), *Moïse* (1827), and *Guillaume Tell* (1829) works of grand spectacle, but they also required vocal forces of a power and flexibility that heretofore had been impossible to find at the Salle le Peletier. In 1827, while Hugo's Preface to *Cromwell* called for greater historical truth on the stage, the Salon of the same year demonstrated in the clearest possible terms that Romanticism had invaded the world of painting. The year 1827 also saw the arrival of a troupe of English actors who performed the plays of Shakespeare to enthusiastic Parisian audiences. The historical settings, Romantic contrasts, and convincing performance style of the Shakespeareans were not lost on those involved in the revitalization of the French stage.

In 1827, as well, the formation of a Comité de Mise en Scène at the Opéra, and with it the appointment of Solomé, then Duponchel, as *metteur en scène,* demonstrated that the Académie Royale de Musique was serious in its increasingly frequent attempts to improve the quality of its productions. At last Ciceri felt free to direct the full strength of his imagination to the creation of innovative stage designs, a process that led to the colorful Neapolitan locales of *La muette de Portici* and the clever *practicables* of *Guillaume Tell.* With the cloister scene in *Robert le diable,* French grand opera displayed a true synthesis of the arts. Outstanding in dramatic conception, musical realization, and scenic presentation, it was also unique in that it was suggested not by the librettist or the composer, but by Duponchel, the *metteur en scène.*[35]

Finally, in 1828, came *La muette de Portici,* the Opéra's most nearly complete expression to date of the ideals of Romantic *mise en scène* and of its distinctive combination with literary drama and music to produce a new genre—French grand opera. The Salle le Peletier had been standing for seven years, some of its personnel had been working for the Opéra even longer, and the innovations of the boulevard theaters had arisen before their eyes. Yet it took this convergence of heavenly bodies at the end of the decade to build up the gravitational force necessary to pull the Opéra away from its antiquated traditions and forward into the age of Romanticism. Marvin Carlson has observed that "the story of the

French theater from 1800 to 1830 is more than anything else the story of the defeat of the Neoclassical vision of Napoleon and the triumph of the melodrama."[36] The Opéra, in its transition from the Gluck-based Classicism to vision-based Romanticism, demonstrates the essential truth of this statement.

The Operas

Clear illustrations of the emergence and development of Romantic ideals and practices on the stage of the Opéra can be found in scenes from *La muette de Portici,* grand opera's standard-setter; *La Juive* (1835), representing the mature style of the mid 1830s; and *Le prophète* (1849), a product of the master-composer of the genre, Giacomo Meyerbeer, and its most important librettist, Eugène Scribe.[37] In choosing these works, we have essentially limited ourselves to the period when, according to Carlson, Romanticism truly flourished on the French stage.[38] Though many of the innovations of the 1830s and early '40s lingered on, little can be cited after Carlson's watershed date of 1843 that adds a great deal to the Romantic tradition already established. The years of greatest creative ferment for French grand opera were those of the late 1820s and the '30s; later works demonstrate the perfection of techniques that had already acquired a firm grounding.

La muette de Portici and the Scenic-Musical Tableau

When Louis Véron took over as director of the Académie Royale de Musique in 1831, he was told in no uncertain terms that "new works are to be mounted with new sets and costumes."[39] This provision of Véron's contract directly contradicted the regulation previously in force that commanded the reuse of such items whenever possible. During the transition, however, old customs died hard, and *La muette de Portici* had only two sets that were entirely new.[40] Yet the reworkings were cleverly done, for the image of sunny Naples is revealed in all of Ciceri's designs.

More important for the development of grand opera as a distinctive genre, however, are the musico-dramatic-scenic tableaux that occur at least once in every act. These tableaux are characterized by large numbers of people on the stage, a flexible approach to stage composition that allows the chorus to become an active character in the drama, and a slow but steady motion in real time that contrasts strongly with the musical or stage time in sections of the opera devoted to self-contained, nearly outmoded arias and small ensembles. For these tableaux Auber created large-scale forms that eschewed the expected repeat structures and numbers organization in favor of a continuously evolving set of contrasting musical vignettes, each specific to its context. This confluence of real-time dramatic movement and structural freeing-up of the musical framework occurs only in scenes involving large groups of people on the stage, as in the second scene of Act III or the conclusion of Act V. Hence the nature of the stage movement becomes an important component of the opera's visual side. The essential qualities of the scenic-musical tableau result from exactly the sort of dramaturgy that forsakes the traditional soloist-emphasis of opera for an emphasis on the group, and that reveals the interdependence of action, spectacle, and music.

The second scene of Act III shows both how grand opera exploited the principle of contrast and how machinists might take advantage of this principle. Act III's opening scene is set in "an apartment in the palace . . . quite a small salon," where Elvire and Alphonse perform a duet.[41] Unknown to the audience, however, the stagehands have already set up, behind and at the sides of the salon, the much grander set that is to serve for the market scene to follow (figure 7.6). Once the set pieces for the salon and the masking borders have been removed,[42] the marketplace is revealed in all its color.

> The scene represents the grand marketplace of Naples.
>
> At the rear, a *ferme* across the stage. Upstage, one sees several small carts which pass from right to left and from left to right. In front of the *ferme,* somewhat to the left, a stage on two trestles. A Neapolitan

Figure 7.6. *La muette de Portici*, Act III, scene ii, engraving by Lemaître from *Album Léger-Larbouillat* (Bibliothèque de l'Opéra).

Pulcinella, a Pantalone, and a Columbine are doing their act; groups of
children watch them. At the right and the left, along a line from the
rear of the stage up to the salon [i.e., the set for the preceding duet],
which has disappeared, one sees a group of women from the second act.
They are seated on stools and have in front of them the provisions they
carried in. As soon as the set is changed, they move forward in the same
order up to the apron, where others join them.[43] Fishermen enter from
all sides and arrange themselves in three lines. Others, with large baskets of fish, form a line in the back, facing the public. When everyone
is on stage, the chorus begins. Fenella has arrived with Pietro, who seats
her stage right at the head of the women. She is seated on a stool. She
is sad, pensive, and takes no part in what is going on around her.

As the chorus begins one sees inhabitants of Naples arriving,
followed by their attendants or their porters (*facchini*). The women
with their maids pass down the rows of the market, bargaining, making
purchases. The merchants show their joy. One merchant carries hams at
the top of a long pole; another carries chickens; a third has hazelnuts
threaded on strings, etc. They stroll down the rows to sell their
merchandise. A seller of watermelons, another of ices and sorbets, two
with a basket of cheeses, etc. The words the chorus sings indicate all
that is necessary for the execution of a tableau that must be varied and
above all very animated.[44]

The church in center stage and probably the buildings to its left were part
of the *ferme* mentioned in the second sentence of the description. This *ferme*
would have been brought up from the *dessous,* while the small stage and its
canopy, a *practicable,* was brought in from the wings. The rest of the buildings
would have been painted on a drop cloth, as these cloths generally took over at
the point where the perspective of a scene began to indicate a receding into the
background. Both the *ferme* and *practicable* lent a three-dimensional look to the
scenery.

Though a tableau that opens with a straightforward if animated chorus may
seem to contradict the possibility of action that moves more or less in real
time, the stage activity, as represented in the text, already reflects the real-time
experience of a lively marketplace.

Come running, hasten to the market which has just opened. Look! here
are flowers, fruits, golden raisins, exquisite lemons, fine oranges from
Meta and Rosolio, wine from Somma, new citron from Portici. Come
to me, come here![45]

These words, combined with the lively, colorful stage movement described in
the scenic libretto and the quick patter of the music, form a sharp contrast to

the preceding duet. Near the end of the chorus, the buyers disperse, the merchants cart away leftover wares, and the women remain on stage to view the dancers' market-day entertainment, a lively tarantella. But time does not stand still even here: "During the *divertissement* the sellers of refreshments return to sell [the women] something to drink, etc."[46]

Even the poses held by the dancers at the end of the tarantella become part of an ongoing drama as Fenella, during a quiet, nine-bar, instrumental transition, tries to slip in among the dancers in order to avoid being caught by Selva and the soldiers. During the same nine measures,

> The soldiers in the first platoon (they have muskets) enter from all sides, in no particular order, as if they were taking a walk. The male dancers leave their partners and exit. Only the women remain on stage. [After Selva sees Fenella and calls to the soldiers,] the soldiers move as if to approach [her]. The women who are near them surround them, bar their way, grab their muskets with both hands, and fight with them.[47]

The fight lasts for thirty-two bars of agitated but not particularly interesting music. The chorus, a character in its own right, engages in dialogue with the captain, and the action continues, always in real time, as Masaniello enters and calls his friends to help him free Fenella. During the brief chorus that ensues ("Courons à la vengeance"), stage movement continues at the same realistic pace. "The unarmed men loot the shops of the armorers. . . . Others go to the shops of the torch-sellers. Everything presents the appearance of a general revolt. All make as if to leave."[48] At this point the work's creators, knowing the value of dropping back from a high point of activity in order to prepare for one that is still higher, have Masaniello call the people to prayer. Though the serene, *a cappella* segment that follows seems to stop the work's forward motion in its tracks, the pause is again realistic: people show respect for things sacred, even in real time on the operatic stage.

> During the *ritournelle* all people fall respectfully to their knees; the men remove their hats. (Night begins to fall.) Care must be taken to distribute the people over the whole plaza, with torches here and there. . . .
> At the end of the prayer the tocsin is heard. Everyone rises and moves about furiously.[49]

"Courons à la vengeance" returns as "daggers and other arms are held aloft. . . . People run off in all directions to burn and loot the city."[50]

Save for the market chorus and the prayer, none of the music in this tableau has much value except as enhancement of the drama and the stage action, and its pace differs noticeably from that of the music in the traditional numbers (e.g., the preceding duet). Even the market chorus and the prayer have some claim to be considered part of the real-time continuum, since the activities they accompany could easily take up the musical time allotted. Hence the musical logic of the scene is in good part derived from or reflective of its visual side, and Auber shows himself to be in tune with the progressive forces moving toward change in French opera.

The tableau as mimed stage-picture reaches new heights in the final act of *La muette*. At the same time, the tableau as dramatic unit here reflects most clearly its derivation from the popular *mélodrames* and optical spectacles. As early as 1818, Pixérécourt had staged a volcanic eruption in his *Le Belvéder* at the Ambigu-Comique. More recently, both Pixérécourt and Daguerre had featured volcanoes in their work: Pixérécourt in his *La tête de mort* and Daguerre at his Diorama.[51] Both of these spectacles, as well as the model usually cited for Ciceri's Vesuvius—Sanquirico's work for Pacini's *L'ultimo giorno di Pompei*— were less than a year old, hence fresh in people's minds. Yet audiences were still impressed with the Vesuvius of *La muette*.

Unlike the market scene of Act III, Act V's spectacle makes considerable use of stage machinery, sound effects, and special lighting. The technical crescendo in the course of the act represents a kind of Scribean preparation for the climactic eruption of the volcano (figure 7.7). Yet there is enough random activity on the stage that the crowd fails to realize the significance of the lightning, thunder claps, and gradual darkness creeping out from the wings onto the sides of the playing area.[52] The volcano's activity is not lost on Fenella, how-ever. Mounting the staircase stage right, she throws herself into the flow of the lava.

> During this scene the cloud curtain has disappeared, uncovering Vesuvius in fury. [The volcano] throws up eddies of flame and smoke. The lava runs down to the bottom of the staircase. The music must be timed so that the chorus begins as soon as Fenella has disappeared into the lava.
>
> After the final chorus, everyone moves about with the greatest fright. A man arrives at the top of the staircase. The roof of the terrace, with a sound like an explosion, collapses and overwhelms him and his three children—two holding his hand, one on his back. All see this scene of horror and form themselves into the following groups: Alphonse in the middle of the stage; Elvire, her head buried in his breast; the pages and ladies-in-waiting surround them, variously grouped.
>
> The people fill the entire stage. Mothers carry their children; husbands support their wives. Some fall to the ground, others lean on the columns.

Figure 7.7. *La muette de Portici,* Act V, engraving by Lemaître from *Album Léger-Larbouillat* (Bibliothèque de l'Opéra).

Those who enter by way of the terrace die on the steps. Finally, the terror in everyone's movements cannot be portrayed too strongly. Subterranean noises continue. . . . everything goes off at once. Almost at the moment when the curtain falls, from the flies, and reaching from Vesuvius to the staircase, comes a shower of stones of all sizes which are understood to be coming from the crater. You will need a lot of them.[53]

Such a concentrated show of stage effects required the coordinated efforts of many stagehands. The Opéra regularly called on as many as sixty *machinistes* and a crew of at least forty men to produce a single work on the stage. The most complex works might use more than eighty *machinistes* and a proportionally larger crew.[54] These men would already have shifted the large, often ungainly *fermes* from the previous act to the wings or the *dessous* and set in place the equally large *fermes* that framed the backcloth on which the volcano appeared. Lower *fermes* representing the gardens had also been moved into place, and would soon be covered with the "lava" already prepared by stagehands stationed behind them. They would also have secured the *practicable* staircase stage left and the floor drape, which had been painted to resemble a mosaic. Others, working in the *cintre,* would have lowered the new backdrop into position and would be preparing to regulate the departure of the clouds that partially hid Vesuvius at the beginning of the act. Still others, from behind the set pieces on stage, would create the illusion of collapsing buildings by releasing hinges that held the upper portions of the *fermes* in place. Lights at different intensities, combined with various colored filters, would yield the requisite fiery atmosphere, while the lava flow would result from the manipulation of rippling, gossamer cloths by the hidden crewmen. Later, a second backdrop would descend from the *cintre* to represent the erupting volcano, and new *fermes* showing smoke and flames would be moved in from the wings.[55]

Meanwhile, workers in the *dessous* were creating ominous rumblings by means of thunder sheets and similar devices,[56] while crewmen above the stage were preparing to release a shower of stones into the area of the stage between the backcloth and the staircase, once it was free of the chorus members and supers who had rushed onto the stage earlier.[57] The effect of such technical virtuosity must have been overwhelming. Yet it is less important to know how these matters were accomplished than to realize that their effectiveness depended on the arts of designer, machinist, crewman, librettist, and composer alike.

La Juive: Luxury and Authenticity

Nothing could have been more splendid than the premiere of *La Juive*.[58] Spectators on that February evening in 1835 began their imaginary journey to the fifteenth century at an intersection in the city of Constance, filled with representatives of all classes and métiers. Before the first act ended, they would see soldiers, horses, trumpeters, ecclesiastics, and banner-carriers, authentically and luxuriously costumed, parade before their eyes (figure 7.8). Cutting to the interior of a Jewish home, they witnessed a Seder in progress, accompanied by *a cappella* music in a responsorial style recalling that of the Vienna synagogue as described with wonder and admiration by Joseph Mainzer in the *Gazette musicale*.[59] The third act returned to the stage the festive trappings of the Council of Constance, where "magnificent gardens" and "lovely views" of the "rich countryside" formed the backdrop for the emperor's banquet, with its troubadour-fantasy ballet and its troubling pronouncement of anathema.[60]

Figure 7.8. Lithograph (originally in color) of the set for *La Juive*, Act I (Bibliothèque de l'Opéra).

Act IV took the audience to a reception hall, only three *plans* deep, outside the council chamber. Even this small set, however, was magnificent, its Gothic arches and carved oak furniture a testimony to the luxury of the whole production. Returning to the out-of-doors, the audience beheld a huge tent, held aloft by gilt-topped columns, which opened onto a plaza surrounded by people and reached by means of a ramp to a false floor built at the first substage level. A panoramic view of the city that included a *ferme* of the cathedral on the rear-most *plan* and dozens of additional spectators painted onto the backdrop finished the perspective (see figure 7.9). In the middle of this immense space stood a large cauldron, supported by a brick furnace in which a lively fire already danced. Here, in a conclusion that never especially pleased the public, the Jewess Rachel would be cast to her death during the final pages of the score.

La Juive's staging was the culmination of the major tendencies observable in operatic *mise en scène* during the July Monarchy.[61] First and most important, it

Figure 7.9. The city of Constance, lithograph of the set for Act V of *La Juive* (Bibliothèque de l'Opéra).

demonstrated superbly the move toward increasing scenic and historical truth and monumentality, the desire to produce the feeling of actually being at a given place during a specific time, an overarching *couleur du temps*. Théophile Gautier was among those who praised *La Juive* for its recreation of reality. "The Middle Ages in their entirety are unfolded before us. . . . It is the medieval period itself in all the infinite variety of its dress and its hierarchy."[62] The *Courrier français* agreed, observing that "nothing is missing in this prodigious resurrection of a distant century,"[63] and *Le ménestrel* commented on the work's "historical fidelity without example in the pageantry of the theater."[64]

Within this trend toward authenticity, designers concentrated on architecture, reproducing single buildings or cityscapes in great detail. Figure 7.8, for example, shows the center of town, with churches, homes, and public buildings, while the panorama in figure 7.9 reveals the entire public square, including Constance's grand cathedral. Yet for all its architectural magnificence and its desire to recreate past realities, *mise en scène* would still be a clever mixture of realism and fantasy: the prominent building silhouetted against the sky in the right half of figure 7.8 stood not in Constance but in Gand, where it served as the city hall.[65]

Reading the *livret de mise en scène,* one soon becomes aware of the two major areas where stage movement is frequent and is prescribed in great detail: in scenes of pure spectacle, such as at the beginning or at the finale of Act I, at the banquet of Act III, or at the entry procession of Act V; and in scenes in which major dramatic *coups* occur—the encounters between Jews and Christians in Act I, Rachel's accusation of Léopold in Act III, or the finale of Act V. By contrast, little prescribed stage movement occurs in arias or small ensembles, and most of this movement takes place either during the instrumental *ritournelles* or in the recitatives. Finally, several places in the work use freeze-frame technique to stunning effect: the a cappella "Te Deum" (Act I), Eléazar's prayer (Act II), Brogni's virtually unaccompanied pronunciation of anathema (Act IV), and the conclusions of every act except the fourth. In all these cases the drama provides for and the music intensifies the kind of stage activity required, as examples from the first act will demonstrate.

The stage movement prescribed in *La Juive'*s scenes of pure spectacle is largely that of masses of people, the "compact crowds" that first appeared on the Opéra's stage in this production.[66] In such crowds a small number of people, appropriately costumed, were intended to suggest the presence of larger groups. Musically, the crowd scenes generally take the form of choruses with broad repeat structures and, at times, extended orchestral introductions and postludes. Such, for example, is the impressive cortège that ends Act I. The procession starts down the street represented at stage left in figure 7.8, comes forward to face the public, then turns and exits up the street shown under the arch at stage right.[67] The set itself makes creative use of *fermes* that face the audience directly and *fermes* constructed with one or more wings that could be positioned at various angles. (Eléazar's house, the prominent building placed across *plans* 2 and 3 at stage right, is a good example of the latter type of structure.) Set pieces have been painted using skillful chiaroscuro techniques that are in effect substitutes for subtleties of lighting that could not yet be accomplished. The glimmer of sunlight on the walls of Eléazar's house owes its existence not to the way it is lit, but to the way it is painted.

The setting for the cortège also illustrates the greatest difference between Romantic and Classical scene design: the use or absence of a vanishing point. Whereas Classical stage settings most often assumed a vanishing point at the center back of the stage and arranged their series of symmetrical flats in relation to that point, Romantic designers conceived their settings as three dimensional, with no given end to the vista presented. In figure 7.8, expert use of *fermes,* chiaroscuro, and backdrops suggests not a limited space but a segment of a large area, an entire city. The setting for Act V (figure 7.9) also suggests more than it presents—not just the city square but the rest of the town as well, viewed from the more limited area of a portico that takes up only the first three *plans*. This suggestion is given not just by creating a three-dimensional stage picture, but by using a rounded panorama drop instead of a flat cloth, and by painting numbers of spectators onto the backdrop. In addition, both the Act I and Act V sets use *practicable* staircases and ramps to create a multilevel playing area and decorative borders to frame the stage picture.

The chorus "De ces nobles guerriers" covers the first part of the cortège:[68]

1. The emperor's trumpeters, preceded by three guards on horseback, richly armed and equipped. 2. A banner-carrier. 3. Twenty crossbow-men. 4. A banner-carrier. 5. Two cardinals followed by two clerks. 6. Two other cardinals followed by two clerks. 7. A banner-carrier accompanied by bishops and masters of different crafts.

The music then moves from a 6/8 *allegro brillante* to a 2/4, and the chorus drops out for a time as Rachel, then Eléazar, utter brief prayers ("O mon Dieu que j'implore"). During this passage we see only a small number of new faces in the cortège:

8. A banner-carrier accompanied by two other bishops and some father-superiors. 9. Three sheriffs.

The larger body of the cortège recommences at the choral entrance "Non, jamais dans ces lieux" and consists of:

10. A hundred and twenty soldiers richly armed and wearing short coats, their bodies covered with gold mail. 11. Six trumpeters. (Their instruments are adorned with richly encrusted banners.) . . . 12. Six trumpeters. 13. Six banner-carriers. 14. Twenty guards bearing cross-bows. 15. Three cardinals followed by their pages and their clerks. 16. Under a magnificent baldachin carried by four heralds (a fifth carries the horse's bridle), Cardinal Brogni on horseback, followed by his pages and his gentlemen and preceded by heralds bearing the pontifical vestments on rich velvet cushions. 17. Ten soldiers. 18. Three heralds-at-arms on horseback. 19. Twenty pages of the emperor. 20. Emperor Sigismond, in the most stunning armor with all the luxury imaginable.[69]

During this movement both the chorus and the ensemble of soloists have been singing in place. As earlier in the act, however, all movement stops when the "Te Deum" resounds from within the church. Doubtless this is a practical move—the shuffling of feet and the sounds of horses' hooves on stage would hardly have allowed an offstage chorus to be heard—but it also highlights the distinctive texture of the "Te Deum" and brings it into sharp relief against the full choral-orchestral sound that has heretofore characterized most of this scene. In a musical way, the "Te Deum" also broadens the scene's visual dimensions, as it extends the audience's perception of stage space to include the wings—i.e., the church's interior.[70]

> During the "Te Deum": choirboys (at least eight) on the church steps . . . swing illuminated censers toward the emperor. The emperor stops and bows before God's house.

Then, shouting "Hosanna, gloire à l'Empereur," chorus and orchestra resume their song of joy.

Unlike the cortège just described, encounters between Jews and Christians in Act I show both a discontinuous musical profile and an amount of individual stage movement that far exceeds anything prescribed for the set numbers. In such scenes the chorus becomes more active as a character, its interjections limited to a few phrases, and the scene as a whole operates in something close to the sort of real time represented by similar examples in *La muette de Portici*.

The chorus "Hosanna, plaisir, ivresse," which covers the mass movement on stage in the opera's Introduction, yields to solo voices as Ruggiero, then the crier, announces the forthcoming public celebration of Léopold's victory over the Hussites. These announcements, performed partly in a reciting tone, divide the large, musically static crowd scene from the events to follow. The crowd's rejoicing is interrupted by the sound of anvils coming from the home of Eléazar, and the people immediately identify the impious culprit: "the heretic, . . . the Jew Eléazar, the rich jeweler." At Ruggiero's orders the guards enter the house, arrest Eléazar and his daughter, and bring them before the crowd.

The amount of individual stage movement and a constantly changing stage picture set this segment of the scene apart from both the solo set-numbers and from the crowd scenes with chorus, and "depict with striking truth the terrifying outbreak of the passions of a rebellious crowd."[71] In fewer than eight pages of orchestral score, we find more movement of individuals than in the first forty pages of music or in the final cortège. When the guards come out of the house, "brutally dragging Rachel and the Jew," the stage picture resolves to that outlined in figure 7.10.

At this point:

> The soldiers, on Ruggiero's order, want to take Rachel and Eléazar off, when Brogni, followed by his pages and three other cardinals, emerges from the church and stops for an instant on the stairs.

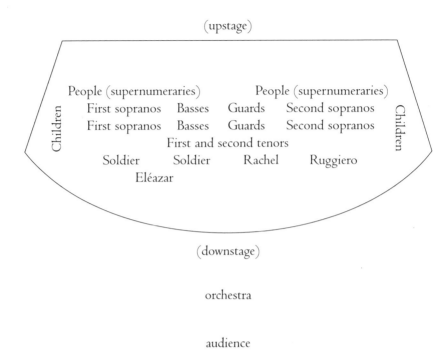

Figure 7.10. The stage as Rachel and Ruggiero are brought before the crowd.

In a single phrase the chorus identifies Brogni as "the supreme president of the Council [of Constance]." As he asks, "Where are you taking them?" (*Où les conduisez-vous ainsi?*) the characters are arranged as shown in figure 7.11.

Brogni then moves downstage to view the prisoners, identified by Ruggiero as Jews, who are being led to their execution. Though Brogni calls Eléazar forward, he finds that neither can conduct a reasoned conversation with the other. Yet Brogni plays the peacemaker. With the beginning of his *cavatine* "Si la rigueur et la vengeance," all movement on stage ceases until, having blessed the assembly, the cardinal and his pages exit. This exciting encounter between Jews and Christians, placed between the "Hosanna" chorus and Brogni's aria, is accompanied by music that is varied, constantly changing in texture, melody, and rhythm, but of little value in itself. Its function is rather to underscore the rapid, real-time motion in the drama.[72] That contemporary audiences recognized the real-time aspect of these scenes is implied in Stoepel's comment that, in the Act I example, "the music pursues its course rapidly, while characterizing the elements of the drama as they develop."[73]

The recurring use of freeze-frame technique in *La Juive* highlights certain key moments in the plot by means of scenic and, at times, musical emphasis. One such freeze frame occurs in the scene just described, when Brogni

(upstage)

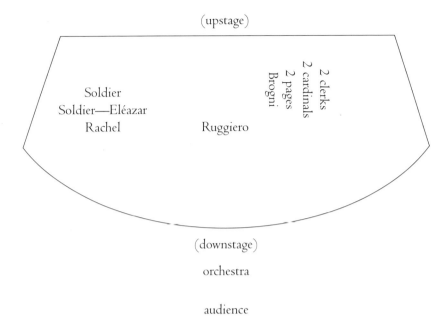

Soldier
Soldier—Eléazar
Rachel

Ruggiero

2 clerks
2 cardinals
2 pages
Brogni

(downstage)

orchestra

audience

Figure 7.11. The configuration of characters on the stage as Brogni speaks.

confronts the Jews and begins to take an interest in them. Similarly, after Léopold gives orders that the Jews are to be set free, a freeze frame is indicated in the scenic libretto by the word "TABLEAU." Here the music highlights the "surprise général" with a short, static ensemble ("O surprise nouvelle") which produces the effect of stunned silence before the people, noticing that the cortège is approaching, turn their attentions elsewhere.

To be sure, such frozen stage pictures were commonplace in grand opera, but their being labeled in the scenic libretto of *La Juive* indicates that the *metteur en scène* was conscious that this device at specific points in the work intensified dramatic moments in a visual way. The resulting stage pictures moved Mrs. Trollope to remark that their subjects were arranged "not merely in combinations of grace and beauty, but in such bold, easy, and picturesque variety, that one might fancy Murillo had made the sketches for them."[74]

Another unusual feature of *La Juive*'s scenic libretto is its specification of some basic lighting cues.[75] In Act II, changes in lighting from the *rampe* or footlights—the row of gaslights that lined the apron below floor level—underscore important dramatic turning points. When Eudoxie and her attendants interrupt the Seder with loud knocking at the door, Eléazar orders the candles extinguished and the scenic libretto notes *nuit à la rampe*—the footlights dimming to represent the sudden darkness in the room. Léopold's recognition of Eudoxie is emphasized by a sudden brightening of the lights (*jour à la rampe*), but the original light levels are restored once Eléazar has escorted Eudoxie out the door. Halévy underscores these lighting changes by virtually eliminating the orchestra for ten bars after the candles are extinguished, by the crescendo of tremolo chords that marks Léopold's recognition of his wife, and by returning to a kind of musical stability, a six-bar orchestral postlude, after the trio for Eudoxie, Léopold, and Eléazar.

The magic of *La Juive* cannot be overestimated. Even when, soon after the premiere, the work was reduced to "more rational proportions,"[76] its magnificence remained undisputed until it was outdone by the greater magnificence of *Le prophète*. Mrs. Trollope, who attended the premiere, noted that though some individual scenes in other works might be the equals of those in *La Juive,* there was about the whole of Halévy's opera "the extraordinary propriety and perfection of all accessaries [*sic*] which makes this part of the performance worthy of a critical study from the beginning to the end of it."[77]

Le prophète: The Triumph of the Grandiose

In 1850, the year following the premiere of Meyerbeer's *Le prophète,* Georges Kastner wrote a series of eight analytical articles about the opera for the *Revue et gazette musicale de Paris.* This detailed attention in just one of the many Paris publications of the day is evidence of the adoration for grand opera in general and for *Le prophète* in particular. Kastner suggests just how important this opera was to his contemporaries.

> Thus ends the drama, the curtain falls, and the friends of [opera] gather to review their impressions [and] to consider the great significance and the value of such a work. What principally characterizes this vast production is the brilliance, the precision, the grandeur and originality of ideas . . . the rich means of expression, and especially the power of truth in the dramatic representation.[78]

Clearly, the artistic ideals and the presentation of *Le prophète* had met with complete success in the writer's opinion.

This premiere had been eagerly anticipated. It had been thirteen years since Paris had witnessed a new work by Meyerbeer. The Opéra had experienced some difficulties in the years before the 1848 revolution, relying upon overworked warhorses and singers of flagging appeal. Meyerbeer's fanatic attention to detail and his relentless concern for quality were part and parcel of his new opera. Perhaps only this composer could have brought the designers, the chorus, the orchestra, and the *corps de ballet* to a pitch of excitement that drew them to peak form. The critic and musicologist François-Joseph Fétis confirmed a verdict of success for *Le prophète.*

With regard to the ballet, the *mise en scène,* the sets, the exactitude and the freshness of the costumes, [and] finally of the general effect of the work, there is no exaggeration in saying that nothing as beautiful, as complete, as striking, has been given at the Opéra. The third act, with its picturesque countryside, its ice-covered lake, and its lively dances, offers a charming ensemble. There has been nothing as beautiful and as novel as the interior of Munster Cathedral, nothing as intelligently managed as the *mise en scène* of the great spectacle offered by the crowd that has assembled there, nothing more magnificent than the great hall of the palace in the fifth act or more striking than the scene of destruction that ends the work. With *Le Prophète,* the Opéra has rediscovered its great days.[79]

A veil of secrecy had been imposed over all aspects of the work while it was in rehearsal, and all of the insiders seem to have been remarkably compliant. A spy for *Le ménestrel,* referred to as *notre petit démon,* did manage a few details for the 25 March 1849 issue of the journal.

The opera is clothed in a series of sets of fabulous beauty. The *mise en scène* is sworn to out-distance all local traditions; there is a piquant tableau of skaters and a sunrise of great impact. In order to make these effects even more dazzling, they have tried this week the use of electric lighting. The result is a profusion of light which is truly frightful: the sun of the Opéra threatens to eclipse the sun of the Good Lord.[80]

It was noted earlier in this chapter that few technical innovations resulted from the move to the Salle le Peletier and that most advances that did occur had been achieved by the 1830s. *Le prophète*'s use of electricity is a significant exception and it has a place not only in the annals of theater but also in the history of electricity itself.[81]

This use of electric lighting for the sun created a sensation. There is even a footnote in the *livret de mise en scène,* presumably in order to allow other producers access to the magical effect: "At the Opéra, the sunrise is carried out by means of an electrical apparatus by M. Lormier, 13 Rue du Delta in Paris."[82] (See figure 7.12.) Lighting in general is a feature of the third act, which progresses through an entire night to the following midday, hence the stunning effect of the sunrise. The *livret de mise en scène* dictates the progression of the sun as the action unfolds: "It is nearly morning"; "Day dawns little by little"; "Munster is illuminated more and more . . . already the rays of the rising sun appear on the horizon"; and finally, at the scene's climax, "The sun appears in all its splendor and soars above the city." This sun was a successful addition to the technical means used to realize the dramatic vision.

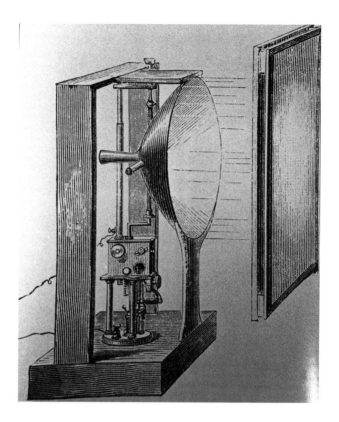

Figure 7.12. An electric arc instrument used to represent the sun in Act III of *Le prophète*, from Pougin, *Dictionnaire historique et pittoresque du théâtre*.

The third act of the opera illustrates links among words, music, and staging. An implicit link—the mood—is effectively realized in the setting for this act. The wintry outdoor camp of the Anabaptists near the city of Munster is carefully described in the *livret de mise en scène* which, fortunately, was the work of a fastidious individual. The act takes advantage of the full playing area of the stage. The city of Munster is represented in silhouette on a backdrop at the extreme rear of the stage, probably on the eleventh or twelfth *plan*. Individual trees, clumps of trees, and a forest entrance (constructed as both *fermes* and painted canvases brought to the stage as canvas drops from the *cintre*, flats on *chariots* from the wings, and *fermes* raised through the *rues* from below) provide vertical as well as horizontal interest. The trees and the ground are covered with snow. Fog (a scrim hanging in front of the backdrop) somewhat obscures the view of the city. The fog, i.e., the scrim, will finally lift at the end of the act, when the sun is at its brightest. The atmosphere for the evening and early morning portions of the act is enriched by the lighting from the gas cylinders suspended above the stage and filtered through blue glass. An ice-covered pond, represented by means of stretched canvas, occupies a considerable portion of the playing area extending to the horizon. As an aid to perspective, the *livret* calls for small children to skate at the rear, larger children to occupy the middle, and adults to appear at the front. Their skates were, of course, special roller skates.[83]

Contrast, sometimes striking contrast, was a hallmark of Giacomo Meyerbeer's musical style. This set facilitates contrast as well with moods of both winter barrenness and joyous frolicking. The former is evident in the first tableau of the act. A number of nobles have been taken prisoner by the Anabaptists and are led onto the stage for execution:

> The murderers move toward their victims; the latter draw back, some terrified, others patiently awaiting death. The Confessor . . . protects a woman and her daughter. This pantomime occupies all of the chorus "Frappez l'épi quand il se lève" to the "Te Deum laudamus," at the beginning of which everyone kneels. At the end of the 6/8 all rise, take some steps forward, and brandish their arms: "Dansons, dansons sur leur tombe," etc. During this reprise, the prayer of the Confessor, the women, and the girls is even more expressive. At the words "Du sang! . . . du sang! du sang!" all arms are raised to strike. Tableau.[84]

The setting, lighting, and stage movement have focused and amplified the dramatic events and the music.

The *divertissement* of the famous "Patineurs" or "Skaters' Waltz" later in the act highlights quite an opposite mood and demonstrates not only an explicit connection between music and staging but also the ability of the opera's *metteur en scène* to evoke a *couleur du temps*. At the beginning of the piece, the children skate across the far reaches of the stage with trays of food and pots of milk on their heads. Horse-drawn wagons and carriages cross the ice. Soldiers, peasants, farmers, and children move about forming various groups to eat and drink. The skating continues throughout the lively chorus "Voici les fermières lestes" with its illustrative woodwind figures. Kastner describes the scene and music.

> The glowing tableau that the scene presents upon the arrival of the skaters reflects the music of Meyerbeer. The elusive turns of the gliding sextuplets from one part to another, the *rinforzando* placed in other parts at the beginnings of each measure, the appoggiaturas of the bassoons and the violoncellos . . . the simple yet elegant and graceful motive, the detached syllables of the voices . . . this picturesque instrumental foundation is so true a reproduction of the serpentine movements of the skaters. . . . In order to be a good painter, one must be a great musician.[85]

In the tent scene of the third act, two of the Anabaptist leaders (Zachaire and Jonas) interrogate a stranger who has been discovered near the camp. Night is falling and it is dark inside the tent. The stranger proclaims his desire to join the Anabaptists and is nearly accepted when Jonas decides to light a lamp: "Why should we keep sitting in the dark like this?" (*Mais pourquoi dans l'ombre demeurer ainsi?*)

> Jonas, in the middle of the stage, strikes the flint and steel that he had brought to the table. (He must strike the steel in time to the notes of the triangle.)[86]

A notated part in the full score for the flint and steel (the *briquet*) duplicates the triangle part above it—a moment of minor significance, perhaps, but clear illustration of the composer's linking of action and sound. The set used for this scene resembles that for the duet that begins Act III of *La muette de Portici*. As in Auber's opera, borders from the sides and from above narrowed the proscenium opening while a backdrop descended across the first *plan*. The box set also generated an intimacy that permitted the admission of subtle humor in the exchanges of the Anabaptist leaders and the stranger. A rapid return to the plain near Munster would be accomplished by the relatively simple removal of the components of the box set. The day could then proceed with the remarkable rise in the pitch of excitement as the Anabaptists prepare for the assault on Munster and the rising sun feeds a climactic frenzy.

The fourth-act Coronation Scene represents the very heart of the popular conception of grand opera. This scene (figure 7.13) is part of an elite class of monumental stage creations that includes the street procession in *La Juive,* the *auto da fé* in Verdi's *Don Carlos,* and the triumphal march from *Aïda.* Imagery and invention run rampant, but the keystone is the grandeur of it all: the grandeur in the dramaturgy, the music, and the staging.

In the opinion of Fétis, "It is for this scene that the master has reserved his most beautiful effects."[87] The famous "Coronation March," the *Marche du Sacre*, made extraordinary musical demands, and Meyerbeer knew it. A page of possible substitutions of instruments in the score was intended to assist when the ideal forces were not available.[88] Meyerbeer alternates martial *ritournelles* with contrasting sections of more lyrical character to provide variety and contrast in the unfolding spectacle. The musical dimensions match the visual dimensions as the following description will show.

Rather than rely on a straightforward view of Munster Cathedral with the high altar front and center on the stage, the designers chose a much more dynamic and complex approach (figures 7.13 and 7.14). The high altar is not even visible to the audience, since the principal nave of the cathedral runs in a perpendicular fashion, leading upstage and toward stage left. The backdrop, visible above the more forward scene components, captures the body of the

Figure 7.13. Lithograph of the Coronation Scene from *Le prophète*, Act IV (Bibliothèque de l'Opéra, Collection des estampes).

nave. Once again, as in *La Juive*, the lack of a fixed vanishing point allows the designer to suggest a space far more vast than that represented by the set itself.

1.) The backdrop represents the principal nave of the church—The perspective leads back to the distance, stage left. —2.) Ornamented balustrade. —3.) One ascends to the choir by three marble steps, which can only be seen in part by the audience, and the high altar which is completely out of sight. —4.) Principal nave. —5.) Three steps supposedly give access to a corridor which leads to the choir and the high altar. —6.) Cloth drops. —7.) *Chassis* that comprise the church. —One of the *chassis*, stage right "B," allows a part of the backdrop to be seen above it as well as those *chassis* which are situated on upstage *plans*. —The column (*chassis* "A") is copied on the backdrop.

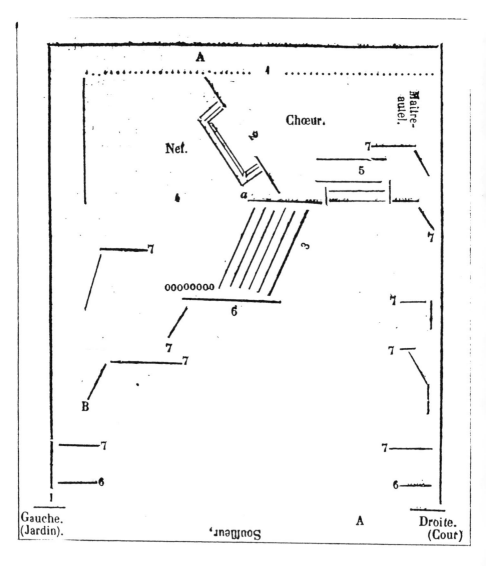

Figure 7.14. Act IV of *Le prophète*, diagram from the *livret de mise en scène*.

—The figuration [on the cloth drops] "6" is repeated, painted on the column (*chassis* "A"). —The stage band is situated at the top of the steps, designated [on the floor plan] with "ooooooooo."[89]

Presented in the *livret* is a simplified description of a set that clearly observed the greatest detail in its execution at the Opéra. The purpose of this simplification is, of course, to facilitate understanding of the stage directions which follow in the *livret*. It would be up to the designers and craftsmen of provincial and foreign theaters to examine their own resources and to adapt them to the overall requirements of the scene, both aesthetic and functional.

It is fascinating to see the concept of layering outlined in such an explicit manner. There are suggestions of coherence in the repetition of designs and representations of architectural components (e.g., columns) but there is little in the description that prepares one for the image we have in the engraving by Henri Valentin for *L'illustration* (shown above as figure 7.13). We know some of the tricks of the trade in the layering, the shading, the lighting, and the devices that rise from below, descend from above, and close in from the wings. Yet we must, in the end, see the art far more than the craft.

All of the March participants enter from the rear steps and proceed up the center-stage steps to the nave (figure 7.14): twenty soldiers, two by two, preceded by a leader; twelve children of the choir; four monks in violet robes, square caps, lace surplices, hooded capes, etc.; twelve more children of the choir, carrying censers; a herald-at-arms carrying the banner of the Prophet; eight pages; twelve grand electors carrying on velour cushions a crown, a scepter, the hand of justice, the seal of state, and other imperial ornaments; a baldachin carried over the Prophet, bare-headed and dressed in white, by the two heralds-at-arms; the three principal Anabaptists; three grand dignitaries followed by their pages; twelve magistrates in great cloaks of gold and ermine; three other dignitaries of the army followed by their pages; twelve buglers carrying instruments decorated with armorial aprons; soldiers to complete the march. In addition, there are other soldiers and large crowds of people filling the church to witness the event.

All possible resources are called into play to intensify display and diversity. For example, a dozen children of the choir move downstage to face the prompter's box. They sing a melody of appropriate simplicity, "Le voilà, le Roi Prophète," to organ accompaniment. Two of the children sing solos to the crowd, calling upon them to kneel. The simple melody introduced by the children becomes the foundation upon which a full choir builds, the orchestra enters, and the organ is augmented to four-hand scoring. Fétis wrote about the means and the ends of this portion of the scene:

> On the last note of the [children's] theme, a chorus of women is heard and joins with the song of the children; as it continues to develop, this melody is repeated by the choir of people; the organ offers all its riches . . . and the orchestra adds all its power with energetic chords. There is in this ensemble a grandeur, a solemnity, which seizes, surprises, and captivates the listener.[90]

The setting now provides the sublime vessel for the denouement. Integrated into this massive visual and musical creation is a dramatic focus in the person of Fidès, the mother of the Prophet. The figure of Fidès was one of Scribe's and Meyerbeer's greatest contributions to the pantheon of operatic characters. Fidès recognizes the Prophet, supposedly of divine origin, as her son. Freeze frames (both musical and dramatic climaxes) flow in succession as Fidès confronts Jean, and then reacts to each new insult and shock as her son proclaims her to be mad and coerces her into confessing her error. When their eyes meet, she falls onto one knee. Jean spreads his arms above her, a moment immortalized by the lithographers of the day.[91] It is Fidès who dominates the climax of the act vocally and dramatically, transforming her angry denunciation "I no longer have a son, alas!" (*je n'ai pas de fils, hélas!*) into an emotional complex of reactions. Suddenly the same phrase expresses the pain of her son's rejection, her anger, and her effort to convince the people of her error and thereby save her son's life. The stage setting, the arrangement and movement of the people, the music, and the dramatic developments all revolve around Fidès; she is the sum of the parts and arguably much more. Fétis voices the contemporary reaction.

> Passing alternatively through all of the parties in the massed chorus, and enriched by degrees with all the resources of instrumentation and all the art of composing, this theme, which was at first only a heartfelt cry, becomes an idea which leaves a profound emotion in the soul.[92]

Perhaps his words will be ours again when the vision, the complete *mise en scène*, receives the same respect in performance as the musical score.

Conclusion

One can scarcely overestimate the influence of French grand opera on the entire operatic scene of nineteenth-century Europe. Here lie the roots not only of further developments in France itself (some of them in reaction to what many came to consider grand opera's excesses) but of the concern Verdi showed over the production of his mature works too. Verdi's own participation in decisions affecting the décors and stage movement for *Aïda*, for example, is amply demonstrated by the way in which summaries printed in its scenic libretto reflect notes in Verdi's own hand concerning these matters.[93] Surely it is significant that *livrets de mise en scène* for Verdi's works began to appear only after the staging of his first French opera, *Les Vêpres siciliennes*.

It is also significant that the creators of French grand opera in effect produced the prototype of the Wagnerian *Gesamtkunstwerk*. Though not the product of a single creative genius, French grand opera nonetheless refused to give short shrift to any single element of the production in favor of any other element. Though the French "opera by committee" was strongly criticized even in its own time, Wagner was to prove that its fundamental principle— equality of the arts—was sound. Among his early works, *Rienzi* is the most Meyerbeerian, though it exaggerates grand opera characteristics in ways typical of an imitator rather than a generator. The seascapes and choral scenes of *The Flying Dutchman*, the processions and historically genuine sets and costumes of *Tannhäuser* and *Lohengrin*, the enlarged choral forces of *Parsifal,* and the whole of *Die Meistersinger* hearken back to the lessons of Paris of the 1830s. Meyerbeer posed the question—where but in Paris could one produce works like these?— and Wagner answered: Bayreuth.

CHAPTER EIGHT

Verdi's Operas
and Giuseppe Bertoja's Designs
at the Gran Teatro la Fenice, Venice

Evan Baker

> "Oh, the scenery could be so beautiful!"
> *Oh le decorazioni potrebbero essere così belle!*
>
> — Giuseppe Verdi,
> letter of 3 September 1856 to F. M. Piave

Among the Italian operatic composers of the nineteenth century, Verdi stands out as one of the few who possessed an extraordinary understanding of the visual elements in the creation of an opera. During the compositional process, Verdi often envisioned the locale in which the opera was set. This "scenic imagination" was a useful tool to him when he sketched out scenes and shaped the dramaturgy of the opera. Yet even with this gift, Verdi needed people of remarkable skill and talent who were able to put his ideas into practice.

During what he called his "years of the galleys," Verdi composed for theaters throughout Italy as well as in Paris, thus incrementally gaining much experience in the physical elements of operatic production. Several scenic designers collaborated with Verdi during the first two decades of his career in Italy, but only one was to give consistently excellent results. This designer was Giuseppe Bertoja (1808–1873), based at the Gran Teatro la Fenice in Venice. Under Verdi's direct supervision, Bertoja designed settings for nine different operas: seven for La Fenice, one for the Teatro Gallo, and one for the Teatro Grande in Trieste.[1]

The overt influences that Bertoja may have exerted on Verdi cannot be documented with absolute precision. Any influences, therefore, must be accounted as subtle. No correspondence between the composer and the designer appears to have survived, nor is Bertoja specifically mentioned in any other published documents relating to Verdi.[2] Bertoja's designs successfully realized the visual images that Verdi communicated through his librettist, Francesco Maria Piave, who functioned not only as his liaison to the theaters in Venice but also as stage director at the Gran Teatro la Fenice. It seems that Verdi was satisfied with Bertoja's first results presented on stage, beginning with *Ernani* in 1843. Bertoja's *Ernani* settings, however, were made for the Teatro Gallo's production that opened several months after the actual premiere at the Teatro la Fenice. After this successful production, Bertoja was to work with Verdi for fourteen years. This personal collaboration concluded with *Simon Boccanegra* in 1857, the last production personally supervised by Verdi at La Fenice.

Because of this successful collaboration, Verdi was able to express his visual ideas, in both general and specific terms, with the full knowledge that his intentions would be effectively translated into a living stage picture. Moreover, Bertoja provided Verdi with his first Italian opera in which plastic elements, such as stairs, platforms, and balconies, were to play an integral part of a production; these elements combined to create several distinct and separate acting spaces within the setting. The opera was *Rigoletto,* produced at La Fenice in 1850, and it included a house with a balcony in the first act and a tavern with two stories in the last scene of the opera. The use of platforms and balconies was to figure prominently once more with the production of *Simon Boccanegra* in 1857.

In no other theater did Verdi ever work with the same designer on so many operas. Not until Verdi began his collaboration with Girolamo Magnani for a production of *Simon Boccanegra* in Reggio Emilia shortly after the Venetian premiere did he find another genial collaborator who would satisfy his expectations of high standards in aesthetic tastes and in the quality of operatic production.

Although Verdi worked with other designers at La Scala (Milan), San Carlo (Naples), and the Teatro Argentina (Rome), they did not exert the same subtle influence as Bertoja did. None of these other theaters, except perhaps La Scala, had a scenographic team that was consistent in personnel and stylistic approach, so that working conditions were consequently less than ideal. Filippo Peroni, chief designer at the Teatro alla Scala from 1849 to 1868, never had the opportunity to work directly with Verdi. Pietro Venier first worked with Verdi in 1843 during the summer season in Sinigaglia and at La Fenice in Venice. In 1844 Venier collaborated again with the composer at the Teatro Argentina in Rome, this time for *I due Foscari.* At the same time, Venier joined the production staff at the Teatro San Carlo in Naples. He did not again work with Verdi since conditions never permitted him to work directly with the composer at the San Carlo after *Luisa Miller* in 1849.[3]

One team remained constant and ongoing, and that was in Venice with Bertoja. Verdi's continued exposure to Bertoja's work and his interaction with the technical team during the rehearsal process planted seeds of scenic experience that would blossom fully with his later great works produced at La Scala: *Aïda*, the revision of *Simon Boccanegra* (both designed by Girolamo Magnani, 1872 and 1881 respectively) and *Don Carlo* (designed by Carlo Ferrario, 1884), *Otello* (codesigned by Carlo Ferrario and Giovanni Zuccarelli, 1887), and *Falstaff* (Adolfo Hohenstein, 1893).[4]

Stage Design in Italy

In 1839, at the beginning of Verdi's operatic career, the scenic arts were in a state of flux in terms of artistic and technological development. The illustrious scenic designers and painters of the eighteenth century—the dynasties of the Galliari and Galli-Bibiena families, who revolutionized the scenic arts with their unique use of perspective—were either dead or retired from the profession. Alessandro Sanquirico, the great designer at the Teatro alla Scala, had retired in 1832.[5] Antonio Niccolini reigned supreme at the Teatro San Carlo in Naples with his designs, but followed Sanquirico into retirement ten years later.[6] Both Sanquirico and Niccolini generated a neoclassical style for the scenic arts—one that stressed realism and simple historical accuracy. Decoration with baroque ornamentation was no longer in fashion. Ferdinando Galli-Bibiena's invention of *veduta per angolo* (i.e., the placement of the vanishing perspective in various places within the scene rather than in one focal point at the center) was now standard practice. The art of perspective suggested through a series of flats on both sides of the stage leading to the central image of the backdrop was used to delineate and clarify the settings, rather than purely as a device to deceive the eye and to amaze the beholder.[7]

In the 1820s new artistic and aesthetic values began to shift the scenic styles from neoclassicism to Romanticism. The dependency upon historical verisimilitude for locales was reduced in favor of generalizations suggesting through form and color not only the locales but also the emotional atmosphere. Rigid control, clarity of form, and dependency on the sharpness of color were lessened. The backdrop remained the key visual point and, other than for an occasional piece of furniture, many details of the locales represented by settings were painted onto the same drop as well as onto the flats situated in the wings. Plastic elements, such as furniture, stairs, and practical units of balconies and platforms, did not, with certain exceptions, come into widespread use until the mid nineteenth century.[8]

The mechanisms of theatrical production had remained essentially unchanged since the construction of numerous Italian opera houses in the eighteenth century. Such theaters include the Teatro alla Scala, (1776; figure 8.1), the Teatro San Carlo, (constructed 1737 and rebuilt after a fire in 1817; figure 8.2), and the Gran Teatro la Fenice (1792; figure 8.3) to name only the largest houses. These, as well as the smaller theaters, all followed the same basic format in theatrical architecture and technology.[9] Each theater possessed a stage clearly demarcated by a proscenium arch with a forestage and an auditorium usually laid out in a horseshoe or oval shape with up to six galleries of boxes. The orchestra pit was placed at the front of the forestage and, it is important to note, at the same level as the parterre seats. This design obstructed sightlines, and problems were caused by the illumination from the oil-burning lamps of the music stands. The practice of sinking the pit below the level of the auditorium floor did not come into widespread use until the latter part of the nineteenth century.

All forms of drops could be placed in view of the audience, or, either through flying or rolling them up, they could be taken completely out of sight. The backdrops as well as "cutdrops" (painted drops cut into shapes such as trees,

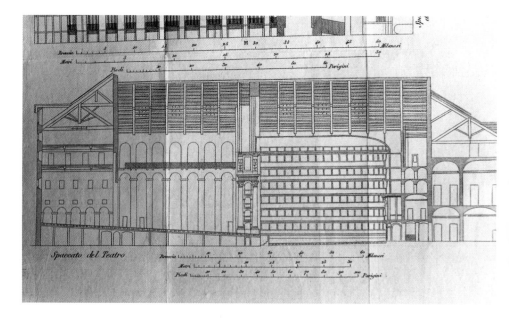

Figure 8.1. Cross-section of the Teatro alla Scala, Milan (1776). From Giulio Ferrario, *Storia e descrizione de'principali teatri antichi e moderne corredata di tavole col saggio sull'architettura teatrale di Mr. Patte illustrato con erudite osservazioni del chiarissimo architetto e pittore scenico Paolo Landriani* (Milan: dalla tipografia del dottor Giulio Ferrario, 1830).

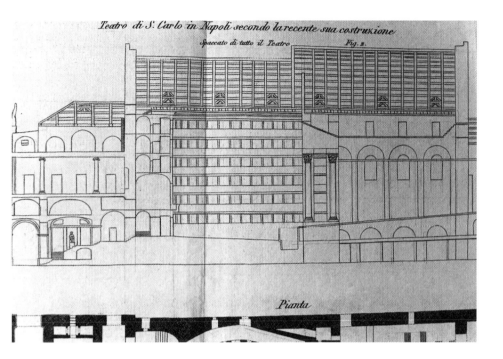

Figure 8.2. Cross-section of the Teatro San Carlo, Naples (constructed 1737 and rebuilt after a fire in 1817). From Ferrario, *Storia e descrizione de'principali teatri*.

foliage, caverns, or architectural forms such as arches, columns, gateways, to name several of many possibilities) were painted either on the floor of the stage between rehearsals or in a large room above the foyer of the auditorium. In many instances, the scenery was painted in a location outside the theater.[10] Upon the completion of the painting of the canvases, they were folded or rolled up and brought to the stage. Strips of wood (known as battens) were attached to the entire length of the top and bottom of the painted canvas thereby reducing wrinkles and rippling caused by wafts of air drifting across the stage. Rope lines were hung from the drums in the fly towers above the stage floor and threaded through pulleys to provide the means for raising, or "flying," the drops. These rope lines (usually four) were attached to the top battens.

To assist in the creation of the illusory perspective and in order to mask the offstage areas from the view of the public, flats (painted canvas on large vertical frames) were mounted onto wagons (also called chariots; see figure 8.4) that could slide into view from either side of the stage through slots in the stage floor. These painted flats served to extend the architectural vista or to delineate an area of nature within which, for example, an encampment might be seen. The

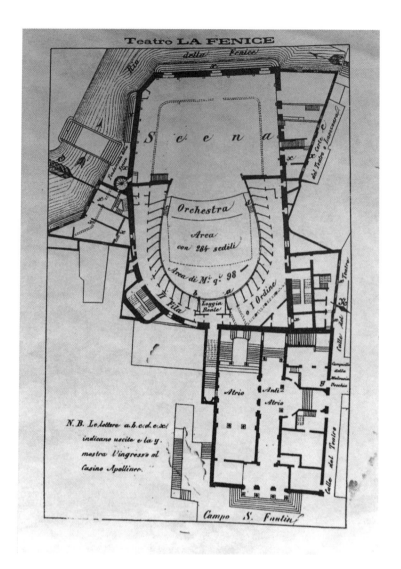

Figure 8.3. Plan of Gran Teatro la Fenice, Venice (1792). From [Giuseppe Civelli], *I teatri di Venezia* (Milan: Giuseppe Civelli, 1869).

mechanisms to which the flats were attached served a critical function: they concealed the lighting apparatus attached to the rear of the chariot. When gas lighting was introduced into Italian theaters during the 1840s, strips of gas lamps were flown above the stage floor between the wings; consequently, painted canvas borders were flown to perform a masking function as well. Strips of gas lamps also were placed on the edge of the forestage (footlights).[11]

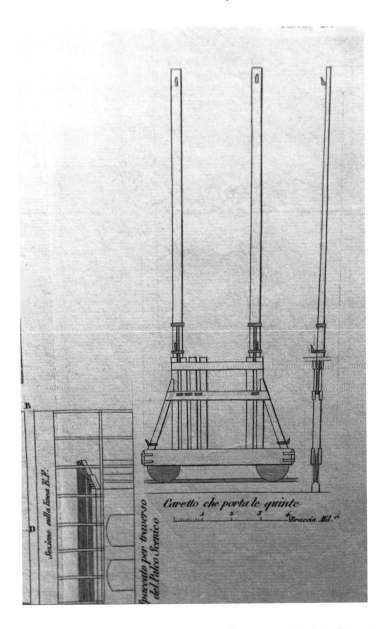

Figure 8.4. "Chariot" from Ferrario, *Storia e descrizione de'principali teatri.*

All changes of scenery and settings during the course of an act took place in full view (*a vista*) of the public. It was not until Wagner used the curtain, permitting hidden changes of settings without disturbing the mood already created, that the raising and lowering of the curtain during the act became a standard practice. The technique was first used regularly at his Festival Theater in Bayreuth.

Verdi's Early Operatic Productions

With the exception of the extraordinary documentation pertaining to the planning for the production of *Macbeth* at the Teatro alla Pergola in 1847, little original material seems to have survived from Verdi's supervision of early operatic productions at the Teatro alla Scala in the years from 1839 through 1845.[12] These operas were *Oberto, conte di San Bonifacio* (1839), *Un giorno di regno* (1840), *Nabucodonosor* (1842), and *I Lombardi alla prima crociata* (1843).[13] No designs for the operas prior to *I Lombardi* are known to exist. The productions up to and including *Nabucco* were probably prepared using existing generic scenery taken from the impresario's warehouse, with retouches provided by local scenic artists. This practice was used in the first series of performances for new operas whose fates were uncertain.[14] *I Lombardi* was Verdi's first opera to receive completely new settings—a locale for a setting is specified in the libretto: the Piazza San Ambrogio in Milan with a view of the church of the same name.

According to the libretti for these first performances, the painters were Baldassare Cavallotti and Domenico Menozzi, who succeeded the great Alessandro Sanquirico as primary scenic designers and artists for La Scala.[15] Unfortunately, little is known about Cavalotti and Menozzi.

Eyewitness accounts of the early Verdian productions are lacking. The decorations were probably taken from generic drops, wings, and borders. For Verdi's *Nabucco,* it appears that, for reasons of economy, the settings from Antonio Cortesi's ballet of the same name were extensively refurbished and reused with apparent success by the same designers. One review noted:

> The scenery, costumes, and decorations were magnificent, worthy of the opera, the composer, La Scala, and worthy of the proud Babylonians. The triumph was singular, resounding, and experienced to the fullest by everyone.[16]

In his autobiographical sketch, Verdi recalled a conversation with Bartolomeo Merelli, the impresario of the Teatro alla Scala:

> [Merelli said] "we will give this *Nabucco*: However, you must consider that I will have very heavy expenses for the other new operas; I cannot have costumes or sets specially made for *Nabucco*!...and I'll have to patch up as best I can the most suitable material I find in the storeroom." . . .
> The costumes, patched together in haste, proved splendid!...

Old sets, repaired by the painter Perroni [*sic*], have an extraordinary effect: the first scene of the temple in particular produces such a great effect that the applause of the audience lasts for a good ten minutes![17]

Some of this narrative is a good story albeit erroneous and nothing more than an embellishment of selective memories on Verdi's part. The painter Peroni was not engaged at La Scala until 1849, and he never worked directly with Verdi during his career at the opera house. That the opera production was based entirely on the earlier ballet is doubtful. The ballet settings were used only for the 1838 season and, given Merelli's notorious parsimony, it is difficult to believe that in the intervening four years the settings were not painted over and recycled for other productions in the theater. In those days, four years was an extraordinarily long time for a production to remain in storage. Merelli was likely to have reused and painted over the scenery for other operas and ballets.[18]

Merelli attempted to cut costs too often, and artistic liberties were taken with Verdi's operas. These included the reordering of scenes and acts, and the ignoring of explicit directions for the staging of the operas. As early as 1842, problems appeared in the quality of stagings to such an extent that rumblings of discontent were noted in a review: "If Verdi had been present at the mounting of his opera, without doubt things would have gone better and the applause would have been greater and he would have won greater glory."[19] Production standards continued to drop and became so low that, after hearing of a wretched production of *Attila* on 26 December 1846, Emanuele Muzio wrote in a letter the following day to Verdi's patron Antonio Barezzi in Busseto:

Furore! Furore! Furore! *Attila* raised the roof, as the journalists say. . . .
    The *mise en scène* was wretched. The sun rose before the music indicated the sunrise. The sea, instead of being stormy and tempestuous, was calm and without a ripple. There were hermits without any huts; there were priests but no altar; in the banquet scene Attila gave a banquet without any lights . . . and when the storm came the sky remained serene and limpid as on the most beautiful spring day. Everyone (aloud and in our hearts) cursed Merelli for having treated *Attila* so badly.[20]

Consequently, Verdi was enraged, and in a letter to his publisher Ricordi dated 29 December 1846, he expressed his anger over poorly staged productions of his works.

I have more than enough examples to persuade me that here [Scala] they do not know how, or do not want, to mount operas—my operas in particular—in a suitable manner. I cannot forget the wretched staging of *I Lombardi, Ernani, I due Foscari...* etc.... I have another proof of this before my eyes with *Attila*.[21]

At the same time, he prohibited the immediate production of his newest creation, *Macbeth*, at La Scala. As long as Merelli remained impresario of La Scala, Verdi refused to enter the opera house again or personally to supervise the stagings of his works. Merelli was already having difficulties with the governing authorities, for they cited him for not "having control" over the various departments dealing with production.[22]

Quality at La Scala continued to suffer. During Verdi's self-exile, which lasted until 1869, he never worked with Filippo Peroni, the leading scenographer of the theater. Peroni retired in 1867 and was succeeded by his assistant, Carlo Ferrario.[23] By this time, Giulio Ricordi, Verdi's publisher, had secured complete control over the production process at La Scala. Ricordi created an ideal environment in which the composer could stage his newly revised version of *La forza del destino.* Verdi relented, and reentered La Scala, which then became the center for his future artistic creations.

Verdi's primary theater in southern Italy was the Teatro San Carlo. During Verdi's affiliation with the Teatro San Carlo, a single production team remained in control. The chief designer, Pietro Venier, was already known to the composer from previous collaborations, first in Sinigaglia during the summer of 1843, and then at La Fenice with another production of *I Lombari* followed by *Ernani* in 1844. *I due Foscari* provided another collaboration with Verdi, this time at the the Teatro Argentina in Rome in November 1844. Shortly thereafter, Venier became chief designer at the San Carlo and collaborated with the composer for the settings of *Luisa Miller* in 1849. The conditions were unfavorable for Verdi, and he did not return to stage any of his operas in Naples until 1858.[24]

Gran Teatro la Fenice, Venice

Verdi made his first appearance at the Gran Teatro la Fenice in Venice in 1843. Counted today as one of the grandest and greatest Italian opera houses, the Gran Teatro la Fenice was constructed in the Venetian quarter of San Fantin to the designs of Giannantonio Selva and opened in 1792.[25] Verdi knew La Fenice in two forms: after a major conflagration gutted the theater in 1836, and after extensive renovations in 1854 (illustrated with a scene from what appears to be the final act of *La traviata;* figure 8.5).

Seating more than 1,900 persons, the auditorium of La Fenice consisted of five galleries and followed the form of a typical Italian opera house, the horseshoe shape. From the rail of the orchestra pit to the back of the auditorium measured 44.3 feet (13.5 meters); the width at its widest (from gallery rail to rail) was 59.1 feet (18 meters). The ceiling was 49.3 feet (15 meters) from the sloping floor of the auditorium. The orchestra pit (not to be lowered until the 1880s), on the same level as the parterre, could seat up to seventy musicians and had a space of 8.2 feet (2.5 meters) between the audience and the forestage.[26]

XVI   LA FENICE AI TEMPI DEL « SIMON BOCCANEGRA »

Figure 8.5. Interior view of Gran Teatro la Fenice (1854).

The stage had six sets of wings. The width from wall to wall measured 88.7 feet (27 meters), and the depth upstage from the proscenium arch 59.1 feet (18 meters). The forestage spanned the width of the proscenium opening, 42.7 feet (13 meters), and extended downstage 11.5 feet (3.5 meters). The height of the proscenium opening measured 36.1 feet (11 meters). A distance of 49.3 feet (15 meters) spanned the space from the stage floor to the fly gallery (figure 8.6).[27]

It is important to note that the entire theater was constructed well above the ground level; this required that all the scenery, which was brought in by gondolas and small barges, be hoisted above into the stage area. Consequently, large pieces of scenery were avoided for reasons of economy and practicality.

The backstage contained all the latest theatrical machinery, including traps, and the flies had ample room to allow the raising of canvas drops. The floor was equipped with sliding wagons mounted on tracks in the subbasement and extending through seven sets of slots in each wing on both sides of the stage. Following the convention of the period, the floor was raked to enhance the illusion of perspective. When Verdi began his career, stage lighting consisted of oil and candles.[28] Gas lighting was installed at the end of 1844, in time for the opening of the winter season with Bellini's *Norma* on 26 December.[29]

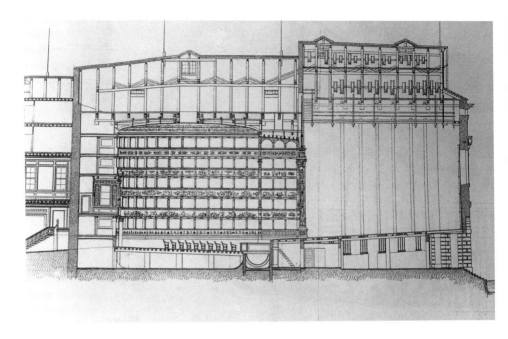

Figure 8.6. Cross-section of La Fenice (1846). From Meduna, *Il Teatro la Fenice.*

Prior to Verdi's arrival in 1843, the chief designer of La Fenice was Francesco Bagnara, assisted by Pietro Venier. After Venier departed in 1844 for Rome and Naples, Giuseppe Bertoja took over the assisting position. Bagnara remained as supervising designer for several years and retired in favor of Bertoja, who already did all the designing and the supervising of the painting of the drops and scenery.[30] Luigi Caprara was the chief machinist, and he was responsible for the construction of the sets, the setup and takedown of the production, and the management of the production during the performances. He was also responsible for the lighting, the special effects, and the maintenance of the stage machinery.

While they were creating the designs and scenery, the production team had little guidance from the music until well after Verdi had arrived in Venice, since they did not hear much, if any, of it. Verdi completed his orchestration after the rehearsals were well underway. It is unlikely that Bertoja cared, since the librettist Piave was the one who told him what the settings should look like. A manuscript of the libretto probably was available when needed. A detailed listing (scenario) of the settings, props, and costumes prepared by Piave for the impresarios, the local authorities, and the production team sufficed.

The settings must have been prepared at breakneck speed since many of the scenarios were written only a month before the premiere of the opera. The scenic artists had to work quickly, if they were to paint the large drops required for La Fenice's stage in time for the final stage rehearsals. An average of four to seven new productions had to be prepared for the primary season of the theatrical year, carnival, which opened on 26 December and ran in repertory until late March.[31] Piave was certainly in constant touch with the production team, particularly in planning for the new works. Not every new opera received a completely new production; certainly several important scenes may have had new pieces of scenery while the remainder of the production was fleshed out with generic settings. This was necessary for saving both time and, most importantly, money.[32]

At the time of the premiere of *Ernani* in 1844, there were three working theaters in the immediate vicinity of the Gran Teatro la Fenice: (1) the Apollo (figure 8.7), (2) the Malibran (formerly the San Giovanni Gristostomo, figure 8.8), and (3) the Gallo (formerly the Teatro San Benedetto, figure 8.9).[33] The last named theater was managed by Antonio Gallo, Verdi's friend and business colleague, who produced short seasons that included revivals of Verdi's works, thereby competing with La Fenice.

Verdi and the Teatro la Fenice

Verdi composed and personally staged five operas for the Teatro la Fenice: *Ernani* (1843), *Attila* (1845), *Rigoletto* (1851), *La traviata* (1853), and *Simon Boccanegra* (1857).[34] For each of these works, Francesco Maria Piave not only prepared the libretto but also functioned for the most part as Verdi's personal liaison with the board of directors (*presidenza*) and with the production staff of La Fenice: that staff consisted chiefly of the same Francesco Maria Piave, who also served as the stage director; Giuseppe Bertoja, the designer and scenic artist; and Luigi Caprara, the *macchinista* responsible for the actual production.

What is not so well known, however, is that Verdi supervised several other operas in Venice as well as one further production with the same production team in Trieste. These productions included the first Venetian performances of *Giovanna d'Arco* at La Fenice, as well as *I Lombardi* and *I due Foscari* at the Teatro Gallo.[35] With the same team, Verdi staged *Stiffelio* on the other side of the Adriatic in the Teatro Grande at Trieste during 1850.[36]

Prior to Verdi's arrival in Venice, *Nabucco* (26 December 1842) and *I Lombardi* (which followed exactly one year later) had been staged at La Fenice. Both productions were designed by Pietro Venier. Neither Bertoja nor Piave was associated with the Venetian team until early 1844 when Venier left for Rome and Naples.[37] Press reports were favorable for both new productions, and *I Lombardi* received additional notice owing to the novelty of the gas lighting system installed in La Fenice during the summer of 1843.

Verdi was already known to Bertoja, who had created the settings (together with Giuseppe Badiale) for the successful revival on 11 January 1840 of Verdi's

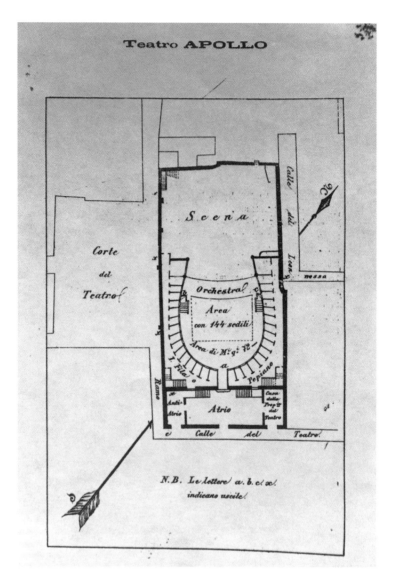

Figure 8.7. Teatro Apollo, Venice (1864). From Civelli, *I teatri di Venezia.*

first work, *Oberto, conte di San Bonifacio,* and for a new production of *I Lombardi* on 26 December 1843. Both were given at the Teatro Regio in Turin.[38] Of the Verdi operas produced in Venice from 1843 through 1857, Bertoja designed more than seventeen productions for La Fenice and the Teatro Gallo.[39] Although Verdi was involved with only eight, he nevertheless was aware of other productions through correspondence, theatrical newspapers, and word of mouth from friends in Venice.

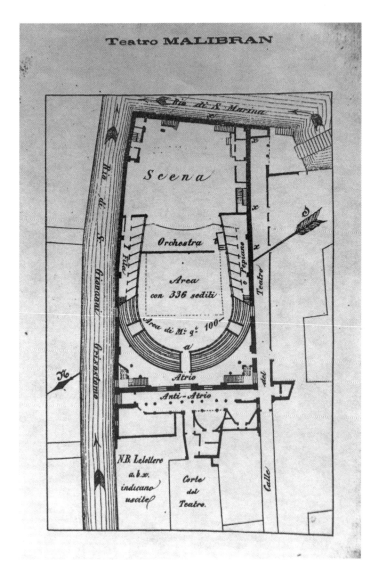

Figure 8.8. Teatro Malibran, Venice (1864). From Civelli, *I teatri di Venezia.*

The first Verdi opera to be produced in Venice after its phenomenal success at La Scala was *Nabucco*, which was given for the first time at La Fenice on 26 December 1842. In Sinigaglia, Verdi worked with the impresario Alessandro Lanari on the production of *I Lombardi* (29 July 1843) with stage settings by Pietro Venier.[40] From this collaboration, correspondence between La Fenice and Verdi regarding future possibilities began.[41] It is probable that during this time Verdi discussed the staging and settings of *I Lombardi* with Venier in prepa-

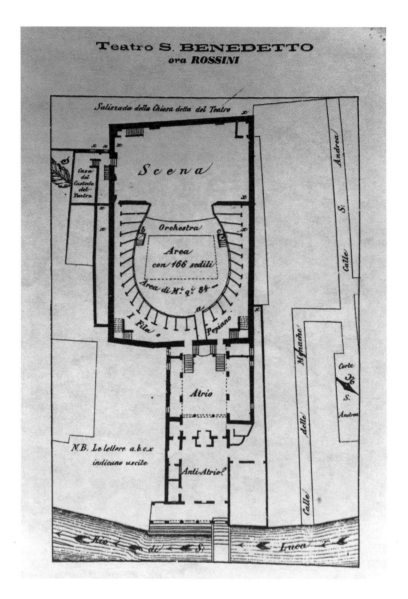

Figure 8.9. Teatro Gallo, Venice (1864). From Civelli, *I teatri di Venezia*.

ration for its Venetian premiere five months later. Through this contact, Verdi developed an understanding of the scenic possibilities for La Fenice. At the same time, he most likely laid down the groundwork for the production that would open the 1843–44 carnival season at the Gran Teatro la Fenice.

Verdi arrived in Venice 23 November 1843 to supervise the musical and staging rehearsals for *I Lombardi,* which opened on 26 December.[42] Though the reaction of the press was negative, the opera received a total of seventeen performances (twelve in the space of twenty-two days).[43] During this time, Verdi continued to work on his first new opera for La Fenice, *Ernani*.

The settings for *Ernani* were probably planned and executed sometime after the premiere of *I Lombardi*.[44] Difficulties with the production ensued during the final rehearsals, and Verdi and Piave were displeased with the results. On 1 March they signed a letter of protest to the *presidenza*. As a consequence, the posters that had been printed to advertise the premiere noted that several of the settings were not finished in time and begged the indulgence of the public. Despite these difficulties, the opera premiered on 6 March and was a resounding success. Unfortunately, the reviews of the performances offer only sparse observations relating to the settings.[45]

Bertoja worked on this particular production as an assistant; Venier created most of the settings. For a revival in 1846, Bertoja interleaved several new decorations for the production.[46] It is probable that these designs were first used for a production of the same opera at the Teatro Gallo several months after the premiere of the opera at La Fenice in 1844. Bertoja's work for that production was praised by the *Gazzetta musicale di Milano:*

> Antonio Gallo . . . has without regard to expense provided everything to contribute to a great success, and care was given to the magnificent costumes and scenery for which the skillful Signor Bertoja was invited to display his rare and beautiful talent.[47]

Verdi returned to Venice to stage a production of *I due Foscari* for his friend Antonio Gallo at the theater of the same name. The production opened successfully on 30 March 1845. Bertoja again was engaged to create the settings, for which one design exists in the Museo Correr. Verdi was pleased with the results, and so was the leading critic in Venice, Tommaso Locatelli:

> The production has been staged with much honor; Bertoja produced not only two beautiful backdrops—one of a hall of the Foscari with excellent effect and the other a small piazza—in which the small [stage] space did not interfere with the perfect illusion of perspective.[48]

Attila

Bertoja's direct relationship with Verdi began with the preparations for the production of the composer's second new opera for La Fenice, *Attila*. After the signing of the contracts and the selecting of the story of Attila, Verdi engaged in intense discussions about the visual aspects of the opera. Before Piave began writing the libretto, Verdi demonstrated his visual acuity in a letter to the poet dated 12 April 1845:

The curtain must go up to reveal Aquileja in flames, with a chorus of people, and a chorus of Huns. . . .

The first act should open in Rome, and instead of doing the banquet on stage, let it be off stage, and on stage, Azzio [Ezio] meditates on the events, etc..., etc...,

It would be magnificent in the third act that the whole scene have [Pope] Leo on the Aventine hills and the battle below. . . .

I recommend that you study this subject hard, and keep everything clearly in mind; the period, the characters, etc..., etc....[49]

Verdi wrote to Lanari, who was functioning as the impresario for La Fenice, stressing the importance of the scenery, saying: "Don't leave anything out regarding the decorations."[50] In a letter dated 29 September 1845, Lanari wrote to the directors of La Fenice passing on Verdi's specific wishes for the decorations and his request that the manuscript of the libretto be sent to the design team.

Maestro Verdi, who feels especially strongly, advises me that for several of the scenes he would like to fill the entire stage and, to use his own words, he says, "what I would like to be sublime is the second of scene six [second part of the Prologue], which is the beginning of the city of Venice. Let the sunrise be done well, since I want to express it with the music."[51]

On 8 October, the administration of La Fenice passed these instructions on to Bertoja. Amidst what must have been exhausting work for the new production of Verdi's *Giovanna d'Arco*, a revival of *Ernani* (for which the designer contributed a new setting), two new operas, and five ballets, Bertoja began the designing and painting of the settings for *Attila*. All the works required new or recycled settings, flats, and drops.

In mid November the detailed description of the settings arrived from Piave, and formal approval from the theater directors was given to Bertoja to commence work on the designs for the opera. The Prologue, in two parts, is described in the libretto:

Piazza of Aquileja. Night, which is almost over, is illuminated by a great number of torches. Everywhere there is a miserable pile of ruins. Here and there flames can be seen rising up, the terrible remains of four days of fire.

Rio-alto in the Adriatic lagoon. Here and there are shanties rising on pile-dwellings, interconnecting by long wooden boards propped up on boats. Downstage is an altar, in the guise of a stone pile, dedicated to San Giacomo. Farther upstage can be discerned a bell attached to a wooden cabin, which later became the belfry of San Giacomo. The darkness is dissipating amidst stormy clouds. A rosy glow is gradually increasing until (up to the end of the scene) the rays of sunlight suddenly inundate everything, adorning a serene, calm blue sky. Slow bell strokes greet the morning [figure 8.10].

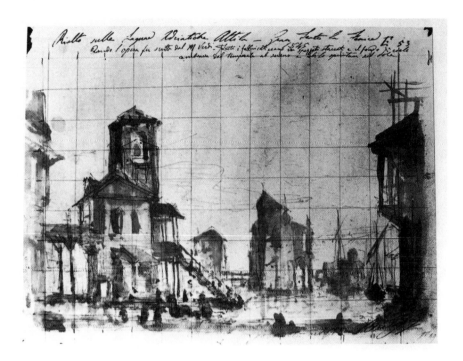

Figure 8.10. Rio-alto in the Adriatic lagoon, *Attila* (Prologue, part 2). Design by Giuseppe Bertoja, 1846 (Venice, Museo Correr).

For these scenes of destruction and desolation in the Prologue, Bertoja drew two designs. One was definitely used for the production (that shown in figure 8.10), and it was noted by the designer, *Rialto sulle Lagune Adriatiche Attila—Gran teatro la Fenice*. Below this inscription, another hand recorded:

> As written in the opera by Maestro Verdi—All the buildings were [constructed] in separate pieces, and the background of the sky changed from the storm to the serene sunrise.[52]

This observation reflected Verdi's instructions noted above in the letter from Lanari to the directors of La Fenice.

Verdi arrived in Venice on 6 December to complete the composition of *Attila*. Although ill much of the time, and though he later claimed not to have participated in any of the rehearsals for *Giovanna d'Arco,* the composer must have exercised at least some nominal supervision over the production.[53] Certainly his closest collaborator, Piave, functioned as his representative during the staging rehearsals of the opera, and Bertoja probably had some discussions with Verdi about the settings and lighting for *Giovanna, Ernani,* and *Attila.* *Giovanna* opened the carnival season on 26 December 1845, and *Ernani* was revived two weeks later. Bertoja's new setting for the tomb scene in *Ernani* was interleaved into the production from the previous year by Pietro Venier.

The next two months found Verdi recovering from bouts of bad health and completing the composition of *Attila.* Staging rehearsals began in late February, and the final dress rehearsal took place on the afternoon of 16 March. The premiere of *Attila* the following night was a rousing success, although there was a small hitch in the production. During the banquet scene in the second act, something went wrong with the candles on stage. Before they were extinguished at the conclusion of the act, a horrendous odor permeated the stage and drifted into the auditorium. Tommaso Locatelli, critic for the *Gazzetta priviliegata di Venezia,* commented that "The scourge of God ought not be the scourge of the nose." (*Il flagello di Dio non si faccia il flagello de'nasi.*)[54]

Bertoja's skills and talents were tacitly acknowledged through the publication in early 1847 of a colored lithograph (albeit without attribution) of the second scene of the Prologue, complete with a stage floor plan (simplified in figure 8.11), in *L'Italia musicale.*[55] The first scene was primarily represented by a single, large painted backdrop hanging behind the third set of wings in the stage. Behind the drop stood the second scene (that shown in figure 8.10).

The design sought to recreate the sense of desolation and destruction both through its pictorial reproduction of ruined and burned out structures and through its effective combination of the painted earth colors and the flickering, yellowish glow cast by the gas lighting. Bertoja juxtaposed expressive colors and a chiaroscuro effect to suggest the illusion of smoldering ruins. The decorations for both parts of the Prologue benefited greatly from the flickering gas lights. These scenic effects assisted not only in augmenting the sense of despair in the text and in Verdi's music, but also in projecting the cold brutality of Attila himself.

Stiffelio and *Rigoletto*

Verdi next collaborated with Bertoja on his new opera, *Stiffelio.* With Piave's assistance, Verdi personally staged *Stiffelio,* which premiered on 16 November 1850 at the Teatro Grande in Trieste. Although Pietro Pupilli was the house designer for the Teatro Grande, Bertoja was brought in to design and paint the churchyard scene in Act II, scene ii.[56] During this period Verdi doubtless discussed with Piave the forthcoming production of his *Luisa Miller* (26 December 1850) at La Fenice, and perhaps with Bertoja as well. At the

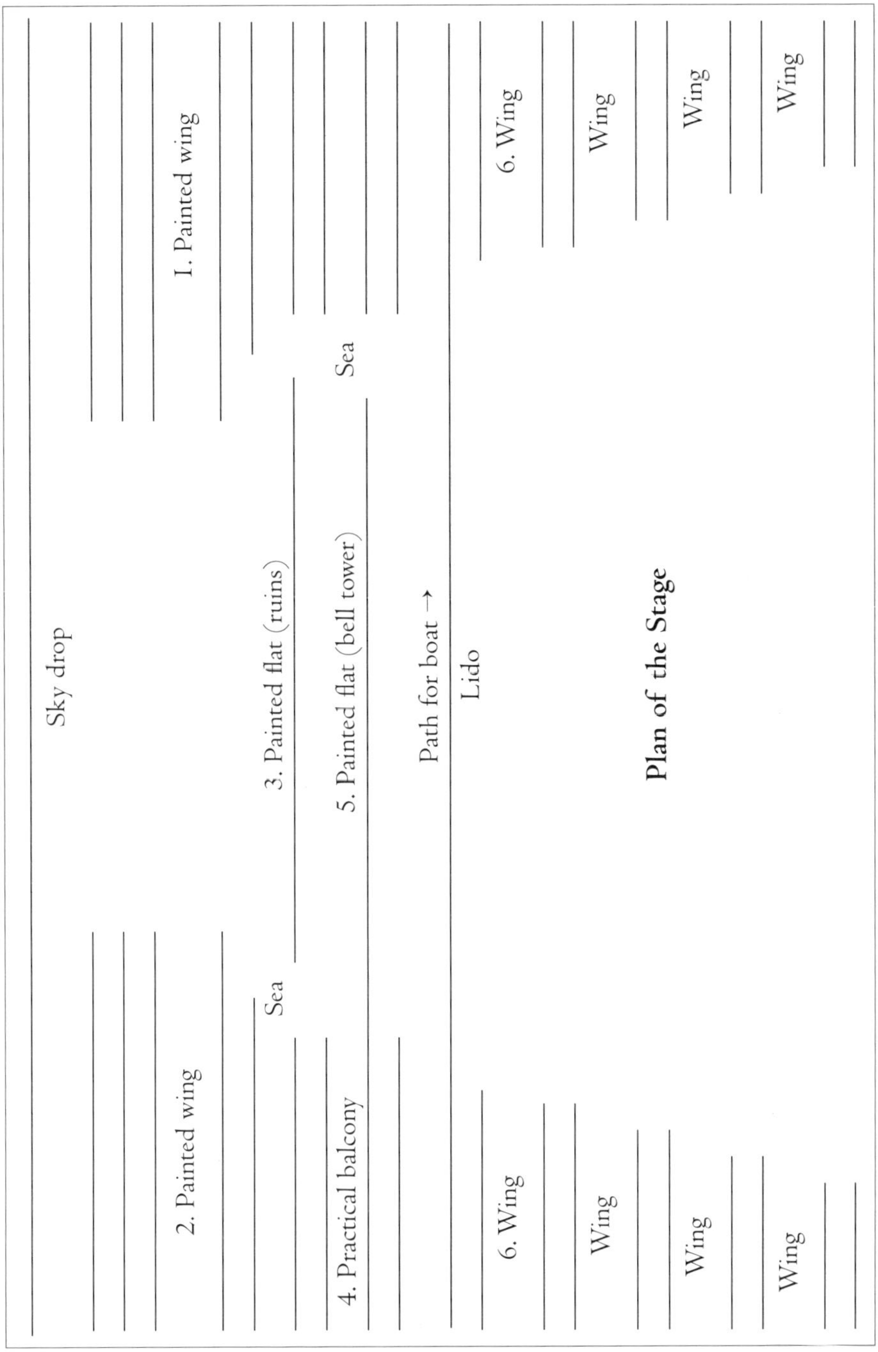

Sky drop

1. Painted wing

2. Painted wing

Sea

3. Painted flat (ruins)

Sea

4. Practical balcony

5. Painted flat (bell tower)

Path for boat →

Lido

6. Wing

6. Wing

Wing

Wing

Wing

Wing

Wing

Wing

Plan of the Stage

Figure 8.11. Floor plan for *Attila* (Prologue, part 2).

same time, Verdi was in the midst of composing *Rigoletto,* and it seems likely that he would have also discussed with them the staging and design possibilities for this opera.

The use of settings in a multilevel format as an integral part of staging probably stemmed from the composer's conferences with the Venetian production team. Verdi's scenic art, in Venice at least, began to evolve with the enlargement of settings.

On 5 October 1850, the directors of La Fenice met to finalize plans for the upcoming carnival season. In that meeting, it was confirmed that the third new opera of the season would be by Verdi. After all the difficulties with censorship were overcome, that opera was to be *Rigoletto.* It was further decided that Bertoja would continue his work for the theater as designer and painter.[57]

Several weeks later, Verdi passed through Venice on his way to Trieste for rehearsals of *Stiffelio.* As Piave was to join him, it is probable that Bertoja spoke directly with Piave and Verdi about his ideas for what, at first, was to have been an opera set in fifteenth-century Paris and entitled *La maledizione.* Plans for the opening production of the season, *Luisa Miller,* were discussed as well. During this time Bertoja had his hands full: he was busily preparing new drops for several ballets, retouching and repainting the settings for the revivals of *Lucia di Lammermoor* and *Allan Cameron,* and creating the settings for another new opera, *Fernando Cortez.*[58] In addition, Bertoja created one setting for the new opera at the Teatro Grande in Trieste, Verdi's *Stiffelio.*

Preparations for the production of what was to become *Rigoletto* certainly began with Piave's informing Bertoja in mid November of the requirements for the settings. Even during the difficult period for the transformation of the libretto from *La maledizione* to *Il duca di Vendome* in the beginning of December, the description of the settings remained consistent, except for minor differences. When the libretto finally evolved into *Rigoletto* in late January 1851, as far as Bertoja was concerned, the settings remained consistent as well. The only noticeable change was for the concluding scene, in which the city of Mantua (instead of Paris) was to be seen in the distance.

With the production of *Rigoletto* on 14 March 1851 at La Fenice, the scenic styles for Verdi's operas evolved through the use of plastic decorations. Multilevel platforms and stairs became an integral part of the stage settings, specifically for Rigoletto's house in the second scene of the first act and for Sparafucile's tavern in the final scene of the opera.[59] The production team were confident in their ability both to create splendid settings for the new opera and to construct and set up the multilevel pieces of scenery in the theater. Piave wrote to Verdi on 21 January 1851: "I have already given all the specifications for the decorations which will be magnificent, and the young Caprara wants to prove his ability with the practical [scenic units], etc. etc."[60]

Several days later on 26 January, after the final approval for the libretto of *Rigoletto* was granted by the authorities, Piave joyfully wrote about the news to Verdi. By this time, the final instructions for the settings had been given to

Bertoja and Caprara, and Piave indicated that "neither he nor Verdi needed to concern themselves any longer" (*non abbiamo più pensieri*) with the requirements of the settings.[61]

Verdi remained concerned, however, not simply about the settings but about the lighting as well. The sound and lighting effects, of which thunder and lightning played a significant role for the final scene of the opera, were vitally important for they had to be coordinated with the music. In response to Piave's previous letter, Verdi wrote on 31 January:

> I don't need you to do any more verses. What needs to be done are the changes in the scenic indications, above all the tempest in the third act, because I have written for the thunder, lightning flashes, and the thunderbolts etc... etc... all to take place precisely, and I was not always able to follow your indications. Our friend of the "wood nymphs" [nickname for the stage machinist Caprara] will have to accept my ideas and make the thunder and lightning occur precisely according to the music and not (as usually done) by chance. I would like the lightning bolts to transpire as a "zigzag" on the upstage drop, etc... etc... and many other such things. You will tear your hair out (as usual) but on the evening of the performance, you will say "he was right" provided there not be a fiasco.[62]

Verdi was referring to the thunder and lightning flashes which were to occur throughout the final scene of the opera. Each lightning flash and stroke of thunder—even the rain—received a specific place in the score, particularly during the great trio of Gilda-Maddalena-Sparafucile. The final flashes of lightning were scored upon Rigoletto's discovery of Gilda:

> A human body! [*lightning flash*] My daughter! God! My daughter! Ah no! It's impossible! She's on her way to Verona! It was a vision! [*final lightning flash*]

> (*È umano corpo! Mia figlia! Dio! mia figlia! Ah no! è imposibil! per Verona è in via! Fu vision!*)

By this time, Bertoja was completing whatever work was required for *Lucia di Lammermoor* as well as supervising the assembling of generic settings for a ballet that premiered on 6 February. Only then could he devote his full attention to designing and painting the settings for *Rigoletto.*

The final version of the two scenes in the libretto reads as follows:

> Act I, scene 2: *The end of a blind alley. To the left, a modest-looking house with a little courtyard surrounded by walls. In the courtyard a tall, thick tree and a marble bench; in the wall a door giving on the street; above the wall, a usable balcony,*

supported by arches. The door of the upper floor opens on this balcony, which one reaches by a stairway opposite us. To the right of the street are the very high wall of the garden of Ceprano's palace and one flank of the building. It is night.

Act III, scene 2: *The right bank of the Mincio. To the left, a half-ruined, two-story house; the front of it, facing the spectator, has a great arch, through which one can see a rustic inn on the ground floor, and a rough stair that leads to the loft, where a bed can be seen, beyond a balcony without shutters. In the side toward the road there is a door that opens in; the wall is full of crevices, so that from outside one can easily see what is going on within. The rest of the scene represents a deserted part of the Mincio, which flows in the back beyond a half-ruined parapet; beyond the river lies Mantua. It is night.*[63]

Bertoja drew several sketches for each scene. For Rigoletto's house, there exists a preparatory study that included on the left side of the sheet a small sketch indicating the height requirements for constructing the street-level and balcony-level platforms.[64] Comparing this scene with the final scene showing Sparafucile's tavern reveals striking similarities (figures 8.12 and 8.13).[65] Each house is positioned on stage right, each with an extended balcony. The "wall" appears in each scene as well.

Figure 8.12. Rigoletto's house. *Rigoletto* (Act I, scene ii). Design by Giuseppe Bertoja, 1850 (Venice, Museo Correr).

Figure 8.13. Sparafucile's inn. *Rigoletto* (Act III, scene ii). Design by Giuseppe Bertoja, 1850 (Venice, Museo Correr).

For Rigoletto's house in the cul-de-sac, a painted tree on a cutout canvas drop hung from the flies in front of the house. The archway providing the entry into Rigoletto's house as well as the windows were all painted onto either one or two flats attached to the front of the platform. The balcony trellises and railing were painted onto a separate flat. To the left of the house, two painted wing flats provided the illusion of adjoining buildings. Another set of painted wing flats, using the illusion of perspective, provided more buildings to the right of the house. A blue sky drop farther upstage completed the scene.

For the final scene, the platforms and steps used for the house were utilized for the tavern. A painted flat provided an arch that opened into the tavern itself; upstage was another flat with a painted fireplace, dishes, and cabinets. To the right was a doorway to the steps leading to the second story of the tavern. The right side of the structure was another set of painted wall flats with a door attached to the structure. A low and long painted flat to the right and upstage of the tavern depicted a wall on the bank of the Mincio river. On the wing flats (stage left) were painted trees, foliage, and perhaps a ruined building. Several large trees were painted onto a large, cutout drop hanging from the flies adjacent to the tavern. Farther upstage was a drop depicting Mantua and the bridge leading into the town itself.

Verdi continued to be concerned about the preparations for the rehearsals of *Rigoletto.* He wrote to Piave on 5 February regarding the music for the singers but also ordered him to "check the settings, costumes, and the machinery" to ensure all was in order.[66] Upon arrival in Venice on 19 February, Verdi immediately began rehearsals, and the triumphant premiere followed on 12 March 1851. The reviews were positive, and one reported that the impresario Lasina "spared no expense for the production of this opera, which was accompanied with every precision and magnificence."[67] Again, Bertoja's style augmented Verdi's music and, together with Caprara's lighting effects in the third act, brought out many of the opera's dramatic effects. A fairly accurate reproduction of the scene is the famous representation printed on the title page of the first edition of the piano-vocal score published in 1851 (figure 8.14).

Figure 8.14. *Rigoletto.* Vignette from Act III, scene ii as part of the title page of the first edition of piano-vocal score published by Ricordi in 1851.

La traviata

The next opera staged by Verdi at La Fenice was *La traviata* on 7 March 1853. It was not a success. Several sketches by Bertoja exist, for which the ballroom in Act II was signed by Verdi as "seen by me."[68] A print from 1854 offers an interior view of La Fenice complete with the auditorium and stage. On the stage is a performance of an opera with settings strikingly suggestive of the final scene of *La traviata* (shown above as figure 8.5). It is probable that this setting was created by Bertoja. One year later, Bertoja participated in a revival of the opera at the Teatro Gallo on 6 May 1854. For the new production, he contributed two designs. It was this production at Gallo's theater that propelled the opera into the permanent operatic repertory after its initial failure at La Fenice.

Simon Boccanegra

The subsequent years brought Verdi to Paris where he staged *Les Vêpres siciliennes* at the Opéra on 13 June 1855. This experience gave Verdi greater exposure and confidence in working with new and different scenic ideas. Many of these ideas were to have an important influence on his scenic imagination during the creation of his next work for La Fenice.[69]

For the 1857 carnival season, the management of La Fenice engaged Verdi for what was to be his last new opera for the theater, the first version of *Simon Boccanegra*. The schedule of performances was, as in the previous years, intense and unrelenting. Five operas were planned, though only one was a new production. Nevertheless, the scenery for the revivals needed to be inspected, retouched, and replaced wherever necessary. The settings for all four ballets then in repertory also needed to be designed and painted.

After the contracts were signed and the selection of *Simon Boccanegra* was settled, Verdi gave much thought during the course of the composition to the visual needs of the staging. In expressing his requirements for *Simon Boccanegra,* Verdi wrote to Piave in early February 1857: "Take great care over the sets. The directions are exact enough; nevertheless I will permit myself some observations." Verdi did just that and more, revealing in this and several other letters his visual thoughts, which would guide the production team of Piave, the stage director, Bertoja, the set designer, and his Venetian scenic artists and lighting technicians for the premiere of the opera at the Gran Teatro la Fenice. One letter came from Enghien (near Paris), 3 September 1856:

> Think about the scenery and the costumes. Oh, the scenery could be so beautiful in this *Simone!* In three especially, a painter should and could do very well. But the sets should have double and triple drops, and the platforms should not be stools like those in *Guglielmo Tell,* but real platforms.[70]

Bertoja continued to refine the application of platforms, balconies, and stairs for Verdi's works.

Again, Verdi's visual astuteness worked with the music to create the dramatic effect. His letter to Piave, mentioned a moment ago, continues:

In the first scene, if the Fieschi Palace is on the side [of the stage], it must be in clear view to the entire audience, because it is necessary that everybody see Simone when he enters the house, when he goes to the balcony, and takes the little lantern [into the palace]; I think I have a musical effect [here], which I don't want to lose because of the set. Furthermore, I would like to see in front of the Church of San Lorenzo a small staircase, a real one with three or four steps, with some columns, which would serve now Paolo, now Fiesco, etc., to lean against and to hide behind.

This scene must have great depth.[71]

The Grimaldi Palace in the first act does not need to have much depth. Instead of one window I would have several down to the ground, and a terrace; I would put in a second backdrop with the moon whose rays reflect on the sea, which should be seen by the audience. The sea would be a shimmering, slanted drop, etc.

If I were a painter, I would certainly make a beautiful scene: simple and very effective.

I beg you to take great care with the final scene: when the doge orders Pietro to open the balconies, we should see a rich, broad illumination which takes up a great deal of space, so that one can clearly see the lights little by little, one after the other being extinguished, until at the doge's death everything is in deepest darkness. This is a moment, I think, of grand effect, and there will be trouble if the scene is not well done. It's not necessary to have the first drop very far upstage, but the second, the drop with the illumination, needs to be well upstage.[72]

The scenarios for the settings, costumes, and props were approved by the Presidenza on 2 February 1857 and were received the following day by Bertoja's son, Pietro.[73] During this time the production staff were occupied with the final preparations for the production of Ferrari's new opera, *Ultimo giorni a Suli* (which opened 10 February) as well as with several ballets.[74] The painting of the canvases for *Simon* would not have started until later in the week, although the preparatory work, such as designing the settings themselves, was well underway.

The final act of the opera was described by Piave in his scenario thus:

Daytime toward sunset. Salon of the Genoa ducal palace. Upstage left is a door that opens directly into the forum. At the proscenium a hidden exit. On the right a large door which leads to the interior salons. Straight ahead a long broad practical balcony beyond which one can see the Piazza Doria. In front of the balcony let there be hanging curtains that open and close by means of ropes. It needs therefore to be solidly supported. It will be necessary to give in time the commands to [the stagehands]. The walls of the salon can be decorated by historical paintings in which the genealogy of the republic of Genoa will stand out.

The final scene uses the same setting at nighttime, illuminated by a single lamp hanging over a table. The curtain in front of the balcony is pulled open so the public can see the view of the illuminated buildings around the Piazza Doria. This illumination is gradually extinguished.[75]

For the final scene with the view of the harbor and its lights (figure 8.15), Bertoja used perspective as an optical illusion. Lighting became an extraordinarily important tool in creating the mood implied by the music in the short span before the death of the doge. The final act was simple to reproduce on the stage, as Bertoja this time used the standard configuration of wings painted in perspective with three upstage painted drops. The first two were cutout drops for passages of arches and the balcony; the third provided the view of Genoa— the "double and triple drops" that Verdi referred to in his letter to Piave quoted

Figure 8.15. Salon in the Ducal Palace. *Simon Boccanegra* (Act III, scene iii). Design by Giuseppe Bertoja, 1857 (Venice, Museo Correr).

earlier. In the last scene, set at night, the illumination of the "buildings" was provided by gas lamps or possibly by individual oil lamps glowing at specific places positioned behind this drop. According to the libretto, the individual lamps are to be slowly and randomly extinguished when Fiesco begins to sing:[76]

> By the glimmer of the festive torches
> you will perceive odd, fatal omens.
> The hand of God has written
> your fate upon these walls.
> The light of your star is eclipsed;
> your purple is already deteriorating into tatters;
> you, the conqueror, shall die amid the shades
> of those to whom your lackey denied burial.

Though Verdi's final Venetian opera was not regarded as a success, this scene remained firmly in his thoughts. For the 1881 revision of the opera, Verdi expanded this scene both textually and musically—and the gradual extinguishing of the lights in the nighttime view of Genoa was retained as an important dramatic element with great success.[77]

It is difficult to document Verdi's feelings about the scenic designs of Giuseppe Bertoja, but if the composer had been dissatisfied with any aspect of a production, he would have initiated steps to correct the problem or would have threatened to leave the theater. Eight different productions were staged by Verdi in Venice: seven at La Fenice and one at the Teatro Gallo—all with the same designer—a record equaled nowhere else, not even at the Teatro alla Scala.

The artistic styles of Giuseppe Bertoja's scenic designs emphasized the atmosphere created by the dramatic situations in Verdi's operas. Realism was the dominant style, but without a need for sharp, clear delineation of form. Colors were used to illustrate mood, time, and locale. In addition to the positive (albeit sometimes difficult) working conditions of the Gran Teatro la Fenice, these styles served to sharpen Verdi's dramatic imagery and played a subtle role in his evolving compositional processes during the creation of his new works. The strength of Bertoja's designs resided in their ability to augment the dramatic moods and atmospheres created by Verdi's incomparable music.

• • • • •

Postscript

The Gran Teatro la Fenice, Venice's principal opera house and the subject of chapter eight, was destroyed by fire on Monday, 29 January 1996, long after our chapter was written. *La Fenice* means *the phoenix:* the theater rose like a phoenix from the ashes of the Teatro San Benedetto, which burned to the ground in 1773. The second theater was designed by Giannantonio Selva and completed in 1792. The new opera house opened on 16 May of that year with a gala performance of Giovanni Paisiello's *I giochi d'agrigento,* which was composed specifically for the occasion. Disaster struck again on 13 December 1836, but in keeping with the theater's tradition, a new theater was soon built on the same site. Premiere performances of operas by Rossini, Donizetti, Verdi, Stravinsky, and Britten took place there.

Despite its venerable heritage, La Fenice never became fossilized: renovations were undertaken in 1854 and, more recently, in 1937 in order to update and improve the facilities. According to Giuseppe Pavanello, who with Manlio Brusatin wrote the monograph *Il teatro la Fenice,* the majority of the decorations in the theater were neo-rococo ornaments added in 1854, the light fixtures dated from after World War II, and many other details from the theater were not part of the 1836 design.

Massimo Cacciari, the mayor of Venice, affirmed that the theater would be "rebuilt," but the question during the months following the fire concerns the degree to which the building will be modified from the 1836 blueprints that, according to news reports, have been preserved in a savings bank in Venice.[1] The architects and engineers who would eventually take charge of the restoration were not yet identified as of mid 1996, although Mayor Cacciari proposed recruiting Mario Messinis, a musicologist, as the chief artistic advisor in the project.[2]

The cause of the conflagration had not been determined as of this writing, but Claudio Pasqualetto, the Venetian correspondent who covered the incident in several articles that appeared in the *Corriere della sera,* indicated that it seems to have started in the coffee machine, which was always on, at the bar on the second floor of the theater.[3] Arson is also being considered as a possible cause. Firefighting efforts to control the nine-hour blaze were under the direction of Sandro Furlan, who indicated that work was hampered by inaccessibility of water: two canals near the theater had been drained as part of a citywide dredging project.[4]

By the time the fire had been extinguished, the roof and ceiling with its 1854 decorations by Leonardo Gavagnin[5] had been destroyed along with various salons and public areas, including the Dante salon and the Apollinaire salon with decorations from 1937 by Giacomo Casa and Nino Barbantini respectively.[6] Also destroyed were the imperial box, the galleries with their ornamental designs by Giuseppe Borsato (1828), and the atrium of the main floor, which was remodeled and enlarged after the 1937 renovation. Nothing remained of the scenic stage area (*palcoscenico*), but the façade, the exterior main wall, and most of the rooms to the right of the scenic stage were spared the total devastation of the flames.[7]

Christiano Chiarot, a spokesman for La Fenice, expressed the hope that the reconstruction would take place quickly; however, Judge Felice Casson "sealed" the building until investigations into the blaze could be concluded, and Livio Ricciardi, the city's superintendent of architectural landmarks (*Beni architettonici*), insisted that all materials that could be salvaged from the original structure should be reused in the reconstruction.

Ironically, the Comune of Venice is considering prosecution of Ricciardi for criminal negligence, since he was the person directly in charge of the restoration work being done on La Fenice, work that may have contributed to the devastating consequences of the blaze.[8] Evidence concerning the day-to-day progress has been preserved by Giuseppe Bonamini, who took photographs of the work as it progressed. These photos will doubtless be helpful in recreating the details of the theater as it was at the time of its destruction.

—Mark A. Radice

CHAPTER NINE

Richard Wagner and His Search for the Ideal Theatrical Space

Evan Baker

The everlasting work is ended!
On mountain peak the gods' abode;
resplendent shines
the proud-standing hall!

Vollendet das ewige Werk;
auf Berges Gipfel
die Götterburg,
prächtig prahlt
der prangende Bau!

—*Das Rheingold,* scene ii[1]

Richard Wagner was greeted with these words on 1 August 1875 during the staging rehearsal in his new theater, known as the Festspielhaus (the Festival Theater) in Bayreuth, a small town in the state of Bavaria. The text was sung by the baritone Franz Betz at the rehearsals during the preparations for the first complete cycle of *Der Ring des Nibelungen* that was to take place the following year. Shortly after the rehearsal, Cosima Wagner wrote in her diary, "On the afternoon of Sunday the 1st, rehearsal to test the orchestra tone quality; R[ichard] received by the orchestra with cheers, Betz sings Vollendet das Bau [*sic*], heavenly sound, overwhelming impression, R. very moved."[2]

This particular text from *Das Rheingold* had special significance and emotional meaning both to the cast of *Der Ring des Nibelungen* and to Richard Wagner in particular. Wagner's theatrical enterprise was to make an overt

241

and subtle impact on the entire evolution of the theatrical and operatic genres. Truly unique was the construction of the Festspielhaus, of which the auditorium still stands in nearly its original form, solely according to the designs and intentions of one man, Richard Wagner.[3]

Wagner's conceptions of his Festival Theater did not arise in a vacuum. The dynamics of politics; the financial pressures inherent in theatrical production; and the various caprices of artists, administrators, and the general public exerted influences on the composer's theoretical formulations of the ideal theatrical space. These ideas evolved in consequence of both Wagner's years of participation in the practical affairs of operatic production and his observation of theatrical practices not only during his own early career as a conductor and stage director but also during his sojourns in Paris, Dresden, Zurich, Munich, and Lucerne. *Das Kunstwerk der Zukunft* (Artwork of the future, 1849) was the first of several theoretical works propagating a revolutionary change in operatic production. This change consisted primarily in turning away from the luxurious, Baroque theatrical structure and its horseshoe-shaped auditorium with numerous balconies and its hierarchical seating plans serving only a bourgeois public. Instead, Wagner called for a physical structure that would function exclusively as a place for theatrical performance without any distractions caused by the audience or by the theatrical edifice. Over the years, Wagner refined his theories. These are stated with particular clarity in his foreword to the 1863 edition of his libretto to *Der Ring des Nibelungen*. After more than twenty-five years of planning, theorizing, and raising funds, and with polemics, construction, delays, uncertainty, and plain luck, the Festspielhaus opened in August 1876. The full extent of Wagner's theatrical skills was manifested in 1882 during the first performances of *Parsifal*.

Wagner's Early Practical Experiences

The cultivation of Wagner's theoretical vision for the future Festspielhaus began with his formative theatrical experiences. These included his first engagement, as chorusmaster in Würzburg (1833), followed by conducting in Bad Lauchstädt (1834), Magdeburg (1834 to 1836), Königsberg (1837), and finally, his post as music director in Riga (1837 to 1839). Each of these theaters provided Wagner with experiences not only as a conductor, but also as a stage director. This background evolved into practical uses much later.

The theater in Bad Lauchstädt, a small and popular holiday spot near Halle for the aristocracy, was built at the insistence of Johann Wolfgang von Goethe in 1802.[4] Judging from the available documents, the theater, with a small parterre and a semicircular balcony, was rather intimate and could hold a total of about 400 persons.[5] No auditorium boxes can be detected in the records. The backstage, albeit small, was fairly well equipped with sliding wings and with traps at the center of the stage. It was in this theater that Wagner first conducted an opera, Mozart's *Don Giovanni*.

In 1837 Wagner accepted the conducting position in the city theater (*Stadttheater*) at the flourishing North Sea port Riga (located in present-day Latvia). Several reminiscences of the theater survive. One is significant as it describes the particular features of the auditorium that planted seeds in Wagner's mind, producing theatrical and technical ideas for the Festspielhaus.[6] The theater was small: the auditorium was only 59.1 feet (18 meters) deep with two galleries of boxes. The stage was about 46 feet (14 meters) wide and 36.1 feet (11 meters) deep; the proscenium opening measured not quite 42.7 feet (13 meters). Because only 27.9 feet (8.5 meters) of fly space were available, it was impossible to fly objects completely out of view from the audience.[7]

C. F. Glasenapp, Wagner's biographer, a native of Riga, remembered the theater well. He recounted from the memoirs of a Rigan musician a conversation in which Wagner discussed his activities in Riga:

> In fact the . . . [auditorium of the] old Riga Stadttheater in the Königstrasse was, by today's standards, a pretty gloomy place. It had only one balcony [with boxes], immediately above which was the gallery, which was much frequented by middle-class families. Both younger and older ladies, equipped with their knitting and the necessary refreshments, could be seen arriving early to assure themselves of a comfortable seat, the places being unnumbered, preferably next to the balustrade, and there to await what was to follow. With regard to this auditorium, the cellist Arved Poorten, who was born in Riga, interrupted [Wagner] to call it a stable, a barn, and asked, "How on earth, Master, were you able to conduct there?" To which Wagner replied very seriously: three things had stuck in his memory as being particularly remarkable about this "barn." First, the steeply rising parterre, rather like an amphitheater; second, the darkness of the auditorium; and third, the surprising depth of the orchestra pit. If he ever succeeded in building a theater to his own plans, he would have regard to these three features, and that was something he had already decided on at that time.[8]

This makes a good story, but how many of these memories are based in actual fact is not known, since the theater no longer exists. A small plan of the theater has survived, and it confirms the observation of the "steeply rising" parterre.[9]

Taken together, these early experiences gave Wagner much insight in terms of staging and acoustics, particularly when he worked with singers on the stage. He was able to grasp the essence, albeit in small theaters, of theatrical production especially from the perspective of the audience.[10] It was also during this time that he experienced (and much to his dismay) both the frequent slovenliness and the low standards of theatrical production that were considered the norm of the time. These impressions were to remain with Wagner for the rest of his life.

Paris

After much frustration in the provincial German theaters, Wagner moved to Paris, then the theatrical capital of Europe. On 17 September 1839, Wagner began a sojourn that lasted almost three years—a sojourn that would introduce him to many of the marvels and, at the same time, weaknesses of theatrical architecture, staging, design, and production techniques for both opera and spoken theater.

In France's capital, more than twenty theaters were in operation, including the Académie Royale de Musique (Opéra), the Opéra Comique, and other stages both large and small.[11] Most theaters provided a varying mixture of opera, ballets, plays, and vaudevilles. The theater also was a gathering place for social displays and entertainments, for assignations, as well as for flaunting one's economic status.

Paris was a laboratory for experimentation with a number of operatic elements—scenic design, stagecraft, orchestral instrumentation, and the use of offstage orchestras and bands. The Opéra was the focal point for opera in Europe with respect to music, singing, orchestral playing, stage and costume design, and stage direction. Wagner experienced there a high *niveau* of theatrical production he had only dreamed of previously. The production techniques of the Opéra made a lasting impression on Wagner—as did both the behavior of its audiences and other social aspects. Wagner encountered a perpetual conflict: the attention demanded from the audience by the drama and music of the opera versus the often superficial musical and visual spectacle demanded by the public from the same opera. The ostentatious display of luxury, the hunger of the public for spectacle, and the behavior of the audience alienated Wagner. The public was unable, or unwilling, to devote its full attention to all aspects of opera: music, text, staging, and production. Thus the audience left with only a partial impression of what purported to be a complete work of art.

The staging techniques and the scenic styles of the Paris Opéra have already been discussed in chapter seven of this book. Here it is sufficient to note that Wagner was intrigued by the scenic possibilities in a theater with a well-equipped stage. Despite his always precarious financial situation, he attended many of the new creations at the Opéra, and at other theaters, where he observed diverse styles in staging and design.[12] At the same time, Wagner struck up a friendship with Edouard Despléchin, one of the chief designers and scenic artists at the Opéra, who was to influence some of Wagner's visual precepts for theatrical design.

Much of the public attending the performances at the Opéra did not necessarily do so with the wish to experience solely the aesthetic pleasures of a genre that incorporated music, text, and spectacle. Recent researches have shown that attendance was widely treated as purely a social event: the Opéra was attended primarily by those who could afford a subscription either for boxes or for individual seats.[13] Hector Berlioz remarked that the fashionable patrons never entered their boxes before nine o'clock. An important function of the boxes was to facilitate the public display of luxury by the box-owner, showing his current social and financial stature. Auditoriums remained fully lit during performances, and audiences frequently engaged in other social activities such as conversation, eating, drinking, and visiting other boxes. Attention was given to the stage only if the favorite singer of the moment was performing or if a new scenic effect made a particular impact with its novelty. Wagner grew to detest such attitudes.

Despite these public attitudes and Wagner's growing distaste for the genre of "grand opera," he continued to attend performances and to observe staging practices at the Opéra. One work lay very near his heart: Weber's *Der Freischütz*. It was presented at the Opéra on 7 June 1841 in a version prepared by Berlioz. In his review of the production, Wagner ridiculed the staging and mocked the Parisians' lack of understanding of the relationships among the Romantic elements in German music and theater.[14] Much of this lack in understanding resulted from the audience's tastes and from their demand for superficial spectacle in operatic production.

With the increasing success of spectacle in French grand opera, attention became focused chiefly upon selected moments within the production. The processions, large choral scenes, and elaborate effects became the favorites of stage directors and designers, and these elements were overly used. In 1852 Berlioz mocked this abuse in his *Les soirées de l'orchestre* (Evenings with the orchestra) where he commented about the 1841 production of his version of *Der Freischütz*:

the staging of [*Der Freischütz*] the masterpiece, the costumes being naturally put under the supervision of Duponchel.[15]

"Duponchel!" simultaneously exclaim five or six musicians; "do you mean the celebrated inventor of the canopy, the man who introduced the canopy into opera as the principal element of success? The author of the canopy in *La Juive*, in *La reine de Chypre*, in *Le prophète*, the creator of the floating canopy, the miraculous canopy, the canopy of canopies?"

"The very same, gentlemen. And so, as Duponchel was once more in charge of the costumes, processions, and canopies, I called on him to find out his plans for the properties in the infernal scene, wherein his canopy, unfortunately, could have no place."[16]

During his stay in Paris, Wagner completed the score to what would be his first popular success, *Rienzi*. On 29 June 1841, the opera was accepted for production at the Dresden Court Theater. Wagner then turned his thoughts toward the staging, production, and musical capabilities of that theater. Some months later, he received information from Ferdinand Heine, a designer and stage director at the Court Theater, regarding the rehearsals and staging plans for *Rienzi*. In mid January 1842 Wagner responded with some concern in a letter to Heine:

> All that I have heard from various quarters concerning the beauty of the Dresden Theatre, its splendid furnishings, its admirable band and the excellence of its ensemble fills me with a great sense of joy. . . .
> . . . But how do things stand with the scenery? Much of it will have to be built specially, and even though the Dresden stage sets are in good condition, so that it would be senseless of me to demand that the existing stock should not be put to the appropriate use, there are nonetheless some individual sets, e.g., (Act I) the church of St. John Lateran in the background, (Act IV) the same in the foreground and to one side, (Act II) the view of Rome through the main door, and (Act V) the Capitol itself in the background, which cannot be adequately and characteristically assembled without new and additional sets being provided. Is anyone thinking about this and working on it?[17]

It is clear that Wagner desired specific images in the settings and that using recycled scenery from earlier productions of other operas was unacceptable.

Despite the acceptance of *Rienzi* by the Dresden Opera, success for Wagner in Paris was out of his reach. With the impending preparations of *Rienzi* in Dresden, Wagner left Paris in April 1842. The sum of his contacts and experiences in Paris would prove to be among his most valuable assets during his forthcoming residence in Dresden.

Dresden

The Dresden Court Theater (Dresden Hoftheater) was constructed to the designs of Gottfried Semper and opened with a performance of Goethe's *Torquato Tasso* on 12 April 1841.[18] It was counted among the grander German court theaters, which included those at Berlin and Munich. The Dresden Hoftheater could seat 1,750 persons. The audience was seated in the parquet and five levels of balconies, complete with private boxes (figure 9.1). Semper was unique among the theater architects of his time. In his designs he gave careful consideration to each aspect of the auditorium and to the practical and aesthetic relationships to the performances on the stage.[19] These aspects included the sightlines from the audience to the stage, the acoustics of the auditorium, and

Figure 9.1. Interior view of Dresden Court Theater.

the size of the orchestra pit. The results included excellent sightlines, a favorable acoustic, and a pit large enough for more than seventy musicians.

Decoration in the auditorium was kept modest. Semper wished the public to become absorbed with the theatrical events unfolding on the stage, not with the auditorium. Proscenium arch boxes—a feature common to virtually all other opera houses—were lacking. Hanging in the upper part of the proscenium opening were "draperies" painted by the Parisian scenic studio of Despléchin, who later created the settings for the Dresden premiere of Wagner's *Tannhäuser.* In the stage area, the newest equipment allowed for rapid changes of scenery on wagons in the wings as well as flying drops out of view from the audience. Both spoken drama and opera were produced in the theater throughout the year. Opera was performed on the average of three to four times a week. Only the court theaters in Berlin and Munich could rival the Dresden Court Theater with their repertory, architecture, and staging capabilities.

Rienzi, Wagner's first great operatic success, received its premiere on 20 October 1843. Set in five acts, the opera required a multitude of stage decorations, grand choruses, processions, horses for the leading singers, and other paraphernalia of the grand opera that Wagner professed to dislike intensely. These elements contributed to its success with the public, but it was a success which an embarrassed Wagner later disavowed.[20] The scenic styles were typical for the nineteenth century, centering on realism produced by painted flats mounted on wagons situated in the wings. Painted drops, some with a series of cutout cloths giving the illusion of depth and others spanning the width of the stage, were used as well. For *Rienzi,* all these elements were employed along with short platforms replicating steps. Several months after the premiere of *Rienzi,* the *Leipzig Illustrierte Zeitung* published an illustration of the finale to Act IV as viewed from the center box in the rear of the auditorium of the Dresden Court Theater (figure 9.2).

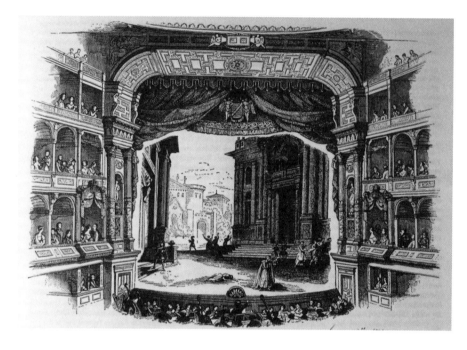

Figure 9.2. *Rienzi,* Finale, Act IV. From *Leipzig Illustrierte Zeitung,* 12 August 1843.

Wagner's next two operas, *Der fliegende Holländer* (2 January 1843) and *Tannhäuser* (19 October 1845), stood in contrast to *Rienzi.* The opening performances were not a success, even though the operas were conducted and staged by Wagner himself. Wagner admitted that the audience, used to grand works in the French manner or Italian showpieces, was not prepared for such a "gloomy work."[21] Because of the poor reception from the public, the *Holländer* received only three more performances before it was dropped in favor of *Rienzi. Tannhäuser,* Wagner's next opera, fared somewhat better, but Wagner continued to encounter difficulties, this time from the theater administration. The settings were designed by Eduoard Despléchin, Wagner's colleague from Paris.[22] Even though some of the settings were reminiscent of the grand works found in

Paris, the first scene did not meet the specifications and had to be repainted. For the Hall of Song, the administration ordered that the settings from another new production (Weber's *Oberon*) be recycled in order to reduce costs. Wagner strenuously fought against this order, and the administration finally relented. The settings were commissioned, but much to everyone's disappointment, they did not arrive in time for the premiere. The issues of audience tastes, meddling by theater administrators, and poor production qualities were already apparent to Wagner, and dealing with these issues was to play an important part in his artistic development.

Wagner was long dissatisfied with the Dresden Opera, especially with its productions, and with its relationships to the public's tastes in opera. Throughout Wagner's engagement in Dresden, he made numerous attempts to reform the administrative structure of the theater management, its method of production, as well as the public's tastes in opera. Most of these efforts proved futile, given the resistance to change on the part of the administration, personnel (especially the orchestra musicians), and the public itself.[23] Many letters and documents from Wagner reveal not only the depths of his artistic convictions but, if we read between the lines, his frustrations with the current artistic milieu of the Dresden Opera as well.[24] Too much meddling in theatrical and musical affairs by unqualified persons irritated Wagner no end. In another attempt to reform the administrative structure of the Court Opera, Wagner heaped sarcasm on the use of patronage by the royal court:

> Have we ever experienced, for example, that an art-loving major of the Hussars would be placed at the head of an art academy? No, and our "theater friend" appears to admit that the orchestra should be directed by a musician and not by a lawyer. Should only a theater company be led by an educated chamberlain, by an experienced banker, or perhaps by a clever journalist?[25]

Despite the shortcomings of the Court Opera, Wagner continued—in Dresden, Berlin, and elsewhere—to conduct and to stage productions of works by other composers as well as of his own.[26] During the summer of 1848, Wagner began intensive study of the ancient Greeks. He read and pondered many sagas and epic works by Aeschylus, Aristotle, Plato, Euripides, Homer, and Sophocles. The importance of drama and of theatrical production as presented by the Greeks was not lost on Wagner:

> My ideas about the significance of drama, and especially of the theater itself, were decisively molded by these impressions. [From these studies I] gained such an insight into the wonderful beauty of Greek life that I felt myself palpably more at home in ancient Athens than in any circumstances afforded by the modern world.[27]

Given Wagner's voracious reading habit and his intellectual curiosity, it seems more than likely that he became familiar with Greek architecture through the writings of the Roman Vitruvius, active in the first century A.D., and through other early tracts that discuss theatrical spaces. He would have known, for example, the layout of seating in the amphitheater of Epidauros in ancient Greece.[28]

At the same time, Wagner developed a personal friendship with Gottfried Semper, the architect of the Court Theater. They had numerous meetings to discuss their concepts for the ideal theatrical structures. This was a friendship that was to have great consequences in the history of theater architecture, acoustics, and theatrical technology. These meetings and their discussions laid the conceptual foundation for what would become the Festspielhaus in Bayreuth.

Exile and the First Theories of an Ideal Theater

After fleeing the consequences of his participation in the political uprisings in Dresden, Wagner took refuge in Switzerland at the end of May 1849.[29] Despite his difficult personal and financial circumstances, Wagner continued his creative work, most importantly with "Siegfrieds Tod," which ultimately was to become *Der Ring des Nibelungen*. During his exile, Wagner penned a number of important essays expostulating his theories on aesthetics, music, operatic production, visual arts, and theater. Several were to have profound influences upon the various aspects of Wagnerian operatic production: *Kunst und Revolution* (Art and revolution, 1849), *Das Kunstwerk der Zukunft* (Artwork of the future, 1849), and *Oper und Drama* (Opera and drama, 1851), as well as his autobiographical *Eine Mitteilung an meine Freunde* (A message to my friends, also 1851). Of these, *Das Kunstwerk der Zukunft* best articulates Wagner's early thoughts on the ideal theatrical space.

In this treatise, Wagner argued for a unity of the arts. All must concentrate and work together towards the common goal: a utilization of every aspect of the performing, written, and visual arts that would coalesce into a complete and unified work of art. Wagner made no aesthetic pronouncements about the balance of artistic elements—only that they should all blend into a seamless whole. As a part of that artistic entity, architecture was extraordinarily important. Wagner noted that ancient architecture had a public function, as both a temple and a theater that must serve the public. The public utility of an edifice prevented its degeneration into mere luxury.

> Luxury is as heartless, inhuman, insatiable, and egotistic as the "need" which called it forth, but which, with all its heaping-up and over-reaching, it never more can still. For this need itself is no natural and

therefore satisfiable one; by very reason that, being false, it has no true, essential antithesis in which it may be spent, consumed, and satisfied.[30]

The ancient theater of the Greeks—simple, without luxury and ornate decoration—served several purposes, including the bringing together of a community. The theater also was intended to serve a didactic purpose. Wagner proposed to use these ideas as a justification for his future Festival Theater.

Under the fair-ceiled roof, and amid the symmetry of marble columns of the God's temple, the art-glad Lyrist led the mazes of his dance, to strains of sounding hymns,—and in the Theatre, which reared itself around the God's altar—as its central point—on the one hand to the message-giving stage, on the other to the ample rows where sat the message-craving audience, the Tragedian brought to birth the living work of consummated Art.

Thus did artistic Man, of his longing for artistic commune with himself, rule Nature to his own artistic needs and bid her serve his highest purpose. Thus did the Lyrist and Tragedian command the Architect to build the artistic edifice which should answer to their art in worthy manner.[31]

Wagner goes on to say:

The highest conjoint work of art is the Drama: it can only be at hand in all its possible fullness, when in it each separate branch of art is at hand in its own utmost fullness.

The true drama is only conceivable as proceeding from a common urge of every art toward the most direct appeal to a common public. In this drama, each separate art can only bare its utmost secret to their common public through a mutual parleying with the other arts; for the purpose of each separate branch of art can only be fully attained by the reciprocal agreement and cooperation of all the branches in their common message.[32]

In other words, there must be a semblance of "give and take" in the arts, an osmotic quality in which one element of operatic production supports the other. Wagner continues his discussion of architecture and his observations of the effect of the orchestra:

Architecture can set before herself no higher task than to frame for a fellowship of artists, who in their own persons portray the life of man, the special surroundings necessary for the display of the Human

Artwork. Only that edifice is built according to Necessity, which
answers most befittingly an aim of man: the highest aim of man is the
highest artistic aim; the artistic aim—the Drama. . . . In a perfect
theatrical edifice, Art's need alone gives law and measure, down even
to the smallest detail. This need is twofold, that of giving and that of
receiving, which reciprocally pervade and condition one another. The
Scene has firstly to comply with all the conditions of "space" imposed
by the joint (*gemeinsam*) dramatic action to be displayed thereon: but
secondly, it has to fulfill those conditions in the sense of bringing this
dramatic action to the eye and ear of the spectator in an intelligible
fashion. In the arrangement of the space for the spectators, the need for
optic and acoustic understanding of the artwork will give the necessary law, which can only be observed by a union of beauty and fitness
in the proportions; for the demand of the collective (*gemeinsam*) audience is the demand for the artwork, to whose comprehension it must
be distinctly led by everything that meets the eye. Thus the spectator
transplants himself upon the stage, by means of all his visual and aural
faculties; while the performer becomes an artist only by complete
absorption into the public. Everything, that breathes and moves upon
the stage, thus breathes and moves alone from eloquent desire to impart,
to be seen and heard within those walls which, however circumscribed
their space, seem to the actor from his scenic standpoint to embrace the
whole of humankind; whereas the public, that representative of daily
life, forgets the confines of the auditorium, and lives and breathes now
only in the artwork which seems to it as life itself, and on the stage
which seems the wide expanse of the whole world.[33]

In these consequential passages, Wagner laid down the theoretical groundwork
that would guide him to the creation of the ideal theatrical space. It would be
another thirteen years, however, before Wagner was able to formulate concisely
the layout of the auditorium and the placement of the orchestra in that
ideal space.

The Search for the Ideal Space

Wagner expressed his first thoughts on the ideal performance space in a
letter from Paris, dated 14 September 1850, to Ernst Benedikt Kietz:

I am genuinely thinking of setting Siegfried to music, only I cannot
reconcile myself with the idea of trusting to luck and of having the
work performed by the very first theater that comes along: on the contrary, I am toying with the boldest of plans. . . . I would have a theater

erected here [in Zurich] on the spot, made of planks, and have the most suitable singers join me here, and arrange everything necessary for this one special occasion, so that I could be certain of an outstanding performance of the opera . . . and give three performances . . . in a space of a week, after which the theater would then be demolished and the whole affair would be over and done with. Only something of this nature can still appeal to me.[34]

This is the first documented instance of Wagner's idea for what would become the Bayreuth Festival. The concept of constructing a temporary theater is an old one, deriving from wandering theater troupes and, in Wagner's time, choral festivals in Germany that would take place in town squares or in a large field. In Switzerland, Wagner saw many street festivals during Lent, where provisional stages were quickly set up for several days and, just as quickly, dismantled. What Wagner grasped was that a festival, under temporary conditions, would serve not only his needs but also those of the public. In Wagner's eyes, the public was not merely seeking entertainment but, in a subtle manner, fulfillment of a dialectical need as well.[35]

During all his polemical activities while in exile, Wagner did not withdraw from musical and theatrical work. He became involved in the theatrical affairs of the local opera company, the Theater Aktiengesellschaft.[36] Between October 1850 and April 1851, he staged and conducted Boieldieu's *Die weisse Dame* (*La dame blanche*), Bellini's *Norma,* Beethoven's *Fidelio,* and Mozart's *Die Zauberflöte* and *Don Giovanni.*[37] But Wagner soon withdrew from the theater, for it was much too small for his ambitions, it lacked organization, and its financial situation was too precarious.[38]

These experiences spurred Wagner to write *Ein Theater in Zürich* (A theater in Zurich) in April 1851.[39] This valuable work sets forth Wagner's thinking about production and staging, emphasizing originality rather than the imitation of production styles associated with grand opera. He castigated the opera public for being interested in only the spectacle of a production rather than in the drama and music of the opera. This reflected the continuing lust of audiences for productions in the style of grand opera. Among his key recommendations were that theaters (not just Zurich's alone) should employ a permanent stage director and that the director must seek a close collaboration of the scenic artists and designers. Wagner's letters during this time reveal his growing conviction that only he could properly stage his own works.

Wagner continued to consider the current architectural format of opera houses. He desired to move away from the standard theatrical space consisting chiefly of an auditorium with multitiered balconies, private boxes, and hierarchical seating schemes modeled after the Baroque, decorative, horseshoe format. At the same time, the ramifications of the enormous practical requirements necessary for any future production of "Siegfrieds Tod" began to dawn on

Wagner. He concluded that the opera needed to be staged over a period of several days, and under festival conditions. Instead of attempting to produce the opera in a standard repertory-based opera house, he considered constructing only a simple and temporary space, similar to those constructed for carnivals and street fairs he encountered in Zurich.[40] Singers and an orchestra would be brought together solely for the purposes of performing the future *Ring*.

Consideration of the practical application of Wagner's ideas continued, particularly after Gottfried Semper took up his appointment in 1855 as a professor at the Technical University of Zurich. He and Wagner met numerous times, picking up their discussions about the ideal theatrical space for the production of opera. These meetings, together with the sum of Wagner's practical theater experience, would contribute greatly to the evolution of the Bayreuth Festspielhaus.

The *Ring* Preface (1863)

In 1863 Richard Wagner was rehearsing what was to be an abortive production of *Tristan und Isolde* for the court opera in Vienna. At that time, a new version of the libretto for *Der Ring des Nibelungen* was published. For this edition, Wagner wrote "Vorwort zur Herausgabe der Dichtung des Bühnenfestspiels *Der Ring des Nibelungen*" (Preface to the publication of the poem of the stage festival, *Der Ring des Nibelungen*), some of which specifically outlined his thoughts for a future festival theater where he would produce the *Ring* totally under his own artistic control.

This Preface served as a summation not only of Wagner's earlier correspondence on the topic of theatrical performance, but it was also a distillation of his previous theoretical writings, especially of the essay *Das Kunstwerk der Zukunft*. Wagner ruled out basing his future festival endeavors in any large city, preferring instead to seek a small town without any of the distractions of a large urban setting. Wagner then indicated for the first time the shape that his ideal theatrical space would take. Two extraordinary points were proposed. First, the auditorium was to follow the form of the Grecian amphitheater with the rows of seats rising toward the rear. Secondly, the orchestra pit (from whence the auditorium itself begins) was to be hidden from the view of the audience. Wagner further wrote:

> I next should lay especial stress on the invisibility of the orchestra—to be effected by an architectural illusion quite feasible with an amphitheatric plan of auditorium. The importance of this will be manifest to anybody who attends our opera performances with the notion of getting the true impression of a work of dramatic art; through the inevitable sight of the mechanical movements of the musicians and their

conductor, he is made an unwilling witness of technical evolutions which should be almost as carefully concealed from him as the cords, ropes, laths and scaffoldings of the stage decorations—which, seen from the wings, as everyone knows, destroy all vestige of illusion.[41]

With this statement of the premise that stage mechanics be hidden from the audience, Wagner foresaw the end of the practice of changing pieces of scenery or complete stage settings in full view of the public. Up to this time, the main curtain in the theater was raised and lowered only at the beginning and close of each act. The implications of this statement are clear: no longer was the audience to be distracted by the surroundings within the theater or by other competing theatrical events outside; nor would their own antics in the auditorium be permitted to draw attention from the art work unfolding on the stage. Thus the force of the illusion created by the visual events on the stage and the aural elements of the music during the course of the performance would not be shattered by anything unrelated to the opera.

Wagner realized, however, that a theater of the kind he envisioned required an enormous sum of money. With the knowledge that only a wealthy prince would have the wherewithal to support such a project, Wagner asked plaintively at the end of the essay, "In the beginning was the deed. Will such a prince be found?" (*Wird dieser Fürst sich finden? Im Anfang war die That.*)[42]

Munich—The Semper Theater

That prince who answered Wagner's call was Ludwig II, the young king of Bavaria.[43] With an official commission given on 7 October 1864, Ludwig made it possible for Wagner to concentrate on completing the *Ring*. At the same time, Ludwig placed the royal court theater and its orchestra at the composer's disposal for the first performances of *Tristan und Isolde* (10 June 1865), *Die Meistersinger von Nürnberg* (21 June 1868), *Das Rheingold* (22 September 1869), and *Die Walküre* (26 June 1870).[44] In a letter to Wagner dated 26 November 1864, Ludwig announced his decision to have a grand festival theater constructed for the first performances of Wagner's completed *Ring*. On Wagner's suggestion, Ludwig engaged the services of Gottfried Semper to draw up plans that would incorporate many of the composer's concepts for the ideal theatrical space.

While Wagner awaited the construction and completion of the Festival Theater, the Hof- und Nationaltheater (Court and National Theater) served as the primary theater for his works. The court theater first opened in 1818 but was destroyed by fire in 1823; it was rebuilt and opened again two years later.[45] The Nationaltheater, in comparison to other theaters, could be counted as one of the grander German court theaters, equaling Schinkel's Schauspielhaus in

Berlin and Semper's Hoftheater in Dresden for the excellence of its facilities. The auditorium, an almost circular format (rather than the usual horseshoe shape favored in the Baroque theaters), was capable of seating more than 2,000 spectators spread over a parterre and five galleries of boxes.[46] The orchestra pit space was generous, allowing up to about ninety musicians (figure 9.3).

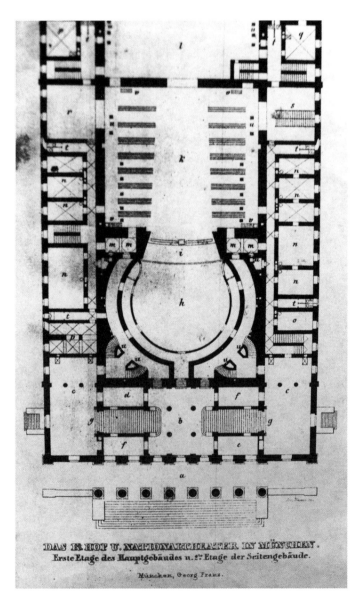

Figure 9.3. Hof- und Nationaltheater, floor plan, Munich. Print by G. Franz.

The stage area was extremely well equipped, with nine sets of movable wings for scenery. Each wing was attached to a winch that could simultaneously or separately slide the scenic units in or out. Several wings were constructed to traverse the width of the entire stage (figure 9.4). Drops could be flown up completely out of sight of the audience. Traps in the stage floor were available as well. In short, the production capabilities of the court theater were in keeping with Wagner's requirements, despite the auditorium's still being set in a hierarchical fashion with the parterre and boxes.

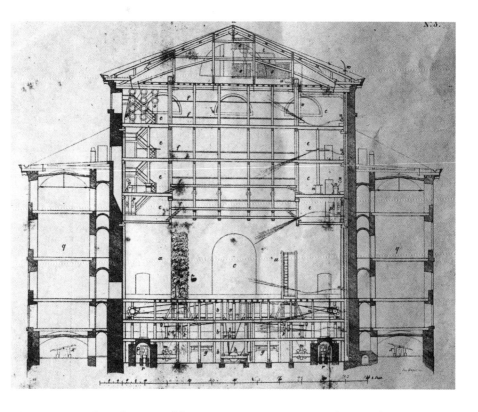

Figure 9.4. Hof- und Nationaltheater, cross-section, Munich. Print by G. Franz.

While most of Wagner's works were staged in the court theater, several under the direct supervision of the composer, the artistic results were mixed. *Tristan und Isolde* was a success as was *Die Meistersinger von Nürnberg*—the latter rapturously received by the public. The rehearsals for most of the works were, nevertheless, difficult, and often the theater and court officials impeded Wagner's wishes both artistically and financially. These frustrations strengthened his ambition to construct his own theater, in which he would have the final say in all matters. Wagner's difficulties were exacerbated beginning with the first productions of *Das Rheingold* and *Die Walküre*, which were staged in his absence. He had concluded months before that the court theater could not or would not provide the ideal working conditions.

In the meantime Semper's grand project of the Festival Theater building for King Ludwig was underway, and the architect was commissioned to draw up the plans. Two important letters from Semper to Wagner outline some of his ideas with respect to the ideal form of the theater sought by Wagner. For the design, the architect incorporated many of the composer's ideas from the 1863 *Ring* Preface. Semper's first letter dates from 10 May 1865 and discusses the basic layout of the auditorium that takes a "comfortable amphitheatrical" shape capable of seating more than 1,000 persons. This required the placing of the orchestra under the forestage and a significant increase in the rake of the auditorium floor at the rear. The placement of the orchestra would assist greatly in "separating the real world from that of the theater."[47] In another letter dated 26 November 1865, Semper emphasizes the practicality of a second proscenium arch, which functions as a "bridge" to distance the audience from the "outside world" and bring it closer to the theatrical experience. The proscenium will greatly assist in completely masking the orchestra pit without having to sink it too deeply into the forestage area.[48]

For Wagner and Semper, two issues were of primary importance. First, the orchestra was to be completely hidden from view. This led to the second issue: the "separation" of the theater from the world of reality represented by the audience. These two objectives were to be achieved by the use of two separate proscenium arches, between which the orchestra pit was hidden. The crucial result from this separation was, according to Semper's reasoning, that

> It creates between the two what may be called a neutral space, whose boundaries in every direction, upwards, downwards and sideways, are not visible to the spectator, so that the eye can no longer measure the true distance of the stage area rising on the far side of the neutral space, for lack of points of reference, especially if the eye is further deceived as to the distance by appropriate use of perspective and optical illusion.[49]

The Greek and Roman amphitheaters provided a model for the layout of the seating for the audience. Galleries surrounding the parterre, a standard feature in contemporary theater construction, were to be eliminated.

After all the discussions, debates, and planning were said and done, nothing (and somewhat to Wagner's own relief) came out of this grand project. By this time, it was clear to him that only he could create the ideal circumstances for the production and performance of his operas; only he could provide the ideal theatrical space in which these future productions could take place without outside artistic and political interference as well as without fiscal constraints. Nonetheless, Semper's contribution toward the eventual construction of the Festspielhaus was considerable.

Bayreuth

During Wagner's residency in Lucerne, he searched for a site on which to build his ideal theater. In early 1871 the town of Bayreuth, located in the province of Franconia in the kingdom of Bavaria, suited several of Wagner's conditions for a possible festival site: small, with no year-round repertory theater to distract or compete with the festival, and close to transportation from neighboring larger towns and cities, of which Nuremberg was the nearest. Wagner, together with his wife, Cosima, visited Bayreuth between the 16th and the 20th of April 1871 and surveyed possible sites for the future Festival Theater. Bayreuth did have an existing theater: the magnificent Baroque Markgräfliches Opernhaus (Margrave's Opera House), designed by Giuseppe Galli-Bibiena and constructed in 1748.[50] Owing to constraints on existing stage and orchestral space, aesthetics, and general considerations, this theater was deemed ill-suited for Wagner's needs.[51] Furthermore, Bibiena's Baroque decoration ran counter to Wagner's proposal of a simple and bare space in the auditorium. Nevertheless, the locale suited Wagner not only for his future theater but for his permanent domicile as well.

Wagner then took steps that were to initiate the Festspielhaus project. After his first visit to Bayreuth, he traveled on to Berlin. There, amidst other activities, he engaged the architect Wilhelm Neumann to design the theater. On 14 May 1871, Wagner visited Darmstadt, where Carl Brandt was the *Maschinenmeister* (master machinist, or, in current theater parlance, technical director) of the local court theater. Brandt was among the best and most experienced of theater technicians of the time. His work at Darmstadt had been augmented by experience at Munich and elsewhere. He became Wagner's technical director, responsible for planning all aspects of theatrical production, which included the selection and installation of the new stage machinery; his trusted influence was also to affect the designs for the auditorium.[52] At the same time, Wagner decided to use the Semper designs from the ill-fated Munich Festival Theater as the basis for his Festspielhaus. From May through December, preliminary planning and discussions took place in Wagner's residence in Lucerne.

On 1 November 1871 Wagner wrote his first letter to Friedrich Feustel, a banker, a city councilor, and one of Bayreuth's prominent citizens, proposing that the town be the site for his future festival.[53] Wagner outlined the economic benefits of a festival to the town and suggested that a piece of land be given to him in return. Wagner further indicated that he would be responsible for raising the necessary funds for the construction of the Festspielhaus and for the organization of the festival itself. Together with Neumann and Brandt, Wagner traveled to Bayreuth to survey possible sites and to enter final discussions with Feustel and other officials of Bayreuth. The town council voted to accept Wagner's proposals and selected an agreed-upon location for the theater; however the owner refused to sell the property. Another site was selected and offered to Wagner, who accepted after initial reluctance. This property was to become the site of the future festival, in an area known locally as Bürgerreuth, highly regarded for its scenic vistas. Wagner visited Bayreuth once more, from 31 January until 3 February 1872. On 1 February, he visited the site and, according to his friend Emil Heckel, he cried out that "this view is charming and enchanting!"[54]

Problems beset the enterprise in the first months of the new year: Neumann, the architect, proved dilatory and undependable. His suggestions for the project were expensive and they did not follow Wagner's desires for a "provisional" theater. He was subsequently dropped from the project.[55] In a letter to Feustel dated 12 April, Wagner reiterated his intentions regarding the theater building:

> 1. The theater building to be *provisional* only; I should be quite content for it to be only of wood, like the halls used for gymnastic displays and choral festivals; it should be no more solid than is necessary to prevent it from collapsing. Therefore economize here, economize—no ornamentation. With this building we are offering only the outline of our idea, and hand it over to the *nation for completion* as a monumental edifice.
> 2. Stage machinery and scenery, and everything that relates to the ideal inner work of art—*perfect* in every way. *No economies here: everything as though designed to last a long time, nothing provisional.*[56]

This letter is significant in several details. Two points are clear: great emphasis was to be given to visual aspects of theatrical production; theatrical machinery and ideal stage conditions were of greatest importance. Furthermore, in previously unpublished passages, the letter reveals that Wagner had refused any direct financial contributions from King Ludwig, fearing political and artistic interference from the Bavarian Royal Court.[57] Wagner placed equal value upon complete freedom in artistic and political matters relating to the festival; he would not be beholden to any government or public authority. Such were the fruits of his bitter experiences in Dresden and Munich.

On 22 April Wagner traveled again to Darmstadt to confer with Brandt regarding possible replacements for Neumann. Brandt suggested an architect in Leipzig, Otto Brückwald. Two days later, telegrams from Wagner and Brandt were sent to Brückwald offering him the job. The architect, then only thirty-one years old, accepted the commission. Brückwald traveled to Bayreuth, and on 1 May the first discussions between Wagner, Brandt, and the architect took place. On 22 May 1872, Wagner's fifty-ninth birthday, the foundation stone for the Festspielhaus was laid during a festive ceremony. The first plans, adapted in part from Semper's Munich designs, were sent on 29 May to Wagner and the town officials. After further meetings, discussions, problems, and final official approvals, construction began in the spring of 1873. The raising of the roof supports to the stage-house was celebrated on 2 August. It is interesting to note, from the reports and photographs made at that time, that there had been greater progress in the construction of the stage area in contrast to the auditorium.[58]

Word on the construction of Wagner's Festspielhaus had spread throughout Germany. As early as February 1873, Wagner was preparing an essay, discussing the Festspielhaus, for publication. On 2 April 1873, Wagner wrote Brückwald asking him to prepare six plans which would then accompany the essay describing in detail the purpose and the specifics of the Festspielhaus.[59] That essay was published as *Das Bühnenfestspielhaus zu Bayreuth: Nebst einem Bericht über die Grundsteinlegung desselben* (The stage festival theater in Bayreuth: With a report of the laying of the foundation stone).[60]

The essay is a remarkable document. Wagner explains clearly not only the purpose of the theater but also how the theater will appear and why he has specified the particular layout of the auditorium and the stage areas. It is worth reproducing at length the parts of the essay that elucidate some of his thinking regarding theatrical architecture, aesthetics, and operatic production.

You will find an outer shell constructed of the very simplest material, which at best will remind you of those wooden structures which are knocked together in German towns for gatherings of singers and the like, and pulled down again as soon as the festival is over. How much of this building is reckoned for endurance, shall become clearer to you when you step inside. Here too you will find the very humblest material . . . . In the proportions and arrangement of the room and its seats, however, you will find expressed a thought which once you have grasped it, will place you in a new relation to the play you are about to witness, a relation quite distinct from that in which you had always been involved when visiting our theaters. Should this first impression have proved correct, the mysterious entry of the music will next pre-pare you for the unveiling and distinct portrayal of scenic pictures that seem to rise from an ideal world of dreams, and which are meant to set before you the whole reality of a noble art's most skilled illusion. Here at last you are spoken to no more in provisional hints and outlines; so far as lies within the power of the artists of the present, the most accomplished scenery and miming shall be offered you.

To explain the plan of the festival theater now in course of erection at Bayreuth I believe I cannot do better than to begin with the need I felt at the first, that of rendering invisible the mechanical source of its music, to wit the orchestra; for this one requirement led step by step to a total transformation of the auditorium of our neo-European theater.

I hope that a subsequent visit to the Opera will have convinced you of my rightness in condemning the constant visibility of the mechanism for tone-production as an aggressive nuisance. . . . With a dramatic representation, on the contrary, it is a matter of focusing the eye itself upon a picture; and that can only be done by leading it away from any sight of real objects lying in between, such as the technical apparatus for projecting the picture.

Without being actually covered, the orchestra was to be lowered so that the spectator would look right over it and onto the stage. This at once supplied the principle that the seats for the audience must be ranged in gradually ascending rows, their ultimate height to be governed solely by the possibility of a distinct view of the scenic picture. Our whole system of tiers of boxes was accordingly excluded . . . .

Hence we were strictly bound by the laws of perspective, according to which the rows of seats might widen as they mounted higher, but must always face the stage in a straight line. From this point forward, the proscenium, the actual framing of the scenic picture, becomes the starting point for all further arrangements. My demand that the orchestra should be made invisible had at once inspired the genius of the famous architect [Semper] to provide an empty space between the proscenium and the front row of seats. This space — which we called the mystic gulf, because it had to part reality from ideality — . . . framed in a second, wider proscenium, from whose relation to the narrower proscenium proper [Semper had] anticipated the marvelous illusion of an apparent receding of the scene itself, making the spectator imagine it as quite far away. Although [the spectator] still beholds it in all the clearness of proximity, it yet gives rise to the illusion that the persons figuring upon the stage are of larger, superhuman stature.

The success of this arrangement would alone suffice to give an idea of the spectator's completely changed relation to the scenic picture. His seat once taken, he finds himself in an actual "theatron," i.e., a room intended for no other purpose than his looking in, and that for looking straight in front of him. Between him and the picture to be looked at there is nothing plainly visible, merely a floating atmosphere of distance, resulting from the architectural adjustment of the two proscenia; whereby the scene is removed as it were to the unapproachable world of dreams, while the spectral music sounds from the "mystic gulf." . . .

Now, to mask the blanks immediately in front of our double proscenium, the ingenuity of [Semper] had already hit on the plan of inserting a third and still broader proscenium. Seized with the excellence of this thought, we soon went further in this direction, and found that, to do full justice to the idea of an auditorium narrowing in true perspective toward the stage, we must extend the process to the entire auditorium by adding one proscenium after another until they reach the highest gallery, and thus enclosing the entire audience in the vista, no matter where they sit. For this we devised a system of columns, beginning at the first proscenium and widening with the rows of seats they framed; thus appearing to cover the square walls behind them and hiding the intervening doors and steps.[61]

The theater was nothing less than a revolution in design. First and foremost, the entire attention of the audience is to be focused on nothing other than what is being performed on the stage. Social events have no place in the theater; the activities of the orchestra and its conductor are kept out of sight; and the magical illusion of the theater is preserved by masking all the mechanical effects and changes of scenery occurring on the stage.

During the course of construction, Wagner watched carefully over the development of the theatrical space, giving particular attention to the orchestra pit (figures 9.5 and 9.6). Twice he found the orchestra pit too small and had it expanded. Wagner placed such great importance on the size of the pit that the first two rows of the parterre (and its potential financial income) were sacrificed to accommodate the expansion. In its final form, the pit could accommodate up to 115 players.

The pit of the Festspielhaus is unique—even today no other theater has an orchestra pit configuration of a similar design. The concept of lowering the pit was not a new one, having been proposed as early as 1775 by de Marette, by Schinkel for his Schauspielhaus in 1818, and by di Benevello in 1841.[62] However, only Wagner actually put the idea of the sunken and hidden orchestra into practice. Up to this time, most opera house orchestra pits were constructed either on the same level or only very slightly below the parterre. The Festspielhaus orchestra pit led the way for other theaters in sinking the pit out of the direct view of the audience.

The Bayreuth pit descends below the forestage, and is constructed with six descending levels (figures 9.6 and 9.7). The pit was originally planned with three levels, but during the course of expansion, an additional three levels were installed. The pit itself spans in an oval form almost the entire width of the front of the auditorium at 46 feet (14 meters); from the front to the rear measures 37.1 feet (11.3 meters). The strings occupied the first three levels, with the winds, brass, and percussion taking the last three levels.[63] A cowl hides the front of the pit and arches over toward the stage. At the center is an open space of

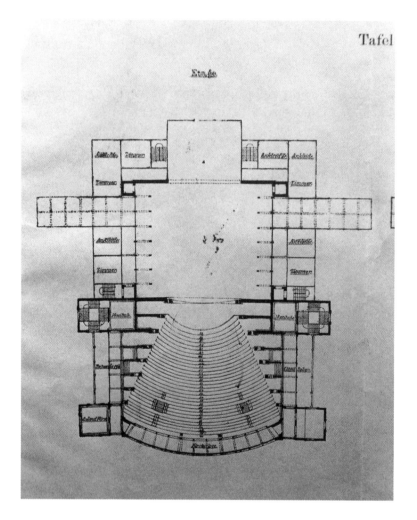

Figure 9.5. Wagner Festspielhaus, floor plan, detail. Published in Richard Wagner, *Gesammelte Schriften und Dichtungen*, vol. 9, pl. 1, 1873.

9.9 feet (3 meters) from the edge of the cowl to the lip of the stage. Overhanging from the lip of the stage is a sound "damper" which was added in 1882 for *Parsifal*. Flanking both sides of the pit are the two prosceniums that create the "mystic gulf" from which emanates—apparently from nothingness—the orchestral sound. The effect, even today, is magnificent.

A "third" proscenium in front of the pit was added at Brandt's suggestion. This proscenium served two functions: first, and foremost, to assist with the illusion of the scenic perspective. Secondly, the canvas ceiling was affixed to the proscenium, providing the first full frame leading toward the stage and the "mystic gulf."

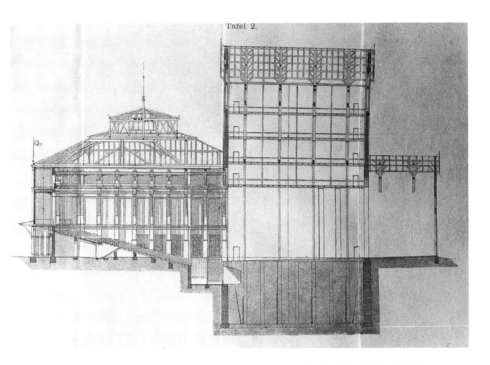

Figure 9.6. Wagner Festspielhaus, side cross-section. Published in Richard Wagner, *Gesammelte Schriften und Dichtungen,* vol. 9, pl. 2, 1873.

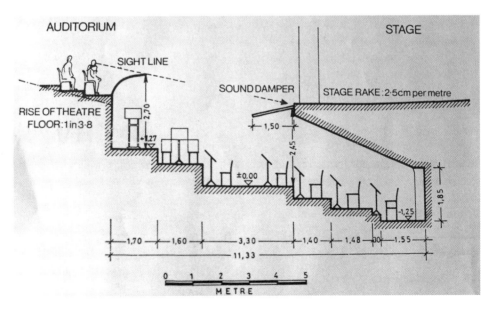

Figure 9.7. Wagner Festspielhaus, side cross-section and current configuration of orchestra pit.

The theatrical complex was deliberately designed in two separate physical parts: the auditorium (which includes the orchestra pit), and the stage-house which encompasses the backstage areas. As Wagner indicated in his letter to Feustel, as well as in his earlier writings, the auditorium was envisioned as a temporary structure. The stage-house, however, should be a permanent structure that could be reused after the conclusion of the first festival.

The auditorium had a width of 108.4 feet (33 meters) and a depth of 85.4 feet (26 meters) to the front of the balcony. The main floor was constructed on a steep rake with thirty rows of seats laid out in the shape of a fan, a reflection of a Grecian amphitheater. The last row of seats stood at a height of 52.5 feet (16 meters) above the front row. Each seat was permanently fixed directly toward the center at the front of the stage, and each afforded a clear view of the stage without any obstruction from persons in front. Access to the seats was from either side of each row through six doors. Between the doors on both sides of the auditorium were six plain extensions perpendicular to the walls reaching into the seating area and ending with a classical column on the upper half of the extension (figure 9.8). In essence, as noted in Wagner's essay *Das Festspielhaus,* these extensions functioned as additional proscenia, thus assisting the viewers to focus their perspective toward the stage. The extensions also served to mask the exit doors from the public.

Figure 9.8. Wagner Festspielhaus, interior view. Published in Richard Wagner, *Gesammelte Schriften und Dichtungen,* vol. 9, pl. 4, 1873.

Two small balconies were placed directly at the rear of the auditorium. One was planned for royalty, the other for artists and participants of the festival. There were no boxes, no decorations, and all the walls were austere and bare. In its own way, the seating layout reflects a democratic plan (other than cost of admission): originally, every member of the audience was an equal, and there was no display of social status or luxury—a complete contrast to other contemporary theatrical and social practices.[64]

The ceiling was an innovation, for it consisted of one giant canvas sail painted by the scenic artists—the brothers Max and Gotthold Brückner—and it spanned the width and length of the auditorium.[65] No chandelier was hung from the ceiling, and auditorium lighting was provided by gas lamps in sconces mounted on each of the columns at the sides and rear of the auditorium. Almost by accident, due to difficulties with regulating the gas lamps, the levels of the auditorium lights were lowered during the first performance of *Das Rheingold* in 1876. Wagner was pleased with this effect, for it was another aid in focusing the attention of the audience on the stage. Subsequently he decided to keep the house lights at the lowered intensity for all performances during the entire festival. Contrary to popular belief, however, Wagner never intended to have the auditorium in total darkness. He stated as much in his report to the festival patrons after the conclusion of the first *Ring* cycle. This particular practice did not come into its own until the turn of the century.[66]

The stage was among the best equipped in any theater. The proscenium opening was 42.7 feet (13 meters) wide and 39.4 feet (12 meters) high. The stage measured 91.9 feet (28 meters) wide and 75.5 feet (23 meters) deep. Seven sets of wings were installed, and traps were placed in the middle of each wing space at the center of the stage. Within the traps were machines that allowed objects or persons to be raised to the stage level and above, or to be lowered from the stage to the basement area 32.8 feet (10 meters) deep. The fly tower was constructed to an enormous height of 95.2 feet (29 meters), enough to allow any drop or other scenic unit to be flown completely out of sight. (The exterior views of the fly tower from the side and front respectively are shown in figures 9.9 and 9.10.) Illumination for the stage area was provided by more than 3,000 gas lamps.[67]

An important technical innovation popularized by Wagner was the multiple use of the act curtain hung directly behind the proscenium arch. Instead of merely raising and lowering the curtain as a single horizontal unit, it could be split vertically into two parts and opened to and closed from the sides of the proscenium. In addition—and perhaps the most striking effect—the curtain could also be split vertically into two parts and gathered diagonally toward the upper corners of the proscenium. This type of curtain became known as the *Raffvorhang*—otherwise known simply as the "Wagner" curtain.[68]

One interested observer wrote of his visit to the backstage during the 1876 festival:

Figure 9.9. Wagner Festspielhaus, exterior side view. Published in Richard Wagner, *Gesammelte Schriften und Dichtungen*, vol. 9, pl. 5, 1873.

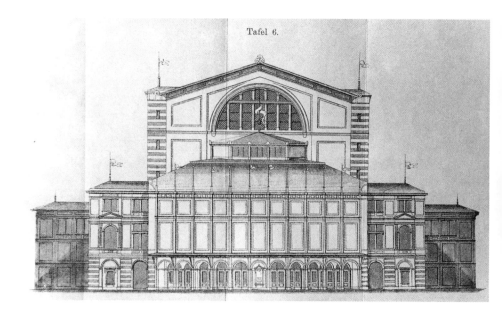

Figure 9.10. Wagner Festspielhaus, exterior front view. Published in Richard Wagner, *Gesammelte Schriften und Dichtungen*, vol. 9, pl. 6, 1873.

Herr Brandt, the master machinist, from the Royal Theater at Darmstadt, offered politely to explain the mysteries of the stage apparatus. The roof above my head was composed apparently of a hazy myriad of ropes, sticks, pulleys and canvases, and I could see the sides of some snow-clad hill in what seemed sad juxtaposition with the glowing interiors of princely palaces. In fact, above me were the pieces and sections of many a wonderland Herr Brandt will produce in the coming festival. There is a height of 108 feet [32.9 meters] from the stage to the flies, and the sides are occupied by five machine galleries, the first being 45 feet [13.7 meters] from the boards. The bowels of the stage have a depth of 40 feet [12.2 meters], a descent to which discovered a most distressing labyrinth of ropes and traps and awkward elbowed joists that resembled a section of some universal motor. There were, in addition, two immense long wooden drums for working the machinery by means of a steam pump, and other requisites for the production of vapor, which in some portions of the *Nibelungen* drama covers the scene from sight, so that while the fleecy clouds are radiant with reflected colored lights, the transformation necessary to the story will take place. The nymphs who swim from rock to rock in the Rhine do so with the most perfect of motions apparently without support from above or below.[69]

Twenty-five years were to pass from Wagner's first idea for a festival producing his works to the realization of an ideal space completely under his control. The *Bühnenfestspiele* in his own theater were presented to the public beginning on 13 August 1876 with the first complete production of *Der Ring des Nibelungen*.

Parsifal

Parsifal was Wagner's only opera written expressly for the Festspielhaus, and it was to take full advantage of the scenic and acoustical capabilities of the theater. Wagner began composing the preliminary musical drafts for *Parsifal* in September 1877. As in his earlier operas, Wagner was acutely aware of the visual aspects of production during the compositional process. The second scene of the first act, the Hall of the Grail, presented possibilities for great artistic and scenic effect. On 23 January 1878, Cosima wrote in her diary, "In the morning we discussed the scenery for the Hall of the Grail, and I suggested a Basilica, two naves leading through pillars to doors hidden behind them."[70] Thus the seeds for the second scene of the first act were planted.

Shortly after this discussion, Wagner completed the compositional drafts for the first act. Cosima took the initiative in finding an artist to create designs for the settings in time for Wagner's birthday on 22 May. By letter on 2 February, she approached a Swiss artist, Arnold Böcklin, but without success.[71] Later Wagner attempted to interest other prominent artists such as Camillo Sitte and Rudolf Seitz, but again without success. In the months before May 1880, Paul Joukowsky, a member of Wagner's inner circle of friends, was commissioned to create the designs.

Over an extended period, Joukowsky labored with the designs. In time Wagner approved four that became the basis for the forest and the temple of the Grail in the first act as well as the glade in the third act. During a trip to Italy at the end of August 1880, the Wagners and Joukowsky visited the cathedral in Siena. Upon viewing the interior of the cathedral, particularly the high dome supported by mighty columns, the composer was moved to tears. Joukowsky wrote in his memoirs that these impressions of the cathedral became a model for the temple of the Grail: "I had to make a sketch of the interior of the dome, which later would be very useful for the design of the Grail temple."[72]

For one important episode in the first act, the scenic artists Gotthold and Max Brückner were engaged to create the scenic effect of the change from the forest to the temple of the Grail. This was to become the basis for a "change of scene" in view of the audience and coordinated with the music. This effect, the so-called *Verwandlungsszene*, was to be achieved through the mechanical means of moving canvas drops.[73]

Carl Brandt, Wagner's technical director during the production of the first *Ring,* was to supervise the construction of the machinery required to effect the change of scene. Long before the score was completed, Wagner was aware—although perhaps not to the full extent—of the potential pitfalls relating to the time required to accomplish the change of scenery. He conferred with Brandt first on 13 and 14 January 1881, together with Joukowsky, about achieving the desired scenic effect with a minimum of technical difficulty.[74] Designs and models were examined and discussed. Out of that conference, Wagner and Brandt optimistically concluded that the change could be completed in fewer than four minutes. In March Wagner composed the music to fit the duration of the change of scene. Cosima noted in her diary: "R. writes some additional music for 'Parsifal'—4 minutes of music." She noted several days later, "He works on his 3-minute music, literally with his watch in hand."[75] Unwittingly, Wagner was to give himself many a headache with this figure of four minutes. The preparations suffered a great setback when Brandt died unexpectedly in 1881; however, his son Fritz took over the position and fulfilled his appointment to great praise.

The setting for the first scene of Act I is described in the libretto:

> *A forest, shadowy and solemn, but not gloomy. A rocky landscape. A clearing in the center. Rising up to the left is taken to be a path leading to the castle of the Grail. In the background at the center, the ground slopes down to a lake deep in the forest. Daybreak.*[76]

After Kundry departs from the scene, Gurnemanz notes that Amfortas is returning to the castle and invites Parsifal to accompany him to the feast of the Grail: "Now let me accompany you to the hallowed meal, for you are pure." (*Nun lass' zum frommen Mahle mich dich geleiten, denn du bist rein.*) It is here that Wagner specifically noted in the full score that the "Verwandlung" should already be underway, but it must be imperceptible (*unmerklich*).[77] Gurnemanz takes Parsifal by the arm, and both begin to "walk in place." The decorations begin to move from left to right: Parsifal asks—"Who is the Grail?" (*Wer ist der Gral?*)—Gurnemanz does not answer directly other than to say that the Grail has guided Parsifal's steps to this otherwise hidden land. At that moment, Parsifal remarks, "I have hardly walked, but seem to have gone far." (*Ich schreite kaum, doch wähn ich mich schon weit.*) Gurnemanz answers him: "You see, my son, here space is one with time." (*Du siehst mein Sohn, zum Raum wird hier die Zeit.*) At this point, the *Verwandlungsmusik* begins its solemn march in E-flat major.

The libretto describes the change of scene:

> *While Gurnemanz and Parsifal appear to be walking, the scene gradually changes in an imperceptible manner from left to right; thus the forest disappears. In rock walls, a gateway opens and then closes upon the two. Both become visible in a rising passageway, through which they appear to be walking. Long held trombone tones gently rise up; sounds of ringing bells come closer. Finally, they enter a mighty hall, [the height] of which disappears up into a high, vaulted, dome through which a single source of light penetrates. From high above the dome one hears the bells ringing ever louder.*[78]

This entire visual transformation takes place in full view of the audience. The effect was accomplished by the seemingly simple means of moving from left to right one very long painted drop 39.4 feet (12 meters) in height. Four separate sets of drops were used to achieve the complete effect (figure 9.11).[79] Each drop was already in its place from the beginning of the act to assist in creating a perspective view of the forest scene. The second and third drops were in two parts, each with a cutout of a wooded scene, then a continuation of woods to mask the actual change of scenery upstage of the drops themselves. The fourth drop upstage depicted the woodland along with the forest lake in the distance, as described in the libretto. This drop remained in place until the change of the scenery to the Hall of the Grail, whereupon it flew up into the flies.

The key to the entire *Verwandlung* was the first downstage drop. This was the longest of the three drops that traveled the width of the stage, for it contained all of the painted vistas that Gurnemanz and Parsifal walk through to reach the castle of the Grail. The tops of the first, second, and third drops were attached to a hanging rail and pulled from the left side of the stage to the right. Each drop was rolled onto a vertical drum. The turning of the three drums was, of course, carefully coordinated. More than 27,000 square feet (2,500 square meters) of painted canvas were required for the four drops in achieving this effect.[80]

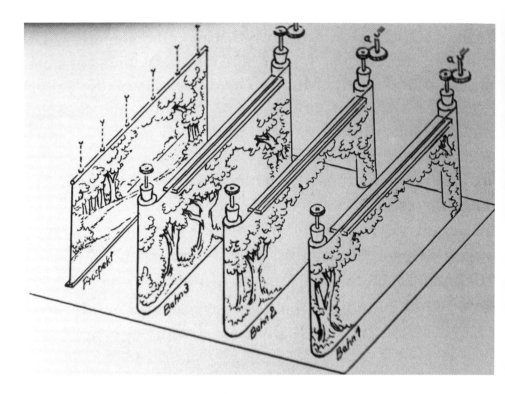

Figure 9.11. Kurt Söhnlein, reconstruction of machinery for the *Verwandlung* in Act I, *Parsifal*.

A document with a running commentary on the action from the first performances exists, and might be considered akin to a staging manual somewhat similar to the French *livrets de mise en scène* (staging manuals). This document was prepared by G. Philipp, a stage manager at the first performances of the opera, at the behest of the singer Anton Schittenhelm. The stage action during the *Verwandlung* is described as follows:

> At this point begins the slow change of scene from left to right, as seen from the perspective of the auditorium, under a "greenish white" lighting on the stage. The train [of Amfortas and his knights] has disappeared, and Gurnemanz and Parsifal upon reaching the path A remain in position a´ [center stage; figure 9.12]. Both seemingly sway from side to side on the balls of their feet. The decorations display rock grottos of which one leads upwards to sheltered stone steps with short but mighty columns supporting slabs of stone. In the course of the change of scene, which now stretches across the entire stage, Parsifal

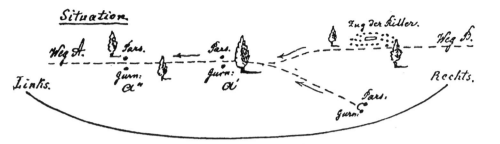

Figure 9.12. Anton Schittenhelm, *Parsifal*. Staging plan of the Forest scene before the *Verwandlung,* Act I.

and Gurnemanz disappear for a short time; they then appear again at position a″ before disappearing completely shortly thereafter. The final [portion] of the changing scenery reveals two enormous and mighty pillars with an entry gate, through which the path should lead to the castle of the Grail. This final piece then disappears through the traps, and at the same moment the stage changes into the hall of columns with the vaulted dome [figure 9.13]. One hears the chiming of bells.[81]

Figure 9.13. Gotthold and Max Brückner, *Parsifal,* Hall of the Grail.

During all this, the stage behind the first drop was being changed over into the Hall of the Grail. Properties such as the tables, benches, and altar were placed into position. Cutout drops depicting the painted columns, dome, and upstage halls were lowered from the flies. The "entry gate," as described by Schittenhelm, apparently consisted of enormous stone walls painted on large flats which became visible when the first drop completed its movement across the stage. Now the temple is completely set. The E-flat fanfare of the trumpets and trombones rings out from behind the scenes, leading into the majestic C-major chord with the bells ringing softly in the background.[82] Gurnemanz says to Parsifal, "Now observe well, and let me see: if you are the pure fool; what knowledge will be given you" (*Nun achte wohl, und lass mich seh'n: bist du ein Thor und rein, welch' Wissen dir auch mag beschieden sein*). The two large flats then sink down into the traps. At first, Wagner was disappointed with this phase of the change, for Cosima noted in her diaries:

> The discrepancy between the transformation scenes and the music provided for them becomes clearly apparent; R. at first jokes about it, saying that usually conductors make cuts, now they have to compose additional music for him. But it saddens him to see that even here his ideas are not realized in practice. The forest scenery in the first transformation is not at all the way he wanted it, and it is also bad that at the end the rocks sink into the ground.[83]

Only later, and after many more rehearsals and adjustments, did Wagner approve of the change.

Schittenhelm continued the description of the *Verwandlung*:

> The forestage shows two large pillars and the same upstage. These four pillars support the dome. On either side of the pillars, both downstage and upstage are corresponding pillars for the passages. Under the vaulted dome is the main dining hall, from which both sides lead to the halls of the castle. A golden partition upstage encloses the space. From the right hall enter the knights of the Holy Grail two by two in measured steps. At the center of the dining area stands, almost altar-like, the Grail chest with four octagonal steps leading up to it (upon which the closed Grail will later be placed). The dining table of the knights is drawn up in the shape of a half-circle reaching from one of the downstage pillars to the other around the chest. [Here follows the order of entry for the knights, squires, etc. along with Amfortas.]
>
> After the change of scene is complete, Gurnemanz and Parsifal enter from the upstage right hall ("C") and after several more steps

come to downstage right in front of the hall and remain standing at position "A." They observe the entries of the knights, squires, and youths [figure 9.14].[84]

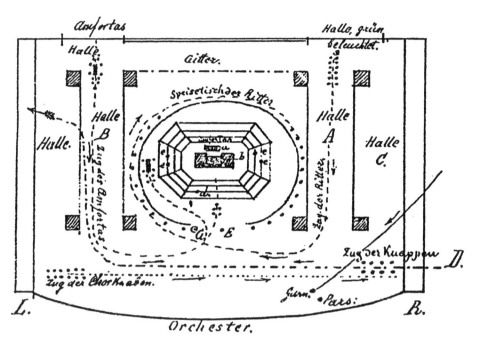

Figure 9.14. Anton Schittenhelm, *Parsifal*. Staging plan for the entry into the Hall of the Grail, Act I.

The entire change of scene lasted a little more than five minutes: seventy-two measures of the score passed before the C-major fanfare rang out.

Executing the change turned out to be far more difficult than anticipated. In June 1882 during the first staging rehearsals with the music and with Wagner present, the complications arising from the timing of the change of scene nearly derailed any chance of success.[85] On 21 June the actual rehearsal using the completed decorations for the *Verwandlung* began, and the result was a disaster. It was clear that the technical staff had completely miscalculated the time necessary for the change of settings. Engelbert Humperdinck—best known for his opera *Hänsel und Gretel*—was a music assistant. He left this priceless description of the rehearsal:

It became apparent during the piano rehearsal that [the scene change] was taking far too long. "Yes, there must be more music added," calmly said Master [Fritz] Brand[t] from Darmstadt with his watch in hand. He needs so and so many minutes in order to unreel all of the scenery.

"What! Now I must compose by the meter?" shouted Wagner, enraged.

Yes [said Brandt], it can't be done otherwise. The machinery can't run any faster, and the decorations can no longer be changed, it would cost a king's ransom, and besides, there's not enough time.

Wagner was beside himself, swore over and over not to have anything more to do with the rehearsals and performances, and, in high dudgeon, quickly left.[86]

Hermann Levi, the conductor of the first performances, quietly suggested that some of the music be repeated. Humperdinck saved the situation by composing several very short passages which were discreetly added to the full score to give the stage machinery the additional necessary time. One week later rehearsals were improving, and Humperdinck showed the additions to Wagner who was mollified and accepted the changes with good humor.[87] After all the problems with the *Verwandlung* were corrected, Humperdinck's additions were removed from the score.

Still, during the first performances, Levi required some latitude with the music during the *Verwandlung*—the most likely place for this was near the end of the transformation when, after the fanfare, the offstage bells are ringing without any additional musical accompaniment. In the full score, the conductor is instructed to let the bells ring to a crescendo for four measures and, when needed, to repeat the measures until the transformation is completed.[88] Levi's music stand was also constructed with an electrical device that communicated the beat to the backstage musical staff who were not only supervising the backstage orchestra players but also watching over the cranking of the canvas rollers during the *Verwandlung*.

At the end of June although the first-act change seemed finally to pull itself together, problems with the *Verwandlung* in the third act continued. After a difficult rehearsal on 18 July, it was decided that the third-act *Verwandlung* was to be dropped. Instead, the stage lighting was dimmed and a neutral curtain lowered to permit the change of scenery hidden from view of the audience.[89]

Wagner, in his essay *Das Bühnenweihfestspiel in Bayreuth 1882,* reported the difficulties of both the first- and third-act *Verwandlung* scenes:

Only on one point we had to make a tiresome compromise, on this occasion. By a still inexplicable misreckoning, the highly-gifted [Brandt]—to whom I owe the whole stage-mounting of the "Parsifal," as formerly of the Nibelungen pieces, and who was torn from us by

sudden death before the completion of his work—had calculated the
speed of the so-called Wandeldekoration (moving scenery) in the first
and third acts at more than twice as fast as was dictated by the interest
of the dramatic action. In this interest I had never meant the passing of
a changing scene to act as a decorative effect, however artistically
carried out; but, with the help of the accompanying music, we were to
be led quite imperceptibly, as if in a dream, along the "pathless" trails
to the Gralsburg, whose legendary inaccessibility to the non-elect was
thus to be brought within the bounds of dramatic portrayal. When we
discovered the mistake, it was too late to alter the unusually complicated mechanism so as to reduce the rolling scenery to half its length;
for this time I had to decide not only on repeating the orchestral inter-
lude [Act I] in full, but also upon introducing tedious retards in its
tempo: the painful effect was felt by us all, yet the mounting itself was
so admirably executed that the entranced spectator was compelled to
shut one eye to criticism.[90]

The final arbiter of the *Verwandlung*'s success was the public. Felix von
Weingartner, later to become a distinguished conductor and opera administra-
tor, reported his reactions from his visit to the first performances in 1882:

The auditorium grew completely dark. Like a voice from another
world, the first expansive theme of the prelude begins. This impression
is incomparable. . . .
    The curtain parted fairly slowly. A beautiful setting unrolled before
the eyes: Gurnemanz awakened by the distant trombone tones. . . .
    When Gurnemanz was ready to accompany Parsifal to the Grail
castle, I was seized by a slight dizziness. What was happening? It seemed
to me that the theater with its entire audience began to move. The
scene had started to change by means of moving the backcloth. The
illusion was complete. One did not walk, one was carried along. "Here
space is one with time." On two or three columns, one behind another
facing each other on either side of the stage, were drops that unrolled
[together], until the last stone walls moved away and the noble dimensions of the interior of the Grail castle stood before us. Exactly at the
C-major chord, light poured over the majestic scene. An incomparable
effect was produced with the simplest means.[91]

This production by Richard Wagner, with the designs of Paul Joukowsky and
the Brückner brothers, was a great success and remained in the repertory of the
Festival until 1933. Other than for refurbishing and retouching the scenic units,
the settings of the Temple of the Grail and the *Verwandlungen* in their entirety
remained unchanged for fifty years.[92]

Fine

From the years of his own practical experiences in the theater and in opera houses, Wagner gathered knowledge, sagacity, and ideals. With his sheer force of personality and stubbornness, he created a theater with its own unique environment, one that has had repercussions in theater, opera, and all branches of the performing arts. These repercussions continue to be felt to this day. That the theater was constructed at all is a tribute to Wagner's theatrical genius, to his persistence, and these mixed with sheer luck. The Festspielhaus is a model theater: its primary focus is to bring the attention of the audience solely to events unfolding on the stage without other distractions. Anything less is unacceptable. At the conclusion of his essay on the Festspielhaus, Wagner wrote: "There may it stand, on the beautiful hill near Bayreuth" (*Dort stehe es, auf dem lieblichen Hügel bei Bayreuth*). For as long as the Festspielhaus continues to stand on that hill, it will continue to exert influence, both subtle and overt, on the continuing evolution of the operatic arts in all their forms.

CHAPTER TEN

Realism on the Opera Stage: Belasco, Puccini, and the California Sunset

Helen M. Greenwald

> Light, like music, can express to me
> whatever belongs to the "inner essence of
> all appearances."
>
> *Das Licht kann, gleich der Musik, mir das
> ausdrücken was dem 'inneren Wesen aller
> Erscheinung' angehört.*
>
> —Adolphe Appia,
> *Die Musik und die Inscenierung*

The Demise of "Number Opera"

The late nineteenth century witnessed a literary and musical revolution in which efforts to dramatize realistic life situations became the objective of novelists, playwrights, librettists, and composers. In the Italian opera house, one arm of the movement became known as *verismo*. While inspired locally by the literary efforts of Giovanni Verga and his contemporaries, *verismo* had its principal source in French literature: first, in the works of Dumas (*fils*) and later, fully realized by Émile Zola.[1] This revolution was itself the product of revolutions, both political and technological, and reflected, consequently, not only the social problems arising out of the rapid industrialization of Europe (especially France), but also the rapid "industrialization" of the theater itself.

279

As a literary movement, *verismo* sought to represent truthfully the characters and situations of "real" life, couching itself in the milieu, most often, of the lower classes, who were considered "'more natural' men and women, whose emotions were closer to the surface and hence more intense than those of effete upper class city dwellers."[2] The romantic view, once characterized by formalized structures and polished styles, was thus exchanged for a more objective and positivistic presentation of what was considered observable fact.[3]

In America, the movement toward naturalism spawned a genre of drama— melodrama—that, while lacking "psychological insight and artistic depth,"[4] compensated for it pictorially by means of new technological skills that were to overtake the theater in the late nineteenth century as a direct result of the advent of electricity. The most important consequence of this invention and the *sine qua non* of its expression would be film, all the better to produce "more faithfully train wrecks, fires, snow-storms, steamship explosions and avalanches" then popular in the theater.[5]

In the opera house, however, the most profound effect of this move toward realism was the eventual dissolution of what is generally called *number opera*, a type of opera that consisted of essentially independent numbers that could be strung together in a sequence to construct larger act complexes. The rejection of number opera resulted from a long process of evolution, already begun in the era of Verdi's first works.[6] This new veristic style was also influenced by Wagner, whose works, while by no means realistic, placed greater emphasis upon the orchestra. The symphonic nature and continuous texture of Wagner's operas led, in Italian opera, to a new rapport between vocal and instrumental music.[7] Also inherent in this change was the gradual realization that continuous and "realistic" works must have a unified interpretation. Thus, number opera's old reliance upon singers to work out the specific difficulties of their roles on their own, while rehearsals were held primarily to complete the details of the staging, was abandoned during the course of the nineteenth century in favor of a more integrated conception. Even rehearsal and staging techniques had, of necessity, to be altered. This was also true in the spoken theater, as severely limited rehearsal time also had to give way to new techniques of preparation, and a director could no longer be someone who merely directed traffic.[8]

The Aesthetics of Lighting

By the end of the nineteenth century, the desire for a unified interpretation fundamentally engaged all aspects of production. No aspect of production was more critical in this role than lighting. Even though stage lighting is a thoroughly modern concept (before the nineteenth century both the playing area and the viewing area shared the available lighting in the theater), two principles were evident to those involved with the theater from early on: that light plays a role in communicating and shaping the drama; and that it is desirable to make the playing area lighter and brighter than the viewing area.[9] The effect of the nineteenth century's technological advances was extraordinary, for not only was the new ability to plunge the audience into darkness a powerful method for quieting them, but it also defined more clearly the playing area and brought into new perspective all other aspects of production such as scenery, costumes, and makeup. As the great nineteenth-century stage designer Adolphe Appia once said:

> Light is the most important plastic medium on the stage. . . . Without its unifying power our eyes would be able to perceive what objects were but not what they expressed. . . . What can give us this sublime unity which is capable of uplifting us? Light! . . . Light and light alone, quite apart from its subsidiary importance in illuminating a dark stage, has the greatest plastic power, for it is subject to a minimum of conventions and so is able to reveal vividly in its most expressive form the eternally fluctuating appearance of a phenomenal world.[10]

The dramatic illusion thus had to be restyled at every level. It is, therefore, no small coincidence that the technological innovations in the theater corresponded with the new move toward realism in literature and performance practice. Indeed, light became essential to the establishment of mood, time, and place, and new approaches to acting (by Stanislavski, for example) as well as to rehearsing and staging were consequently developed.[11] The impact upon musical theater, specifically opera, was even more profound, however, because time is quintessential in any musical creation, and any modulation of it—either technical or dramatic—affects musical composition as well as libretto construction. Indeed, time in opera is marked primarily through music, as the basic durational elements—rhythm and meter—propel the work forward in the most regular and systematic way. These measurable elements are in turn enriched by aria and song, elements that tend to control the larger sense of pacing: aria, a reflective function, analogous to that of the soliloquy in spoken drama, generally suspends time,[12] while song consumes "real" time.

In both real life and the theater (be it sung or spoken), time is not accessible to direct observation.[13] It is perceived only through its manifestations: natural phenomena such as the changes from light to dark or from winter to spring; signs such as the calendar and the clock; or activities such as meals, courtship and marriage, and seasonal rituals. The re-creation of these manifestations in the theater (and opera house) provides a chronology for the drama, while the semantic connotations that certain seasons of the year or times of day seem to possess establish both a mood and a set of expectations.[14] For example,

tragedy is commonly associated with night and winter, whereas comedy is traditionally associated with day and springtime. Night is often perceived as
being the realm of the supernatural, while day is thought of as the realm of
the rational.[15] In both spoken drama and opera, the passage of time may be
suggested explicitly through aural signals such as offstage chimes or verbal
references to time, each of which either concretely establishes the present or
stimulates movement by suggesting the future. Visual cues, however, constitute
a more subtle means of creating a temporal illusion, and these are created on
stage through lighting and physical activity.

In the nineteenth century, no opera composer's art was more thoroughly
modern in its emphasis on the detailed re-creation of specific times and places
than that of Giacomo Puccini (1858–1924). Puccini was known to go to great
lengths to provide a correct ambience, whether it be through the chimes of the
Castel Sant' Angelo in *Tosca* or through the use of authentic Japanese melodies
in *Madama Butterfly*. Moreover, there are numerous examples of direct references
to time in Puccini's works, including the Bohemians' anticipation of their
Christmas Eve celebration at the Café Momus (looking ahead to the Latin
Quarter Scene) or the distant chimes proclaiming the hour in *Il tabarro*, which,
while designating a specific hour, also set an ominous tone for what is to come.
The structure of his works also reflects a radical rethinking of conventions, as
his operas unfold primarily through a more or less continuous sequence of
arioso exchanges and musically accompanied "action" scenes. This is nowhere
more evident than in *Tosca*, where the curtain rises on what is basically an action
piece despite the very few lines of dialogue, as Angelotti seeks the key to the
Attavanti Chapel. Indeed, a *primo ottocento* composer most likely would have
had Angelotti sing an aria in which he explained his predicament. Puccini's conception, on the other hand, is a cinematically contrived tableau that strikingly
parallels the kind of effects the American playwright, producer, director, and
innovator David Belasco (1853–1931) sought to achieve in his plays.

Foundations for a Collaboration

It is remarkable that Puccini and Belasco, residing an ocean apart, should
have crossed paths at all, much less become collaborators. Both men were considered consummately theatrical and withstood enormous criticism for their
individual pursuits.[16] From the earliest stages of their careers, each was obsessed
with controlling every aspect of his creative output, making countless revisions
in the process. Indeed, Puccini drove away one librettist after another in the
genesis of *Manon Lescaut* with his demands for rewrites,[17] and then went on to
aggravate to distraction both Giacosa and Illica during the creation of *La
bohème*, as their letters of protest to Giulio Ricordi reveal.[18] It is not surprising,
then, that Belasco's remarks on the evolution of a play seem almost to hint

at a conspiracy with his European counterpart, Puccini: "The exceptionally successful play is not written, but rewritten."[19]

The most remarkable parallels in Puccini's and Belasco's work are to be found in matters of production. Puccini demanded that the motivation and action of the drama be self-explanatory, insisting, as Carner has noted, "on what he called *L'evidenza della situazione*, which should enable the spectator to follow the drama even without understanding the actual words."[20] Given this attitude toward theater, it is no surprise that Puccini, while not understanding a word of English, would be taken with the work of a man, who, independently and thousands of miles away, developed his own art form from a similar point of view.

Belasco was a pioneer of modern staging and keenly sensitive, in particular, to the dramatic potential of stage lighting. He once said:

> Lights are to drama what music is to the lyrics of a song. No other factor that enters into the production of a play is so effective in conveying its mood and feeling. They are as essential to every work of dramatic art as blood is to life.[21]

Puccini, though he rarely spoke about it, also considered stage lighting as both a narrative and artistic element, but independently of Belasco. His structural use of lighting is clearly evident in his scores, especially in *La fanciulla del West*, in which he adopted nearly wholesale not only Belasco's play, but also details of production, including a special lighting effect—a sunset—that Belasco had tried desperately to achieve but had ultimately discarded. David Belasco's play *The Girl of the Golden West* and Puccini's opera based upon it, *La fanciulla del West*, thus stand as the conflation of the idioms of these two men and as exemplars of live theater at the threshold of film.

Puccini's First Contact with Belasco: *Madame Butterfly*

Puccini first viewed David Belasco's one-act play, *Madame Butterfly*, in London in 1900.[22] Even though he could not understand the English dialogue, he was struck by the effectiveness of the production in which the play was couched, in particular the scene of Butterfly's vigil. For its time, this scene, as staged and lighted by Belasco, was a theatrical coup, as a time lapse of twelve hours from sunset to the following morning was unfolded magnificently through changing lighting effects achieved through the use of colored silks. Belasco even claimed that his production of *Madame Butterfly* was "the first play to develop electricity in its use for stage effects, from the merely practical to the picturesque and poetical."[23] Louis Hartmann, for years Belasco's lighting technician, describes the process:

The several colors of silk were in long strips. These strips were attached to tin rollers; the rollers were set into bearings fastened to a wooden frame that slid into the color groove of the lamp. The turning of the rollers passed the colors in front of the light and they were projected on the windows in a series of soft blends. As the orange deepened into blue, floor lanterns were brought on the scene and lighted; as the pink of the morning light was seen the lanterns flickered out one by one. The light changes were accompanied by special music. Music and lights were perfectly timed and the entire change consumed less than three minutes. By the manipulation of lights and music David Belasco made it convincing to an audience that a period of twelve hours had passed.[24]

In his opera *Madama Butterfly* (1904), Puccini translated this scene into an extended and uniquely tinted window in which Butterfly's vigil is underscored by sound—a humming chorus as ethereal as the lighting—and sight. Thus even though Puccini suspended both action and dialogue insofar as they are traditionally understood in opera, he did *not* stop them. Rather, he abstracted them by substituting visual time for action, unfolding it through the gradual changes in light adopted from Belasco, and substituting an unseen humming chorus for dialogue. It is all the more compelling, then, that after a dry spell of six years, Puccini found his inspiration once more in another Belasco effort, *The Girl of the Golden West*. The inspiration neither ended nor climaxed with this production, however, since the impact of Belasco's influence would reach well into Puccini's final works, most vividly in *Il trittico* and in *Turandot*, the composer's most visually exciting efforts.

Light and Music in Puccini's Operas

The shape of many internal components in Puccini's operas can be discerned through lighting cues—annotations in the score that reveal a temporal framework that is both progressive and closed. In these works the lighting modulates perceptibly over the course of an act and thereby provides visual housing for the large-scale musical and dramatic motion.[25] While not all of Puccini's operas have a completely realized temporal course, most of them take place in a definable season or time of day. Six of them observe the classical unities of time and place: *Tosca*, *La fanciulla del West*, *Il tabarro*, *Suor Angelica*, *Gianni Schicchi*, and *Turandot*. Table 10.1 displays the time of day and season or month of Puccini's first acts and one-act operas. It reveals these features to be consistent and career-long.

Table 10.1. Temporal settings of first acts and one-act operas

Opera	Time of day beginning—end	Season or month
Le villi	afternoon—sunset	spring
Edgar	morning	spring
Manon Lescaut	sunset—evening	spring
La bohème	afternoon—evening	Christmas Eve
Tosca	midday	June
Madama Butterfly	afternoon—evening	spring
La fanciulla del West	sunset—evening	January
	lanterns on—lanterns off	
La rondine	sunset	spring
Il tabarro	sunset—evening	September
Suor Angelica	sunset—evening	May
Gianni Schicchi	9:00 A.M.	spring (?)
Turandot	sunset—evening	?

Clearly, sunset held a particular fascination for Puccini. Not only do seven of the twelve operas specifically begin at sunset, but two more—*La bohème* and *Madama Butterfly*—may also begin at or near sunset. In literature and in the theater (especially during the nineteenth century), the setting sun traditionally suggested either malaise or foreboding or, by contrast, provided a cover for lovers such as Tristan and Isolde.[26] Moreover, as a purely visual phenomenon, sunset is the most colorful time of day, and it provides the maximum opportunity for creating special effects on stage. Puccini's sunsets gather in all these conventional associations. While he found the sunset a rich source of varying moods, he also found it to be a good starting place, and most often used it to initiate a temporal progression that provides a physical framework as well as a particular ethos for the scenario. This purposeful selection of the time of day is especially clear in *Le villi, Manon Lescaut, La bohème, La fanciulla del West, Il tabarro, Suor Angelica*, and *Turandot*, all of which not only begin with the setting sun, but also follow a temporal course that is tied in with the psychology of the drama and closely coordinated with both the physical action and the large-scale musical gestures.

Of all Puccini's sunsets, that in *Le villi*[27] is the one most fraught with conventional foreboding. The first act takes place in spring, at a party celebrating the betrothal of Anna and Roberto. The setting sun becomes an issue only as the peasants exhort Roberto to make haste before the sun fades into the western sky (for one does not want to be caught alone in the Black Forest after dark). The gloom of the wintry night of the second act is forecast in this warning, and

almost nowhere else in Puccini's works are time and season so clearly and traditionally defined as here. These contrasts are realized musically in the opposition
of major and minor tonalities, of triple and duple rhythms, and even in the
opposing dances of the two acts.

Table 10.2. Coordination of light and music in *Le villi*

Act I (Part I)	*Act II* (Part II)
Harmony: Life	Conflict: Death
Light: afternoon—sunset	Dark: nighttime
Spring	Winter
Betrothal dance	Witches' dance
3/4	2/4
C major	C minor

Puccini returned to a quasi-supernatural setting only at the end of his
career, in *Turandot,*[28] which not only begins with a fairy-tale sunset, but also
adopts time as a condition of plot. This visual aspect of the plot is very carefully measured out (especially in the first act) through the modulating hue of the
setting sun and the various stages of the moonrise. Closely coordinated with
these visual changes are the most important, large-scale, tonal changes in Act I:

Table 10.3. Coordination of light and music in *Turandot*

	Part I		*Part II*
Light:	sunset/golden moonrise—moonrays		dimness
Tonal motion:	(F#)–B$\flat$———————E$\flat$		A$\flat$–E$\flat$

The parallels between *Le villi* and *Turandot* are especially interesting, not only
because they are Puccini's first and last efforts, but also because they are his only
fairy-tale operas. In each of them, Puccini draws heavily on the semantic associations of day and night and of light and dark: in *Le villi* evil triumphs in the dark,
as Roberto is vanquished, while in *Turandot* goodness triumphs with the dawn,
as the Princess is overwhelmed by Calaf's kiss.[29] Thus, by the time of *Turandot*,
Puccini's ability to engage and integrate light into his works is highly enriched.
    The first act of *Manon Lescaut*[30] opens on a sunset that has a different but
equally conventional association. Here it signals the coming of night, which is

a time for partying and for making love. The curtain rises on a group of students reveling at the end of the school term. Edmondo praises the approaching night as the time in which pleasure seekers thrive: "Hail, gentle evening, you who descend with your cortege of breezes and stars; hail, beloved of poets and lovers." (*Ave, sera, gentile, che discendi col tuo corteo di zeffiri e di stelle; Ave, cara ai poeti ed agli amanti.*) The text is most meaningful, as it anticipates the after-dark elopement of Manon and Des Grieux and reaches across the opera to the fourth act,[31] in which the cover of darkness has quite a different role. The final scene of the opera is compelling, as Manon's life fades away with the descent of night, a stark contrast to the lusty anticipation with which darkness was first greeted in Act I. The pleasurable imagery of Act I is thus shattered as Manon cries (Act IV, *18-16*), "I'm dying: darkness descends. . . . the night envelops me." (*Muoio: scendon le tenebre. . . . su me la notte scende.*) Of course, the equating of darkness with death is not an original idea, but the contrast between the image of darkness as a desideratum at the opening of the opera and the image of darkness that embraces the dying Manon at the end is very powerful, and it mollifies some of the more stringent criticism about the usefulness of the fourth act.

In yet another sense entirely, nightfall is linked to the theme of fate and fortune in *Manon Lescaut,* as the students anticipate the beginning of a serious card game with the coming of evening. It is this card game that forms a scenic and psychological backdrop for the entire second half of the first act. Indeed, as evening takes over and the lamps are lit onstage, the game intensifies, and the dialogue of the gambling students and of their companion, Lescaut, is periodically heard as a commentary on the main action, much in the manner of a Greek chorus (*45-2*). Moreover, the card game is an action that one associates specifically with an evening's entertainment, the intensity and potential danger of gambling being inappropriate to the quite literally more enlightened daylight hours.[32] A visual realization of the motif of chance and adventure permeates the drama nearly from the time the curtain goes up, Manon having gambled and lost by the end of the opera. The descending fifth between the two parts of the act emphasizes this change in both intensity and lighting, as does the rhythmic quickening from 3/4 to 3/8:

Table 10.4. Coordination of light and music in *Manon Lescaut*

	Part I	*Part II*
Light:	sunset	nightfall
Action:	songs	cards
Tonal motion:	A	D
Meter:	3/4	3/8

Belasco's *Girl* and Puccini's *La fanciulla*

The sunset at the beginning of *La fanciulla del West* is divorced entirely from any nineteenth-century supernatural or sexual ethos. The temporal setting of this work is especially interesting because it is among the few things that Puccini altered from Belasco's original play.[33] Belasco's 1905 production of *The Girl of the Golden West* was considered a landmark in the playwright's *oeuvre* for its naturalistic décor.[34] Of particular interest in connection with this change is that Belasco himself had spent three months trying to achieve "the soft, changing colors of a California sunset over the Sierra Nevada."[35] No doubt because Belasco was a native Californian (born in San Francisco), he had firsthand knowledge and sensitivity to the kind of light that defined his home.[36] He ultimately "turned to another method," while noting that "It was a good sunset, but it was not Californian."[37] The other "method" to which he refers included a complete revision of the play's opening, which, after a series of "pictures," ultimately leads to the midnight setting of the final version of the first act. Belasco created his pictures on a "painted canvas rolled vertically on drums across the proscenium opening; the scenes depicted on it gave a moving map-like panorama of the entire setting of the drama."[38] Nevertheless, even though he abandoned his "California" sunset, Belasco was very particular about the lighting effects that opened his production. Indeed, even as the house was opened for the public to enter, the lowered curtain was to be highlighted in a very specific way. The opening instructions to the text describe the state of the auditorium and lowered curtain at the opening of the house: "When the theatre opens and is lighted up there is a lens from the second balcony on sun effect on the Act Curtain, also thirty-two-candle-power lamps on in foots."[39] Thus, Belasco's drama begins the moment the audience enters the theater and unfolds to the opening scene through a musical prelude[40] and two "pictures" provided by painted panorama drops. The first of these, seen when the curtain is raised, presents a mountaintop panorama in which the Girl's cabin is featured. The sun is now replaced by moonlight which floods the tableau. The "picture" reveals the exterior of the "Polka" saloon, silhouetted against a dark mountainside. Light is provided by kerosene lamps and interior lighting which shines through the cracks of the door. Thus, even as Belasco unfolded his prelude in what today would be called, in cinematic terms, a pan down, it was in fact a device that he had used before, one that was characteristic of nineteenth-century theater in general, which used "'tableaux vivants,' panoramas, [and] dioramas" to enhance the spectacle.[41] Belasco's own use of such techniques dates to the 1878 staging in San Francisco of his play, *The Octoroon,* in which, as he wrote to William Winter,

> I used a panorama, painted on several hundred yards of canvas, and I introduced drops, changing scenes in the twinkling of an eye, showing,

alternately and in quick succession, pursued and pursuer,—Jacob McCloskey and the Indian,—making their way through the canebrake and swamp, and ending with the life and death struggle and the killing of McCloskey.[12]

Moreover, if Puccini was thinking in clearly Belasco-like terms, Belasco's individual scenes are eminently Pucciniesque, especially the opening scene of *The Girl* which merges group activity and drama by a "natural method of allowing the dialogue and the action to fade slowly into motion."[43] This technique was already part and parcel of Puccini's *oeuvre*, almost from the start, but most obviously so from *Manon Lescaut* on, particularly in such scenes as the tavern scene at Amiens and the Latin Quarter scene, both "crowd" scenes, unique in opera and that predate Belasco's *Girl*.[44]

Puccini retained the skeleton of Belasco's opening two pictorial tableaux, replacing the first with a prelude, heard with the curtain down, and using the second as a curtain raiser and backdrop to a musically supported dumb show. Puccini's scenario as the curtain rises, however, abandons the "pictures," compresses the outdoors and the indoors into one scene, and replaces the midnight setting with a sunset:

> *The big door in the background and the window command a view of the valley with its wild vegetation of elders, oaks and dwarf pines, all bathed in sunset-glow. In the distance the snow-mountains are tinted with gold and violet. The very strong light outside, which is rapidly fading, makes the inside of the "Polka" seem all the darker. In the gloom the outlines of things can scarcely be distinguished. On the left, almost to the proscenium,* [i.e., close to the footlights] *near the chimney-piece, the glimmer of Jack Rance's cigar is seen.*[45]

Puccini's sunset provides a frame of reference for the opera that is completely different from that of the play. For one thing, a sunset is a kinetic phenomenon, a part of a progression, whereas a nighttime setting is perceptually static. The saloon is already open at the beginning of Belasco's play, and even though Nick also closes the saloon in the original play, putting out candles and closing the shutters, this "closing" action does not mirror any previous action—his opening up at sunset—as does the closing of the saloon in the opera. Thus the actual progression of time in the opera, together with the symmetry of Nick's opening and closing of the Polka (lighting and extinguishing the lanterns), provides a temporal framework for the act,[46] with the opening sequence allowing Puccini more time to establish local color and create a mood. He accomplished this with the brief musical prelude and the dumb show, deepening the perspective of the tableau with the offstage minstrel's song and miners' calls, while establishing a timetable for the action: the end of the work day and the beginning of the evening's entertainment. Furthermore, whereas

Belasco's curtain rises on the action *in medias res*, Puccini creates a rather different scenario by beginning the action at the onset of the men's evening, rather than catching it in progress. It is an interesting adjustment, because Puccini had already dealt successfully with an opening *in medias res* in the first act of *La bohème*. Moreover, the combination of Belasco's midnight opening and his reveling miners projects a more obviously coarse image, whereas Puccini's early-evening time and long-distance shouts of "hello" seem to romanticize and soften the same setting and characters. Perhaps it is a foreigner's image of the American West.

Puccini's opera begins with an immensely vital, upward-sweeping motif that catapults the work into action and is the musical realization of the vast California setting that he described in his letter of 26 August 1907 to Giulio Ricordi as "a grand scenario, a clearing in the great Californian forest, with some colossal trees" (*uno scenario grandioso, un spianata nella grande foresta californiana cogli alberi colossali*).[47] The opening musical gesture is thus an onomatopoeic statement that evokes the gusts of wind blowing in the mountains surrounding the Polka Saloon and Minnie's cabin. The effectiveness of the gesture is reinforced by the held note at the top of the upward sweep, which, when released to (descending) *détaché* quarter notes, heightens, by contrast, the suddenness of the opening motion. The sweeping figure is articulated at different pitch levels four times in the Prelude, but Puccini then used it sparingly within the opera. In Act I it is heard again only at the end, just as the posse prepares to search for Ramirrez (Johnson).[48] This moment is also articulated in Belasco's play in his lighting design, at the point the men depart to find the outlaws. The exit of the posse is noted as

> *Six of the MEN pass from L. to R. in back of window. Three with lighted torches, two with lighted candle lights, white, and one with lighted candle lantern, red.*[49]

In both the play and the opera, Nick eventually puts out most of the lights and closes the shutters, but stops short as he sees that Johnson and the girl are remaining. Of course, Puccini picks up on this detail in the opera, but the moment has an even greater impact because the act itself had begun in daylight. It initiates the close of the act (*95*), as Nick, the bartender, wishes the men good luck and begins to close the Polka Saloon (by extinguishing the lights!), leaving Minnie and Johnson alone to carry on a more intimate conversation. Finally, because the setting of Act I of *La fanciulla* is interior rather than exterior, lamplight serves as the main visual indicator of time (i.e., lights on at the beginning and lights off at the end).[50]

It would appear, then, that Puccini was following Belasco's original intention with his sunset, especially since the playwright himself assisted in the staging of the New York premiere of the opera.[51] Whether or not Puccini actually achieved what Belasco could not is unclear. Puccini had never seen a sunset in the Sierra Nevada, and, perhaps, he was simply not as concerned with the shade and hue of it as was Belasco. On the other hand, the sunset opening was, without a doubt, stylistically consistent with what Puccini had done in his previous operatic scores. Perhaps, then, Puccini's alteration of the opening is relevant to the size and equipment of the theaters in which the play and the opera were each presented.

Belasco and Lighting

David Belasco's drama is intricately tied to the Victory Theatre, which still stands on 42nd Street in New York City and is currently undergoing renovation as part of the 42nd Street Inc. Renovation Project. It was here that Puccini first saw the play, which had opened on 14 November 1905 after a brief run in Pittsburgh.[52]

The Victory had originally opened as the Theatre Republic on 27 September 1900 with Lionel Barrymore in his Broadway debut in James Herne's *Sag Harbor*. This new house, with its two balconies, proscenium boxes, and concealed dome lighting, was seen by Oscar Hammerstein (the elder) as a monument to "all that is best in dramatic and lyric art."[53] David Belasco was the manager of the theater, but within two years he leased it himself, and, after renaming it the "Belasco," set upon a massive renovation that concentrated on the tiny backstage area. He equipped this anew with the most up-to-date machinery: elevator lifts, turntables, and trapdoors, all features intended to enlarge and expand the space of the house enough to compensate for the small distance between the audience and the stage as well as for the small space backstage.[54] Belasco, however, was known for seeking out small spaces, once remarking:

> I like a moderate sized, even a small theatre, for most plays, because of the intimacy, the close contact which permits the closest observation, so that the most delicate and subtle touches, intonations and glances, the fluttering of an eyelid, the trembling of a lip, the tense tremor of nervous fingers shall not be lost or obscured.[55]

Most important among Belasco's additions, however, was a special lighting lab he installed in the dome of the theater.[56] It was here that he could turn his attention to what he considered the "all-important factor in a dramatic production—the lighting of the scenes."[57] Lighting was more than spectacle to Belasco, and like Puccini, he was extremely sensitive to its value as a psychological tool, even upon his actors, who responded instinctively, he believed, to changes in the light cast upon them during the course of a play.[58] In order to achieve these effects, Belasco conducted experiments during the years from 1900 to 1930 with his electrician, Louis Hartmann, often with a model miniature theater, "evolving colors by transmitting white light through gelatin or silk of various hues."[59]

Belasco was very conscientious about concealing the mechanism of his lighting effects, often doing away with footlights or inventing reflectors to create a special hue, making his electricians "become as familiar with the play as the actors themselves."[60] The lighting in this theater was quite modern, with most of the equipment hidden so that the audience could not identify the source of certain special effects. As Winter has noted,

> all the lamps in the house, whether upon the stage or in the auditorium, were connected "on resistance,"—that is, so connected with the electric current feed wires that the lights could be (as invariably they were) turned up or down, as required, gently by degrees.[61]

More importantly, Belasco's goal with lighting was to enhance the very structure of the drama itself, as opposed to the work of at least one of his contemporaries, Lincoln J. Carter, whom Hartmann calls, "a clever showman whose sole offering to the theatre was the illusion he created by light."[62]

At the time of Belasco's *Girl* (1905), the vast majority of homes in the United States were still lit by means of candle or gas flame.[63] Yet the transition in American theaters from gas to electric sources came much earlier, beginning in 1879 with the introduction of Edison's carbon filament lamps. By the turn of the century, the transition was virtually a *fait accompli*. It can be no small coincidence that the first recorded attempt to use electric light in an American theater, made at the California Theatre, San Francisco, 21–28 February 1879, was observed by David Belasco.[64] Here works were first presented under "flickering candles and smelly oil-lamps,"[65] eventually illuminated by gas, and ultimately electric light. As Belasco notes:

> It was inevitable that I should utilize to the fullest extent every new means by which the true effects of nature could be more closely reproduced in the theatre. So it is upon applying to the stage's art electric lighting, and the more perfect use of color which it has made possible, that a great part of my thought and energies as a dramatic producer has been concentrated.[66]

Moreover, Belasco even claimed responsibility for one of the most meaningful developments in theater lighting—the introduction of the incandescent filament lighting source into theatrical spotlights and floodlights.[67]

The basic equipment in most theaters included footlights, wing lighting, battens, and movable light sources.[68] The most striking innovations in this area, however, were the resistance plate dimmer and the lensed spotlight, which allowed the manipulation of the actual fields of light themselves into various shapes—linear, round, or square as needed with soft- or hard-edge beams.[69] The very important so-called baby lens, allegedly invented by Louis Hartmann,[70] was used in a decidedly artificial way by some directors, Marker notes, as "a kind of sculptural spotlight."[71] Hartmann describes the baby lens as

> a lamp in which I combined several pieces of apparatus then in common use as separate units. In brief, it was a lens box housing an incandescent lamp that had a concentrated filament. Each unit was fitted with a dimmer so that I could control the amount of light in easy stages from full brilliancy to out. They were the first lens lamps that could be placed anywhere on the scene.[72]

In Belasco's hands it "produced a lifelike, plastic, yet essentially imperceptible effect."[73] It was this flexibility that seemed to be Belasco's trademark, as many of his unique lighting effects stem from a "flexible system of movable spots and projectors," which, "counteracting the flattening effect produced by the normal footlights and border lights, [was] used to achieve an atmospheric, plastic illumination of the scenery by means of constantly varying, delicately natural shades of brightness and shadow."[74]

It would seem, then, that the only building that rivaled Belasco's theater was the Metropolitan Opera House, which, by 1892, after a devastating fire, was newly renovated and actually maintained both electric and gas powered border lights and footlights. It was not until 1903, however, with the total renovation of the house, that all the stage equipment was completely updated.[75] Before this the house had to employ a "gas man" who sat at a gas table set into the proscenium wall.[76]

Among the most important features of the lighting system in the Met was a " 'V' shaped reflector section placed between adjacent [border] lamps so as to prevent intermingling of the colors of light."[77] The border lights (eight in all), made of galvanized iron, "were wired for three colors and white, each of the eight containing a total of 72-50 c[andle] p[ower] lamps, white, and 48-32 cp lamps each of red, blue, and amber."[78] The single feature which seems most striking, however, is the switchboard itself; while based upon control of three colors—red, blue, and amber—the switchboard was divided into left and right sides in such a way that "it was possible to dim or switch the lights of one color on one side of the stage independently from the same color on the other side of the stage."[79] It was, as Rubin notes, "a real and substantial development in the art of dimming control when compared to the noninterlocking dimmers in use only a few years before."[80] The switchboard contained ninety-six rheostats for stage lighting and twenty for auditorium lighting. By contrast, Belasco's renovation of the Republic Theater included fewer than half as many dimmers, a total of forty-five in all.[81]

The renovated stage space was, undoubtedly, larger than that of the Belasco Theatre. This was in stark contrast to the second Belasco Theatre (the Stuyvesant), with its proscenium opening width of 32 feet (9.8 meters), height of 30 feet (9.1 meters), and distance from curtain line to back wall standing at a mere 27 feet (8.2 meters) which, according to Marker, was comparable to the first Belasco Theatre (the Republic-Victory).[82] Rubin describes the dimensions of the Metropolitan Opera House stage and its lighting equipment:

> The over-all dimensions of the stage were unchanged during the recon-struction, remaining at slightly over 100 feet [30.5 meters] across and approximately 73 feet [22.3 meters] from curtain line to the back wall, 86 feet [26.2 meters] from footlights to the back wall; the proscenium opening being 54 feet [16.5 meters]. Into this space were placed eight border lights for lighting the stage and backdrops, and a ninth border light for lighting the paint frame at the rear of the stage. These border lights were 64 feet long [19.5 meters], thus extending approximately five feet [1.5 meters] past the proscenium opening at either side, according to the recommendations of the day.[83]

As in the remodelling of the first Belasco Theatre before it, a principal aim of the 1903 renovation of the old Met was to hide the source of the lights as well as to prevent any light spill or glare that might distract the audience or obscure its lines of sight. To this end the footlights were placed in such a manner that they conformed to the curve of the stage. Baffles between the lamps prevented intermingling of the light. The notion of adapting the lighting to suit the shape of the stage was also followed through as "additional strips of lights were placed immediately upstage of the proscenium arch, and arranged to follow the curve of the arch in a continuous inverted 'U' shape."[84] Additional lighting equipment was portable, and the arrangement of pockets in various locations in the stage and backstage area — on the fly floors at either side of the stage, on the circumference of the stage floor, in the orchestra pit, and so on — reveals that all the "light on the stage originated from behind the proscenium arch, with absolutely no provision for lighting equipment to be connected ahead of the arch."[85] Rubin notes that there were also "10,000 other lamps, mostly 16 c[andle] p[ower], used in lighting the auditorium, public areas, and dressing rooms," all of which "was controlled from the main switchboard located under-neath the stage apron."[86] All in all, the Met facilities constituted an expansion of Belasco's concept of lighting.

Belasco's Influence on Puccini after *The Girl*

Undoubtedly, the magnificence of this technology together with Puccini's newly acquired experience with David Belasco set the stage for the remainder of the composer's career. Thus, nearly eight years after *La fanciulla del West*, Puccini would find himself premiering yet another work at the Metropolitan Opera House, this time the three, one-act operas known collectively as *Il trittico*. Perhaps it is no small coincidence that the very opening of this three-part evening—*Il tabarro*—is what Kimbell calls "the supreme example of Belasco-like *ambientismo*."[87]

Il tabarro,[88] like *La fanciulla del West*, begins at the end of a working day—that of Michele and his longshoremen. Time and light in this work are all-important, but not only as a frame in which to surround the action. The text is riddled with both direct and indirect references to time and light, many of them very specific. For example, Giorgetta notes both the sunset and the season in her remarks to Michele near the beginning of the opera (*21*): "Already night is falling. . . . Oh, what a red September sunset! An autumn shiver! Doesn't the sun look like a great orange dying in the Seine!" (*Già discende la sera. . . . Oh che rosso tramonto di settembre! Che brivido d'autunno! Non sembra un grosso arancio questo sole che muore nella Senna!*) Light is also a property in *Il tabarro,* as Giorgetta's very first words focus not only on the mesmerizing sunset but more importantly on Michele's unlit pipe, which, when relighted, will quite literally "ignite" the opera's brutal denouement (*3*): "O Michele, aren't you tired of staring at the sunset? Do you find it such a great show? I see that your pipe has gone out." (*O Michele? Michele? Non sei stanco d'abbacinarti al sole che tramonta? Ti sembra gran spettacolo? Lo vedo bene: dalla tua pipa il fumo bianco non sbuffa più.*) Light comes into play even more subtly later on as Giorgetta considers the pleasure she has had (and will have again) in lighting the match that signals Luigi to come (*68-7*): "It seemed to me I had lit a star, the flame of our love, a star that never will set!" (*Mi pareva d'accendere una stella, fiamma del nostro amore, stella senza tramonto!*) Even Michele recalls, as Giorgetta refuses his advances, that, to him, night is also a time for love (*La notte è bella!, 83-1*). At this moment a distant church bell strikes the hour (precisely eight o'clock; *83+6*), and two lovers are heard offstage in the shadows (*84+6*): "O perfumed night . . . There is the moon. . . . the moon that spies on us." (*O profumata sera . . . C'è la luna. . . . la luna che ci spia. . . .*) Darkness has now taken over, and the presence of lovers in the shadows seems to mock Michele. The mystery of his wife's lover is, he says, a darkness that must be torn away (*87+5*): *Squarciare le tenebre!* Of course, the mystery is solved as Michele lights his pipe: the opera ends brutally under the darkness of Michele's cloak, a place that once embraced a wife and child. It is the most profound integration of scenario, libretto, and music in Puccini's *oeuvre*.

The Architecture of Mood, Time, and Place

Light provided Puccini with a unique architectural tool, something visible but untouchable, stable but kinetic. He used it to define the macrostructure of his works and to express the drama as he expanded his musical ideas from within. Exemplary of this is *La fanciulla del West*, Puccini's most dissonant work to date and the one that relies least on memorable tunes or arias. Here most of the set pieces—the Minstrel's song and the waltz—take place in the first act and function as musical properties, mainly to establish local color. It is arguably Puccini's first truly continuous and thoroughly integrated music drama, a piece that eschews almost entirely the conventions of traditional opera. It is a turning point for him both musically and scenically, inspired, no doubt, by his contact with David Belasco and the space and technology available to him in the Metropolitan Opera House in New York. Despite a brief digression to operetta with *La rondine*, the four operas that followed it—the three one-act operas of *Il trittico* and the full-scale *Turandot*—are of the same suit, works that reflect a rich and detailed musical imagination and an unfailing sense of mood, time, and place.

Notes

Chapter One

I wish to thank Anne MacNeil (University of Chicago) for her suggestions and Edmond Strainchamps (State University of New York at Buffalo) for commenting on a draft of this essay and for allowing me access to his library.

1. "Dalle macchine adunque la maraviglia, che è la prima cagione dello imparare . . . dalla nobile e graziosa favola la moralità e 'l costume divino e l'umano; il quale con bel decoro essendovi espresso, ne purgava le menti degli uditori, traendoli a giustizia e a dirittura di vero amore; come ancora si potette trarre dallo 'ntessimento di parole ottime, che immagini sono de' pensieri interni, e dalla squisita e rara musica e varia, ottimamente a' personaggi e a' concetti adattata." Michelangelo Buonarroti, *Descrizione delle felicissime nozze della Cristianissima Maestà Madama Maria Medici Regina di Francia e di Navarra*, modern edition in Angelo Solerti, *Gli albori del melodramma* (Milan, 1904; reprint, Hildesheim: G. Olms, 1969) vol. 3, pp. 27–28. The author (1568–1642) was a grand-nephew of the painter. See Silvio d'Amico, s.v. "Buonarroti, Michelangelo il giovine (o il nepote)," *Enciclopedia dello spettacolo* (Rome: Le Maschere, 1954), vol. 2, cols. 1331–1333.

2. *Il corago, o vero alcune osservazioni per metter bene in scena le composizioni drammatiche*, ed. Paolo Fabbri and Angelo Pompilio (Florence: Olschki, 1983), pp. 23–24. A partial English translation of *Il corago* may be found in Roger Savage and Matteo Sansone, "*Il corago* and the staging of early opera: four chapters from an anonymous treatise circa 1630," *Early Music* 17 (1989), 494–511.

3. Cesare Molinari, *Le nozze degli dèi: Un saggio sul grande spettacolo italiano nel seicento* (Rome: Bulzoni, 1968), p. 43.

4. See Lorenzo Bianconi, "Scena, musica e pubblico nell'opera del seicento," in *Illusione e pratica teatrale: proposte per una lettura dello spazio scenico dagli Intermedi fiorentini all' opera*

297

comica veneziana. Catalogo della mostra, ed. Franco Mancini, Maria Teresa Muraro, and Elena Povoledo (Venice: Neri Pozza, 1975), p. 19.

5. See Nino Pirrotta, *Li due Orfei da Poliziano a Monteverdi: Con un saggio critico sulla scenografia di Elena Povoledo* (Turin: Einaudi, 1975), p. 322 n. 3, as well as pp. 230 and 268 n. 102.

6. "è avvenuto che in una medesima sala dove un principe la mattina è stato ricevuto con publiche accoglienze, non senza funzioni sacre, di lì a quattro ore, avendo detto principe altrove in quel mentre pranzato, vi comparve il palco e le scene come per incanto edificate e vi si recitò l'azione con giusta maraviglia di quel personaggio e di chiunque vi si ritrovò." *Il corago,* p. 32.

7. Robert Lamar Weaver and Norma Wright Weaver, *A Chronology of Music in the Florentine Theater, 1590–1750,* Detroit Studies in Music Bibliography, no. 38 (Detroit: Information Coordinators, 1978), p. 61.

8. Ibid.

9. In spite of its smallish size, the *sala delle commedie* could accommodate fairly elaborate stagings: *L'Euridice* required a full infernal scene, and in 1613 a *Mascherata di ninfe di Senna* required a seascape, machines emerging from below the stage, and dancing in the orchestra. See Solerti, *Gli albori del melodramma,* vol. 2, pp. 113 and 263.

10. A drawing of the banquet can be found in A[lois] M. Nagler, *Theatre Festivals of the Medici, 1539–1637* (New Haven, Connecticut: Yale University Press, 1964), plate 66.

11. Solerti, *Gli albori del melodramma,* vol. 2, pp. 337 and 348. On sacred representations in Florence, sometimes staged and costumed, see the catalog of the exhibition *Il luogo teatrale a Firenze: Brunelleschi, Vasari, Buontalenti, Parigi,* ed. Mario Fabbri, Elvira Garbero Zorzi, and Anna Maria Petrioli Tofani (Milan: Electa, 1975), pp. 55–69, which offers ample documentation of the kinds of productions that were possible in churches. See also John Walter Hill, "Oratory Music in Florence, I: Recitar Cantando, 1583–1655," *Acta musicologica* 51 (1979), 108–136.

12. Bastiano de' Rossi, *Descrizione del magnificentiss. apparato e de' meravigliosi intermedi fatti per la commedia rappresentata in Firenze nelle felicissime nozze degl'Illustrissimi, ed Eccellentissimi Signori il Signor Don Cesare D'Este, e la Signora Donna Virginia Medici* (Florence: Marescotti, 1585 [1586 new style]) indicates: "in the aforementioned room . . . Grand Duke Francesco ordered that the play be produced" (*In detta sala . . . volle il . . . granduca Francesco, che si facesse questa rappresentazione di commedia*). Pirrotta doubts that the room was permanently set up as a theater, and argues that the aesthetics of the "theatrical game" required the construction, *ex novo,* of the structures necessary for each production. He cautions, therefore, against interpreting the word "teatro" as indicating a permanent structure. See *Li due Orfei,* p. 268 n. 102. Others disagree, among them Povoledo (*Li due Orfei,* p. 458 n. 57). There is good evidence to support the hypothesis that the 1586 conversion may have been permanent: from then on the *salone* was under Buontalenti's supervision; it was the site of major productions in 1586, 1589, 1600, and later; and chroniclers like Furttenbach speak of the room's technical setup as permanent. It was at about this time (in the 1580s) that permanent theaters were being erected elsewhere in Italy: see for example the theater at Sabbioneta and Palladio's celebrated Teatro Olimpico at Vicenza.

13. Weaver, *Chronology,* p. 111. Povoledo suggests that Filippo Baldinucci, who wrote a biography of Buontalenti at the end of the seventeenth century, may have seen the theater personally.

14. Joseph Furttenbach the Elder, *Newes Itinerarium Italiae,* quoted in George R. Kernodle, "Joseph Furttenbach the Elder, 1591–1667," in Barnard Hewitt, *The Renaissance Stage: Documents of Serlio, Sabbatini, and Furttenbach,* trans. Allardyce Nicoll, John McDowell, and George R. Kernodle (Coral Gables, Florida: University of Miami Press, 1958), p. 180. The illustration to which Furttenbach refers appears on p. 181 and is also reproduced in Nagler, *Theatre Festivals,* plate 101.

15. De' Rossi, *Descrizione* (1586) and *Descrizione dell' apparato e degl'intermedi fatti per la commedia rappresentata in Firenze. Nelle nozze de' Serenissimi Don Ferdinando Medici, e Madama Cristina di Loreno, Gran Duchi di Toscana* (Florence: Padovani, 1589). Nagler, *Theatre Festivals,* p. 70 n. 1, lists other, nonofficial, descriptions of the 1589 wedding. Extracts from de' Rossi's 1589 account can be found, together with editions of the surviving scores, in D. P. Walker, *Musique des intermedes de* La pellegrina: *Les fêtes de Florence, 1589* (Paris: Éditions du Centre National de la Recherche Scientifique, 1986); a planned companion volume, including a modern edition of de' Rossi's *Descrizione* of 1589 has not come to fruition. To date there is no modern edition of either the 1586 or 1589 volumes.

16. Michelangelo Buonarroti, *Descrizione delle felicissime nozze della Cristianissma Maestà di Madama Maria Medici Regina di Francia e di Navarra* (Florence: Marescotti, 1600). Buonarroti's description of the performance of Chiabrera's *Il rapimento di Cefalo,* excerpted from the *Descrizione,* is edited, together with Chiabera's libretto, in Solerti, *Gli albori del melodramma,* vol. 3, pp. 11–58. The libretto was published separately as *Il rapimento di Cefalo rappresentato nelle nozze della Christianiss. Regina di Francia e di Navarra Maria Medici* (Florence: Marescotti, 1600).

17. Jacques Callot's engraving, based on Giulio Parigi's design for the first *intermedio* of *La liberazione di Tirreno e d'Arnea autori del sangue toscano,* is reproduced in Mark S. Weil, *Baroque Theater and Stage Design* (St. Louis: Washington University, 1983), as plate 10a; it is also on the frontispiece of Nagler, *Theatre Festivals,* and in Pirrotta and Povoledo, *Li due Orfei,* plate 33. For a description of the *intermedii* and the *balletto* that followed, see Solerti, *Gli albori del melodramma,* vol. 3, p. 121.

18. The Uffizi theater has been described by Povoledo in *Li due Orfei,* pp. 432–435, by Nagler in *Theatre Festivals,* pp. 59–61, and by Sara Mamone in *Il teatro nella Firenze medicea* (Milan: Mursia, 1981), pp. 59–64. Povoledo bases her description on the two accounts left by de' Rossi, the drawing by Callot, and a late seventeenth-century biography of Buontalenti by Filippo Baldinucci, who may have seen the theater, probably highly modified, sometime in the last quarter of the century. Nagler's description relies on the same sources and does not take into account Buonarroti's *Descrizione,* although he does make use of it in the chapter on "Buontalenti and the New Opera," pp. 93–100. Ludovico Zorzi discusses the theater briefly in "Il teatro medicea degli Uffizi e il teatrino detto della Dogana," in *Il potere e lo spazio: La scena del principe,* ed. Franco Borsi (Florence: Edizioni Medicee, 1980), pp. 355–357. Illustrations 5.53 and 5.25 in the catalog show photographs of a hypothetical reconstruction of the theater based on de' Rossi's 1589 *Descrizione.* De' Rossi's proportions were given in *bracci:* 95 long, 35 wide, and 24 high. The *braccio* was not a precise unit of measurement, and this perhaps accounts for some discrepancies between the dimensions given by de' Rossi and those reported by Buonarroti, who estimates the height of the last set for *Il rapimento di Cefalo* (see below) at 25 *bracci* (47.5 feet)—clearly an impossibility. Modern scholarship reflects the imprecision of the *braccio* as a measurement: Elena Povoledo

converts it at 22.83 inches (58 cm); Hewitt at 18 inches (45.7 cm). The discrepancy does make a difference in calculating the actual dimensions of the room, which can vary from 142.5 feet (43.3 meters) to 180 feet (54.9 meters) in length, with significant consequences for estimating the size of the audience it could hold. I follow Povoledo's more generous conversion throughout.

19. Mauro Bini, ed. *Il Teatro all'Antica di Sabbioneta* (Modena: Il Bulino, 1991). A plan and cross-section of the theater, copied in 1588 and signed by Vincenzo Scamozzi, appears on p. 14 and, magnified, on the endpapers of the book. Povoledo, in "Il teatro da sala in Italia," part of the entry on "Teatro" in the *Enciclopedia dello spettacolo* (Rome: Le Maschere, 1954), vol. 9, cols. 760–762, draws the distinction between theaters like the Salone grande in the Uffizi in Florence and the *sala delle commedie* in Mantua (where Monteverdi's *Ballo delle ingrate* was performed in 1608), which focused on a large orchestra accessible to the performers, primarily for *balli,* and had bleacher-like seats along three sides, and theaters like Sabbioneta and the Teatro Olimpico in Verona, built on the Vitruvian model, which had a small, non-functional orchestra and fixed or semi-fixed architectural scenes. The Uffizi theater had certain features in common with Sabbioneta and other houses, such as the curved arrangement of the seats, the sloping floor, and—at least for the earlier productions—no access to the orchestra from the stage.

20. "It was given this slope so that the spectators in front did not block the view of the entertainments for those behind them . . . " (*Le fu data cotal pendenza, acciocchè le persone dinanzi, à quelle di dietro, la veduta degli spettacoli non impedissero. . . .*), de' Rossi, *Descrizione* (1586) as quoted in Pirrotta, *Li due Orfei,* p. 268 n. 102. Sebastiano Serlio, in his *Second Book of Architecture* (1545), shows a cross-section and floor plan of a *teatro da sala,* with a flat floor, a flat proscenium at floor level, a raised orchestra, and steeply raked, semi-circular seats, in a solution that is quite different from that employed in the Uffizi. His term for "orchestra" was originally "proscenio." In later editions of the treatise, the term was changed to "piazza della scena," reflecting the fact that the action spilled over onto it from the stage. By the term "orchestra," Serlio identified an empty, raised (by .5 foot [15 cm]) area shaped like a half circle, bounded at the front by the *piazza della scena* and all around by the amphitheater-like bleacher seats. See Hewitt, *The Renaissance Stage,* p. 22 nn. 5 and 6. Serlio's design reflects the influence of Vitruvius's *De architectura* and is in some ways closer to the Teatro Olimpico and Sabbioneta than to the Uffizi.

21. "The room was given the shape of a theater by that ingenious creator [Buontalenti]. . . ." (*Fu da questo ingegnoso artefice [Buontalenti] dato forma di teatro alla detta sala. . . .*), de' Rossi, *Descrizione,* in Pirrota, *Li due Orfei,* p. 268 n. 102.

22. The room today has an apparently original marble and tile floor. I am grateful to Edmond Strainchamps for this information.

23. Povoledo, *Li due Orfei,* p. 434.

24. The extreme foreshortening of the theater in Callot's engraving distorts somewhat the proportions of the room, making it appear wider and grander than it was. Nevertheless, the relative width and height, measured at the stage opening, are not far removed from the dimensions given by de' Rossi. Callot's representation should not, therefore, be entirely dismissed and does indicate the relative proportions of elements that, because of their placement in relation to one another, can suggest size and layout. Callot shows four tiers of seats rising to a level just about even with the stage. This agrees roughly with the scale of the seats in the theater at Sabbioneta.

25. *Il corago,* p. 35. Nicola Sabbatini, *Pratica di fabricar scene e machine ne' teatri* (Ravenna: Pietro de' Paoli and Giovanni Battista Giovannelli, 1638), facsimile ed. in *Anleitung*

Dekorationen und Theatermaschinen Herzustellen von Nicola Sabbattini [*sic*], ed. Willi Flemming (Weimar: Gesellschaft der Bibliophilen, 1926); trans. in Hewitt, *The Renaissance Stage*, pp. 43–177. For his instructions on stage construction, see pp. 44–46. On the place of the *Pratica* in the history of theatrical treatises, see Marotti, *Lo spazio scenico: Teorie e tecniche scenografiche in Italia dall'età barocca al settecento* (Rome: Bulzoni, 1974), pp. 61–68.

26. I have taken the height of the stage at Sabbioneta from Scamozzi's drawing.

27. Sebastiano Serlio, writing in his *Second Book of Architecture* (1545), finds a sloping stage "effective," and his drawing of a cross-section of a theater shows a flat forestage and sloping inner stage; see Hewitt, *The Renaissance Stage*, pp. 22–25; Sabbatini, *Pratica*, pp. 44–46, suggests a slope of one-half inch to the foot if there is to be dancing and two-thirds of an inch if none is required. *Il corago*, p. 35, recommends a two-degree slope.

28. Nagler, *Theatre Festivals*, p. 61.

29. Hewitt, *The Renaissance Stage*, pp. 44 and 158–162. Sabbatini does offer alternative solutions—such as anchoring the supports for clouds to the back wall—when not enough space is available.

30. The catalog for the exhibition *Illusione e pratica teatrale*, edited by Franco Mancini, Maria Teresa Muraro, and Elena Povoledo (Venice: Neri Pozza, 1975), p. 42, describes the stage as being "organized on three levels" and as having machines both below the stage and in the rafters.

31. Sabbatini suggested the construction of balconies along the side walls behind the stage opening so that they would be hidden from view. See Hewitt, *The Renaissance Stage*, pp. 89–90. *Il corago*, pp. 17–18, also recommended hiding the musicians, either behind the stage in an enclosed area between the stage and the spectators or in enclosed spaces along the sides of the theater. On the placement of instruments in the theater, see Pirrotta, "The Orchestra and Stage in Renaissance Intermedii and Early Opera," in *Music and Culture in Italy from the Middle Ages to the Baroque: A Collection of Essays* (Cambridge, Massachusetts: Harvard University Press, 1984), pp. 210–16. Pirrotta, p. 214, notes that it was in Mantua in 1607, for Monteverdi's *L'Orfeo*, that the "orchestra pit" was first adopted because of space limitations. There is no evidence to suggest that this "pit" was a sunken area: on the contrary, it was simply a portion of the parterre set apart for the musicians.

32. Pirrotta, ibid., p. 213, suggests that for dancing and other action in the *piazza di scena*, the musicians were placed on balconies or scaffolds within the hall, the better to keep the action together.

33. Palisca, "Musical Asides in the Correspondence of Emilio de' Cavalieri," *Musical Quarterly* 49 (1963), 350–351.

34. Cited in Solerti, *Le origini del melodramma*, pp. 5–6 and 84.

35. Marco da Gagliano is quite explicit on the question of communication between those on stage and their accompanists (see Solerti, *Le origini del melodramma*, pp. 83 and 88). *Cefalo*, which was performed on 9 October 1600, was in rehearsal from at least the middle of August and was still ragged at the performance. On the rehearsal process for the festivities, see Palisca, "The First Performance of *Euridice*," pp. 7–10, and "Musical Asides in the Diplomatic Correspondence of Emilio de' Cavalieri," 349–355. Probably because of both the novelty of the style and the difficulty of coordinating onstage singing and accompaniment, other early operas required extensive rehearsal, none perhaps more than Monteverdi's *Arianna*, which had "five months of strenuous rehearsal" and which the composer remembered as having nearly cost him his health.

See *The Letters of Claudio Monteverdi*, ed. and trans. by Denis Stevens (Cambridge University Press, 1980), pp. 104 and 160. On the other hand, Filippo Vitali's *L'Aretusa*, performed in Rome at the Corsini Palace in 1620, needed only forty-four days to produce, including the writing of the libretto, the composition of the music, and the rehearsals. See Solerti, *Le origini del melodramma*, p. 93.

36. Buonarroti, in Solerti, *Gli albori del melodramma*, vol. 3, p. 13.

37. Sabbatini's instructions cover both rising and falling curtains. He preferred the former, although it was more expensive and labor-intensive, because a falling curtain could create "confusion and fright [as] when part of the curtain sometimes falls on the audience." Hewitt, *The Renaissance Stage*, pp. 90–91. Pirrotta, *Li due Orfei*, p. 268 n. 102, underscores the novelty of the curtain at the Uffizi.

38. Neither Nagler nor Povoledo remarks on the "half-oval" shape of the room as described by Buonarroti. A floor plan of the Teatro Farnese is reproduced in Nagler, *Theatre Festivals*, plate 128.

39. On the role of the dance in early opera, see Marian Hannah Winter, "Il balletto e lo spazio scenico," in *Illusione e pratica teatrale*, pp. 147–151.

40. Hewitt, *The Renaissance Stage*, p. 3.

41. Sabbatini, "How and in What Order to Accommodate an Audience," in Hewitt, *The Renaissance Stage*, p. 97.

42. Sabbatini, "How to Place the Prince's Seat," in Hewitt, *The Renaissance Stage*, pp. 87–88.

43. Pirrotta, *Li due Orfei*, p. 268 n. 102.

44. I estimate a maximum of 1,400 linear feet (426.7 meters) of seating space, allowing about 21 inches (53.3 cm) per spectator.

45. Callot's engraving shows the projecting stands leaving about 60 percent of the floor space open, a little more than 39 feet (11.9 meters).

46. Assuming each spectator could have fit into a meager 1.5 square feet (.14 square meters) of space.

47. Povoledo, *Li due Orfei*, pp. 434–435.

48. Buonarroti, in Solerti, *Gli albori del melodramma*, vol. 3, p. 13. The outdoor paintings and classical statues of the *salone* in the Uffizi recall the decorations for the theater at Sabbioneta, where sweeping landscape vistas are frescoed on the north and south walls, and the pantheon of Greek gods looks onto the stage from the *loggia* behind the seats. See Bini, *Il Teatro all'Antica di Sabbioneta*, 87–101.

49. Buonarroti, in Solerti, *Gli albori del melodramma*, vol. 3, p. 13.

50. Povoledo, *Li due Orfei*, pp. 434–435.

51. "il nostro Architettore è stato il primiero, che abbia trovato il modo d'illuminarlo." Quoted in Nagler, *Theatre Festivals*, p. 61 n. 14.

52. Povoledo, *Li due Orfei*, pp. 434–435, summarizes the distribution of the lights as given in de' Rossi's descriptions. In 1600 the footlights were a noteworthy innovation; by 1628 they seem to have become relatively common. Indeed, Sabbatini described their placement, while expressing some doubt regarding their usefulness.

53. Sabbatini dwells at length on the dangers posed by fire on the stage and in the hall, as well as on other problems, such as smoke, caused by the various oil lamps, torches, and other lights. See, for example, "How to Place the Lights outside the Stage" and "How to Place the Lamps within the Stage," with particular emphasis on the smoke caused by the footlights, and "How to Light the Lamps," in Hewitt, *The Renaissance Stage*, pp. 93–96 and 97–98. Povoledo, *Li due Orfei*, p. 434, describes the placement of vents in the ceiling and below the stage.

54. Buonarroti, in Solerti, *Gli albori del melodramma*, vol. 3, p. 22.

55. "Nessun movimento di macchine così traversanti circolarmente, e discendenti e saglienti come venenti innanzi, e chiudentisi per vari modi, mancovvi, dismisurati pesi reggendo sopra . . . quale avesse veduto l'ascoso luogo dove elle locate erano e si maneggiavano . . . quivi altresia avria veramente veduto, ciascuna apertura, o componimento, picciolo o grande, di ferro o legname, a maraviglia rendere, oprare con agevolezza non più creduta, benchè per loro quantità ad usarli uomini moltissimi rechiedessero, regolati in un certo modo da note e terminazioni di musica." Solerti, *Gli albori del melodramma,* vol. 3, p. 27.

56. From the *Traicté du mariage de Henry IIII. Roy de France et de Navarre avec la Serenissime Princesse de Florence* (Paris: Jean Petit, 1601), p. 17, cited in Palisca, "The First Performance of *Euridice,*" in *Queens College Department of Music: Twenty-fifth Anniversary Festschrift,* ed. Albert Mell (New York: Queens College Press, 1964), p. 4.

57. Buonarroti, in Solerti, *Gli albori del melodramma,* vol. 3, p. 18.

58. Reports of the festivities, including those of Emilio de' Cavalieri and Cardinal Pietro Aldobrandini in his diary, record negative judgments on both counts. See Palisca, "Musical Asides," 350–351; Sara Mamone, "Feste e spettacoli a Firenze e in Francia per le nozze di Maria de' Medici con Enrico IV," in *Quaderni di teatro 2* (1980), *Il teatro dei Medici,* ed. Ludovico Zorzi, p. 218; and Tim Carter, "A Florentine Wedding of 1608," *Acta musicologica* 55 (1983), 93.

59. Both cited in Carter, "A Florentine Wedding," 92.

60. Palisca, "Musical Asides," 350–355.

61. Savage and Sansone, "*Il corago* and the Staging of Early Opera," 505.

62. The 1628 wedding entertainments in Parma, to which *Il corago* makes reference, were plagued with technical problems, including a poorly executed seascape, a visible supporting beam, and another that had not been sufficiently lubricated. See Nagler, *Theatre Festivals of the Medici,* p. 150, and Savage and Sansone, "*Il corago* and the Staging of Early Opera," 505, especially n. 52.

63. This is one of Tim Carter's main points in "A Florentine Wedding."

64. A scene-by-scene synopsis of the plot can be found in Nagler, *Theatre Festivals,* pp. 96–100.

65. The design of the second *intermedio* for *La pellegrina,* a representation of Mount Helicon complete with Pegasus, Apollo, and the Muses, might have served as the prototype for this later and much larger version of the mountain. See Nagler, *Theatre Festivals,* plates 48–51.

66. Streams did not necessarily flow with water: Sabbatini's method was to use a continuous belt of blue cloth, as wide as the stream and studded with silver, and to make it "flow" by pulling it from beneath the stage at one end. See "How to Represent a River That Seems to Flow Continuously," in Hewitt, *The Renaissance Stage,* pp. 144–145.

67. "Ecco in un tratto il gran monte tutto avvallare, e quasi in un certo modo sgonfiandosi, come se leggerissima cosa si fosse stato, che pure così grave peso sostenea sopra, sinfoniando sempre le Muse, nascondersi sotto, nè più vedersi: e le deretane nugole che 'l circondavano velocissimamente rifuggirsi suso nel cielo. Onde il piano della scena, e le prime prospettive scopertesi, larghe pianure, antri aperti e profondi, e alte e ombrose selve allor si videro verdeggianti." Solerti, *Gli albori del melodramma,* vol. 3, p. 15.

68. There has been some question as to whether the Uffizi theater used flats or the revolving triangular sets called *periaktoi,* which took up more space but, because they turned on a fixed axis rather than sliding out of the way, required less wing area. Povoledo argues, quite rightly, in favor of flats; see *Li due Orfei,* p. 442. For a description of both flats and *periaktoi,* see Sabbatini, in Hewitt, *The Renaissance Stage,* pp. 98–109.

69. Sabbatini's methods for enlarging, reducing, and dividing a cloud are found in Hewitt, *The Renaissance Stage,* pp. 162–164, and 166–168.

70. Nagler, *Theatre Festivals*, plate 136.
71. "innalzando fuori in prima sole le molli teste . . . poco appresso, battendo frequente-
    mente le zampe, parendone di grado in grado ascendere alla superficie dell'acque, si
    dimostrarono interi. Anelavano spumanti, scotevano le crinite fronti, e non potevano
    esser frenati." Buonarroti, in Solerti, *Gli albori del melodramma,* vol. 3, p. 17.
72. Nagler, *Theatre Festivals,* plates 36 and 88.
73. Ibid., plate 135.
74. "Sopra nel cielo, e per l'aria veggendosi nuvole, e d'intorno mutabili scene, e sotto
    grandissimo allagamento tramezzato da altre moli, che si aggitavano." In Solerti, *Gli
    albori del melodramma,* vol. 3, p. 18.
75. Both Sabbatini and Furttenbach describe ways of constructing multilayered paradise or
    glory machines. See Hewitt, *The Renaissance Stage,* pp. 173–174 and 224–227.
76. Sabbatini describes three methods for creating a sea, and a way of making a calm sea
    become stormy. The first two use painted cloth, while the third—the best in his opin-
    ion—consists of several wave-shaped rollers, covered with painted cloth and turned to
    give the impression of perpetually moving and shifting waves. Although neither of the
    first two designs as given permits actors and machines to appear from below, they could
    have been modified to accommodate gaps or lanes in which props could be moved. The
    third method has built-in gaps. Sabbatini allows about a foot (30.5 cm) between rollers
    for actors to move around. However, this method seems more cumbersome for scene
    changes than either of the first two. Whereas the cloths and their supports could easily
    be made to disappear into slots on the stage floor, the rollers do not lend themselves to
    quick storage, and they are less likely to produce the shimmering effect that Buonarroti
    describes. See Hewitt, *The Renaissance Stage,* pp. 130–135.
77. For Sabbatini's method for darkening lamps without turning them off, by using tin
    cylinders that are slid onto the lamp to cover it and then lifted when light is needed
    again, see Hewitt, *The Renaissance Stage,* pp. 111–112.
78. "veggendo tanto di voto sotto la scena, non sapevano essi rinvenire ove le tante altre
    macchine, ad ogni ora sorgenti e moventisi, si potessero avere auto lor luogo e lor
    movimento." Buonarroti, in Solerti, *Gli albori del melodramma,* vol. 3, p. 21.
79. See Pirrotta, "The Orchestra and Stage in Renaissance *Intermedi* and Early Opera,"
    p. 211.
80. The final chorus is not included in the libretto.
81. This was true in the earlier *intermedii,* but in *Il rapimento di Cefalo,* it became the central
    strategy.
82. At times the *corago* found it necessary to distract the audience in order to hide the
    mechanics of a scene change. See Sabbatini, in Hewitt, *The Renaissance Stage.*
83. Buontalenti had reportedly built a mechanical *crèche* scene as a youth. See Molinari,
    Le nozze degli dèi, p. 15.
84. Puppets were used to animate backgrounds (as in the views of Florence and Pisa in
    1586 and 1589) and to simulate musicians and actors in heavenly views. Molinari,
    Le nozze degli dèi, pp. 16–17, and Pirrotta, "Orchestra and Stage in Renaissance
    Intermedi and Early Opera," pp. 211–212.
85. Buontalenti's interest in light, as well as in shadow games, was apparently lifelong: at
    fifteen, according to Baldinucci, he had invented a revolving magic lantern for
    Francesco de' Medici. See Povoledo, *Li due Orfei,* p. 460 n. 71.
86. *Le nozze degli dèi,* pp. 47–49.
87. "Con mirabil ordine s'accesero in un tratto da loro le torce che facevano ghirlanda
    all'anfiteatro, senza conoscersi da nessuno alcuno aiuto di fuoco lavorato o di sì fatti

artifici, ed ebbe subito incominciamento la bellissima commedia." In Solerti, *Gli albori del melodramma*, vol. 2, p. 17.

88. Molinari, *Le nozze degli dèi*, p. 48.

89. Ibid., p. 46, and "Les rapports entre la scène et les spectateurs dans le théâtre italien du XVI siècle," in *Le lieu théâtral à la Renaissance* (Paris: Éditions du Centre National de la Recherche Scientifique, 1964), pp. 61–71.

90. The scene changes are indicated in the published scores. Peri indicates that "the scene changes to the underworld" (*la scena si muta in inferno*). Caccini describes the scene with the words: "turned back" (*si rivolge*) suggesting the use of *periaktoi*. See *Le Musiche di Iacopo Peri . . . sopra L'Euridice* (Florence: Marescotti, 1600; reprint in *Monuments of Music and Music Literature in Facsimile*, First Series, no. 27, New York: Broude Brothers, 1973), p. 28; and *L'Euridice composta in musica in stile rappresentativo da Giulio Caccini detto Romano* (Florence: Marescotti, 1600; reprint in *Bibliotheca musica Bononiensis*, Sezione iv, no. 3, Bologna: Forni, 1976), p. 41.

91. Nicolò da Molin, Venetian ambassador to Florence, cited in Solerti, *Musica, ballo e drammatica alla corte medicea*, p. 27.

92. Molinari, *Le nozze degli dèi*, p. 51.

93. Carter emphasizes the connections between the *intermedii* of 1608 and those of 1589, arguing that Buonarroti and Bardi intentionally harked back to a successful model, bypassing the more embarrassing precedent of the productions of 1600. See "A Florentine Wedding of 1608," 90–95. This de-emphasizes the links between *Cefalo* and the *intermedio* tradition.

94. Povoledo, *Li due Orfei*, pp. 436–451, has noted that the *intermedii* of 1589 were, with the exception of the scene in hell, less violent overall than those of 1586, and that the elimination of all violence from *Il rapimento di Cefalo*, including the infernal scene, seems to continue this trend.

95. See Molinari, *Le nozze degli dèi*, pp. 13–49, and Povoledo, *Li due Orfei*, pp. 442–451, for analyses of the structure of the earlier *intermedii*.

96. Buontalenti's inventions loom particularly large in light of the abandonment in the seventeenth century of fixed models for stage design in favor of a greater variety of action and of solutions for dividing the dramatic space. See Franco Mancini, ed. *Illusione e pratica teatrale*, pp. 41–42.

Chapter Two

I would like to thank Professor John S. Powell for reading a draft of this paper and for providing additional information and source materials relating especially to the Salle des Machines.

1. Some of the many sources on French theaters and on their musical repertoire include eyewitness reports from the *Gazette;* from the *Mercure;* in Loret, *La muse historique: Ou recueil des lettres en vers, 1650–1665* (Paris: P. Daffis, 1857–1878); and in Dangeau, *Mémoires de la cour de France* (Paris: Didot Frères, 1854). Treatises on theater construction in the seventeenth century were written primarily by Italians, such as Sabbatini, *Pratica di fabricar scene, e machine ne' teatri* (Ravenna, 1638); and Motta, *Trattato sopra la structtura de' theatri e scene* (1676); but in the eighteenth century, several collections of architectural drawings including some of the French theaters appeared, such as Blondel, *L'architecture française: Ou recueil de plans, d'elevations, coupes, et profils des églises, maisons royales,*

palais, hôtels, et édifices les plus considérables (Paris: C. A. Jomberteur, 1752–1756; reprint, Paris: Librairie Centrale des Beaux-Arts, 1904–1905), and Dumont, *Parallele de plans des plus belles salles de spectacles d'Italie et de France* (1774; reprint, New York: Benjamin Blom, 1968)—this last is especially good for comparison of French buildings to Italian.

The modern criticism of repertoire includes commentary relating to performance sites, for example, Prunières, *L'opéra italien en France avant Lulli* (Paris: E. Champion, 1913; reprint, Paris: Honoré Champion, 1975) and *Le ballet de cour avant Benserade et Lully* (Paris: H. Laurens, 1914; reprint, New York: Johnson Reprint, 1970); Silin, *Benserade and His Ballets de cour* (Baltimore: Johns Hopkins Press, 1940); and Bjurström, *Giacomo Torelli and Baroque Stage Design* (Stockholm: Nationalmuseum, 1961). The best survey of the music of the period is Anthony, *French Baroque Music from Beaujoyeulx to Rameau;* rev. and expanded ed. (Portland, Oregon: Amadeus Press, 1997).

Architectural studies usually do not address music *per se,* but offer good descriptions of spaces: Lawrenson, *The French Stage in the XVIIth Century* (Manchester University Press, 1957); see also Marie, "Les théâtres du château de Versailles," *Revue d'histoire du théâtre* 2 (1951), 133–152; Boucher, "Les théâtres des Palais Royaux," *Les monuments historiques de France* 4 (1978), 16–21; and Beauvert, *Les temples de l'opéra* (Paris: Gallimard, 1990). Forsythe, *Buildings for Music: The Architect, the Musician, and the Listener from the Seventeenth Century to the Present Day* (Cambridge, Massachusetts: MIT Press, 1985) gives a general overview of buildings for music. Izenour, *Theater Design* (New York: McGraw Hill, 1977) provides some of the best discussion of the technical aspects involved in theater architecture.

2. Carlson, *Places of Performance: The Semiotics of Theatre Architecture* (Ithaca, New York: Cornell University Press, 1989) examines the range of meanings afforded by a study of theaters. Isherwood, *Music in the Service of the King* (Ithaca, New York: Cornell University Press, 1973) is the best discussion to date of the repertoire in a political context.

3. Lawrenson, *The French Stage in the XVIIth Century* offers one of the best overviews of French seventeenth-century theaters.

4. A drawing of the room in Heuzey, "Notes sur un dessin représentant la Salle des Machines au XVIIᵉ siècle," *Revue d'histoire du théâtre* 6 (1954), plate 7, emphasizes the large, communal aspect of the hall.

5. The hall discussed in this essay burned on 6 April 1763. See Lesure, *L'opéra classique français* (Geneva: Minkoff, 1972), plate 10, for an often-reproduced view of the burning building. Another theater built on the same site operated from 1770 until 1781, when it too was destroyed by fire. At that point the Paris Opera moved from the Palais Royal for good. See La Salle, *Les treize salles de l'opéra* (Paris: Librairie Sartorius, 1875); and Gourret, *Histoire des salles de l'opéra de Paris* (Paris: Guy Trédaniel, 1985) for comprehensive histories of the theaters of the Paris opera.

6. Bapst, *Essai sur l'histoire du théâtre* (Paris: Librairie Hachette, 1893), p. 209, points out that seventeenth-century French theaters and their theatrical life were defined by court standards. La Grave, *Le théâtre et le public à Paris de 1715 à 1750* (Paris: Librairie C. Klincksiek, 1972), p. 129, views theater in court, at least under Louis XV's reign, as generating very different conditions from public theaters, *en cas tout à fait particulier.*

7. Repertoire lists for these and other theaters can enhance our understanding of opera reception. The repertoire for the Salle des Machines' limited life and for the Palais Royal as a court site (up to 1674) appear in my work in progress, *Performances of Musical Theater in the Court of the Sun King: 1643–1715.* For the Palais Royal as the home of the

Paris Opera, the best lists of repertoire are those in Durey, *Histoire du théâtre de l'Académie Royale de Musique en France* (Paris: Duchesne, 1757; reprint, Geneva: Minkoff, 1972); and in LaJarte, *Théâtre de l'opéra: Catalogue* (Paris: Librairie des Bibliophiles, 1878).

8. A "chicken-and-egg" situation exists in theater production: do sites influence the repertoire therein, or does repertoire drive builders and designers to respond with new structural features? The French delay in developing well-designed buildings may have been caused by their difficulty in establishing a French national opera. Musical theater played catch-up not only with Italian opera but also with French spoken theater: for example, the literary Académie Française was established in 1635, but the Académie Nationale de Musique did not come into being until 1669.

The history of French theaters—even after the founding of a national opera—was marked by irony and coincidence. By 1700 it seemed that the Paris Opera had more or less caught up with theatrical practice in other cities, but during the eighteenth century, other theaters in France (Bordeaux and Lyon) and in Italy soon left Paris behind the times once again. Carlson, *Places of Performance,* pp. 73–76, discusses Voltaire's concern over the poor image that Paris's theaters offered. Riccoboni, *A General History of the Stage from Its Origin,* facsimile of the English trans. *Music and Theatre in France in the 17th and 18th Centuries* (W. Owen, 1754; reprint, New York: AMS Press, 1978), p. 144, asserts that French style consistently ran behind Italian practice. Perhaps not until the Garnier Opera house of the 1860s did Paris become a leader rather than a follower in buildings for opera.

9. Ballrooms were created by placing a portable floor over the seats to the level of the stage. The Palais Royal theater, particularly during the regency of Louis XV, was the site for many public balls.

10. The influence of politics on seventeenth-century French theater deserves much more examination by modern scholars. Political and artistic influences on theater can easily become confused: too often historians look for artistic answers for questions that are fundamentally political.

11. Bapst, *Essai sur l'histoire du théâtre,* p. 372, notes that during the era of Henry IV and Louis XIII, audience areas in French settings had mostly equalized seating, as the interplay between performers and audience was quite fluid, but during the reign of Louis XIV, hierarchical seating based on social class increased.

12. A well-known exception to this horseshoe plan is seen in the views of the 1745 production of Rameau's *Princesse de Navarre* in the Grand Ecurie at Versailles, showing the parallel side balconies meeting the rear balconies at right angles. See Lesure, *L'opéra classique français* or Marie, *Versailles au temps de Louis XV* (Paris: Éditions Jacques Freal, 1984), figures 208, 211.

13. Beijer, "Vigarani et Bérain au Palais-Royal" *Revue d'histoire du théâtre* 8 (1956), 192, suggests that the Palais Royal was a crowded theater relative to its stage capacity. Its stage was almost the same size as the stage in the court theater in Drottningholm, Sweden. The Palais Royal probably accommodated up to 1,400 spectators, in comparison with the Swedish hall, which holds about 350 persons.

14. Riccoboni, *A General History of the Stage,* p. 145, suggests a maximum capacity of only 500 to 600 in most French theaters. Of course actual seating varied greatly from hall to hall, but Riccoboni's numbers seem quite low.

15. Riccoboni, *A General History of the Stage,* pp. 144–145. I remain unclear about how Riccoboni distinguished "pit" from "orchestra." Architectural plans I have consulted suggest that only musicians, not spectators, occupied the "orchestra." Jeffrey Ravel has

discussed the area called the parterre in French theaters in an unpublished conference paper, "From Royal Gardens to Commercial Theaters: The 'Parterre' in Seventeenth-Century France."

16. Riccoboni, *A General History of the Stage*, p. 151, and Bapst, *Essai sur l'histoire du théâtre*, p. 372, discuss spectators on stage, a practice which apparently started about 1650. For the most critical modern discussion of spectators on the public stage, see Mittman, *Spectators on the Paris Stage in the Seventeenth and Eighteenth Centuries*, in Theater and Dramatic Studies, No. 25 (Ann Arbor, Michigan: UMI Research Press, 1984).

17. The question of social interaction during the course of a production has been examined by James H. Johnson, *Listening in Paris* (Berkeley and Los Angeles: University of California Press, 1995). Some time must have elapsed between the acts of an opera, if only to change candles. The reports of French operas lasting for up to six hours suggest that some of this time must have been devoted to activities other than the *tragédie-lyrique* itself.

18. Does this indicate that private boxes may have been the setting for much of the social interaction at the theater? Even the huge Salle des Machines had relatively small corridors and lobbies. The Palais Royal as the Paris Opera included a cafe on the lower level under the stage. Bapst, *Essai sur l'histoire du théâtre*, chap. 4, pp. 371 ff., discusses public areas in the theaters. Also see Johnson, "The French Musical Experience from the Old Regime to Romanticism" (Ph.D. dissertation, University of Chicago, 1988).

19. De Pure, *Idée des spectacles anciens et nouveaux* (Paris: M. Brunet, 1668; reprint, Geneva: Minkoff, 1972), p. 315.

20. Riccoboni, *A General History of the Stage*, p. 150. Throughout his discussion of repertoire, Prunières, *L'opéra italien en France avant Lulli*, also includes many comments about theater machinery.

21. For example, machines from *Orfeo* in 1647 at the Palais Royal were reused for *Andromède* in 1650 at the Petit Bourbon.

22. Regarding performance sites, see Marie, "Les théâtres du château de Versailles"; Rice, "The Court Theater at Fontainebleau," *Theatre Research International* 9 (1982), 127–139; Coeyman, "Theatres for Opera and Ballet during the Reigns of Louis XIV and Louis XV," *Early Music* 18 (February 1990), 22–37, and "Sites of Indoor Musical-Theatrical Productions at Versailles," *Eighteenth-Century Life* 17 (May 1993), 55–67. For the overall environment of court performance, see Isherwood, *Music in the Service of the King*. The introduction to Rouchès, *Inventaire des lettres et papiers manuscrits de Gaspare, Carlo et Lodovico Vigarani* (Paris: H. Champion, 1913), includes a summary of Parisian theaters in the seventeenth century.

23. Several of these *châteaux* hosted performances as early as the sixteenth century. For example, Bapst, *Essai sur l'histoire du théâtre*, p. 131, describes a wooden theater built at the Tuileries in 1573 for a ballet presented during a visit of the Polish ambassador to Henri III. Bapst shows the ballet in an often-reproduced engraving. Two significant influences on the development of court theaters were the theaters for street fairs and the theaters constructed in tennis courts, subjects which we cannot pursue in this essay.

24. See Lawrenson, *The French Stage in the XVIIth Century*, pp. 135 ff.; Bapst, *Essai sur l'histoire du théâtre*, pp. 150–163; and Rouchès, *Inventaire des lettres et papiers*, p. x.

25. Bapst, *Essai sur l'histoire du théâtre*, p. 171. Concerning the 1674 remodeling, see S. Wilma Deierkauf-Holsboer, *Le Théâtre de l'Hôtel de Bourgogne* (Paris: A. G. Nizet, 1968–1970), vol. 1, pp. 182–183.

26. See, for example, Wickham, *A History of the Theatre* (Cambridge University Press, 1985), p. 151, for a view of the room during this 1614 meeting. The Petit Bourbon

theater was exceptionally large, approximately 49 feet (14.9 meters) wide and 115 feet (35 meters) long, included in that length a stage 49 by 49 feet (14.9 meters by 14.9 meters), 6 feet (1.8 meters) off the floor. Beyond the stage, an additional 44 feet (13.4 meters) formed an apse in which the king sat. Sauval, *Histoire et recherches des antiquités de la ville de Paris* (1724; reprint, Paris, 1969), vol. 2, p. 209, reported that the height of the building was similar to the nearby church of St. Germain l'Auxerrois. (Sauval gives dimensions as 16 to 17 meters by 70 meters [52.5 to 55.8 feet by 229.8 feet].) The room included a vaulted ceiling decorated with *fleurs de lis* and two rows of balconies parallel to the side walls. Also see Bapst, *Essai sur l'histoire du théâtre,* pp. 150 ff., and pp. 172–174; Horn-Monval, "Le théâtre du Petit Bourbon," *Revue d'histoire du théâtre* 1–2 (1948), 46–48; and Bjurström, *Giacomo Torelli and Baroque Stage Design,* p. 122, for further description of the room.

27. See Horn-Monval, "Le théâtre du Petit Bourbon" for a more extensive list of repertoire.

28. Bapst, *Essai sur l'histoire du théâtre,* p. 170, discusses Richelieu's role in transforming the room into a theater. Bapst, p. 181, indicates Richelieu's knowledge of Italian machinery.

29. Ibid., p. 168.

30. Sauval, *Histoire et recherches des antiquités de la ville de Paris,* vol. 3, pp. 161–163; Coeyman, "Theatres for Opera and Ballet during the Reigns of Louis XIV and Louis XV," 31–34.

31. Bapst, *Essai sur l'histoire du théâtre,* p. 187, regards *Mirame* as an important development in machine plays, an influence on later productions such as *Psiché, Toison d'or, Andromède,* and others produced through the end of the Fronde.

32. The Barberini theater held about 3,000 spectators.

33. Italian artists in Paris is a subject well-examined in studies such as Prunières, *L'opéra italien en France avant Lulli* or Anthony, *French Baroque Music from Beaujoyeulx to Rameau,* chap. 4.

34. Lawrenson, *The French Stage in the XVIIth Century,* p. 170.

35. Prunières, *L'opéra italien en France avant Lulli,* p. 296 reports a letter of 8 July 1659 from Mazarin to the queen mother stating that no money would be spared for the production. France would solicit the greatest artists in the world. Christout, "*Ercole amante, L'Hercule amoureux* à la Salle des Machines des Tuileries," 9, reports that it took some persuading to get Cavalli to leave Italy, where he had already established a successful career as an opera composer in theaters such as Venice's San Giovanni and San Paolo, and San Cassiano.

36. See Rouchès, *Inventaire des lettres et papiers,* pp. ii–iv; and Prunières, *L'opéra italien en France avant Lulli,* pp. 214 ff. Ludovico, born in 1588, was 71 and had officially retired when the call came from Paris. He had been in the employment of the duke of Modena from 1636 to 1658, the year of the duke's death. Ludovico also built a theater in Carpi in 1640 and another in Mantua in 1651, and he worked on wedding festivities for Francis I, Duke of Modena in 1631 and again for the duke's third wedding, with Lucrezia Barberini (niece of Urban VIII), in 1654. His sons were age 36 (Carlo) and 33 (Ludovico) in 1659. Lawrenson, *The French Stage in the XVIIth Century,* p. 135, points out that they were known primarily as landscape artists, machinists, and decorators, not as architects. These additional skills were utilized to full advantage over the next twenty years in Carlo's numerous court productions. Hautecoeur, *Histoire de l'architecture classique en France;* vol. 2, *Le règne de Louis XIV* (Paris: Picard, 1948), p. 234, called Gaspare "un homme universal." Their theater in Modena was destroyed in 1780.

Systematic research on this important family has not been done. The most extensive documentation of their activities in Paris is Rouchès's compilation of their letters, *Inventaire des lettres et papiers.*

37. Ibid., p. xvi.

38. There was much discussion about these critical decisions, as indicated by the many letters to and from Mazarin. Prunières, *L'opéra italien en France avant Lulli,* pp. 215–216, summarizes the issues. De Pure, *Idée des spectacles,* p. 311, critiques the choice of site and praises the Vigaranis for their decisions. Babeau, "Le théâtre des Tuileries sous Louis XIV, Louis XV et Louis XVI," *Bulletin de la société de l'histoire de Paris et de l'Ile-de-France* 22 (1895), 133, suggests that Le Vau, as builder, had greater responsibility for many aspects of the theater than Vigarani, as machinist, did. Among other issues, the size of the theater was a source of disagreement between the Vigarani family and Le Vau (as indicated in a letter of August 1659). See Rouchès, *Inventaire des lettres et papiers,* p. 12 n. 5.

39. Prunières, *L'opéra italien en France avant Lulli,* pp. 215–220; Rouchès, *Inventaire des lettres et papiers,* p. 30. Louis was in Paris in July 1660. The entire court left Paris for two months at the end of September.

40. Work ceased frequently because of cold weather, as on 19 December 1659.

41. *Xerxes* premiered in Venice in 1654 and then played in Florence, Bologna, and other Italian cities to great success. In Paris, the opera was reworked from three to five acts in accordance with French taste, and Lully added interludes of French dance music. Only professional dancers appeared in the production, possibly because there was insufficient time to prepare courtiers. During carnival in 1661, the *Ballet de l'impatience* appeared in the same *galerie* after another theater site suspiciously burned on 11 February. According to a letter of 28 October given in Rouchès, *Inventaire des lettres et papiers,* p. 39, Gaspare prepared the theater, Carlo handled machines, and Ludovico the décor for that production. The *Ballet de l'impatience,* totally French in content and musical style, enjoyed much more success than did *Xerxes.* The *Ballet des saisons* played at Fontainebleau in July 1661.

42. *Gazette de France,* September 1661, p. 1038; Rouchès, *Inventaire des lettres et papiers,* p. 63, letter of 23 September. A letter in Rouchès, p. 45, 31 December 1660, indicates that two hundred men worked on the theater. The two queens (i.e., Louis's mother and wife) inspected the site on 21 January 1662.

43. Christout, "*Ercole amante, L'Hercule amoureux* à la Salle des Machines des Tuileries," 10.

44. Rouchès, *Inventaire des lettres et papiers,* p. xvii, reports that the acoustics were deplorable and the machines noisy. Prunières, *L'opéra italien en France avant Lulli,* p. 274; Loret, *La muse historique,* p. 465; and de Pure, *Idée des spectacles,* p. 313; *Gazette* 7 February 1662, all include favorable reports, describing the ballet, costumes, dancers, machines, scenery, concerts, and theater. The *Gazette* on 14 February gives even more details, with equal attention to sights and sounds, and much notice to the theater itself. Reasons for the negative criticism are not as readily apparent as many histories report. Theoretically, the production should have worked well, composed as it was with the performance site in mind. Perhaps political factors were as powerful as artistic ones in creating the negative reports. We must be careful to distinguish criticism of the hall from criticism of the opera, and criticism of both from displeasure with Mazarin and the Italian art he promoted. Even the artist Giovanni Bernini criticized the theater and the Vigaranis, who, according to Bernini, did not have enough talent to build a theater. See Hautecoeur, *Le règne de Louis XIV,* p. 235.

45. Particularly grand were the three celebrations of military victories known as the *Fêtes de Versailles* (1664, 1668, and 1674), in which eight different stage productions appeared. The festivities in 1674 marked the end of outdoor musical productions during Louis XIV's reign, as opera—a genre not at all conducive to large, open-air settings—assumed a more important role.

46. The single member of the Italian company remaining in Paris was Anna Bergerotti. See Christout, "*Ercole amante, L'Hercule amoureux* à la Salle des Machines des Tuileries," 15. Lully seems to have been the only musician who profited from the affair. Arriving in Modena in June 1662, Gaspare completed one more building project before his death in September 1663 at the age of 75.

47. Carlo was naturalized a French citizen in 1673. He received an annual pension of 6,000 *livres*, a sizable sum, and also was given an apartment in the Louvre. He continued to work for the court even after his partnership with Lully ended: see Rouchès, *Inventaire des lettres et papiers*, p. xxiv, for productions that he worked on at Saint German-en-Laye. He apparently returned to Italy, but never went back to Modena. His greatest accomplishments included inventing machinery, building provisional theaters and triumphant arches, and creating settings for fireworks and other illuminations. His last noted activity was in 1683, and the exact date of his death is not known. Jean Bérain succeeded Vigarani, signaling the final stage of the French musical theater's dissociation from Italian influences. See Rouchès, *Inventaire des lettres et papiers;* Tessier, "Bérain: Créateur du pays d'opéra," *La revue musicale* (1925), 56–73; Weigert, *Jean I Bérain: Dessinateur de la chambre et du cabinet du roi (1640–1711);* 2 vols. (Paris: Éditions d'Art et d'Histoire, 1937); Beijer, "Vigarani et Bérain au Palais-Royal"; and La Gorce, *Bérain: Dessinateur du Roi Soleil* (Paris: Éditions Herscher, 1986).

48. Torelli returned to Fano, where he built another theater. He died in 1678. See Bjurström, *Giacomo Torelli and Baroque Stage Design,* pp. 212–215.

49. La Grange, *Le registre de La Grange 1659–1685;* with a preface by Bert Edward Young and Grave Philputt Young (Paris: Librairie E. Droz, 1947), pp. 26–27. Bjurström, *Giacomo Torelli and Baroque Stage Design,* p. 137. *L'estat de France* 1663, p. 230.

50. How much the Salle des Machines was used in the 1660s after *Hercule* is unclear. Babeau, "Le théâtre des Tuileries sous Louis XIV," 139, reports that Louis lived in the Tuileries during the winters of 1667–1668 and 1668–1669 and that comedies played in his apartment. Comedies also played in the gallery, and ballets in the Grand Salon du Dome. However, no productions in the theater are recorded. Babeau, 139, also reports caretaker fees for the hall during 1662 to 1671.

51. Babeau, "Le théâtre des Tuileries sous Louis XIV," 140, reports the cost of *Psiché.* These costs included 21,000 *livres* for workers; 10,000 for decoration by painters; 1,200 for carpenters and 5,100 for wood merchants. Lully received 1,400 *livres* for overseeing the copying of music. Bapst, *Essai sur l'histoire du théâtre,* p. 387, seems to read the production as the best test of visual effects held in the theaters, calling the production "a paradigm for pieces using machines" (*l'ideal des pièces à machines*).

   Psiché opened on 17 January 1671. The *Gazette* reported a second performance on 24 January, but this may have been only of the ballet segments. Consequently, accounts of the production disagree about the number of performances in the Salle des Machines. Some, such as Christout, "*Ercole amante, L'Hercule amoureux* à la Salle des Machines des Tuileries," indicate that the performance on the 24th was in the Palais Royal. Curiously, Babeau, 142, reports five performances in the Tuileries. Molière's company repeated the work in the Palais Royal in March, at which time Molière built new machinery for that theater. Babeau, 142, indicates minor repairs to the Salle des Machines in 1672 and 1689 and payments of 500 to 1,000 *livres* annually for regular maintenance. The usual historical explanation of the hall's poor acoustics is not the whole story of why it fell from use: politics must have been at work as well.

52. Costs are given in "Comptes de la maison du roi," documents in the Archives Nationales, O' 2851, fol. 63–85; fol. 166–219; and O' 2852, fol. 56–79, fol. 174–234. These records refer to decorative, not structural, repairs in the auditorium and suggest that stage machinery was not included in repair work. Although acoustics in previous productions were reported as poor, there is no evidence of attempts to modify the situation. Perhaps the room was not as "deplorable" as some historians lead us to believe. There was never any suggestion that the remodeled Salle des Machines threatened the monopoly of the Palais Royal.

53. See Coeyman, "Theatres for Opera and Ballet during the Reigns of Louis XIV and Louis XV," 25, for a plan of the reworked theater. A new theater for the Opera opened at the Palais Royal in 1770 when the Comédie-Française moved into the Salle des Machines. The Salle des Machines burned down during a civil revolt in 1871.

54. See La Salle, *Les treize salles de l'opéra*, pp. 27 ff.; Rouchès, *Inventaire des lettres et papiers*, p. 194; Mélèse, *Le théâtre et le public à Paris sous Louis XIV: 1659–1715* (Paris: Librairie E. Droz, 1934), p. 158; and Cordey, "Lully installe l'Opéra dans le théâtre de Molière: La décoration de la salle," *Bulletin de la société historique de l'architecture française* (1950), 137–142.

55. In sources consulted for this essay, dimensions are often given in old French measurements, the principal ones being *pieds* and *toise*, with 6 *pieds* = 1 *toise*. Here we have converted to the metric system at the equivalent of 1 *toise* = 1.974 meters, except in quotations from contemporary sources, where measurements are left as in the original. Diverse primary sources have been consulted to corroborate dimensions, but Blondel, *L'architecture française*, remains the principal source of information relating to both theaters. Only documents vastly different from his will be discussed at length even though a variety of drawings and written descriptions are cited. Terminology for indicating floors corresponds to the French: ground (*rez de chausée*), first (*premier étage*), second (*deuxième étage*), and so on.

56. For the most part, research on these sites conducted at the end of the nineteenth and the beginning of the twentieth centuries remains the most reliable. It is indeed remarkable that no comprehensive critical study of the Palais Royal theater has been conducted to date. Our essay here marks a step toward that history.

57. It is curious that the Salle des Machines was documented so often and yet used so little. One of the best sources for a description of the hall, contemporary with performances, is the *livret* of *Psiché* published by Ballard in 1671: the copy used for this study is located in the Bibliothèque de l'Opéra Liv 17 [R6(10)]. Others include Brice, *Description de la ville de Paris et de tout ce qu'elle contient de plus remarquable;* 9th ed. (Paris: Chez les Librairies Associes, 1752; reprint, Geneva: Librairie Droz, 1971), pp. 134–152, especially 151–152; Sauval, *Histoire et recherches des antiquités de la ville de Paris,* vol. 2, pp. 52 ff., vol. 3, pp. 46 ff.; de Pure, *Idée des spectacles,* pp. 311–318; Menestrier, *Des ballets anciens et modernes selon les règles du théâtre* (Paris: R. Guignard, 1682; reprint, Geneva: Minkoff, 1972), pp. 195–207; and *Gazette* 1662, pp. 147 ff., 170 ff. Plans of the room include: one of 1668 by Israel Silvestre in the set of engravings of the Cabinet du roy; an anonymous plan of c. 1700 in the National Archives, figure 2.3 above, which records great detail on three levels of the theater; and the most detailed coverage, in Blondel,

L'architecture française, vol. 4, pp. 89–90 and plates 20, 23, 27 and 30, which offer many details about the auditorium but virtually ignore the stage [note: *three* plates are assigned the single number "30"]. An undated plan, as in BN Cabinet des Estampes, Va219c fol: Paris 1er quarter, Tuileries, published in Diderot, *Theater Architecture and Stage Machines* from the *Encyclopédie: Ou dictionnaire raisonné des sciences, des arts, et des métiers* (1762–1772; excerpts trans. and reprinted New York: Benjamin Blom, 1969) may have been inspired by Blondel's view, since it too excludes details of the stage. See also the plates in Dumont, *Parallele de plans des plus belles salles de spectacles d'Italie et de France* and, among modern editions, in Wickham, *A History of the Theatre*, and in Izenour, *Theater Design*. It is difficult to know what state of the hall most of these drawings represent, since they are not precisely dated. In particular, I have not discovered any documentation about the hall for Servandoni's pantomime theater from 1738 on.

Modern research appears in Bapst, *Essai sur l'histoire du théâtre*, pp. 367–369; in Babeau, "Le théâtre des Tuileries sous Louis XIV"; in Rouchès, *Inventaire des lettres et papiers*, pp. xvi–xx; in Heuzey, "Notes sur un dessin représentant la Salle des Machines au XVIIe siècle"; in Christout, "*Ercole amante, L'Hercule amoureux* à la Salle des Machines des Tuileries"; and in Coeyman, "Theatres for Opera and Ballet during the Reigns of Louis XIV and Louis XV." There is surprisingly little written to date about the Vigaranis, the best work being the collected letters, Rouchès, *Inventaire des lettres et papiers*. De Pure, *Idée des spectacles*, p. 312, says he obtained his information about the Salle des Machines from Carlo Vigarani, but he does not explain how. Hautecoeur, *Le règne de Louis XIV*, p. 235, reproduces Silvestre's drawing, and on p. 236, a maquette of the hall made by M. Charles Nuitter for the Paris Exhibition of 1889, property of the Musée de l'Opéra, Paris.

58. See Coeyman, "Theatres for Opera and Ballet during the Reigns of Louis XIV and Louis XV," 24, for all three levels. Blondel, *L'architecture française*, did not include information about the stage; nevertheless, his drawings of the auditorium are quite detailed. Blondel (p. 88) contended that descriptions of the stage were properly the subject matter of treatises about practical stage craft. The omission from his study of this aspect of theater design and construction suggests that by the mid eighteenth century he, at least, did not regard the technical aspects of theaters as valid for inclusion in a study of architecture.

59. See n. 26 for measurements of the Petit Bourbon theater. Heuzey, "Notes sur un dessin représentant la Salle des Machines au XVIIe siècle," 64 n. 16, points out that Vigarani referred to the Salle des Machines as "room for the populace" (*sala del popolo*). Among the many seventeenth- and eighteenth-century sources listing measurements of the room are de Pure, *Idée des spectacles*, and Blondel, *L'architecture française*. De Pure's measurements are given in French feet rather than in *toise*.

60. This entrance from the outside is almost as cumbersome as the famous cul-de-sac at the Palais Royal theater. The absence in such a large building of any places outside the auditorium for socializing is curious and suggests that this may be a particularly French trait in theater design during the seventeenth century. As will be seen below, one of the difficulties with the Paris Opera in the Palais Royal was its lack of public area. The social space was presumably sacrificed because all available room was needed for the stage and auditorium. The Salle des Machines had plenty of room, yet still no lobbies. Does this feature of French theaters suggest that socializing (talking, drinking, eating, whatever else the imagination can allow) occurred within the boxes and balconies of the auditorium?

61. Blondel, *L'architecture française*, p. 87.
62. De Pure, *Idée des spectacles*, pp. 315–318. Does this description suggest that he regarded the theater largely as a place in which to present court productions? Also, the theater was the site for the weekly rehearsals of the Académie de Danse. De Pure, p. 315.
63. Blondel, *L'architecture française*, p. 88.
64. *. . . le coup d'oeil le plus eclatant*. Ibid., p. 87. Blondel also reported that the room had lost much of its glory since the time of its building. We must remember that the theater had been standing largely unused for at least ninety years by the time of the publication of Blondel's treatise.
65. Blondel, *L'architecture française*, p. 88. Why the décor was changed is unclear, since the room was hardly being used.
66. De Pure, *Idée des spectacles*, p. 314. See also Babeau, "Le théâtre des Tuileries sous Louis XIV," 134 n. 3.
67. Babeau, "Le théâtre des Tuileries sous Louis XIV," 133 n. 2, and Heuzey, "Notes sur un dessin représentant la Salle des Machines au XVIIᵉ siècle," 66.
68. This suggests that by the time of Blondel's work, *L'architecture française*, the stage may have fallen into such disrepair that there was little information for eyewitnesses to evaluate. The exact date of Blondel's description is not clear, although he certainly could have known the theater for many years before his treatise was published. On the other hand, de Pure obviously would have been able to witness the theater just after its completion, yet he says hardly anything truly revealing about the mechanical effects on stage.
69. The area for the musicians was not sunken as in most modern theaters. The orchestra also was separated from the parterre by a partition wall about forty inches (one meter) high. The area where the musicians sat (figure 2.2) is on line with the inside pair of columns on stage, behind which is the proscenium arch. Blondel, *L'architecture française*, says nothing about musicians who used the pit. An orchestra of twenty-four, the average size of the King's Violins in the 1660s and 1670s, would have fit into the space with a bit more than thirty-two square feet (three square meters) per player.
70. One can clearly see this decoration in Blondel's side elevation of the theater, "L'architecture française," vol. 6, no. 1, plate 30. Another drawing of the side elevation appears in Coeyman, "Theatres for Opera and Ballet during the Reigns of Louis XIV and Louis XV," 25.
71. Curiously, Blondel depicts this box only on his rear elevation. He reports the attractive grillwork on the box, which made it beautiful as well as safe.
72. Boxes in the Salle des Machines were not built as in Italian theaters: there were no partition walls separating the boxes in the Tuileries theater. This open plan gave the room a sense of even greater spaciousness and a more communal feeling, since audience members could watch one another much more easily than in the Italian arrangement. From this viewpoint, the hall harkens back to the communal great hall settings of court ballets.
73. See Babeau, "Le théâtre des Tuileries sous Louis XIV," 141. Archival documents of the 1720 remodeling include many references to candles.
74. La Grave, *Le théâtre et le public à Paris*, pp. 91–92, reports several other sources but does not offer his own estimate. Sauval, *Histoire et recherches des antiquités de la ville de Paris*, vol. 3, p. 47, says 7,000; the *Mercure galant* of 1749 says 8,000; Brice, *Description de la ville de Paris*, p. 152, reports 7,000–8,000.

75. During the reign of Louis XIV, the population of Paris was approximately 450,000; in 1762 it reached 600,000; and under Louis XVI, 700,000. Loret was one observer who attended multiple times, but certainly he was not the typical spectator. Some research in this area has been undertaken, as in Johnson, *Listening in Paris*, but much more research on ethnographic and demographic aspects of Baroque theaters remains to be done. The issue of the frequency in attendance requires further study and could shed light on the question of how the repertoire was received. The repeated attendance of any individual at a particular production may indicate that one went to the theater as much for social engagement as for artistic edification. This is particularly true for court ballets. We can speculate even further by asking what percentage of French society ever attended theater in the seventeenth century.

76. These measurements reveal that this stage and auditorium approximated normal proportions of French theaters and that they were not inordinately large as some sources suggest. I suspect that some modern criticism about the excessive size of the stage may have been in reaction to the plan published in Diderot's *Encyclopédie*, which does not include details of the stage and backstage area. By comparison, the stage in the Palais Royal measured 56 feet by 30 feet (17.8 meters by 9.1 meters), only one third the area of the stage of the Salle des Machines.

77. That it was used for *Psiché* in 1671 is suggested by a tapestry representing the production and showing the use of an upper stage. See Heuzey, "Notes sur un dessin représentant la Salle des Machines au XVIIe siècle," 68. Unfortunately Heuzey did not identify his illustration carefully: we cannot know which performance this tapestry depicts, since *Psiché* also played in the Palais Royal.

78. Menestrier, *Des ballets anciens et modernes*, p. 218. Prunières, *L'opéra italien en France avant Lulli*, p. 220, also discusses this machinery, which he says held one hundred performers.

79. See Lawrenson, *The French Stage in the XVIIth Century*, p. 174, and Rouchès, *Inventaire des lettres et papiers*, p. 228, for comments on how Vigarani was forced to work within Le Vau's structure. Christout, "*Ercole amante, L'Hercule amoureux* à la Salle des Machines des Tuileries," 11, accepts unconditionally that acoustics were bad because of the large dimensions of the hall. Also, she comments (14) that the audiences loved the machines.

80. See the *Gazette*, (February 1662), 147, 170. Also, La Grave, *Le théâtre et le public à Paris*, p. 91, who cites Brice's 1713 edition, p. 105. Brice, in the 1757 edition, discusses the hall on p. 151. La Grave also notes the *Mercure galant* (March 1722), 152.

81. Blondel, *L'architecture française*, p. 87. "Because of the vastness of the stage, from which one must comprehend the voices of the actors, it is difficult to hear. This [circumstance] led to the abandonment of the theater to mute shows given to those present under the auspices and management of the Chevalier Servandoni." (*D'ailleurs le lieu de la scene est si vaste, que la voix des Acteurs à ce qu'on prétend, avoit peine à se faire entendu. Ce que n'a pas peu contribué à faire abandonner ce théâtre aux spectacles muets qui s'y donnent à présent sur les desseins et sous la conduite du Chevalier Servandoni.*) Prunières, *L'opéra italien en France avant Lulli*, pp. 221, 282, mentions that the music could hardly be heard.

82. What was described as an ignominious retreat from Paris by Cavalli was probably due not to the quality of his music but to the political bind into which he was thrust by the changed direction of French culture during the two-year delay in staging *Hercule*.

83. Lawrenson, *The French Stage in the XVIIth Century*, p. 143, discusses sites built on the communal approach. Early ballets were undifferentiated (i.e., there was little or no distinction between performer and audience member) spectacles. Ballets on a proscenium

stage turned performances into very different events: performers, including nobles, were distinguished from observers by virtue of the proscenium separating the hall into stage and auditorium.

84. In all its extended reporting on the production, the *Gazette de France* never mentioned Cavalli. See *Gazette* 1662, 147 ff., 170 ff., 196 ff., 412 ff., 435 ff., 459 ff. Loret focused largely on the ballet, not the opera. It might be instructive to study the source of negative criticism, noticing any distinctions along national lines. See Babeau, "Le théâtre des Tuileries sous Louis XIV," 135 n. 3. Louis LeClerc (= Ludovic Celler), *Les décors, les costumes, et la mise en scène au XVIIᵉ siècle 1615–1680* (Paris: Liepmannssohn et Dufour, 1869), pp. 124–128, describes the opera. The production may have been a failure simply because French audiences did not like the music. For example, Cavalli did not include a French overture, which Lully had popularized a few years earlier. See Prunières, *Cavalli et l'opéra vénitien au XVIIᵉ siècle* (Paris: Éditions Rieder, 1931), p. 85. Babeau, "Le théâtre des Tuileries sous Louis XIV," 135 n. 3, cites reports that do not even mention the location of *Hercule*. Other reports avoid real issues about the hall or unfairly discredit the Italian designer. The hall is not cited at all by Loret in his extended verse about the production. Even some of our more perceptive modern critics have repeated unqualified reports about acoustics.

85. My descriptions of repertoire focus on interpreting visual and spatial conditions experienced by performers and audiences. The reader who prefers longer or more detailed descriptions of the dramatic or musical contents of repertoire may consult the original or the modern editions of repertoire. A carrousel in June 1662 was held on the ground of the Tuileries Palace very near the site of the Salle des Machines. The *Gazette de France* 1662, pp. 554–556, reports (how accurately we cannot say) that 10,000 people attended this outdoor presentation. Are we to consider the theater as being a comparable place, indoors, to accommodate a crowd of equal or near-equal size? The gardens of the Tuileries did include an outdoor Salle de la Comédie, not very large, as shown in Blondel, *L'architecture française*, vol. 4, plate 21.

86. In this essay we refer to this opera by its French rather than by its Italian title—the way it was known in France and also the way most French historians refer to it. Our designation should not lead the reader to think of the work as a French-style opera or an opera in French. Dates for these and other productions are based on a conflation of sources reporting productions, including the *Gazette de France*, Loret's verse, and the title pages of *livrets*.

87. Because Cavalli composed *Hercule* specifically for Paris, we cannot gain much information about how a production for French audiences may have altered the creators' concept of the opera. On the other hand, his ballet *Xerxes* could furnish such information, since it played originally in Italy before the performances in Paris in 1660. For example, Cavalli reworked *Xerxes* from three to five acts and added a prologue and six *entrées* of dance. If complaints about acoustics were justified, could some of the negative criticism have resulted from the noises of the machines covering up the singing? Perhaps it was not that the *room* was too soft but that the *machines* were too loud.

88. No images of the production were ever engraved, as they were for many other Italian operas. Louis apparently proposed a set of plates which never were realized. The opera deserves much more research.

89. In my opinion, some secondary reports, as de Pure's (*Idée des spectacles*) and Loret's (*La muse historique*), depict a much grander production than the *livret* suggests. Could they have had reasons to fabricate, other than the usual honoring of anything royal? Was it

necessary to pad the numbers to increase the impression of a magnificent hall? They may have wanted to represent *Hercule* as grandly as possible in order to contrast it with the 1660, apartment production of *Xerxes*, which had no scene changes or dancing nobles.

90. See Babeau, "Le théâtre des Tuileries sous Louis XIV," 138.

91. Loret, *La muse historique*, 1662, vol. 3, p. 470, usually given to exaggeration, reports a total of 730 performers. See also Babeau, "Le théâtre des Tuileries sous Louis XIV," 136 n. 1.

92. Not knowing the exact size of the orchestra or of the chorus hinders our speculation about how their sound filled the hall.

93. Information about how French and Italian casts got along together might shed some light on the success of Italian opera in France. I have not seen this topic discussed in research to date.

94. Here I am not attempting to analyze reasons for presenting the cast in this way, instead simply trying to describe the use of the stage. I suspect, however, that the relatively *un*spectacular presentation of *Hercule*—at least, by French standards—may have contributed to the disappointment with the hall.

95. The *Gazette de France* and Loret also focus their reports on the Prologue. A summary of the contents of the complete ballet appears in Babeau, "Le théâtre des Tuileries sous Louis XIV," 138.

96. *Entrée* 9 presented fifteen dancing grand captains of antiquity, including the king and Monsieur le Prince; *entrée* 10, the moon and ten pilgrims; *entrée* 11, Mercure and sixteen charlatans with eleven guitars; *entrée* 12, Jupiter and four nations depicted by twenty-two dancers; *entrée* 13, the eleven guitars and ten dancing pleasures; *entrée* 14, twelve delights; *entrée* 15, the twelve hours of the night; *entrée* 16, Aurora alone (danced by Mlle. Verpré); *entrée* 17, the twelve hours of the day, with Louis as the sun; and *entrée* 18, sixteen stars.

97. See Hautecoeur, *Le règne de Louis XIV,* especially chap. 2, for a discussion about the Tuileries Palace.

98. Additionally, politics may have heavily entered into the decision to discontinue the use of the hall again. Lully's takeover of the Paris Opera in 1672 and his moving of the Opera to the Palais Royal after Molière's death may have been the strongest factors in the closing of the Salle des Machines once again. Louis preferred a site other than one associated with Mazarin, as the young king set out to define his rule after Mazarin's death. Holding the next big production after *Psiché*, the *Fête de Versailles* of 1674, outside Paris further deflected interest in the Salle des Machines.

99. I know of no other *livret* of court repertoire that describes an architectural entity in such detail. The preface is reproduced by P. Mesnard in the complete works of Molière in *Grands écrivains de la France,* vol. 8, pp. 362–384.

100. There is some ambiguity about the number of performances in the Salle des Machines. My source documenting the two performances is the *Gazette de France.* See also Babeau, "Le théâtre des Tuileries sous Louis XIV," n. 7. Whether Molière used machinery from the Salle des Machines is unclear.

101. Overall *Psiché* was a much grander production than *Hercule.* See Babeau, "Le théâtre des Tuileries sous Louis XIV," 140 nn. 6, 7, where he notes that singers were recruited from Gascogne for the Académie Royale.

102. Costs reached 115,000 *livres* for repairs to the hall and the production of the ballet. Details are included in the reports of the *Menus plaisirs* (i.e., records of the king's house-

hold). Also, see Coeyman, "The Stage Works of Michel-Richard Delalande in the Musical-Cultural Context of the French Court, 1680–1726" (Ph.D. dissertation, City University of New York, 1987), pp. 320 ff., for more on the ballet.

103. Sauval, *Histoire et recherches des antiquités de la ville de Paris,* vol. 2, pp. 161–163; vol. 3, p. 47, is the best source contemporary with the theater. Some modern sources relating to the Palais Royal theater include Bapst, *Essai sur l'histoire du théâtre,* pp. 180–189, 339–346; Prunières, *L'opéra italien en France avant Lulli;* Bjurström, *Giacomo Torelli and Baroque Stage Design;* Gourret, *Histoire des salles de l'opéra de Paris,* pp. 25–36; and Coeyman, "Theatres for Opera and Ballet during the Reigns of Louis XIV and Louis XV." We will use the name "Palais Royal" throughout this section, even though some references to the building relate to the time when it would have been known officially as the "Palais Cardinal."

104. Sauval, *Histoire et recherches des antiquités de la ville de Paris,* p. 163.

105. It is ironic that the history of the Salle des Machines is recorded in much greater detail than is that of the Palais Royal theater. In particular, Blondel's choice to depict the larger hall (*L'architecture française*) is curious, especially since the Palais Royal hall would have been the public opera theater he knew and possibly used for many years.

106. See Lawrenson, *The French Stage in the XVIIth Century,* p. 169.

107. For the *Mirame* view, see ibid., figure 56; Bjurström, *Giacomo Torelli and Baroque Stage Design,* p. 118. For *Le soir,* see Bapst, *Essai sur l'histoire du théâtre,* p. 217; or Lawrenson, *The French Stage in the XVIIth Century,* figure 87.

108. In various drawings, musicians appear in many places around the hall, sometimes on the stage, sometimes in the audience area, and, of course, in the orchestra area in front of the stage.

109. Lawrenson (*The French Stage in the XVIIth Century*) suggests that the engraving may depict the theater before seat banks were installed, or simply reflects artistic license to incorporate the monarchs in the view. Based on Sauval's measurements (*Histoire et recherches des antiquités de la ville de Paris*), the flat area on the floor measured about 8 meters by 20 meters (26.3 feet by 65.7 feet), not nearly as deep as the space suggested in *Le soir.*

110. Sauval's measurements (*Histoire et recherches des antiquités de la ville de Paris*) are in *toise.* The length is 18 *toise,* and of that, the amphitheater is 10 to 11 *toise* long.

111. See Bjurström, *Giacomo Torelli and Baroque Stage Design,* p. 123. Recall that the Petit Bourbon stage measured roughly 49 feet by 49 feet (14.9 meters by 14.9 meters). See n. 26 in this essay.

112. See Lawrenson, *The French Stage in the XVIIth Century,* p. 169.

113. Bjurström, *Giacomo Torelli and Baroque Stage Design,* p. 117.

114. More works may have played there. McGowan, *L'art du ballet de cour en France: 1581–1643* (Paris: Éditions du Centre National de la Recherche Scientifique, 1978), pp. 307–308, lists many more court ballets that were staged during the first phase of the theater's history, but she has not indicated the location of most of these.

115. Bjurström, *Giacomo Torelli and Baroque Stage Design,* pp. 123–124.

116. See LeClerc, *Les décors, les costumes, et la mise en scène au XVIIe siècle,* p. 75; Bapst, *Essai sur l'histoire du théâtre,* pp. 210–211; and Prunières, *L'opéra italien en France avant Lulli,* p. 104.

117. The original plan was to open the hall on 26 February, but it was not finished. Bjurström, *Giacomo Torelli and Baroque Stage Design,* pp. 124–125, says there were six per-

formances. In his discussion of the production, Prunières, *L'opéra italien en France avant Lulli*, pp. 86–150, also contends that there were six; however, my records indicate five. Both Prunières and Bjurström describe problems with the machinery on the first day.

118. Prunières, *L'opéra italien en France avant Lulli*, pp. 110–111; Bjurström, *Giacomo Torelli and Baroque Stage Design*, p. 125.

119. Bjurström, *Giacomo Torelli and Baroque Stage Design*, p. 126.

120. Torelli's productions in France probably totaled nine. After those in the Palais Royal, he probably also worked on the *Ballet du nuit* in 1653; on *Les noces de Pelée et de Thétis* in 1654; on *Psiché* in 1656; and on *Le rosaure* in 1658, all presented in the Petit Bourbon; and on *Les fâcheux* of 1661 at Vaux-le-Vicomte.

121. See the *Gazette* (1647), #27 (the entire issue), 201 ff.; Ménestrier, *Des ballets anciennes et modernes selon les règles du théâtre*, pp. 195 ff.; LeClerc, *Les origines de l'opera et le ballet de la reine (1581)*, (Paris: Didier, 1868) pp. 340–343; and Prunières, *L'opéra italien en France avant Lulli*, pp. 103, 110, 351. Also, many personal letters include accounts of the opera. There is also a summary in Bjurström, *Giacomo Torelli and Baroque Stage Design*, pp. 143–147, based on the report in the *Gazette*. The *Gazette* report is more detailed than the *livret*.

122. See Bjurström, *Giacomo Torelli and Baroque Stage Design*, p. 124. In these and other reports, distinctions between remodeling costs and production costs are not clear.

123. *Gazette*, (1662), 360, 362.

124. The *livret* points out that the work contains new visual images not seen before in French theater, with machines, scenery changes, and various other views. Does this suggest comparable talents between Torelli and the Vigaranis? Bjurström, *Giacomo Torelli and Baroque Stage Design*, p. 147, says no iconographic documentation of *Orphée* has been identified.

125. *Gazette* (1647), 208.

126. Bjurström, *Giacomo Torelli and Baroque Stage Design*, p. 145, says a tapestry probably was lowered during Venus's scene to prepare the background of clouds.

127. Cordey, "Lully installe l'Opéra dans le théâtre de Molière," 137, reports a comment from La Grange, *Le registre de La Grange 1659–1685*, p. 122, that an item in the accounts of Molière's troupe says that ten years earlier the installation had been "in haste and without due consideration" (*à la haste et à la legere*).

128. See La Grange, *Le registre de La Grange 1659–1685*, pp. 25–26, record of 10 October 1660.

129. See Cordey, "Lully installe l'Opéra dans le théâtre de Molière," 137.

130. Mittman, *Spectators on the Paris Stage*, p. 7.

131. Gourret, *Histoire des salles de l'opéra de Paris*, p. 30.

132. The set of drawings, found in Archives Nationales N III Seine 545, is reproduced in La Grave, *Le théâtre et le public à Paris*, figures 7 to 12. The project, Archives Nationales N III Seine 566, is reproduced in Coeyman, "Theatres for Opera and Ballet during the Reigns of Louis XIV and Louis XV," 32. Blondel's plan of the theater appears in his view of the complete Palais Royal, *L'architecture française*, vol. 5, no. 9, plates 2 and 3.

133. See Zaslaw, "At the Paris Opera in 1747," *Early Music* 12 (1983).

134. Coeyman, "Theatres for Opera and Ballet during the Reigns of Louis XIV and Louis XV," 33.

135. See La Grave, *Le théâtre et le public à Paris*, p. 82. Riccoboni, *A General History of the Stage*, p. 152, observed the diminutive proportions of most French theaters in contrast with

Italian sites. Blondel, *L'architecture française,* (1754), vol. 2, p. 14, reported that in 1742, all plans to that date for building a larger hall were discontinued. The *Mercure galant* of March 1678 and of June 1732 each discuss actual remodeling on the theater.

136. In contrast, the new opera house built by Moreau in 1770 drew much more attention from critics and illustrators. For example, see the plates in Dumont, *Parallele de plans des plus belles salles de spectacles d'Italie et de France,* and in Diderot, *Theater Architecture and Stage Machines.*

137. Cordey, "Lully installe l'Opéra dans le théâtre de Molière," 138 ff.

138. See Coeyman, "Theatres for Opera and Ballet during the Reigns of Louis XIV and Louis XV," n. 46, citing Anthony, *French Baroque Music from Beaujoyeulx to Rameau,* quoting an ordinance of 1713 that lists forty-eight members of the Opera orchestra. There is still no evidence to suggest that the musicians sat in a sunken pit.

139. See Cordey, "Lully installe l'Opéra dans le théâtre de Molière," 140.

140. Rouchès, *Inventaire des lettres et papiers,* p. 194, says Vigarani was again occupied with the theater in February. We lack further details: a single letter of 22 February is the only correspondence from 1674 that Rouchès reprints.

141. See Coeyman, "Theatres for Opera and Ballet during the Reigns of Louis XIV and Louis XV," 37, where I concluded that La Grave (*Le théâtre et le public à Paris*) allowed roughly two square feet (.19 square meter) per person.

142. Several eighteenth-century drawings studying seat bank design in French theaters, complete with human subjects, indicate that audience comfort became increasingly important to designers. See *Lully, Musicien Soleil. Exposition 1987* (Paris: ADIAM, 1987), plate 44, for a drawing that may depict the boxes of the Palais Royal.

143. Sauval, *Histoire et recherches des antiquités de la ville de Paris,* p. 163, discusses the ceiling and roof.

144. See Coeyman, "Theatres for Opera and Ballet during the Reigns of Louis XIV and Louis XV," 34, for a more detailed illustration than in Blondel's plan in *L'architecture française.*

145. Moreau's hall of 1770 may have profited from the model of some better-functioning theaters in Lyon and Bordeaux. It included an entrance and public foyer along *Rue St. Honoré,* which, however, reduced the area of the auditorium. Moreau apparently filled in the cul-de-sac with off-stage rooms for actors.

146. See catalogues such as Durey, *Histoire du théâtre de l'Académie Royale de Musique;* or Lajarte, *Théâtre de l'opéra: Catalogue.*

Chapter Three

1. These works include *The Prophetess, or, The History of Dioclesian,* Z. 627, *King Arthur,* Z. 628, *The Fairy Queen,* Z. 629, *The Indian Queen,* Z. 630, *The Tempest,* Z. 631, and *Timon of Athens,* Z. 632. The numbers used here to identify Purcell's works are those assigned by Franklin B. Zimmerman, *Henry Purcell, 1659–1695: An Analytical Catalogue of His Music* (New York: St. Martin's Press, 1963). Questions about the authenticity of Z. 631 are not germane to the present discussion.

2. Diana De Marly, "The Architect of Dorset Garden Theatre," *Theatre Notebook* 29/3 (1975), 124.

3. John R. Spring, "The Dorset Garden Theatre: Playhouse or Opera House?" *Theatre Notebook* 34/2 (1980), 60 – 69.

4. John Genest, ed. *Some Account of the English Stage from the Restoration in 1660 to 1830*, 10 vols. (New York: Burt Franklin; originally published in Bath, 1832), vol. 1, p. 43.

5. Leslie Hotson, *The Commonwealth and Restoration Stage* (New York: Russell and Russell, 1962), p. 256. Regarding Wren's role in the design of the Dorset Garden Theatre, see De Marly, "The Architect of Dorset Garden Theatre," 119–124.

6. See Hamilton Bell, "Contributions to the History of the English Playhouse," *The Architectural Record* 33 (1913), 359 ff.

7. Hotson, *Restoration Stage*, p. 113.

8. Cibber is the author of *An Apology for the Life of Mr. Colley Cibber* (1740). John Loftis has characterized this work as "a good autobiography, which is in fact a comprehensive though not unbiased account of theatrical affairs from about 1690, when he became an actor, until 1738. . . . the *Apology* is the closest approximation to a satisfactory contemporary account of the theaters in the period just before Garrick." See John Loftis, "The Social and Literary Context: Theatrical Records and the Rise of Theatrical Scholarship," in *The Revels History of Drama in English* (London: Methuen, 1976), vol. 5, pp. 78–79.

9. Dimensions of other theaters have also been preserved, but many of these are of rural theaters or so-called nursery theaters (i.e., theaters used primarily for the training of young actors and actresses). These theaters were quite a bit smaller than the major London houses. For example, according to the contract of 1671 between John Perin and Thomas Duckworth, the latter agreed to build upon "a certain piece of ground of the said Perin's situate in Finsbury Fields, commonly called Bun hill, one booth or playhouse: to contain in length threescore foot, and in breadth forty foot from out to out." Cited in Hotson, *Restoration Stage*, p. 189.

10. On the basis of Ogilby and Morgan's scale map of 1677, Hotson has suggested dimensions of 140 feet by 57 feet (42.7 meters by 17.4 meters). See ibid., p. 233. Robert D. Hume puts a finer point on the exterior dimensions at 148 feet by 57 feet (45.1 meters by 17.4 meters). See his article "The Dorset Garden Theatre. A Review of Facts and Problems," *Theatre Notebook* 33/1 (1979), 4. Edward A. Langhans puts the dimensions at 147 feet by 57 feet. See his article "The Dorset Garden Theatre in Pictures," *Theatre Survey* 4/2 (1965), 143. The exterior view of the Dorset Garden Theatre is reproduced in *The Revels History*, vol. 5, plate 7.

11. These memoirs are B.L., Add. Ms. 35,177. The portion in question is reproduced in Hotson, *Restoration Stage*, pp. 234–235.

12. This accords with another plan found among Wren's sketches.

13. This layout is seen in Wren's plan for Drury Lane (see figure 3.6), which shows entrances to the pit only in the front of the theater to the left and right of the stage.

14. In his article "Platforms and Picture Frames: A Conjectural Reconstruction of the Duke of York's Theatre, Dorset Garden, 1669–1709," in *Theatre Notebook* 31/3 (1977), 6–19, Spring suggests (p. 16) that Dorset Garden's seating capacity was analogous to Drury Lane's—about 1,200. Hume ("Review of Facts and Problems," p. 13) puts the capacity at 820.

15. Although Puritan rulings closed the theaters during the Commonwealth, when the theaters reopened in 1660, some actors who had known Shakespeare personally were still alive. Among these were William Beeston, who led two theater troops, as well as Sir William D'Avenant, who was reputed to have been—of all things—an illegitimate son of Shakespeare's. See Allardyce Nicoll, *The English Theatre: A Short History* (London: Thomas Nelson and Sons, 1936), pp. 76–80.

16. Colley Cibber, *An Apology for the Life of Mr. Colley Cibber,* in *Days of the Dandies* (London: The Grolier Society, 1888), vol. 2, pp. 86–87.

17. W. J. Macqueen-Pope has stated, "There were no footlights when the [Drury] Lane [Theatre of 1663] first opened. They appeared nearly forty years later as little oil lamps." (*Theatre Royal Drury Lane* [London: W. H. Allen, 1945], p. 34.) There can be no doubt that footlights were known well before the date that Macqueen-Pope gives. A bill dated February 1671 for work done by carpenters in the Hall Theatre mentions "making a trough at ye foote of the stage for the lights to stand in." The bill is cited in full in Eleanore Boswell, *The Restoration Court Stage: 1660–1702* (Cambridge, Massachusetts: Harvard University Press, 1932), p. 250.

18. Some of the diverse dramatic functions served by these theater doors and balconies are discussed in Collin Viser's two-part study "The Anatomy of the Early Restoration Stage: *The Adventures of Five Hours* and John Dryden's 'Spanish Comedies,'" *Theatre Notebook* 29/2 (1975), 56–69; part II, 29/3 (1975), 114–119. Montague Summers also examined numerous Restoration plays and analyzed their stage directions in order to discover the precise functions that the stage doors and balconies served: "The usual entrances and exits employed on the Restoration stage were the proscenium doors, that is to say the permanent doors, set on either side of the apron stage, between the oval front of the stage which faced the pit and the proscenium arch. As the error has been more than once made and is yet repeated, it must be emphasized that there were no such doors, indeed there could not be, on the further side of the proscenium arch, behind the curtain line. Actually the evidence concerning the number of proscenium doors employed in Restoration times is most contradictory and confusing if we attempt to generalize, and the safest plan is to prove the precise number employed in each theatre, so far as the known details admit." See Summers, *Restoration Theatre* (New York: Macmillan, 1934), p. 126.

   In keeping with the last bit of advice given by Summers, note that Richard Southern, using the engravings from *The Empress of Morocco,* has created a tentative reconstruction of these doors as they appeared in the Dorset Garden Theatre. See his *Revels History,* figure 2, p. 97. According to Macqueen-Pope, "In the first Drury Lane Theatre, there were six of them, three on each side. In the second they were reduced to four. . . . These proscenium doors lasted for many years and were very useful." See his *Drury Lane,* p. 35.

19. Summers, *Restoration Theatre,* p. 239.

20. Edward A. Langhans, "A Conjectural Reconstruction of the Dorset Garden Theatre," *Theatre Survey* 13/2 (November 1972), 78.

21. Samuel Pepys, *The Diary of Samuel Pepys,* ed. Robert Latham and William Matthews (Berkeley and Los Angeles: University of California Press, 1976), vol. 4, p. 128. Another early instance of modern placement of the orchestra occurred in *The Siege of Rhodes* (1656), which was presented at Rutland House. Here the musicians were placed in that position primarily for lack of space elsewhere. See Dennis Arundell, *The Critic at the Opera* (London: Ernest Benn, 1957) pp. 56–57.

22. In his article "The Dorset Garden Theatre: Playhouse or Opera House," 64–65, Spring argues against Hume's estimation of the scenic stage depth.

23. Nicoll, *Short History,* p. 60.

24. Boswell, *Court Stage,* pp. 149–150.

25. Richard Southern, "Flat," *The Oxford Companion to the Theatre,* ed. Phyllis Hartnoll (London: Oxford University Press, 1951), p. 265.

26. Spring, "Platforms and Picture Frames," 14.

27. Langhans, "Conjectural Reconstruction," figure 1, 82–83.

28. In this study I have referred to the areas behind the shutters as "inner stages" rather than as "discovery areas." I have deliberately avoided this terminology since it presupposes that this space was used for scenic purposes exclusively.

29. Samuel Pepys, *The Diary of Samuel Pepys,* vol. 9, p. 434. John Evelyn, another diarist of the period, also commented upon Streeter's work. Concerning a performance of *The Conquest of Granada* [10–11 February 1671] he says "there were indeed very glorious scenes and perspectives, the work of Mr. Streeter, who well understands it."

30. Killigrew's bill and Fuller's reply are reproduced in Hotson, *Restoration Stage,* pp. 348–355. Other scene painters of the period known by name include John Webb (a pupil of Inigo Jones), Robert Aggas (or Angus), Samuel Towers, Robert Robinson, and one painter known only as "Mr. Stephenson," who provided scenery for the productions of Shadwell's *Psyche* at the Dorset Garden Theatre in February 1675.

31. Summers, *Restoration Theatre,* p. 101.

32. Boswell, *Court Stage,* p. 155.

33. See ibid., p. 43.

34. "No less than ninety-six tin sconces and tin plates for reflectors were supplied for the masque . . . *Calisto.*" Ibid., p. 160.

35. In Pepys's entry for 1 May 1668, we read: "To the King's playhouse and there saw *The Surprizall;* and a disorder in the pit by its raining in from the Copulo at top." (Pepys, *The Diary of Samuel Pepys,* vol. 9, p. 182.)

36. Nicoll, *Short History,* p. 85.

37. Boswell, *Court Stage,* pp. 168–169.

38. This engraving is in volume six of the 1711 complete works edition. In Nicoll, *Short History,* p. 39, it is incorrectly identified as the frontispiece to *The Honest Man's Fortune.*

39. The date was 23 May 1656. Music for the entertainment was provided by Henry Lawes, Matthew Locke, Captain Cooke, George Hudson, and Charles and Edward Coleman (father and son).

40. Cited in Hotson, *Restoration Stage,* p. 150. See also Dennis Arundell, *The Critic at the Opera* (London: Ernest Benn, 1957), p. 56.

41. Pepys, *Diary* (19 March 1666), vol. 7, p. 76.

42. Cited in Summers, *Restoration Theatre,* p. 111.

43. Pepys, *Diary,* vol. 8, pp. 521–522. The air in question was Ferdinand's "Go thy way," which was set to music by John Banister.

44. According to Genest, "There was no Queen's Theatre from the Restoration till the accession of James the 2d. to the crown—in the *second* edition of the play (i.e., *The Forced Marriage*) in 1688, it is said to have been acted at the Queen's Theatre, as in that year Dorset Garden became the Queen's Theatre." See Genest's *Some Account of the English Stage,* vol. 1, p. 146. One further point to be borne in mind is that the union of the two companies (i.e., the Duke's men and the King's men) took place in 1682. At this time, Drury Lane became the main house. Dorset Garden was used only for presentations—such as operas—requiring extensive scenery and a large stage. This remained so until well after the death of Purcell in 1695.

45. See Edward J. Dent, *Foundations of English Opera: A Study of Musical Drama in England during the Seventeenth Century* (Cambridge University Press, 1928), pp. 139–140.

46. Spring ("Platforms and Picture Frames," 15) calculates the proscenium opening as 24 feet (7.3 meters). Hume ("Review of Facts and Problems," 10–11) argues for a wider opening.

Chapter Four

1. "To recover them [Betterton's company], therefore, to their due estimation, a new project was formed, of building them a stately theatre in the Haymarket, by Sir John Vanbrugh." Colley Cibber, *An Apology for the Life of Mr. Colley Cibber,* ed. Edmund Bellchambers (London: W. Simpkin and R. Marshall, 1822), p. 294.

2. C. P. M. Dumont, *Paralléle de plans des plus belles salles de spectacles d'Italie et de France* (Paris, 1764).

3. "This does not include the stage wings, adjoining dressing rooms and scene shops, hallways, or foyer. Nor does it include the vista stage area, which was added in 1719 or earlier when John James Heidegger, then manager of the opera, purchased this adjoining house." *Survey of London* 29 (London: Athlone Press, 1960), 226. The vista stage room added 29 feet (8.8 meters) to the depth of the stage. Graham Barlow, in "Vanbrugh's Queen's Theatre in the Haymarket, 1703–9," *Early Music* 17 (1989), 518, lists the width of the auditorium as 54 feet 8 inches (16.7 meters), but this appears to include the side passages. Comparison with the Dumont plan (figure 4.1) and the 1776 plan (Barlow's illustration 6, Public Record Office LRRO63/70, p. 200; also in *Survey of London* 30, plate 27a) shows an auditorium width closer to 52 or 53 feet (15.8 to 16.2 meters).

4. Nicodemus Tessin measured the theater during a visit to Hamburg in the year 1687. His description is quoted in Hellmuth Christian Wolff, *Die Barockoper in Hamburg (1678–1738)* (Wolfenbüttel: Möseler, 1957), p. 352. Whether the 80-foot (24.4-meter) stage depth included the forestage is unclear. Paris's seventeenth-century Salle des Machines, discussed by Barbara Coeyman in chap. 2 of this book, and the Salle des Ballets in that same city were also exponentially larger than the London opera house. See also T. E. Lawrenson, *The French Stage in the XVIIth Century* (Manchester University Press, 1957), p. 179.

5. At the present Covent Garden opera house, the rear wall of the main floor of seating is nearly 85 feet (25.9 meters) from the front of the stage. The rear of the top gallery is upwards of 40 feet (12.2 meters) farther from the stage. The ceiling over the auditorium is domed, reaching 65 feet (19.8 meters) above the main floor. This is a considerably larger space for performing. (Measurements taken from *Survey of London* 35 [London: Athlone Press, 1970], pp. 106–107, plan of "existing state" of the theater.)

6. Including the space on stage from the proscenium arch to the rear-most scenery-grooves adds only 32 feet (9.8 meters) to the depth of the principal performing space on stage.

7. Cibber, *Apology,* p. 296.

8. Side boxes were added to boost ticket revenue, and the ceiling was lowered over the audience. A significant change in the forestage architecture may also have been undertaken. See Graham Barlow, "Vanbrugh's Queen's Theatre," 515–521. His reconstruction of the pre-1709 proscenium arch is tantalizing, but remains speculative. The proposal of an extendable forestage appears groundless.

9. The monopoly on opera granted the theater on 31 December 1707 prohibited the presentation of plays (*Survey of London* 29, 225). The only other form of theater commonly presented in the Haymarket Theatre was French Harlequin comedies. These broad-brush bits of situation comedy relied less on verbal finesse than did the plays at other theaters; hence, the booming acoustics of the Haymarket, which garbled normal speech, could do no significant damage to these works (which incorporated dancing acts, tumbling acts, or "Entertainments").

10. This led one early anonymous poet to pen the following bit of doggerel:
> When I their Boxes, Pit and Stage did see,
> Their Musick Room, and Middle Gallery,
> In Semi Circles all of them to be,
> I well perceiv'd they took especial care
> Nothing to make or do upon the Square.
> (*Diverting Post,* 14 April 1705).

11. The plan of the theater made by C. P. M. Dumont in 1764 confirms the dual function of benches as seats and stairs, for it shows the semicircular benches extending without aisles, yet there are traffic paths indicated on the benches, leading directly from the entrances at the back and sides of the main floor down to the front rows.

12. Judith Milhous, "The Capacity of Vanbrugh's Theatre in the Haymarket," *Theatre History Studies* 4 (1984), 39. The second gallery, as Milhous points out, was in all likelihood largely filled with the footmen of the richer folk seated down below.

13. Even considerations of fashion enter into this discussion, since the girth of clothing affected the number of people possible in a given bench-length. An advertisement for a charity performance by Handel of *Messiah* at the Foundling Hospital in 1750 shows a contemporary awareness of this: "The Gentlemen are desired to come without Swords, and the Ladies without Hoops." Otto Erich Deutsch, *Händel-Handbuch* 4 (Kassel: Bärenreiter, 1985), p. 439.

14. Milhous, "Capacity of Vanbrugh's Theatre," 44–45. She lists a wide variety of previous estimates on p. 38 of the same.

15. Ibid., 45.

16. Barlow, "Vanbrugh's Queen's Theatre," 517–518. This argument also presumes that the 1707–1708 renovations failed to add chandeliers.

17. "Les bords du théâtre sont ornez de colones, le longs desquels sont attachez des miroirs avec des bras et plusieur de bougies, ainsi qu'aux pilastres qui soutienent la gallerie du fond de la salle. Au lieu de lustres ce sont de vilains chandeliers de bois, soutenus de cordes comme on en voit aux danseurs de cordes. Rien n'est plus vilain, ce sont pourtant des bougies par tout." Winton Dean, "A French Traveller's View of Handel's Operas," *Music and Letters* 55 (1974), 177–178.

18. I have not yet found any listing of accounts for candle sales at Handel's theaters.

19. For an overview of the stagecraft of the time, see Colin Visser's "Scenery and Technical Design," in *The London Theatre World,* ed. Robert D. Hume (Carbondale: Southern Illinois University Press, 1980), pp. 66–118.

20. Barlow, "Vanbrugh's Queen's Theatre," 519–520.

21. The last-mentioned scene, being on a mountain, may have been accomplished with a raked piece of machinery in the shape of a mountain. During the stage action, the mountain opens to swallow several soldiers. There may then have been room inside of this machine for the spirits, etc., to disappear and reappear without using the floor traps. Additional information will be given in the discussion of *Rinaldo* at the end of this essay.

22. In Act III, spirits fly away with Arcane's sword. In Act IV, Medea enters on a cloud, and later, Theseus descends from above while sleeping. In Act V, Medea flies away, and later reenters on a dragon-drawn chariot. Minerva enters at the end of the fifth act, descending "on a Machine."

23. In Act II, Hecate enters on a dragon-drawn chariot (possibly the same set piece used for *Teseo*). Later in the same act, four specters descend from above and fly around Claudio's statue. The statue sinks, and a cypress tree rises in its place. In Act III, Mars enters on a cloud (again probably the same cloud used in *Teseo*).

24. Given that the theater was designed with Thomas Betterton's company in mind, an ambitious fly system would be requisite since his extravaganzas at Dorset Garden in the 1670s and 1680s used "the most spectacular machines for descents." Visser, "Scenery," p. 102.

25. Philip H. Highfill, Jr., "Rich's 1744 Inventory of Covent Garden Properties," *Restoration and 18th Century Theatre Research* 6/1 (May 1967), 31. Visser points out that accounts at Drury Lane indicate the use of under-stage carriages at that theater in 1714—much closer to the time of the building of the Haymarket Theatre. See Visser, "Scenery," p. 77.

26. See Visser, "Scenery," pp. 75–78, for a description and illustration as well as for some evidence of this system in other theaters.

27. Dean, "French Traveller," 177. Even with the under-stage carriages, the drops and shutters at the back of the scene had to be changed by hand, requiring coordination with the movement of the wings.

28. See the stage designs in Lowell Lindgren, "The Staging of Handel's Operas in London," in *Handel Tercentenary Collection,* ed. Stanley Sadie and Anthony Hicks (Ann Arbor: UMI Research Press, 1987), pp. 93–119.

29. Interestingly, late seventeenth-century productions in England using elaborate scenery designed in perspective were known as operas, regardless of their musical content. We know the names of some of the stage designers for the Haymarket during Handel's time there, but only two depictions of the stage with sets exist. See Lindgren, "Staging," pp. 93–112.

30. See Judith Milhous and Robert D. Hume, "A Prompt Copy of Handel's *Radamisto,"* *Musical Times* 127 (1986), 319, for prompting notes for this effect. In modern parlance, this copy would more accurately be described as a stage manager's copy, since the notations refer to entrance preparations and to prop and set changes. This is quite different from the modern role of a prompter in opera performance, where he serves as a safety net for the singers' memory. Prompting, as we understand it, was likely provided by Handel, while also directing the orchestra.

31. *The London Stage, 1660–1800,* ed. Emmett L. Avery, (Carbondale: Southern Illinois University Press, 1960), vol. 2, pp. 249, 251.

32. It is also possible that the footlights were floating wick units in a tray of oil, as described by Mark A. Radice in chap. 3 of this volume.

33. The chandeliers partially blocked the audience's view of the stage. These forestage chandeliers, possibly the only ones in front of the proscenium arch, would have been the "ugly wooden" ones mentioned by Fougeroux. During David Garrick's tenure as the manager of Drury Lane (1747–1776), he initiated important reforms, among them, the concealment of stage lighting from the audience: the chandeliers above the forestage were gone. Though other English theaters soon followed Garrick's lead, Handel's audience had had to endure the "ugly wooden chandeliers" throughout the composer's career.

34. See Visser, "Scenery," p. 114.

35. The Covent Garden inventory lists "86 thunder balls 6 baskets to d[itt]o." The baskets containing the thunder balls were rolled down a ramp or across the ceiling. See Highfill, "Rich's 1744 Inventory," 30.

36. The libretto for this production is reprinted in *The Librettos of Handel's Operas,* ed. Ellen T. Harris (New York: Garland Publishing, 1989), vol. 2. Plot and scene descriptions are also given in Winton Dean and J. Merrill Knapp, *Handel's Operas: 1704–1726* (Oxford: Clarendon Press, 1987), pp. 168–171.

37. Milhous and Hume, "Prompt Copy," 317, 321.
38. See Visser, "Scenery," pp. 105–108.
39. Steele hints that the actual staging did not live up to the promise of the libretto: "The Undertakers of the *Hay-Market,* having raised too great an Expectation in their printed Opera [libretto], very much disappoint their Audience on the Stage." A literal depiction of every detail of the stage directions in the libretto was not perhaps seen by Handel's audience.
40. He follows this with a comment indicating the access some audience members had to the machinery: "I was not a little astonished to see a well-dressed young Fellow, in a full bottom'd Wigg, appear in the midst of the Sea, and without any visible Concern taking Snuff." For the 1712 revival, it was advertised that "by her Majesty's Command no Persons are to be admitted behind the Scenes." (*Händel-Handbuch,* vol. 4, p. 57).

Chapter Five

1. Andrew Steptoe, *The Mozart–Da Ponte Operas: The Cultural and Musical Background to* Le nozze di Figaro, Don Giovanni, *and* Così fan tutte. (Oxford: Clarendon Press, 1988), p. 142. James Webster, "Mozart's Operas and the Myth of Musical Unity," *Cambridge Opera Journal* 2 (July 1990), 199, finds Steptoe's treatment "a refreshing change from the usual art-for-art's sake approach to a genre that was explicitly rooted in social relations and was covertly (if not indeed overtly) political."
2. Among the spate of recent volumes devoted to Mozart's Viennese decade are: H. C. Robbins Landon, *1791: Mozart's Last Year* (New York: Schirmer Books, 1988); and his *Mozart: The Golden Years, 1781–1791* (New York: Schirmer Books, 1989); as well as his *Mozart and Vienna* (New York: Schirmer Books, 1991); Volkmar Braunbehrens, *Mozart in Vienna, 1781–1791,* trans. Timothy Bell (First HarperPerennial Edition, 1991; hardcover, New York: Grove Weidenfeld, 1990); and John A. Rice, "Vienna under Joseph II and Leopold II," *Man and Music—The Classical Era: From the 1740s to the End of the 18th Century,* ed. Neal Zaslaw (Englewood Cliffs, New Jersey: Prentice Hall, 1989), pp. 126–165.
3. Ernst Wangermann, *The Austrian Achievement, 1700–1800* (London: Thames and Hudson, 1973), p. 88, a translation of Alfred Ritter von Arneth, ed. *Maria Theresia und Joseph II: Ihre Correspondenz* (Vienna, 1867–1868), vol. 3, pp. 360–361.
4. Significant areas of reform included education, the penal system, and a drastic limiting of the role of the Catholic church in imperial lands.
5. Michael Kelly, *Reminiscences of Michael Kelly of the King's Theatre, and Theatre Royal Drury Lane* (London: Henry Colburn, 1826), vol. 1, p. 197.
6. Johann Pezzl, *Skizze von Wien: Ein Kultur- und Sittenbild aus der josefinischen Zeit,* ed. Gustav Gugitz and Anton Schlossar (Graz: Leykam-Verlag, 1923), as translated in Landon, *Mozart and Vienna,* pp. 109–110.
7. Pezzl, 1786, in Landon, *Mozart and Vienna,* p. 177.
8. Wangermann, *Austrian Achievement,* p. 118.
9. The court also controlled the Kärntnertor Theater.
10. Pezzl, 1787, in Landon, *Mozart and Vienna,* pp. 136–137.
11. Lorenzo Da Ponte, *Memoirs of Lorenzo Da Ponte,* trans. Elisabeth Abbott, ed. Arthur Livingston (Philadelphia: J. B. Lippincott, 1929), p. 130. For the original Italian of this and other remarks by Da Ponte, see *Memorie di Lorenzo da Ponte da Ceneda scritte da esso,* ed. Cesare Pagnini (Milan: Rizzoli, 1971).

12. Concerning this attachment, see, for example, Landon, *Mozart: The Golden Years*, p. 212, and Braunbehrens, *Mozart in Vienna*, pp. 163–172, especially p. 167: "The letters indicate a secret admiration" [for Joseph].

13. For Mozart's political awareness, see Neal Zaslaw, *Mozart's Symphonies: Context, Performance Practice, Reception* (Oxford: Clarendon Press, 1989), pp. 526–528.

14. Höslinger's view is reported by Landon, *Mozart: The Golden Years*, p. 170. Focusing on its political implications, Julian Rushton *W. A. Mozart: Don Giovanni* (Cambridge University Press, 1981), pp. 15–16 and p. 140 n. 1, offers a different interpretation.

15. Concerning this "true father of Viennese *Volkskomik* and therewith the Viennese *Volkstheater*" (*eigentliche Vater der Wiener Volkskomik und damit des Wiener Volkstheaters*), see, for example, Otto Rommel, ed. *Die Maschinenkomödie* (Leipzig: Philipp Reclam, jun., 1935), p. 10.

16. Franz Hadamowsky, *Wien Theater Geschichte von den Anfängen bis zum Ende des ersten Weltkriegs* (Vienna and Munich: Jugend und Volk, 1988), p. 453.

17. Wangermann, *Austrian Achievement*, p. 124.

18. While the two theaters of concern are long gone, the third, the Theater in der Josefstadt, continues to operate.

19. Kurt Honolka, *Papageno: Emanuel Schikaneder, Man of the Theater in Mozart's Time*, trans. Jane Mary Wilde (Portland, Oregon: Amadeus Press, 1990), p. 79. [*Papageno* (Salzburg and Vienna: Residenz Verlag, 1984)]

20. Elisabeth Grossegger, *Freimaurerei und Theater 1770–1800: Freimaurerdramen an den k.k. privilegierten Theatern in Wien* (Vienna: Hermann Böhlaus, Nachf., 1981), p. 63.

21. John A. Rice, "Emperor and Impresario: Leopold II and the Transformation of Viennese Musical Theater, 1790–1792" (Ph. D. dissertation, University of California, Berkeley, 1987), p. 321.

22. Emily Anderson, *The Letters of Mozart and His Family*, 3rd ed. (New York: W. W. Norton, 1989), 30 January–3 February 1768, p. 80. For the original German texts, consult *Mozart: Briefe und Aufzeichnungen*, coll. and ed. Wilhelm A. Bauer, Otto Erich Deutsch, and Joseph Heinz Eibl (Kassel: Bärenreiter, 1962–75), 7 vols.

23. For this felicitous turn of phrase, I am indebted to Rice, "Emperor and Impresario," p. 321.

24. Gustav Zechmeister, *Die Wiener Theater nächst der Burg und nächst dem Kärntnerthor von 1747 bis 1776* (Vienna: Hermann Böhlaus Nachf., 1971), p. 299.

25. Anderson, *Letters*, 1 August 1781, p. 755. See also Mozart's letter of 16 June 1781, p. 745, in which he discusses the rumors of Stephanie's reputation: "Whether he has written his plays alone or with the help of others, whether he has plagiarized or created, he still understands the stage, and his plays are invariably popular."

26. Da Ponte, *Memoirs*, p. 130.

27. For a delightful account of his remarkable apprenticeship, see ibid., beginning p. 130.

28. This oft-cited confession appeared in Schikaneder's preface to *Der Spiegel von Arkadien* (Vienna, 1795). For a recent reprint of the original German, see Gernot Gruber, "Schaffensgeschichte und Uraufführung der *Zauberflöte*," *Wolfgang Amadeus Mozart, Die Zauberflöte: Texte, Materialien, Kommentare*, ed. Attila Csampai and Dietmar Holland (Reinbek bei Hamburg: Rowohlt Taschenbuch, 1982 [Ricordi]), p. 141 n. 24. Peter Branscombe, *W.A. Mozart: Die Zauberflöte* (Cambridge University Press, 1991), p. 90, offers a different translation.

29. The phrase appears in the *Allgemeine Literaturzeitung* (Jena [1792]), as reported, among other places, in Honolka, *Papageno*, p. 150.

30. Branscombe, *Mozart: Die Zauberflöte*, p. 101, and also Otto Erich Deutsch, *Mozart: A Documentary Biography*, trans. Eric Blom, Peter Branscombe, and Jeremy Noble (London: Adam and Charles Black, 1965), p. 522, reproduce the complete quotation from Johann Peter Eckermann, *Gespräche mit Goethe*, vol. 3, 23 April 1823. Less complimentary in sum, it begins, "The text . . . is full of improbabilities and jokes that not everyone is capable of understanding and appreciating."

31. Otto Jahn, *W. A. Mozart*, 2nd ed. (Leipzig: Breitkopf und Härtel, 1867), vol. 2, pp. 464–465; Otto Jahn, *Life of Mozart*, trans. Pauline Townsend (London: Novello, 1891), vol. 3, pp. 283–284. "He was addicted to sensual gratification, a parasite and a spendthrift," Jahn / Townsend elaborate, p. 283. Georg Nikolaus von Nissen, *Biographie W. A. Mozarts*, ed. Constanze Nissen / Mozart (Leipzig: Breitkopf und Härtel, 1828), pp. 548–549, contains already many elements that cast Schikaneder in a poor light.

32. Honolka, *Papageno*, p. 9. Komorzynski's first Schikaneder biography appeared in 1901. Two world wars notwithstanding, articles and books issued in a steady stream, capped by *Emanuel Schikaneder: Ein Beitrag zur Geschichte des deutschen Theaters* (Vienna: Ludwig Doblinger, 1951).

33. For a striking, one-sentence appraisal, see Rommel, *Maschinenkomödie*, p. 59. For recent assessments, see Malcolm S. Cole, s.v. "Schikaneder, Emanuel," *International Dictionary of Opera*, ed. C. Steven LaRue (Detroit: St. James Press, 1993), vol. 2, pp. 1191–1193, and Judith A. Eckelmeyer, *The Cultural Context of Mozart's* Magic Flute: *Social, Aesthetic, Philosophical* (Lewiston, New York: The Edwin Mellen Press, 1991), 2 vols.

34. Given what we know of Mozart and Schikaneder as accomplished theater professionals, I find no compelling reason to support Ingmar Bergman's "idiosyncratic mishandling" of the original Act II finale of *Zauberflöte* (Branscombe, *Mozart: Die Zauberflöte*, p. 177). Of greater interest is the dramatic and psychological problem presented by the original position of the Act II terzetto, "Soll ich dich, Teurer, nicht mehr sehn?" (No. 19), addressed by Branscombe, pp. 209–212.

35. As an example of rearrangement, in 1965 Christopher Raeburn and Robert Moberly proposed a hypothesis about *Figaro*, Act III. Invoking reasons of dramatic continuity, theatrical convention, and tonal planning, they argued that the original order of scenes must have been altered to accommodate the double-cast Bussani's need to change costumes from Bartolo to Antonio. With the Act III–IV autograph then inaccessible, the hypothesis proved so attractive that Colin Davis recorded the act that way for Philips (6707–014), that is, with the Countess's "Dove sono" (No. 19) preceding the Sextet (No. 18). With the reappearance of the autograph, Alan Tyson, "*Le nozze di Figaro*: Lessons from the Autograph Score," *Musical Times* 122 (July 1981), 456–461, demonstrated that its layout "precludes the possibility of there having been a late change in the order." The quotation is from Tim Carter, *W. A. Mozart: Le nozze di Figaro* (Cambridge University Press, 1987), pp. 73–74.

36. Anderson, *Letters*, 4 July 1781, p. 751.

37. The fragment appears in Jahn, *Mozart*, vol. 2, pp. 676–680, and in *Mozart: Briefe und Aufzeichnungen*, vol. 4, pp. 168–173.

38. Da Ponte, *Memoirs*, pp. 177–178. In connection with this Martín y Soler / Da Ponte collaboration, Otto Michtner, *Das alte Burgtheater als Opernbühne von der Einführung des deutschen Singspiels (1778) bis zum Tod Kaiser Leopolds II. (1792)* (Vienna: Hermann Böhlaus Nachf., 1970), pp. 238–241, calls attention to a document unlike any that has yet surfaced for a Mozart production. Conveying a graphic account of this opera in performance is an anonymous pamphlet entitled "Lettre d'un habitant de Vienne à son

ami à Prague, qui lui avait demandé ses réflexions sur l'opéra intitulé L'arbore di Diana" [reprinted in Michtner, pp. 435–439]. Among the numerous topics addressed is stage machinery, for example: "An ugly hand, foul and filthy, which seems [that] of an obstetrician, is seen emerging from below the stage." (*On voit sortir de dessous le théâtre une vilane main sale et crasseuse, qui semble celle d'un accoucheur.*) In a similar vein, Salieri's preface to *Axur, rè d'Ormus* (1788), yet another Da Ponte collaboration (after Beaumarchais), invites careful study because it confirms concern by a composer active in the Burgtheater for a powerful coordination of drama, spectacle, and music. In this seventeen-page document, in essence a production book, Salieri discusses a host of issues, including character portraits reinforced by appropriate costumes and décor (Michtner, pp. 246–250; the complete preface, entitled "Il mio parere sopra la musica di quest'opera," is preserved with the score in the music collection of the Austrian National Library [17049]). I limit the mention of the preface to this note because this French-influenced, largely serious work is "an opera *sui generis,* rendering useless the conventional genre distinctions of 18th-century opera" (John A. Rice, s.v. "Salieri, Antonio," *New Grove Dictionary of Opera,* vol. 4, p. 143). Further, to paraphrase Michtner, it fell outside the scope of opera production then customary in Vienna. For additional coverage of this important work, see Rudolph Angermüller, "Salieris Vorbemerkungen zu seinen Opern," *Mitteilungen der Internationalen Stiftung Mozarteum,* 25 (3–4, 1977), 15–33; and his "Salieris *Tarare* (1787) und *Axur re d'Ormus* (1788): Vertonung eines Sujets für Paris und Wien," *Hamburger Jahrbuch für Musikwissenschaft* 5 (1981), 211–217.

39. This passage, too, comes from Schikaneder's *Der Spiegel von Arkadien.* The translation is by Branscombe, *Mozart:* Die Zauberflöte, p. 89.

40. Drawn from Ignaz Franz Castelli, *Memoiren meines Lebens,* ed. Joachim Schondorff (Munich: Winkler, 1969), p. 71. This quotation appears in Donald G. Henderson, "The *Magic Flute* of Peter Winter," *Music and Letters* 64 (July–October 1983), 197.

41. Anderson, *Letters,* 13 October 1781, p. 773.

42. *Wolfgang Amadeus Mozart, Neue Ausgabe sämtlicher Werke,* ed. Internationale Stiftung Mozarteum Salzburg (Kassel: Bärenreiter, 1955–), ser. 2, work group 5: *Die Entführung aus dem Serail,* vol. 12, ed. Gerhard Croll (1982); *Le nozze di Figaro,* vol. 16:1–2, ed. Ludwig Finscher (1973); *Don Giovanni,* vol. 17, ed. Wolfgang Plath and Wolfgang Rehm (1968); *Così fan tutte,* vol. 18:1–2, ed. Faye Ferguson and Wolfgang Rehm (1991); *Die Zauberflöte,* vol. 19, ed. Gernot Gruber and Alfred Orel (1970). For a striking example of how loss of the dialogue can prevent dramatic comprehension, see the sadly jumbled Schikaneder / Winter collaboration, *Das Labyrinth, oder: Der Kampf mit den Elementen* (part II of *The Magic Flute,* 1798). Only the text of the vocal numbers survives, as *Arien und Gesänge zum Zweyten Theil der Zauberflöte* (Berlin, 1803). Appearing too late for consultation in the preparation of this chapter, a new libretto series promises to be extremely useful: *The Librettos of Mozart's Operas,* ed. Ernest Warburton (New York: Garland Publishing, 1992).

43. Thomas Bauman, *W.A. Mozart:* Die Entführung aus dem Serail (Cambridge University Press, 1987), p. 107. See also p. 128 n. 12. "The revised version of the text has maintained its hold down to the present day."

44. Julian Rushton, *Mozart:* Don Giovanni, p. 61. He continues, "Some were already missing from the 1788 (Vienna) libretto, although nothing replaced them."

45. Emmanuel [*sic*] Schikaneder, *Die Zauberflöte: Eine grosse Oper in zwey Aufzügen* (Vienna: Ignaz Alberti, 1791), pp. 4–5 [Facsimile, Vienna: Wiener Bibliophilen-Gesellschaft, 1942].

46. Anderson, *Letters,* 19 September 1781, p. 766.

47. For a discussion of this vogue, see Thomas Bauman, *Mozart:* Die Entführung, chap. 3 ("Oriental opera"). The Near East, India, Egypt, Central and South America, and even moorish Spain were all fair game.

48. For Mozart's account of his working relationship with Stephanie, see Anderson, *Letters,* 26 September 1781, p. 770. For general background, consult Rice, "Vienna under Joseph II and Leopold II," pp. 135–138. Thomas Bauman, *Mozart:* Die Entführung, pp. 24–25, prints the twelve specific points of Stephanie's paradigm.

49. Bauman, *Mozart:* Die Entführung, pp. 12–26, thoroughly discusses the reasons.

50. Ibid., p. 4.

51. Rice, "Vienna under Joseph II and Leopold II," p. 138.

52. Landon omits Pezzl's citation of Schubart's descriptive phrase. See Pezzl, *Skizze von Wien: Ein Kultur- und Sittenbild,* p. 318.

53. For an excellent overview of the genre, consult Michael F. Robinson, "Mozart and the *opera buffa* Tradition," in Carter, *Mozart:* Le nozze di Figaro, pp. 11–32.

54. Anderson, *Letters,* 21 May 1783, p. 849.

55. I paraphrase Rudolph Angermüller, s.v. "Da Ponte, Lorenzo," *New Grove Dictionary of Music and Musicians,* ed. Stanley Sadie (London: Macmillan, 1980), vol. 5, p. 238.

56. Da Ponte, *Memoirs,* p. 151.

57. Deutsch, *Mozart:A Documentary Biography,* p. 274, from Da Ponte's preface to the libretto.

58. John Platoff, "The *buffa* Aria in Mozart's Vienna," *Cambridge Opera Journal* 2 (July 1990), 99. For a persuasive argument in support of the aria's ongoing centrality in Mozart's conception of opera, see James Webster, "The Analysis of Mozart's Arias," *Mozart Studies,* ed. Cliff Eisen (Oxford: Clarendon Press, 1991), pp. 101–199.

59. John Platoff, "Musical and Dramatic Structure in the *opera buffa* Finale," *Journal of Musicology* 7 (Spring 1989), 191–230.

60. For two versions of this humorous yet accurate account, see Da Ponte, *Memoirs,* p. 133, and Daniel Heartz, "Constructing *Le nozze di Figaro,*" in *Mozart's Operas,* ed., with contributing essays, Thomas Bauman (Berkeley and Los Angeles: University of California Press, 1990), pp. 133–134, from *Extract* (New York, 1819).

61. Rommel, *Maschinenkomödie,* pp. 57–58.

62. Ibid., p. 58. See also Cole, s.v. "Schikaneder, Emanuel" and s.v. "Die Zauberflöte," *International Dictionary of Opera,* vol. 2, p. 1193; and vol. 2, p. 1474.

63. Branscombe, *Mozart:* Die Zauberflöte, p. 146.

64. Ibid., p. 7.

65. Malcolm S. Cole, "*The Magic Flute* and the Quatrain," *Journal of Musicology* 3 (Spring 1984), 157–176.

66. Anderson, *Letters,* 26 September 1781, p. 769; 13 October 1781, p. 772.

67. The translations of these insults are by Lionel Salter in *W.A. Mozart:* Die Zauberflöte [*and*] Die Entführung aus dem Serail, intro. Brigid Brophy (New York: Universe Books, 1971). Joachim Kaiser, *Who's Who in Mozart's Operas: From Alfonso to Zerlina,* trans. Charles Kessler (New York: Schirmer Books, 1987), pp. 127–130, includes a summary and interpretation of these unpleasant traits. [*Meine Name ist Sarastro* (Munich: Piper, 1984).]

68. Anderson, *Letters,* 26 September 1781, p. 768.

69. Pierre Augustin Caron de Beaumarchais, *La folle journée ou le mariage de Figaro,* pub. J. B. Ratermanis. Vol. 63 of Studies on Voltaire and the Eighteenth Century, ed. Theodore Besterman (Geneva: Institut et Musée Voltaire, 1968), p. 561. The translation is by Wye Jamison Allanbrook, *Rhythmic Gesture in Mozart:* Le nozze di Figaro *and* Don

Giovanni (University of Chicago Press, 1983), p. 355. For broad coverage of the Beaumarchais plays and the Mozart / Da Ponte opera, see Rudolph Angermüller, Figaro: Le nozze di Figaro *auf dem Theater* (Salzburg: Internationale Stiftung Mozarteum, 1986), a source rich in information but plagued with incorrect dates.

70. Again, translations of the insults are by Lionel Salter in *W. A. Mozart: Le Nozze di Figaro* [*and*] Così fan tutte, intro. Dennis Arundell (New York: Universe Books, 1971). The quotation is from Allanbrook, *Rhythmic Gesture,* p. 163.

71. Rushton, *Mozart: Don Giovanni,* p. 54. Perhaps she merits a closer look. Allanbrook, *Rhythmic Gesture,* p. 160, writes: "Taking up the cause of women in his play Beaumarchais made Marceline . . . his chief crusader." Agreeing with Allanbrook, Carter, *Mozart: Le nozze di Figaro,* p. 65, advocates the aria's inclusion for another reason: "it does seem necessary to reinforce a character that has shifted awkwardly from being an enemy of Figaro and Susanna to being an ally."

72. Ibid.

73. Should the Moor's name properly be "Manostatos"? For a fascinating theory, including a double-entendre that connects Mozart, Myslivecek, and Manostatos, see Hans-Josef Irmen, *Mozart, Mitglied geheimer Gesellschaften* (Neustadt/Aisch: Prisca, 1988), pp. 312–313. More recently, Irmen's theory is reported by Hartmut Krones, "Mozart gibt uns selbst die Antworten: Zur Musiksprache der *Zauberflöte,*" Österreichische *Musikzeitschrift* 46 (January–February 1991), 26–27.

74. Christoph Martin Wieland, "Adis und Dahy," *Dschinnistan oder auserlesene Feen- und Geistermärchen,* vol. 11 (18, 20) of the *Gesammelte Schriften,* ed. Siegfried Mauermann (Berlin: Weidmann, 1987 [orig. pub. 1786]), pp. 36–63.

75. Egon Komorzynski, "*Die Zauberflöte* und *Dschinnistan,*" *Mozart-Jahrbuch* (1954), 187.

76. Turned into a frog, Torgut is banished to a swamp along with Farsana, the woman he had sought to seduce. Their only remaining hope is to torment one another forever.

77. Thomas Bauman, *Mozart: Die Entführung,* pp. 62–65, offers a fine overview of "'Turkish' music in oriental opera." For Myslivecek's theme, see the postscript of Leopold Mozart's letter of 22 December 1770, in Anderson, *Letters,* p. 176. Cole, "*The Magic Flute* and the Quatrain," 166, examines Monostatos's aria specifically.

78. Brophy, *W. A. Mozart: Die Zauberflöte* [*and*] Die Entführung, p. 104.

79. Giorgio Pestelli, *The Age of Mozart and Beethoven,* trans. Eric Cross (Cambridge University Press, 1984), p. 158.

80. Allanbrook, *Rhythmic Gesture,* p. 1.

81. Braunbehrens, *Mozart in Vienna,* p. 215.

82. David J. Buch, "Fairy-Tale Literature and *Die Zauberflöte,*" *Acta musicologica* 64 (January–June 1992), 30–49, develops the theme of *The Magic Flute* as a fairy tale.

83. Steptoe, *The Mozart–Da Ponte Operas,* pp. 245–246.

84. Deutsch, *Mozart: A Documentary Biography,* p. 344.

85. Clearly a point, Constanze's great aria "Martern aller Arten" from *Entführung* is prefaced by an extraordinarily long ritornello in *sinfonia concertante* style. What, if anything, should the singer do during this time? William Mann, *The Operas of Mozart* (New York: Oxford University Press, 1977), p. 307, would have her "indulging in a spit and adjustment of her costume, some *plastik* gesturing, advancing to the footlights, composing herself and fixing the spectators with a beady, imperious eye." See also Bauman, *Mozart: Die Entführung,* p. 81, who views the ritornello as "a perfect medium for a preliminary instrumental-pantomimetic exposition of the struggle" [between Constanze and Selim].

86. Da Ponte's "Rules" are reprinted in Michtner, *Burgtheater als Opernbühne*, pp. 439–440, in the original Italian; they are translated in Heartz, *Mozart's Operas*, pp. 104–105. Schikaneder's "Instructions" appear in Komorzynski, *Emanuel Schikaneder*, pp. 162–164. Branscombe, *Mozart: Die Zauberflöte*, p. 145, discusses them. For an instructive cross-check, consult Friedrich Ludwig Wilhelm Meyer, ed. *Friedrich Ludwig Schröder: Beitrag zur Kunde des Menschen und des Künstlers*, pt. 2, sec. 1 (Hamburg: Hoffmann und Campe, 1819), pp. 242–243: "Die Oper besonders betreffend," drawn from XXII. *Gesetze des Hamburgischen Deutschen Theaters* (1798). As Oscar Brockett reports in *History of the Theatre*, 5th ed. (Boston: Allyn and Bacon, 1987), pp. 407–408, the organization and procedures of the Imperial and National Theater in Vienna were modelled on the Comédie-Française.

87. Cliff Eisen, *New Mozart Documents: A Supplement to O. E. Deutsch's Documentary Biography* (Stanford, California: Stanford University Press, 1991), pp. 76–77. Owen also remarks, "The scenery was varied in a thousand grotesque forms."

88. Steptoe, *The Mozart–Da Ponte Operas*, pp. 145–146, stresses the youth of the Italian troupe; Branscombe, *Mozart: Die Zauberflöte*, p. 145, remarks similarly about Schikander's Freihaus Theater company.

89. A more detailed discussion of the theaters' proportions follows below.

90. Steptoe, *The Mozart–Da Ponte Operas*, pp. 145–146.

91. Among the several commentators who make this point is Dennis Arundell, *W. A. Mozart: Le Nozze di Figaro [and] Così fan tutte*, p. 19. The singer Lucia Popp, for one, agrees. See Helena Matheopoulos, *Diva: Great Sopranos and Mezzos Discuss Their Art* (Boston: Northeastern University Press, 1992), p. 149: "It is important for Susanna and the Countess to be physically and vocally somewhat similar."

92. Anderson, *Letters*, 28 February 1778, p. 497. Strangely enough, a near-contemporary chided Mozart for writing to suit specific voices. See the letter by J. B. Schaul, *Briefe über den Geschmack der Musik* (1809), printed in Karl Gustav Fellerer, "Zur Mozart-Kritik im 18./19. Jahrhundert," *Mozart-Jahrbuch* (1959), 93: "Whoever writes an opera, like Mozart, must also bear in mind at the same time that he must not write solely for *the* place in which *he* finds himself and for *its* personnel, but so that it is performable everywhere." (*Wer eine Oper schreibt, wie Mozart, muss auch dabey bedenken, dass er nicht für* den Ort und für die Subjekte wo er sich befindet, allein schreiben darf, sondern so, dass es überall ausführbar ist.)

93. Fischer has already been mentioned. Four representative sources of concise accounts and criticisms by contemporaries, often accompanied by pictorial representations or silhouettes, are: Michtner, *Burgtheater als Opernbühne*; Marshall, *Mozart Speaks*; *New Grove Dictionary of Opera*, ed. Stanley Sadie (London: Macmillan, 1992), 4 vols.; and—a fascinating cooperative venture in general—*Zaubertöne: Mozart in Wien, 1781–1791*, *Ausstellung des Historischen Museums der Stadt Wien im Künstlerhaus, 6. Dezember 1990–15. September 1991* (Vienna: Agens-Werk Geyer und Reisser, n.d.).

94. Kelly, *Reminiscences*, vol. 1, p. 255. He continues, "I have seen it performed at different periods in other countries, . . . but no more to compare with its original performance than light is to darkness."

95. For Kelly, see ibid., vol. 1, p. 194; Pezzl, as translated in Heartz, *Mozart's Operas*, p. 125. Landon, *Mozart and Vienna*, p. 137, translates the passage somewhat differently.

96. Wilhelm Deutschmann, *Zaubertöne*, p. 220. For model coverage of an eighteenth-century singer, see Thomas Bauman, "Mozart's Belmonte," *Early Music* 19 (November 1991), 557–563.

97. Patricia Lewy Gidwitz, s.v. "Cavalieri, Caterina," *New Grove Dictionary of Opera,* vol. 1, p. 779. In his letter of 26 September 1781, Mozart had mentioned sacrificing Constanze's aria a little to the flexible throat of Mlle. Cavalieri ["Trennung war mein banges Los"], Anderson, *Letters,* p. 769.

98. Heartz, *Mozart's Operas,* p. 126.

99. Ibid., p. 125.

100. Patricia Lewy Gidwitz and Betty Matthews, s.v. "Storace, Nancy," *New Grove Dictionary of Opera,* vol. 4, p. 554.

101. Ibid.

102. *Zaubertöne,* p. 317. Drawn from Franz Kazinczy's *Selbstbiographie* (May 1786). Angermüller, Figaro: Le nozze di Figaro *auf dem Theater,* p. 77, gives this more extensive citation: *Denkwürdigkeiten meiner Laufbahn* (new edition, Budapest: Ladislaus Orosz, 1956).

103. Heartz, *Mozart's Operas,* p. 135.

104. Christopher Raeburn and Dorothea Link, s.v. "Benucci, Francesco," *New Grove Dictionary of Opera,* vol. 1, pp. 410–411.

105. Platoff, "The *buffa* Aria," p. 101.

106. Ibid., p. 112.

107. Branscombe, *Mozart: Die Zauberflöte,* p. 147. Linda Tyler, s.v. "Schack, Benedikt," *New Grove Dictionary of Opera,* vol. 4, pp. 210–211, translates this letter of 26 May 1786 a bit differently. Swept away by his enthusiasm, Egon Komorzynski, "Sänger und Orchester des Freihaustheaters," *Mozart-Jahrbuch* (1951), 141, claims that for Mozart, Tamino "became not merely a 'role,' but matched the personal character of the actor" (*nicht eine 'Rolle' wurde, sondern dem persönlichen Wesen des Darstellers entsprach*).

108. Meyer, F. L. *Schröder,* p. 85. Schröder judged Josepha Weber-Hofer "A very disagreeable singer, [she] lacks sufficient upper register for this role and shrieks them out [the high notes]." (*Eine sehr unangenehme Sängerin, hat nicht Höhe genug zu dieser Rolle [Oberon], und erquiekt sie.*) As a postscript to the companies, the intersection of a singer's personal and professional lives can perhaps have affected Mozart's music and career. Did Cavalieri, for example, for whose flexible throat Mozart tailored so much glorious music, join the alleged cabal against *Figaro* because she was Salieri's mistress? In 1789, was Mozart particularly enthusiastic about altering Susanna's part for Da Ponte's mistress, Adriana Ferrarese del Bene? He had once reported from Dresden, "The leading woman singer, Madame Allegranti, is far better than Madame Ferraresi, which, I admit, is not saying very much" (Anderson, *Letters,* 16 April 1789, p. 924).

109. Suzanne Julia Beicken, "Johann Adam Hiller's *Anweisung zum musikalischen-zierlichen Gesange,* 1780: A Translation and Commentary" (Ph. D. dissertation, Stanford University, 1980). Offered in the Peters Reprint Series (1976) is a facsimile edition: Johann Adam Hiller, *Anweisung zum musikalisch-zierlichen Gesange* (Leipzig: Johann Friedrich Junius, 1780).

110. Ibid., p. 48.

111. A representative list of recent efforts would have to include: Jean-Pierre Marty, *The Tempo Indications of Mozart* (New Haven, Connecticut: Yale University Press, 1988); Frederick Neumann, *Ornamentation and Improvisation in Mozart* (Princeton, New Jersey: Princeton University Press, 1986); Neal Zaslaw, *Mozart's Symphonies;* R. Larry Todd and Peter Williams, eds., *Perspectives on Mozart Performance* (Cambridge University Press, 1991); and "Performing Mozart's Music I," the special issue of *Early Music* 19 (November 1991).

112. Among the readily available performances on CD that incorporate period instruments are *Die Entführung aus dem Serail,* Christopher Hogwood (L'oiseau-lyre, 430 339-2, 1990); also John Eliot Gardiner (Archiv, 435 857-2, 1992); *Le nozze di Figaro,* Arnold Östman (L'oiseau-lyre, CD 421-333-2, 1987); *Don Giovanni,* Östman (L'oiseau-lyre, 425 943-2, 1990); also Roger Norrington (EMI CDS 7-54859-2, 1993); *Così fan tutte,* Östman (L'oiseau-lyre, 414 316-2, 1985); and *Die Zauberflöte,* Norrington (EMI, CDS 7-54287-2, 1990).

113. Else Spiesberger, *Das Freihaus* (Vienna: Paul Zsolnay, 1980), p. 59.

114. Suggested readings outside the Viennese orbit include: "The Auditorium of the Comédie Française," A. M. Nagler, *A Source Book in Theatrical History* (New York: Dover Publications, 1959), pp. 285–288; *Gustavian Opera: An Interdisciplinary Reader in Swedish Opera, Dance and Theatre 1771–1809,* ed. Inger Mattsson (Uppsala: Almqvist och Wiksell, 1991); Géza Staud, *Adelstheater in Ungarn: 18. und 19. Jahrhundert* (Vienna: Österreichische Akademie der Wissenschaften, 1977); H. C. Robbins Landon, *Haydn at Esterháza 1766–1790,* vol. 2 of *Haydn: Chronicle and Works* (Bloomington: Indiana University Press, 1978).

115. Fred Hennings, *Zweimal Burgtheater: Vom Michaelerplatz zum Franzensring* (Vienna: Kremayr und Scheriau, 1955), p. 10, likens the façade "rather to a Theresian garden house than a theater" (*eher einem Theresianischen Gartenstöckl als einem Theater glich* [*sic*]).

116. An enormous literature deals with the Burgtheater. See, for example, Margret Dietrich, ed. *Das Burgtheater und sein Publikum, Festgabe zur 200-Jahr-Feier der Erhebung des Burgtheaters zum Nationaltheater* (Vienna: Österreichische Akademie der Wissenschaften, 1976); Ernst Haeusserman, *Das Wiener Burgtheater* (Vienna: Fritz Molden, 1975); Daniel Heartz, "Nicolas Jadot and the Building of the Burgtheater," *Musical Quarterly* 68 (January 1982), 1–31; Fred Hennings, *Zweimal Burgtheater;* Otto Michtner, *Burgtheater als Opernbühne;* Otto G. Schindler, "Der Zuschauerraum des Burgtheaters im 18. Jahrhundert: Eine baugeschichtliche Skizze," *Maske und Kothurn* 22 (1976, 1/2), 20–53; and Gustav Zechmeister, *Die Wiener Theater nächst der Burg und nächst dem Kärntnerthor von 1747 bis 1776* (Vienna: Hermann Böhlaus, 1971).

117. Ernst Moritz Arndt, *Bruckstücke aus einer Reise von Baireuth bis Wien im Sommer 1798* (Leipzig: Heinrich Gräff, 1801), p. 250, quoted in Mary Sue Morrow, *Concert Life in Haydn's Vienna: Aspects of a Developing Musical and Social Institution* (Stuyvesant, New York: Pendragon Press, 1989), p. 75. Leopold II had reached an identical conclusion some years earlier. As reported in Rice, "Emperor and Impresario," pp. 63–65, in 1791 the emperor wrote an *Entwurf* proposing a renovation or replacement of the Burgtheater. A mysterious architect named Moretti constructed a model seen by Zinzendorf on 12 November 1791. The stage was to be 80 feet (24.4 meters) deep and 45 feet (13.7 meters) wide, while the ceiling was to arch 65 feet (19.8 meters) above the parterre.

118. The term is borrowed from Brockett, *History of the Theatre,* p. 176.

119. Fred Hennings, *Zweimal Burgtheater,* p. 12, is one of several writers who have remarked upon the "two stone spiral staircases" (*zwei steinerne Wendeltreppen*), which scarcely allowed two persons to ascend or descend side by side: "consequently, the clearing of a full house lasted one hour" (*Infolgedessen dauerte die Leerung des Hauses bei vollem Besuch eine Stunde*).

120. The term "architectural mishap" [literally "cripple"] appears in an affectionate tribute to the Burgtheater, its intimacy, and its singular historical significance, in Fred Hennings, *Zweimal Burgtheater,* p. 19. The quotation stems from Michael Forsyth,

Buildings for Music: The Architect, the Musician, and the Listener from the Seventeenth Century to the Present Day (Cambridge, Massachusetts: the MIT Press [1985]), p. 94.

121. Anderson, *Letters,* 8–9 October 1791, p. 969.

122. Forsyth, *Buildings for Music,* p. 94.

123. Herta Singer, "Die Akustik des alten Burgtheaters: Versuch einer Darstellung der Zusammenhänge zwischen Aufführungsstil und Raumakustik," *Maske und Kothurn* 4 (1958, 2/3), 220–229. In W. C. Sabine's formula—T = 0, 16 V/A—T equals reverberation time in seconds; V equals room volume in cubic meters; A equals the sum of all acoustic absorptions of the individual surfaces in this space.

124. Ibid., p. 229; Michtner, *Burgtheater als Opernbühne,* p. 143.

125. Hennings, *Zweimal Burgtheater,* pp. 14–16, reechoed in Verena Keil-Budischowsky, *Die Theater Wiens* (Vienna and Hamburg: Paul Zsolnay, 1983), p. 106.

126. For coverage of the Kärntnertor Theater, frequently accompanied by reproductions of iconographic materials, see Evan Baker, "Theaters in Vienna during Mozart's Lifetime," *Mozart-Jahrbuch* (1991), vol. 2, pp. 984–992; Keil-Budischowsky, *Die Theater Wiens,* pp. 81–101; Morrow, *Concert Life in Haydn's Vienna,* pp. 68–71, 78–82; and Zechmeister, *Die Wiener Theater,* pp. 183–185, with generous quotations from Johann Heinrich Friedrich Müller, *Genaue Nachrichten von beyden k.k. Schaubühnen . . . in Wien* (Vienna: Ghelen, 1772).

127. *An Eighteenth-Century Musical Tour in Central Europe and the Netherlands,* vol. 2 of *Dr. Burney's Musical Tours in Europe,* ed. Percy A. Scholes (London: Oxford University Press, 1959), p. 75.

128. See n. 31. For coverage of the Freihaus Theater, consult Otto Erich Deutsch, *Das Freihaustheater auf der Wieden, 1787–1801,* 2nd ed. (Vienna: Deutscher Verlag für Jugend und Volk, 1937) and Spiesberger, *Das Freihaus,* chap. 4, "Das Theater im Freihaus."

129. The inventory appears in Spiesberger, *Das Freihaus,* pp. 50–51, as:

Das Podium
das Portale
das Parterre noble bestehend aus
    18 Bänken mit Lehnen, und rothen Tuch
    5 Detto ohne Lehnen mit Detto
    1 Wand von Holz mit Tuch zwischen Parterre und Parterre noble
    1 Detto am Orchestre
Am Parterre
    28 gefütterte Bänke ohne Lehnen
    4 ungefütterte Detto ohne Lehnen
Auf der noble Gallerie
    8 Bänke mit Lehnen und rothen Tuch gefüttert
Auf der 2ten Gallerie
    12 weiche Bänke auf die Seiten
    5 Detto lange auf der Mitte
Ferners 20 Logen
    Rechts 6 kleine
        3 grosse
    Links 10 kleine
        1 grosse.

130. Tendered in prose, a somewhat different translation appears in Evan Baker, "September, 1791: The Burgtheater and the Theater im Starhembergschen Freihaus auf der Wieden," an unpublished paper delivered at the 1991 RMA Mozart Conference, p. 12.

131. Translated from Ignaz Franz Castelli, *Memoiren meines Lebens,* ed. J. Bindtner (Munich: G. Müller [1913]), vol. 1, pp. 232–233. [originally pub. 1861]. This recollection appears in numerous secondary sources, for example, in Spiesberger, *Das Freihaus,* pp. 39–40.

132. Included in Edward A. Langhans and Robert Benson, s.v. "Lighting," *New Grove Dictionary of Opera,* vol. 2, p. 1267, is an anonymous painting (after 1791) of the interior of the National Theatre, Warsaw. Chandeliers and sconces are ablaze during a performance of Paisiello's *Pirro.* See also Ture Rangström, "The Stage Machinery at Drottningholm," *Gustavian Opera,* pp. 101–103: "How to Darken the Stage."

133. The translation appears in Heartz, "Nicolas Jadot," 17. Schindler, "Zuschauerraum," pp. 48–51, is drawing his material from Brandes, "Bemerkungen über das Pariser und Wiener Theater," *Litteratur- und Theater-Zeitung* 4:3 (Berlin, 1781), 681; and Friedel in *Vertraute Briefe zur Charakteristik von Wien* (Görlitz, 1793), vol. 2, p. 45.

134. Heartz, *Mozart's Operas,* p. 130. For particulars of the Richter satire, see below and n. 171.

135. For these accounting lists, complete with the players' names, see Dexter Edge, "Mozart's Viennese Orchestras," *Early Music* 20 (February 1992), especially 71–79. Augmenting the thirty-five musicians of 1782/83, *Entführung* would have required two trumpets, a timpanist, and a harpsichordist, plus four instrumentalists to execute the Turkish music. Similarly, *Figaro* would have required a timpanist and a harpsichordist. Each musician, it must be remembered, played an instrument different from its present-day counterpart. Neal Zaslaw, *Mozart's Symphonies,* beginning p. 449, offers superb coverage of Classical orchestras and seating plans. For eighteenth-century opera houses, the term "pit" is problematic because it implies a depression. In the Burgtheater and the Freihaus Theater, the orchestra simply occupied the space between the stage and the *parterre noble,* with a partition separating the areas in the Freihaus Theater.

136. Ibid., beginning p. 463. For his *Zauberflöte* recording using period instruments, Roger Norrington adopts a seating plan which is neither exactly that of Dresden nor exactly that of Turin. Printed on p. 12 of the accompanying booklet is a diagram of his disposition. For yet another seating arrangement, consult Johann Joachim Quantz, *On Playing the Flute,* trans. Edward R. Reilly (London: Faber and Faber, 1966), pp. 211–212.

137. *The Autobiography of Karl von Dittersdorf: Dictated to His Son,* trans. A. D. Coleridge (London: Richard Bentley, 1896), p. 252. See also Karl Ditters von Dittersdorf, *Lebensbeschreibung: Seinem Sohne in die Feder diktiert,* ed. Norbert Miller (Munich: Kösel-Verlag, 1967), p. 227 [originally pub. Leipzig: Breitkopf und Härtel, 1801].

138. Baker, "September, 1791," p. 6.

139. Rangström, "The Stage Machinery at Drottningholm," p. 88. Enriching this entry are several magnificent diagrams of the machinery and its placement. Edward A. Langhans, s.v. "Machinery," *New Grove Dictionary of Opera,* vol. 3, pp. 120–132, discusses machinery by category: rolling or sliding devices, flying devices, elevating devices, revolving devices, and special effects.

140. Rushton, *Mozart: Don Giovanni,* beginning p. 10, with his "Synopsis."

141. Rangström, "Stage Machinery," pp. 90–91. The paragraph concludes, "Such alternations are often stipulated in contemporary playbooks and libretti." Schikaneder, too, "used a backdrop behind which he could change the old sets while a new scene was being played in front of it" (Angermüller, *Mozart's Operas,* pp. 226–229).

142. "Das Innere des Hauses ist gut eingerichtet, die Maschinieren beim Theater gut angebracht, so dass grosse Verwandlungen können bewürckt werden." Anonymous, *Vertraute Briefe zur Charakteristik von Wien* (Görlitz: Hermsdorf und Anton, 1793), vol. 2, pp. 50–53. Angermüller in *Mozart's Operas,* p. 226, prints this particular quotation,

attributing it to Knüppel, *Intimate Letters on the Characteristics of Vienna*. Branscombe in *Mozart: Die Zauberflöte*, pp. 158–159, republishes this entire review for the first time. See also Wolfgang Greisenegger, *Zaubertöne*, pp. 506–507: "*The Magic Flute* proves its [the Freihaus Theater's] technically excellent equipment. On its 15 × 12 meter [49 × 39.4 feet] stage, machine comedies also were mounted, with all their intricate transformation effects. (*Zauberflöte erweist seine technisch gute Ausstattung. Auf der 15 × 12 Meter grossen Kulissenbühne wurden auch Maschinenkomödien mit all ihren komplizierten Verwandlungseffekten aufgeführt.*)

143. For the total of thirteen, see Anthony Besch, "A Director's Approach;" Branscombe, *Mozart: Die Zauberflöte*, p. 183. In June 1783, the Montgolfier brothers had first ascended at Versailles. A celebrated ascent had occurred in Vienna in 1791. See, for example, Braunbehrens, *Mozart in Vienna*, pp. 383–385.

144. For corroboration of my observation, see Sidney Jackson Jowers, s.v. "Costume," *New Grove Dictionary of Opera*, vol. 1, p. 981. For an example of the kind of written commentary to which I allude, see Deutsch, *Mozart: A Documentary Biography*, pp. 433–434, an anonymous report found in the *Allgemeines Theaterjournal* (Frankfurt and Mainz, 1792): "But one must give Hr. Schikaneder credit for sparing no expense with his new productions of works, and, where necessary, for having new sets and costumes made. The expenditure on Mozart's last opera, *Die Zauberflöte*—Mozart's swansong—is said to have amounted to 5,000 fl., but he is in return well repaid, for only by satisfying the desire for beautiful sets and appropriately grand costumes of those who bring their eyes rather than their feelings into the theatre, and by sparing no expense, can one perform the works more often."

145. See Wolfgang Greisenegger, *Zaubertöne*, p. 275. For more extensive coverage of Cantini's sets and scenic reform, see Michtner, *Burgtheater als Opernbühne*, p. 39.

146. Selections from these engravings, by Jean-Baptiste Liénard after Jacques Philippe Joseph de Saint-Quentin, and the equally celebrated etchings of Daniel Nikolaus Chodowiecki are commonly reproduced, as in Angermüller, Figaro: Le nozze di Figaro *auf dem Theater*, pp. 27, 30–31.

147. This engraving, too, appears often, for example, in *Mozart und seine Welt in zeitgenössischen Bildern*, Maximilian Zenger and O. E. Deutsch (Kassel: Bärenreiter, 1961), no. 460. For a combination of reproduction and interpretation, see Angermüller, *Mozart's Operas*, pp. 164–165.

148. Landon, *Haydn at Esterháza 1766–1790*, p. 28, accompanied by a reproduction of the *gouache* in question.

149. Ibid., p. 28 n. 2. For extensive coverage of *Le cadi dupé*, Gluck's first "Turkish" opera, see Bruce Alan Brown, *Gluck and the French Theatre in Vienna* (Oxford: Clarendon Press, 1991), pp. 384–397.

150. "In Wien war es Noverre, der auf die individuelle Aussagekraft der stilechten Kostüme hinwies, genau sowie Friedr. Ludwig Schröder 1781 die Bühnenbekleidung als Wesensausdruck in ein individuelles und wirklichkeitsnahes Spiel einbezog." Michtner, *Burgtheater als Opernbühne*, p. 38.

151. See Beaumarchais, *Le mariage de Figaro*, p. 561.

152. Michael Raeburn and Alan Kendall, eds. *Heritage of Music: Classical Music and Its Origins* (Oxford University Press, 1989), vol. 1, p. 264.

153. Reproductions, in order, may be found in: Alberti frontispiece in Schikaneder, *Die Zauberflöte*, between pp. 4–5; Branscombe, *Mozart: Die Zauberflöte*, p. 99; Csampai and Holland, *Mozart, Die Zauberflöte*, p. 200; Zenger and Deutsch, *Mozart und seine Welt*, no. 554 [also in Angermüller, *Mozart's Operas*, p. 228]; Zenger and Deutsch, no. 555.

154. See Brophy, *W.A. Mozart, Die Zauberflöte* [and] Die Entführung, p. 148.

155. The translation, with minor editorial emendations, is that of Lionel Salter in Arundell, *W. A. Mozart*, Le nozze di Figaro [*and*] Così fan tutte, p. 52.
156. Rommel, *Maschinenkomödie*, p. 68.
157. Siegfried Morenz, *Die Zauberflöte: Eine Studie zum Lebenszusammenhang Aegypten–Antike–Abendland* (Münster and Cologne: Böhlau, 1952), pp. 40–41.
158. Baker, "September, 1791," pp. 13–18.
159. *Allgemeines Europäisches Journal* ([today] Brno, January–July 1795). The six engravings are reproduced in color in Angermüller, *Mozart's Operas*, p. 227.
160. Working from basically the same body of evidence, Baker, "September, 1791," 13; Gisela Jaacks, "Das Bühnenbild der Maschinenkomödie *Die Zauberflöte*," Csampai and Holland, *Mozart: Die Zauberflöte*, pp. 201–216; and Roger Norrington, booklet accompanying his performance of *Die Zauberflöte* (EMI Records, CDS 7-54287-2), p. 25, connect the Schaffer engravings, however loosely, with the Freihaus Theater production. Komorzynski, *Emanuel Schikaneder*, pp. 226–232; Angermüller, *Mozart's Operas*, p. 229; and Branscombe, *Mozart: Die Zauberflöte*, p. 175 (critical of the Holland Festival production of 1982, based on these very engravings) suggest that they relate to an early production in some other place, possibly present-day Brno. Adelbert Schusse, *Zaubertöne*, p. 508, chooses a middle road: "Indeed, many details speak for the original performance of *The Magic Flute* in the Viennese Freihaus Theater. Still, the stage in the engravings appears extraordinarily small. . . . For that reason, the copper engravings probably reproduce the performance practice in Brno, where Mozart's *The Magic Flute* was given in June 1793." (*Zwar sprechen manche Details für die Uraufführung der* Zauberflöte *im Wiener Freihaustheater, doch erscheint die Bühne auf den Stichen ausserordentlich klein. . . . Die Kupferstiche geben daher wahrscheinlich die Aufführungspraxis in Brünn wieder, wo Mozart's* Zauberflöte *im Juni 1793 gegeben wurde.*)
161. W. A. Mozart, *The Magic Flute: 1791 Libretto by Emanuel Schikaneder,* trans. Judith A. Eckelmeyer (New York: The Edwin Mellen Press, 1979), p. 51. See also Emmanuel [*sic*] Schikaneder, *Die Zauberflöte: Eine grosse Oper in zwey Aufzügen* (Vienna: Ignaz Alberti, 1791), p. 95 [Facsimile edition, Vienna, 1942].
162. Baker, "September, 1791," 15.
163. "Die nächste Generation [hingegen], gipfelnd in K. Fr. Schinkel (1815) [sic; should read: 1816], ist um historische Stiltreue im Sinne des strengen Klassizismus bemüht. . . . Weil das so ist, scheint es müssig, für die Schöpfer der Zauberflöte selbst nach bestimmten antiken Vorbildern der Dekoration zu suchen." Morenz, *Die Zauberflöte: Eine Studie,* pp. 40–41. See also Anke Schmitt, *Der Exotismus in der deutschen Oper zwischen Mozart und Spohr* (Hamburg: Karl Dieter Wagner, 1988), p. 58: "décor and theater costumes profited also from the opening up of exotic realms" (*Auch Bühnenbild und Theaterkostüm profitierten von der Erschliessung fremder Länder*) around the turn of the century.
164. For recent Mozart studies with commendable production histories, see Angermüller, *Mozart's Operas*, pp. 222–259; Branscombe, *Mozart: Die Zauberflöte,* chaps. 7 (by Branscombe) and 8 (by Anthony Besch); Jaacks, "Bühnenbild," pp. 201–216; and various contributors in *Zaubertöne*, pp. 508–513, who include playing cards and figurines.
165. Morrow, *Concert Life in Haydn's Vienna,* p. 227.
166. For detailed coverage of the Burgtheater's public, see Otto G. Schindler, "Das Publikum des Burgtheaters in der Josephinischen Aera: Versuch einer Strukturbestimmung," *Das Burgtheater und sein Publikum,* vol. 1, ed. Margret Dietrich, pp. 11–95. Compact summaries appear in Bauman, *Mozart: Die Entführung,* p. 100, and in Rice, "Vienna under Joseph II and Leopold II," p. 128.
167. Keil-Budischowsky, *Die Theater Wiens,* p. 61.

168. Concerning the cabals attending *Entführung*, see Mozart's caution in Anderson, *Letters*, 1 August 1781, pp. 755–756; also 20 July 1782, pp. 807–808, when, at its second performance, "the whole first act was accompanied by hissing." Three days before the premiere of *Figaro*, Leopold Mozart direly forecasts to his daughter that "Salieri and all his supporters will again try to move heaven and earth to down his opera," 28 April 1786, p. 897. Kelly, *Reminiscences*, vol. 1, pp. 254–255, contends that he alone was "a stickler for Mozart." Deutsch, *Mozart: A Documentary Biography*, pp. 278–279, prints the entire review of 11 July 1786.

169. Deutsch, *Mozart: A Documentary Biography*, p. 278.

170. The translation of this enjoyable continuation of Leopold's account appears in Eva Badura-Skoda, "The Influence of the Viennese Popular Comedy on Haydn and Mozart," *Journal of the Royal Musical Association* 100 (1973–74), 196. For the original German, consult Bauer, Deutsch, Eibl, *Mozart: Briefe*, vol. 1, p. 254.

171. "Ein Kavalier sieht mit unverwandten Perspectiv nach der schönen Predigerinn, um ja kein Wort von ihrer Moral zu verlieren." [Joseph Richter], *Bildergalerie weltlicher Misbräuche: Ein Gegenstück zur Bildergalerie katholischer und klösterlicher Misbräuche, von Pater Hilarion, Exkapuzinern* (Frankfurt and Leipzig, 1785), p. 258. [Facsimile ed. *Die bibliophilen Taschenbücher* (Dortmund: Druckerei Karl Hitzegrad, 1977)]

172. Anderson, *Letters*, 15 January 1787, p. 904.

173. Ibid., 26 September 1781, pp. 769–770.

174. Ibid., p. 770.

175. See Schindler, "Das Publikum des Burgtheaters," p. 56.

176. Deutsch, *Mozart: A Documentary Biography*, p. 275.

177. Anderson, *Letters*, 7–8 October 1791, p. 967.

178. Ibid., 21 June 1783, p. 853; 13 October 1781, p. 773.

179. Ibid., 26 September 1781, p. 769.

180. Leonard G. Ratner, *Classic Music: Expression, Form, and Style* (New York: Schirmer Books, 1980); Allanbrook, *Rhythmic Gesture in Mozart*.

181. Allanbrook, *Rhythmic Gesture in Mozart*, p. 22.

182. Ibid., pp. 79–82.

183. Ibid., p. 81.

184. John Eliot Gardiner in the booklet accompanying his recorded performance of *Idomeneo* (Archiv, 431674-2, 1990), p. 16.

185. Alan Tyson, "Some Variant Versions," in the booklet accompanying Arnold Östman's recorded performance of *Le nozze di Figaro* (L'oiseau-lyre, CD 421 333-2, 1987), pp. 17–21. Östman includes six of the seven variants. See also Alan Tyson, *Mozart: Studies of the Autograph Scores* (Cambridge, Massachusetts: Harvard University Press, 1987), chap. 10, "*Le nozze di Figaro*: Lessons from the Autograph Score," pp. 114–124.

186. Alan Tyson, "Some Problems in the Text of *Le nozze di Figaro*: Did Mozart Have a Hand in Them?" *Journal of the Royal Musical Association* 112 (Pt. I, 1987), 101.

187. Appended to Alessandra Campana, "Mozart's Italian *buffo* Singers," *Early Music* 19 (November 1991), 582, is a transcript of the discussion that followed the author's presentation. I have drawn the Heartz quotation from that discussion.

188. Rushton, *Mozart: Don Giovanni*, p. 57, a sentence cobbled from Da Ponte's *Memoirs* and Mozart's correspondence concerning *Entführung* and Cavalieri. See also William Mann, *The Operas of Mozart*, p. 395: "Un moto di gioia" Mann finds "musically uninteresting, dramatically and texturally a hindrance to the plot." More problematic than the *Figaro* numbers, which at least are known, is the tantalizing issue raised by a promise on

Schikaneder's playbill for the first staging of *Zauberflöte* at the new Theater an der Wien (5 January 1802): "I shall perhaps pleasantly surprise the respected public today with two pieces of music of Mozart's composition which he bequeathed to me alone." For a discussion of what they might have been, see Branscombe, *Mozart:* Die Zauberflöte, pp. 207–209.

189. Anderson, *Letters,* 19 August 1789, pp. 933–934.

190. Heartz's discussion of the Campana article appeared in *Early Music* 19 (November 1991), 582. The quotation is from Rice, "Emperor and Impresario," p. 126.

191. Rushton, *Mozart:* Don Giovanni, pp. 53–57.

192. Ibid., p. 57.

193. Ibid., p. 141 n. 4; see also Rushton's observation that the Epilogue may well strike a modern audience as "too neat, a trivialization of the action" (pp. 64–65).

194. The term *Herzstück* appears in Hennings, *Zweimal Burgtheater,* p. 19. My summary owes much to Michtner, *Burgtheater als Opernbühne,* p. 343.

195. A Freihaus Theater performance began at 7:00 P.M. On two occasions, Mozart was home starting letters to Constanze by 10:30 P.M. Considering the dialogue, the three customary encores, some delay at the theater, and the walk home, Branscombe, *Mozart:* Die Zauberflöte, p. 154 (followed by Norrington on his EMI recording), concludes that the musical numbers must have moved at a very fair pace, about an hour and forty-five minutes in all. Like Mozart and Schikaneder, modern directors too should envision a swiftly moving drama.

196. "(Man hört den stärksten Accord, Donner, Blitz, Sturm. Sogleich verwandelt sich das ganze Theater in eine Sonne.)" Schikaneder, *Die Zauberflöte,* p. 106; Eckelmeyer, *The Magic Flute,* p. 106. As Gisela Jaacks, "Das Bühnenbild der Maschinenkomödie *Die Zauberflöte,*" writes in Csampai and Holland, *W. A. Mozart:* Die Zauberflöte, p. 201: "The fire- and water trials in Act II, however, and above all the finale of the opera, . . . can be made presentable and credible only with difficulty." (*Die Feuer- und Wasserprobe im zweiten Akt aber und vor allem das Finale der Oper, . . . sind nur schwer darstellbar und glaubhaft zu machen.*). As found frequently in German stage directions of the eighteenth century, the word *Theater* is puzzling. Does the librettist really mean "theater" or, more probably, simply "stage"?

197. Mozart quoted in Anderson, *Letters,* 7–8 October 1791, p. 967; Wangermann, *Austrian Achievement,* p. 155.

Chapter Six

This research was supported in part by a Provost's Project Grant from Ithaca College.

1. Friedrich Wilhelm Jähns, *Carl Maria von Weber in seinen Werken: Chronologisch-thematisches Verzeichniss seiner sämmtlichen Compositionen* (Berlin, 1871; reprint, Berlin: Lienau, 1967), p. 309. For further information on Weber's work in establishing German opera in Dresden, see Wolfgang Becker, *Die deutsche Oper in Dresden unter der Leitung von Carl Maria von Weber: 1817–1826* (Berlin: Colloquium, 1962).

2. *Carl Maria von Weber: Briefe an den Grafen Karl von Brühl,* ed. Georg Kaiser (Leipzig: Breitkopf und Härtel, 1911), p. 20 n. 2.

3. Carl Maria von Weber, Der Freischütz: *Nachbildung der Eigenschrift aus dem Besitz der preussischen Staatsbibliothek,* ed. Georg Schünemann (Berlin: n. p., 1942), p. 18.

4. The diary is part of the Weber Familien-Nachlaß, Staatsbibliothek zu Berlin—Preußischer Kulturbesitz, Musikabteilung. The entries pertaining to the composition of *Der Freischütz* are quoted in full in Jähns, *Carl Maria von Weber in seinen Werken,* p. 309.

5. *Weber an von Brühl,* p. 20.

6. This information is from an 1817 pamphlet of which a significant portion is reprinted in Adalbert Behr and Alfred Hoffmann, *Das Schauspielhaus in Berlin* (Berlin: VEB Verlag für Bauwesen, 1984), pp. 33–34.

7. Ibid., p. 34.

8. For Schinkel's detailed drawings of the proposed renovation, see ibid., pp. 40–41.

9. The fire was described in detail by E. T. A. Hoffmann (1776–1822), who lived directly behind the theater: "I could tell you that during the burning of the theater, from which I live only fifteen or twenty steps, I came under the most manifest danger, since the roof of my apartment was already on fire, still more! That the credit of the state wavered, there, as the wig room was in flames and five thousand wigs flew up, Unzelmann's wig from the *Dorfbarbier* with a long pigtail like an ominous fiery meteor soared over the bank building—. . . and as it so happened, both were saved, I and the state. I through the strength of three hosemen for one of whom I bound a nasty wound with one of my wife's silk petticoats; the state through a courageous guardsman on Taubenstraße, who as several hoses were pointed in vain at the rising wigs, brought down the above-mentioned monstrosity with a well-aimed musket shot. Fatally wounded, it sank whizzing and roaring into the piss pot of the Schonert wine house—upon which fell immediately the government bonds! Is that not epic stuff?" E. T. A. *Hoffmanns Briefwechsel,* 2 vols., ed. Friedrich Schnapp (Munich: Winkler, 1967–68), vol. 2, p. 147.

10. For extensive discussions of Schinkel's reform ideas, see Hans von Wolzogen, "Karl Friedrich Schinkel und der Theaterbau: Betrachtungen nebst Mittheilungen aus nachgelassenen Papieren," *Bayreuther Blätter* 10/3 (March 1887), 65–90; Franz Benedikt Biermann, *Die Pläne zur Reform des Theaterbaues bei Karl Friedrich Schinkel und Gottfried Semper* (Berlin: Gesellschaft für Theatergeschichte, 1928), pp. 29–50; Ulrike Harten, *Die Bühnenbilder K. F. Schinkels 1798–1834* (Ph.D. dissertation, Kiel, 1974), pp. 77–103; and Behr and Hoffmann, *Das Schauspielhaus in Berlin,* pp. 38–48.

11. The most important of these documents are the letter to Iffland and the longer of the two drafts, both of which are reprinted in Behr and Hoffmann, *Das Schauspielhaus in Berlin,* pp. 42–49. The drawings and the sketches are reproduced in facsimile: see pp. 40–41 and 47.

12. Harten, *Die Bühnenbilder K. F. Schinkels,* p. 88.

13. Marvin Carlson, *Places of Performance: The Semiotics of Theatre Architecture* (Ithaca, New York: Cornell University Press, 1989), pp. 146–147.

14. Klaus Wever, "Karl Friedrich Schinkels Position und Beitrag zur Reform des Theaterraums," in *Karl Friedrich Schinkel: Werke und Wirkungen,* ed. Hans Joachim Arndt et al. (Berlin: Nicolaische Buchhandlung, 1981), pp. 190–193.

15. Behr and Hoffmann, *Das Schauspielhaus in Berlin,* p. 45.

16. "das von oben fallende Licht [wird] weit natürlicher wirken als das von unten aufsteigende." Quoted in ibid., p. 46.

17. For more on Gilly's ideas on theater reform, see Biermann, *Die Pläne zur Reform,* pp. 1–28.

18. "Die Senkung des Orchesters um zwei Fuß tiefer ist für die Wirkung der Musik vom größten Nutzen. Die einzelnen Instrumente schmelzen durch den eingeschlossenen

Raum, in dem sie sich zusammenfinden, mehr zusammen und kommen als eine vollständige Harmonie heraus. . . . . Vorzüglich wird der Gesang auf der Szene mehr dominieren, der jetzt sehr häufig durch das Übertönen des näher liegenden Orchesters ganz verdeckt wird. Auch wirken die vor der Szene arbeitenden Musiker nicht so störend, sondern ein sehr vorteilhaft trennender Raum wird zwischen Publikum und Theater dadurch gebildet." Quoted in Behr and Hoffmann, *Das Schauspielhaus in Berlin,* p. 46.

19. See his *Stammbaum* (flow chart) in Wever, "Karl Friedrich Schinkel's Position," p. 184.

20. Alfred von Wolzogen, *Aus Schinkels Nachlass: Reisetagebücher, Briefe und Aphorismen,* 4 vols. (Berlin, 1862–64; reprint, Mainz: Mäander, 1981), vol. 3, p. 170 n. 1.

21. Reprinted in ibid., vol. 3, pp. 170–174.

22. Ibid., vol. 3, p. 170 n. 1. Schinkel's memoranda to Brühl and the king are reprinted on pp. 170–174 and pp. 175–182 respectively.

23. In his history of German theater, Eduard Devrient characterizes Brühl as a highly educated nobleman with less practical experience than his predecessors. Despite this, he possessed the "self-confidence of a noble dilettante" (*Selbstvertrauen eines vornehmen Dilettantismus*), which led him to immerse himself in every aspect of the theater.

24. Quoted in Hans von Wolzogen, "Karl Friedrich Schinkel und der Theaterbau," 80.

25. Alfred von Wolzogen, *Aus Schinkels Nachlaß,* vol. 3, pp. 180–181.

26. Carl Friedrich Schinkel, *Sammlung architektonischer Entwürfe, neue vollständige Ausgabe in CLXXIV Tafeln* (Berlin, 1866; reprint, Chicago: Baluster Books, 1984), [3].

27. Alfred von Wolzogen, *Aus Schinkels Nachlaß,* vol. 3, p. 177.

28. Ibid., vol. 3, p. 176. A comparison between figures 6.3 and 6.5 shows that the square footage was lost because of the relative shallowness of the new stage.

29. This difference is shown for the three royal theaters in a seating chart, dating from 1825, that is reproduced in Ruth Freydank, *Theater in Berlin* (Berlin: Henschelverlag Kunst und Gesellschaft, 1988), p. 226.

30. Carlson, *Places of Performance,* p. 146.

31. The letters relating to this sequence of events are published in *Weber an von Brühl,* pp. 26–28.

32. Schünemann, Der Freischütz: *Nachbildung,* p. 58.

33. Ibid., pp. 56–57.

34. In the published version (see n. 36 below), Kind changed this figure to 28,000.

35. A letter to the editor printed in the 26 May edition of the *Königliche privilegierte Berlinische Zeitung (Vossische)* chastised the audience for its poor response to this second performance, stating, "The formerly so celebrated artists may be certain that no lack of recognition of the excellence of their work is to blame; rather, that unlucky star whose accidental occurrence has no reason."

36. Letters, 27 May 1821 and 31 May 1821, Staatsbibliothek zu Berlin—Preußischer Kulturbesitz, Musikabteilung; reprinted in Friedrich Kind, *Der Freischütz: Ausgabe letzter Hand* (Leipzig: Göschen, 1843), pp. 158, 160.

37. Weber's diary [Notizen und Ausgabe Buch für das Jahr 1821. C. M. von Weber. Dresden], housed in the Staatsbibliothek zu Berlin—Preußischer Kulturbesitz, Musikabteilung, gives detailed information on Weber's activities during the frenetic two months he and his wife spent in Berlin.

38. Letter, 6 December 1819, *Weber an von Brühl,* p. 21.

39. A review of the opening-night performance noted that *Olympia* was rehearsed for two months, as opposed to the eight or nine months that had been necessary for the Paris

premiere. "Vorbericht über die Oper *Olimpia*," *Königliche privilegierte Berlinische Zeitung* (*Vossische*) No. 59 (17 May 1821).

40. Carl von Ledebur, *Tonkünstler-Lexikon Berlins von den ältesten Zeiten bis auf die Gegenwart* (Berlin, 1861; reprint, Tutzing and Berlin: Hans Schneider, 1965), p. 545.

41. Ibid., p. 581.

42. Ibid., p. 62.

43. Ibid., p. 63.

44. Schünemann, Der Freischütz: *Nachbildung*, pp. 67–68. In addition to providing more rehearsal time, the postponement was fortuitous for another reason. The 18th of June 1821 was the eighth anniversary of the battle of Waterloo, and therefore was a date with special significance for those of a nationalistic bent. The distinctly German character of *Der Freischütz*, particularly when contrasted with *Olympia*, was seen as uniquely appropriate for this day.

45. Max Maria von Weber, *Carl Maria von Weber: The Life of an Artist*, 2 vols., trans. J. Palgrave Simpson (Boston: Oliver Ditson [1865]), vol. 2, pp. 164–168. Among the spectators on opening night were Heinrich Heine, E. T. A. Hoffmann, Carl Friedrich Zelter, and the twelve-year-old Felix Mendelssohn. Since Max von Weber was not yet born at the time of this premiere, he relied on the recollections of others, most notably those of Sir Julius Benedict, a student of the composer's who was present at the first performance.

46. Julius Kapp, "Die Uraufführung des *Freischütz*," *Blätter der Staatsoper* 1/8 (18 June 1921), 13.

47. Diary, p. 28; also reprinted in Schünemann, Der Freischütz: *Nachbildung*, p. 68.

48. Carl Wilhelm Gropius (1793–1870).

49. "Nun sollen auf S. Majestät ausdrücklichen Befehl, alte Sachen gegeben werden, bis meine Oper in Szene gehen kann. Dies wird schwerlich vor dem 8–10 Juny geschehen können, da die Wolfsschlucht gar zu viel Spanischen Apparat fordert. Übrigens sind des Maschinen Meister und Dekorateur Gropius Ansichten und Plane [sic] davon ganz herrlich und phantasiereich, und es wird wohl in seiner Art einzig dargestellt werden." Kind, *Der Freischütz*, p. 158.

50. Ibid., p. 160.

51. The original manuscript is in the Staatsbibliothek zu Berlin—Preußischer Kulturbesitz, Musikabteilung. The text is reprinted in Schünemann, Der Freischütz: *Nachbildung*, pp. 64–65.

52. Ph. J. Düringer and H. Barthels, eds., *Theater-Lexicon: Theoretisch-practisches Handbuch für Vorstände, Mitglieder und Freunde des deutschen Theaters* (Leipzig: Otto Wigand, 1841).

53. Ibid., p. 146.

54. Ibid., pp. 326–327.

55. Ibid., pp. 347–348.

56. Ibid., p. 918. The subtlety and variety of available sound effects indicates that this aspect of theater production had become crucial by the nineteenth century. While it is certainly impractical to recreate the most complex of these machines, modern theater directors must devote the same care and attention to the subtleties of sound, no matter what the medium of production.

57. In his letter to the king outlining his plans and describing his accompanying drawings, Schinkel had discussed four main points: function, beauty, fire safety, and economy (Alfred von Wolzogen, *Aus Schinkels Nachlaß*, vol. 3, pp. 176–182.).

58. Weber's costs and income for *Der Freischütz* during his lifetime are recorded in a book now held by the Staatsbibliothek zu Berlin—Preußischer Kulturbesitz, Musikabteilung and reproduced in Schünemann, Der Freischütz: *Nachbildung,* p. 73. Weber had purchased the libretto from Kind for a flat fee—contrary to the librettist's wishes—and the unparalleled success of the opera led to bitter feelings from Kind.

59. The whereabouts of this book are not known, but the costume drawings were later published in Carl Gropius, *Dekorationen auf den beiden königl[ichen] Theatern in Berlin, unter Generalintendantur des Herrn Grafen Brühl* (Berlin: Wittich, 1827).

60. Weber's estimate was low by almost 7,000 talers, according to Johann V. Teichmann, *Literarischer Nachlaß,* ed. Franz Dingelstedt (Stuttgart: Cotta, 1863), p. 145.

61. *Weber an von Brühl,* p. 38.

62. Julius Kapp, ed. *185 Jahre Staatsoper: Festschrift zur Wiedereröffnung des Opernhauses Unter den Linden am 28. April 1928,* (Berlin: Atlantic [1928]), p. 110. *Der Freischütz* had by this time been performed 756 times at the Berlin opera. The second most-performed work was Wagner's *Lohengrin,* with 706 performances.

63. "Die Musik findet großen Beifall und ist in der Tat so gut, daß das Publikum den vielen Kohlen- und Pulverdampf nicht unerträglich findet." *Der Briefwechsel zwischen Goethe und Zelter,* ed. Max Hecker (Leipzig: Insel, 1915), vol. 2, p. 127.

Chapter Seven

1. Letter from Meyerbeer to Nicolas Levasseur, quoted in William L. Crosten, *French Grand Opera: An Art and a Business* (New York: King's Crown Press, 1948), p. 107.

2. Michael Walter, *Hugenotten-Studien* (Frankfurt am Main: Peter Lang, 1987), p. 91 ff.

3. Victor Hugo, *Préface de Cromwell,* ed. Michel Cambien (Paris: Librairie Larousse, 1971), p. 68.

4. Ibid., p. 81.

5. Ibid., p. 84.

6. For more information on the structural elements of grand opera librettos, see Karin Pendle, *Eugène Scribe and French Opera of the Nineteenth Century* (Ann Arbor: UMI Research Press, 1971). For a discussion of the boulevard influences on grand opera, see Karin Pendle, "Boulevard Theatres and Continuity in French Opera of the Nineteenth Century," *Music in Paris in the 1830s,* ed. P. Bloom (Stuyvesant, New York: Pendragon Press, 1987), pp. 509–535.

7. Louis Véron, *L'Opéra de Paris, 1820–1835* (Paris: Éditions Michel de Maule, 1987), pp. 134–135.

8. See Nicole Wild, *Décors et costumes du XIXe siècle.* Vol. I: *L'Opéra de Paris* (Paris: Bibliothèque National, Département de la Musique, 1987). *Maquettes* are paper models of stage settings which served as models for those building and painting the set.

9. For further information, see H. Robert Cohen, with Sylvia L'Ecuyer, *Les gravures musicales dans l'illustration (1843–1899)* (Québec: Université Laval, 1982–83), 3 vols.

10. An example of such an inventory, covering materials for *Robert le diable,* is given in Rebecca Wilberg, "The *mise en scène* at the Paris Opéra-Salle Le Peletier (1821–1873) and the Staging of the First French 'Grand Opéra': Meyerbeer's *Robert le diable*" (Ph.D. dissertation, Brigham Young University, 1990), Appendix B.

11. See H. Robert Cohen, *The Original Staging Manuals for Twelve Parisian Opera Premieres* (Stuyvesant, New York: Pendragon Press, 1990) and Hellmuth Christian Wolff, "Die Regiebücher des Louis Palianti für die Pariser Opera 1830–1870," *Maske und Kothurn* 26 (1980), 74–84. According to Gösta Bergman, in "Les agences théâtrales et l'impression des mises en scène aux environs de 1800," *Revue d'histoire du théâtre* 8 #2–3 (1956), 228–240, printed production books for spoken dramas began to appear by the end of the eighteenth century. The scenic libretto for *La muette de Portici* is the first known example to deal with an opera. It is important to realize that the *livret* was, to a large extent, intended to assist other producers in mounting a work. Since the collective stage resources of the Opéra were unique in all of Europe, explicit instructions based upon the *plan* (layout) of the stage or references to the machinery housed there would have been of little use to imitators. It is, therefore, often necessary to draw conclusions about the means used to achieve various settings and effects based upon our knowledge of the house resources in general.

12. Examples of both types are reprinted in H. Robert Cohen, *Original Staging Manuals*.

13. Alexis Donnet, *Architectonographie des théâtres de Paris* (Paris: De Lacroix-Comon, 1840–57), p. 276.

14. In fact, this *salle provisoire* was used until October of 1873, when it was destroyed by fire. See *Revue et gazette musicale de Paris* 40 #44 (2 November 1873), 345–346, for information about the fire. The Palais Garnier, which was then under construction, opened in 1875.

15. Adolphe Jullien, "Inauguration de la Salle de l'Opéra," *Chronique musicale* 2 (1873), 169.

16. For details about the construction of the facility, see Jullien, "Inauguration," 171 ff.

17. Ibid., 170–172.

18. For example, contemporaries were as yet unaccustomed to such an amalgamation of styles that included Corinthian, Ionic, and Doric columns.

19. Edouard Devrient, *Briefe aus Paris* (Berlin, 1840), p. 34, quoted in Germain Bapst, *Essai sur l'histoire du théâtre* (Paris: Librairie Hachette, 1893), p. 535.

20. Spire Pitou, *The Paris Opéra: An Encyclopedia of Operas, Ballets, Composers, and Performers: Genesis and Glory, 1671–1715* (Westport, Connecticut: Greenwood Press, 1983), p. 44.

21. Donnet, *Architectonographie*, p. 295.

22. Véron, *L'Opéra de Paris*, p. 22.

23. When forced into a recessed pit at the inauguration of the Palais Garnier in 1875, the orchestra members retaliated by playing excerpts from the grand opera repertoire *pianissimo* throughout the evening. Wilberg, "The *mise en scène* at the Paris Opéra," p. 72.

24. Ibid., p. 71.

25. Véron, *L'Opéra de Paris* (pp. 130, 135), in the early 1830s, cites as well: eighty choristers, seventy dancers, and sixty machinists. Wilberg, "The *mise en scène* at the Paris Opéra"(p. 310), says that the chorus in 1831 numbered between sixty and seventy.

26. Bapst, *Essai sur l'histoire du théâtre*, p. 536.

27. References to "depth" measurements in this discussion refer to front-to-back (downstage to upstage) distances.

28. Information on the size of the theater and its stage varies, although usually only slightly, from source to source. For a detailed yet patient and intelligent examination of the dimensions and resources of the Salle le Peletier, see Wilberg, "The *mise en scène* at the Paris Opéra." The interested reader may also wish to consult Cecil Ault, "Operation

and Organization of Stage Machinery at the Paris Opéra" (Ph.D. dissertation, University of Michigan, 1983).

29. Bapst, *Essai sur l'histoire du théâtre*, p. 330.

30. Catherine Join-Diéterle, "Cicéri et la décoration théâtrale à l'Opéra de Paris," *Victor Louis et le théâtre* (Paris: Centre National de la Recherche Scientifique, 1982), p. 142.

31. For a full explanation of the diorama, see Gösta M. Bergman, *Lighting in the Theatre* (Stockholm: Almqvist och Wiksell, 1977), p. 323 ff.; and Helmut and Alison Gernsheim, *L.-J.-M. Daguerre* (New York: Dover, 1968).

32. André-Jean-Jacques Deshayes, *Idées générales sur l'Académie Royale de Musique* (Paris, 1822), quoted in Nicole Wild, "Un demi-siècle de décors à l'Opéra de Paris," *Regards sur l'Opéra* (Paris: Presses Universitaires de France, 1976), p. 18.

33. Bergman, *Lighting*, pp. 204–205.

34. For more detailed coverage of the influences of the boulevard theaters on French grand opera, see Karin Pendle, "Boulevard Theatres."

35. Wild, "Un demi-siècle," p. 19.

36. Marvin Carlson, *The French Stage in the Nineteenth Century* (Metuchen, New Jersey: Scarecrow Press, 1972), p. 13.

37. For a thorough discussion of the production of Meyerbeer's *Robert le diable*, see Wilberg, "The *mise en scène* at the Paris Opéra."

38. "The full flowering of Romanticism in the French theater was extremely brief, lasting from the triumph of *Hernani* in 1830 to the failure of Hugo's *Burgraves* in 1843." Carlson, *The French Stage*, p. 5. By 1843 the score of *Le prophète* was essentially complete, though it would undergo revisions later in the decade.

39. Véron, *L'Opéra de Paris*, p. 75. Véron is known to have had trouble with the officials overseeing the Opéra when he attempted to reuse set pieces and costumes in ways that seemed too obvious to them.

40. Catherine Join-Diéterle, *Les décors de scène de l'Opéra de Paris à l'époque Romantique* (Paris: Picard, 1988), p. 194. The printed *mise en scène* also includes an appendix, "Moyens de simplifier l'exécution" (Ways to simplify the production), which closes with the following advice: "The directors who had [Carafa's] *Masaniello* performed at the Feydeau [Theater in 1827] ought to have some of the things necessary for the execution of *La Muette*, whether in sets, costumes, props, etc., since they are on the same subject. For the rest, *La Neige, Mme de Sévigné, Le Chevalier de Canale, Cendrillon, Le Petit Chaperon Rouge, Joconde* [all *opéras-comiques* of recent vintage] can furnish the materials necessary for any given part of this opera." Hence the smaller theaters were being encouraged to reuse sets and costumes in order to produce Auber's opera on their own terms. See Solomé, *Indications générales et observations pour la mise en scène de* La muette de Portici (n.p.: Duverger, n.d.), p. 59.

41. Solomé, *Indications générales*, p. 39.

42. Those mounted on *chariots* would be slid off to the wings, while others would disappear into the substage.

43. An appendix to the scenic libretto notes: "In order to form the market scene, place at the head of each line of merchants those who sing, and extend the lines with supernumeraries" (Solomé, *Indications générales*, p. 56). Earlier, Solomé suggests (I, i) that the chorus be "as near as possible to the first *plan* so that they can be heard" (p. 5). Hence, though the people, whether chorus members or supers, move all over the stage in the examples under discussion, care was taken that the singers should always be audible.

44. Solomé, *Indications générales*, pp. 27–29.
45. "Au marché qui vient de s'ouvrir, / Venez, hâtez-vous d'accourir, / Voilà des fleurs, voilà des fruits, / Raisins vermeils, limons exquis, / Oranges fines de Méta, / Rosolio, vin de Somma, / Nouveaux cédrats de Portici, / Venez à moi, venez ici." *La muette de Portici,* Act III, scene ii.
46. Solomé, *Indications générales*, p. 29.
47. Ibid., pp. 29–30.
48. Ibid., p. 31.
49. Ibid., pp. 31–32.
50. Ibid., p. 32. One might well ask why the French government did not fear the effect on audiences of this musically and scenically enhanced revolution. Perhaps the fact that the rulers in *La muette* represent a foreign power was enough to convince anyone that such a revolution could not happen in France. If not, then surely Act V, in which the revolutionaries prove to be just as corrupt as those they are fighting against, would settle the matter.
51. For a description of the volcano tableau in *La tête de mort,* see Pendle, "Boulevard Theatres," 532.
52. Solomé, *Indications générales*, p. 47.
53. All descriptions of the workings of stage effects are drawn from Solomé.
54. Jean-Pierre Moynet, *L'envers du théâtre* (Paris: Hachette, 1888), 136–138; Arthur Pougin, *Dictionnaire historique et pittoresque du théâtre* (Paris: Firmin-Didot, 1885), p. 490.
55. See Bergman, *Lighting,* pp. 271–272, for a detailed description of the way this scene was accomplished in a Stockholm theater.
56. According to Wilberg, "The *mise en scène* at the Paris Opéra," pp. 311–312, a "distant rumble of thunder was achieved . . . by the vigorous agitation of a large piece of sheet-iron." Also, Solomé, *Indications générales,* p. 66, lists a tam-tam among the props required for Act V. For a sudden clap of thunder, says Wilberg, stagehands used "a thunder apparatus . . . made of numerous long planks of sheet-iron strung on top of each other by a cord at each end and separated from each other by knots at even distances in the cords." When this suspended apparatus was dropped from one level in the *cintre* to the next, the result was "a loud crack and a series of irregular, echoing crashes." Flames from the volcano were likely created in a way resembling that used in the third act of *Robert le diable:* "A pipe was laid on the stage floor. . . . This pipe had an alcohol lamp attached to the front end with the opposite end filled with lycopodium powder—a highly flammable fine yellowish powder made of vegetable moss spores. A crewman then blew through the pipe, sending some of the lycopodium across the flame of the lamp, producing sudden yet quickly dissipated flames."
57. Solomé, *Indications générales,* p. 32, shows groupings of chorus members (people and nobility, plus five guards), supers (three platoons of soldiers, pages, and sentinels), and leading characters asymmetrically arranged over the frontmost *plans* of the stage.
58. According to Allévy, the designers for *La Juive* were Ciceri, Charles Séchan, Jules-Pierre-Michel Diéterle, Edouard Despléchin, Léon Feuchère, Humanité-René Philastre, and Charles Cambon. Hence, like most grand operas of the mid 1830s, *La Juive* used more than one designer. The costumer, Paul Lormier, based his designs on the work of seventeenth-century historiographer Pierre Paillot. See Marie-Antoinette Allévy, *La mise en scène en France dans la première moitié du XIXe siècle* (Paris: E. Droz, 1936), p. 108.
59. Joseph Mainzer, "Vienne et la synagogue juive pendant les années 1826, 1827, et 1828," *Gazette musicale de Paris* 1 #16 (20 April 1834), 125–128; and #18 (4 May 1834), 143–146. Judging by Mainzer's comments, no such music was in use in Paris at the time.

60. F. Palianti, *La Juive. Opéra en 5 actes* (Paris: E. Brière [1835]), p. 9.

61. See Join-Diéterle, *Les décors,* p. 224 ff.

62. Théophile Gautier, *Les beautés de l'Opéra* (Paris, 1845), p. 3, quoted in Crosten, *French Grand Opera,* p. 66.

63. *Le courrier français* (27 February 1835), quoted in Crosten, *French Grand Opera,* p. 65.

64. *Le ménestrel* 2 #14 (1 March 1835), unnumbered page.

65. Join-Diéterle, *Les décors,* caption to plate 20.

66. Bapst, *Essai sur l'histoire du théâtre,* p. 552.

67. The *livret de mise en scène* indicates stage right and stage left from the audience's perspective. Since modern usage considers stage directions from the actor's perspective, all references to stage left or stage right in the scenic libretto have been transposed to agree with current practice.

68. All descriptions of stage movement are from Palianti. The chorus, which Wilberg, "The *mise en scène* at the Paris Opéra," p. 310, numbers at 60–70 voices as of 1831, would remain onstage for the entire cortège, which was made up of nonsinging extras. Hence the number of people onstage at any one time would have been 85–90 for most of the scene.

69. The *Courrier français* (27 February 1835) described the emperor as "a glittering ingot from head to foot." Quoted in Crosten, *French Grand Opera,* p. 65.

70. A similar extension of space beyond the visible stage occurs when sounds from Eléazar's shop cause an adverse reaction among those on stage in the early scenes of Act I. These noises extend into the orchestra as the simultaneous use of valved and natural horns in octaves reflects the disturbing sounds of the jeweler's anvils.

71. F. Stoepel, "Académie Royale de Musique. *La Juive,* opéra en 5 actes. . . ," *Gazette musicale de Paris* 2 #10 (8 March 1835), 82.

72. Similar passages occur between the people's celebration and the arrival of the cortège, when the Jews are once more threatened by the crowd and saved by the intervention of a powerful figure (Prince Léopold), and at the end of Act V, where Rachel's fate is decided and carried out in real time.

73. Stoepel, "Académie Royale de Musique. *La Juive,*" 82.

74. Frances Trollope, *Paris and the Parisians in 1835* (London: Richard Bentley, 1836), vol. 2, p. 151.

75. Other lighting effects, though not indicated in the scenic libretto, were achieved by the use of gas. Bapst, *Essai sur l'histoire du théâtre,* p. 552, for example, mentions that the Act I cortège was "lit by gas projections."

76. *Le ménestrel* 2 #14 (1 March 1835), unnumbered page.

77. Trollope, *Paris and the Parisians,* p. 149.

78. *Revue et gazette musicale de Paris* 17 #15 (14 April 1850), 128.

79. *Revue et gazette musicale de Paris* 16 #16 (22 April 1849), 126.

80. *Le ménestrel* (22 March 1849), 126.

81. The first patent for the incandescent lamp had been granted only in 1841.

82. *Mise en scène* [*sic*] *Le prophète, Opéra en cinq actes* (reproduced in Cohen, *The Original Staging Manuals for Twelve Parisian Opera Premiers,* 151–182), p. 165.

83. The *livret* identifies the purveyor of the skates: "The roller skates are the invention of M. Legrand, 8, rue des Jardins, at Chaillot" (*Mise en scène,* p. 160).

84. *Mise en scène,* p. 160.

85. *Revue et gazette musicale de Paris* 17 #11 (17 March 1850), 87.

86. *Mise en scène,* p. 163.

87. *Revue et gazette musicale de Paris* 16 #22 (3 June 1849), 172.

88. The ideal instrumentation included eighteen saxhorns, two cornets, two trumpets, and drums for the stage band; and piccolo, two flutes, two oboes, two clarinets, two bassoons, four horns, five trombones, ophicleide, four trumpets, timpani, cymbals, bass drum, snare drum, and strings for the "pit" orchestra.

89. *Mise en scène,* p. 168. The numbers and letters in the description refer to the diagram in figure 7.14.

90. *Revue et gazette musicale de Paris* 16 #22 (3 June 1849), 172.

91. Praise for Pauline Viardot, the creator of the role, was utterly extraordinary and completely unanimous.

92. *Revue et gazette musicale de Paris* 16 #22 (3 June 1849), 173.

93. See Hans Busch, *Verdi's* Aïda: *The History of an Opera in Letters and Documents* (Minneapolis: University of Minnesota Press, 1978), which includes copies of the printed scenic libretto and the textual libretto containing Verdi's annotations concerning staging.

Chapter Eight

Nineteenth-century Italian prose—particularly Verdi's own writings—frequently contains suspension points, indicated here by ellipsis points that are not spaced. Omissions made for the purposes of this essay are indicated by spaced ellipses.

1. In the period spanning 1843 through 1857, Bertoja created designs for more than seventeen Verdi operas at the Teatro la Fenice.

2. To my knowledge, the only correspondence that Verdi carried out with a designer was that with Girolamo Magnani. See the exhibit catalog, Maurizia Bonatti Bacchini, *Il teatro di Girolamo Magnani: Scenografo di Verdi* (Parma: [La civiltà musicale di Parma], 1989). Documents may exist in the archives of Bertoja's descendants in Pordenone, however. Ten volumes of Bertoja's designs are in Museo Correr, Venice, and one further volume was recently given to the Museo Civico, Pordenone. See Natalia Grilli, "Le immagini per il *Simon Boccanegra* di Verdi," in Marcello Conati and Natalia Grilli, *Simon Boccanegra* (Milan: Ricordi, 1993), published as part of the series, *Musica e Spettacolo: Collana di disposizioni sceniche.*

3. For Verdi's earlier works at the San Carlo (*I due Foscari* and *Alzira,* both 1845), the designs were created by Angelo Belloni and Domenico Ferri. Details regarding the productions are mentioned by Franco Mancini, *Il Teatro di San Carlo. 1737–1987: Le scene, i costumi* (Naples: Electa, 1987), vol. 3, p. 114, *passim.*

4. Many of the designs have been reproduced in William Weaver, *Verdi: A Documentary Study* (London: Thames and Hudson, 1977), and in Marzio Pieri, *Verdi: L'immaginario dell'ottocento* (Milano: Electa, 1981).

5. See the entries on Alessandro Sanquirico in *New Grove Dictionary of Opera* (London: Macmillan, 1992), vol. 4, pp. 168–169, and Mercedes Viale-Ferrero, *La scenografia della Scala nell'età neoclassica* (Milan: Polifilo, 1983), pp. 77–81, 91–103.

6. Mancini, *Il Teatro di San Carlo,* and his *Scenografia napoletana dell'ottocento: Antonio Niccolini e il neoclassico* (Naples: Edizione scientifiche italiana, 1980).

7. Bibiena's theories have been translated and briefly discussed in Dunbar Ogden, *The Italian Baroque Stage: Documents by Giulio Troili, Andrea Pozzo, Ferdinando Galli-Bibiena, Baldassare Orsini* (Berkeley and Los Angeles: University of California Press, 1978).

8. There were always notable exceptions, such as Sanquirico's production of Bellini's *La sonnambula* at the Teatro Carcano in 1831.

9. Theaters in Italy numbered well into the hundreds, particularly after the "boom" in construction that began toward the end of the eighteenth century and continued into the first decades of the nineteenth century.

10. In the Teatro Regio of Parma (constructed in 1823), the drops were painted in a space above the foyer, which today is used as a rehearsal hall. The original sink, stove, and preparatory areas are still preserved in their original state.

11. Full electric stage-lighting (including, for example, overhead strip lights, footlights, etc.) was not installed in most theaters until the mid 1880s.

12. A detailed history and documents relating to *Macbeth* can be found in David Rosen, Andrew Porter (eds.), *Verdi's* Macbeth: *A Sourcebook* (New York: W. W. Norton, 1984).

13. For the purposes of this essay, all the operas will be referred to by short titles.

14. It must be made clear that the physical elements of the operas—sets, properties, costumes, and lighting—were the properties of either the impresarios managing the theater or the private contractors. The idea of the physical production being the property of the theater itself is a concept that did not come into practice until the end of the nineteenth century, when the municipalities gained ownership of the opera houses.

15. The librettos reported thus: *Le Scene sono d'inventione ed esecuzione del signor Cavallotti Baldassare.* Menozzi was also reported as part of the production team in Guido Marangoni, *La Scala: Studi e ricerche* (Bergamo: Istituto Italiano d'Arte Grafiche, 1922), pp. 64–65.

16. *La moda* (10 March 1842). Facsimile reproduced in program book "*Nabucco,* Teatro alla Scala," season 1986/1987, p. 88.

17. Verdi's autobiographical narrative to Giulio Ricordi, Sant'Agata, 19 October 1879. Quoted in Weaver, *Verdi,* p. 14. See also Arthur Pougin, *Giuseppe Verdi: Vita aneddotica con note ed aggiunte di Folchetto (Jacobo Caponi)* (Milan: Ricordi, 1881), pp. 45–46.

18. If anything were to be "in stock," it would be the costumes since these could easily be rented for profit to other opera companies. Drops and wings were more difficult to rent, since these were usually cut and painted to the sizes of specific theaters. The stage of the Teatro alla Scala at that time was among the largest in existence; only the stage of the San Carlo in Naples was equivalent in size. John Rosselli examines much of this in his study *The Opera Industry in Italy from Cimarosa to Verdi: The Role of the Impresario* (Cambridge University Press, 1984).

19. *La moda.* See n. 16.

20. "Furore! Furore! Furore! *L'Attila* è andato alle stelle, come dicono I giornalisti...La 'mise en scène' è perfida; il sole si era alzato prima che fosse segnato dalla musica. Il mare, invece di essere burrascoso ed in tempesta, era placido e senza un'onda increspata. Vi erano i solitari senza capanne; vi erano i sacerdoti senza altare; nella scena del convito Attila ha fatto banchetto senza lumi, . . . ed il temporale il cielo è rimasto sereno e limpido come in un più bel giorno di primavera. Tutti (a voce ed in cuore) maledicevano Merelli per aver trattato Attila sì malamente." Quoted in Frank Walker, *The Man Verdi* (New York: Alfred A. Knopf, 1963), p. 154. Original in Luigi Garibaldi, *Giuseppe Verdi nelle lettere di Emanuale Muzio ad Antonio Barezzi* (Milan: Fratelli Treves, 1931), pp. 302–303.

21. G. Cesari and A. Luzio, *I copialettere di Giuseppe Verdi* (Milan: Commune, 1913), p. 34.

22. In 1847 some complaints had already been registered from the authorities regarding the qualities of the costumes. Merelli subsequently created an advisory group to pass judgment on future costume designs. Among the members was the noted portraitist Francesco Hayez. Many of his comments are found in the Museo Teatrale alla Scala, Milan. See Remo Giazotto, *Le carte della Scala: Storie di impresari e appaltatori teatrali 1778–1860* (Pisa: Akademos, 1990), p. 129, and Maria Christina Gozzoli and Fernando Mazzocca, *Hayez* (Milan: Electa, 1983).

23. Exhibition catalog of Museo Scala ed. Natalia Grilli, Filippo Peroni. *Scenografo alla Scala 1849–1867* (Milan: Museo Teatrale alla Scala, 1985).

24. See Mancini's study of the designs for the Teatro San Carlo in: *Il Teatro di San Carlo,* vol. 3, pp. 111–169.

25. For a detailed history of the edifice, see Manlio Brusatin and Giuseppe Pavanello, *Il Teatro la Fenice: I progetti, l'architettura, le decorazioni* (Venice: Albrizzi, 1987). Regarding the reconstruction of the opera house after its disastrous fire in 1836, see Tommaso and Giambattista Meduna, *Il Teatro la Fenice in Venezia edificato dall'Architetto Antonio Selva nel 1792 e ricostruito in parte in 1836* (Venice: Imp. Reg. Privil. Stabilimento Antonelli, 1849).

26. All measurements are necessarily approximate. The dimensions for La Fenice are taken from the plans published by Meduna, *Il Teatro la Fenice,* plates 1, 2, and 4.

27. Both La Scala and the Teatro San Carlo were considerably larger.

28. Details in Gösta M. Bergman, *Lighting in the Theatre* (Stockholm: Almqvist och Wiksell, 1977).

29. Michele Girardi and Franco Rossi, *Il Teatro la Fenice. Cronologia degli spettacoli 1792–1936* (Venice: Albrizzi, 1989), p. 172. Electricity was first used for the auditorium there in 1878; it was not installed for full use on stage until December 1886. Girardi indicates the availability of the equipment for the 1886–87 season, *Forn. della luce elettrica in scena* (p. 283)—around the same time most other major European theater stages were electrified.

30. More details on Bertoja can be found in an exhibition catalog edited by Gino Damerini, *Scenografi veneziani dell'ottocento* (Venice: Neri Pozza, 1962).

31. While there were other, shorter seasons in the spring, occasionally in the summer, and in the fall, carnival was the main season in which most of the new operas and stagings were produced.

32. Administrative records of the Teatro la Fenice exist, and they are now housed in the Fondazione Levi, Venice. Financial records documenting the costs of the productions have yet to be fully studied. Several documents relating to Verdi's works have been published in Marcello Conati, "La disposizione scenica per il *Simon Boccanegra* di Verdi. Studio critico," in Conati and Grilli, *Simon Boccanegra.*

33. A general summary of theaters is found in Nicola Mangini, *I teatri di Venezia* (Milan: Mursia, 1974).

34. For complete details, including relevant documents from the Teatro la Fenice, see Marcello Conati's magnificent study, *La bottega della musica: Verdi e la Fenice* (Milan: Saggiatore, 1983). Maria Teresa Muraro gives an introductory overview, with reproductions of designs, "Le scenografie delle cinque 'prime assolute' di Verdi alla Fenice di Venezia" in *Atti del I° congresso internazionale di studi verdiani* (Parma: Istituto di studi verdiani, 1969), pp. 328–334. Many of Bertoja's works have been reproduced in color in Weaver, *Verdi.*

35. Gallo produced a revival of *La traviata* at his theater. Its ensuing success reversed the fortunes of the opera after its disastrous premiere at La Fenice.

36. Premieres and revivals supervised by Verdi between 1839 and 1857.

Date	Opera	City	Theater	Designer
17 November 1839	Oberto, conte di San Bonifacio	Milan	Scala	Baldassare Cavallotti / Domenico Menozzi
5 September 1840	Un giorno di regno	Milan	Scala	Cavallotti / Menozzi
9 January 1841	Oberto, conte di San Bonifacio	Genoa	Carlo Felice	Michele Canzio
9 March 1842	Nabucodonosor	Milan	Scala	Cavallotti
11 February 1843	I Lombardi alla prima crociata	Milan	Scala	Cavallotti
4 April 1843	Nabucco	Vienna	Hofoper	Giuseppe Brioschi
29 July 1843	I Lombardi	Sinigaglia	Fenice	Pietro Venier
26 December 1843	I Lombardi	Venice	Fenice	Venier / Giuseppe Bertoja
9 March 1844	Ernani	Venice	Fenice	Venier
3 November 1844	I due Foscari	Rome	Argentina	Venier
15 February 1845	Giovanna d'Arco	Milan	Scala	Alessandro Merlo / Giovanni Fontana
30 March 1845	I due Foscari	Venice	Gallo	Bertoja
8 August 1845	Alzira	Naples	San Carlo	Angelo Belloni / Domenico Ferri
26 December 1845	Giovanna d'Arco	Venice	Fenice	Bertoja
17 March 1846	Attila	Venice	Fenice	Bertoja
14 March 1847	Macbeth	Florence	Pergola	Giovanni Gianni
22 July 1847	I Masnadieri	London	Majesty's	Charles Marshall
26 November 1847	Jérusalem	Paris	Opéra	Séchan / Dieterle / Despléchin / Cambon / Thierry
25 October 1848	Il corsaro	Trieste	Grande	Pietro Pupilli
27 January 1849	La battaglia di Legnano	Rome	Argentina	Venier / Vincenzo Scarabellotto
8 December 1849	Luisa Miller	Naples	San Carlo	Venier
16 November 1850	Stiffelio	Trieste	Grande	Bertoja / Pupilli
15 March 1851	Rigoletto	Venice	Fenice	Bertoja
19 January 1853	Il trovatore	Rome	Apollo	Carlo Bazzani / Prampolini / Antonio Fornari
6 March 1853	La traviata	Venice	Fenice	Bertoja
26 December 1854	Il trovatore	Paris	Théâtre Italien	Charles Cambon
13 June 1855	Les Vêpres siciliennes	Paris	Opéra	Cambon / Thierry / Lavastre / Despléchin / Nolau / Rubé / Chaperon
12 January 1857	Le trouvère	Paris	Opéra	Cambon / Thierry / Lavastre / Despléchin / Nolau / Rubé
12 March 1857	Simon Boccanegra	Venice	Fenice	Bertoja

37. *I Lombardi* was already known to Bertoja from his work at the Teatro Regio, Turin. Coincidentally, the opera premiered at the same time as the Venetian production on 26 December 1843.

38. The originals are in Museo Correr, Venice. Reproduced in Weaver, plate 54, and Mercedes Viale-Ferrero, *La scenografia dalle origini al 1936: Storia del Teatro Regio di Torino* (Turin: [Cassa di risparmio], 1980), vol. 3, p. 378, plates 63–66.

39. Bertoja designed productions at the Teatro Apollo as well, but specific documentation presently is not available.

40. Giuseppe Radiciotti, *Teatro, musica e musicisti in Sinigaglia* (Milan: Ricordi, 1893), p. 87.

41. Conati, *Bottega*, p. 60.

42. It is not known if the designs survive among the large holdings of Venier's works now located in the Theater Collection at the University of Cologne. Mercedes Viale-Ferrero's discussion in "*Ernani* di Verdi: Le critiche del tempo. Alcune considerazioni," in *Verdi: Bolletino dell'istituto di studi verdiani numero 10, Ernani. Ieri e oggi. Atti* (Parma: Istituto di studi verdiani, 1987), focuses primarily upon Bertoja's later contributions, as does Muraro.

43. *Lombardi* was revived in the spring season (April) for a total of six additional performances. See Girardi, *Cronologia*, p. 175.

44. Mercedes Viale-Ferrero discussed the designs in "*Ernani* di Verdi," pp. 195–206, and included several reproductions of the designs.

45. The visual aspects of the production were rarely discussed in newspaper reviews. It was not until much later in the century that productions would be reported in greater detail.

46. Over the years numerous historians have noted that Bertoja created a subterranean setting for the 1844 production, but there is no documentation to support this claim.

47. Peretti, "*L'Ernani* di Verdi al Teatro S. Benedetto in Venezia" in *Gazzetta musicale di Milano,* 26 May 1844; transcribed in *Bollettino 10,* p. 228. It is surprising that neither Muraro nor Viale-Ferrero has made any reference to this point in their discussions of Bertoja's designs for *Ernani*.

48. Tommaso Locatelli, *Gazzetta di Venezia* (3 April 1845).

49. "Bisogna alzar la tenda e far vedere Aquileja incendiata con coro di popolo e coro di Unni. . . . Apriva il primo atto in Roma e invece di far la festa in scena farla interna ed Azzio pensoso in scena a meditare sulli avvenimenti ect..., ect..., Sarebbe magnifico nel terzo atto tutta la scena di Leone sull'Avventino mentre sotto si combatte. . . . Ti raccomando di studiare molto questo soggetto ed avere bene in mente tutto, l'epoca, i caratteri etc..., etc...." Conati, *Bottega*, p. 143.

50. Verdi to Lanari, 6 August 1845; cited in Conati, *Bottega*, p. 155.

51. "così mi previene il Maestro Verdi, il quale poi particolarmente raccomanda sono le Scene di cui alcune le brama a tutto Teatro, e per valermi della sua espressione, dice 'quelle che desidererei sublime e la Seconda alla Scena VI. che e il principio della Città di Venezia: Sia ben fatto l'alzare del Sole, che io voglio esprimere colla Musica. Nella Scena VI. del prim'Atto nel finale, guarda che quella Scena si più lontana che sia possibile, e la tenda d'Attila sia fatta in modo da potersi aprire spaccattamente per intero.'" Reproduced in ibid., p. 159.

52. "Quando l'opera fu scritto dal M. Verdi. Tutti I fabbricati erano in spezzata staccati e il fondo di cielo cambrava dal temporale al sereno e cielo spintare del sole." Reproduced in Viale-Ferrero, *Ernani*, plate 4.

53. So stated Verdi in a letter to Giuseppina Appiani, 22 December 1845. See Conati, *Bottega,* p. 167.
54. Locatelli, *Gazzetta di Venezia* (18 March 1846).
55. Reproduced by Viale-Ferrero, *Ernani,* plate 5.
56. See the reproduction in Giuseppe Stefani, *Verdi e Trieste* (Trieste: Commune, 1951), plate 23 of the poster from the premiere where the names are specified. Among Bertoja's surviving designs is one for the cemetery scene in the second act. For the staging at La Fenice on 13 January 1852, Bertoja recycled his graveyard scene and created new designs for the remainder of the opera. Verdi did not participate in the preparations for this production.
57. Albeit under the nominal supervision of Bagnara. The protocol is transcribed in Conati, *Bottega,* p. 218.
58. Details in Girardi, *Cronologia,* p. 194.
59. For the chronology of the changes, see Julian Budden, *The Operas of Verdi: From* Oberto *to* Rigoletto (Oxford University Press, 1992), vol. 2, as well as Conati, *Bottega.* Maria Teresa Muraro discussed some of Bertoja's designs in her study "Giuseppe Bertoja e le scene per la prima di *Rigoletto* alla Fenice," in *Verdi. Bolletino dell'istituto di studi verdiani* (Parma: Istituto di studi verdiani, 1982), vol. 9, pp. 1582–1588.
60. Conati, *Bottega,* pp. 246–247.
61. Ibid., p. 249.
62. "Non ho più bisogno di te per far versi. Bisognerà cambiare alcune indicazioni di scena soprattutto nella tempesta del terz' atto perché io ho messo tuoni, saette, lampi et... et... tutti a tempo e non ho potuto seguire sempre le tue indicazioni. Bisognerà che 'l'amico delle amadriadi' secondi le mie idee e facci i tuoni ed i lampi non a caso (secondo il solito) ma a tempo: deside[er]rei che i lampi trasparissero dal fondo della scena facendo dei 'zigzag' nella tela et... et... e tante altre cose. Bisognerà secondarmi in tutto perché io ho fatto della musica con molte intenzioni. Tu prenderai dei capelli (secondo il solito) ma alla scena della recita tu dirai: *Egli aveva ragione,* ammesso non si faccia fiasco." The full text of the letter can be found in Evan Baker, "Lettere di Giuseppe Verdi a Francesco Maria Piave, 1843–1865. Documenti della Frederick R. Koch Foundation Collection e della Mary Flagler Cary Collection presso la Pierpont Morgan Library di New York" in *Studi verdiani* 4 (1986–1987), pp. 158–159.
63. Translation taken from William Weaver, *Seven Verdi Librettos* (New York: W. W. Norton, 1975), pp. 17–20 and 42–45 respectively.
64. This design is illustrated in Muraro, *Giuseppe Bertoja,* plate 9.
65. An additional study is in the Museo Correr, Venice, and the finished design is in Museo Ricchieri, Pordenone. See Muraro, *Giuseppe Verdi,* plates 11 and 12.
66. This sentence was omitted from the standard but flawed biography of Verdi by Franco Abbiati, *Verdi* (Milan: Ricordi, 1963), vol. 2, p. 105. Consequently, later transcriptions and translations of this letter do not contain this sentence. The original of the letter is in the Pierpont Morgan Library.
67. *Teatri, arte e letteratura,* 19 March 1851.
68. This design is now in the Museo Ricchieri, Pordenone. It was published in the program book of the Teatro la Fenice, *La traviata,* 1992 season, p. 125.
69. It was after the premiere of his *Les Vêpres siciliennes* at the Opéra on 13 June 1855 and the subsequent publication of the staging manual by Louis Palianti that Verdi began applying many of the practical aspects of staging to his works in the Italian theaters.

Verdi had sent a copy of the staging manual to Piave from Paris for his use in the premiere of the Italian version, *Giovanna de Guzman,* on 16 February 1856 at La Fenice. See David Rosen, "The Staging of Verdi's Operas: An Introduction to the Ricordi 'Disposizione sceniche,'" in *Report of the Twelfth Congress of the International Musicological Society, Berkeley 1977* (Kassel: Bärenreiter, 1981), pp. 444–453.

70. "Pensi alle decorazioni ed ai costumi. Oh le decorazioni potrebbero essere così belle in questo Simone! In tre specialmente un pittore dovrebbe e potrebbe fare molto bene. Ma le scene dovrebbero essere a doppi e tripli teloni, ed i <u>praticabili</u>, non sgabelli come quegli del Guglielmo Tell ma veri praticabili." Conati, *Bottega,* p. 383.

71. Emphasis Verdi's. In other words, the entire depth of the stage should be utilized.

72. Conati, *Bottega,* p. 401.

73. Each scenario has been transcribed in Conati, "La disposizione scenica per il *Simon Boccanegra* di Verdi."

74. Girardi, *Cronologia,* p. 218.

75. "A giorno, verso il tramonto. Salone del palazzo ducale in Genova. A sinistra in fondo è una porta che mette direttamente al foro; presso al proscenio un'uscio nascosto. Alla destra una grande porta la quale conduce ad interni saloni. Di fronte largo e lungo poggiolo praticabile, fuor del quale si vede la piazza Doria. Davanti il poggiolo vi sieno cortinaggi di tappezzeria da chiudersi e aprirsi a vista a mediante cordoni. Bisogna quindi, che sieno solidamente sostenuti. Bisogna darne a tempo le ordinazioni a chi spettano. Le pareti della sala potrano [essere] decorate da quadri storici; spiccherà nel soppalco lo stemma della repubblica Genovese.

"La suddetta scena a notte illuminata da una lucerna posta sopra un tavolo. Le cortine davanti al poggiolo saranno tirate, ed aprendole a vista del pubblico lasceranno vedere la piazza Doria architettonicamente illuminata. Tale illuminazione si spegnerà gradatamente." Original in La Fenice archives. Transcription in Conati, "La disposizione scenica per il *Simon Boccanegra* di Verdi," pp. 47–48.

76. For a specific musical analysis, see Julian Budden's *Operas of Verdi,* vol. 2, pp. 322–328.

77. See Conati's "La disposizione scenica per il *Simon Boccanegra* di Verdi" for further details.

Postscript

1. Celestine Bohlen, "A Stunned Venice Surveys the Ruins of a Beloved Hall," *The New York Times,* (31 January 1996), C11. Pros and cons of rebuilding according to the 1836 plan are reviewed in Franco Zeffirelli, "Zeffirelli: 'Prendiamo esempio dalla Scala, deve rinascere come prima,'" *Corriere della sera* (31 January 1996), 3.

2. Alan Riding, "Venice Opera's Rebirth: As It Was or Might Be," *The New York Times,* (1 April 1996), B1.

3. Claudio Pasqualetto, "La Fenice perduta," *Corriere della sera* (2 February 1996), 10. "L'ultima imputata per il rogo, intanto, sembra essere la macchina per il caffè del bar al secondo piano del Teatro, che restava perennemente accesa."

4. Bohlen, "Stunned Venice," C11.

5. "Preziosi affreschi?," *Corriere della sera* (2 February 1996), 10.

6. Ibid.

7. Claudio Pasqualetto, "La Fenice risorgerà a tempo di record," *Corriere della sera* (31 January 1996), 3.

8. See Claudio Pasqualetto, "La Fenice perduta," *Corriere della sera* (2 February 1996), 10.

Chapter Nine

1. Translation from Stewart Spencer, *Wagner's* Ring of the Nibelung (New York: Thames and Hudson, 1993), p. 70.
2. *Cosima Wagner's Diaries,* trans. Geoffrey Skelton (New York: Harcourt, Brace, Jovanovich, 1978), vol. 1, p. 858. Hereafter cited as *Diaries.* See also Cosima Wagner, *Die Tagebücher* (Munich: Piper, 1976), vol. 1, p. 930. Hereafter cited as *Tagebücher.*
3. The entire backstage area, particularly after the 1920s, has undergone numerous renovations. Two publications survey the construction of the Festspielhaus and its evolution up to the present: Heinrich Habel, *Festspielhaus und Wahnfried* (Munich: Prestel, 1985) and *Baugeschichte des Bayreuther Festspielhauses.* "Dort stehe es, auf dem lieblichen Hügel bei Bayreuth" (Bayreuth: Bayerische Vereinsbank Munich, 1994).
4. An early photograph of the stage is reproduced in Herbert Barth, Dietrich Mack, and Egon Voss (eds.), *Wagner: A Documentary Biography* (New York: Oxford University Press, 1975), plate 26.
5. Eduard Genast, *Aus Weimars klassischer Zeit: Erinnerungen eines alten Schauspielers* (Stuttgart: R. Lutz, 1905), p. 84. Cited in Ernest Newman, *Richard Wagner* (New York: Alfred A. Knopf, 1933), vol. 1, p. 174.
6. See C. F. Baumann, *Bühnentechnik im Festspielhaus Bayreuth* (Munich: Prestel, 1980), p. 18. Hereafter cited as *Bühnentechnik.*
7. More detailed information is available in Baumann, *Bühnentechnik,* p. 19.
8. "In Wahrheit, . . . des alten Rigaschen Stadttheaters in der Königstrasse nach unseren heutigen Begriffen ein ziemlich düsterer Raum, mit nur einem einzigen Rang versehen, über welchem sich sofort die Galerie erhob, von bürgerlichen Familien häufig benützt, indem sich jüngere und ältere Damen, mit ihrem Strickstrumpf und den nötigen Erfrischungen versehen, frühzeitig daselbst einfanden, um auf den unnummerierten Sitzen möglichst an der Brüstung behaglich Platz nehmen zu können und der kommenden Dinge zu harren. Mit Bezug auf diesen Raum interpellierte der aus Riga gebürtige Violoncellist Arved Poorten den Meister, indem er ihn einen Stall, eine Scheune nannte: 'wie haben Sie denn, Meister, darin dirigieren können?' Da habe ihm Wagner ernsthaft erwidert: drei Dinge seien ihm aus dieser 'Scheune' als merkwürdig in der Erinnerung geblieben: erstlich das stark aufsteigende, nach Art eines Amphitheaters sich erhebende Parkett, zweitens die Dunkelheit des Zuschauerraumes und drittens das ziemlich tief liegende Orchester. 'Wenn er je einmal dazu käme, sich ein Theater nach seinen Wünschen zu errichten, so werde er diese drei Dinge in Betracht ziehen, das habe er sich schon damals gedacht.'" C. F. Glasenapp, *Das Leben Richard Wagners* (Leipzig: Breitkopf und Härtel, 1923), vol. 1, pp. 288–289.
9. Baumann, *Bühnentechnik,* pp. 18–22. Baumann discounted the effect Riga may have played, claiming it "incredible" that Wagner would have placed such an emphasis upon this theater without having taken into account other theaters, particularly in Paris. Nonetheless, some aspects of this story contain grains of truth.
10. As a youth Wagner had much exposure to theatrical practices; several members of his immediate family were involved in spoken theater at Leipzig.
11. For an excellent overview of theaters in nineteenth-century Paris, see Nicole Wild, *Dictionnaire des théâtres parisiens au XIXe siècle* (Paris: Aux amateurs de livres, 1989).
12. It is not known exactly which operas Wagner may have seen or when. Given Wagner's passion for the theater, one can only surmise he attended, saw, and heard much during his residence in Paris. It is inconceivable that he wrote his articles on Halevy's *La reine*

de Chypre (premiered at the Opéra on 22 December 1841) or Weber's *Le Freyschütz* (Berlioz's adaptation for the Opéra; 7 June 1841) without having attending the respective performances.

13. A brief but excellent survey of audiences may be found in Steven Huebner's "Opera Audiences in Paris 1830–1870," *Music and Letters* 50 (1989), 206–225.

14. A translation of the review is in R. Jacobs and G. Skelton, eds. and trans., *Wagner Writes from Paris: Stories, Essays and Articles by the Young Composer* (London: George Allen and Unwin, 1973), pp. 138–155.

15. Edmond Duponchel was director of the Paris Opéra (1837 to 1843, 1847 to 1849) and its chief stage director. *Der Freischütz* was revised by Berlioz as *Le Freyschütz* and staged by Duponchel at the Opéra in 1841.

16. Hector Berlioz, *Evenings with the Orchestra,* "Fourth Evening," trans. and ed. Jacques Barzun (New York: Alfred A. Knopf, 1956), pp. 54–55. See also Hector Berlioz, *Les soirées de l'orchestre* (Paris: Calmann-Lévy, 1922), "Quatrième Soirée," p. 59.

17. Wagner to Ferdinand Heine [end of January, 1842]. Translation in Stewart Spencer and Barry Millington, *Selected Letters of Richard Wagner* (New York: W. W. Norton, 1988), no. 43. See also Richard Wagner, *Sämtliche Briefe.* Herausgegeben im Auftrage der Richard-Wagner-Stiftung Bayreuth (Leipzig: Deutscher Verlag für Musik, 1983), vol. 1, pp. 586–587, no. 192. Hereafter cited as *Sämtliche Briefe.*

18. It stood in this form until its destruction by fire in 1869. It was rebuilt again by Semper in 1878.

19. Twelve illustrated plates detailing the plans of the theater were published by Gottfried Semper as *Das königliche Hoftheater zu Dresden* (Braunschweig: F. Wiewig, 1849).

20. The newspaper reviews made much of the horses.

21. For this essay, Ellis's translations occasionally have been modified slightly for ease of reading. See Wagner's "A Communication to My Friends," in *Richard Wagner: Prose Works,* vol. 1, *The Art-Work of the Future, etc.,* trans. William Ashton Ellis (London: Kegan Paul, Trench, Trübner, 1895). Hereafter cited as *Art-Work of the Future,* Ellis.

22. Despléchin recreated part of the settings for the first performances at the Paris Opéra on 13 March 1861.

23. Much documentation survives detailing not only Wagner's aesthetic points of view towards the text and towards the production of music and theater but also his superb organizational skills particularly when given (if ever) complete freedom to place his plans into effect.

24. Wagner was also disappointed in other German theaters, especially in Berlin, both with their attempts to produce his works and with the attitudes of the court, its ministries, and the Berlin public.

25. From Richard Wagner, "Theaterreform (1849)" in *Sämtliche Schriften und Dichtungen* (Leipzig, n.d.), vol. 12, p. 234.

26. See Wagner's anecdotes about Spontini at rehearsals for his *La vestale* in Dresden.

27. Richard Wagner, *My Life,* trans. Arnold Witthall (Cambridge University Press, 1991), pp. 342–343. See also Wagner, *Mein Leben* (Munich: Paul List, 1963), p. 356.

28. The Royal Library in Dresden probably owned architectural works of Vitruvius in a German translation. One such work was *Des aller namhafftigsten und Hocherfarnesten Romischen Architecti . . . Zehen Bücher . . . Erst verteuscht . . .* (Basel: S. Henricpetri, 1575). In his capacity as court conductor, Wagner certainly had access to its library.

29. For a detailed chronology of Wagner's activities during his residence in Zurich, see Werner G. Zimmermann, *Richard Wagner in Zürich: Eine Chronik* (Zürich: Präsidialabteilung der Stadt Zürich, 1983).

30. Wagner's writing is not easy to read, even for native German speakers. Ashton Ellis's translations often reflect Wagner's tortuous syntax. From *Art-Work of the Future,* trans. Ellis, vol. 1, p. 76. See also Richard Wagner, *Das Kunstwerk der Zukunft* in *Gesammelte Schriften und Dichtungen* (Leipzig: Fritsch, 1888), vol. 3, p. 49 (hereafter cited as *Das Kunstwerk der Zukunft*): "Der Luxus ist ebenso herzlos, unmenschlich, unersättlich und egoistisch, als das Bedürfnis, welches ihn hervorruft, das er aber, bei aller Steigerung und Überbietung seines Wesens nie zu stillen vermag, weil das Bedürfnis eben selbst kein natürliches, deshalb zu befriedigendes ist, und zwar aus dem Grunde, weil es als ein unwahres, auch keinen wahren, wesenhaften Gegensatz hat, in dem es aufgehen, sich also vernichten, befriedigen könnte."

31. *Art-Work of the Future,* Ellis, vol. 1, pp. 157–158. See also *Das Kunstwerk der Zukunft,* p. 125.

32. *Art-Work of the Future,* Ellis, vol. 1, p. 184. See also *Das Kunstwerk der Zukunft,* p. 150.

33. *Art-Work of the Future,* Ellis, vol. 1, pp. 184–185. See also *Das Kunstwerk der Zukunft,* pp. 150–152.

34. Spencer and Millington, *Selected Letters,* no. 116. See also Wagner, *Sämtliche Briefe,* vol. 3, pp. 404–405, no. 105: "Ich denke daran, den Siegfried wirklich noch in Musik zu setzen, nur bin ich nicht gesonnen, ihn auf's geradewohl vom ersten besten Theater aufführen zu lassen: im Gegenteil trage ich mich mit den allerkühnsten Plänen. . . . Dann würde ich nämlich hier [in Zürich], wo ich gerade bin, nach meinem Plane aus brettern ein Theater errichten lassen, die geeignetsten Sänger dazu mir kommen und Alles nötige für diesen einen besonderen fall mir so herstellen lassen, daß ich einer vortrefflichen Aufführung der Oper gewiß sein könnte . . . drei Vorstellungen in einer Woche hintereinander geben, worauf dann das Theater abgebrochen wird und die Sache ihr Ende hat. Nur so etwas kann mich noch reizen."

35. This particular issue is a tricky one for study and discussion; reams of paper have been used in analyses of this aspect of Wagnerian aesthetics. For overall discussion see Dieter Borchmeyer, *Theory and Theatre* (Oxford: Clarendon Press, 1991), part 1.

36. Information from Gottfried Kummer, *Beiträge zur Geschichte des Zürcher Aktientheaters 1843–1890* (Zurich: Leemann, 1938). Iconographic material for the interior of the theater apparently has not survived. Exterior views can be found in Herbert Barth, Dietrich Mack, and Egon Voss (eds.), *Wagner: A Documentary Biography* (New York: Oxford University Press, 1975), plate 82.

37. Chronology from Zimmermann, *Wagner in Zürich.*

38. Nonetheless, Wagner returned the following year to conduct his *Holländer* (1852) and again for *Tannhäuser* (1855). Zimmermann, *Wagner in Zürich.*

39. *Ein Theater in Zürich,* in *Gesammelte Schriften und Dichtungen,* vol. 5, pp. 20–52. "A Theater in Zurich," Ellis, vol. 2, pp. 23–58.

40. See Borchmeyer, *Theory and Theatre.*

41. "The Preface to the Publication of the Poem of the Stage Festival, *Der Ring des Nibelungen,*" Ellis, vol. 5, pp. 276–277. A modern translation may be found in Barth, *Wagner,* pp. 199–200. See also "Vorwort zur Herausgabe der Dichtung des Bühnenfestspiels *Der Ring des Nibelungen,*" in *Gesammelte Schriften und Dichtungen,* vol. 6, p. 275: "würde ich dann noch besonders die Unsichtbarkeit des Orchesters, wie sie durch eine, bei amphitheatralischer Anlage des Zuschauerraumes mögliche, architektonische Täuschung zu bewerkstelligen wäre, von großem Werte halten. Jedem wird die Wichtigkeit hiervon einleuchten, der mit der Absicht, den wirklichen Eindruck einer dramatischen Kunstleistung zu gewinnen, unseren Opernaufführungen beiwohnt, und durch den unerläßlichen Anblick der mechanischen Hilfsbewegungen beim

Vortrage der Musiker und ihrer Leitung unwillkürlich zu Augenzeugen technischer Evolutionen gemacht wird, die ihm durchaus verborgen bleiben sollten, fast ebenso sorgsam, als die Fäden, Schnüre, Leisten und Bretter der Theaterdekorationen, welche, aus den Kulissen betrachtet, einen bekanntlich alle Täuschung störenden Eindruck machen."

42. "Vorwort," in *Gesammelte Schriften und Dichtungen,* vol. 6, p. 281.
43. To track the ups and downs of this relationship, see Newman vols. 3 and 4 for biographical material. Further material is in Otto Strobel's five-volume compilation *König Ludwig II. und Richard Wagner: Briefwechsel.* (Karlsruhe: G. Braun, 1936–1939) of which generous portions are translated in Spencer and Millington.
44. During Wagner's sojourn in Munich, Ludwig's generosity extended also toward new productions of *Der fliegende Holländer* (4 December 1865), *Lohengrin* (16 June 1867), and *Tannhäuser* (1 August 1867). The settings from each of these productions were to be the standards by which other productions were measured before Bayreuth extended its influence. Later new productions also included *Rienzi* (21 June 1871) and *Siegfried* (10 June 1878). For exhaustive details of Wagner's operatic productions in Munich, see Detta and Michael Petzet's extraordinary *Die Richard Wagner Bühne Ludwigs II* (Munich: Prestel, 1970), with a complete iconography of more than 700 illustrations!
45. An early history of the edifice as found in Wagner's time, including technical descriptions, is F. Meiser, *Das königliche neue Hof- und Nationaltheater Gebäude zu München* (Munich: Georg Franz, 1840).
46. The following table lists comparative dimensions for theater stages (measurements rounded off to nearest half-meter).

Stage Dimensions for Major Theaters of Wagner's Day

column key:
1 = Theater, *2* = Proscenium width, *3* = Proscenium height, *4* = Stage width wall to wall, *5* = Stage depth curtain line to back, *6* = Wings, *7* = Stage height floor to grid

1	*2*	*3*	*4*	*5*	*6*	*7*
Bayreuth Festspielhaus (1876)	13	12	28	23	7	29.5
Dresden Hoftheater (1842–1869)	12	14	30	23.5	9	24
Milan Teatro alla Scala (1776)	14	12	26	23	10	25
Munich Court Opera (1825)	12	14	29	25.5	9	31
Paris, Opéra Palais Garnier (1875)	15.5	14	53	26.5	10	36
Paris, Opéra Rue le Peletier (1821)	13	14	24	30	12	22
Venice Teatro la Fenice (1792)	13	12	18	17	6	17
Vienna Court Opera (1869)	14.5	12	30	26	9	26
Vienna Kärntnertor Theater (1763–1869)	13	11	20	12	5	16

47. Habel, *Festspielhaus,* p. 38.
48. Ibid., p. 41.
49. Semper codified his conceptions in an essay dating from 1867, which was first published in 1906. A partial English translation is in Barth, *Wagner,* pp. 206–207. See also Habel,

Festspielhaus, p. 630: "Es entsteht zwischen beiden ein gleichsam neutraler Zwischenraum, dessen Abschluß nach allen Seiten hin, nach oben, unten und seitwärts vom Auge des Zuschauers nicht verfolgt werden kann, so daß die wahre Entfernung der Einfassung der Bühne, die sich jenseits dieses Zwischenraumes erhebt, für das abschätzende Auge aus Mangel an Haltpunkten nicht wohl ermeßbar ist, besonders, wenn letzteres noch außerdem durch passend angebrachte perspektivische und optische Mittel über diese Entfernung getäuscht wird."

50. The Margrave's opera house is today among the few surviving Baroque theaters. The original Baroque stage, along with its machinery, unfortunately no longer exists. A brief history of the theater may be found in Luisa Hagen and Lorenz Seelig, *Markgräfliches Opernhaus* (Munich: Bayerische Verwaltung der Staatlichen Schlösser, Gärten und Seen, 1991).

51. Spencer and Millington, no. 400, Petzet, *Wagner Bühne,* p. 808. Wagner led a performance of Beethoven's Ninth Symphony in the theater.

52. Nicknamed by Wagner "Theaterbrand," a pun meaning "theater fire." Wagner thought very highly of Brandt, calling him "a brilliant stage technician" in a letter to King Ludwig dated 1 October 1874. See Hermann Kaiser, *Der Bühnenmeister Carl Brandt* (Darmstadt: Eduard Roether, 1968) for further details on the life and works of Brandt.

53. Spencer and Millington, no. 402.

54. "*Entzückend, bezaubernd ist dieser Punkt!*"

55. It has been suggested that Neumann, being involved in large building projects occurring in Berlin, simply lost interest in the Bayreuth undertaking.

56. Last sentence emphasis mine. Spencer and Millington, no. 407. See also Habel, *Festspielhaus,* p. 340: "1. Das Theatergebäude durchaus nur als *provisorisches* halten: mir wäre es recht, wenn es ganz nur aus Holz wäre, wie Turner- und Sängerfesthallen: keine andere Solidität, als die welche es vor Einsturz sichert; Deshalb hier sparen—sparen, keine Verzierung. Wir geben mit diesem Bau nur den Schattenriß der Idee, und übergeben diesen der *Nation zur Ausführung* als monumentales Gebäude. 2. Maschinerie und Decoration, Alles auf das ideale, innere Kunstwerk Bezügliche—ganz vollkommen. Hier nichts sparen: Alles wie für lange Dauer berechnet, nichts provisorisches." Another letter to Feustel two days later reiterates these points.

57. Spencer and Millington, no. 407. Spencer restored a number of passages from the original letter that were previously censored. These passages do not shed a positive light on the court.

58. Illustrated in Habel, *Festspielhaus,* plate B 63.

59. Ibid., p. 351.

60. Richard Wagner, *Das Bühnenfestspielhaus zu Bayreuth: nebst einem Bericht über die Grundsteinlegung desselben* (Leipzig, Fritsch, 1873); republished in *Gesammelte Schriften und Dichtungen,* vol. 9, pp. 322–344 with six plates. Ellis's translation, "The Festival-Playhouse at Bayreuth with an Account of the Laying of its Foundation-Stone," appeared in vol. 5, pp. 320–340, but without the plates.

61. Ellis, vol. 5, pp. 321–338, passim. See also *Bühnenfestspielhaus,* in *Gesammelte Schriften und Dichtungen,* vol. 9, pp. 326–339, passim.

62. A brief historical overview of the "invisible orchestra" is offered by C. Kipke, "Das unsichtbare Orchester: Eine historisch-kritische Studie," *Bayreuther Blätter,* 12 (9/10, 1889), pp. 324–347.

63. Illustrations of the orchestral seating plans from *Parsifal* are reproduced in Habel, *Festspielhaus,* plates B 91, B 92.

64. Nowadays, tickets to the Wagner festival are extremely difficult to obtain, and there is a five-year waiting list. In keeping with democratic ideals, a lottery is held for the distribution of available tickets.

65. The Brückner brothers painted the scenery and designed most of Wagner's later Bayreuth productions. Detailed information may be found in an exhibition catalogue, *Die Bühnenwerkstatt der Gebrüder Brückner* (Bayreuth: Bayerische Vereinsbank, 1989).

66. A complete discussion of the pros (primarily artistic reasons) and cons (inability to read libretti during performances, lack of safety, and the possibility of jeopardizing morals) may be found in Baumann, *Bühnentechnik*, pp. 256–261.

67. Ibid., p. 123, for detailed listing and discussion. Although electric lighting for the stage in general was not introduced until 1886, some special effects used electric lighting (gold in the Rhine for *Das Rheingold;* the illuminated grail in the Temple scenes for *Parsifal*), albeit in a limited fashion.

68. *Raffen,* i.e., to gather up.

69. *Manchester Guardian,* 9 August 1876. Cited in *Bayreuth: The Early Years* (Cambridge University Press, 1991), pp. 95–96 and attributed to George Freemantle. The measurements are not entirely accurate.

70. *Diaries,* vol. 2, p. 21. See also *Tagebücher,* vol. 2, p. 39.

71. Cosima's letter is reprinted in *Neben meiner Kunst: Flugstudien, Briefe und persönliches von und über Arnold Böcklin* (Berlin: Vita, 1909), pp. 223–224.

72. See Glasenapp, *Leben,* vol. 6, p. 383: "Ich mußte eine Zeichnung vom Innern des Domes machen, welche mir später für den Entwurf des Gralstempel sehr nützlich wurde."

73. The idea of the moving scenery on painted drops was not new. In Paris, moving panoramas were seen at Daguerre's Diorama establishment; the Odeon Théâtre in the 1830s was another popular place using moving scenery. Wagner certainly saw these scenic effects in the boulevard theaters during his Parisian sojourn. This effect was shown in Vienna during the 1840s at the Josefstädter Theater in a wildly popular musical piece, *Der Zauberschleier* (The magic veil). The moving decoration depicted views of the Danube river from Valhalla (!) to Vienna. Wagner's technical director, Carl Brandt, had used such devices in his own theater in Darmstadt.

74. Cosima reported the details 13–14 January in her diaries. *Diaries,* vol. 2, p. 597; *Tagebücher,* vol. 2, pp. 664–665. Earlier discussions about the scenery, with other designers who did not participate in the final version, had taken place in November 1878 at Munich. See *Diaries,* vol. 2, p. 194.

75. Entries of 6 and 12 March respectively. *Diaries,* vol. 2, pp. 636, 639; *Tagebücher,* vol. 2, p. 709.

76. "Wald, schattig und ernst, doch nicht düster. Felsiger Boden. Eine Lichtung in der Mitte. Links aufsteigend wird der Weg zur Gralsburg angenommen. Der Mitte des Hintergrundes zu senkt sich der Boden zu einem tiefer gelegenen Waldsee hinab. Tagesanbruch." "Parsifal," in *Gesammelte Schriften und Dichtungen,* vol. 10, p. 324. For reproductions of the designs and photographs for the stage settings, see Petzet, *Wagner Bühne.*

77. See the first edition of the full score. *Parsifal* (Mainz: Schott, 1882), p. 83.

78. "Allmählich, während Gurnemanz und Parsifal zu schreiten scheinen, verwandelt sich die Bühne, von links nach rechts hin, in unmerklicher Weise: es verschwindet so der Wald; in Felsenwänden öffnet sich ein Tor, welches nun die Beiden einschließt; dann wieder werden sie in aufsteigenden Gängen sichtbar, welche sie zu durchschreiten scheinen. Lang gehaltene Posaunentöne schwellen sanft an: näher kommendes Glockengeläute. Endlich sind sie in einem mächtigen Saale angekommen, welcher nach

oben in eine hochgewölbte Kuppel, durch die einzig das Licht hereindringt, sich verliert. Von der Höhe über der Kuppel her vernimmt man wachsendes Geläute." "Parsifal," in *Gesammelte Schriften und Dichtungen,* vol. 10, p. 339.

79. The settings for this production remained in the repertory of the Festival until 1933 when it was replaced by a new production. This particular discussion is based on Kurt Söhnlein's personal reminiscences as a technical assistant with the Festival, 1924–1931. Details in Baumann, *Bühnentechnik,* pp. 157–161.

80. Ibid.

81. "Nun geht langsam die Verwandlung der Szene von links nach rechts, vom Zuschauerraum aus gesehen vor sich, bei einer weißlich grünen Beleuchtung der Bühne. Der Zug ist verschwunden und Gurnemanz und Parsifal bleiben auf dem Wege A bei der Stelle a´ stehen. Beide wiegen sich bloß auf den Fußballen hin und her. Die Decorationen bilden: Felsengrotten, eine nach aufwärts führende gedeckte Treppe, Säulen, niedrig und stark, welche helfen stützen. Parsifal und Gurnemanz verschwinden infolge der Wandeldekoration, welche sich jetzt über die ganze Szene erstreckt, auf kurze Zeit, und erscheinen dann wieder bei der Stelle a´´, da sie der durchbrochenen Dekoration wegen sichtbar werden und verschwinden hierauf vollends. Das letzte Stück der Dekoration stellt ein großes, zwischen enorm starken Pfeilern befindliches Eingangstor dar, durch das man in die Gralsburg gelangen soll. Dieses letzte Stück verschwindet nach abwärts in die Versenkung und ist von diesem Augenblicke an die Bühne in die Säulenhalle mit dem Kuppelgewölbe verwandelt. Man hört Glockengeläute." From *Nach stenografischen Notierungen verfaßt von Anton Schittenhelm, K.K. Hofopernsänger in Wien (Meinem lieben Kollegen Herrn The. Reichmann, Premier Amfortas). Nach dem Original autografiert von G. Philipp, 7. Juni, 1883, Inspizient am K.K. Hofopern-Theater in Wien. Lithografie von H. Schlittke.* The entire text, with its diagrams, was reproduced in *Richard Wagner: Sämtliche Werke,* vol. 30, *Dokumente zur Entstehung und ersten Aufführung des Bühnenweihfestspiels* Parsifal, pp. 139–155. According to the available documentation, Schittenhelm was not officially associated with the Festival.

82. Engelbert Humperdinck, one of the musical assistants, noted in his diary the location of the instruments during the rehearsals.

83. 21 June 1882. *Diaries,* vol. 2, p. 877. See also *Tagebücher,* vol. 2, p. 966.

84. "Den Vordergrund der Bühne bilden zwei große Pfeiler und zwei gleiche den Hintergrund. Von diesen vier Pfeilren wird die Kuppel getragen. Zu beiden Seiten der Hauptpfeiler vorne und hinten befinden sich die korrespondierenden Pfeiler für die Gänge. Unter dem Kuppelgeländе liegt der Speiseraum, zu dessen beiden Seiten Gänge in die Hallen der Burg führen. Rückwärts schließt ein goldenes Gitter den Raum ab. Durch die rechte Halle treten die Ritter des heiligen Gral 2 und 2 in den Vordergrund, die Schritte taktmäßig markierend. In dem Speiseraum steht in der Mitte desselben, erhöht und–fast–altarartig die Gralslade, (auf die der verschlossene Gral später gestellt wird), zu der 4 achteckige Stufen führen. Der Speisetisch der Ritter zieht sich halbkreisförmig von einem Pfeiler des Vordergrundes zum andern um die Gralslade. . . .

     "Gurnemanz und Parsifal sind sofort nach vollzogenem Wechsel der Szene von der Halle C her, rechts in den Vordergrund getreten und mehrere Schritte vor der Halle A stehen geblieben. Sie betrachten den Aufzug der Ritter, Knappen und Jünglinge." In *Richard Wagner, Dokumente,* p. 144.

85. The reports of problems with the scenery were leaking out to the press. The *Neue Zeitschrift für Musik* carried detailed reports of the rehearsals in each weekly issue throughout the rehearsal period of June and July 1882.

86. From Engelbert Humperdinck, *Briefe und Tagebücher.* vol. 2, *(1881–1883),* ed. Hans-Josef Irmen. (Cologne: Arno Volk, 1975), p. 135.

87. Ibid. See also Cosima's comments in the *Diaries,* vol. 2, p. 882.

88. The first edition of the full score (p. 92) states: "This passage from the growing and then diminishing of the ringing of bells may be repeated, according to the score, four times — if necessary, still more — so that the orchestra will again join in only at the cue from the conductor, as after a fermata." (*Dieser Takt wird, als anwachsendes und dann abnehmendes Glockengeläute, nach der Notenvorschrift viermal — wenn nötig, auch öfters — wiederholt, so daß das Orchester erst auf das Zeichen des Dirigenten, wie nach einer Fermate, wieder einfällt.*)

89. See *Tagebücher,* vol. 2, pp. 981, 982; *Diaries,* vol. 2, pp. 891, 892 respectively.

90. "The Sacred Stage Festival in Bayreuth 1882," Ellis, vol. 6, pp. 309–310, with slight modifications in the translation. In a letter to King Ludwig on 8 September 1882, Wagner gave a similar report, as the essay did not appear until later. The letter is published in Spencer and Millington, pp. 926–927; original in Strobel, vol. 3, pp. 248–249. The third act *Verwandlung* was discarded only for the first performances; in subsequent years it was reinstated. See also *Das Bühnenweihfestspiel in Bayreuth 1882,* in *Gesammelte Schriften und Dichtungen,* vol. 10, p. 305.

91. "Der Zuschauerraum verdunkelt sich vollständig. Wie eine Stimme aus einer andern Welt setzt das erste grosslinige Thema des Vorspiels ein. Dieser Eindruck ist unvergleichlich. . . .

"Der Vorhang teilt sich mäßig langsam. Ein schönes ernstes Bühnenbild entrollt sich dem Auge: Gurnemanz erwacht von den fernen Posaunentönen. . . .

"Als Gurnemanz sich anschickte, Parsifal zur Gralsburg zu geleiten, ergriff mich ein leiser Schwindel. Was geschah? Mir war es, als ob sich das Haus mit allen Zuhörern in Bewegung setzte. Die durch eine Wandeldekoration bewerkstelligte Umgestaltung der Szene hatte begonnen. Die Illusion war vollkommen. Man schritt nicht, man wurde getragen. 'Zum Raum wird hier die Zeit.' Auf je zwei oder drei beiderseits der Bühne hintereinander aufgestellten Säulen wickelten sich entsprechend abgestimmte Prospekte ab, bis die letzte Felswand sich hinwegschob und das in edelsten Dimensionen gemalte Innere der Gralsburg vor uns stand. Genau auf den C-dur Akkord ergoß sich Licht über das majestätische Bild. Eine beispiellose Wirkung war mit den einfachsten Mitteln hervorgebracht." Felix von Weingartner, *Lebenserinnerungen* (Zurich: Orell Füssli, 1923), vol. 1, pp. 131–132.

92. Gradually scenes were replaced, and Wagnerites were outraged when the entire production was retired in 1934 in favor of new designs by Alfred Roller. For details, see Frederic Spotts, *Bayreuth: A History of the Wagner Festival* (New Haven, Connecticut: Yale University Press, 1994).

Chapter Ten

1. Two thorough discussions of this literary movement as it ultimately relates to *verismo* are to be found in Dona De Sanctis, "Literary Realism and *verismo* Opera" (Ph.D. dissertation, The City University of New York, 1983); and in Adriana Guarnieri Corazzol, "Opera and *verismo*: Regressive Points of View and the Artifice of Alienation," trans. by Roger Parker, *Cambridge Opera Journal* 5/1 (1993), pp. 39–53. Luigi Capuana and, eventually, Gabriele d'Annunzio would number among Verga's contemporaries in the movement. French sources range from Dumas's (*fils*) *La dame*

aux camélias, which became Verdi's *La traviata,* to Zola's *La faute de l'Abbé Mouret,* which, according to Mosco Carner, *Puccini: A Critical Biography,* 2nd edition (New York: Holmes and Meier, 1974; reprint, 1988), p. 99, Puccini had once considered for an opera libretto. See, also, David Kimbell, *Italian Opera,* in National Traditions of Opera, ed. John Warrack (Cambridge University Press, 1991), p. 625. Kimbell, p. 623, notes additionally that "veristic" works were less political than the corresponding works in France, since the newly unified Italy was to its intellectuals still more a source of pride than discontent.

2. De Sanctis, "Literary Realism," pp. 9–10.

3. See Kimbell, *Italian Opera,* pp. 621–624, who cites D. Grant, *Realism,* The Critical Idiom 9 (London, 1970), especially pp. 20–40.

4. See Daniel C. Gerould, Introduction to *American Melodrama,* ed. by Daniel C. Gerould (New York: Performing Arts Journal Publications, 1983), pp. 8–9. Gerould notes that American melodrama was a particular "child" of France and its political upheaval. He cites (p. 9) the Russian playwright Adrian Piotrovsky, who notes that, "Melodrama is the child of transitional epochs. Chance and relative morality, these are its driving forces. Melodrama by its very nature is individualistic."

5. See Gerould, Introduction to *American Melodrama,* especially p. 9, and the plays in this volume, Belasco's *The Girl of the Golden West;* Boucicault's *The Poor of New York;* Aiken's and Stowe's *Uncle Tom's Cabin;* and Daly's *Under the Gaslight.*

6. Relevant studies include Scott Balthazar, "Evolving Conventions in Italian Serious Opera: Scene Structure in the Works of Rossini, Bellini, Donizetti, and Verdi, 1810–1850," (Ph.D. dissertation, University of Pennsylvania, 1985), and Jay Nicolaisen, *Italian Opera in Transition, 1871–1893* (Ann Arbor: UMI Research Press, 1980). See, also, Greenwald, "Dramatic Exposition and Musical Structure in Puccini's Operas," (Ph.D. dissertation, The City University of New York, 1991).

7. See Corazzol, "Opera and *verismo,*" p. 42.

8. See Lise-Lone Marker, *David Belasco: Naturalism in the American Theatre* (Princeton: Princeton University Press, 1975), p. 19, who discusses rehearsal techniques at the California Theatre in San Francisco in the 1870s, when David Belasco was first learning his craft. She notes that its routinely abbreviated rehearsal period was "an intrinsic factor in the earlier theatrical practice, in accordance with which each actor prepared his part independently and resented or distrusted interference and advice from others. Under these conditions, a director was plainly a superfluity, useful only for informing the players about sets, entrances and exits, handling of props, and positions on stage in crowded scenes requiring more complicated blocking."

9. See, for example, Sebastiano Serlio, *Regole generali di archittetura* (Paris, 1545), excerpted in A. M. Nagler, *Sources of Theatrical History* (New York, 1952), pp. 73–81, who defines a difference in lighting for the three "standard" dramatic genres: tragedy, comedy, and satire; and Leone Ebreo di Somi, *Dialoghi* (Mantua, 1565), also excerpted in Nagler, pp. 107–110. Both are cited by Edward A. Langhans and Robert Benson, s.v. "Lighting," *New Grove Dictionary of Opera* (New York: Macmillan, 1992), pp. 1265–1266.

10. Adolphe Appia, *Die Musik und die Inscenierung* (Munich: Verlagsanstalt F. Bruckmann, 1899), trans. in Lee Simon, *The Stage Is Set* (New York: Harcourt, Brace, 1932), p. 358, and partially quoted by Langhans and Benson, "Lighting," p. 1269. Appia discusses the relationship between light and music in great detail in his original tract. See, especially, pp. 81–88.

11. Pioneers in this area included Adolphe Appia and Gordon Craig.

12. See Manfred Pfister, *The Theory and Analysis of Drama,* trans. John Halliday, European Studies in English Literature (Cambridge University Press, 1988; originally published as *Das Drama* [Munich: Wilhelm Fink, 1977]), p. 285.

13. Bernard Beckerman, *Dynamics of Drama: Theory and Method of Analysis* (New York: Drama Book Specialists, 1979), pp. 38–44.

14. See Pfister, *The Theory and Analysis,* p. 282.

15. Among Puccini's operas, *Le villi,* in particular, is geared to these conventional associations.

16. Puccini, in particular, suffered not only for his own unique art, which was at the time perceived to be *un*-Italian, but also for being in the shadow of Verdi. For a discussion of criticism by Puccini's contemporaries see my "Recent Puccini Research," *Acta musicologica* 65/1 (1993), especially pp. 23–25. See, also, William Winter, *The Life of David Belasco,* 2 vols. (New York: Moffat, Yard and Company, 1918; reprint, Freeport, New York: Books for Libraries Press, 1970), vol. 1, pp. 155 ff.

17. See William Ashbrook, *The Operas of Puccini* (New York: Oxford University Press, 1968; reprint, with foreword by Roger Parker, Ithaca, New York: Cornell University Press, 1985), p. 32, who notes that "A libretto that took three years and seven men to complete is no laughing matter." The final authorship may actually be credited to eight men: Ricordi, Giacosa, Illica, Puccini, Leoncavallo, Praga, Oliva, and Adami, the last supplying a single line in Act IV (see Ashbrook, p. 32 n. 47).

18. See, for example, Giacosa's letter of 6 October 1893, letter no. 92 in Eugenio Gara, ed. *Carteggi pucciniani* (Milan: Ricordi, 1958).

19. David Belasco, *The Theatre through Its Stage Door,* ed. Louis V. Defoe (New York: Benjamin Blom, 1919; reprint, 1969), p. 46. Belasco gives numerous examples of his revisions, citing (p. 47) "The Rose of the Rancho" (seen by Puccini), which was changed at least a dozen times.

20. Carner, *Puccini,* p. 284.

21. Belasco, *The Theatre,* p. 56.

22. According to Carner, *Puccini,* p. 126, the play was first produced at the Herald Theatre in New York on 5 March 1900, with Blanche Bates in the starring role. She later took on the role of the Girl in Belasco's *The Girl of the Golden West.*

23. Quoted by Gösta M. Bergman, *Lighting in the Theatre* (Totowa, New Jersey: Rowman and Littlefield; Stockholm: Amqvist och Wiksell International, 1977), p. 306, from Belasco's article, "Poetry in Light—a Prophesy for the Drama," *New York Herald* 1903.

24. See Louis Hartmann, *Theatre Lighting: A Manual of the Stage Switchboard,* foreword by David Belasco (New York: D. Appleton, 1930; reprint, New York: Drama Book Specialists, 1970), pp. 17–18.

25. Many of the musical points made here have been discussed in greater detail in chapter three of Greenwald, "Dramatic Exposition."

26. Such associations seem to be more German or eastern European than Italian. See, for example, the Dracula legends or *Grimm's Fairy Tales,* in which the setting sun is often a condition of the plot, and most of the action (usually evil) occurs after dark. Charles Rosen and Henri Zerner, *Romanticism and Realism: The Mythology of Nineteenth-Century Art* (New York: Viking Press, 1984), p. 61, note, however, that such symbols are so deeply rooted in ancient tradition, so pervasive in the entire culture, that their artificiality is no longer felt and they appear to be part of human nature. See also, Beckerman, *Dynamics of Drama,* pp. 38–44, and Pfister, *Theory and Analysis of Drama,* pp. 282–285.

27. See Giacomo Puccini, *Le villi* (Milan: G. Ricordi, 1956, plate no. 49457).

28. See Giacomo Puccini, *Turandot* (Milan: G. Ricordi, 1987, plate no. 121329).

29. The Prince even remarks upon the time of day as he claims his victory (Act III, *40*+7): "It is morning! And love is born with the sun!" (*E l'alba! E amor nasce col sole!*). I have indicated locations in the score by using rehearsal numbers in italics plus or minus a certain number of measures. Thus, if the measure to which I refer is five bars before rehearsal number 12, it will be indicated as follows: *12*-5. If it is five bars after, the reference is *12*+5. All translations are mine unless otherwise indicated.

30. See Giacomo Puccini, *Manon Lescaut* (Milan: G. Ricordi, 1980, plate no. P.R. 113).

31. "Sola, perduta, abbandonata!" was originally cut, but Puccini wrote to Carlo Clausetti in December 1920 (Gara, *Carteggi,* letter no. 781), to have it reinstated. Ashbrook, *The Operas,* p. 34, who calls Act IV a "miscalculation," notes further (p. 35 and, also, n. 54) that "Sola, perduta, abbandonata" was restored for the thirtieth anniversary production of the opera, conducted by Toscanini, and reinstated into the printed scores about 1923.

32. Of several card games in Puccini's operas (including the one in *Manon Lescaut* and three in *La fanciulla*) only Billy Jackrabbit, in *La fanciulla del West,* plays cards in the daytime. He begins a game of "Patience" at dawn and plays for the duration of Act III, oblivious to all (see the stage directions beginning at Act III, *6*-5). See Giacomo Puccini, *La fanciulla del West* (Milan: G. Ricordi, 1980, plate no. 113483).

33. Puccini also compressed the action into less than a twenty-four hour period, while Belasco's fourth act takes place a week later. One other significant change is the transferal of Belasco's third-act academy scene to Puccini's first act.

34. Marker, *David Belasco: Naturalism,* p. 139.

35. Belasco, *The Theatre,* p. 56. Belasco notes that the sunset was perfectly good, but not "Californian," a typology he never really defines. Never to let hard work go to waste, especially when it had cost him five thousand dollars, Belasco ultimately sold the formula for this particular sunset "to the producers of 'Salomy Jane,'" where "it proved very effective and perfectly adjusted to the needs of that play."

36. It is not surprising, then, that Belasco created a string of "wild" West settings—*The Girl I Left Behind Me* and *The Rose of the Rancho,* followed by *The Girl of the Golden West*— all generated, no doubt, from his youthful memories.

37. Belasco, *The Theatre,* p. 57.

38. Gerould, *American Melodrama,* p. 24. This "moving" panorama, a precursor to film, was a standard "entertainment" in America from at least the 1830s. Belasco changed it slightly by moving it from the back of the stage to the front.

39. See David Belasco, *The Girl of the Golden West,* (New York: Samuel French, 1915), p. 11.

40. Music for the prelude and entr'actes in the original production was composed by William (Wallace) Furst, who also had been the music director and composer of incidental music for Belasco's *Madame Butterfly.* See Allan W. Atlas, "Belasco and Puccini: 'Old Dog Tray' and the Zuni Indians," *The Musical Quarterly* 75 (1991), n. 19, who cites Gerald Bordman, *American Musical Theatre: A Chronicle* (New York: Oxford University Press, 1978); and Ken Bloom, *American Song: The Complete Musical Theatre Companion, 1900–1984* (New York: Facts on File Publications, 1985), vol. 1, nos. 2130, 3151.

41. Marker, *David Belasco: Naturalism,* p. 143.

42. Winter, *The Life of David Belasco,* vol. 1, p. 257, and quoted (in part) by Marker, *David Belasco: Naturalism,* p. 143.

43. Marker, *David Belasco: Naturalism,* p. 147.

44. Ibid., p. 147, points out that directors such as Antoine, Stanislavski, and Bloch, were also employing such techniques on the stage, although no opera composer prior to Puccini is known to have done so.

45. "Dalla grande porte del fondo e attraverso la finestra si scorge la valle, con la sua vegetazione selvaggia di sambuchi, quercie, conifere basse, tutta avvolta nel fiammeggiare del tramonto. Lontano, le montagne nevose si sfumano di toni d'oro e di viola. La luce violenta dell'esterno, che va calando rapidamente, rende anche più oscuro l'interno della 'Polka.' Nel buio appena si scorgono i contorni delle cose. A sinistra, quasi al proscenio, presso il camino, si vede rosseggiare la gragia del sigaro di Jack Rance." Trans. R. H. Elkin in Carlo Zangarini and Guelfo Civinini, *The Girl of the Golden West* (New York: Belwin, n.d.), p. 8. These and other lighting instructions do not appear in any of the available early sketches (NYpm, Koch 989, Koch 282) and continuity drafts (Acts I and II, only; NYpm, Lehman deposit [without number]) for *La fanciulla,* now housed in the Pierpont Morgan Library in New York. Clearly, these kinds of details were added later on.

46. See Greenwald "Dramatic Exposition," p. 101, especially example 17, in which the key of C major, especially as it relates to Nick's opening and closing of the saloon is illustrated. Puccini carries the lighting effect a step further at the very end of the act, as Minnie comes down to the footlights "and pauses under the only light which is still burning and which sheds a strong light on her face." At this point she reiterates in wonderment Johnson's observation about her face's being that of an angel. The scene is accompanied by an offstage humming chorus. Puccini first explored this sonority in *Madama Butterfly,* his only other directly Belasco-inspired creation.

47. Gara, *Carteggi,* letter no. 521. See, also, Greenwald, "Dramatic Exposition," pp. 34–36.

48. The gust of wind returns in Act II in a similarly intimate moment, as it blows open the door during Minnie's and Johnson's first kiss (Act II, 27-3 and 29), contrasting their physical closeness with the infinity of the outdoors. Puccini's musical mimicry of nature corresponds to Belasco's grand theatrical storm in Act II of the play, which Winter (*The Life of David Belasco,* vol. 2, p. 207) says "required a force of thirty-two trained artisans—a sort of mechanical orchestra, directed by a centrally placed conductor who was visible from the special station of every worker."

49. Belasco, *The Girl,* p. 47.

50. In such exterior settings as those of *Manon Lescaut* or *Turandot,* time is manifested more naturalistically through the gradual descent of darkness.

51. Belasco's participation in this event, however, seems to have been somewhat *ex officio,* as the opening night program acknowledges his contribution to the staging of the opera, without actually listing him with a specific title. As confirmation of this more or less advisory role—but one much appreciated—the Metropolitan's board of directors presented Belasco with a souvenir certificate. A reproduction of this may be found in Winter, *The Life of David Belasco,* vol. 2, opposite p. 218. Belasco, *The Theatre,* p. 103, provides some details of his direction of the opera, mostly, however, having to do with the difficulty of getting singers to act.

52. As Atlas, "Belasco and Puccini," n. 6, points out, the exact date of Puccini's first encounter with the play is uncertain. He was in New York to supervise a festival of his operas at the Metropolitan. His letter to Tito Ricordi of 18 February 1907 (Gara, *Carteggi,* letter no. 500) suggests that he had seen it already: "I have found good ideas in Belasco. . . ." Puccini's letter to Belasco, dated 7 March 1907, indicates that the viewing was fairly fresh and that he had seen it at Belasco's own theater. Atlas notes, however, that by 1907 it was running at the Academy of Music and had been replaced at the Belasco (Victory) Theatre by *The Rose of the Rancho* on 27 November 1906.

53. See Deborah Grace, "Reversal of Fortune," *Opera News* 57/12 (27 February 1993), p. 19, who claims that the theater had 1,100 orchestra seats. Winter, *The Life of David*

Belasco, vol. 2, p. 58, however, notes the capacity of the theater to have been 950: "300 in the gallery, 200 in the balcony, and 450 on the orchestra, or main, floor."

54. See Hartmann, *Theatre Lighting,* pp. 12–13 and Winter, *The Life of David Belasco,* vol. 2, p. 56.

55. *New York Morning Telegraph* (9 August 1925), quoted by Marker, *David Belasco: Naturalism,* pp. 37–38.

56. Grace, "Reversal of Fortune," p. 20. See, also, Hartmann, *Theatre Lighting,* p. 3.

57. Belasco, *The Theatre,* p. 55.

58. Ibid., p. 74.

59. Ibid., p. 56. See, also, "Stage Lighting," *Cambridge Guide to American Theatre,* ed. Don B. Wilmeth and Tice L. Miller (Cambridge University Press, 1993), p. 442.

60. Belasco, *The Theatre,* pp. 55–57, 80. Belasco eventually eliminated footlights. According to Marker, *David Belasco: Naturalism,* p. 83, his 1889 production of Sophocles's *Electra* at the Lyceum theater was the first run *sans* footlights.

61. Winter, *The Life of David Belasco,* vol. 2, p. 57.

62. Hartmann, *Theatre Lighting,* p. 3.

63. "Stage Lighting," in *Cambridge Guide,* p. 442.

64. See Winter, *The Life of David Belasco,* vol. 2, p. 245. See also, Bergman, *Lighting in the Theatre,* p. 288, who notes that the first lighting fixtures in the California Theatre were probably Swan lamps, the invention of the Englishman, Swan.

65. Belasco, *The Theatre,* p. 163.

66. Ibid., p. 164.

67. Joel Rubin, "The Technical Development of Stage Lighting Apparatus in the United States, 1900–1950," (Ph.D. dissertation, Stanford University, 1959), p. 79. Yet, as Rubin points out, pp. 82–83 n. 48, Belasco's claims have been proven false—incredibly—in the playwright's own theater programs which state, "The electrical equipment and effects are furnished by Kliegl Brothers."

68. See Bergman, *Lighting in the Theatre,* p. 290.

69. See Langhans and Benson, "Lighting," p. 1270.

70. Hartmann, *Theatre Lighting,* p. 26.

71. Marker, *David Belasco: Naturalism,* p. 83.

72. Hartmann, *Theatre Lighting,* p. 23.

73. Marker, *David Belasco: Naturalism,* p. 83.

74. Ibid., p. 82.

75. "Stage Lighting," in *Cambridge Guide,* p. 442.

76. See the illustration in Hartmann, *Theatre Lighting,* p. 46, which shows the "Gas" man at the Metropolitan Opera House with an "emergency" oil lantern hanging behind his head. According to Langhans and Benson, "Lighting," p. 1269, the Metropolitan did not employ a full-time "resident lighting designer" until 1976.

77. It was patented by Anton T. Kliegl, the brother of John Kliegl who was the chief electrician for the house. See Rubin, "Development of Stage Lighting," pp. 37–38.

78. Ibid., p. 37.

79. Ibid., p. 41. It is illustrated in Willmeth and Miller, *Cambridge Guide,* p. 443.

80. Ibid., p. 41.

81. Ibid., pp. 121–122.

82. Marker, *David Belasco: Naturalism,* p. 38.

83. Rubin, "Development of Stage Lighting," p. 37. While the immensity of the house may indeed have had an impact on the production of *La fanciulla del West,* it seems also to have had an impact on certain revisions in the score made specifically for the premiere.

Puccini, a skilled orchestrator and by this time a composer in his full maturity, was, nevertheless, used to the smaller scale of the European opera houses in which his works to date had been premiered. Thus, as Gabriele Dotto, "Opera, Four Hands: Collaborative Alterations in Puccini's *Fanciulla*," *Journal of the American Musicological Society* 42 (1989), 612–613, points out, the Metropolitan Opera House in New York with its 3,600 seats dwarfed La Scala in Milan with its 2,300 seats. Moreover, again perhaps owing to its size, the old house resonated quite differently. Thus, as Dotto notes, "While the distribution of sound in the old Met was fairly even, it suffered from two specific acoustical shortcomings . . . both tied to the vastness of the space: the distance between the stage and the reflecting surfaces in the hall meant that the sound was sapped of brilliance and sonority; and the low reverberation time dulled the sound." Among the many levels of changes made, according to Dotto (609–610), one set of rescorings in which the orchestration has been thinned and lightened and the doublings eliminated suggests that they were actually "alterations in the original timbral equilibrium" made to suit the abilities of the hall, and which, more important, became part of the definitive text.

84. Rubin, "Development of Stage Lighting," p. 38.
85. Ibid., p. 39.
86. Ibid., p. 39.
87. Kimbell, *Italian Opera,* p. 629.
88. See Giacomo Puccini, *Il tabarro* (Milan: G. Ricordi, 1984, plate no. 129782).

Bibliography

General Works

Appia, Adolphe. *Die Musik und die Inscenierung.* Munich: Verlagsanstalt F. Bruckmann, 1899.

Arundell, Dennis. *The Critic at the Opera.* London: Ernest Benn, 1957.

Badenhausen, Rolf, and Harald Zielske. *Bühnenformen, Bühnenräume, Bühnendekorationen—Beiträge zur Entwicklung des Spielorts.* Berlin: Erich Schmidt, 1974.

Bapst, Germain. *Essai sur l'histoire du théâtre.* Paris: Librairie Hachette 1983.

———. *Essai sur l'histoire des panoramas et des dioramas.* Paris: G. Masson, 1891.

Bergman, Gösta M. *Lighting in the Theatre.* Totowa, New Jersey: Rowman and Littlefield; Stockholm: Almqvist och Wiksell International, 1977.

Boll, André. *Les spectacles à travers les âges: Théâtre, cirque, music-hall, cafés-concerts, cabarets artistiques.* Paris: Éditions du Cygne, 1931.

Brockett, Oscar. *History of the Theatre.* 5th ed. Boston: Allyn and Bacon, 1987.

Brown, Van Dyke. *Secrets of Scene Painting and Stage Effects.* 6th ed. London: George Routledge and Sons, 1913.

Carlson, Marvin. *Places of Performance: The Semiotics of Theatre Architecture.* Ithaca, New York: Cornell University Press, 1989.

———. *Theatre Semiotics: Signs of Life.* Bloomington: Indiana University Press, 1990.

Chandler, Dean. *Outline of the History of Lighting by Gas.* London: S. Metropolitan Gas Company, 1936.

Claudon, Francis, Jean Mongrédien, Carl de Nys, and Karlheinz Roschitz. *Histoire de l'opéra en France.* N.p.: Fernand Nathan, 1984.

Contant, Clément. *Parallèle des principaux théâtres modernes de l'Europe et des machines théâtrales françaises, allemandes et anglaises.* Paris: Chez l'auteur, 1842.

Decugis, Nicole, and Suzanne Reymond. *Le décor de théâtre en France du Moyen-Age à 1925.* Paris: Compagnie Française des Arts Graphiques, 1953.

Dictionnaire critique et documentaire des peintres, sculpteurs, dessinateurs et graveurs de tous les temps et de tous les pays. 10 vols. New edition, ed. E. Bénézit. Paris: Librairie Grund, 1976 ff.

Dictionnaire de biographie française. 14 vols. Ed. M. Prévost and R. d'Amat. Paris: Letouzey et Ane, 1933 ff.

Dictionnaire universel des contemporains. Ed. G. Vapereau. 6th ed. Paris: Hachette, 1893.

Enciclopedia dello spettacolo. 9 vols. Rome: Le Maschere, 1954–62.

Filippi, Joseph de. *Parallèle des principaux théâtres modernes de l'Europe et des machines théâtrales françaises, allemandes et anglaises.* Illustrated Clément Contant. Paris: Chez l'auteur, 1860. Reprint, New York: Benjamin Bloom, 1968.

Forsyth, Michael. *Buildings for Music: The Architect, the Musician, and the Listener from the Seventeenth Century to the Present Day.* Cambridge, Massachusetts: the MIT Press [1985].

Gourret, Jean. *Histoire des salles de l'opéra de Paris.* Paris: Guy Trédaniel, 1985.

Hartnoll, Phyllis, ed. *The Oxford Companion to the Theatre.* London: Oxford University Press, 1951.

Hume, Robert D., ed. *The London Theatre World.* Carbondale: Southern Illinois University Press, 1980.

International Dictionary of Opera. Ed. by Steven LaRue. 2 vols. Detroit: St. James Press, 1993.

Izenour, George C. *Theater Design.* New York: McGraw Hill, 1977.

Johnson, James. "The French Musical Experience from the Old Regime to Romanticism." Ph.D. dissertation, University of Chicago, 1988.

Join-Diéterle, Catherine. "Evolution de la scénographie à l'Académie de Musique à l'époque Romantique." *Romantisme* 38 (1982), 65–76.

Jullien, Adolphe. *Histoire du costume au théâtre depuis les origines du théâtre en France jusqu'en nos jours.* Paris: G. Charpentier, 1880.

Kimbell, David. *Italian Opera.* In National Traditions of Opera. Ed. John Warrack. Cambridge University Press, 1991.

Lacy, Robin Thurlow. *A Biographical Dictionary of Scenographers.* New York: Greenwood Press, 1990.

Lange, Hans. *Vom Tribunal zum Tempel: Zur Architektur und Geschichte deutscher Hoftheater zwischen Vormärz und Restauration.* Marburg: Jonas, 1985.

Langhans, Edward A., and Robert Benson. "Lighting." *New Grove Dictionary of Opera.* New York: Macmillan, 1992. Vol. 2, pp. 1265–1277.

LaRue, Steven, ed. *International Dictionary of Opera.* 2 vols. Detroit: St. James Press, 1993.

Leacroft, Richard. *The Development of the English Playhouse.* Ithaca, New York: Cornell University Press, 1973.

Lecomte, Louis Henry. *Histoire des théâtres de Paris, 1402–1904.* 9 vols. Paris: H. Daragon, 1905–12. Reprint, Geneva: Slatkine, 1973.

Matheopoulos, Helena. *Diva: Great Sopranos and Mezzos Discuss Their Art.* Boston: Northeastern University Press, 1992.

Matthews, William. *A Historical Sketch of the Origin, Progress and Present State of Gas Lighting.* London: Rowland Hunter, 1827.

Nagler, A[lois] M. *A Source Book in Theatrical History.* New York: Dover Publications, 1959. Originally pub. 1952 as *Sources of Theatrical History.*

New Grove Dictionary of Music and Musicians. Ed. by Stanley Sadie. 20 vols. London: Macmillan, 1980.

New Grove Dictionary of Opera. Ed. by Stanley Sadie. 4 vols. London: Macmillan, 1992.

Nicoll, Allardyce. *The English Theatre: A Short History.* London: Thomas Nelson and Sons, 1936.

Oxford Companion to the Theatre. Ed. Phyllis Hartnoll. London: Oxford University Press, 1951.

Penzel, Frederick. *Theatre Lighting before Electricity.* Middletown, Connecticut: Wesleyan University Press, 1978.

Pestelli, Giorgio. *The Age of Mozart and Beethoven.* Trans. Eric Cross. Cambridge University Press, 1984.

Quantz, Johann Joachim. *On Playing the Flute.* Trans. Edward R. Reilly. London: Faber and Faber, 1966.

Raeburn, Michael, and Alan Kendall, eds. *Heritage of Music,* vol. 1: *Classical Music and Its Origins.* Oxford University Press, 1989.

Ratner, Leonard G. *Classic Music: Expression, Form, and Style.* New York: Schirmer Books, 1980.

Rosen, Charles. *The Classical Style: Haydn, Mozart, Beethoven.* New York: Viking Press, 1971.

Sachs, Edwin O. *Modern Opera Houses and Theatres.* 3 vols. London: Batsford, 1896–98.

Sadie, Stanley, ed. *New Grove Dictionary of Music and Musicians.* 20 vols. London: Macmillan, 1980.

———, ed. *New Grove Dictionary of Opera.* 4 vols. London: Macmillan, 1992.

Solerti, Angelo. *Gli albori del melodramma.* Milan, 1904. Reprint, Hildesheim: G. Olms, 1969.

———. *Le origini del melodramma.* Turin: Fratelli Bocca, 1903. Reprint, Hildesheim: G. Olms, 1969.

Southern, Richard. "Flat." *Oxford Companion to the Theatre.*

Survey of London. 42 vols. London: Athlone Press, 1900–.

Weaver, Robert Lamar, and Norma Wright Weaver. *A Chronology of Music in the Florentine Theater, 1590–1750.* Detroit Studies in Music Bibliography, no. 38. Detroit: Information Coordinators, 1978.

Weil, Mark S. *Baroque Theater and Stage Design.* St. Louis: Washington University, 1993.

Wickham, Glynne. *A History of the Theatre.* Cambridge University Press, 1985.

Zaslaw, Neal, ed. *Man and Music—The Classical Era: From the 1740s to the End of the 18th Century.* Englewood Cliffs, New Jersey: Prentice Hall, 1989.

Specialized Bibliographies

Chapter One

d'Amico, Silvio. "Buonarroti, Michelangelo il giovine (o il nepote)." *Enciclopedia dello spettacolo.* Rome: Le Maschere, 1954.

Bini, Mauro, ed. *Il teatro all'antica di Sabbioneta.* Modena: Il Bulino, 1991.

Borsi, Franco. *Il potere e lo spazio: La scena del principe.* Florence: Edizioni Medicee, 1980.

Buonarroti, Michelangelo. *Descrizione delle felicissime nozze della Cristianissma Maestà di Madama Maria Medici Regina di Francia e di Navarra.* Florence: Marescotti, 1600.

Carter, Tim. "A Florentine Wedding of 1608." *Acta musicologica* 55 (1983), 89–107.

Cavicchi, Adriano. "Teatro monteverdiano e tradizione teatrale ferrarese." In *Congresso internazionale sul tema Claudio Monteverdi e il suo tempo.* Ed. Raffaello Monterosso, 139–156. Verona: Stamperia Valdonega, 1969.

Fabbri, Mario, Elvira Garbero Zorzi, and Anna Maria Petrioli. *Il luogo teatrale a Firenze: Brunelleschi, Vasari, Buontalenti, Parigi.* Milan: Electa, 1975.

Fabbri, Paolo. *Monteverdi.* Turin: E. D. T., 1985.

———. *Monteverdi.* Trans. Tim Carter. Cambridge University Press, 1994.

Fabbri, Paolo and Angelo Pompilio, eds. *Il corago, o vero alcune osservazioni per metter bene in scena le composizioni drammatiche.* Florence: Olschki, 1983.

Ghisi, Federico. "Le Feste medicee, gli spettacoli teatrali, gli intermedi e la nascita dell'opera in musica." S.v. "Firenze." *Enciclopedia dello spettacolo.* Rome: Le Maschere, 1954.

Hewitt, Barnard. *The Renaissance Stage. Documents of Serlio, Sabbattini, and Furttenbach.* Trans. Allardyce Nicoll, John H. McDowell, and George R. Kernodle. Coral Gables: University of Miami Press, 1958.

Hill, John Walter. "Oratory Music in Florence, I: Recitar Cantando, 1583–1655." *Acta musicologica* 51 (1979), 108–136.

Mamone, Sara. "Feste e spettacoli a Firenze e in Francia per le nozze di Maria dei Medici con Enrico IV." *Quaderni di teatro* 2 (1980), *Il teatro dei Medici.* Ed. Ludovico Zorzi, 218.

——. *Il teatro nella Firenze medicea.* Nuova edizione aggiornata. Milan: Mursia, 1981.

Mancini, Franco, Maria Teresa Muraro, and Elena Povoledo, eds. *Illusione e pratica teatrale: Proposte per una lettura dello spazio scenico dagli intermedi fiorentini all'opera comica veneziana. Catalogo della mostra.* Venice: Neri Pozza, 1975.

Marotti, Ferruccio. *Lo spazio scenico: Teorie e tecniche scenografiche in Italia dall'età barocca al settecento.* Rome: Bulzoni, 1974.

Molinari, Cesare. "Les rapports entre la scène et les spectateurs dans le théâtre italien du xvi siècle." In *Le lieu théâtral à la Renaissance. Royaumont, 22–27 mars 1963. Colloques internationaux du Centre National de la Recherche Scientifique. Sciences humaines.* Ed. Jean Jacquot with Elie Konigson and Marcel Oddon. Paris: Éditions du Centre National de la Recherche Scientifique, 1964, pp. 61–71.

——. *Le nozze degli dèi. Un saggio sul grande spettacolo italiano nel seicento.* Rome: Bulzoni, 1968.

Muraro, Maria Teresa. *Studi sul teatro veneto fra Rinascimento ed età Barocca.* Florence: Olschki, 1971.

Nagler, A[lois] M. *Theatre Festivals of the Medici, 1539–1637.* New Haven, Connecticut: Yale University Press, 1964.

Palisca, Claude. "Musical Asides in the Diplomatic Correspondence of Emilio de' Cavalieri." *The Musical Quarterly* 49 (1963), 339–355.

——. "The First Performance of *L'Euridice.*" In *Queens College Department of Music: Twenty-fifth Anniversary Festschrift.* Ed. Albert Mell, pp. 1–23. New York: Queens College Press, 1964.

Pirrotta, Nino. *Music and Theater from Poliziano to Monteverdi.* Trans. [of *Li due Orfei*] by Karen Eales. Cambridge University Press, 1982.

——. "The Orchestra and Stage in Renaissance Intermedi and Early Opera." In *Music and Culture in Italy from the Middle Ages to the Baroque: A Collection of Essays.* Cambridge. Massachusetts: Harvard University Press, 1984. pp. 210–216.

——. "Theater, Sets, and Music in Monteverdi's Operas." In *Music and Culture in Italy from the Middle Ages to the Baroque: A Collection of Essays.* Cambridge, Massachusetts: Harvard University Press, 1984. pp. 254–270.

Pirrotta, Nino, and Elena Povoledo. *Li due Orfei da Poliziano a Monteverdi: Con un saggio critico sulla scenografia di Elena Povoledo.* Torino: Giulio Einaudi, 1975.

Povoledo, Elena. "Parigi, Giulio." *Enciclopedia dello spettacolo.* Rome: Le Maschere, 1954.

——. "Teatro." *Enciclopedia dello spettacolo.* Rome: Le Maschere, 1954.

de' Rossi, Bastiano. *Descrizione dell' apparato e degl'intermedi fatti per la commedia rappresentata in Firenze. Nelle nozze de' Serenissimi Don Ferdinando Medici, e Madama Cristina di Loreno, Gran Duchi di Toscana.* Florence: Padovani, 1589.

——. *Descrizione del magnificentis. apparato e de' meravigliosi intermedi fatti per la commedia rappresentata in Firenze nelle felicissime nozze degl'illustrissimi, ed eccellentissimi Signori il Signor Don Cesare D'Este, e la Signora Donna Virginia Medici.* Florence: Marescotti, 1585 [1586 new style].

Sabbatini, Nicola. *Pratica di fabricar scene e machine ne' teatri.* Ravenna, Pietro de' Paoli and Giovanni Battista Giovannelli, 1638. Reprint, Weimar, Gesellschaft der Bibliophilen, 1926.

Savage, Roger, and Matteo Sansone. "*Il corago* and the staging of early opera: four chapters from an anonymous treatise circa 1630." *Early Music* 17 (1989), 495–511.

Solerti, Angelo. *Musica, ballo e drammatica alla corte medicea dal 1600 al 1637: Notizie tratte da un diario con appendice di testi inediti e rari.* Florence: Bemporad, 1905. Reprint, Bibliotheca Musica Bononiensis, Sezione III n. 4. Bologna: Forni, 1969, and New York: Broude Brothers, 1968.

Turchetti, Piero. "Buontalenti, Bernardo." *Enciclopedia dello spettacolo.* Rome: Le Maschere, 1954.

Worsthorne, Simon Towneley. *Venetian Opera in the Seventeenth Century.* Oxford: Clarendon Press, 1954.

Chapter Two

Anthony, James R. *French Baroque Music from Beaujoyeulx to Rameau.* Rev. and expanded ed. Portland, Oregon: Amadeus Press, 1997. Original edition N.Y.: W. W. Norton, 1978.

Apostolidès, Jean-Marie. *Le Prince Sacrifié: Théâtre et politique au temps de Louis XIV.* Paris: Les Éditions de Minuit, 1985.

———. *Le Roi-Machine: Spectacle et politique au temps de Louis XIV.* Paris: Les Éditions de Minuit, 1981.

Babeau, Albert. "Le Théâtre des Tuileries sous Louis XIV, Louis XV et Louis XVI." *Bulletin de la société de l'histoire de Paris et de l'Ile-de-France* 22 (1895), 130–188.

Beauvert, Thierry, and Michel Parouty. *Les temples de l'opéra.* Paris: Gallimard, 1990.

Beijer, Agne. "Vigarani et Bérain au Palais-Royal." *Revue d'histoire du théâtre* 8 (1956), 184–196.

Bianconi, Lorenzo. *Music in the Seventeenth Century.* Trans. David Bryant. Cambridge University Press, 1987.

Bjurström, Per. *Giacomo Torelli and Baroque Stage Design.* Stockholm: Nationalmuseum, 1961.

Blondel, Jacques François. *L'architecture Française: Ou recueil de plans, d'elevations, coupes, et profils des églises, maisons royales, palais, hôtels, & édifices les plus considérables.* Paris: C. A. Jomberteur, 1752–56. Reprint, Paris: Librairie centrale des beaux-arts, 1904–5.

Bluche, François. *Louis XIV.* Trans. Mark Greengrass. New York: Franklin Watts, 1990.

Boucher, Thierry. "Les théâtres des Palais Royaux." *Les monuments historiques de France* 4 (1978), 16–21.

Brice, Germain. *Description de la ville de Paris et de tout ce qu'elle contient de plus remarquable.* 9th ed. Paris: Chez les libraires associes, 1752. Reprint, Geneva: Librairie Droz, 1971.

Burke, Peter. *The Fabrication of Louis XIV.* New Haven: Yale University Press, 1992.

Chappuzeau, Samuel. *Le théâtre français.* Lyon: Michel Mayer, 1674. Reprint, Paris: Éditions d'Aujourd'hui, 1985.

Christout, Marie-Françoise. *Le ballet de cour au XVIIe siècle.* Geneva: Minkoff, 1987.

———. "*Ercole amante, L'Hercule amoureux* à la Salle des Machines des Tuileries." *XVIIe Siècle* 36 (January–March 1984), 5–15.

Coeyman, Barbara. "Sites of Indoor Musical-Theatrical Productions at Versailles." *Eighteenth-Century Life* 17 (May 1993), 55–67. Special issue on the Art and Architecture of Versailles.

———. "Theatres for Opera and Ballet During the Reigns of Louis XIV and Louis XV." *Early Music* 18 (February 1990), 22–37.

———. "The Stage Works of Michel-Richard Delalande in the Musical-Cultural Context of the French Court, 1680–1726." Ph.D. dissertation: City University of New York, 1987.

Cordey, Jean. "Lully installe l'Opéra dans le théâtre de Molière: La décoration de la salle." *Bulletin de la société historique de l'architecture française* (1950), 137–142.

Dangeau, Philippe de Courcillon de. *Mémoires de la cour de France.* Paris: Didot Frères, 1854.

Deierkauf-Holsboer, S. Wilma. *Le Théâtre de l'Hôtel de Bourgogne.* 2 vols. Paris: A. G. Nizet, 1968–70.

Diderot, Denis, and Jean le Rond d'Alembert. *Theater Architecture and Stage Machines* from the *Encyclopédie: Ou dictionnaire raisonné des sciences, des arts, et des métiers.* Extracts edited and trans. New York: Benjamin Blom, 1969.

Dumont, Gabriel-Pierre-Martin. *Parallele de plans des plus belles salles de spectacles d'Italie et de France.* 1774. Reprint, New York: Benjamin Blom, 1968.

Durey de Noinville, J. B. *Histoire du théâtre de l'Académie Royale de Musique en France.* Paris: Duchesne, 1757. Reprint, Geneva: Minkoff, 1972.

Gazette de France. Paris, 1643–1672.

Hautecoeur, Louis. *Histoire de l'architecture classique en France.* Vol. 2, *Le règne de Louis XIV.* Paris: Picard, 1948.

Heuzey, Jacques. "Notes sur un dessin représentant la Salle Des Machines au XVIIe siècle." *Revue d'histoire du théâtre* 6 (1954), 60–69.

Horn-Monval, Madeleine. "La grande machinerie théâtrale et ses origines." *Revue d'histoire du théâtre* 9 (1957), 291–308.

———."Le théâtre du Petit Bourbon." *Revue d'histoire du théâtre,* 1–2 (1948), 46–48.

Isherwood, Robert M. *Music in the Service of the King.* Ithaca, New York: Cornell University Press, 1973.

Johnson, James H. *Listening in Paris: A Cultural History.* Berkeley and Los Angeles: University of California Press, 1995.

La Gorce, Jérôme de. *Bérain: Dessinateur du Roi Soleil.* Paris: Éditions Herscher, 1986.

———. "Les costumes d'Henry Gissey pour les représentations de 'Psyché.'" *Revue de l'art* 66 (1984), 39–52.

La Grange. *Le registre de La Grange 1659–1685.* With a preface by Bert Edward Young and Grave Philputt Young. Paris: Librairie E. Droz, 1947.

La Grave, Henri. *Le théâtre et le public à Paris de 1715 à 1750.* Paris: Librairie C. Klincksiek, 1972.

La Salle, Albert. *Les treize salles de l'opéra.* Paris: Librairie Sartorius, 1875.

LaJarte, Théodore de. *Bibliothèque musicale du Théâtre de l'Opéra: Catalogue.* Paris: Librairie des Bibliophiles, 1878. Reprint, Hildesheim: Olms, 1969.

Lavin, Irving. "On the Unity of the Arts and the Early Baroque Opera House," *Art and Pageantry in the Renaissance and Baroque.* In Papers in Art History from The Pennsylvania State University, vol. 6, pp. 519–579.

Lawrenson, T. E. *The French Stage in the XVIIth Century.* Manchester University Press, 1957.

LeClerc, Louis (Celler, Ludovic). *Les décors, les costumes, et la mise en scène au XVIIe siècle 1615–1680.* Paris: Liepmannssohn et Dufour, 1869. Reprint, Geneva: Slatkine, 1970.

———. *Les origines de l'opéra et le ballet de la reine (1581).* Paris, Didier, 1868.

Lesure, François. *L'opéra classique français.* Geneva: Minkoff, 1972.

Loret, Jean. *La muse historique: Ou recueil des lettres en vers (1650–1665).* Paris: P. Daffis, 1857–1878.

Lully, Musicien Soleil. Exposition 1987. Exposition Catalog ed. Jérôme de La Gorce. Paris: ADIAM, 1987.

Marie, Alfred. "Les théâtres du chasteau de Versailles." *Revue d'histoire du théâtre* 2 (1951), 133–152.

Marie, Alfred and Jeanne. *Versailles au temps de Louis XIV.* Paris: Éditions Jacques Freal, 1976.

McGowan, Margaret. *L'art du ballet de cour en France: 1581–1643.* Paris: Éditions du Centre National de la Recherche Scientifique, 1978.

Mélèse, Pierre. *Le théâtre et le public à Paris sous Louis XIV: 1659–1715.* Paris: Librairie E. Droz, 1934.

Ménestrier, Claude-François. *Des ballets anciens et modernes selon les règles du théâtre.* Paris: R. Guignard, 1682. Reprint, Geneva: Minkoff, 1972.

———. *Des représentations en musique anciennes et modernes selon les règles du théâtre.* Paris: R. Guignard, 1681. Reprint, Geneva: Minkoff, 1972.

Le Mercure galant, contenant plusieurs histoires véritables et tout ce qui s'est passé depuis le premier janvier jusques au départ du roy. Paris: Girard, 1672–74; 1677–1715.

Mittman, Barbara G. *Spectators on the Paris Stage in the Seventeenth and Eighteenth Centuries.* In Theater and Dramatic Studies, No. 25. Ann Arbor, Michigan: UMI Research Press, 1984.

Motta, Fabrizio Carini. *Costruzione de teatri e machine teatrali 1688.* Trans. Orville K. Larson. Carbondale: Southern Illinois University Press, 1987.

———. *Trattato sopra la structtura de'theatri e scene 1676.* Trans. Orville K. Larson. Carbondale: Southern Illinois Press, 1987.

Prunières, Henry. *Le ballet de cour avant Benserade et Lully.* Paris: H. Laurens, 1914. Reprint, New York: Johnson Reprint, 1970.

———. *Cavalli et l'opéra vénitien au XVIIe siècle.* Paris: Éditions Rieder, 1931.

———. *L'opéra italien en France avant Lulli.* Paris: E. Champion, 1913. Reprint, Paris: Honoré Champion, 1975.

Pure, Michel de. *Idée des spectacles anciens et nouveaux.* Paris: M. Brunet, 1668. Reprint, Geneva: Minkoff, 1972.

Riccoboni, Luigi. *A General History of the Stage from Its Origin.* Facsimile of 1754 English trans. *Music and Theatre in France in the 17th and 18th Centuries.* New York: AMS Press, 1978.

Rice, Paul. "The Court Theater at Fontainebleau." *Theatre Research International* 9 (1982), 127–139.

Rouchès, Gabriel. *Inventaire des lettres et papiers manuscrits de Gaspare, Carlo et Lodovico Vigarani.* Paris: H. Champion, 1913.

Sabbatini, Nicola. *Pratica di fabricar scene, e machine ne'teatri.* Ravenna, 1638.

Sauval, Henri. *Histoire et recherches des antiquités de la ville de Paris.* 3 vols. Paris: C. Moette, 1724. Reprint, Franbarough, England: Gregg, 1969.

Silin, Charles. *Benserade and His Ballets de Cour.* Baltimore: Johns Hopkins Press, 1940.

Southorn, Janet. *Power and Display in the Seventeenth Century: The Arts and Their Patrons in Modena and Ferrara.* In Cambridge Studies in the History of Art. Cambridge University Press, 1988.

Stein, Louise K. "Opera and the Spanish Political Agenda." *Acta musicologica* 43 (1991), 125–167.

Tessier, André. "Bérain: Créateur du pays d'opéra." *La revue musicale* (1925), 56–73.

———. "Giacomo Torelli a Parigi e la messa in scena delle 'Nozze di Peleo e Teti' di Carlo Caprolo" *La rassegna musicale* 1 (November 1928), 573–590.

Walker, Thomas. "Cavalli." In *New Grove Dictionary of Music and Musicians.* 6th ed., 24–34. London: MacMillan, 1980.

Weigert, R. A. *Jean I Bérain: Dessinateur de la chambre et du cabinet du roi (1640–1711).* 2 vols. Paris: Éditions d'Art et d'Histoire, 1937.

Zaslaw, Neal. "At the Paris Opera in 1747," *Early Music* 12 (1983), 515,

Chapter Three

Beaumont and Fletcher. *Wit at Severall Weapons.* London, 1711. Vol. 6.

Bell, Hamilton. "Contributions to the History of the English Playhouse." *The Architectural Record* 33 (March–April 1913), 262–267; 359–368.

Boswell, Eleanore. *The Restoration Court Stage: 1660–1702.* Cambridge, Massachusetts: Harvard University Press, 1932.

Cibber, Colley. *An Apology for the Life of Mr. Colley Cibber, Comedian* (1740). Vol. 2 *Days of the Dandies.* London: The Grolier Society, 1888.

De Marly, Diana. "The Architect of Dorset Garden Theatre." *Theatre Notebook* 29/3 (1975), 119–124.

Dent, Edward J. *Foundations of English Opera: A Study of Musical Drama in England during the Seventeenth Century.* Cambridge University Press, 1928.

Genest, John, ed. *Some Account of the English Stage from the Restoration in 1660 to 1830.* 10 vols. New York: Burt Franklin. Originally. pub. Bath, 1832.

Hotson, Leslie. *The Commonwealth and Restoration Stage.* New York: Russell and Russell, 1962.

Hume, Robert D. "The Dorset Garden Theatre: A Review of Facts and Problems." *Theatre Notebook* 33/1 (1979), 4–17.

Langhans, Edward A. "The Dorset Garden Theatre in Pictures." *Theatre Survey* 4/2 (1965).

Macqueen-Pope, W. J. *Theatre Royal Drury Lane.* London: W. H. Allen, 1945.

Pepys, Samuel. *Diary.* Ed. Robert Latham and William Matthews. Berkeley and Los Angeles: University of California Press, 1976.

Spring, John R. "Platforms and Picture Frames: A Conjectural Reconstruction of the Duke of York's Theatre, Dorset Garden, 1669–1709." *Theatre Notebook* 31/3 (1977), 6–19.

———. "The Dorset Garden Theatre: Playhouse or Opera House?" *Theatre Notebook* 34/2 (1980), 60–69.

Summers, Montague. *Restoration Theatre.* New York: Macmillan, 1934.

Viser, Collin. "The Anatomy of the Early Restoration Stage: *The Adventures of Five Hours* and John Dryden's 'Spanish Comedies.'" *Theatre Notebook* part 1, 29/2 (1975), 56–69; part 2, 29/3, 114–119.

Chapter Four

Barlow, Graham. "Vanbrugh's Queen's Theatre in the Haymarket, 1703–9." *Early Music* 17 (1989), 515–521.

Cibber, Colley. *An Apology for the Life of Mr. Colley Cibber.* Ed. Edmund Bellchambers. London: W. Simpkin and R. Marshall, 1822.

Dean, Winton. *Handel and the opera seria.* Berkeley: University of California Press, 1969.

———. "A French Traveller's View of Handel's Operas." *Music and Letters* 55 (1974): 172–178.

Dean, Winton, and John Merrill Knapp. *Handel's Operas: 1704–1726.* Oxford: Clarendon Press, 1987.

Deutsch, Otto. *Händel-Handbuch* 4. Kassel: Bärenreiter, 1985.

Dumont, C. P. M. *Parallele de plans des plus belles salles de spectacle d'Italie et de France.* Paris, 1764.

Harris, Ellen T., ed. *The Librettos of Handel's Operas.* 13 vols. New York: Garland Publishing, 1989.

Highfill, Philip H., Jr. "Rich's 1744 Inventory of Covent Garden Properties." *Restoration and 18th Century Theatre Research.* 5/1 (May 1966), 7–17; 5/1 (November 1966), 17–26; 6/1 (May 1967), 27–35.

Visser, Colin. "Scenery and Technical Design." In *The London Theatre World*. Ed. Robert D. Hume. Carbondale: Southern Illinois University Press, 1980.

Langhans, Edward. "The Theatres." In *The London Theatre World*. Ed. Robert D. Hume. Carbondale: Southern Illinois University Press, 1980.

Lindgren, Lowell. "The Staging of Handel's Operas in London." In *Handel Tercentenary Collection*. Ed. Stanley Sadie and Anthony Hicks. Ann Arbor, Michigan: UMI Research Press, 1985.

Milhous, Judith. "The Capacity of Vanbrugh's Theatre in the Haymarket." *Theatre History Studies* 4 (1984), 38–46.

—— and Robert D. Hume. "A Prompt Copy of Handel's *Radamisto*." *Musical Times* 127 (1986), 316–321.

Nalbach, Daniel. *The King's Theatre*. London: The Society for Theatre Research, 1972.

Chapter Five

Allanbrook, Wye Jamison. *Rhythmic Gesture in Mozart:* Le nozze di Figaro *and* Don Giovanni. Chicago: University of Chicago Press, 1983.

Anderson, Emily. *The Letters of Mozart and His Family*. 3rd ed. New York: W. W. Norton, 1989.

Angermüller, Rudolph. "Da Ponte, Lorenzo." *New Grove Dictionary of Music and Musicians,* vol. 5, pp. 236–238.

——. *Figaro:* Le nozze di Figaro *auf dem Theater*. Salzburg: Internationale Stiftung Mozarteum, 1986.

——. *Mozart's Operas*. Trans. Stewart Spencer. New York: Rizzoli, 1988; originally pub. as *Mozart—Die Opern von der Uraufführung bis Heute*. Frankfurt am Main: Propyläen Verlag, 1988.

——. "Salieri's *Tarare* (1787) und *Axur re d'Ormus* (1788): Vertonung eines Sujets für Paris und Wien." *Hamburger Jahrbuch für Musikwissenschaft* 5 (1981), 211–217.

——. "Salieri's Vorbemerkungen zu seinen Opern." *Mitteilungen der Internationalen Stiftung Mozarteum* 25 (Heft 3/4, 1977), 15–33.

Anon. *Vertraute Briefe zur Charakteristik von Wien*. Görlitz: Hermsdorf und Anton, 1793.

Arndt, Ernst Moritz. *Bruchstücke aus einer Reise von Baireuth bis Wien im Sommer 1798*. Leipzig: Heinrich Gräff, 1801.

Arundell, Dennis. *W. A. Mozart:* Le Nozze di Figaro [*and*] Così fan tutte. New York: Universe Books, 1971.

Badura-Skoda, Eva. "The Influence of the Viennese Popular Comedy on Haydn and Mozart." *Journal of the Royal Musical Association* 100 (1973–74), 185–199.

Baker, Evan. "September, 1791: The Burgtheater and the Theater im Starhembergschen Freihaus auf der Wieden." Paper presented at the 1991 RMA Mozart Conference, London.

——. "Theaters in Vienna during Mozart's Lifetime." *Mozart-Jahrbuch* (1991), vol. 2, pp. 984–992.

Batley, Edward M. *A Preface to the Magic Flute*. London: Dennis Dobson, 1969.

Bauman, Thomas. "Mozart's Belmonte." *Early Music* 19 (November 1991), 557–563.

——. *W. A. Mozart:* Die Entführung aus dem Serail. Cambridge University Press, 1987.

Beaumarchais, Pierre Augustin Caron de. *La folle journée ou le mariage de Figaro*. Pub. J. B. Ratermanis; ed. Theodore Besterman. Vol. 63 of *Studies on Voltaire and the Eighteenth Century*. Geneva: Institut et Musée Voltaire, 1968.

Beicken, Suzanne Julia. "Johann Adam Hiller's *Anweisung zum musikalisch-zierlichen Gesange, 1780:* A Translation and Commentary." Ph.D. dissertation, Stanford University, 1980.

Besch, Anthony. "A Director's Approach." Peter Branscombe, *W.A. Mozart:* Die Zauberflöte. Cambridge University Press, 1991, pp. 178–204.

Blümml, Emil Karl and Gustav Gugitz. *Alt-Wiener Thespiskarren: Die Frühzeit der Wiener Vorstadtbühnen.* Vienna: Anton Schroll, 1925.

Branscombe, Peter. "Mozart and the Theatre of His Time." *The Mozart Compendium: A Guide to Mozart's Life and Music.* Ed. H. C. Robbins Landon. New York: Schirmer Books, 1990, pp. 358–370.

———. *W.A. Mozart:* Die Zauberflöte. Cambridge University Press, 1991.

Braunbehrens, Volkmar. *Mozart in Vienna, 1781–1791.* Trans. Timothy Bell. First HarperPerennial [*sic*] Ed., 1991; hardcover, New York: Grove Weidenfeld, 1990.

Brophy, Brigid. *W.A. Mozart:* Die Zauberflöte [*and*] Die Entführung aus dem Serail. New York: Universe Books, 1971.

Brown, Bruce Alan. *Gluck and the French Theatre in Vienna.* Oxford: Clarendon Press, 1991.

Buch, David J. "Fairy-Tale Literature and *Die Zauberflöte.*" *Acta musicologica* 64 (January–June 1992), 30–49.

Burney, Charles. *Dr. Burney's Musical Tours in Europe.* Vol. 2, *An Eighteenth-Century Musical Tour in Central Europe and the Netherlands.* Ed. Percy Scholes. London: Oxford University Press, 1959.

Campana, Alessandra. "Mozart's Italian *buffo* Singers." *Early Music* 19 (November 1991), 580–583.

Carter, Tim. *W.A. Mozart:* Le nozze di Figaro. Cambridge University Press, 1987.

Castelli, Ignaz Franz. *Memoiren meines Lebens.* Ed. Josef Bindtner. 2 vols. Munich: G. Müller, 1914. Another ed. by Joachim Schondorff. Munich: Winkler, 1969. [Die Fundgrube, No. 43]

Cole, Malcolm S. "*The Magic Flute* and the Quatrain." *Journal of Musicology* 3 (Spring 1984), 157–176.

———. "Schikaneder, Emanuel." *International Dictionary of Opera,* vol. 2, pp. 1191–1193.

———. "Die Zauberflöte [The Magic Flute]." *International Dictionary of Opera,* vol. 2, pp. 1473–1476.

Csampai, Attila and Dietmar Holland, eds. *Wolfgang Amadeus Mozart,* Die Zauberflöte: *Texte, Materialien, Kommentare.* Reinbek bei Hamburg: Rowohlt Taschenbuch [Ricordi], 1982.

Da Ponte, Lorenzo. *Memoirs.* Trans. Elisabeth Abbott. Ed. Arthur Livingston. Philadelphia: J. B. Lippincott, 1929. *Memorie di Lorenzo da Ponte da Ceneda scritte da esso.* New York, 1823–27. Ed. Cesare Pagnini. Milan: Rizzoli, 1971.

Deutsch, Otto Erich. *Das Freihaustheater auf der Wieden, 1787–1801.* 2nd ed. Vienna: Deutscher Verlag für Jugend und Volk, 1937.

———. *Mozart: A Documentary Biography.* Trans. Eric Blom, Peter Branscombe, and Jeremy Noble. London: Adam and Charles Black, 1965; originally pub. as *Mozart: Die Dokumente seines Lebens.* Kassel: Bärenreiter, 1961.

Dietrich, Margret, ed. *Das Burgtheater und sein Publikum, Festgabe zur 200-Jahr-Feier der Erhebung des Burgtheaters zum Nationaltheater.* Vienna: Österreichische Akademie der Wissenschaften, 1976. [Veröffentlichungen des Instituts für Publikumsforschung, No. 3]

Dittersdorf, Karl Ditters von. *The Autobiography of Karl von Dittersdorf: Dictated to his Son.* Trans. A. D. Coleridge. London: Richard Bentley and Son, 1896.

———. *Lebensbeschreibung: Seinem Sohne in die Feder diktiert.* Ed. Norbert Miller. Munich: Kösel-Verlag, 1967. Originally. pub. Leipzig: Breitkopf und Härtel, 1801.

Eckelmeyer, Judith A. *The Cultural Context of Mozart's* Magic Flute: *Social, Aesthetic, Philosophical.* 2 vols. Lewiston, New York: The Edwin Mellen Press, 1991. [*Studies in the History and Interpretation of Music,* vol. 34A–B]

——, trans. *Wolfgang Amadeus Mozart,* The Magic Flute: *1791 Libretto by Emanuel Schikaneder.* New York: The Edwin Mellen Press, 1979.

Edge, Dexter. "Mozart's Viennese Orchestras." *Early Music* 20 (February 1992), 64–88.

Eisen, Cliff, ed. *Mozart Studies.* Oxford: Clarendon Press, 1991.

——. *New Mozart Documents: A Supplement to O. E. Deutsch's Documentary Biography.* Stanford: Stanford University Press, 1991.

Fellerer, Karl Gustav. "Zur Mozart Kritik im 18./19. Jahrhundert." *Mozart-Jahrbuch* (1959), 80–94.

Gidwitz, Patricia Lewy. "Cavalieri, Caterina." *New Grove Dictionary of Opera,* vol. 1, p. 779.

—— and Betty Matthews, "Storace, Nancy." *New Grove Dictionary of Opera,* vol. 4, pp. 553–554.

Grossegger, Elisabeth. *Freimaurerei und Theater 1770–1800: Freimaurerdramen an den k.k. privilegierten Theatern in Wien.* Vienna: Hermann Böhlaus, 1981.

Gruber, Gernot. "Schaffensgeschichte und Uraufführung der 'Zauberflöte.'" *Wolfgang Amadeus Mozart:* Die Zauberflöte. Ed. A. Csampai and D. Holland, Reinbek bei Hamburg: Rowohlt, [Ricordi] 1982, pp. 137–148.

Hadamowsky, Franz. *Wien Theater Geschichte von den Anfängen bis zum Ende des ersten Weltkriegs.* Vienna: Jugend und Volk, 1988.

Haeusserman, Ernst. *Das Wiener Burgtheater.* Vienna: Fritz Molden, 1975.

Heartz, Daniel. *Mozart's Operas.* Ed. with contributing essays, by Thomas Bauman. Berkeley and Los Angeles: University of California Press, 1990.

——. "Nicolas Jadot and the Building of the Burgtheater." *Musical Quarterly* 68 (January 1982), 1–31.

Henderson, Donald G. "The 'Magic Flute' of Peter Winter." *Music and Letters* 64 (July–October 1983), 193–205.

Hennings, Fred. *Zweimal Burgtheater vom Michaelerplatz zum Franzensring.* Vienna: Verlag Kremayr und Scheriau, 1955.

Hiller, Johann Adam. *Anweisung zum musikalisch-zierlichen Gesange.* Leipzig: Johann Friedrich Junius, 1780. Reprint facsimile ed., Leipzig: Peters, 1976. [Peters Reprints]

Honolka, Kurt. *Papageno: Emanuel Schikaneder, Man of the Theater in Mozart's Time.* Trans. Jane Mary Wilde. Portland, Oregon: Amadeus Press, 1990. Originally pub. as *Papageno.* Salzburg: Residenz Verlag, 1984.

Irmen, Hans-Josef. *Mozart: Mitglied geheimer Gesellschaften.* Neustadt/Aisch: Prisca-Verlag, 1988.

Jaacks, Gisela. "Das Bühnenbild der Maschinenkomödie 'Die Zauberflöte.'" *W.A. Mozart:* Die Zauberflöte, pp. 201–216.

Jahn, Otto. *W.A. Mozart.* 2nd ed. 2 vols. Leipzig: Breitkopf und Härtel, 1867.

——. *Life of Mozart.* Trans. Pauline Townsend. 3 vols. London: Novello, 1891.

Jowers, Sidney Jackson. "Costume." *New Grove Dictionary of Opera,* vol. 1, pp. 971–998.

Kaiser, Joachim. *Who's Who in Mozart's Operas: From Alfonso to Zerlina.* Trans. Charles Kessler. New York: Schirmer Books, 1987. Originally pub. as *Mein Name ist Sarastro: Die Gestalten in Mozarts Meisteropern von Alfonso bis Zerlina.* Munich: Piper, 1984.

Kazinczy, Franz. *Selbstbiographie* [*Denkwürdigkeiten meiner Laufbahn*]. New ed., Budapest: Ladislaus Orosz, 1956.

Keil-Budischowsky, Verena. *Die Theater Wiens.* Vienna: Paul Zsolnay, 1983. [Wiener Geschichtsbücher, vols. 30/31/32. Ed. Peter Pötschner.]

Kelly, Michael. *Reminiscences of Michael Kelly, of the King's Theatre, and Theatre Royal Drury Lane.* 2 vols. London: Henry Colburn, 1826.

Komorzynski, Egon. *Emanuel Schikaneder: Ein Beitrag zur Geschichte des deutschen Theaters.* Vienna: Ludwig Doblinger, 1951.

———. "Sänger und Orchester des Freihaustheaters." *Mozart-Jahrbuch* (1951), 138–150.

———. "*Die Zauberflöte* und *Dschinnistan.*" *Mozart-Jahrbuch* (1954), 177–194.

Krones, Hartmut. "Mozart gibt uns selbst die Antworten: Zur Musiksprache der *Zauberflöte.*" *Österreichische Musikzeitschrift* 46 (January–February 1991), 24–33.

Landon, H. C. Robbins. *Haydn: Chronicle and Works.* Vol. 2, *Haydn at Esterháza 1766–1790.* Bloomington: Indiana University Press, 1978.

———. *1791: Mozart's Last Year.* New York: Schirmer Books, 1988.

———, ed. *The Mozart Compendium: A Guide to Mozart's Life and Music.* New York: Schirmer Books, 1990.

———. *Mozart: The Golden Years, 1781–1791.* New York: Schirmer Books, 1989.

———. *Mozart and Vienna.* New York: Schirmer Books, 1991.

Langhans, Edward A. and Robert Benson. "Lighting." *New Grove Dictionary of Opera,* vol. 2, pp. 1265–1277.

———. "Machinery." *New Grove Dictionary of Opera,* vol. 3, pp. 120–132.

The Librettos of Mozart's Operas. Ed. Ernest Warburton. New York: Garland Publishing, 1992.

Mann, William. *The Operas of Mozart.* New York: Oxford University Press, 1977.

Marshall, Robert. *Mozart Speaks: Views on Music, Musicians, and the World.* New York: Schirmer Books, 1990.

Marty, Jean-Pierre. "Mozart's Tempo Indications and the Problems of Interpretation." *Perspectives on Mozart Performance.* Ed. R. Larry Todd and Peter Williams. Cambridge University Press, 1991, pp. 55–73.

———. *The Tempo Indications of Mozart.* New Haven: Yale University Press, 1988.

Mattsson, Inger, ed. *Gustavian Opera: An Interdisciplinary Reader in Swedish Opera, Dance and Theatre 1771–1809.* Uppsala: Almqvist och Wiksell, 1991.

Meyer, Friedrich Ludwig Wilhelm, ed. *Friedrich Ludwig Schröder: Beitrag zur Kunde des Menschen und des Künstlers.* Hamburg: Hoffmann und Campe, 1819.

Michtner, Otto. *Das alte Burgtheater als Opernbühne von der Einführung des deutschen Singspiels (1778) bis zum Tod Kaiser Leopolds II. (1792).* Vienna: Hermann Böhlaus Nachf., 1970. [*Theatergeschichte Österreichs,* 3:1]

Morenz, Siegfried. Die Zauberflöte: *Eine Studie zum Lebenszusammenhang Aegypten–Antike– Abendland.* Münster: Böhlau-Verlag, 1952.

Morrow, Mary Sue. *Concert Life in Haydn's Vienna: Aspects of a Developing Musical and Social Institution.* Stuyvesant, New York: Pendragon Press, 1989.

Mozart: Briefe und Aufzeichnungen. Collected and ed. Wilhelm A. Bauer, Otto Erich Deutsch, and Joseph Heinz Eibl. 7 vols. Kassel: Bärenreiter, 1962–75.

Mozart, Wolfgang Amadeus. *Neue Ausgabe sämtlicher Werke.* Series 2, Group 5, Vol. 12, *Die Entführung aus dem Serail.* Ed. Gerhard Croll. Kassel: Bärenreiter, 1982.

———. Series 2, Group 5, Vol. 16 (1–2), *Le nozze di Figaro.* Ed. Ludwig Finscher. Kassel: Bärenreiter, 1973.

———. Series 2, Group 5, Vol. 17, *Don Giovanni.* Ed. Wolfgang Plath and Wolfgang Rehm. Kassel: Bärenreiter, 1968.

———. Series 2, Group 5, Vol. 18 (1–2), *Così fan tutte.* Ed. Faye Ferguson and Wolfgang Rehm. Kassel: Bärenreiter, 1991.

———. Series 2, Group 5, Vol. 19, *Die Zauberflöte.* Ed. Gernot Gruber and Alfred Orel. Kassel: Bärenreiter, 1970.

Neumann, Frederick. *Ornamentation and Improvisation in Mozart.* Princeton: Princeton University Press, 1986.

Nissen, Georg Nikolaus von. *Biographie W. A. Mozarts.* Ed. Constanze Nissen / Mozart. Leipzig: Breitkopf und Härtel, 1828.

"Performing Mozart's Music I." Special issue of *Early Music* 19 (November 1991). "Performing Mozart's Music II." *Early Music* 20 (February 1992).

Pezzl, Johann. *Skizze von Wien: Ein Kultur- und Sittenbild aus der josefinischen Zeit.* Ed. Gustav Gugitz and Anton Schlossar. Graz: Leykam-Verlag, 1923.

Platoff, John. "The *buffa* Aria in Mozart's Vienna." *Cambridge Opera Journal* 2 (July 1990), 99–120.

———. "Musical and Dramatic Structure in the *opera buffa* Finale." *Journal of Musicology* 7 (Spring 1989), 191–230.

Raeburn, Christopher and Dorothea Link. "Benucci, Francesco." *New Grove Dictionary of Opera,* vol. 1, pp. 410–411.

Rangström, Ture. "The Stage Machinery at Drottningholm." *Gustavian Opera.* Ed. Inger Mattsson, pp. 87–103.

Rice, John A. "Axur, re d'Ormus ('Axur, King of Ormus')." *New Grove Dictionary of Opera,* vol. 1, pp. 263–264.

———. "Emperor and Impresario: Leopold II and the Transformation of Viennese Musical Theater, 1790–1792." Ph.D. dissertation, University of California, Berkeley, 1987.

———. "Salieri, Antonio." *New Grove Dictionary of Opera,* vol. 4, pp. 141–144.

———. "Vienna under Joseph II and Leopold II." *Man and Music—The Classical Era: From the 1740s to the End of the 18th Century.* Ed. Neal Zaslaw, pp. 126–165.

Richter, Joseph. *Bildergalerie weltlicher Misbräuche: Ein Gegenstück zur Bildergalerie katholischer und klösterlicher Misbräuche, von Pater Hilarion, Exkapuzinern.* Frankfurt, 1785. Reprint facsimile ed., Dortmund: Harenberg Kommunikation, 1977. [Die bibliophilen Taschenbücher]

Robinson, Michael F. "Mozart and the *opera buffa* Tradition." Tim Carter. *Mozart: Le nozze di Figaro,* pp. 11–32.

Rommel, Otto, ed. *Die Maschinenkomödie.* Leipzig: Philipp Reclam, jun., 1935. [*Barocktradition im österreichisch-bayrischen Volkstheater,* vol. 1]

Rushton, Julian. *W. A. Mozart: Don Giovanni.* Cambridge University Press, 1981.

Schikaneder, Emmanuel [*sic*]. *Die Zauberflöte: Eine grosse Oper in zwey Aufzügen.* Vienna: Ignaz Alberti, 1791. [Facsimile, Vienna: Wiener Bibliophilen-Gesellschaft, 1942]

Schindler, Otto G. "Das Publikum des Burgtheaters in der Josephinischen Aera. Versuch einer Strukturbestimmung." *Das Burgtheater und sein Publikum.* Ed. Margret Dietrich, pp. 11–95.

———. "Der Zuschauerraum des Burgtheaters im 18. Jahrhundert, Eine baugeschichtliche Skizze." *Maske und Kothurn* 22 (1976, 1/2), 20–53.

Schmitt, Anke. *Der Exotismus in der deutschen Oper zwischen Mozart und Spohr.* Hamburg: Karl Dieter Wagner, 1988.

Singer, Herta. "Die Akustik des alten Burgtheaters, Versuch einer Darstellung der Zusammenhänge zwischen Aufführungsstil und Raumakustik." *Maske und Kothurn* 4 (1958, 2/3), 220–229.

Spiesberger, Else. *Das Freihaus.* Vienna: Paul Zsolnay, 1980. [Wiener Geschichtsbücher, vol. 25. Ed. Peter Pötschner]

Staud, Géza. *Adelstheater in Ungarn (18. und 19. Jahrhundert).* Vienna: Österreichische Akademie der Wissenschaften, 1977. [*Theatergeschichte Österreichs,* 10:2]

Steptoe, Andrew. *The Mozart—Da Ponte Operas: The Cultural and Musical Background to* Le nozze di Figaro, Don Giovanni, *and* Così fan tutte. Oxford: Clarendon Press, 1988.

Teuber, Oscar. *Die Theater Wiens.* Vienna: Gesellschaft für vervielfältigende Kunst, 1903.

Todd, R. Larry and Peter Williams, eds. *Perspectives on Mozart Performance.* Cambridge University Press, 1991.

Tyler, Linda. "Schack, Benedikt." *New Grove Dictionary of Opera,* vol. 4, pp. 210–211.

Tyson, Alan. *Mozart: Studies of the Autograph Scores.* Cambridge, Massachusetts: Harvard University Press, 1987.

——. "'Le nozze di Figaro': Lessons from the Autograph Score." *Musical Times* 122 (July 1981), 456–461.

——. "Some Problems in the Text of *Le nozze di Figaro:* Did Mozart Have a Hand in Them?" *Journal of the Royal Musical Association* 112 part I (1987), 99–131.

Wangermann, Ernst. *The Austrian Achievement, 1700–1800.* London: Thames and Hudson, 1973.

Webster, James. "The Analysis of Mozart's Arias." *Mozart Studies.* Ed. Cliff Eisen. Oxford: Clarendon Press, 1991, pp. 101–199.

——. "Mozart's Operas and the Myth of Musical Unity." *Cambridge Opera Journal* 2 (July 1990), 197–218.

Wieland, Christoph Martin. "Adis und Dahy." *Dschinnistan oder auserlesene Feen- und Geistermärchen.* Vol. 11 (18, 20) of the *Gesammelte Schriften.* Ed. Siegfried Mauermann. Berlin: Weidmann, 1987, pp. 36–63.

Zaslaw, Neal. *Mozart's Symphonies: Context, Performance Practice, Reception.* Oxford: Clarendon Press, 1989.

Zaubertöne. Mozart in Wien, 1781–1791, Ausstellung des Historischen Museums der Stadt Wien im Künstlerhaus, 6. Dezember 1990–15. September 1991. Vienna: Agens-Werk Geyer + Reisser, n.d.

Zechmeister, Gustav. *Die Wiener Theater nächst der Burg und nächst dem Kärntnerthor von 1747 bis 1776.* Vienna: Hermann Böhlaus Nachf., 1971. [*Theatergeschichte Österreichs,* 3:2]

Zenger, Maximilian and Otto Erich Deutsch. *Mozart und seine Welt in zeitgenössischen Bildern.* Kassel: Bärenreiter, 1961.

Chapter Six

Altmann, Wilhelm. "Spontini an der Berliner Oper," *Sammelbände der internationalen Musik-gesellschaft* 4/2 (January–March 1903), 244–292.

Arndt, Hans Joachim et al., eds., *Karl Friedrich Schinkel: Werke und Wirkungen.* Berlin: Nicolaische Buchhandlung, 1981.

Bartlitz, Eveline, comp. *Carl Maria von Weber: Autographenverzeichnis.* Berlin: Deutsche Staatsbibliothek, 1986.

Bauakademie der DDR, ed., *Karl Friedrich Schinkel: Sein Wirken als Architekt.* Berlin: Verlag für Bauwesen, 1981.

Becker, Wolfgang. *Die deutsche Oper in Dresden unter der Leitung von Carl Maria von Weber 1817–1826.* Berlin: Colloquium, 1962.

Behr, Adalbert and Alfred Hoffmann. *Das Schauspielhaus in Berlin.* Berlin: Verlag für Bauwesen, 1984.

Biermann, Franz Benedikt. *Die Pläne zur Reform des Theaterbaues bei Karl Friedrich Schinkel und Gottfried Semper.* Berlin: Gesellschaft für Theatergeschichte, 1928.

Brachvogel, Albert Emil. *Die Geschichte des königlichen Theaters zu Berlin.* 2 vols. Berlin: Otto Janke, 1878.

Cornelissen, Thilo. *Carl Maria von Weber's Freischütz als Beispiel einer Opernbehandlung.* Berlin: Matthiesen, 1940.

Csampai, Attila and Dietmar Holland, eds. *Der Freischütz: Texte, Materialien, Kommentare.* Reinbek: Rowohlt, 1981.

[Dorn, Heinrich Ludwig Egmont.] *Spontini in Deutschland: oder unparteiische Würdigung seiner Leistungen während seines Aufenthalts daselbst in den letzten zehn Jahren.* Leipzig: Steinacker und Hartknoch, 1830.

Duault, Alain, ed. *Le freischütz.* Whole issue of *L'avant scène opéra* 105/106 (January/February 1988).

Düringer, Ph. J. and H. Barthels, eds. *Theater-Lexicon: Theoretisch-practisches Handbuch für Vorstände, Mitglieder und Freunde des deutschen Theaters.* Leipzig: Otto Wigand, 1841.

Finscher, Ludwig. "Weber's *Freischütz*: Conceptions and Misconceptions," *Proceedings of the Royal Music Association* 110 (1983–84), 79–90.

Freydank, Ruth. *Theater in Berlin.* Berlin: Henschelverlag Kunst und Gesellschaft, 1988.

Gropius, Carl. *Dekorationen auf den beiden königl. Theatern in Berlin, unter der General-Intendantur des Herrn Grafen Brühl.* Berlin: Wittich, 1827.

Guhl, Ernst. "Schinkel's Schauspielhaus," *Zeitschrift für Bauwesen* 9 (1859), 431–439.

Harten, Ulrike. *Die Bühnenbilder K. F. Schinkels 1798–1834.* Ph.D. dissertation, Kiel, 1974.

Hecker, Max, ed. *Der Briefwechsel zwischen Goethe und Zelter.* Leipzig: Insel, 1915, vol. 2, pp. 1819–1827.

Jähns, Friedrich Wilhelm. *Carl Maria von Weber in seinen Werken: Chronologisch-thematisches Verzeichniss seiner sämmtlichen Compositionen.* Berlin, 1871. Reprint, Berlin: Lienau, 1967.

Kapp, Julius, ed. *185 Jahre Staatsoper: Festschrift zur Wiedereröffnung des Opernhauses Unter den Linden am 28. April 1928.* Berlin: Atlantic [1928].

———. *200 Jahre Staatsoper im Bild.* Berlin: Max Hess, 1942.

———. "Die Uraufführung des *Freischütz*," *Blätter der Staatsoper* 1/8 (18 June 1921), 9–15.

Kind, Friedrich. *Freischütz: Ausgabe letzter Hand.* Leipzig: G. J. Göschen, 1843.

Kindermann, Heinz. *Bühne und Zuschauerraum—ihre Zueinanderordnung seit der griechischen Antike.* Vienna: Hermann Böhlaus Nachfolger, 1963.

Ledebur, Carl von. *Tonkünstler-Lexicon Berlin's von den ältesten Zeiten bis auf die Gegenwart.* Berlin, 1861. Reprint, Tutzing and Berlin: Hans Schneider, 1965.

Maecklenburg, Albert. "Der Fall Spontini-Weber," *Zeitschrift für Musikwissenschaft* 6 (1926), 449–465.

Neue Kostüme auf den beiden Königlichen Theatern in Berlin unter der General-Intendantur des Herrn Grafen von Brühl. Vol. 2. Berlin, 1823.

Nohl, Ludwig. *Beethoven's Leben.* 3 vols. Leipzig: Ernst Julius Günther, 1867.

Schinkel, Karl Friedrich. *Briefe, Tagebücher, Gedanken.* Ed. Hans Mackowsky. Berlin: Propyläen, 1922.

———. *Collection of Architectural Designs: New Complete Edition in CLXXIV Plates.* Berlin, 1866. Chicago: Baluster Books, 1984.

———. *Decorationen auf den kgl. Hoftheatern zu Berlin,* ed. K[arl] F[riedrich] M[oritz] Graf zu Brühl. Berlin: Wittich, 1819–1824.

———. *Sammlung architektonischer Entwürfe.* 28 vols. Berlin, 1819–40.

Schnapp, Friedrich, ed. *E. T. A. Hoffmanns Briefwechsel.* 2 vols. Munich: Winkler, 1967–68.

Schneider, Louis. *Geschichte der Oper und des königlichen Opernhauses in Berlin.* Berlin: Duncker und Humblot, 1852.

Spitta, Philipp. "Spontini in Berlin," in *Zur Musik.* Berlin, 1892. Reprint, Hildesheim and New York: Georg Olms, 1976.

Stoverock, Dietrich and Thilo Cornelissen, eds. *Der Freischütz von Carl Maria von Weber.* Berlin: Robert Lienau, 1959.

Teichmann, Johann V. *Literarischer Nachlaß.* Ed. Franz Dingelstedt. Stuttgart: Cotta, 1863.

"Vorbericht über die Oper Olimpia." *Königliche priviligierte Berlinische Zeitung (Vossische)* No. 59 (17 May 1821).

Waltershausen, Hermann Wolfgang von. *Der Freischütz: Ein Versuch über die musikalische Romantik.* Munich: Hugo Bruckmann, 1920.

Weber, Carl Maria von. *Briefe an den Grafen Karl von Brühl.* Ed. Georg Kaiser. Leipzig: Breitkopf und Härtel, 1911.

Weber, Carl Maria von. *Der Freischütz: Nachbildung der Eigenschrift aus dem Besitz der Preussischen Staatsbibliothek.* Ed. Georg Schünemann. Berlin: n.p., 1942.

Weber, Max Maria von. *Carl Maria von Weber: The Life of an Artist.* 2 vols. Trans. J. Palgrave Simpson. Boston: Oliver Ditson [1865].

Wolzogen, Alfred von. *Aus Schinkels Nachlass: Reisetagebücher, Briefe und Aphorismen.* 4 vols. Berlin, 1862–64. Reprint, Mainz: Mäander, 1981.

Wolzogen, Hans von. "Karl Friedrich Schinkel und der Theaterbau: Betrachtungen nebst Mittheilungen aus nachgelassenen Papieren." *Bayreuther Blätter* 10/3 (March 1887), 65–90.

Zadow, Mario. *Karl Friedrich Schinkel.* Berlin: Rembrandt, 1980.

Chapter Seven

"Académie Royale de Musique. Première Représentation. *La Juive.*" *Courrier des Théâtres* (24 February 1835), 3.

Albert, Maurice. *Les théâtres des boulevards, 1789–1848.* Paris: Société Française d'Imprimerie et de Librairie, 1902.

Allévy, Marie-Antoinette. *La mise en scène en France dans la première moitié du XIXe siècle.* Paris: E. Droz, 1936.

Arvin, Neil Cole. *Eugène Scribe and the French Theatre.* Cambridge, Massachusetts: Harvard University, 1924.

Armstrong, Alan. "Meyerbeer's *Le prophète:* A History of Its Composition and Performance." Ph.D. dissertation, Ohio State University, 1983.

Bapst, Germain. *Essai sur l'histoire des panoramas et des dioramas.* Paris: G. Masson, 1891.

Barbier, Patrick. *La vie quotidienne à l'opéra au temps de Rossini et de Balzac, 1800–1850.* Paris: Hachette, 1987. Translated by Robert Luoma under the title *Opera in Paris, 1800–1850.* Portland, Oregon: Amadeus Press, 1995.

Becker, Heinz and Gudrun. *Giacomo Meyerbeer: A Life in Letters.* Trans. Mark Violette. Portland, Oregon: Amadeus Press, 1989.

———. *Giacomo Meyerbeer: Briefwechsel und Tagebücher.* 4 vols. Berlin: W. de Gruyter, 1960–85.

———. "Giacomo Meyerbeers Mitarbeit an den Libretti seiner Opern." Gesellschaft für Musikforschung. *Bericht über den internationalen musikwissenschaftlichen Kongress Bonn 1970.* Kassel: Bärenreiter, 1971, pp. 155 ff.

Bergman, Gösta M. "Les agences théâtrales et l'impression des mises en scène aux environs de 1800." *Revue d'histoire du théâtre* 8 nos. 2–3 (1956), 228–240.

Berlioz, Hector. *A travers chants.* Paris: Michel Lévy Frères, 1862.

———. *Correspondance générale.* 4 vols. Ed. Pierre Citron *et al.* Paris: Flammarion, 1972.

———. *Memoirs.* Ed. David Cairns. London: Gollancz, 1969.

———. *Les musiciens et la musique.* Paris: Calmann Lévy, 1903. Reprint, Farnborough, England: Gregg, 1969.

———. *Evenings in the Orchestra.* Trans. Charles E. Roche. New York: Knopf, 1929.

Blaze de Bury, Henri. "De l'esprit du temps à propos de musique: M. Meyerbeer." *Revue des deux mondes* 23 (1859), 645–673.

———. "Giacomo Meyerbeer: Sa vie et ses oeuvres." *Le ménestrel* 32 (1865), 193–196, 201–203, 209–212.

———. *Meyerbeer et son temps.* Paris: Michel Lévy Frères, 1865.

Bloom, Peter, ed. *Music in Paris in the 1830s.* La vie musicale en France au XIXe siècle, vol. 4. Stuyvesant, New York: Pendragon, 1987.

Bonnefon, Paul. "Scribe sous l'empire et sous la restauration d'après des documents inédits." *Revue d'histoire littéraire de la France* 28 (1921), 60–99, 241–260.

Brockett, O. G. "Pixérécourt and Unified Production." *Educational Theatre Journal* 11 (1959), 181–187.

Carlson, Marvin. "French Stage Composition from Hugo to Zola." *Educational Theatre Journal* 23 (1971), 363–378.

———. "Hernani's Revolt from the Tradition of French Stage Composition." *Theatre Survey* 13 no. 1 (May 1972), 1–27.

———. *The French Stage in the Nineteenth Century.* Metuchen, New Jersey: Scarecrow Press, 1972.

Chorley, Henry F. *Thirty Years' Musical Recollections.* 2 vols. London: Hurst and Blackett, 1862. Reprint, New York: Da Capo, 1984.

Cohen, H. Robert. "Les gravures musicales dans *L'illustration* de 1843 à 1899." *Revue de musicologie* 62 (1976), 125–131.

———. "On the Reconstruction of the Visual Elements of French Grand Opera: Unexplored Sources in Parisian Collections." *Report of the Twelfth Congress of the International Musicological Society. Berkeley 1977.* Kassel: Bärenreiter, 1981, pp. 463–481.

———, ed. *The Original Staging Manuals for Twelve Parisian Opera Premieres.* New York: Pendragon, 1990.

—— and Marie-Odile Gigou. "La conservation de la tradition scenique sur la scène lyrique en France au XIXe siècle: Les livrets de mise en scène et la bibliothèque de l'Association de la Régie Théâtrale." *Revue de musicologie* 64 (1978), 253–267.

—— and Marie-Odile Gigou. *100 Years of Operatic Staging in France (c. 1830–1930).* Stuyvesant, New York: Pendragon, 1986.

—— and Sylvia L'Ecuyer. *Les gravures musicales dans* l'illustration. 3 vols. Quebec: Université Laval, 1982–83.

Contant, Clément, and Joseph de Filippi. *Parallèle des principaux théâtres modernes de l'Europe et des machines théâtrales.* Paris: A. Lévy Fils, 1860.

Coudroy, Marie-Hélène. "Le grand opéra Meyerbeerien: Synthèse de l'imaginaire Romantique." *L'avant-scène opéra* 76 (1985), 12–18.

Crosten, William L. *French Grand Opera: An Art and a Business.* New York: King's Crown Press, 1948. Reprint, New York: Da Capo, 1972.

Daguerre, Louis-Jacques. *An Historical Descriptive Account of the Various Processes of the Daguerréotype and the Diorama.* London: McLean, 1839. Reprint, New York: Winter House, 1971.

Dauriac, Lionel. "La dramaturgie de Meyerbeer." *Revue des études juives* 62 (1911), vi–xxvii.

Döhring, Sieghart. "Die Autographen der vier Hauptopern Meyerbeers: Ein erster Quellenbericht." *Archiv für Musikwissenschaft* 39 (1982), 32–63.

———. "Multimediale Tendenzen in der französischen Oper des 19. Jahrhunderts." *Report of the Twelfth Congress of the International Musicological Society. Berkeley 1977.* Kassel: Bärenreiter, 1981, pp. 497–500.

Doin, Jeanne. "Charles Séchan et son atelier de décoration théâtrale pendant le Romantisme." *Gazette des beaux-arts* 11 (1925), 344–360.

Donnet, Alexis. *Architectonographie des théâtres de Paris.* 2 vols. Paris: De Lacroix-Comon, 1840–57.

Dumas, Alexandre. "La Juive." *Gazette musicale de Paris* 2 #17 (26 April 1835), 141–146; #18 (3 May 1835), 149–154.

Ferrière, Théophile. "Le Château de Chenonceaux." *Revue et gazette musicale de Paris* 3 #11 (13 March 1836), 83–86.

Fétis, François. "Le Prophète." *Revue et gazette musicale de Paris* 16 #16 (22 April 1849), 121–126; #17 (29 April 1849), 129–134; #18 (6 May 1840), 137–140; #20 (20 May 1849), 153–157; #22 (3 June 1849), 169–174.

Finscher, Ludwig. "Aubers *La muette de Portici* und die Anfänge der Grand Opéra." *Festschrift Heinz Becker.* Ed. Jürgen Schläder and Reinhold Quandt. Laaber: Laaber-Verlag, 1982, pp. 87–105.

Forbes, Elizabeth. "The Age of Scribe at the Paris Opera." *Opera* 19 (1968), 7–12.

Frese, Christhard. *Dramaturgie der grossen Opern Giacomo Meyerbeers.* Berlin: Lienau, 1970.

Fulcher, Jane. "Meyerbeer and the Music of Society." *Musical Quarterly* 67 (1981), 213–229.

——. *The Nation's Image: French Grand Opera as Political and Politicized Art.* Cambridge University Press, 1987.

Gautier, Théophile. *Histoire de l'art dramatique depuis vingt-cinq ans.* 6 vols. Paris: Magnin-Blanchard, 1858–59.

——. *Les beautés de l'opéra.* Paris: Soulié, 1845.

Gernsheim, Helmut and Alison. *L. -J. -M. Daguerre.* New York: Dover, 1968.

Guest, Ivor. "Stage Designers—VI. Pierre Ciceri." *Ballet* 8 (July 1949), 20–28.

Halévy, Léon. *F. Halévy. Sa vie et ses oeuvres.* 2nd ed. Paris: Heugel, 1863.

Hogarth, George. *Memoirs of the Musical Drama.* 2 vols. London: Richard Bentley, 1851. Reprint, New York: Da Capo, 1972.

Hugo, Victor. *Préface de Cromwell.* Ed. Michel Cambien. Paris: Librairie Larousse, 1971.

Jacquot, Jean, and André Veinstein. *La mise en scène des oeuvres du passé.* Paris: Centre National de la Recherche Scientifique, 1957.

Join-Diéterle, Catherine. "Ciceri et la décoration théâtrale à l'opéra de Paris pendant la première partie du XIXe siècle." *Victor Louis et le théâtre: scénographie, mise en scène, et architecture théâtrale aux XVIIIe et XIXe siècles.* Paris: Éditions du Centre National de la Recherche Scientifique, 1982, pp. 141–151.

——. "Les décors de l'opéra de Paris à l'époque Romantique." *Revue internationale de musique française* 4 (1981), 57–73.

——. *Les décors de scène de l'opéra de Paris à l'époque Romantique.* Paris: Picard, 1988.

——. "Evolution de la scénographie à l'Académie de Musique à l'époque Romantique." *Romantisme* 38 (1982), 65–76.

Jullien, Adolphe. "Inauguration de la Salle de l'Opéra, 16 Août 1821." *La chronique musicale* 2 (1873), 168–176.

Kastner, Georges. "Le Prophète de Meyerbeer." *Revue et gazette musicale de Paris* 17 #5 (3 February 1850), 33–35; #6 (10 February 1850), 41–43; #7 (17 February 1850), 52–55; #9 (3 March 1850), 69–72; #10 (10 March 1850), 80–82; #11 (17 March 1850), 87–90; #14 (7 April 1850), 115–118.

Kirchmeyer, Helmut. "Psychologie des Meyerbeer-Erfolges." *Neue Zeitschrift für Musik* 125 (1964), 471–476.

Krafft, Jean-Charles. *Traité sur l'art de la charpente: Plans, coupes et élévations de diverses productions, executées tant en France que dans les pays étrangers.* 2 vols. 3rd ed. Paris: Bancé, Sr., 1840.

La Gournerie, Jules de. *Traité de perspective linéare contenant les traces pour les tableaux, plans et courbes, les bas-reliefs, et les décorations théâtrales.* Paris: Dalmont et Dunod, 1859.

Lasalle, Albert de. *Les treize salles d'opéra.* Paris: Sartorius, 1875.

Longyear, Rey Morgan. "La muette de Portici." *Music Review* 19 (1958), 37–46.

Maehder, Jürgen. "Historienmalerei und Grand Opéra: Zur Raumvorstellung in den Bildern Géricaults und Delacroix' und auf der Bühne der Académie Royale de Musique." Paper presented at the colloquium "Perspektiven der Opernforschung," Bad Homburg, Germany, 18–20 May 1987.

Mainzer, Joseph. "Vienne et la synagogue juive pendant les années 1826, 1827, et 1828." *Gazette musicale de Paris* 1 #16 (20 April 1834), 125–128; #18 (4 May 1834), 143–146.

Mason, James Frederick. *The Melodrama in France from the Revolution to the Beginnings of Romantic Drama, 1791–1830.* Baltimore: J. H. Furst, 1912.

Matthews, J. Brander. "Eugène Scribe." *Atlantic Monthly* 47 (1881), 678–690.

———. *The Theaters of Paris.* New York: Charles Scribner's Sons, 1880.

Matthews, William. *A Historical Sketch of the Origin, Progress and Present State of Gas Lighting.* London: Rowland Hunter, 1827.

Mongrédien, Jean. *La musique en France des lumières au Romantisme, 1789–1830.* Paris: Flammarion, 1986. Translated by Sylvain Frémaux under the title *French Music from the Enlightenment to Romanticism, 1789 to 1830* (Portland, Oregon: Amadeus Press, 1996).

———. "Variations sur un Thème: Masaniello." *Jahrbuch für Opernforschung* 1 (1985), 90–121.

Montdejoli. *La nouvelle Salle de l'Opéra, telle qu'elle est.* Paris: Bachelier, 1821.

Moynet, Georges. *La machinerie théâtrale: Trucs et décors.* Paris: Librairie Illustrée [1893].

Moynet, Jean-Pierre. *L'envers du théâtre.* Paris: Hachette, 1888. Reprint, New York, B. Blom, 1972.

———. *French Theatrical Production in the Nineteenth Century.* Trans. and augmented by A. S. Jackson and J. G. Wilson. [Binghamton, New York] Max Reinhardt Foundation, 1976.

Nuitter, Charles. "Les décors et les machines de l'Opéra." *La chronique musicale* 2 (1873), 76–83.

Paul, Charles Robert. "An Annotated Translation: *Theatrical Machinery, Stage Scenery and Devices* by Georges Moynet." Ph.D. dissertation, University of Southern California, 1970.

Pendle, Karin. "Boulevard Theatres and Continuity in French Opera of the Nineteenth Century." *Music in Paris in the 1830s.* Ed. Peter Bloom. Stuyvesant, New York: Pendragon, 1987, pp. 509–535.

———. *Eugène Scribe and French Opera of the Nineteenth Century.* Ann Arbor: UMI Research Press, 1971.

Perrin, Emile. "Etude sur la mise en scène." *Annales du théâtre et de la musique* 8 (1882), i–lxxii.

Pierre, Constant. *Le magasin des décors de l'Opéra, rue Richier, son histoire (1781–1894).* Paris: Bibliothèque de la Revue Dramatique et Musicale, 1894.

Pistone, Danièle. "L'Opéra de Paris au siècle Romantique." *Revue internationale de musique française* 4 (1981), 6–56.

Pougin, Arthur. "Décors et décorateurs." *Revue d'art dramatique* 33 (January–March 1894), 65–84.

———. *Dictionnaire historique et pittoresque du théâtre.* Paris: Firmin-Didot, 1885.

Ricks, Clyde. "A Survey of Theatrical Machines and Stage Devices Used in the Production of Melodrama in the Nineteenth Century." MA thesis, Brigham Young University, 1956.

Scherle, Arthur. "Eugène Scribe und die Oper des 19. Jahrhunderts." *Maske und Kothurn* 3 (1957), 141–158.

Schlesinger, Kathleen. "The Machinery of Grand Opera." *World Work* 2 (1903), 25–33.

Scribe, Eugène. *Oeuvres complètes.* 76 vols. Paris: E. Dentu, 1874–85.

Séchan, Charles. *Souvenirs d'un homme de théâtre, 1831–1855.* Ed. Adolphe Badin. Paris: Calmann Lévy, 1883.

Sonneck, Oscar G., and F. H. Martens. "Heinrich Heine's Musical Feuilletons." *Musical Quarterly* 8 (1922), 119–159, 273–295, 435–468.

Soubies, Albert. *Costumes et mise en scène.* Paris: Fischbacher, 1910.

Stoepel, F. "Académie de Musique. *La Juive.* Opéra en 5 actes . . . (Première Représentation)." *Gazette musicale de Paris* 2 #9 (1 March 1835), 72–75; #10 (8 March 1835), 82–83; #11 (15 March 1835) 91–92; #14 (5 April 1835), 117–119.

Strunk, Oliver. "Musical Life in Paris (1817–1848), A Chapter from the Memoirs of Sophie Augustine Leo." *Musical Quarterly* 17 (1931), 259–271, 389–403.

Thomson, Joan Lewis. "Meyerbeer and His Contemporaries." Ph.D. dissertation, Columbia University, 1972.

Tiersot, Jules. "Le centenaire du Romantisme et la musique: *La muette de Portici.*" *Le ménestrel* 90 #11 (16 March 1928), 117–118.

Trollope, Frances. *Paris and the Parisians in 1835.* 2 vols. London: Richard Bentley, 1836.

Véron, Louis. *Mémoires d'un bourgeois de Paris.* 5 vols. Paris: E. de Gonet, 1853–55.

———. *L'Opéra de Paris, 1820–1835.* Paris: Éditions Michel de Maule, 1987.

Walter, Michael. *Hugenotten-Studien.* Frankfurt am Main: Peter Lang, 1987.

Wilberg, Rebecca. "The *mise en scène* at the Paris Opéra-Salle le Peletier (1821–1873) and the Staging of the First French 'Grand Opéra': Meyerbeer's *Robert le diable.*" Ph.D. dissertation, Brigham Young University, 1990.

Wild, Nicole. *Décors et costumes du XIXe siècle.* Vol. I: *L'Opéra de Paris.* Paris: Bibliothèque Nationale Département de la Musique, 1987.

———. "Un demi-siècle de décors à l'Opéra de Paris." *Regards sur l'Opéra.* Paris: Presses Universitaires de France, 1976, 11–22.

———. "La recherche de la précision historique chez les décorateurs de l'Opéra de Paris au XIXe siècle." *Report of the Twelfth Congress of the International Musicological Society. Berkeley 1977.* Kassel: Bärenreiter, 1981, 453–463.

Winter, Marian-Hannah. *The Theatre of Marvels.* Trans. C. Meldon. New York: B. Blom [1964].

Wolff, Hellmut Christian. *Oper, Szene und Darstellung.* Leipzig: V. E. B. Deutscher Verlag für Musik, 1968.

———. "Die Regiebücher des Louis Palianti für die Pariser Opera 1830–1870." *Maske und Kothurn* 26 (1980), 74–84.

Chapter Eight

For a detailed bibliography, see the entry on Giuseppe Verdi by Roger Parker in vol. 4 of *New Grove Dictionary of Opera.* London: Macmillan, 1992.

Abbiati, Franco. *Verdi.* Milan: Ricordi, 1963.

Bacchini, Maurizia Bonatti. *Il teatro di Girolamo Magnani: Scenografo di Verdi.* Parma: La civiltà musicale di Parma, 1989.

Baker, Evan. "Lettere di Giuseppe Verdi a Francesco Maria Piave. 1843–1865: Documenti della Frederick R. Koch Foundation Collection e della Mary Flagler Cary Collection presso la Pierpont Morgan Library di New York." In *Studi verdiani* 4 (1986–1987), 136–166.

Brusatin, Manlio, and Giuseppe Pavanello. *Il Teatro la Fenice. I progetti, l'architettura, le decorazioni.* Venice: Albrizzi, 1987.

Budden, Julian. *The Operas of Verdi: From* Oberto *to* Rigoletto. Oxford University Press, 1991.

Conati, Marcello. "La disposizione scenica per il *Simon Boccanegra* di Verdi: Studio critico." In Conati and Grilli, *Simon Boccanegra.* Milan: Ricordi, 1993.

———. *La bottega della musica: Verdi e la Fenice.* Milan: Saggiatore, 1983.

Conati, Marcello, and Natalia Grilli. *Simon Boccanegra.* Milan: Ricordi, 1993. Published as part of the series *Musica e Spettacolo: Collana di disposizioni sceniche.*

Damerini, Gino. *Scenografi veneziani dell'Ottocento.* Venice: Neri Pozza, 1962.

Garibaldi, Luigi. *Giuseppe Verdi nelle lettere di Emanuale Muzio ad Antonio Barezzi.* Milan: Fratelli Treves, 1931.

Giazotto, Remo. *Le carte della Scala: Storie di impresari e appaltatori teatrali 1778–1860.* Pisa: Akademos, 1990.

Girardi, Michele and Franco Rossi. *Il Teatro la Fenice. Cronologia degli spettacoli 1792–1936.* Venice: Albrizzi, 1989.

Grilli, Natalia. "Le immagini per il *Simon Boccanegra* di Verdi." In Conati and Grilli, *Simon Boccanegra.* Milan: Ricordi, 1993.

Grilli, Natalia. *Filippo Peroni — Scenografo alla Scala 1849–1867.* Milan: Museo teatrale alla Scala, 1985.

Mancini, Franco. *Il Teatro di San Carlo: 1737–1987: Vol. III. Le scene, i costumi.* Naples, Electa, 1987.

———. *Scenografia napoletana dell'ottocento: Antonio Niccolini e il neoclassico.* Naples: Edizioni Scientifica, 1980.

Mangini, Nicola. *I teatri di Venezia.* Milano: Mursia, 1974.

Marangoni, Guido, and Carlo Vanbianchi. *La Scala: Studi e ricerche.* Bergamo: Istituto Italiano d'Arte Grafiche, Editore, 1922.

Matz, Mary Jane. *Verdi.* New York: Oxford University Press, 1993.

Meduna, Tommaso, and Giambattista Meduna. *Il Teatro la Fenice in Venezia edificato dall'architetto Antonio Selva nel 1792 e ricostruito in parte il 1836.* Venice: Antonelli, 1849.

Muraro, Maria Teresa. "Giuseppe Bertoja e le scene per la prima di *Rigoletto* alla Fenice." In *Verdi: Bolletino dell'istituto di studi verdiani.* Parma: Istituto di studi verdiani, 1982. Vol. 9, pp. 1582–1588.

———. "Le scenografie delle cinque 'prime assolute' di Verdi alla Fenice di Venezia." In *Atti del I° congresso internazionale di studi verdiani.* Parma: Istituto di studi verdiani, 1969.

Ogden, Dunbar. *The Italian Baroque Stage: Documents by Giulio Troili, Andrea Pozzo, Ferdinando Galli-Bibiena, Baldassare Orsini.* Berkeley and Los Angeles: University of California Press, 1978.

Pieri, Marzio. *Verdi: L'immaginario dell'ottocento.* Milan, Electa, 1981.

Radiciotti, Giuseppe. *Teatro, musica e musicisti in Sinigaglia.* Milan, Ricordi, 1893.

Rosen, David. "The Staging of Verdi's Operas: An Introduction to the Ricordi *Disposizione sceniche.*" In *Report of the Twelfth Congress of the International Musicological Society, Berkeley 1977.* Kassel: Bärenreiter, 1981.

Rosen, David and Andrew Porter, eds. *Verdi's* Macbeth: *A Sourcebook.* New York: W. W. Norton, 1984.

Rosselli, John. *The Opera Industry in Italy from Cimarosa to Verdi: The Role of the Impresario.* Cambridge University Press, 1984.

Stefani, Giuseppe. *Verdi e Trieste.* Trieste: Editore il Commune, 1951.

Viale-Ferrero, Mercedes. "*Ernani* di Verdi. Le critiche del tempo: Alcune considerazioni." In *Verdi: Bolletino dell'istituto di studi verdiani numero 10, Ernani: Ieri e oggi.* Parma: Istituto nazionale di studi verdiani, 1987.

——. *La scenografia dalle origini al 1936: Storia del Teatro Regio di Torino.* Turin: Cassa di risparmio, 1980.

——. *La scenografia della Scala nell'età neoclassica.* Milano: Polifilo, 1983.

Walker, Frank. *The Man Verdi.* New York: Alfred P. Knopf, 1963.

Weaver, William. *Seven Verdi Librettos.* New York: W. W. Norton, 1975.

——. *Verdi: A Documentary Study.* London: Thames and Hudson, 1977.

Chapter Nine

The bibliography on the subject of Richard Wagner is enormous. An extensive and detailed listing may be found in *New Grove Dictionary of Opera.* London: Macmillan, 1992. Listed below are publications which were helpful in the preparation of the present essay.

Barth, Herbert, Dietrich Mack, and Egon Voss, eds. *Wagner: A Documentary Biography.* New York: Oxford University Press, 1975.

Bauer, Oswald Georg. *Richard Wagner: The Stage Designs and Productions from the Premières to the Present.* New York: Rizzoli, 1983.

Baugeschichte des Bayreuther Festspielhauses. "Dort stehe es, auf dem lieblichen Hügel bei Bayreuth." Bayreuth: Bayerische Vereinsbank, 1994.

Baumann, Carl-Friedrich. *Bühnentechnik im Festspielhaus Bayreuth.* Munich: Prestel, 1980.

Borchmeyer, Dieter. *Theory and Theatre.* Trans. by Stewart Spencer. Oxford: Clarendon Press, 1991.

Brand, Hans B. *Aus Richard Wagners Leben in Bayreuth. Nach eigenen Beobachtungen erzählt von einem Zeitgenossen.* Munich: G. Hirth, 1934.

Die Bühnenwerkstatt der Gebrüder Brückner. Bayreuth: Bayerische Vereinsbank, 1989.

Eger, Manfred. *Königsfreundschaft: Ludwig, Wagner, Legende und Wirklichkeit.* Bayreuth: Richard-Wagner-Stiftung, 1987.

Fricke, Richard. *Bayreuth vor dreissig Jahren. Erinnerungen an Wahnfried und aus dem Festspielhause.* Stuttgart: Akademischer Verlag Hans-Dieter Heinz, 1983. Originally pub. in 1876 as *Richard Wagner auf der Probe: Das Bayreuther Tagebuch des Ballettmeisters und Hofregisseurs Richard Fricke.*

Glasenapp, C. F. *Das Leben Richard Wagners;* 5th ed. 5 vols. Leipzig: Breitkopf und Härtel, 1910–1923.

Gottfried Semper zum 100. Todestag. Dresden: Staatliche Kunstsammlung, 1979.

Habel, Heinrich. *Festspielhaus und Wahnfried.* Munich: Prestel, 1985.

Hartford, Robert, ed. *Bayreuth: The Early Years.* Cambridge University Press, 1980.

Huebner, Steven. "Opera Audiences in Paris 1830–1870." *Music and Letters* (1989), 206–225

Humperdinck, Engelbert. *Briefe und Tagebücher.* Vol. 2. *(1881–1883).* Ed. by Hans-Josef Irmen. Cologne: Arno Volk, 1975.

Kaiser, Hermann. *Der Bühnenmeister Carl Brandt und Richard Wagner: Kunst der Szene in Darmstadt und Bayreuth.* Darmstadt: Eduard Roether, 1968.

Kipke, C. "Das unsichtbare Orchester. Eine historisch-kritische Studie." *Bayreuther Blätter,* 12 (1889), 324–347.

Kirchmeyer, Helmut. *Das zeitgenössische Wagnerbild.* Vol. 1. *Wagner in Dresden.* Regensburg: Gustav Bosse, 1967.

Kirchmeyer, Helmut. *Das zeitgenössische Wagnerbild.* Vol. 2. *Dokumente 1842–1845.* Regensburg: Gustav Bosse, 1967.

Mack, Dietrich. *Der Bayreuther Inszenierungsstil: 1876–1976.* Munich: Prestel, 1976.

Millington, Barry, ed. *The Wagner Compendium. A Guide to Wagner's Life and Music.* New York: Schirmer Books, 1992.

Millington, Barry and Stewart Spencer. *Wagner in Performance.* New Haven, Connecticut: Yale University Press, 1992.

Müller, Ulrich and Peter Wapnewski, eds. *Wagner Handbook: The Full Story of the Man, His Music, and His Legacy.* Trans. and ed. by John Deathridge. Cambridge, Massachusetts: Harvard University Press, 1992.

Newman, Ernest. *The Life of Richard Wagner.* 4 vols. New York: Alfred A. Knopf, 1932–1948.

Newman, Ernest. *Wagner Nights.* London: Putnam, 1947.

Noelle, Ekehart, ed. *Richard Wagner 1813–1883: Ur- und Erstaufführungen seiner Werke in München: Eine Austellung aus den Beständen des Deutschen Theater Museums.* Munich: Deutsches Theatermuseum, 1983.

Petzet, Detta and Michael. *Die Richard Wagner Bühne König Ludwigs II.* Munich: Prestel, 1970.

Semper, Gottfried. *Das Königliche Hoftheater zu Dresden.* Braunschweig, 1849.

Spencer, Stewart and Barry Millington. *Selected Letters of Richard Wagner.* New York: W. W. Norton, 1988.

Spencer, Stewart and Barry Millington. *Wagner's Ring of the Nibelung: The Full German Text with a New Translation and Commentaries.* New York: Thames and Hudson, 1993.

Spotts, Frederic. *Bayreuth: A History of the Wagner Festival.* New Haven: Yale University Press, 1994.

Steinbeck, Dietrich. *Richard Wagners Tannhäuser-Szenarium: Das Vorbild der Erstaufführungen mit der Kostümbeschreibung und den Dekorationsplänen.* Berlin: Gesellschaft für Theatergeschichte, 1968.

Strobel, Otto. *König Ludwig II. und Richard Wagner: Briefwechsel mit vielen anderen Urkunden in vier Bänden herausgegeben vom Wittelsbacher Ausgleich-Fonds und von Winifried Wagner. Nachtragsband: Neue Urkunden zur Lebensgeschichte Richard Wagners 1864–1882.* Karlsruhe: G. Braun, 1936–1939.

Wagner, Cosima. *Diaries.* Trans. Geoffrey Skelton. New York: Harcourt, Brace, Jovanovich, 1978.

——. *Die Tagebücher.* Munich: Piper, 1978.

Wagner, Richard. *Gesammelte Schriften und Dichtungen.* Leipzig: Fritsch, 1888. 10 vols.

——. *Mein Leben.* Munich: Paul List, 1963.

—— *My Life.* Trans. by Arnold Whittall. Cambridge University Press, 1991.

——. *Richard Wagner's Prose Works.* Vol. 1. *The Art-Work of the Future, &c.* London: Kegan Paul, Trench, Trübner, 1895. Trans. William Ashton Ellis.

——. *Richard Wagner's Prose Works.* Vol. 3. *The Theatre.* London: Kegan Paul, Trench, Trübner, 1895. Trans. William Ashton Ellis.

——. *Richard Wagner und König Ludwig II. von Bayern: Briefwechsel Auswahl.* Ed. with a postscript by Kurt Wölfel. Stuttgart: Gerd Hatje, 1993.

——. *Sämtliche Briefe.* Issued in conjunction with the Richard-Wagner-Stiftung Bayreuth. Leipzig: Deutscher Verlag für Musik, 1983.

Weingartner, Felix von. *Lebenserinnerungen.* Zürich: Orell Füssli, 1923.

Wieszner, Georg Gustav. *Richard Wagner der Theater-Reformer: Vom Werden des deutschen National-Theaters im Geiste des Jahres 1848.* Emsdetten: H. und J. Lechte, 1951.

Wild, Nicole. *Dictionnaire des théâtres parisiens au XIXe siècle*. Paris: Aux amateurs des livres, 1989.

Zimmermann, Werner G. *Richard Wagner in Zürich: Eine Chronik*. Zurich: Präsidialabteilung der Stadt Zürich, 1983.

Chapter Ten

Appia, Adolphe. *Die Musik und die Inscenierung*. Munich: Verlagsanstalt F. Bruckmann, 1899.

Ashbrook, William. *The Operas of Puccini*. New York: Oxford University Press, 1968. Reprint with foreword by Roger Parker, Ithaca, New York: Cornell University Press, 1985.

Atlas, Allan W. "Belasco and Puccini: 'Old Dog Tray' and the Zuni Indians." *The Musical Quarterly* 75 (1991), 362–398.

Balthazar, Scott. "Evolving Conventions in Italian Opera: Scene Structure in the Works of Rossini, Bellini, Donizetti, and Verdi, 1810–1850." Ph.D. dissertation, University of Pennsylvania, 1985.

Beckerman, Bernard. *Dynamics of Drama: Theory and Method of Analysis*. New York: Drama Book Specialists, 1979.

Belasco, David. *The Theatre through Its Stage Door*. Ed. Louis V. Defoe. New York: Benjamin Blom, 1919. Reprint, 1969.

——. *The Girl of the Golden West*. New York: Samuel French, 1915.

Bloom, Ken. *American Song: The Complete Musical Theatre Companion, 1900–1984*. New York: Facts on File Publications, 1985.

Bordman, Gerald. *American Musical Theatre: A Chronicle*. New York: Oxford University Press, 1978.

Carner, Mosco. *Puccini: A Critical Biography*. 2nd ed. New York: Holmes and Meier, 1974. Reprint, 1988.

Corazzol, Adriana Guarnieri. "Opera and *verismo*: Regressive Points of View and the Artifice of Alienation." Trans. Roger Parker. *Cambridge Opera Journal* 5/1 (1993), 39–53.

De Sanctis, Dona. "Literary Realism and *verismo* Opera." Ph.D. dissertation, The City University of New York, 1983.

Dotto, Gabriele. "Opera, Four Hands: Collaborative Alterations in Puccini's *Fanciulla*." *Journal of the American Musicological Society* 42 (1989), 604–624.

Gara, Eugenio, ed. *Carteggi pucciniani*. Milan: G. Ricordi, 1958.

Gerould, Daniel C., ed. *American Melodrama*. New York: Performing Arts Publications, 1983.

Grace, Deborah. "Reversal of Fortune." *Opera News* 57/12 (27 February 1993), 18 ff.

Greenwald, Helen M. "Dramatic Exposition and Musical Structure in Puccini's Operas." Ph.D. dissertation, The City University of New York, 1991.

——. "Recent Puccini Research." *Acta musicologica* 65/1 (1993), 23–50.

Hartmann, Louis. *Theatre Lighting: A Manual of the Stage Switchboard*. Foreword by David Belasco. New York: D. Appleton, 1930. Reprint, New York: Drama Book Specialists, 1970.

Marker, Lise-Lone. *David Belasco: Naturalism in the American Theatre*. Princeton: Princeton University Press, 1975.

Nicolaisen, Jay. *Italian Opera in Transition, 1871–1893*. Ann Arbor: UMI Research Press, 1980.

Pfister, Manfred. *The Theory and Analysis of Drama*. Trans. John Halliday. In *European Studies in English Literature*. Cambridge University Press, 1988. Originally pub. as *Das Drama*. Munich: Wilhelm Fink, 1977.

Puccini, Giacomo. *Le villi*. Milan: G. Ricordi, 1956. Pl. no. 49457.

——. *Manon Lescaut*. Milan: G. Ricordi, 1980. Pl. no. P.R. 113.

——. *La fanciulla del West*. Milan: G. Ricordi, 1980. Pl. no. 113483.

——. *Il tabarro*. Milan: G. Ricordi, 1984. Pl. no. 129782.

——. *Turandot*. Milan: G. Ricordi, 1987. Pl. no. 121329.

——. Continuity drafts and sketches of *La fanciulla del West,* New York Public Library, music collection, Koch 989, Koch 282, and Lehman (without number).

Rosen, Charles and Henri Zerner. *Romanticism and Realism: The Mythology of Nineteenth-Century Art*. New York: Viking Press, 1984.

Rubin, Joel. "The Technical Development of Stage Lighting Apparatus in the United States, 1900–1950." Ph.D. dissertation, Stanford University, 1959.

Serlio, Sebastiano. *Regole generali di architettura*. Paris, 1545.

Simon, Lee. *The Stage Is Set*. New York: Harcourt, Brace, 1932.

di Somi, Leone Ebreo. *Dialoghi*. Mantua, 1565.

Wilmeth, Don B. and Tice L. Miller, eds. *Cambridge Guide to American Theatre*. Cambridge University Press, 1993.

Winter, William. *The Life of David Belasco*. 2 vols. New York: Moffat, Yard, 1918. Reprint, Freeport, New York: Books for Libraries Press, 1970.

Zangarini, Carlo and Guelfo Civinini. *The Girl of the Golden West*. Trans. R. H. Elkin. New York: Belwin, n.d.

About the Contributors

Evan Baker has worked as a stage director in opera houses in Switzerland and Germany. In 1985 he created, at the Palazzo Ducale Colorno, the first major exhibition in Italy in more than fifty years on the life and works of Giuseppe Verdi. He also created, in 1986, an exhibition for the Teatro alla Scala on the occasion of the return to the repertory of Richard Strauss's *Die Frau ohne Schatten*. In 1991 for the Mozart bicentennial celebrations, Baker curated, for the New York Public Library, a survey on the life, times, and works of the composer. He received his Ph.D. in performance studies from New York University and wrote a dissertation entitled "Alfred Roller's Production of *Don Giovanni:* A Break in the Scenic Traditions of the Vienna Court Opera, 1905." He has lectured at international conferences, and his essays have appeared in *Opera News,* in the *Mozart-Jahrbuch,* and in the *New Grove Dictionary of Opera.* He is now preparing for Yale University Press a book on the history of operatic production, staging, and design.

E. Douglas Bomberger holds a Ph.D. in musicology from the University of Maryland. He is currently on the faculty at the University of Hawaii at Manoa. His articles on nineteenth-century music have appeared in *The Musical Quarterly, The Piano Quarterly, The Journal of the American Liszt Society,* and *American Music.*

Barbara Coeyman is an associate professor of music history at West Virginia University. Her doctoral research at the City University of New York, focusing on sites of performance, established her contextual approach to French Baroque musical theater. She is a national officer in the Society for Seventeenth-Century Music and in the College Music Society. She is currently at work on two major projects: (1) a book examining performance of musical theater in the court of the Sun King and (2) a catalog of musical theater sources in Stockholm. She has recently published work on the viol in the seventeenth century and on feminist pedagogy in college music. She recently completed a master's degree in management in higher education.

Malcolm S. Cole, a native of San Francisco, received his B.A. degree from the University of California, Berkeley. He took his M.F.A. and Ph.D. degrees at Princeton University. With military service completed and with doctorate in hand, he began his professional career as dean of the San Francisco Conservatory of Music and as music director for St. Francis' Episcopal Church (San Francisco). In 1967 he joined the University of California, Los Angeles, where he presently serves as a professor of musicology. Cole's principal research areas are the Classic period, opera (especially Viennese magic opera), performance practice, and emigré studies (in particular, the Austrian-American composer Eric Zeisl). The author of assorted books, articles, and reviews, he is currently coeditor of *Music in Performance and Society: Essays in Honor of Roland Jackson* (forthcoming from Harmonie Park Press). Professor Cole also appears frequently as lecturer, pianist, and organist.

Helen Greenwald's work has appeared in *Nineteenth-Century Music, Acta musicologica,* the *Mozart-Jahrbuch,* the Music Library Association's *Notes, Studi musicali toscani,* and the *Newsletter of the Résource internationale d'iconographie musicale.* She has presented papers at international forums, including the 1991 international Mozart Congress / Salzburg, the Royal Music Association / British Music Analysis Conference (Southampton), the British Nineteenth-Century Music Conference (Surrey), the 1994 Convegno internazionale di studi su Giacomo Puccini (Lucca), and at the conferences of the American Musicological Society, the Society for Music Theory, the New England Conference of Music Theorists, and the Music Theory Society of New York State. She earned her Ph.D. in musicology from the City University of New York and currently teaches musicology at the New England Conservatory of Music in Boston.

Massimo Ossi, currently on the faculty of the University of Rochester, received his Ph.D. from Harvard University in 1989. His dissertation was entitled "Claudio Monteverdi's Concertato Technique and Its Role in the Development of His Musical Thought." His research interests include early seventeenth-century Italian music theory and aesthetics; Italian lyric poetry, 1570–1650, especially Battista Guarini; and the Italian madrigal, 1550–1650. Among his publications are "Claudio Monteverdi's *ordine novo, bello et gustevole:* The Canzonetta as Dramatic Module and Formal Archetype," which appeared in the *Journal of the American Musicological Society;* "L'armonia raddoppiata: On Claudio Monteverdi's 'Zefiro torna,' Heinrich Schütz's 'Es steh Gott auf,' and Other Early Seventeenth-Century *ciaccone,*" which appeared in *Studi musicali.* He is currently working on a study of Monteverdi's *seconda prattica.* Ossi is the general editor of the Broude Brothers series entitled *Music at the Courts of Italy.* He edits *Seventeenth-Century Music,* the newsletter of the Society for Seventeenth-Century Music, and he serves on the editorial board for the collected works of Luca Marenzio, also published by Broude. He was a fellow at the Villa I Tatti in 1991–92 and won the 1993 Alfred Einstein Award of the American Musicological Society for "Claudio Monteverdi's *ordine novo, bello et gustevole.*"

Karin Pendle, a Ph.D. graduate of the University of Illinois, began her study of French opera with her dissertation, "Eugène Scribe and French Opera of the Nineteenth Century," which was published in book form by UMI Research Press in 1979. Since then she has published numerous articles on French opera of the years 1750–1850, and she has edited a textbook, *Women and Music: A History,* for Indiana University Press. Her study of *opéra-comique* during the period 1762–1789 appears in *L'Opéra-comique en France au XVIIIe siècle* (Liege: Mardaga, 1992). She is professor of musicology at the College-Conservatory of Music, University of Cincinnati.

Mark A. Radice completed his Ph.D. in musicology at the Eastman School of Music in 1984. He has published numerous articles on a wide range of subjects in journals such as *Bach: The Journal of the Riemenschneider Bach Institute, The American Organist: The A.G.O. and R.C.C.O. Journal, The Music Review, Choral Journal, Ars Musica Denver, Opera Quarterly,* and *The Musical Quarterly.* Amadeus Press will also publish his history of chamber music. He is Chair of Graduate Studies in Music at Ithaca College.

Mark Stahura received his undergraduate degree in music from Carleton College. In addition to orchestral conducting studies at the Aspen Music School, he completed a master's degree in choral conducting at the Indiana University School of Music. His doctoral studies under Ellen T. Harris at the University of Chicago centered on Handel's orchestrational techniques. He presently resides in St. Paul, Minnesota.

Index

Pages designated in italics include illustrations.